Ford Ranger & Bronco II Automotive Repair Manual

by Alan Ahlstrand, Homer Eubanks and John H Haynes
Member of the Guild of Motoring Writers

Models covered:
Ford Ranger and Bronco II models
1983 through 1992
Does not include diesel engine information

(1A17 – 36070)
(1026)

ABCDE
FGHIJ
KLMN

2

Haynes Publishing Group
Sparkford Nr Yeovil
Somerset BA22 7JJ England

Haynes North America, Inc
861 Lawrence Drive
Newbury Park
California 91320 USA

Acknowledgements

We are grateful to the Ford Motor Company for assistance with technical information, certain illustrations and vehicle photos. Technical writers who contributed to this project include Ed Scott.

© **Haynes North America, Inc.** 1991, 1992, 1993

With permission from J.H. Haynes & Co. Ltd.

A book in the **Haynes Automotive Repair Manual Series**

Printed in the U.S.A.

ISBN 1 56392 066 2

Library of Congress Catalog Card Number 93-77338

While every attempt is made to ensure that the information in this manual is correct, no liability can be accepted by the authors or publishers for loss, damage or injury caused by any errors in, or omissions from, the information given.

Contents

Ford Ranger two-wheel drive (2WD) pickup

A four-wheel drive (4WD) Ford Bronco II

About this manual

Its purpose

The purpose of this manual is to help you get the best value from your vehicle. It can do so in several ways. It can help you decide what work must be done, even if you choose to have it done by a dealer service department or a repair shop; it provides information and procedures for routine maintenance and servicing; and it offers diagnostic and repair procedures to follow when trouble occurs.

We hope you use the manual to tackle the work yourself. For many simpler jobs, doing it yourself may be quicker than arranging an appointment to get the vehicle into a shop and making the trips to leave it and pick it up. More importantly, a lot of money can be saved by avoiding the expense the shop must pass on to you to cover its labor and overhead costs. An added benefit is the sense of satisfaction and accomplishment that you feel after doing the job yourself.

Using the manual

The manual is divided into Chapters. Each Chapter is divided into numbered Sections, which are headed in bold type between horizontal lines. Each Section consists of consecutively numbered paragraphs.

At the beginning of each numbered Section you will be referred to any illustrations which apply to the procedures in that Section. The reference numbers used in illustration captions pinpoint the pertinent Section and the Step within that Section. That is, illustration 3.2 means the illustration refers to Section 3 and Step (or paragraph) 2 within that Section.

Procedures, once described in the text, are not normally repeated. When it's necessary to refer to another Chapter, the reference will be given as Chapter and Section number. Cross references given without use of the word "Chapter" apply to Sections and/or paragraphs in the same Chapter. For example, "see Section 8" means in the same Chapter.

References to the left or right side of the vehicle assume you are sitting in the driver's seat, facing forward.

Even though we have prepared this manual with extreme care, neither the publisher nor the author can accept responsibility for any errors in, or omissions from, the information given.

NOTE

A **Note** provides information necessary to properly complete a procedure or information which will make the procedure easier to understand.

CAUTION

A **Caution** provides a special procedure or special steps which must be taken while completing the procedure where the **Caution** is found. Not heeding a **Caution** can result in damage to the assembly being worked on.

WARNING

A **Warning** provides a special procedure or special steps which must be taken while completing the procedure where the **Warning** is found. Not heeding a **Warning** can result in personal injury.

Introduction to the Ford Ranger and Bronco II

Ford Ranger and Bronco II models are conventional front-engine, rear-wheel drive vehicles.

Engine options include the 2.0L and 2.3L inline four-cylinder engines and the 2.8L, 2.9L, 3.0L and 4.0L V6 engines.

Power is transmitted through either a manual or automatic transmission to a driveshaft and solid rear axle on two-wheel drive (2WD) models. On four-wheel drive (4WD) models, a transfer case transmits power to the front axle by way of a driveshaft. Transmissions used are a four-speed manual, five-speed overdrive manual, three-speed automatic and four-speed overdrive automatic.

2WD models use twin I-beam front suspension with coil springs and radius arms. 4WD models use a similar independent front suspension with a two-piece front driveaxle assembly, coil springs and radius arms. Both types use semi-elliptical leaf springs at the rear.

All models are equipped with front disc and rear drum brakes, with power assist optional.

Vehicle identification numbers

Modifications are a continuing and unpublicized process in vehicle manufacturing. Since spare parts manuals and lists are compiled on a numerical basis, the individual vehicle numbers are necessary to correctly identify the component required.

Vehicle Identification Number (VIN)

This very important identification number is located on a plate attached to the left side of the dashboard, just inside the windshield (**see illustration**). It is visible from outside the vehicle, through the windshield. The VIN also appears on the Vehicle Certificate of Title and Registration. It contains information such as where and when the vehicle was manufactured, the model year and the body style.

SAMPLE VIN NUMBER

1 F T C R 1 O A 5 J U A 0 0 0 0 1

① Position 1, 2, and 3 — Manufacturer, Make and Type (World Manufacturer Identifier)

② Position 4 — Brake System/GVWR

③ Position 5, 6, and 7 — Model or Line, Series, Chassis, Cab Type

④ Position 8 — Engine Type

⑤ Position 9 — Check Digit

⑥ Position 10 — Model Year

⑦ Position 11 — Assembly Plant

⑧ Position 12 — Constant "A" until sequence number of 99,999 is reached, then changes to a constant "B" and so on

⑨ Position 13 through 17 — Sequence number — begins at 00001

The Vehicle Identification Number (VIN) is visible through the driver's side of the windshield

Vehicle Certification Label

The Vehicle Certification label (VC label, also referred to as the Truck Safety Compliance Certification label) is attached to the front of the left (driver's side) door pillar. The upper half of the label contains the name of the manufacturer, the month and year of production, the Gross Vehicle Weight Rating (GVWR), the Gross Axle Weight Rating (GAWR) and the certification statement (see illustration).

The VC label also contains the VIN number, which is used for warranty identification of the vehicle, and provides such information as manufacturer, type of restraint system, body type, engine, transmission, model year and vehicle serial number.

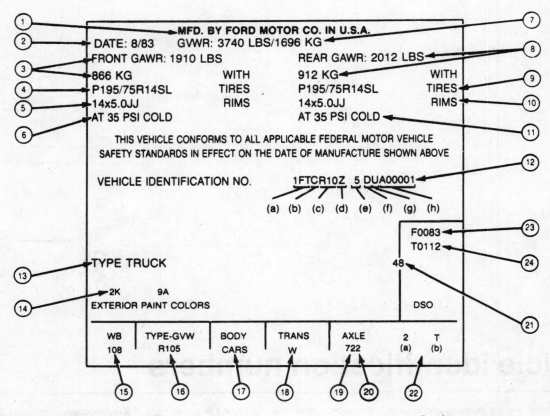

The Truck Safety Compliance Certification label

① Name and Location of Manufacturer	⑩ Rim Size
② Date of Manufacture	⑪ Rear Tire Cold PSI
③ Front Gross Axle Weight Ratings in Pounds (LB) and Kilograms (KG)	⑫ Vehicle Identification Number
④ Front Tire Size	(a) World Manufacturer Identifier
⑤ Rim Size	(b) Brake Type and Gross Vehicle Weight Rating (GVWR) Class
⑥ Front Tire Cold PSI	(c) Model or Line, Series, Chassis and Cab Type
⑦ Gross Vehicle Weight Rating in Pounds (LB) and Kilograms (KG)	(d) Engine Type
	(e) Check Digit
	(f) Model Year
	(g) Assembly Plant Code
⑧ Rear Gross Axle Weight Rating in Pounds (LB) and Kilograms (KG)	(h) Sequential Serial and Model Year
⑨ Rear Tire Size	⑬ Type Vehicle
	⑭ Exterior Paint Codes (two sets of figures designates a two-tone)
	⑮ Wheelbase in Inches

⑯ Model Code and GVW	
⑰ Interior Trim, Seat and Body Cab Type	
⑱ Transmission Code	
⑲ Rear Axle Code	
⑳ Front Axle Code if so equipped	
㉑ District Special Order Codes	
㉒ Suspension Identification Codes	
(a) Front Spring Code	
(b) Rear Spring Code	
㉓ Front Axle Accessory Reserve Capacity in Pounds	
㉔ Total Accessory Reserve Capacity in Pounds	

The Vehicle Certification label, also known as the Truck Safety Compliance Certification label, is attached to the driver's door pillar

Engine numbers

Labels containing the engine code, calibration and serial numbers, as well as the manufacturing plant name, can be found on the timing belt cover or valve cover, as well as stamped on the engine itself **(see illustration)**.

Manual transmission numbers

The manual transmission identification number and serial numbers can be found on a label on the left or right side of the transmission main case **(see illustration)**.

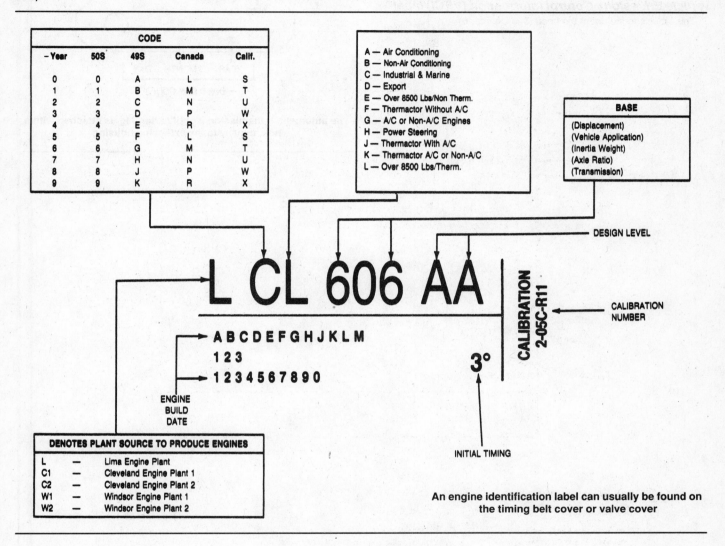

CODE				
– Year	50S	49S	Canada	Calif.
0	0	A	L	S
1	1	B	M	T
2	2	C	N	U
3	3	D	P	W
4	4	E	R	X
5	5	F	L	S
6	6	G	M	T
7	7	H	N	U
8	8	J	P	W
9	9	K	R	X

A — Air Conditioning
B — Non-Air Conditioning
C — Industrial & Marine
D — Export
E — Over 8500 Lbs/Non Therm.
F — Thermactor Without A/C
G — A/C or Non-A/C Engines
H — Power Steering
J — Thermactor With A/C
K — Thermactor A/C or Non-A/C
L — Over 8500 Lbs/Therm.

BASE
(Displacement)
(Vehicle Application)
(Inertia Weight)
(Axle Ratio)
(Transmission)

DESIGN LEVEL

L CL 606 AA

CALIBRATION 2-05C-R11

CALIBRATION NUMBER

A B C D E F G H J K L M
1 2 3
1 2 3 4 5 6 7 8 9 0

ENGINE BUILD DATE

3°

INITIAL TIMING

DENOTES PLANT SOURCE TO PRODUCE ENGINES		
L	—	Lima Engine Plant
C1	—	Cleveland Engine Plant 1
C2	—	Cleveland Engine Plant 2
W1	—	Windsor Engine Plant 1
W2	—	Windsor Engine Plant 2

An engine identification label can usually be found on the timing belt cover or valve cover

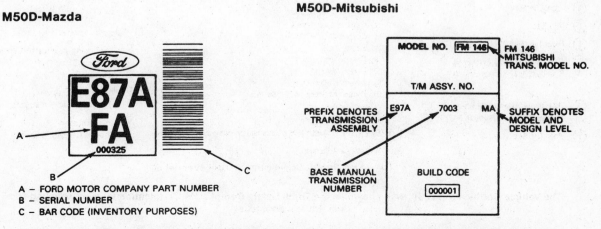

M50D-Mazda

Ford
E87A
FA
000325

A
B
C

A – FORD MOTOR COMPANY PART NUMBER
B – SERIAL NUMBER
C – BAR CODE (INVENTORY PURPOSES)

M50D-Mitsubishi

MODEL NO. FM 146

FM 146 MITSUBISHI TRANS. MODEL NO.

T/M ASSY. NO.

PREFIX DENOTES TRANSMISSION ASSEMBLY

E97A   7003   MA

SUFFIX DENOTES MODEL AND DESIGN LEVEL

BASE MANUAL TRANSMISSION NUMBER

BUILD CODE
000001

The manual transmission identification label is mounted on the left or right side of the transmission case

Automatic transmission numbers

Tags with the automatic transmission serial number, build date and other information are attached with a bolt, usually at the extension housing (see illustration).

Vehicle Emissions Control Information (VECI) label

This label is found under the hood (see Chapter 6).

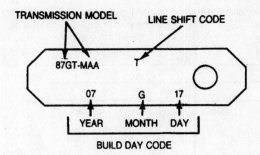

The automatic transmission identification tag is attached with a bolt, usually to the extension housing

Buying parts

Replacement parts are available from many sources, which generally fall into one of two categories – authorized dealer parts departments and independent retail auto parts stores. Our advice concerning these parts is as follows:

Retail auto parts stores: Good auto parts stores will stock frequently needed components which wear out relatively fast, such as clutch components, exhaust systems, brake parts, tune-up parts, etc. These stores often supply new or reconditioned parts on an exchange basis, which can save a considerable amount of money. Discount auto parts stores are often very good places to buy materials and parts needed for general vehicle maintenance such as oil, grease, filters, spark plugs, belts, touch-up paint, bulbs, etc. They also usually sell tools and general accessories, have convenient hours, charge lower prices and can often be found not far from home.

Authorized dealer parts department: This is the best source for parts which are unique to the vehicle and not generally available elsewhere (such as major engine parts, transmission parts, trim pieces, etc.).

Warranty information: If the vehicle is still covered under warranty, be sure that any replacement parts purchased – regardless of the source – do not invalidate the warranty!

To be sure of obtaining the correct parts, have engine and chassis numbers available and, if possible, take the old parts along for positive identification.

Maintenance techniques, tools and working facilities

Maintenance techniques

There are a number of techniques involved in maintenance and repair that will be referred to throughout this manual. Application of these techniques will enable the home mechanic to be more efficient, better organized and capable of performing the various tasks properly, which will ensure that the repair job is thorough and complete.

Fasteners

Fasteners are nuts, bolts, studs and screws used to hold two or more parts together. There are a few things to keep in mind when working with fasteners. Almost all of them use a locking device of some type, either a lockwasher, locknut, locking tab or thread adhesive. All threaded fasteners should be clean and straight, with undamaged threads and undamaged corners on the hex head where the wrench fits. Develop the habit of replacing all damaged nuts and bolts with new ones. Special locknuts with nylon or fiber inserts can only be used once. If they are removed, they lose their locking ability and must be replaced with new ones.

Rusted nuts and bolts should be treated with a penetrating fluid to ease removal and prevent breakage. Some mechanics use turpentine in a spout-type oil can, which works quite well. After applying the rust penetrant, let it work for a few minutes before trying to loosen the nut or bolt. Badly rusted fasteners may have to be chiseled or sawed off or removed with a special nut breaker, available at tool stores.

If a bolt or stud breaks off in an assembly, it can be drilled and removed with a special tool commonly available for this purpose. Most automotive machine shops can perform this task, as well as other repair procedures, such as the repair of threaded holes that have been stripped out.

Flat washers and lockwashers, when removed from an assembly, should always be replaced exactly as removed. Replace any damaged washers with new ones. Never use a lockwasher on any soft metal surface (such as aluminum), thin sheet metal or plastic.

Fastener sizes

For a number of reasons, automobile manufacturers are making wider and wider use of metric fasteners. Therefore, it is important to be able to tell the difference between standard (sometimes called U.S. or SAE) and metric hardware, since they cannot be interchanged.

All bolts, whether standard or metric, are sized according to diameter, thread pitch and length. For example, a standard 1/2 – 13 x 1 bolt is 1/2 inch in diameter, has 13 threads per inch and is 1 inch long. An M12 – 1.75 x 25 metric bolt is 12 mm in diameter, has a thread pitch of 1.75 mm (the distance between threads) and is 25 mm long. The two bolts are nearly identical, and easily confused, but they are not interchangeable.

In addition to the differences in diameter, thread pitch and length, metric and standard bolts can also be distinguished by examining the bolt heads. To begin with, the distance across the flats on a standard bolt head is measured in inches, while the same dimension on a metric bolt is sized in millimeters (the same is true for nuts). As a result, a standard wrench should not be used on a metric bolt and a metric wrench should not be used on a standard bolt. Also, most standard bolts have slashes radiating out from the center of the head to denote the grade or strength of the bolt, which is an indication of the amount of torque that can be applied to it. The greater the number of slashes, the greater the strength of the bolt. Grades 0 through 5 are commonly used on automobiles. Metric bolts have a property class (grade) number, rather than a slash, molded into their heads to indicate bolt strength. In this case, the higher the number, the stronger the bolt. Property class numbers 8.8, 9.8 and 10.9 are commonly used on automobiles.

Strength markings can also be used to distinguish standard hex nuts from metric hex nuts. Many standard nuts have dots stamped into one side, while metric nuts are marked with a number. The greater the number of dots, or the higher the number, the greater the strength of the nut.

Metric studs are also marked on their ends according to property class (grade). Larger studs are numbered (the same as metric bolts), while smaller studs carry a geometric code to denote grade.

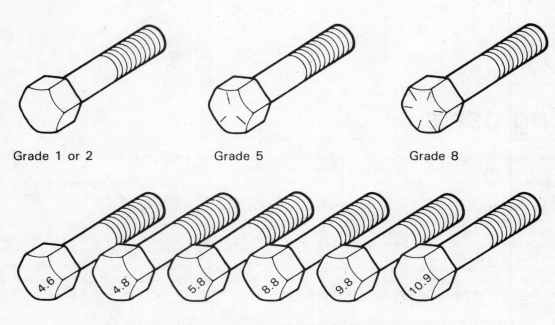

Grade 1 or 2   Grade 5   Grade 8

4.6   4.8   5.8   8.8   9.8   10.9

Bolt strength markings (top – standard/SAE/USS; bottom – metric)

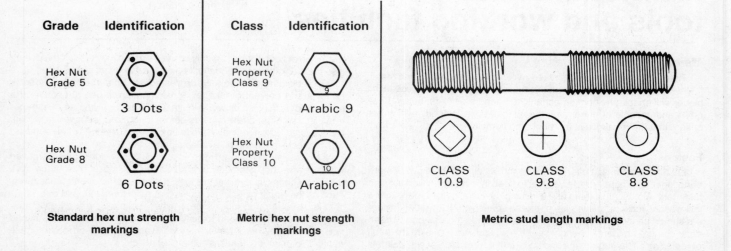

Grade	Identification	Class	Identification
Hex Nut Grade 5	3 Dots	Hex Nut Property Class 9	Arabic 9
Hex Nut Grade 8	6 Dots	Hex Nut Property Class 10	Arabic 10

Standard hex nut strength markings

Metric hex nut strength markings

CLASS 10.9   CLASS 9.8   CLASS 8.8

Metric stud length markings

It should be noted that many fasteners, especially Grades 0 through 2, have no distinguishing marks on them. When such is the case, the only way to determine whether it is standard or metric is to measure the thread pitch or compare it to a known fastener of the same size.

Standard fasteners are often referred to as SAE, as opposed to metric. However, it should be noted that SAE technically refers to a non-metric *fine thread* fastener only. Coarse thread non-metric fasteners are referred to as USS sizes.

Since fasteners of the same size (both standard and metric) may have different strength ratings, be sure to reinstall any bolts, studs or nuts removed from your vehicle in their original locations. Also, when replacing a fastener with a new one, make sure that the new one has a strength rating equal to or greater than the original.

Tightening sequences and procedures

Most threaded fasteners should be tightened to a specific torque value (torque is the twisting force applied to a threaded component such as a nut or bolt). Overtightening the fastener can weaken it and cause it to break, while undertightening can cause it to eventually come loose. Bolts, screws and studs, depending on the material they are made of and their thread diameters, have specific torque values, many of which are noted in the Specifications at the beginning of each Chapter. Be sure to follow the torque recommendations closely. For fasteners not assigned a specific torque, a general torque value chart is presented here as a guide. These torque values are for dry (unlubricated) fasteners threaded into steel or cast iron (not aluminum). As was previously mentioned, the size and grade of a fastener determine the amount of torque that can safely be

Metric thread sizes	Ft-lbs	Nm
M-6	6 to 9	9 to 12
M-8	14 to 21	19 to 28
M-10	28 to 40	38 to 54
M-12	50 to 71	68 to 96
M-14	80 to 140	109 to 154

Pipe thread sizes		
1/8	5 to 8	7 to 10
1/4	12 to 18	17 to 24
3/8	22 to 33	30 to 44
1/2	25 to 35	34 to 47

U.S. thread sizes		
1/4 – 20	6 to 9	9 to 12
5/16 – 18	12 to 18	17 to 24
5/16 – 24	14 to 20	19 to 27
3/8 – 16	22 to 32	30 to 43
3/8 – 24	27 to 38	37 to 51
7/16 – 14	40 to 55	55 to 74
7/16 – 20	40 to 60	55 to 81
1/2 – 13	55 to 80	75 to 108

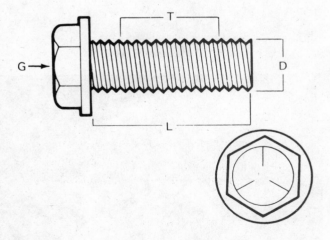

Standard (SAE and USS) bolt dimensions/grade marks

G	Grade marks (bolt length)
L	Length (in inches)
T	Thread pitch (number of threads per inch)
D	Nominal diameter (in inches)

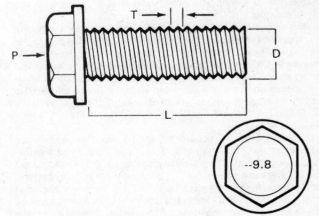

Metric bolt dimensions/grade marks

P	Property class (bolt strength)
L	Length (in millimeters)
T	Thread pitch (distance between threads in millimeters)
D	Diameter

applied to it. The figures listed here are approximate for Grade 2 and Grade 3 fasteners. Higher grades can tolerate higher torque values.

Fasteners laid out in a pattern, such as cylinder head bolts, oil pan bolts, differential cover bolts, etc., must be loosened or tightened in sequence to avoid warping the component. This sequence will normally be shown in the appropriate Chapter. If a specific pattern is not given, the following procedures can be used to prevent warping.

Initially, the bolts or nuts should be assembled finger-tight only. Next, they should be tightened one full turn each, in a criss-cross or diagonal pattern. After each one has been tightened one full turn, return to the first one and tighten them all one-half turn, following the same pattern. Finally, tighten each of them one-quarter turn at a time until each fastener has been tightened to the proper torque. To loosen and remove the fasteners, the procedure would be reversed.

Component disassembly

Component disassembly should be done with care and purpose to help ensure that the parts go back together properly. Always keep track of the sequence in which parts are removed. Make note of special characteristics or marks on parts that can be installed more than one way, such as a grooved thrust washer on a shaft. It is a good idea to lay the disassembled parts out on a clean surface in the order that they were removed. It may also be helpful to make sketches or take instant photos of components before removal.

When removing fasteners from a component, keep track of their locations. Sometimes threading a bolt back in a part, or putting the washers and nut back on a stud, can prevent mix-ups later. If nuts and bolts cannot be returned to their original locations, they should be kept in a compartmented box or a series of small boxes. A cupcake or muffin tin is ideal for this purpose, since each cavity can hold the bolts and nuts from a particular area (i.e. oil pan bolts, valve cover bolts, engine mount bolts, etc.). A pan of this type is especially helpful when working on assemblies with very small parts, such as the carburetor, alternator, valve train or interior dash and trim pieces. The cavities can be marked with paint or tape to identify the contents.

Whenever wiring looms, harnesses or connectors are separated, it is a good idea to identify the two halves with numbered pieces of masking tape so they can be easily reconnected.

Gasket sealing surfaces

Throughout any vehicle, gaskets are used to seal the mating surfaces between two parts and keep lubricants, fluids, vacuum or pressure contained in an assembly.

Many times these gaskets are coated with a liquid or paste-type gasket sealing compound before assembly. Age, heat and pressure can sometimes cause the two parts to stick together so tightly that they are very difficult to separate. Often, the assembly can be loosened by striking it with a soft-face hammer near the mating surfaces. A regular hammer can be used if a block of wood is placed between the hammer and the part. Do not hammer on cast parts or parts that could be easily damaged. With any particularly stubborn part, always recheck to make sure that every fastener has been removed.

Avoid using a screwdriver or bar to pry apart an assembly, as they can easily mar the gasket sealing surfaces of the parts, which must remain smooth. If prying is absolutely necessary, use an old broom handle, but keep in mind that extra clean up will be necessary if the wood splinters.

After the parts are separated, the old gasket must be carefully scraped off and the gasket surfaces cleaned. Stubborn gasket material can be soaked with rust penetrant or treated with a special chemical to soften it so it can be easily scraped off. A scraper can be fashioned from a piece of copper tubing by flattening and sharpening one end. Copper is recommended because it is usually softer than the surfaces to be scraped, which reduces the chance of gouging the part. Some gaskets can be removed with a wire brush, but regardless of the method used, the mating surfaces must be left clean and smooth. If for some reason the gasket surface is gouged, then a gasket sealer thick enough to fill scratches will have to be used during reassembly of the components. For most applications, a non-drying (or semi-drying) gasket sealer should be used.

Hose removal tips

Warning: *If the vehicle is equipped with air conditioning, do not disconnect any of the A/C hoses without first having the system depressurized by a dealer service department or a service station.*

Hose removal precautions closely parallel gasket removal precautions. Avoid scratching or gouging the surface that the hose mates against or the connection may leak. This is especially true for radiator hoses. Because of various chemical reactions, the rubber in hoses can bond itself to the metal spigot that the hose fits over. To remove a hose, first loosen the hose clamps that secure it to the spigot. Then, with slip-joint pliers, grab the hose at the clamp and rotate it around the spigot. Work it back and forth until it is completely free, then pull it off. Silicone or other lubricants will ease removal if they can be applied between the hose and the outside of the spigot. Apply the same lubricant to the inside of the hose and the outside of the spigot to simplify installation.

As a last resort (and if the hose is to be replaced with a new one anyway), the rubber can be slit with a knife and the hose peeled from the spigot. If this must be done, be careful that the metal connection is not damaged.

If a hose clamp is broken or damaged, do not reuse it. Wire-type clamps usually weaken with age, so it is a good idea to replace them with screw-type clamps whenever a hose is removed.

Tools

A selection of good tools is a basic requirement for anyone who plans to maintain and repair his or her own vehicle. For the owner who has few tools, the initial investment might seem high, but when compared to the spiraling costs of professional auto maintenance and repair, it is a wise one.

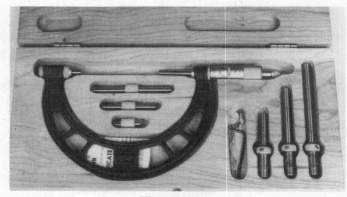

Micrometer set

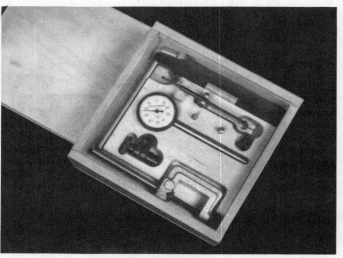

Dial indicator set

Dial Caliper

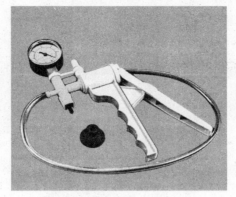

Hand-operated vacuum pump

Timing light

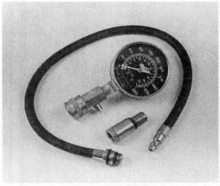

Compression gauge with spark plug hole adapter

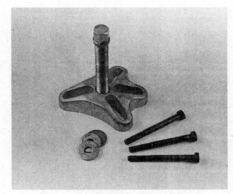

Damper/steering wheel puller

General purpose puller

Hydraulic lifter removal tool

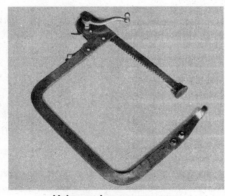

Valve spring compressor

Valve spring compressor

Ridge reamer

Piston ring groove cleaning tool

Ring removal/installation tool

Ring compressor

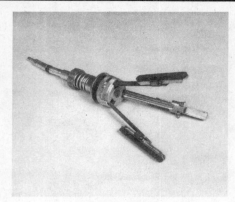

Cylinder hone

Brake hold-down tool

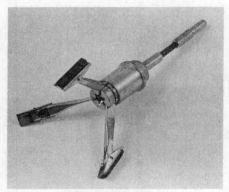

Brake cylinder hone

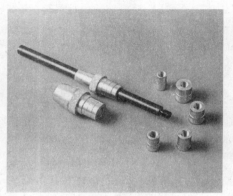

Clutch plate alignment tool

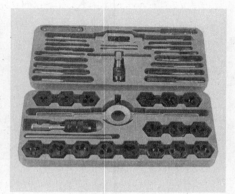

Tap and die set

To help the owner decide which tools are needed to perform the tasks detailed in this manual, the following tool lists are offered: *Maintenance and minor repair, Repair/overhaul* and *Special*.

The newcomer to practical mechanics should start off with the maintenance and minor repair tool kit, which is adequate for the simpler jobs performed on a vehicle. Then, as confidence and experience grow, the owner can tackle more difficult tasks, buying additional tools as they are needed. Eventually the basic kit will be expanded into the repair and overhaul tool set. Over a period of time, the experienced do-it-yourselfer will assemble a tool set complete enough for most repair and overhaul procedures and will add tools from the special category when it is felt that the expense is justified by the frequency of use.

Maintenance and minor repair tool kit

The tools in this list should be considered the minimum required for performance of routine maintenance, servicing and minor repair work. We recommend the purchase of combination wrenches (box-end and open-end combined in one wrench). While more expensive than open end wrenches, they offer the advantages of both types of wrench.

Combination wrench set (1/4-inch to 1 inch or 6 mm to 19 mm)
Adjustable wrench, 8 inch
Spark plug wrench with rubber insert
Spark plug gap adjusting tool
Feeler gauge set
Brake bleeder wrench
Standard screwdriver (5/16-inch x 6 inch)
Phillips screwdriver (No. 2 x 6 inch)
Combination pliers – 6 inch
Hacksaw and assortment of blades
Tire pressure gauge
Grease gun
Oil can
Fine emery cloth
Wire brush

Battery post and cable cleaning tool
Oil filter wrench
Funnel (medium size)
Safety goggles
Jackstands(2)
Drain pan

Note: *If basic tune-ups are going to be part of routine maintenance, it will be necessary to purchase a good quality stroboscopic timing light and combination tachometer/dwell meter. Although they are included in the list of special tools, it is mentioned here because they are absolutely necessary for tuning most vehicles properly.*

Repair and overhaul tool set

These tools are essential for anyone who plans to perform major repairs and are in addition to those in the maintenance and minor repair tool kit. Included is a comprehensive set of sockets which, though expensive, are invaluable because of their versatility, especially when various extensions and drives are available. We recommend the 1/2-inch drive over the 3/8-inch drive. Although the larger drive is bulky and more expensive, it has the capacity of accepting a very wide range of large sockets. Ideally, however, the mechanic should have a 3/8-inch drive set and a 1/2-inch drive set.

Socket set(s)
Reversible ratchet
Extension – 10 inch
Universal joint
Torque wrench (same size drive as sockets)
Ball peen hammer – 8 ounce
Soft-face hammer (plastic/rubber)
Standard screwdriver (1/4-inch x 6 inch)
Standard screwdriver (stubby – 5/16-inch)
Phillips screwdriver (No. 3 x 8 inch)
Phillips screwdriver (stubby – No. 2)

Pliers – vise grip
Pliers – lineman's
Pliers – needle nose
Pliers – snap-ring (internal and external)
Cold chisel – 1/2-inch
Scribe
Scraper (made from flattened copper tubing)
Centerpunch
Pin punches (1/16, 1/8, 3/16-inch)
Steel rule/straightedge – 12 inch
Allen wrench set (1/8 to 3/8-inch or 4 mm to 10 mm)
A selection of files
Wire brush (large)
Jackstands (second set)
Jack (scissor or hydraulic type)

Note: *Another tool which is often useful is an electric drill with a chuck capacity of 3/8-inch and a set of good quality drill bits.*

Special tools

The tools in this list include those which are not used regularly, are expensive to buy, or which need to be used in accordance with their manufacturer's instructions. Unless these tools will be used frequently, it is not very economical to purchase many of them. A consideration would be to split the cost and use between yourself and a friend or friends. In addition, most of these tools can be obtained from a tool rental shop on a temporary basis.

This list primarily contains only those tools and instruments widely available to the public, and not those special tools produced by the vehicle manufacturer for distribution to dealer service departments. Occasionally, references to the manufacturer's special tools are included in the text of this manual. Generally, an alternative method of doing the job without the special tool is offered. However, sometimes there is no alternative to their use. Where this is the case, and the tool cannot be purchased or borrowed, the work should be turned over to the dealer service department or an automotive repair shop.

Valve spring compressor
Piston ring groove cleaning tool
Piston ring compressor
Piston ring installation tool
Cylinder compression gauge
Cylinder ridge reamer
Cylinder surfacing hone
Cylinder bore gauge
Micrometers and/or dial calipers
Hydraulic lifter removal tool
Balljoint separator
Universal-type puller
Impact screwdriver
Dial indicator set
Stroboscopic timing light (inductive pick-up)
Hand operated vacuum/pressure pump
Tachometer/dwell meter
Universal electrical multimeter
Cable hoist
Brake spring removal and installation tools
Floor jack

Buying tools

For the do-it-yourselfer who is just starting to get involved in vehicle maintenance and repair, there are a number of options available when purchasing tools. If maintenance and minor repair is the extent of the work to be done, the purchase of individual tools is satisfactory. If, on the other hand, extensive work is planned, it would be a good idea to purchase a modest tool set from one of the large retail chain stores. A set can usually be bought at a substantial savings over the individual tool prices, and they often come with a tool box. As additional tools are needed, add–on sets, individual tools and a larger tool box can be purchased to expand the tool selection. Building a tool set gradually allows the cost of the tools to be spread over a longer period of time and gives the mechanic the freedom to choose only those tools that will actually be used.

Tool stores will often be the only source of some of the special tools that are needed, but regardless of where tools are bought, try to avoid cheap ones, especially when buying screwdrivers and sockets, because they won't last very long. The expense involved in replacing cheap tools will eventually be greater than the initial cost of quality tools.

Care and maintenance of tools

Good tools are expensive, so it makes sense to treat them with respect. Keep them clean and in usable condition and store them properly when not in use. Always wipe off any dirt, grease or metal chips before putting them away. Never leave tools lying around in the work area. Upon completion of a job, always check closely under the hood for tools that may have been left there so they won't get lost during a test drive.

Some tools, such as screwdrivers, pliers, wrenches and sockets, can be hung on a panel mounted on the garage or workshop wall, while others should be kept in a tool box or tray. Measuring instruments, gauges, meters, etc. must be carefully stored where they cannot be damaged by weather or impact from other tools.

When tools are used with care and stored properly, they will last a very long time. Even with the best of care, though, tools will wear out if used frequently. When a tool is damaged or worn out, replace it. Subsequent jobs will be safer and more enjoyable if you do.

Working facilities

Not to be overlooked when discussing tools is the workshop. If anything more than routine maintenance is to be carried out, some sort of suitable work area is essential.

It is understood, and appreciated, that many home mechanics do not have a good workshop or garage available, and end up removing an engine or doing major repairs outside. It is recommended, however, that the overhaul or repair be completed under the cover of a roof.

A clean, flat workbench or table of comfortable working height is an absolute necessity. The workbench should be equipped with a vise that has a jaw opening of at least four inches.

As mentioned previously, some clean, dry storage space is also required for tools, as well as the lubricants, fluids, cleaning solvents, etc. which soon become necessary.

Sometimes waste oil and fluids, drained from the engine or cooling system during normal maintenance or repairs, present a disposal problem. To avoid pouring them on the ground or into a sewage system, pour the used fluids into large containers, seal them with caps and take them to an authorized disposal site or recycling center. Plastic jugs, such as old antifreeze containers, are ideal for this purpose.

Always keep a supply of old newspapers and clean rags available. Old towels are excellent for mopping up spills. Many mechanics use rolls of paper towels for most work because they are readily available and disposable. To help keep the area under the vehicle clean, a large cardboard box can be cut open and flattened to protect the garage or shop floor.

Whenever working over a painted surface, such as when leaning over a fender to service something under the hood, always cover it with an old blanket or bedspread to protect the finish. Vinyl covered pads, made especially for this purpose, are available at auto parts stores.

Jacking and towing

Jacking

Warning: *The jack supplied with the vehicle should only be used for raising the vehicle when changing a tire or placing jackstands under the frame. Never work under the vehicle or start the engine while the jack is being used as the only means of support.*

The vehicle must be on a level surface with the wheels blocked and the transmission in Park (automatic) or Reverse (manual). Apply the parking brake if the front of the vehicle must be raised. Make sure no one is in the vehicle as it's being raised with the jack.

Remove the jack, lug nut wrench and spare tire (if needed) from stowage. If a tire is being replaced, use the lug wrench to remove the wheel cover (if equipped). **Warning:** *Wheel covers may have sharp edges – be very careful not to cut yourself.* Loosen the lug nuts one-half turn, but leave them in place until the tire is raised off the ground. **Note:** *Some models have one locking lug nut that must be loosened with a special anti-theft wrench adapter.*

Position the jack under the vehicle at the jacking point **(see illustrations)**. Ford recommends positioning the jack under the axles, shock absorber or jacking bracket, as close to the wheel to be removed as possible. Note that on some 2WD models a special jacking pin is provided on the front axle. This pin should only be used with the factory-supplied jack or a jack with a shaft and cap that fit firmly in the bracket.

Turn the jack handle clockwise until the tire clears the ground. Remove the lug nuts and pull the tire off. Clean the mating surfaces of the hub and wheel, then install the spare. Replace the lug nuts with the bevelled edges facing in and tighten them snugly. Don't attempt to tighten them completely until the vehicle is lowered or it could slip off the jack.

Turn the jack handle counterclockwise to lower the vehicle. Remove the jack and tighten the lug nuts in a criss-cross pattern. If possible, tighten the nuts with a torque wrench (see Chapter 1 for the torque figures). If you don't have access to a torque wrench, have the nuts checked by a service station or repair shop as soon as possible.

Stow the tire, jack and wrench and unblock the wheels.

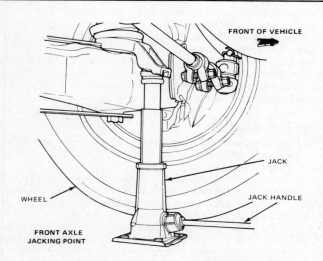

Front axle jacking point – 1983 and 1984 models

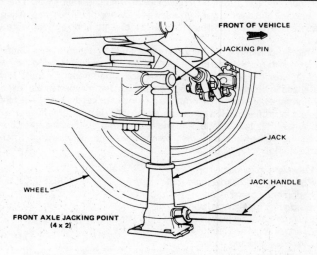

Front axle jacking point – 1985 through 1988 2WD models

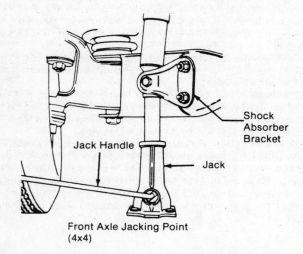

Front axle jacking point – 1985 through 1988 4WD models

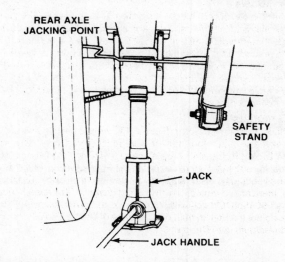

Rear axle jacking and support points (all models)

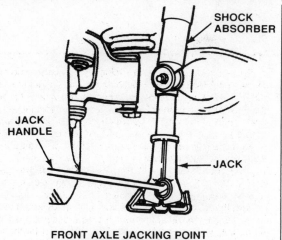

FRONT AXLE JACKING POINT
RANGER AND BRONCO II
BUILT AFTER JAN. 1989

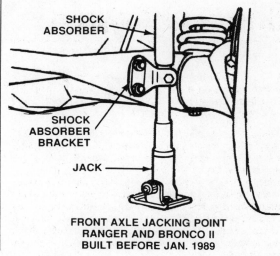

FRONT AXLE JACKING POINT
RANGER AND BRONCO II
BUILT BEFORE JAN. 1989

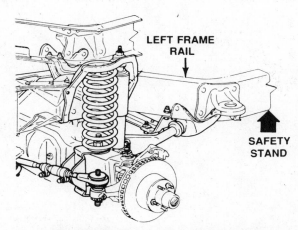

Front axle jacking points – 1989 and later models

Towing

2WD models

The vehicle should be towed with the rear (drive) wheels off the ground, if possible. The transmission must be in Neutral. Do not tow the vehicle faster than 35 mph or farther than 50 miles with the rear wheels on the ground. If the vehicle must be towed with the rear wheels on the ground, and it must be towed more than 50 miles or faster than 35 mph, it is recommended the driveshaft be removed (see Chapter 8). There is not distance limit when towing with the driveshaft removed, but the maximum speed is 50 mph.

4WD models

Place the transmission in Neutral. On vehicles with a lever-operated transfer case, place the transfer case in Neutral. On vehicles with the Touch Drive electric shift transfer case, place the transfer case in 2H. Manual locking hubs should be set in the Free position. Automatic locking hubs should be disenged. On vehicles with a lever-operated transfer case, there are no restrictions on towing distance, but speed should not exceed 50 mph. On vehicles with the Touch Drive electric shift transfer case, do not exceed 35 mph or a distance of 50 miles unless you remove the driveshafts (see Chapter 8).

All models

Be sure the parking brake is released. If the vehicle will be towed with the front wheels on the ground, clamp the steering wheel in the straight-ahead position with a towing clamp designed for the purpose. Do not use the vehicle's steering lock; the ignition key must be in the unlocked position.

The transmission, transfer case (if equipped) and differential must be in working condition. If they are not, the vehicle must be towed with the front wheels on a dolly.

Equipment specifically designed for towing should be used. It should be attached to the main structural members of the vehicle, not the bumpers or brackets. Do not use J-hooks at either end of the vehicle. They will damage steering and suspension components.

While towing, don't exceed 50 mph (35 mph on rough roads).

Safety is a major consideration while towing and all applicable state and local laws must be obeyed. A safety chain system must be used at all times. Route the chain so it does not come into contact with suspension, steering, brake or cooling system components or the air dam. Remember that power steering and power brakes will not work with the engine off.

Booster battery (jump) starting

Observe these precautions when using a booster battery to start a vehicle:

  a) Before connecting the booster battery, make sure the ignition switch is in the Off position.
  b) Turn off the lights, heater and other electrical loads.
  c) Your eyes should be shielded. Safety goggles are a good idea.
  d) Make sure the booster battery is the same voltage as the dead one in the vehicle.
  e) The two vehicles MUST NOT TOUCH each other!
  f) Make sure the transmission is in Neutral (manual) or Park (automatic).
  g) If the booster battery is not a maintenance-free type, remove the vent caps and lay a cloth over the vent holes.

Connect the red jumper cable to the positive (+) terminals of each battery.

Connect one end of the black jumper cable to the negative (–) terminal of the booster battery. The other end of this cable should be connected to a good ground on the vehicle to be started, such as a bolt or bracket on the engine block **(see illustration)**. Make sure the cable will not come into contact with the fan, drivebelts or other moving parts of the engine.

Start the engine using the booster battery, then, with the engine running at idle speed, disconnect the jumper cables in the reverse order of connection.

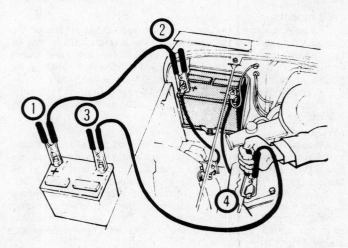

Make the booster battery cable connections in the numerical order shown (note that the negative cable of the booster battery is NOT attached to the negative terminal of the dead battery)

Automotive chemicals and lubricants

A number of automotive chemicals and lubricants are available for use during vehicle maintenance and repair. They include a wide variety of products ranging from cleaning solvents and degreasers to lubricants and protective sprays for rubber, plastic and vinyl.

Cleaners

Carburetor cleaner and choke cleaner is a strong solvent for gum, varnish and carbon. Most carburetor cleaners leave a dry-type lubricant film which will not harden or gum up. Because of this film it is not recommended for use on electrical components.

Brake system cleaner is used to remove grease and brake fluid from the brake system, where clean surfaces are absolutely necessary. It leaves no residue and often eliminates brake squeal caused by contaminants.

Electrical cleaner removes oxidation, corrosion and carbon deposits from electrical contacts, restoring full current flow. It can also be used to clean spark plugs, carburetor jets, voltage regulators and other parts where an oil-free surface is desired.

Demoisturants remove water and moisture from electrical components such as alternators, voltage regulators, electrical connectors and fuse blocks. They are non-conductive, non-corrosive and non-flammable.

Degreasers are heavy-duty solvents used to remove grease from the outside of the engine and from chassis components. They can be sprayed or brushed on and, depending on the type, are rinsed off either with water or solvent.

Lubricants

Motor oil is the lubricant formulated for use in engines. It normally contains a wide variety of additives to prevent corrosion and reduce foaming and wear. Motor oil comes in various weights (viscosity ratings) from 5 to 80. The recommended weight of the oil depends on the season, temperature and the demands on the engine. Light oil is used in cold climates and under light load conditions. Heavy oil is used in hot climates and where high loads are encountered. Multi-viscosity oils are designed to have characteristics of both light and heavy oils and are available in a number of weights from 5W-20 to 20W-50.

Gear oil is designed to be used in differentials, manual transmissions and other areas where high-temperature lubrication is required.

Chassis and wheel bearing grease is a heavy grease used where increased loads and friction are encountered, such as for wheel bearings, balljoints, tie-rod ends and universal joints.

High-temperature wheel bearing grease is designed to withstand the extreme temperatures encountered by wheel bearings in disc brake equipped vehicles. It usually contains molybdenum disulfide (moly), which is a dry-type lubricant.

White grease is a heavy grease for metal-to-metal applications where water is a problem. White grease stays soft under both low and high temperatures (usually from −100 to +190-degrees F), and will not wash off or dilute in the presence of water.

Assembly lube is a special extreme pressure lubricant, usually containing moly, used to lubricate high-load parts (such as main and rod bearings and cam lobes) for initial start-up of a new engine. The assembly lube lubricates the parts without being squeezed out or washed away until the engine oiling system begins to function.

Silicone lubricants are used to protect rubber, plastic, vinyl and nylon parts.

Graphite lubricants are used where oils cannot be used due to contamination problems, such as in locks. The dry graphite will lubricate metal parts while remaining uncontaminated by dirt, water, oil or acids. It is electrically conductive and will not foul electrical contacts in locks such as the ignition switch.

Moly penetrants loosen and lubricate frozen, rusted and corroded fasteners and prevent future rusting or freezing.

Heat-sink grease is a special electrically non-conductive grease that is used for mounting electronic ignition modules where it is essential that heat is transferred away from the module.

Sealants

RTV sealant is one of the most widely used gasket compounds. Made from silicone, RTV is air curing, it seals, bonds, waterproofs, fills surface irregularities, remains flexible, doesn't shrink, is relatively easy to remove, and is used as a supplementary sealer with almost all low and medium temperature gaskets.

Anaerobic sealant is much like RTV in that it can be used either to seal gaskets or to form gaskets by itself. It remains flexible, is solvent resistant and fills surface imperfections. The difference between an anaerobic sealant and an RTV-type sealant is in the curing. RTV cures when exposed to air, while an anaerobic sealant cures only in the absence of air. This means that an anaerobic sealant cures only after the assembly of parts, sealing them together.

Thread and pipe sealant is used for sealing hydraulic and pneumatic fittings and vacuum lines. It is usually made from a Teflon compound, and comes in a spray, a paint-on liquid and as a wrap-around tape.

Chemicals

Anti-seize compound prevents seizing, galling, cold welding, rust and corrosion in fasteners. High-temperature anti-seize, usually made with copper and graphite lubricants, is used for exhaust system and exhaust manifold bolts.

Anaerobic locking compounds are used to keep fasteners from vibrating or working loose and cure only after installation, in the absence of air. Medium strength locking compound is used for small nuts, bolts and screws that may be removed later. High-strength locking compound is for large nuts, bolts and studs which aren't removed on a regular basis.

Oil additives range from viscosity index improvers to chemical treatments that claim to reduce internal engine friction. It should be noted that most oil manufacturers caution against using additives with their oils.

Gas additives perform several functions, depending on their chemical makeup. They usually contain solvents that help dissolve gum and varnish that build up on carburetor, fuel injection and intake parts. They also serve to break down carbon deposits that form on the inside surfaces of the combustion chambers. Some additives contain upper cylinder lubricants for valves and piston rings, and others contain chemicals to remove condensation from the gas tank.

Miscellaneous

Brake fluid is specially formulated hydraulic fluid that can withstand the heat and pressure encountered in brake systems. Care must be taken so this fluid does not come in contact with painted surfaces or plastics. An opened container should always be resealed to prevent contamination by water or dirt.

Weatherstrip adhesive is used to bond weatherstripping around doors, windows and trunk lids. It is sometimes used to attach trim pieces.

Undercoating is a petroleum-based, tar-like substance that is designed to protect metal surfaces on the underside of the vehicle from corrosion. It also acts as a sound-deadening agent by insulating the bottom of the vehicle.

Waxes and polishes are used to help protect painted and plated surfaces from the weather. Different types of paint may require the use of different types of wax and polish. Some polishes utilize a chemical or abrasive cleaner to help remove the top layer of oxidized (dull) paint on older vehicles. In recent years many non-wax polishes that contain a wide variety of chemicals such as polymers and silicones have been introduced. These non-wax polishes are usually easier to apply and last longer than conventional waxes and polishes.

Safety first!

Regardless of how enthusiastic you may be about getting on with the job at hand, take the time to ensure that your safety is not jeopardized. A moment's lack of attention can result in an accident, as can failure to observe certain simple safety precautions. The possibility of an accident will always exist, and the following points should not be considered a comprehensive list of all dangers. Rather, they are intended to make you aware of the risks and to encourage a safety conscious approach to all work you carry out on your vehicle.

Essential DOs and DON'Ts

DON'T rely on a jack when working under the vehicle. Always use approved jackstands to support the weight of the vehicle and place them under the recommended lift or support points.

DON'T attempt to loosen extremely tight fasteners (i.e. wheel lug nuts) while the vehicle is on a jack – it may fall.

DON'T start the engine without first making sure that the transmission is in Neutral (or Park where applicable) and the parking brake is set.

DON'T remove the radiator cap from a hot cooling system – let it cool or cover it with a cloth and release the pressure gradually.

DON'T attempt to drain the engine oil until you are sure it has cooled to the point that it will not burn you.

DON'T touch any part of the engine or exhaust system until it has cooled sufficiently to avoid burns.

DON'T siphon toxic liquids such as gasoline, antifreeze and brake fluid by mouth, or allow them to remain on your skin.

DON'T inhale brake lining dust – it is potentially hazardous (see *Asbestos* below)

DON'T allow spilled oil or grease to remain on the floor – wipe it up before someone slips on it.

DON'T use loose fitting wrenches or other tools which may slip and cause injury.

DON'T push on wrenches when loosening or tightening nuts or bolts. Always try to pull the wrench toward you. If the situation calls for pushing the wrench away, push with an open hand to avoid scraped knuckles if the wrench should slip.

DON'T attempt to lift a heavy component alone – get someone to help you.

DON'T rush or take unsafe shortcuts to finish a job.

DON'T allow children or animals in or around the vehicle while you are working on it.

DO wear eye protection when using power tools such as a drill, sander, bench grinder, etc. and when working under a vehicle.

DO keep loose clothing and long hair well out of the way of moving parts.

DO make sure that any hoist used has a safe working load rating adequate for the job.

DO get someone to check on you periodically when working alone on a vehicle.

DO carry out work in a logical sequence and make sure that everything is correctly assembled and tightened.

DO keep chemicals and fluids tightly capped and out of the reach of children and pets.

DO remember that your vehicle's safety affects that of yourself and others. If in doubt on any point, get professional advice.

Asbestos

Certain friction, insulating, sealing, and other products – such as brake linings, brake bands, clutch linings, torque converters, gaskets, etc. – contain asbestos. *Extreme care must be taken to avoid inhalation of dust from such products, since it is hazardous to health*. If in doubt, assume that they *do* contain asbestos.

Fire

Remember at all times that gasoline is highly flammable. Never smoke or have any kind of open flame around when working on a vehicle. But the risk does not end there. A spark caused by an electrical short circuit, by two metal surfaces contacting each other, or even by static electricity built up in your body under certain conditions, can ignite gasoline vapors, which in a confined space are highly explosive. Do not, under any circumstances, use gasoline for cleaning parts. Use an approved safety solvent.

Always disconnect the battery ground (–) cable *at the battery* before working on any part of the fuel system or electrical system. Never risk spilling fuel on a hot engine or exhaust component.

It is strongly recommended that a fire extinguisher suitable for use on fuel and electrical fires be kept handy in the garage or workshop at all times. Never try to extinguish a fuel or electrical fire with water.

Fumes

Certain fumes are highly toxic and can quickly cause unconsciousness and even death if inhaled to any extent. Gasoline vapor falls into this category, as do the vapors from some cleaning solvents. Any draining or pouring of such volatile fluids should be done in a well ventilated area.

When using cleaning fluids and solvents, read the instructions on the container carefully. Never use materials from unmarked containers.

Never run the engine in an enclosed space, such as a garage. Exhaust fumes contain carbon monoxide, which is extremely poisonous. If you need to run the engine, always do so in the open air, or at least have the rear of the vehicle outside the work area.

If you are fortunate enough to have the use of an inspection pit, never drain or pour gasoline and never run the engine while the vehicle is over the pit. The fumes, being heavier than air, will concentrate in the pit with possibly lethal results.

The battery

Never create a spark or allow a bare light bulb near a battery. They normally give off a certain amount of hydrogen gas, which is highly explosive.

Always disconnect the battery ground (–) cable *at the battery* before working on the fuel or electrical systems.

If possible, loosen the filler caps or cover when charging the battery from an external source (this does not apply to sealed or maintenance-free batteries). Do not charge at an excessive rate or the battery may burst.

Take care when adding water to a non maintenance-free battery and when carrying a battery. The electrolyte, even when diluted, is very corrosive and should not be allowed to contact clothing or skin.

Always wear eye protection when cleaning the battery to prevent the caustic deposits from entering your eyes.

Household current

When using an electric power tool, inspection light, etc., which operates on household current, always make sure that the tool is correctly connected to its plug and that, where necessary, it is properly grounded. Do not use such items in damp conditions and, again, do not create a spark or apply excessive heat in the vicinity of fuel or fuel vapor.

Secondary ignition system voltage

A severe electric shock can result from touching certain parts of the ignition system (such as the spark plug wires) when the engine is running or being cranked, particularly if components are damp or the insulation is defective. In the case of an electronic ignition system, the secondary system voltage is much higher and could prove fatal.

Conversion factors

Length (distance)
Inches (in)	X	25.4	= Millimetres (mm)	X 0.0394	= Inches (in)
Feet (ft)	X	0.305	= Metres (m)	X 3.281	= Feet (ft)
Miles	X	1.609	= Kilometres (km)	X 0.621	= Miles

Volume (capacity)
Cubic inches (cu in; in^3)	X	16.387	= Cubic centimetres (cc; cm^3)	X 0.061	= Cubic inches (cu in; in^3)
Imperial pints (Imp pt)	X	0.568	= Litres (l)	X 1.76	= Imperial pints (Imp pt)
Imperial quarts (Imp qt)	X	1.137	= Litres (l)	X 0.88	= Imperial quarts (Imp qt)
Imperial quarts (Imp qt)	X	1.201	= US quarts (US qt)	X 0.833	= Imperial quarts (Imp qt)
US quarts (US qt)	X	0.946	= Litres (l)	X 1.057	= US quarts (US qt)
Imperial gallons (Imp gal)	X	4.546	= Litres (l)	X 0.22	= Imperial gallons (Imp gal)
Imperial gallons (Imp gal)	X	1.201	= US gallons (US gal)	X 0.833	= Imperial gallons (Imp gal)
US gallons (US gal)	X	3.785	= Litres (l)	X 0.264	= US gallons (US gal)

Mass (weight)
Ounces (oz)	X	28.35	= Grams (g)	X 0.035	= Ounces (oz)
Pounds (lb)	X	0.454	= Kilograms (kg)	X 2.205	= Pounds (lb)

Force
Ounces-force (ozf; oz)	X	0.278	= Newtons (N)	X 3.6	= Ounces-force (ozf; oz)
Pounds-force (lbf; lb)	X	4.448	= Newtons (N)	X 0.225	= Pounds-force (lbf; lb)
Newtons (N)	X	0.1	= Kilograms-force (kgf; kg)	X 9.81	= Newtons (N)

Pressure
Pounds-force per square inch (psi; lbf/in^2; lb/in^2)	X	0.070	= Kilograms-force per square centimetre (kgf/cm^2; kg/cm^2)	X 14.223	= Pounds-force per square inch (psi; lbf/in^2; lb/in^2)
Pounds-force per square inch (psi; lbf/in^2; lb/in^2)	X	0.068	= Atmospheres (atm)	X 14.696	= Pounds-force per square inch (psi; lbf/in^2; lb/in^2)
Pounds-force per square inch (psi; lbf/in^2; lb/in^2)	X	0.069	= Bars	X 14.5	= Pounds-force per square inch (psi; lbf/in^2; lb/in^2)
Pounds-force per square inch (psi; lbf/in^2; lb/in^2)	X	6.895	= Kilopascals (kPa)	X 0.145	= Pounds-force per square inch (psi; lbf/in^2; lb/in^2)
Kilopascals (kPa)	X	0.01	= Kilograms-force per square centimetre (kgf/cm^2; kg/cm^2)	X 98.1	= Kilopascals (kPa)

Torque (moment of force)
Pounds-force inches (lbf in; lb in)	X	1.152	= Kilograms-force centimetre (kgf cm; kg cm)	X 0.868	= Pounds-force inches (lbf in; lb in)
Pounds-force inches (lbf in; lb in)	X	0.113	= Newton metres (Nm)	X 8.85	= Pounds-force inches (lbf in; lb in)
Pounds-force inches (lbf in; lb in)	X	0.083	= Pounds-force feet (lbf ft; lb ft)	X 12	= Pounds-force inches (lbf in; lb in)
Pounds-force feet (lbf ft; lb ft)	X	0.138	= Kilograms-force metres (kgf m; kg m)	X 7.233	= Pounds-force feet (lbf ft; lb ft)
Pounds-force feet (lbf ft; lb ft)	X	1.356	= Newton metres (Nm)	X 0.738	= Pounds-force feet (lbf ft; lb ft)
Newton metres (Nm)	X	0.102	= Kilograms-force metres (kgf m; kg m)	X 9.804	= Newton metres (Nm)

Power
Horsepower (hp)	X	745.7	= Watts (W)	X 0.0013	= Horsepower (hp)

Velocity (speed)
Miles per hour (miles/hr; mph)	X	1.609	= Kilometres per hour (km/hr; kph)	X 0.621	= Miles per hour (miles/hr; mph)

Fuel consumption*
Miles per gallon, Imperial (mpg)	X	0.354	= Kilometres per litre (km/l)	X 2.825	= Miles per gallon, Imperial (mpg)
Miles per gallon, US (mpg)	X	0.425	= Kilometres per litre (km/l)	X 2.352	= Miles per gallon, US (mpg)

Temperature
Degrees Fahrenheit = (°C x 1.8) + 32   Degrees Celsius (Degrees Centigrade; °C) = (°F - 32) x 0.56

*It is common practice to convert from miles per gallon (mpg) to litres/100 kilometres (l/100km), where mpg (Imperial) x l/100 km = 282 and mpg (US) x l/100 km = 235

Troubleshooting

Contents

This Section provides an easy reference guide to the more common problems which may occur during the operation of your vehicle. These problems and possible causes are grouped under various components or systems; i.e. Engine, Cooling System, etc., and also refer to the Chapter and/or Section which deals with the problem.

Remember that successful troubleshooting is not a mysterious black art practiced only by professional mechanics. It's simply the result of a bit of knowledge combined with an intelligent, systematic approach to the problem. Always work by a process of elimination, starting with the simplest solution and working through to the most complex – and never overlook the obvious. Anyone can forget to fill the gas tank or leave the lights on overnight, so don't assume that you are above such oversights.

Finally, always get clear in your mind why a problem has occurred and take steps to ensure that it doesn't happen again. If the electrical system fails because of a poor connection, check all other connections in the system to make sure that they don't fail as well. If a particular fuse continues to blow, find out why – don't just go on replacing fuses. Remember, failure of a small component can often be indicative of potential failure or incorrect functioning of a more important component or system.

Engine

1 Engine will not rotate when attempting to start

1   Battery terminal connections loose or corroded. Check the cable terminals at the battery. Tighten the cable or remove corrosion as necessary.
2   Battery discharged or faulty. If the cable connections are clean and tight on the battery posts, turn the key to the On position and switch on the headlights and/or windshield wipers. If they fail to function, the battery is discharged.
3   Automatic transmission not completely engaged in Park or Neutral or clutch pedal not completely depressed.
4   Broken, loose or disconnected wiring in the starting circuit. Inspect all wiring and connectors at the battery, starter solenoid and ignition switch.
5   Starter motor pinion jammed in flywheel ring gear. If manual transmission, place transmission in gear and rock the vehicle to manually turn the engine. Remove starter and inspect pinion and flywheel at earliest convenience (Chapter 5).
6   Starter solenoid faulty (Chapter 5).
7   Starter motor faulty (Chapter 5).
8   Ignition switch faulty (Chapter 12).

2 Engine rotates but will not start

1   Fuel tank empty.
2   Fault in the carburetor or fuel injection system (Chapter 4).
3   Battery discharged (engine rotates slowly). Check the operation of electrical components as described in the previous Section.
4   Battery terminal connections loose or corroded (see previous Section).
5   Fuel pump faulty or fuel pump inertia switch needs resetting (Chapter 4).
6   Excessive moisture on, or damage to, ignition components (see Chapter 5).
7   Worn, faulty or incorrectly gapped spark plugs (Chapter 1).
8   Broken, loose or disconnected wiring in the starting circuit (see previous Section).
9   Distributor loose, causing ignition timing to change (distributor-equipped models only). Turn the distributor as necessary to start the engine, then set the ignition timing as soon as possible (Chapter 5).
10 Broken, loose or disconnected wires at the ignition coil or faulty coil (Chapter 5).

3 Starter motor operates without rotating engine

1   Starter pinion sticking. Remove the starter (Chapter 5) and inspect.
2   Starter pinion or flywheel teeth worn or broken. Remove the flywheel/driveplate access cover and inspect.

4 Engine hard to start when cold

1   Battery discharged or low. Check as described in Section 1.
2   Fault in the fuel or electrical systems (Chapters 4 and 5).
3   Carburetor (if equipped) in need of overhaul (Chapter 4).
4   Distributor rotor (if equipped) carbon tracked and/or damaged (Chapters 1 and 5).
5   Choke control stuck or inoperative (carbureted models) (Chapters 1 and 4).

5 Engine hard to start when hot

1   Air filter clogged (Chapter 1).

2   Fault in the fuel or electrical systems (Chapters 4 and 5).
3   Fuel not reaching the carburetor or injectors (see Chapter 4).

6 Starter motor noisy or excessively rough in engagement

1   Pinion or flywheel gear teeth worn or broken. Remove the cover at the rear of the engine (if so equipped) and inspect.
2   Starter motor mounting bolts loose or missing.

7 Engine starts but stops immediately

1   Loose or faulty electrical connections at distributor, coil or alternator.
2   Fault in the fuel or electrical systems (Chapters 4 and 5).
3   Insufficient fuel reaching the carburetor (carburetor-equipped models). Check the fuel pump (Chapter 4).
4   Vacuum leak at the gasket surfaces of the intake manifold or carburetor/throttle body. Make sure all mounting bolts/nuts are tightened securely and all vacuum hoses connected to the carburetor and manifold are positioned properly and in good condition.

8 Engine lopes while idling or idles erratically

1   Vacuum leakage. Check the mounting bolts/nuts at the carburetor/throttle body and intake manifold for tightness. Make sure all vacuum hoses are connected and in good condition. Use a stethoscope or a length of fuel hose held against your ear to listen for vacuum leaks while the engine is running. A hissing sound will be heard. A soapy water solution will also detect leaks.
2   Fault in the fuel or electrical systems (Chapters 4 and 5).
3   Leaking EGR valve or plugged PCV valve (see Chapters 1 and 6).
4   Air filter clogged (Chapter 1).
5   Fuel pump not delivering sufficient fuel to the carburetor/fuel injectors (see Chapter 4).
6   Carburetor out of adjustment (Chapter 4).
7   Leaking head gasket. Perform a compression check (Chapter 2).
8   Camshaft lobes worn (Chapter 2).

9 Engine misses at idle speed

1   Spark plugs worn, fouled or not gapped properly (Chapter 1).
2   Fault in the fuel or electrical systems (Chapters 4 and 5).
3   Faulty spark plug wires (Chapter 1).
4   Vacuum leaks at intake or hose connections. Check as described in Section 8.
5   Uneven or low cylinder compression. Check compression as described in Chapter 1.

10 Engine misses throughout driving speed range

1   Fuel filter clogged and/or impurities in the fuel system (Chapter 1).
2   Faulty or incorrectly gapped spark plugs (Chapter 1).
3   Fault in the fuel or electrical systems (Chapters 4 and 5).
4   Incorrect ignition timing (Chapter 5).
5   Cracked distributor cap, disconnected distributor wires or damaged distributor components (distributor-equipped models only) (Chapter 1).
6   Defective spark plug wires (Chapter 1).
7   Faulty emissions system components (Chapter 6).
8   Low or uneven cylinder compression pressures. Remove the spark plugs and test the compression with a gauge (Chapter 2).
9   Weak or faulty ignition system (Chapter 5).
10 Vacuum leaks at the carburetor/throttle body, intake manifold or vacuum hoses (see Section 8).

11   Engine stalls

1   Idle speed incorrect. Refer to the VECI label and Chapter 1.
2   Fuel filter clogged and/or water and impurities in the fuel system (Chapter 1).
3   Distributor components damp or damaged (if equipped) (Chapter 5).
4   Fault in the fuel system or sensors (Chapters 4 and 6).
5   Faulty emissions system components (Chapter 6).
6   Faulty or incorrectly gapped spark plugs (Chapter 1). Also check the spark plug wires (Chapter 1).
7   Vacuum leak at the carburetor/throttle body, intake manifold or vacuum hoses. Check as described in Section 8.

12   Engine lacks power

1   Incorrect ignition timing (Chapter 5).
2   Fault in the fuel or electrical systems (Chapters 4 and 5).
3   Excessive play in the distributor shaft (if equipped). At the same time, check for a damaged rotor, faulty distributor cap, wires, etc. (Chapters 1 and 5).
4   Faulty or incorrectly gapped spark plugs (Chapter 1).
5   Carburetor not adjusted properly or excessively worn (carbureted models) (Chapter 4).
6   Faulty coil (Chapter 5).
7   Brakes binding (Chapter 1).
8   Automatic transmission fluid level incorrect (Chapter 1).
9   Clutch slipping (Chapter 8).
10   Fuel filter clogged and/or impurities in the fuel system (Chapter 1).
11   Emissions control system not functioning properly (Chapter 6).
12   Use of substandard fuel. Fill the tank with the proper octane fuel.
13   Low or uneven cylinder compression pressures. Test with a compression tester, which will detect leaking valves and/or a blown head gasket (Chapter 2).

13   Engine backfires

1   Emissions system not functioning properly (Chapter 6).
2   Fault in the fuel or electrical systems (Chapters 4 and 5).
3   Ignition timing incorrect (Chapter 5).
4   Faulty secondary ignition system (cracked spark plug insulator, faulty plug wires, distributor cap and/or rotor if equipped) (Chapters 1 and 5).
5   Carburetor or fuel injection system in need of adjustment or worn excessively (Chapter 4).
6   Vacuum leak at the carburetor/throttle body, intake manifold or vacuum hoses. Check as described in Section 8.
7   Valves sticking (Chapter 2). Valve clearances incorrectly set (2.8L V6 only).
8   Crossed spark plug wires (Chapter 1).

14   Pinging or knocking engine sounds during acceleration or uphill

1   Incorrect grade of fuel. Fill the tank with fuel of the proper octane rating.
2   Fault in the fuel or electrical systems (Chapters 4 and 5).
3   Ignition timing incorrect (Chapter 5).
4   Carburetor in need of adjustment (carbureted models) (Chapter 4).
5   Improper spark plugs. Check the plug type against the VECI label located in the engine compartment. Also check the plugs and wires for damage (Chapter 1).
6   Worn or damaged distributor components (if equipped) (Chapter 5).
7   Faulty emissions system (Chapter 6).
8   Vacuum leak. Check as described in Section 9.

15   Engine diesels (continues to run) after switching off

1   Idle speed too high. Refer to the VECI label and Chapter 1.
2   Fault in the fuel or electrical systems (Chapters 4 and 5).
3   Ignition timing incorrectly adjusted (Chapter 5).
4   Thermo-controlled air cleaner heat valve not operating properly (Chapter 6).
5   Excessive engine operating temperature. Probable causes of this are a malfunctioning thermostat, clogged radiator, faulty water pump (see Chapter 3).

Engine electrical system

16   Battery will not hold a charge

1   Alternator drivebelt defective or not adjusted properly (Chapter 1).
2   Electrolyte level low or battery discharged (Chapter 1).
3   Battery terminals loose or corroded (Chapter 1).
4   Alternator not charging properly (Chapter 5).
5   Loose, broken or faulty wiring in the charging circuit (Chapter 5).
6   Short in the vehicle wiring causing a continuous drain on battery (refer to Chapter 12 and the Wiring Diagrams).
7   Battery defective internally.

17   Ignition light fails to go out

1   Fault in the alternator or charging circuit (Chapter 5).
2   Alternator drivebelt defective or not properly adjusted (Chapter 1).

18   Ignition light fails to come on when key is turned on

1   Instrument cluster warning light bulb defective (Chapter 12).
2   Alternator faulty (Chapter 5).
3   Fault in the instrument cluster printed circuit, dashboard wiring or bulb holder (Chapter 12).

Fuel system

19   Excessive fuel consumption

1   Dirty or clogged air filter element (Chapter 1).
2   Incorrectly set ignition timing (Chapter 5).
3   Choke sticking or improperly adjusted (carbureted models) (see Chapter 1).
4   Emissions system not functioning properly (Chapter 6).
5   Fault in the fuel or electrical systems (Chapters 4 and 5).
6   Carburetor or fuel injection system internal parts excessively worn or damaged (Chapter 4).
7   Low tire pressure or incorrect tire size (Chapter 1).

20   Fuel leakage and/or fuel odor

1   Leak in a fuel feed or vent line (Chapter 4).
2   Tank overfilled. Fill only to automatic shut-off.
3   Evaporative emissions system canister clogged (Chapter 6).
4   Vapor leaks from system lines (Chapter 4).
5   Carburetor or fuel injection system internal parts excessively worn or out of adjustment (Chapter 4).

Cooling system

21   Overheating

1   Insufficient coolant in the system (Chapter 1).
2   Water pump drivebelt defective or not adjusted properly (Chapter 1).
3   Radiator core blocked or radiator grille dirty and restricted (see Chapter 3).
4   Thermostat faulty (Chapter 3).
5   Fan blades broken or cracked (Chapter 3).
6   Radiator cap not maintaining proper pressure. Have the cap pressure tested by gas station or repair shop.
7   Ignition timing incorrect (Chapter 5).

22   Overcooling

1   Thermostat faulty (Chapter 3).
2   Inaccurate temperature gauge (Chapter 12).

23   External coolant leakage

1   Deteriorated or damaged hoses or loose clamps. Replace hoses and/or tighten the clamps at the hose connections (Chapter 1).
2   Water pump seals defective. If this is the case, water will drip from the weep hole in the water pump body (Chapter 3).
3   Leakage from radiator core or header tank. This will require the radiator to be professionally repaired (see Chapter 3 for removal procedures).
4   Engine drain plug leaking (Chapter 1) or water jacket core plugs leaking (see Chapter 2).

24   Internal coolant leakage

Note: *Internal coolant leaks can usually be detected by examining the oil. Check the dipstick and inside of the valve cover for water deposits and an oil consistency like that of a milkshake.*
1   Leaking cylinder head gasket. Have the cooling system pressure tested.
2   Cracked cylinder bore or cylinder head. Dismantle the engine and inspect (Chapter 2).
3   Leaking intake manifold gasket. Pressure test the cooling system and check for increase in oil level.

25   Coolant loss

1   Too much coolant in the system (Chapter 1).
2   Coolant boiling away due to overheating (see Section 15).
3   External or internal leakage (see Sections 23 and 24).
4   Faulty radiator cap. Have the cap pressure tested.

26   Poor coolant circulation

1   Inoperative water pump. A quick test is to pinch the top radiator hose closed with your hand while the engine is idling, then let it loose. You should feel the surge of coolant if the pump is working properly (see Chapter 1).
2   Restriction in the cooling system. Drain, flush and refill the system (Chapter 1). If necessary, remove the radiator (Chapter 3) and have it reverse flushed.
3   Water pump drivebelt defective or not adjusted properly (Chapter 1).
4   Thermostat sticking (Chapter 3).

Clutch

27   Fails to release (pedal pressed to the floor – shift lever does not move freely in and out of Reverse)

1   Leak in the clutch hydraulic system. Check the master cylinder, slave cylinder and lines (Chapter 8).
2   Clutch fork off ball stud (1983 and 1984 models only). Look under the vehicle, on the left side of the transmission.
3   Clutch plate warped or damaged (Chapter 8).
4   Worn or dry clutch release shaft bushing (Chapter 8).

28   Clutch slips (engine speed increases with no increase in vehicle speed)

1   Clutch plate oil soaked or lining worn. Remove clutch (Chapter 8) and inspect.
2   Clutch plate not seated. It may take 30 or 40 normal starts for a new one to seat.
3   Pressure plate worn (Chapter 8).

29   Grabbing (chattering) as clutch is engaged

1   Oil on clutch plate lining. Remove (Chapter 8) and inspect. Correct any leakage source.
2   Worn or loose engine or transmission mounts. These units move slightly when the clutch is released. Inspect the mounts and bolts (Chapter 2).
3   Worn splines on clutch plate hub. Remove the clutch components (Chapter 8) and inspect.
4   Warped pressure plate or flywheel. Remove the clutch components and inspect.

30   Squeal or rumble with clutch fully engaged (pedal released)

Release bearing binding on transmission bearing retainer. Remove clutch components (Chapter 8) and check bearing. Remove any burrs or nicks; clean and relubricate bearing retainer before installing.

31   Squeal or rumble with clutch fully disengaged (pedal depressed)

1   Worn, defective or broken release bearing (Chapter 8).
2   Worn or broken pressure plate springs (or diaphragm fingers) (Chapter 8).

32   Clutch pedal stays on floor when disengaged

1   Linkage or release bearing binding. Inspect the linkage or remove the clutch components as necessary.
2   Make sure proper pedal stop (bumper) is installed.

Manual transmission

Note: *All the following references are in Chapter 7, unless noted.*

33   Noisy in Neutral with engine running

1   Input shaft bearing worn.
2   Damaged main drive gear bearing.
3   Worn countershaft bearings.
4   Worn or damaged countershaft end play shims.

34   Noisy in all gears

1   Any of the above causes, and/or:
2   Insufficient lubricant (see the checking procedures in Chapter 1).

35   Noisy in one particular gear

1   Worn, damaged or chipped gear teeth for that particular gear.
2   Worn or damaged synchronizer for that particular gear.

36   Slips out of high gear

1   Transmission loose on clutch housing.
2   Dirt between the transmission case and engine or misalignment of the transmission (Chapter 7).

37   Difficulty in engaging gears

1   Clutch not releasing completely (Chapter 8).
2   Loose, damaged or out-of-adjustment shift linkage. Make a thorough inspection, replacing parts as necessary (Chapter 7).

38   Oil leakage

1   Excessive amount of lubricant in the transmission (see Chapter 1 for correct checking procedures). Drain lubricant as required.
2   Driveaxle oil seal or speedometer oil seal in need of replacement (Chapter 7).

Automatic transmission

Note: *Due to the complexity of the automatic transmission, it's difficult for the home mechanic to properly diagnose and service this component. For problems other than the following, the vehicle should be taken to a dealer service department or a transmission shop.*

39   General shift mechanism problems

1   Chapter 7 deals with checking and adjusting the shift linkage on Manual transmission automatic transmissions. Common problems which may be attributed to poorly adjusted linkage are:
    Engine starting in gears other than Park or Neutral.
    Indicator on shifter pointing to a gear other than the one actually being selected.
    Vehicle moves when in Park.
2   Refer to Chapter 7 to adjust the linkage.

40   Transmission will not downshift with accelerator pedal pressed to the floor

    Chapter 7, part B deals with adjusting the throttle cable to enable the transmission to downshift properly.

41   Transmission slips, shifts rough, is noisy or has no drive in forward or reverse gears

1   There are many probable causes for the above problems, but the home mechanic should be concerned with only one possibility – fluid level.
2   Before taking the vehicle to a repair shop, check the level and condition of the fluid as described in Chapter 1. Correct fluid level as necessary or change the fluid and filter if needed. If the problem persists, have a professional diagnose the probable cause.

42   Fluid leakage

1   Automatic transmission fluid is a deep red color. Fluid leaks should not be confused with engine oil, which can easily be blown by air flow to the transmission.
2   To pinpoint a leak, first remove all built-up dirt and grime from around the transmission. Degreasing agents and/or steam cleaning will achieve this. With the underside clean, drive the vehicle at low speeds so air flow will not blow the leak far from its source. Raise the vehicle and determine where the leak is coming from. Common areas of leakage are:
   a)   Pan: Tighten the mounting bolts and/or replace the pan gasket as necessary (see Chapter 7).
   b)   Filler pipe: Replace the rubber seal where the pipe enters the transmission case.
   c)   Transmission oil lines: Tighten the connectors where the lines enter the transmission case and/or replace the lines.
   d)   Vent pipe: Transmission overfilled and/or water in fluid (see checking procedures, Chapter 1).
   e)   Speedometer connector: Replace the O-ring where the speedometer cable enters the transmission case (Chapter 7).

Transfer case

43   Transfer case is difficult to shift into the desired range

1   Speed may be too great to permit engagement. Stop the vehicle and shift into the desired range.
2   Shift linkage loose, bent or binding. Check the linkage for damage or wear and replace or lubricate as necessary (Chapter 7).
3   If the vehicle has been driven on a paved surface for some time, the driveline torque can make shifting difficult. Stop and shift into two-wheel drive on paved or hard surfaces.
4   Insufficient or incorrect grade of lubricant. Drain and refill the transfer case with the specified lubricant. (Chapter 1).
5   Worn or damaged internal components. Disassembly and overhaul of the transfer case may be necessary (Chapter 7).

44   Transfer case noisy in all gears

    Insufficient or incorrect grade of lubricant. Drain and refill (Chapter 1).

45   Noisy or jumps out of 4WD Low range

1   Transfer case not fully engaged. Stop the vehicle, shift into Neutral and then engage 4L.
2   Shift linkage loose, worn or binding. Tighten, repair or lubricate linkage as necessary.
3   Shift fork cracked, inserts worn or fork binding on the rail. Disassemble and repair as necessary (Chapter 7).

46 Lubricant leaks from the vent or output shaft seals

1 Transfer case is overfilled. Drain to the proper level (Chapter 1).
2 Vent is clogged or jammed closed. Clear or replace the vent.
3 Output shaft seal incorrectly installed or damaged. Replace the seal and check contact surfaces for nicks and scoring.

Driveshaft

47 Oil leak at front of driveshaft

Defective transmission rear oil seal. See Chapter 7 for replacement procedures. While this is done, check the splined yoke for burrs or a rough condition which may be damaging the seal. Burrs can be removed with crocus cloth or a fine whetstone.

48 Knock or clunk when the transmission is under initial load (just after transmission is put into gear)

1 Loose or disconnected rear suspension components. Check all mounting bolts, nuts and bushings (see Chapter 10).
2 Loose driveshaft bolts. Inspect all bolts and nuts and tighten them to the specified torque.
3 Worn or damaged universal joint bearings. Check for wear (see Chapter 8).

49 Metallic grinding sound consistent with vehicle speed.

Pronounced wear in the universal joint bearings. Check as described in Chapter 8.

50 Vibration

Note: *Before assuming that the driveshaft is at fault, make sure the tires are perfectly balanced and perform the following test.*
1 Install a tachometer inside the vehicle to monitor engine speed as the vehicle is driven. Drive the vehicle and note the engine speed at which the vibration (roughness) is most pronounced. Now shift the transmission to a different gear and bring the engine speed to the same point.
2 If the vibration occurs at the same engine speed (rpm) regardless of which gear the transmission is in, the driveshaft is NOT at fault since the driveshaft speed varies.
3 If the vibration decreases or is eliminated when the transmission is in a different gear at the same engine speed, refer to the following probable causes.
4 Bent or dented driveshaft. Inspect and replace as necessary (see Chapter 8).
5 Undercoating or built-up dirt, etc. on the driveshaft. Clean the shaft thoroughly and recheck.
6 Worn universal joint bearings. Remove and inspect (see Chapter 8).
7 Driveshaft and/or companion flange out of balance. Check for missing weights on the shaft. Remove the driveshaft (see Chapter 8) and reinstall 180-degrees from original position, then retest. Have the driveshaft professionally balanced if the problem persists.

Axles

51 Noise

1 Road noise. No corrective procedures available.
2 Tire noise. Inspect tires and check tire pressures (Chapter 1).
3 Rear wheel bearings loose, worn or damaged (Chapter 8).

52 Vibration

See probable causes under Driveshaft. Proceed under the guidelines listed for the driveshaft. If the problem persists, check the rear wheel bearings by raising the rear of the vehicle and spinning the wheels by hand. Listen for evidence of rough (noisy) bearings. Remove and inspect (see Chapter 8).

53 Oil leakage

1 Pinion seal damaged (see Chapter 8).
2 Axleshaft oil seals damaged (see Chapter 8).
3 Differential inspection cover leaking. Tighten the bolts or replace the gasket as required (see Chapters 1 and 8).

Brakes

Note: *Before assuming that a brake problem exists, make sure that the tires are in good condition and inflated properly (see Chapter 1), that the front end alignment is correct and that the vehicle is not loaded with weight in an unequal manner.*

54 Vehicle pulls to one side during braking

1 Defective, damaged or oil contaminated disc brake pads or shoes on one side. Inspect as described in Chapter 9.
2 Excessive wear of brake shoe or pad material or drum/disc on one side. Inspect and correct as necessary.
3 Loose or disconnected front suspension components. Inspect and tighten all bolts to the specified torque (Chapter 10).
4 Defective drum brake or caliper assembly. Remove the drum or caliper and inspect for a stuck piston or other damage (Chapter 9).

55 Noise (high-pitched squeal with the brakes applied)

1 Disc brake pads worn out. The noise comes from the wear sensor rubbing against the disc (does not apply to all vehicles) or the actual pad backing plate itself if the material is completely worn away. Replace the pads with new ones immediately (Chapter 9). If the pad material has worn completely away, the brake discs should be inspected for damage as described in Chapter 9.
2 Missing or damaged brake pad insulators (disc brakes). Replace pad insulators (see Chapter 9).
3 Linings contaminated with dirt or grease. Replace pads or shoes.
4 Incorrect linings. Replace with correct linings.

56 Excessive brake pedal travel

1 Partial brake system failure. Inspect the entire system (Chapter 9) and correct as required.
2 Insufficient fluid in the master cylinder. Check (Chapter 1), add fluid and bleed the system if necessary (Chapter 9).

3   Rear brakes not adjusting properly. Make a series of starts and stops while the vehicle is in Reverse. If this does not correct the situation, remove the drums and inspect the self-adjusters (Chapter 9).

57   Brake pedal feels spongy when depressed

1   Air in the hydraulic lines. Bleed the brake system (Chapter 9).
2   Faulty flexible hoses. Inspect all system hoses and lines. Replace parts as necessary.
3   Master cylinder mounting bolts/nuts loose.
4   Master cylinder defective (Chapter 9).

58   Excessive effort required to stop vehicle

1   Power brake booster not operating properly (Chapter 9).
2   Excessively worn linings or pads. Inspect and replace if necessary (Chapter 9).
3   One or more caliper pistons or wheel cylinders seized or sticking. Inspect and rebuild as required (Chapter 9).
4   Brake linings or pads contaminated with oil or grease. Inspect and replace as required (Chapter 9).
5   New pads or shoes installed and not yet seated. It will take a while for the new material to seat against the drum (or rotor).

59   Pedal travels to the floor with little resistance

1   Little or no fluid in the master cylinder reservoir caused by leaking wheel cylinder(s), leaking caliper piston(s), loose, damaged or disconnected brake lines. Inspect the entire system and correct as necessary.
2   Worn master cylinder seals (Chapter 9).

60   Brake pedal pulsates during brake application

1   Caliper improperly installed. Remove and inspect (Chapter 9).
2   Disc or drum defective. Remove (Chapter 9) and check for excessive lateral runout and parallelism. Have the disc or drum resurfaced or replace it with a new one.

Suspension and steering systems

61   Vehicle pulls to one side

1   Tire pressures uneven (Chapter 1).
2   Defective tire (Chapter 1).
3   Excessive wear in suspension or steering components (Chapter 10).
4   Front end in need of alignment.
5   Front brakes dragging. Inspect the brakes as described in Chapter 9.

62   Shimmy, shake or vibration

1   Tire or wheel out-of-balance or out-of-round. Have professionally balanced.
2   Loose, worn or out-of-adjustment rear wheel bearings (Chapter 1).
3   Shock absorbers and/or suspension components worn or damaged (Chapter 10).

63   Excessive pitching and/or rolling around corners or during braking

1   Defective shock absorbers. Replace as a set (Chapter 10).
2   Broken or weak springs and/or suspension components. Inspect as described in Chapter 10.

64   Excessively stiff steering

1   Lack of fluid in power steering fluid reservoir (Chapter 1).
2   Incorrect tire pressures (Chapter 1).
3   Lack of lubrication at steering joints (see Chapter 1).
4   Front end out of alignment.
5   Lack of power assistance (see Section 62).

65   Excessive play in steering

1   Loose front wheel bearings (Chapters 1 and 10).
2   Excessive wear in suspension or steering components (Chapter 10).
3   Steering gearbox damaged or out of adjustment (Chapter 10).

66   Lack of power assistance

1   Steering pump drivebelt faulty or not adjusted properly (Chapter 1).
2   Fluid level low (Chapter 1).
3   Hoses or lines restricted. Inspect and replace parts as necessary.
4   Air in power steering system. Bleed the system (Chapter 10).

67   Excessive tire wear (not specific to one area)

1   Incorrect tire pressures (Chapter 1).
2   Tires out-of-balance. Have professionally balanced.
3   Wheels damaged. Inspect and replace as necessary.
4   Suspension or steering components excessively worn (Chapter 10).

68   Excessive tire wear on outside edge

1   Inflation pressures incorrect (Chapter 1).
2   Excessive speed in turns.
3   Front end alignment incorrect (excessive toe-in). Have professionally aligned.
4   Suspension arm bent or twisted (Chapter 10).

69   Excessive tire wear on inside edge

1   Inflation pressures incorrect (Chapter 1).
2   Front end alignment incorrect (toe-out). Have professionally aligned.
3   Loose or damaged steering components (Chapter 10).

70   Tire tread worn in one place

1   Tires out-of-balance.
2   Damaged or buckled wheel. Inspect and replace if necessary.
3   Defective tire (Chapter 1).

Chapter 1
Tune-up and routine maintenance

Contents

Recommended lubricants and fluids

Note: *For additional information on fluids for your specific vehicle, consult the owner's manual*

Engine oil
  Type .... API grade SG
  Viscosity .... See accompanying chart
Power steering fluid type .... Motorcraft Type F automatic transmission fluid

---

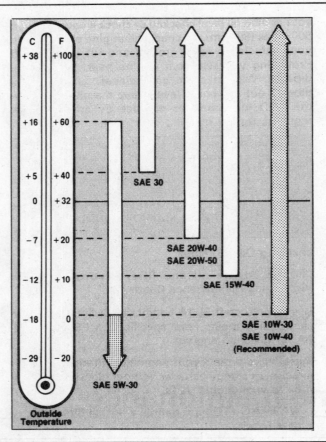

ENGINE OIL VISCOSITY CHART

For best fuel economy and cold starting, select the lowest SAE viscosity grade oil for the expected temperature range

---

Brake fluid type .... DOT 3 heavy-duty brake fluid
Automatic transmission fluid type
  C3 (transmission code V) .... Dexron II automatic transmission fluid
  C5 (transmission code W) .... Motorcraft Type H automatic transmission fluid
  A4LD (transmission code T)
    1983 through 1987 .... DEXRON II automatic transmission fluid
    1988-on .... MERCON automatic transmission fluid
Manual transmission lubricant type
  1983 through 1987 .... SAE 80W standard transmission lubricant (Ford specification ESP-M2C83-C or equivalent)

  1988-on
    Mitsubishi transmission .... SAE 80W standard transmission lubricant (Ford specification ESP-M2C83-C or equivalent)

    Mazda transmission .... MERCON automatic transmission fluid
Transfer case lubricant type
  1983 through 1987 .... Dexron II automatic transmission fluid
  1988-on .... Mercon automatic transmission fluid
Coolant type .... A 50/50 mixture of ethylene glycol-based antifreeze and water
Front wheel bearing grease
  2WD models .... High-temperature wheel bearing grease (Ford part no. C1AZ-19590-BA no. ESA-M1C75-B)

Front wheel bearing grease (continued)
  4WD models
    1983 through 1989 . . . .   High-temperature wheel bearing grease (Ford part no. C1AZ-19590-BA/ spec. no. ESA-M1C75-B)
    1990-on . . . .   High-temperature 4WD front axle and wheel bearing grease (Ford part no. E8TZ-15590-A/spec. no. ESA M1C-198-A)

Automatic locking front hub grease . . . .   High-temperature wheel bearing grease (Ford part no. C1AZ-19590-BA/ spec. no. ESA-MC175-B)

Front spindle and thrust bearing grease (4WD)
    1983 through 1989 . . . .   Multi-purpose grease (Ford part no. C1AZ-19590-BA/spec. no. ESA-MC175-B)
    1990-on . . . .   High-temperature 4WD front axle and wheel bearing grease (Ford part no. E8TZ-15590-A/spec. no. ESA M1C-198-A)

Caliper slide rail grease . . . .   Disc brake caliper slide rail grease (Ford part no. D7AZ-19590-A/spec. no. ESA-M1C172-A)

Chassis grease . . . .   Multi-purpose grease (Ford part no. C1AZ-19590-B/spec. no. ESA-M1C75-A)

Differential lubricant*
  Rear axles . . . .   Hypoid lubricant (Ford part no. E0AZ-19580-AA/spec. no. ESP-M2C154-A)
  Front axles (4WD) . . . .   Hypoid lubricant (Ford part no. C6AZ-19580-E/spec. no. ESW-M2C105-A)

*Trak-Lok axles: add 4 oz. of friction modifier (part C8AZ-19B546-A) when oil is changed.

Capacities (qts)

Engine oil*
  1983
    With filter change 4.5
    Without filter change   4
  1984 through 1986
    2.0L and 2.8L engines
      With filter change   5
      Without filter change   4
    2.3L engine with stamped steel pan
      With filter change   6
      Without filter change   5
    2.3L engine with cast-aluminum pan
      With filter change   5
      Without filter change   4
  1987-on (all engines)
    With filter change   5
    Without filter change   4
Automatic transmission fluid (drain and refill) 3.0
Cooling system**
  2.0L and 2.3L without A/C 6.5
  2.0L and 2.3L with A/C 7.2
  2.8L and 2.9L without A/C 7.2
  2.8L and 2.9L with A/C 7.8
  3.0L without A/C 9.5
  3.0L with A/C 10.2
  4.0L without A/C 7.8
  4.0L with A/C 8.6

*Use dipstick to determine exact fill level.

**Capacity may vary +/- 15% due to equipment variations. Most service refills take only 80% of listed capacity because some coolant remains in the engine. A/C indicates air conditioning.

Drivebelt tension (measured with special tool)

1983 through 1988
  1/4-inch V-belt
    New . . . .   50 to 90
    Used . . . .   40 to 60
    Minimum   40
  3/8-inch V-belt
    New . . . .   90 to 130
    Used . . . .   80 to 100
    Minimum   65
  3/8-inch V-ribbed and all 2.9L belts
    New . . . .   120 to 160
    Used . . . .   110 to 130
    Minimum   70

6K V-ribbed
  New .... 150 to 190
  Used .... 140 to 160
  Minimum 90
1/2-inch V-ribbed
  New .... 120 to 160
  Used .... 110 to 130
  Minimum 65
1989 and 1990
  2.3L engine (all)* ....
  New .... 150 to 190
  Used .... 140 to 160
  Minimum 90
  2.9L engine (all)
  New .... 120 to 160
  Used .... 110 to 130
  Minimum 70
  4.0L engine .... Automatic tensioner – not specified
1991-on
  2.3L engine (all)* ....
  New .... 150 to 190
  Used .... 140 to 160
  Minimum 90
  2.9L engine (all)
  New .... 120 to 160
  Used .... 110 to 130
  Minimum 70
  3.0L engine
  Alternator belt (with air conditioning)
    New .... 150 to 190
    Used .... 140 to 160
    Minimum 90
  Alternator belt (without air conditioning)
    New .... 120 to 160
    Used .... 110 to 130
    Minimum 70
  Power steering belt
    New .... 100 to 140
    Used .... 80 to 100
    Minimum 60
  4.0L engine
  New or used .... 108 to 132
  Minimum 108

*Some 2.3L engines are equipped with a wear indicator. Refer to Section 11.

Brakes

Disc brake pad thickness (minimum) .... 1/8 inch
Drum brake shoe lining thickness (minimum) .... 1/16 inch

Front hub adjustment (4WD models)

Endplay
  1983 through 1989 .... 0.001 to 0.003 inch
  1990-on .... 0.000 to 0.003 inch
Hub turning torque (maximum)
  1983 through 1989 .... Not available
  1990-on .... 25 in-lbs

Ignition system *(refer to page 1–28 and 1–29 for a firing order and cylinder location diagram)*

Spark plug type
  2.0L engine
    1983 and 1984 models .... Champion RS12YC
    1985 through 1990 models .... Champion RS14YC
  2.3L engine
    Early 1983 .... Champion RS12YC
    Late 1983 through 1988 .... Champion RS14LC
    1989 and 1990 .... Champion RS12YC
    1991-on .... Motorcraft AWSF 42 or 42C
  2.8L and 2.9L engines
    Through 1990 .... Champion RS12YC
    1991-on .... Motorcraft AWSF 54

3.0L engines	Motorcraft AWSF 42 or 42C
4.0L engines	Motorcraft AWRF 32-5
Spark plug gap	
Early 1983 2.3L engines and all 1983 2.0L engines	0.035 inch
All others	0.044 inch

Fuel system

Idle speed	Refer to Vehicle Emission Control Information label
Fuel bowl vent travel (dimension A) (1983 and 1984 2.0L and 2.3L models)	0.100 to 0.150 inch
1985 through 1988 2.0L carburetor adjustment	
Closed throttle rpm	700 or less
ISC maximum extension	2000+/-200 rpm
ISC function test rpm	
1985	1200+/-25 rpm
1986 through 1988	1200+/-75 rpm
2.8L V6 carburetor anti-dieseling speed adjustment	
1984	
Manual transmission	750 rpm in Neutral
Automatic transmission	650 rpm in Drive
1985 and 1986	750 rpm in Neutral

Valve clearance (2.8L V6 engine only)

Intake	0.014
Exhaust	0.016

Torque specifications

	Ft-lbs (unless otherwise indicated)
Wheel lug nuts	
1983 through 1985	85 to 115
1986-on	100
Front hub adjusting nut (2WD)	
Step 1	17 to 25
Step 2	Back off 1/2 turn
Step 3	
1983 through 1988	10 to 15 in-lbs
1989-on	18 to 20 in-lbs
Front hub adjusting nut (4WD)	
Manual locking hubs	
Step 1	35
Step 2	Back off 1/4 turn
Step 3	16 in-lbs
Step 4 (outer locknut)	150
Automatic locking hubs	
Step 1	35
Step 2	Back off 1/4 turn
Step 3	16 in-lbs
Spark plugs	
2.0L and 2.3L four cylinder	5 to 10
2.8L and 2.9L V6	18 to 28
3.0L V6	11
Oil pan drain plug	
2.0L and 2.3L four cylinder engines	15 to 25
2.8L and 2.9L V6	15 to 21
3.0L V6	10
Engine block coolant drain plug(s)	
2.3L four cylinder	23 to 38
2.8L and 2.9L V6	14 to 18
3.0L V6	
1/4-18 cylinder block plug	15
3/8-18 cylinder block/intake manifold plug	28
Automatic transmission pan bolts	
C3	12 to 17
C5	12 to 16
A4LD	8 to 10
Automatic transmission filter bolt(s)	
C5	25 to 40 in-lbs

1

Ford Ranger and Bronco II
Maintenance schedule

The following maintenance intervals are based on the assumption that the vehicle owner will be doing the maintenance or service work, as opposed to having a dealer service department do the work. Although the time/mileage intervals are loosely based on factory recommendations, most have been shortened to ensure, for example, that such items as lubricants and fluids are checked/changed at intervals that promote maximum engine/driveline service life. Also, subject to the preference of the individual owner interested in keeping his or her vehicle in peak condition at all times, and with the vehicle's ultimate resale in mind, many of the maintenance procedures may be performed more often than recommended in the following schedule. We encourage such owner initiative.

Because off-road use necessitates more frequent maintenance, a separate schedule is included for vehicles used off road.

When the vehicle is new it should be serviced initially by a factory authorized dealer service department to protect the factory warranty. In many cases the initial maintenance check is done at no cost to the owner (check with your dealer service department for more information).

Every 250 miles or weekly, whichever comes first

Check the engine oil level (Section 3)
Check the engine coolant level (Section 3)
Check the brake fluid level (Section 3)
Check the clutch fluid level (Section 3)
Check the windshield washer fluid level (Section 3)
Check the tires and tire pressures (Section 4)
Perform owner safety checks (Section 5)

Every 3,000 miles or 3 months, whichever comes first

All items listed above, plus . . .
Change the engine oil and oil filter (Section 6)
Check the power steering fluid level (Section 7)
Check the automatic transmission fluid level (Section 8)
Rotate the tires (Section 9)

Every 6,000 miles or 6 months, whichever comes first

All the items listed above, plus . . .
Inspect/replace the underhood hoses (Section 10)
Check/adjust the drivebelts (Section 11)
Check/service the battery (Section 12)
Inspect/lubricate the automatic transmission shift linkage (Section 14)
Lubricate the chassis (Section 15)

Every 12,000 miles or 12 months, whichever comes first

All items listed above, plus . . .
Check/replenish the manual transmission lubricant (Section 16)
Check the differential lubricant level (Section 17)
Check the transfer case lubricant level (Section 18)
Replace the air filter (Section 19)
Check/replace the crankcase vent filter (Section 20)
Check/replace the PCV valve (Section 21)
Check the fuel system (Section 22)
Inspect/replace the fuel filter (Section 23)
Inspect the cooling system (Section 24)
Inspect the exhaust system (Section 25)
Inspect the steering and suspension components (Section 26)
Inspect the brakes and lubricate caliper slide rails (Section 27)
Check/lubricate the front wheel bearings (2WD) (Section 28)
Check/lubricate the hub lock, spindle bearings and front wheel bearings (4WD) (Section 29)
Adjust valve clearances (2.8L V6 engine only) (Section 30)
Inspect/replace the windshield wiper blades (Section 31)

Every 24,000 miles or 24 months, whichever comes first

All items listed above plus . . .
Change the automatic transmission fluid and filter (Section 8)
Service the cooling system (drain, flush and refill) (Section 32)
Replace the spark plugs (except platinum-tipped) (Section 13)*
Check/replace the spark plug wires, distributor cap (if equipped) and rotor (Section 13)
Check the choke and lubricate the linkage (Section 33)
Check idle speed (carbureted models) (Section 34)

Every 30,000 miles or 30 months, whichever comes first

Change the differential lubricant (Section 17)
Change the transfer case lubricant (Section 18)
Lubricate driveshaft slip yokes (Section 35)
Lubricate right front driveaxle slip yoke (4WD) (Section 35)

Every 60,000 miles or 60 months, whichever comes first

Replace platinum-tipped spark plugs (Section 13)*
Replace spark plug wires (Section 13)
Check the thermactor hoses and clamps (Section 10)
Replace emission control components (1986 through 1988 models) (Section 36)

1991 and later 3.0L and 4.0L engines are originally equipped with platinum-tipped spark plugs, which have a recommended replacement interval of 60,000 miles.

Off-road operation

If the vehicle is driven off road, perform the following maintenance items every 1,000 miles. If the vehicle is driven in mud or water, perform the items daily.
Inspect brakes (Section 27)
Inspect front wheel bearings (2WD) (Section 28)
Inspect exhaust system (Section 25)
Lubricate driveshaft slip yoke and U-joints (if equipped with grease fittings) (Sections 15 and 35)

RANGER/BRONCO II (4 x 2) TYPICAL CHASSIS LUBRICATION POINTS

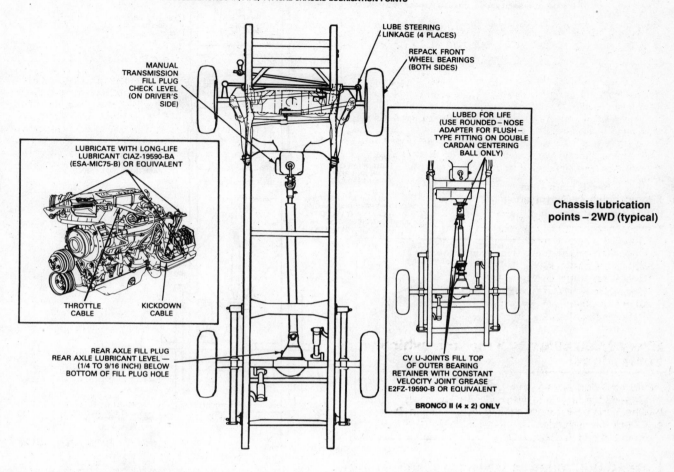

Chassis lubrication points – 2WD (typical)

1

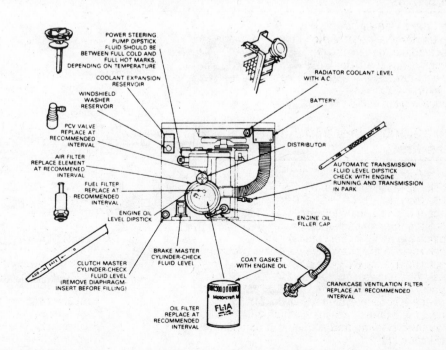

Underhood service points – 2.0L and 2.3L carbureted engines

RANGER/BRONCO II (4 x 4) CHASSIS LUBRICATION POINTS

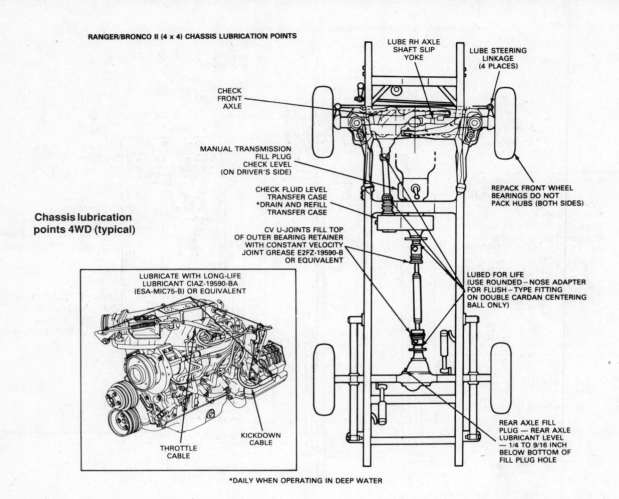

LUBE RH AXLE SHAFT SLIP YOKE

LUBE STEERING LINKAGE (4 PLACES)

CHECK FRONT AXLE

MANUAL TRANSMISSION FILL PLUG CHECK LEVEL (ON DRIVER'S SIDE)

CHECK FLUID LEVEL TRANSFER CASE *DRAIN AND REFILL TRANSFER CASE

REPACK FRONT WHEEL BEARINGS DO NOT PACK HUBS (BOTH SIDES)

Chassis lubrication points 4WD (typical)

CV U-JOINTS FILL TOP OF OUTER BEARING RETAINER WITH CONSTANT VELOCITY JOINT GREASE E2FZ-19590-B OR EQUIVALENT

LUBED FOR LIFE (USE ROUNDED – NOSE ADAPTER FOR FLUSH – TYPE FITTING ON DOUBLE CARDAN CENTERING BALL ONLY)

LUBRICATE WITH LONG-LIFE LUBRICANT C1AZ-19590-BA (ESA-MIC75-B) OR EQUIVALENT

KICKDOWN CABLE

THROTTLE CABLE

REAR AXLE FILL PLUG — REAR AXLE LUBRICANT LEVEL — 1/4 TO 9/16 INCH BELOW BOTTOM OF FILL PLUG HOLE

*DAILY WHEN OPERATING IN DEEP WATER

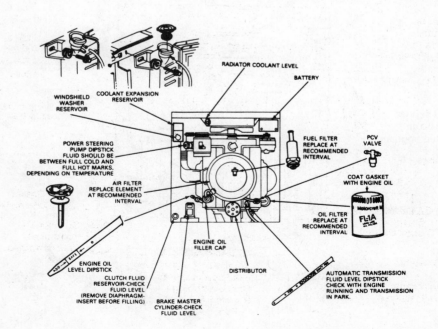

RADIATOR COOLANT LEVEL

BATTERY

WINDSHIELD WASHER RESERVOIR

COOLANT EXPANSION RESERVOIR

FUEL FILTER REPLACE AT RECOMMENDED INTERVAL

PCV VALVE

POWER STEERING PUMP DIPSTICK FLUID SHOULD BE BETWEEN FULL COLD AND FULL HOT MARKS, DEPENDING ON TEMPERATURE

Underhood service points – 2.8L engine

COAT GASKET WITH ENGINE OIL

AIR FILTER REPLACE ELEMENT AT RECOMMENDED INTERVAL

OIL FILTER REPLACE AT RECOMMENDED INTERVAL

ENGINE OIL FILLER CAP

ENGINE OIL LEVEL DIPSTICK

CLUTCH FLUID RESERVOIR-CHECK FLUID LEVEL (REMOVE DIAPHRAGM-INSERT BEFORE FILLING)

BRAKE MASTER CYLINDER-CHECK FLUID LEVEL

DISTRIBUTOR

AUTOMATIC TRANSMISSION FLUID LEVEL DIPSTICK CHECK WITH ENGINE RUNNING AND TRANSMISSION IN PARK.

1

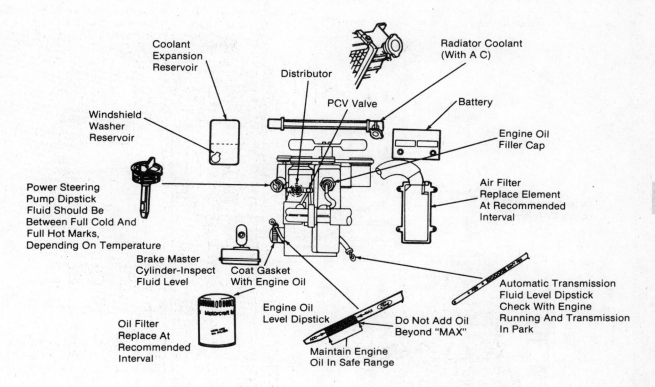

Underhood service points – 2.3L EFI engine (typical)

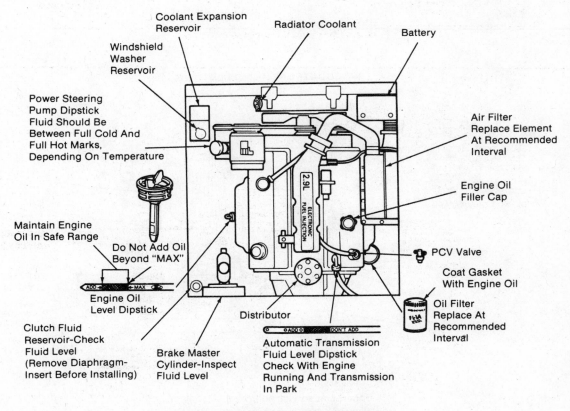

Underhood service points – 2.9L EFI engine

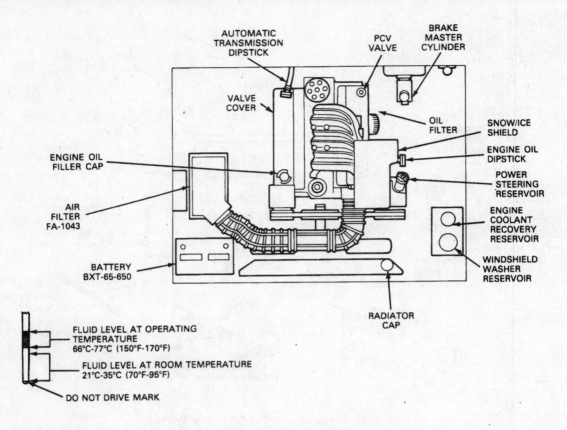

Underhood service points – 3.0L engine

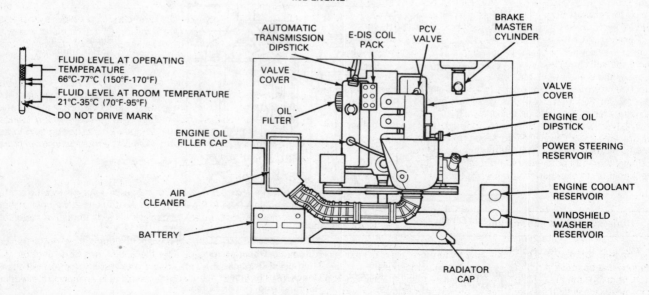

Underhood service points – 4.0L engine

3.4a   Remove the dipstick, wipe it clean, then reinsert it all the way before withdrawing it for an accurate oil level check

1   Introduction

This Chapter is designed to help the home mechanic maintain the Ford Ranger/Bronco II with the goals of maximum performance, economy, safety and reliability in mind.

Included is a master maintenance schedule (page 1-6), followed by procedures dealing specifically with each item on the schedule. Visual checks, adjustments, component replacement and other helpful items are included. Refer to the accompanying illustrations of the engine compartment and the underside of the vehicle for the locations of various components. Servicing the vehicle, in accordance with the mileage/time maintenance schedule and the step-by-step procedures will result in a planned maintenance program that should produce a long and reliable service life. Keep in mind that it is a comprehensive plan, so maintaining some items but not others at specified intervals will not produce the same results.

As you service the vehicle, you will discover that many of the procedures can – and should – be grouped together because of the nature of the particular procedure you're performing or because of the close proximity of two otherwise unrelated components to one another.

For example, if the vehicle is raised for chassis lubrication, you should inspect the exhaust, suspension, steering and fuel systems while you're under the vehicle. When you're rotating the tires, it makes good sense to check the brakes since the wheels are already removed. Finally, let's suppose you have to borrow or rent a torque wrench. Even if you only need it to tighten the spark plugs, you might as well check the torque of as many critical fasteners as time allows.

The first step in this maintenance program is to prepare yourself before the actual work begins. Read through all the procedures you're planning to do, then gather up all the parts and tools needed. If it looks like you might run into problems during a particular job, seek advice from a mechanic or an experienced do-it-yourselfer.

2   Tune-up general information

The term tune-up is used in this manual to represent a combination of individual operations rather than one specific procedure.

If, from the time the vehicle is new, the routine maintenance schedule is followed closely and frequent checks are made of fluid levels and high wear items, as suggested throughout this manual, the engine will be kept in relatively good running condition and the need for additional work will be minimized.

More likely than not, however, there will be times when the engine is running poorly due to a lack of regular maintenance. This is even more likely if a used vehicle, which has not received regular and frequent maintenance checks, is purchased. In such cases, an engine tune-up will be needed outside of the regular maintenance intervals.

The first step in any tune-up or diagnostic procedure to help correct a poor running engine is a cylinder compression check. A compression check (see Chapter 2) will help determine the condition of internal engine components and should be used as a guide for tune-up and repair procedures. If, for instance, a compression check indicates serious internal engine wear, a conventional tune-up will not improve the performance of the engine and would be a waste of time and money. Because of its importance, the compression check should be done by someone with the right equipment and the knowledge to use it properly.

The following procedures are those most often needed to bring as generally poor running engine back into a proper state of tune.

Minor tune-up

Clean, inspect and test the battery (see Section 12)
Check all engine related fluids (see Section 3)
Check and adjust the drivebelts (see Section 11)
Replace the spark plugs (see Section 13)
Inspect the distributor cap and rotor (if equipped) (see Section 13)
Inspect the spark plug and coil wires (see Section 13)
Check and adjust the idle speed (carbureted models only) (see Section 34)
Check the PCV valve (see Section 21)
Check the air filter (see Section 19)
Check the cooling system (see Section 24)
Check all underhood hoses (see Section 10)

Major tune-up

All items listed under minor tune-up, plus:
Check the EGR system (see Chapter 6)
Check the ignition system (see Chapter 5)
Check the charging system (see Chapter 5)
Check the fuel system (see Chapter 4)
Replace the distributor cap and rotor (if equipped) (see Section 13)
Replace the spark plug wires (see Section 13)

3   Fluid level checks

Refer to illustrations 3.4a, 3.4b, 3.9, 3.15, 3.16a, 3.16b, 3.17 and 3.24
Note: *The following are fluid level checks to be done on a 250 mile or weekly basis. Additional fluid level checks can be found in specific maintenance procedures which follow. Regardless of intervals, be alert to fluid leaks under the vehicle which would indicate a fault to be corrected immediately.*

1   Fluids are an essential part of the lubrication, cooling, brake and windshield washer systems. Because the fluids gradually become depleted and/or contaminated during normal operation of the vehicle, they must be periodically replenished. See *Recommended lubricants and fluids* at the beginning of this Chapter before adding fluid to any of the following components. **Note:** *The vehicle must be on level ground when fluid levels are checked.*

Engine oil

2   Engine oil is checked with a dipstick, which is located on the side of the engine (refer to the underhood illustrations at the front of this chapter for dipstick locations). The dipstick extends through a metal tube down into the oil pan.
3   The engine oil should be checked before the vehicle has been driven, or about 15 minutes after the engine has been shut off. If the oil is checked immediately after driving the vehicle, some of the oil will remain in the upper part of the engine, resulting in an inaccurate reading on the dipstick.
4   Pull the dipstick out of the tube (**see illustration**) and wipe all of the oil away from the end with a clean rag or paper towel. Insert the clean dipstick all the way back into the tube and pull it out again. Note the oil at

3.4b   The oil level should appear between the ADD 1 and SAFE marks; do not overfill the crankcase

the end of the dipstick. At its highest point, the oil should be above the ADD mark, in the SAFE range **(see illustration)**.

5   It takes one quart of oil to raise the level from the ADD mark to the FULL or MAX mark on the dipstick. Do not allow the level to drop below the ADD mark or oil starvation may cause engine damage. Conversely, overfilling the engine (adding oil above the FULL or MAX mark) may cause oil fouled spark plugs, oil leaks or oil seal failures.

6   To add oil, remove the filler cap located on the rocker arm cover **(see illustrations at the front of the chapter)**. After adding oil, wait a few minutes to allow the level to stabilize, then pull the dipstick out and check the level again. Add more oil if required. Install the filler cap and tighten it by hand only.

7   Checking the oil level is an important preventive maintenance step. A consistently low oil level indicates oil leakage through damaged seals, defective gaskets or past worn rings or valve guides. The condition of the oil should also be noted. If the oil looks milky in color or has water droplets in it, the cylinder head gasket(s) may be blown or the head(s) or block may be cracked. The engine should be repaired immediately. Whenever you check the oil level, slide your thumb and index finger up the dipstick before wiping off the oil. If you see small dirt or metal particles clinging to the dipstick, the oil should be changed (see Section 6).

Engine coolant

Warning: *Do not allow antifreeze to come in contact with your skin or painted surfaces of the vehicle. Flush contaminated areas immediately with plenty of water. Do not store new coolant or leave old coolant lying around where it's accessible to children or pets – they are attracted by its sweet smell. Ingestion of even a small amount of coolant can be fatal! Wipe up garage floor and drip pan coolant spills. Keep antifreeze containers covered and repair leaks in your cooling system immediately.*

8   All vehicles covered by this manual are equipped with a pressurized coolant recovery system. A white plastic coolant reservoir located at the front of the engine compartment is connected by a hose to the radiator filler neck. If the engine overheats, coolant escapes through a valve in the radiator cap and travels through the hose into the reservoir. As the engine cools, the coolant is automatically drawn back into the cooling system to maintain the correct level.

9   The coolant level in the reservoir **(see illustration)** should be checked regularly. **Warning:** *Do not remove the radiator cap to check the coolant level when the engine is warm! The level in the reservoir varies with the temperature of the engine. When the engine is cold, the coolant level should be at or slightly above the COLD FULL mark on the reservoir. Once the engine has warmed up, the level should be at or near the FULL HOT mark. If it isn't, allow the engine to cool, then remove the cap from the reservoir and add a 50/50 mixture of ethylene glycol-based antifreeze and water.*

10   Drive the vehicle and recheck the coolant level. Don't use rust inhibitors or additives. If only a small amount of coolant is required to bring the

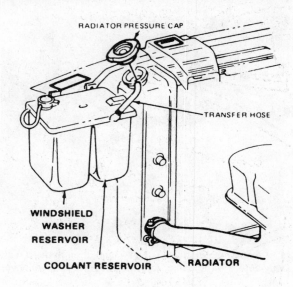

3.9   The coolant reservoir is combined with the front windshield washer fluid reservoir (there are separate compartments for the two fluids)

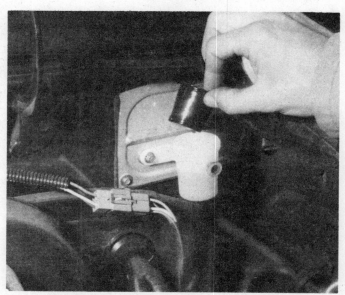

3.15   Clutch fluid is contained in a separate reservoir next to the brake master cylinder – clean the rubber cup before returning it to the reservoir

system up to the proper level, water can be used. However, repeated additions of water will dilute the antifreeze and water solution. In order to maintain the proper ratio of antifreeze and water, always top up the coolant level with the correct mixture. An empty plastic milk jug or bleach bottle makes an excellent container for mixing coolant.

11   If the coolant level drops consistently, there may be a leak in the system. Inspect the radiator, hoses, filler cap, drain plugs and water pump (see Section 24). If no leaks are noted, have the radiator cap pressure tested by a service station.

12   If you have to remove the radiator cap, wait until the engine has cooled completely, then wrap a thick cloth around the cap and turn it to the first stop. If coolant or steam escapes, let the engine cool down longer, then remove the cap.

13   Check the condition of the coolant as well. It should be relatively clear. If it's brown or rust colored, the system should be drained, flushed and refilled. Even if the coolant appears to be normal, the corrosion inhibitors wear out, so it must be replaced at the specified intervals.

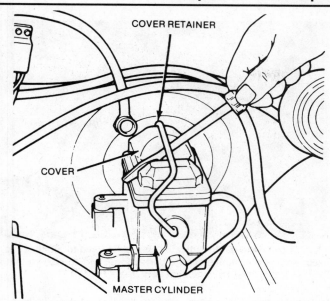

3.16a   On models with a cast-iron master cylinder, clean the area around the cover, pry back the cover clip . . .

3.16b   . . . and lift the cover off to check the level – be sure the rubber gasket seats properly when the cover is reinstalled

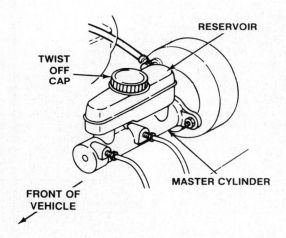

3.17   On models with an aluminum master cylinder, check the fluid level by looking through the translucent plastic reservoir

Brake and clutch fluid

Warning: *Brake fluid can harm your eyes and damage painted surfaces, so use extreme caution when handling or pouring it. Do not use brake fluid that has been standing open or is more than one year old. Brake fluid absorbs moisture from the air, which can cause a dangerous loss of brake effectiveness. Use only the specified type of brake fluid. Mixing different types (such as DOT 3 or 4 and DOT 5) can cause brake failure.*

14   The brake master cylinder is mounted at the left (driver's side) rear corner of the engine compartment. The clutch fluid reservoir (used on models with manual transmissions) is mounted adjacent to it.
15   To check the clutch fluid level, observe the level through the translucent reservoir. The level should be at or near the step molded into the reservoir. If the level is low, remove the reservoir cap to add the specified fluid **(see illustration)**.
16   On 1983 through 1985 models, the brake fluid level is checked by removing the master cylinder cap. The master cylinder is located in the left rear corner of the engine compartment. Clean the area around the

master cylinder so dirt doesn't fall into the brake fluid. Pry back the cap retainer with a screwdriver **(see illustration)**, lift off the cap **(see illustration)** and check the level in both reservoir compartments. It should be 1/4 inch below the top edge of the reservoir. Top up if necessary with the recommended brake fluid, but do not overfill.
17   On 1986 and later models, the brake fluid level is checked by looking through the plastic reservoir mounted on the master cylinder. The fluid level should be between the MAX and MIN lines on the reservoir **(see illustration)**. If the fluid level is low, wipe the top of the reservoir and the cap with a clean rag to prevent contamination of the system as the cap is unscrewed. Top up with the recommended brake fluid, but do not overfill.
Note: *Some models are equipped with a brake fluid level warning system that lights a light on the dashboard when the fluid level is excessively low.*
18   While the reservoir cap is off, check the master cylinder reservoir for contamination. If rust deposits, dirt particles or water droplets are present, the system should be drained and refilled by a dealer service department or repair shop.
19   After filling the reservoir to the proper level, make sure the cap is seated to prevent fluid leakage and/or contamination. On 1983 through 1985 models, make sure the rubber diaphragm inside the cap is seated properly.
20   The fluid level in the master cylinder will drop slightly as the disc brake pads wear. A very low level may indicate worn brake pads. Check for wear (see Section 27).
21   If the brake fluid level drops consistently, check the entire system for leaks immediately. Examine all brake lines, hoses and connections, along with the calipers, wheel cylinders and master cylinder (see Section 27).
22   When checking the fluid level, if you discover one or both reservoirs empty or nearly empty, the brake or clutch hydraulic system should be checked for leaks and bled (see Chapters 8 and 9).

Windshield washer fluid

23   Fluid for the front windshield washer system is stored in a plastic reservoir in the engine compartment. The front windshield washer reservoir is combined with the coolant reservoir (there are separate compartments for the two different fluids) **(see illustration 3.9)**.
24   Fluid for the rear windshield washer system used on Bronco II models is stored in a reservoir on the passenger side of the rear compartment **(see illustration)**. To add fluid, locate the filler tube cap on the quarter panel above the tail light. Open the cap, add fluid and close the cap.

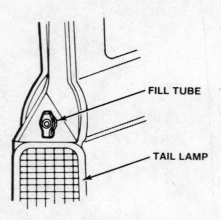

3.24   The rear windshield washer (Bronco II only) is filled through a cap on the quarter panel above the tail light

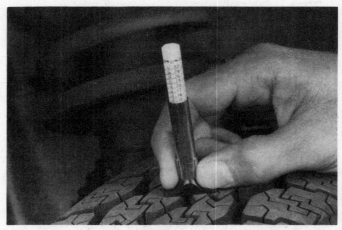

4.2   A tire tread depth indicator should be used to monitor tire wear – they're available at auto parts stores and service stations and cost very little

25   In milder climates, plain water can be used in the reservoir, but it should be kept no more than 2/3 full to allow for expansion if the water freezes. In colder climates, use windshield washer system antifreeze, available at any auto parts store, to lower the freezing point of the fluid. This comes in concentrated or pre-mixed form. If you purchase concentrated antifreeze, mix the antifreeze with water in accordance with the manufacturer's directions on the container. **Caution:** *Do not use cooling system antifreeze – it will damage the vehicle's paint.*

4   Tire and tire pressure checks

Refer to illustrations 4.2, 4.3, 4.4a, 4.4b and 4.8

1   Periodic inspection of the tires may save you the inconvenience of being stranded with a flat tire. It can also provide you with vital information regarding possible problems in the steering and suspension systems before major damage occurs.

2   Tires are equipped with 1/2-inch side bands that will appear when tread depth reaches 1/16-inch, but they don't appear until the tires are worn out. Tread wear can be monitored with a simple, inexpensive device known as a tread depth indicator **(see illustration)**.

3   Note any abnormal tire wear **(see illustration)**. Tread pattern irregularities such as cupping, flat spots and more wear on one side that the other are indications of front end alignment and/or balance problems. If any of these conditions are noted, take the vehicle to a tire shop or service station to correct the problem.

4   Look closely for cuts, punctures and embedded nails or tacks. Sometimes a tire will hold air pressure for a short time or leak down very slowly after a nail has embedded itself in the tread. If a slow leak persists, check the valve stem core to make sure it is tight **(see illustration)**. Examine the tread for an object that may have embedded itself in the tire or for a "plug" that may have begun to leak (radial tire punctures are repaired with a plug that is installed in the puncture). If a puncture is suspected, it can be easily verified by spraying a solution of soapy water onto the puncture **(see illustration)**. The soapy solution will bubble if there is a leak. Unless the puncture is unusually large, a tire shop or service station can usually repair the tire.

Condition	Probable cause	Corrective action	Condition	Probable cause	Corrective action
Shoulder wear	• Underinflation (both sides wear) • Incorrect wheel camber (one side wear) • Hard cornering • Lack of rotation	• Measure and adjust pressure. • Repair or replace axle and suspension parts. • Reduce speed. • Rotate tires.	Feathered edge **Toe wear**	• Incorrect toe	• Adjust toe-in.
Center wear	• Overinflation • Lack of rotation	• Measure and adjust pressure. • Rotate tires.	**Uneven wear**	• Incorrect camber or caster • Malfunctioning suspension • Unbalanced wheel • Out-of-round brake drum • Lack of rotation	• Repair or replace axle and suspension parts. • Repair or replace suspension parts. • Balance or replace. • Turn or replace. • Rotate tires.

4.3   This chart will help you determine the condition of your tires, the probable cause(s) of abnormal wear and the corrective action necessary

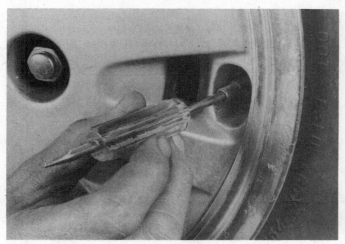

4.4a   If a tire loses air on a steady basis, check the valve core first to make sure it's snug (special inexpensive wrenches are commonly available at auto parts stores)

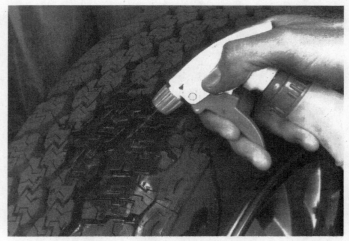

4.4b   If the valve core is tight, raise the corner of the vehicle with the low tire and spray a soapy water solution onto the tread as the tire is rotated – slow leaks will cause small bubbles to appear

4.8   To extend the life of the tires, check the air pressure at least once a week with an accurate gauge (don't forget the spare!)

5   Carefully inspect the inner sidewall of each tire for evidence of brake fluid leakage. If you see any, inspect the brakes immediately.

6   Correct air pressure adds miles to the lifespan of the tires, improves mileage and enhances overall ride quality. Tire pressure cannot be accurately estimated by looking at a tire, especially if it's a radial. A tire pressure gauge is essential. Keep an accurate gauge in the glove compartment. The pressure gauges attached to the nozzles of air hoses at gas stations are often inaccurate.

7   Always check tire pressure when the tires are cold. Cold, in this case, means the vehicle has not been driven over a mile in the three hours preceding a tire pressure check. A pressure rise of four to eight pounds is not uncommon once the tires are warm.

8   Unscrew the valve cap protruding from the wheel or hubcap and push the gauge firmly onto the valve stem **(see illustration)**. Note the reading on the gauge and compare the figure to the recommended tire pressure shown in your owner's manual or on the tire placard on the passenger side door or door pillar. Be sure to reinstall the valve cap to keep dirt and moisture out of the valve stem mechanism. Check all four tires and, if necessary, add enough air to bring them to the recommended pressure.

9   Don't forget to keep the spare tire inflated to the specified pressure (refer to your owner's manual or the placard attached to the door pillar). Note that the pressure recommended for temporary (mini) spare tires is higher than for the tires on the vehicle.

5   Owner safety checks

1   Most of these checks can be easily done while the vehicle is being driven, simply by paying attention to the specified items. The checks are intended to make the vehicle owner aware of potential safety problems before they occur.

2   Check the seatbelts for wear, fraying and cuts. Make sure the buckles latch securely and that the automatic retractors function correctly. Do not try to repair seatbelts; always replace them if any problems are found.

3   Make sure the ignition key cannot be removed when the transmission is in any gear other than Park (automatic) or Reverse (manual). Make sure the steering column locks when the key is removed from the ignition. It may be necessary to rotate the steering wheel slightly to lock the steering column.

4   Check the parking brake. The easiest way to do this is to park on a steep hill, set the parking brake and note whether it keeps the vehicle from rolling.

5   If equipped with an automatic transmission, also check the Park mechanism. Place the transmission in Park, release the parking brake and note whether the transmission holds the vehicle from rolling. If the vehicle rolls while in Park, the transmission should be taken to a qualified shop for repairs.

6   If equipped with an automatic transmission, note whether the shift indicator shows the proper gear. If it doesn't, refer to Chapter 7 for linkage adjustment procedures.

7   If equipped with automatic transmission, make sure the vehicle starts only in Park or Neutral. If it starts in any other gear, refer to Chapter 7 for switch adjustment procedures.

8   On 1985 and later models equipped with manual transmission, the starter should operate only when the clutch pedal is pressed to the floor. If the starter operates when it shouldn't, refer to Chapter 8 for clutch safety switch service.

9   Make sure the brakes do not pull to one side while stopping. The brake pedal should feel firm, but excessive effort should not be required to stop the vehicle. If the pedal sinks too low, if you have to pump it more than once to get a firm pedal, or if pedal effort is too high, refer to Chapter 9 for repair procedures. A squealing sound from the front brakes may be caused by the pad wear indicators. Refer to Chapter 9 for pad replacement procedures.

10   Rearview mirrors should be clean and undamaged. They should hold their position when adjusted.

11   Sun visors should hold their position when adjusted. They should remain securely out of the way when lifted off the windshield.

12   Make sure the defroster blows heated air onto the windshield. If it doesn't, refer to Chapter 3 for heating system service.

1

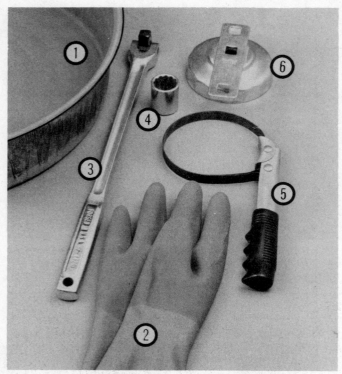

6.2   These tools are required when changing the engine oil and filter

1   **Drain pan** – It should be fairly shallow in depth, but wide to prevent spills
2   **Rubber gloves** – When removing the drain plug and filter, you will get oil on your hands (the gloves will prevent burns)
3   **Breaker bar** – Sometimes the oil drain plug is tight and a long breaker bar is needed to loosen it
4   **Socket** – To be used with the breaker bar or a ratchet (must be the correct size to fit the drain plug – six-point preferred)
5   **Filter wrench** – This is a metal band-type wrench, which requires clearance around the filter to be effective
6   **Filter wrench** – This type fits on the bottom of the filter and can be turned with a ratchet or breaker bar (different size wrenches are available for different types of filters)

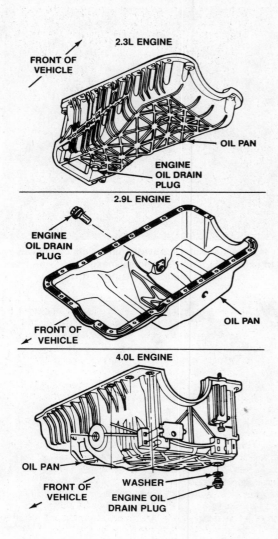

6.7   Engine oil drain plug locations (later 2.3L, 2.9L and 4.0L engines shown, others similar)

13   The horn should sound with a clearly audible tone every time it is operated. If not, refer to Chapter 12.
14   Make sure windows are clean and undamaged.
15   Turn on the lights, then walk around the vehicle and make sure they work. Check headlights in both the high beam and low beam positions. Check the turn indicators for one side of the vehicle, then for the other side. If possible, have an assistant watch the brake lights while you push the pedal. If no assistant is available, the brake lights can be checked by backing up to a wall or garage door, then pressing the pedal. There should be two distinct patches of red light (three for models equipped with a high-mount brake light) when the brake pedal is pressed.
16   Make sure locks operate smoothly when the key is turned. Lubricate locks if necessary with Ford Lock Lubricant or an equivalent product. Make sure all latches hold securely.

6   Engine oil and filter change

Refer to illustrations 6.2, 6.7, 6.12 and 6.16

1   Frequent oil changes are the most important preventive maintenance procedures that can be done by the home mechanic. As engine oil ages, it becomes diluted and contaminated, which leads to premature engine wear.

2   Make sure that you have all the necessary tools before you begin this procedure **(see illustration)**. You should also have plenty of rags or newspapers handy for mopping up oil spills.
3   Start the engine and allow it to reach normal operating temperature— oil and sludge will flow more easily when warm. If new oil, a filter or tools are needed, use the vehicle to go get them and warm up the engine oil at the same time. Park on a level surface and shut off the engine when it's warmed up. Remove the oil filler cap from the valve cover.
4   Access to the oil drain plug and filter will be improved if the vehicle can be lifted on a hoist, driven onto ramps or supported by jackstands. **Warning:** *DO NOT work under a vehicle supported only by a bumper, hydraulic or scissors-type jack – always use jackstands!*
5   If you haven't changed the oil on this vehicle before, get under it and locate the drain plug and the oil filter. The exhaust components will be warm as you work, so note how they are routed to avoid touching them when you are under the vehicle.
6   Raise the vehicle and support it on jackstands. Make sure it is safely supported!
7   Being careful not to touch the hot exhaust components, position a drain pan under the plug in the bottom of the engine **(see illustration)**. Clean the area around the plug, then remove the plug with a socket or box-end wrench. It's a good idea to wear an old glove while unscrewing

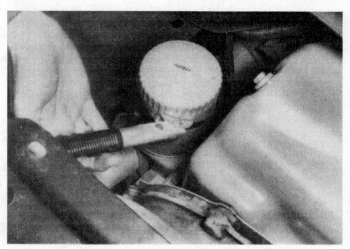

6.12   Removing the oil filter

6.16   Lubricate the oil filter gasket with clean engine oil before installing the filter on the engine

the plug the final few turns to avoid being scalded by hot oil. It will also help to hold the drain plug against the threads as you unscrew it, then pull it away from the drain hole suddenly. This will place your arm out of the way of the hot oil, as well as reducing the chances of dropping the drain plug into the drain pan.

8   It may be necessary to move the drain pan slightly as oil flow slows to a trickle. Inspect the old oil for the presence of metal particles.

9   After all the oil has drained, wipe off the drain plug(s) with a clean rag. Any small metal particles clinging to the plug would immediately contaminate the new oil.

10   Reinstall the plug and tighten it securely, but don't strip the threads.

11   Move the drain pan into position under the oil filter.

12   Loosen the oil filter by turning it counterclockwise with a filter wrench **(see illustration)**. Any standard filter wrench will work.

13   Sometimes the oil filter is screwed on so tightly that it can't be loosened. If it is, punch a metal bar or long screwdriver directly through it, as close to the engine as possible, and use it as a T-bar to turn the filter. Be prepared for oil to spurt out of the canister as it's punctured.

14   Once the filter is loose, use your hands to unscrew it from the block. Just as the filter is detached from the block, immediately tilt the open end up to prevent oil inside the filter from spilling out.

15   Using a clean rag, wipe off the mounting surface on the block. Also, make sure that none of the old gasket remains stuck to the mounting surface. It can be removed with a scraper if necessary.

16   Compare the old filter with the new one to make sure they are the same type. Smear some engine oil on the rubber gasket of the new filter and screw it into place **(see illustration)**. Overtightening the filter will damage the gasket, so don't use a filter wrench. Most filter manufacturers recommend tightening the filter by hand only. Normally, they should be tightened 3/4-turn after the gasket contacts the block, but be sure to follow the directions on the filter or container.

17   Remove all tools and materials from under the vehicle, being careful not to spill the oil in the drain pan, then lower the vehicle.

18   Add new oil to the engine through the oil filler cap in the rocker arm cover. Use a funnel to prevent oil from spilling onto the top of the engine. Pour four quarts of fresh oil into the engine. Wait a few minutes to allow the oil to drain into the pan, then check the level on the dipstick (see Section 3 if necessary). If the oil level is in the SAFE range, install the filler cap.

19   Start the engine and run it for about a minute. While the engine is running, look under the vehicle and check for leaks at the oil pan drain plug and around the oil filter. If either one is leaking, stop the engine and tighten the plug or filter slightly.

20   Wait a few minutes, then recheck the level on the dipstick. Add oil as necessary to bring the level into the SAFE range.

21   During the first few trips after an oil change, make it a point to check frequently for leaks and proper oil level.

22   The old oil drained from the engine cannot be reused in its present

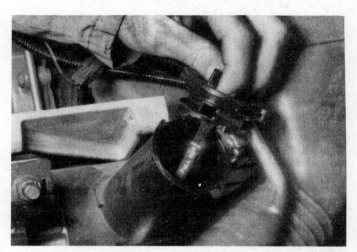

7.2   Take care not to drop any foreign matter into the power steering pump reservoir when you remove the cap

state and should be discarded. Oil reclamation centers, auto repair shops and gas stations will normally accept the oil, which can be recycled. After the oil has cooled, it can be drained into a container (plastic jugs, bottles, milk cartons, etc.) for transport to a disposal site.

7   Power steering fluid level check

Refer to illustrations 7.2 and 7.5

1   Check the power steering fluid level periodically to avoid steering system problems, such as damage to the pump. **Caution:** *DO NOT hold the steering wheel against either stop (extreme left or right turn) for more than five seconds. If you do, the power steering pump could be damaged.*

2   The power steering pump, located at the left front corner of the engine on all models, is equipped with a twist-off cap with an integral fluid level dipstick **(see illustration)**.

3   Park the vehicle on level ground and apply the parking brake.

4   Run the engine until it has reached normal operating temperature. With the engine at idle, turn the steering wheel back-and-forth several times to get any air out of the steering system. Shut the engine off, remove the cap by turning it counterclockwise, wipe the dipstick clean and reinstall the cap (make sure it is seated).

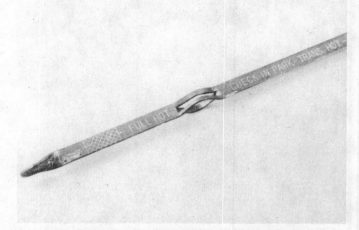

7.5   Check the power steering fluid level with the engine at normal operating temperature – fluid should not go above the Full Hot mark

5   Remove the cap again and note the fluid level. It must be between the two lines designating the FULL HOT range **(see illustration)** (be sure to use the proper temperature range on the dipstick when checking the fluid level – the FULL COLD lines on the reverse side of the dipstick are only usable when the engine is cold).

6   Add small amounts of fluid until the level is correct. **Caution:** *Do not overfill the pump. If too much fluid is added, remove the excess with a clean syringe or suction pump.*

7   Check the power steering hoses and connections for leaks and wear (see Section 10).

8   Check the condition and tension of the power steering pump drivebelt (see Section 11).

---

8   Automatic transmission fluid check/change

Fluid level check

Refer to illustration 8.6

Caution: *The use of transmission fluid other than the type listed in this Chapter's Specifications could result in transmission malfunctions or failure. If you're unsure which type of transmission you have, check the transmission code on the vehicle's Safety Certification Label and compare it with the Specifications.*

1   The automatic transmission fluid should be carefully maintained. Low fluid level can lead to slipping or loss of drive, while overfilling can cause foaming and loss of fluid. Either condition can cause transmission damage.

2   Since transmission fluid expands as it heats up, the fluid level should only be checked when the transmission is warm (at normal operating temperature). If the vehicle has just been driven over 20 miles (32 km), the transmission can be considered warm. **Caution:** *If the vehicle has just been driven for a long time at high speed or in city traffic, in hot weather, or if it has been pulling a trailer, an accurate fluid level reading cannot be obtained. Allow the transmission to cool down for about 30 minutes. You can also check the transmission fluid level when the transmission is cold. If the vehicle has not been driven for over five hours and the fluid is about room temperature (70- to 95-degrees F), the transmission is cold. However, the fluid level is normally checked with the transmission warm to ensure accurate results.*

3   Immediately after driving the vehicle, park it on a level surface, set the parking brake and start the engine. While the engine is idling, depress the brake pedal and move the selector lever through all the gear ranges, beginning and ending in Park.

4   Locate the automatic transmission dipstick tube in the engine compartment (see the illustrations at the front of this chapter for the dipstick location).

8.6   Follow the directions stamped on the transmission dipstick to get an accurate reading

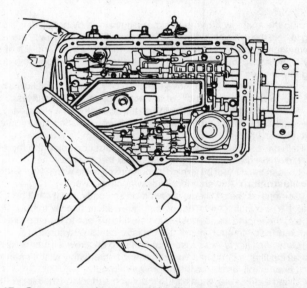

8.17   Once the pan is removed the filter/strainer is accessible

5   With the engine still idling, pull the dipstick away from the tube, wipe it off with a clean rag, push it all the way back into the tube and withdraw it again, then note the fluid level.

6   If the transmission is cold, the level should be in the room temperature range on the dipstick (between the two dots); if it's warm, the fluid level should be in the operating temperature range (between the two lines) **(see illustration)**. If the level is low, add the specified automatic transmission fluid through the dipstick tube – use a clean funnel to prevent spills.

7   Add just enough of the recommended fluid to fill the transmission to the proper level. It takes about one pint to raise the level from the low mark to the high mark when the fluid is hot, so add the fluid a little at a time and keep checking the level until it's correct.

8   The condition of the fluid should also be checked along with the level. If the fluid is black or a dark reddish-brown color, or if it smells burned, it should be changed (see below). If you are in doubt about its condition, purchase some new fluid and compare the two for color and smell.

Fluid and filter change

Refer to illustration 8.17

9   At the specified intervals, the transmission fluid should be drained and replaced. Since the fluid will remain hot long after driving, perform

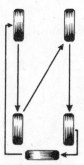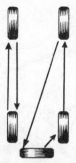

BIAS and BIAS-BELTED TIRES   RADIAL PLY TIRES

9.2   Tire rotation diagram for bias ply and radial tires

this procedure only after the engine has cooled down completely.
10   Before beginning work, purchase the specified transmission fluid (see *Recommended lubricants and fluids* at the front of this Chapter), a new filter and gasket. Never reuse the old filter or gasket!
11   Other tools necessary for this job include jackstands to support the vehicle in a raised position, a drain pan capable of holding at least ten pints, newspapers and clean rags.
12   Raise the vehicle and support it securely on jackstands. DO NOT crawl under the vehicle when it is supported only by a jack!
13   Place the drain pan beneath the transmission.
14   With the drain pan in place, remove the mounting bolts from the front and sides of the transmission oil pan.
15   Loosen the rear pan bolts approximately four turns.
16   Carefully pry the transmission pan loose with a screwdriver. Let the pan hang down so the fluid can drain. Don't damage the pan or transmission gasket surfaces or leaks could develop.
17   Remove the remaining bolts, pan and gasket **(see illustration)**. Carefully clean the gasket surface of the transmission to remove all traces of the old gasket and sealant.
18   Drain the fluid from the transmission pan, clean it with solvent and dry it with compressed air.
19   Remove the bolt (if equipped) and pull the filter from the mount inside the transmission **(see illustration 8.17)**.
20   Install a new filter and gasket. Tighten the mounting bolt securely.
21   Make sure the gasket surface on the transmission pan is clean, then install a new gasket. Put the pan in place against the transmission and install the bolts. Working around the pan, tighten each bolt a little at a time until a final torque (see this Chapter's Specifications) is reached. Don't overtighten the bolts!
22   Lower the vehicle and add automatic transmission fluid through the filler tube. **Caution:** *Refer to the Specifications at the front of this Chapter for the correct amount and type of transmission fluid. Use of the wrong type or the wrong amount can cause transmission damage.*
23   With the transmission in Park and the parking brake set, run the engine at a fast idle, but don't race it.
24   Move the gear selector through each range and back to Park. Check the fluid level. Add fluid if needed to reach the correct level.
25   Check under the vehicle for leaks during the first few trips.

9   Tire rotation

Refer to illustration 9.2

1   The tires should be rotated at the specified intervals and whenever uneven wear is noticed. Since the vehicle will be raised and the tires checked anyway, check the brakes also (see Section 27). **Note:** *Even if you don't rotate the tires, at least check the lug nut tightness.*
2   Radial tires must be rotated in a specific pattern **(see illustration)**.
3   Refer to the information in Jacking and towing at the front of this manual for the proper procedure to follow when raising the vehicle and changing a tire. If the brakes must be checked, don't apply the parking brake as stated.

4   The vehicle must be raised on a hoist or supported on jackstands to get all four tires off the ground. Make sure the vehicle is safely supported!
5   After the rotation procedure is finished, check and adjust the tire pressures as necessary and be sure to check the lug nut tightness.

10   Underhood hose check and replacement

Caution: *Replacement of air conditioning hoses must be left to a dealer service department or air conditioning shop that has the equipment to depressurize the system safely. Never remove air conditioning hoses or components until the system has been depressurized.*

General

1   High temperatures under the hood can cause deterioration of the rubber and plastic hoses used for engine, accessory and emission systems operation. Periodic inspection should be made for cracks, loose clamps, material hardening and leaks.
2   Information specific to the cooling system can be found in Section 24.
3   Most (but not all) hoses are secured to the fitting with clamps. Where clamps are used, check to be sure they haven't lost their tension, allowing the hose to leak. If clamps aren't used, make sure the hose has not expanded and/or hardened where it slips over the fitting, allowing it to leak.

PCV system hose

4   To reduce hydrocarbon emissions, crankcase blow-by gas is vented through the PCV valve to the intake manifold via a rubber hose on most models. The blow-by gases mix with incoming air in the intake manifold before being burned in the combustion chambers.
5   Check the PCV hose for cracks, leaks and other damage. Disconnect it from the rocker arm cover and the intake manifold and check the inside for obstructions. If it's clogged, clean it out with solvent.

Vacuum hoses

6   It's quite common for vacuum hoses, especially those in the emissions system, to be color coded or identified by colored stripes molded into them. Various systems require hoses with different wall thicknesses, collapse resistance and temperature resistance. When replacing hoses, be sure the new ones are made of the same material.
7   Often the only effective way to check a hose is to remove it completely from the vehicle. If more than one hose is removed, be sure to label the hoses and fittings to ensure correct installation.
8   When checking vacuum hoses, be sure to include any plastic T-fittings in the check. Inspect the fittings for cracks and the hose where it fits over each fitting for distortion, which could cause leakage.
9   A small piece of vacuum hose (1/4-inch inside diameter) can be used as a stethoscope to detect vacuum leaks. Hold one end of the hose to your ear and probe around vacuum hoses and fittings, listening for the "hissing" sound characteristic of a vacuum leak. **Warning:** *When probing with the vacuum hose stethoscope, be careful not to come into contact with moving engine components such as drivebelts, the cooling fan, etc.*

Fuel hoses

Warning: *Gasoline is extremely flammable, so take extra precautions when you work on any part of the fuel system. Don't smoke or allow open flames or bare light bulbs near the work area, and don't work in a garage where a natural gas-type appliance (such as a water heater or clothes dryer) with a pilot light is present. If you spill any fuel on your skin, rinse it off immediately with soap and water. When you perform any kind of work on the fuel system, wear safety glasses and have a Class B type fire extinguisher on hand.*

10   The fuel lines are usually under pressure, so if any fuel lines are to be disconnected be prepared to catch spilled fuel. **Warning:** *If your vehicle is equipped with fuel injection, you must relieve the fuel system pressure before servicing the fuel lines. Refer to Chapter 4 for the fuel system pressure relief procedure.*
11   Check all rubber fuel lines for deterioration and chafing. Check especially for cracks in areas where the hose bends and just before fittings,

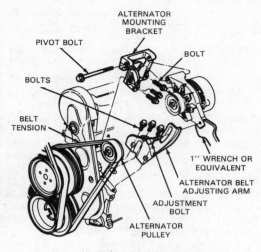

ALTERNATOR W/O POWER STEERING

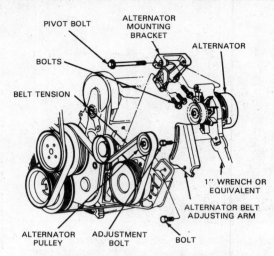

ALTERNATOR WITH POWER STEERING

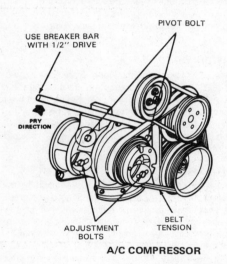

A/C COMPRESSOR

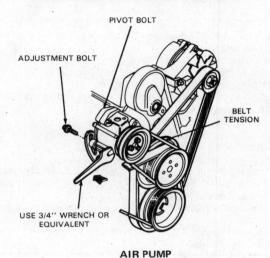

AIR PUMP

11.2a   Drivebelts – 2.0L and 2.3L engines (typical)

such as where a hose attaches to the fuel pump, fuel filter and carburetor or fuel injection system.

12   High quality fuel line, usually identified by the word Fluoroelastomer printed on the hose, should be used for fuel line replacement. Never, under any circumstances, use unreinforced vacuum line, clear plastic tubing or water hose for fuel lines.

13   Spring-type clamps are commonly used on fuel lines. These clamps often lose their tension over a period of time, and can be "sprung" during removal. Replace all spring-type clamps with screw clamps whenever a hose is replaced.

Metal lines

14   Sections of metal line are often used for fuel line between the fuel pump and carburetor or fuel injection system. Check carefully to make sure the line isn't bent, crimped or cracked.

15   If a section of metal fuel line must be replaced, use seamless steel tubing only, since copper and aluminum tubing do not have the strength necessary to withstand the vibration caused by the engine.

16   Check the metal brake lines where they enter the master cylinder and brake proportioning unit (if used) for cracks in the lines and loose fittings. Any sign of brake fluid leakage calls for an immediate thorough inspection of the brake system.

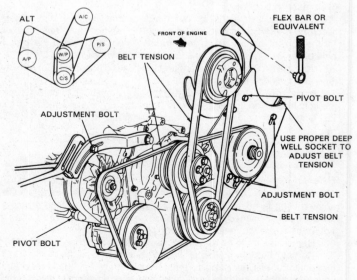

11.2b   Drivebelts – 2.8L V6 engine (2.9L V6 similar)

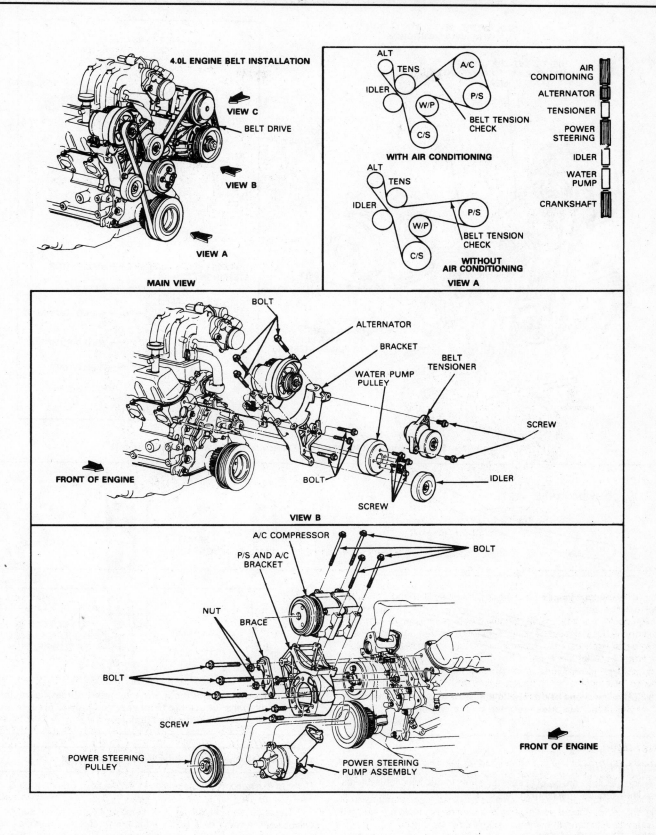

4.0L ENGINE BELT INSTALLATION

VIEW C

BELT DRIVE

VIEW B

VIEW A

MAIN VIEW

ALT

TENS

A/C

IDLER

P/S

W/P

BELT TENSION
CHECK

C/S

WITH AIR CONDITIONING

ALT

TENS

IDLER

P/S

W/P

BELT TENSION
CHECK

C/S

**WITHOUT
AIR CONDITIONING**

VIEW A

AIR
CONDITIONING

ALTERNATOR

TENSIONER

POWER
STEERING

IDLER

WATER
PUMP

CRANKSHAFT

BOLT

ALTERNATOR

BRACKET

WATER PUMP
PULLEY

BELT
TENSIONER

SCREW

FRONT OF ENGINE

BOLT

SCREW

IDLER

VIEW B

A/C COMPRESSOR

P/S AND A/C
BRACKET

BOLT

NUT

BRACE

BOLT

SCREW

POWER STEERING
PULLEY

POWER STEERING
PUMP ASSEMBLY

FRONT OF ENGINE

11.2c   Serpentine belt (4.0L V6 engine)

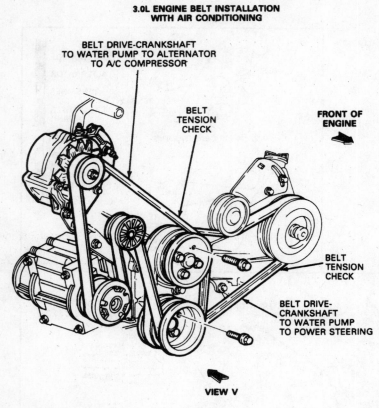

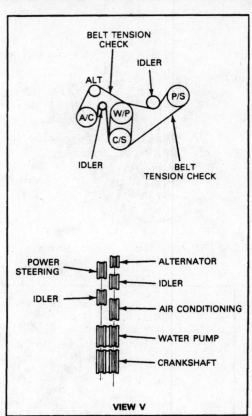

11.2d   Drivebelts – 3.0L V6 engine (model with A/C shown; model without A/C similar)

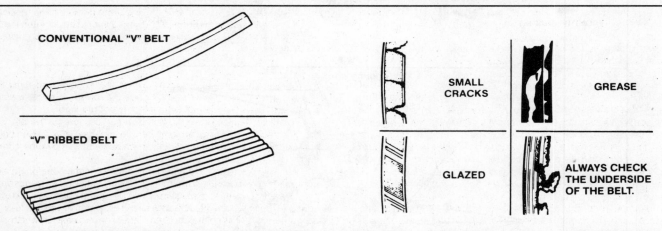

11.3   Different types of drivebelts are used to power the various accessories mounted on the engine

11.4   Here are some of the more common problems associated with drivebelts (check the belts very carefully to prevent an untimely breakdown)

Nylon fuel lines

17   Nylon fuel lines are used at several points in fuel injection systems. These lines require special materials and methods for repair. Refer to Chapter 4 for details.

Power steering hoses

18   Check the power steering hoses for leaks, loose connections and worn clamps. Tighten loose connections. Worn clamps or leaky hoses should be replaced.

11   Drivebelt check, adjustment and replacement

Refer to illustrations 11.2a, 11.2b, 11.2c, 11.2d, 11.3, 11.4, 11.5, 11.6, 11.7 and 11.15

1   The accessory drivebelts are located at the front of the engine. The belts drive the water pump, alternator, power steering pump, air conditioning compressor and thermactor air pump. The condition and tension of the drivebelts are critical to the operation of the engine and accessories. Excessive tension causes bearing wear, while insufficient tension produces

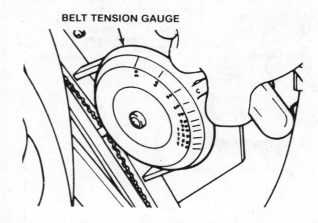

BELT TENSION GAUGE

11.5 A drivebelt tension gauge is recommended for checking the belt tension

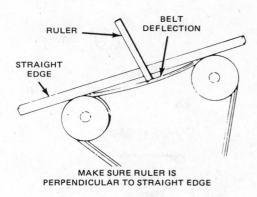

RULER

BELT DEFLECTION

STRAIGHT EDGE

MAKE SURE RULER IS PERPENDICULAR TO STRAIGHT EDGE

11.6 Measuring drivebelt deflection with a straightedge and a ruler

slippage, noise, component vibration and belt failure. Because of their composition and the high stress to which they are subjected, drivebelts stretch and continue to deteriorate as they get older. As a result, they must be periodically checked. Some belts require periodic tension adjustment; others have automatic tensioners and require no adjustment for the life of the belt.

Check

2   The number and type of belts used on a particular vehicle depends on the engine, model year and accessories installed **(see illustrations)**.
3   Various types of drivebelts are used on these models **(see illustration)**. Some components are driven by V-belts. Others are driven by V-ribbed belts. 4.0L and some 2.3L models use a single V-ribbed belt to drive all of the accessories. This is known as a "serpentine" belt because of the winding path it follows between various drive, accessory and idler pulleys.
4   With the engine off, open the hood and locate the drivebelt(s) at the front of the engine. With a flashlight, check each belt for separation of the rubber plies from each side of the core, a severed core, separation of the ribs from the rubber, cracks, torn or worn ribs and cracks in the inner ridges of the ribs. Also check for fraying and glazing, which gives the belt a shiny appearance **(see illustration)**. Cracks in the rib side of V-ribbed belts are acceptable, as are small chunks missing from the ribs. If a V-ribbed belt has lost chunks bigger than 1/2-inch (13 mm) from two adjacent ribs, or if the missing chunks cause belt noise, the belt should be replaced. Both sides of each belt should be inspected, which means you'll have to twist them to check the undersides. Use your fingers to feel a belt where you can't see it. If any of the above conditions are evident, replace the belt as described below.
5   To check the tension of all except the 4.0L and 2.3L serpentine belts in accordance with factory recommendations, install a drivebelt tension gauge (special tool No. T63L-8620-A) **(see illustration)**. Measure the tension in accordance with the tension gauge instructions and compare your measurement to the specified drivebelt tension for either a used or a new belt. **Note:** *A "new" belt is defined as any belt which has not been run; a "used" belt is one which has been run for more than ten minutes.*
6   The special gauge is the most accurate way to check the tension of V-belts. However, if you don't have a gauge, and cannot borrow one, the following "rule of thumb" method is recommended as an alternative (for V-belts only; do not use this method on V-ribbed belts). Lay a straight-edge across the longest free span (the distance between two pulleys) of the belt. Push down firmly on the belt at a point half way between the pulleys and see how much the belt moves (deflects). Measure the deflection with a ruler **(see illustration)**. The belt should deflect 1/8 to 1/4-inch if the distance from pulley center-to-pulley center is less than 12 inches; it should deflect from 1/8 to 3/8-inch if the distance from pulley center-to-pulley center is over 12 inches.

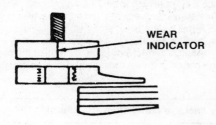

WEAR INDICATOR

11.7 The wear indicator should be between the Min and Max marks on 2.3L engines equipped with an automatic tensioner

7   To check the tension on 2.3L engines with an automatic tensioner, look at the wear indicator **(see illustration)**. It should be between the Min and Max marks. If it is not between the two marks, replace the belt (see Step 13).

Adjustment

8   Adjustment is necessary on all except 4.0L engines and some 2.3L engines. The 4.0L engine's serpentine belt and some 2.3L engines use an automatic tensioner. Manual adjustment is not required.
9   To adjust V-belts, move the belt-driven accessory on the bracket.
10   For each accessory, there will be a locking bolt and a pivot bolt or nut. Both must be loosened slightly to enable you to move the component.
11   After the two bolts have been loosened, move the component away from the engine (to tighten the belt) or toward the engine (to loosen the belt). Many accessories are equipped with a square hole designed to accept a 1/2-inch square drive breaker bar. The bar can be used to lever the component and tension the drivebelt. Others have a cast lug which is designed to accept an open-end wrench, which can be used to pry the accessory. **Caution:** *If it's necessary to pry against an accessory to tighten a drivebelt, be very careful not to damage the accessory or the point the prybar rests against.*
12   Hold the accessory in position and check the belt tension. If it's correct, tighten the two bolts until snug, then recheck the tension. If it's alright, tighten the two bolts completely.

Replacement

13   To replace a V-belt or V-ribbed belt, follow the above procedures for drivebelt adjustment, but loosen the belt until it will slip off the pulleys, then remove it. On some models, it may be necessary to remove forward belts to replace a rearward belt. Since belts tend to wear out at the same time, it's a good idea to replace all of them at the same time. Mark each belt and the corresponding pulley grooves so the belt can be reinstalled properly.

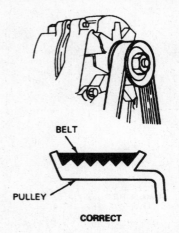 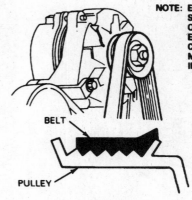

NOTE: ENSURE CORRECT
SEATING ON ALL PULLEYS.
ONE REVLUTION OF THE
ENGINE WITH AN IN-
CORRECTLY SEATED BELT
MAY SNAP TENSILE MEMBERS
IN THE BELT

BELT

PULLEY

CORRECT

BELT

PULLEY

INCORRECT

11.15   V-ribbed drivebelts should be centered on the pulleys, not offset

14   To replace a serpentine belt on 4.0L and some 2.3L engines, rotate the tensioner counterclockwise to lift it off the belt **(see illustration 11.2d)**. Slip the belt off the pulleys.

15   Hold the tensioner in the released position. Install a new belt and make sure it is routed correctly. Be sure the ribs of the new belt engage the pulley ribs correctly **(see illustration)**. Release the tensioner.

12   Battery check, maintenance and charging

Check and maintenance

Refer to illustrations 12.1, 12.4, 12.8a, 12.8b, 12.8c and 12.8d

Warning: *Certain precautions must be followed when checking and servicing the battery. Hydrogen gas, which is highly flammable, is always present in the battery cells, so keep lighted tobacco and all other flames and sparks away from it. The electrolyte inside the battery is actually dilute sulfuric acid, which will cause injury if splashed on your skin or in your eyes. It will ruin clothes and painted surfaces. When removing the battery cables, always detach the negative cable first and hook it up last!*

1   Battery maintenance is an important procedure which will help ensure that you are not stranded because of a dead battery. Several tools are required for this procedure **(see illustration)**.

2   Before servicing the battery, always turn the engine and all accessories off and disconnect the cable from the negative terminal of the battery.

3   A sealed (sometimes called maintenance free) battery is standard equipment. The cell caps cannot be removed, no electrolyte checks are required and water cannot be added to the cells. However, if an aftermarket battery has been installed and it is a type that requires regular maintenance, the following procedures can be used.

4   Check the electrolyte level in each of the battery cells **(see illustration)**. It must be above the plates. There's usually a split-ring indicator in each cell to indicate the correct level. If the level is low, add distilled water only, then install the cell caps. **Caution:** *Overfilling the cells may cause electrolyte to spill over during periods of heavy charging, causing corrosion and damage to nearby components.*

5   If the positive terminal and cable clamp on your vehicle's battery is equipped with a rubber protector, make sure that it's not torn or damaged. It should completely cover the terminal.

6   The external condition of the battery should be checked periodically. Look for damage such as a cracked case.

7   Check the tightness of the battery cable clamps to ensure good electrical connections and inspect the entire length of each cable, looking for cracked or abraded insulation and frayed conductors.

8   If corrosion (visible as white, fluffy deposits) is evident, remove the cables from the terminals, clean them with a battery brush and reinstall them **(see illustrations)**. Corrosion can be kept to a minimum by install-

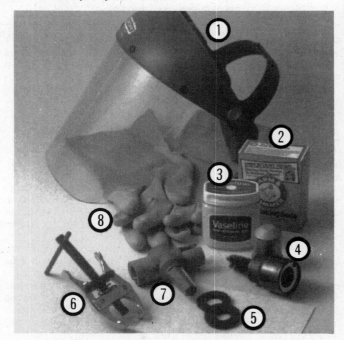

12.1   Tools and materials required for battery maintenance

1   *Face shield/safety goggles – When removing corrosion with a brush, the acidic particles can easily fly up into your eyes*

2   *Baking soda – A solution of baking soda and water can be used to neutralize corrosion*

3   *Petroleum jelly – A layer of this on the battery posts will help prevent corrosion*

4   *Battery post/cable cleaner – This wire brush cleaning tool will remove all traces of corrosion from the battery posts and cable clamps*

5   *Treated felt washers – Placing one of these on each post, directly under the cable clamps, will help prevent corrosion*

6   *Puller – Sometimes the cable clamps are very difficult to pull off the posts, even after the nut/bolt has been completely loosened. This tool pulls the clamp straight up and off the mpost without damage.*

7   *Battery post/cable cleaner – Here is another cleaning tool which is a slightly different version of number 4 above, but it does the same thing*

8   *Rubber gloves – Another safety item to consider when servicing the battery; remember that's acid inside the battery!*

12.4   Remove the cell caps to check the water level in the battery – if the level is low, add distilled water only

12.8a   Battery terminal corrosion usually appears as light, fluffy powder

12.8b   Removing the cable from a battery post with a wrench – sometimes a special pliers is required for this procedure if corrosion has caused deterioration of the nut hex (always remove the ground cable first and hook it up last!)

12.8c   Regardless of the type of tool used on the battery posts, a clean, shiny surface should be the result

ing specially treated washers available at auto parts stores or by applying a layer of petroleum jelly or grease to the terminals and cable clamps after they are assembled.

9   Make sure that the battery carrier is in good condition and that the hold-down clamp bolt is tight. If the battery is removed (see Chapter 5 for the removal and installation procedure), make sure that no parts remain in the bottom of the carrier when it's reinstalled. When reinstalling the hold-down clamp, don't overtighten the bolt.

10   Corrosion on the carrier, battery case and surrounding areas can be removed with a solution of water and baking soda. Apply the mixture with a small brush, let it work, then rinse it off with plenty of clean water.

11   Any metal parts of the vehicle damaged by corrosion should be coated with a zinc-based primer, then painted.

12   Additional information on the battery, charging and jump starting can be found in Chapter 5 and the front of this manual.

Charging

13   Remove all of the cell caps (if equipped) and cover the holes with a clean cloth to prevent spattering electrolyte. Disconnect the negative battery cable and hook the battery charger leads to the battery posts (positive to positive, negative to negative), then plug in the charger. Make sure it is set at 12 volts if it has a selector switch.

12.8d   When cleaning the cable clamps, all corrosion must be removed (the inside of the clamp is tapered to match the taper on the post, so don't remove too much material)

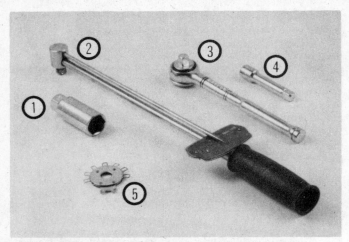

13.2   Tools required for changing spark plugs

1   **Spark plug socket** – This will have special padding inside
to protect the spark plug's porcelain insulator
2   **Torque wrench** – Although not mandatory, using this tool is
the best way to ensure the plugs are tightened properly
3   **Ratchet** – Standard hand tool to fit the spark plug socket
4   **Extension** – Depending on model and accessories, you may
need special extensions and universal joints to reach one or
more of the plugs
5   **Spark plug gap gauge** – This gauge for checking the gap
comes in a variety of styles. Make sure the gap for your
engine is included.

14   If you're using a charger with a rate higher than two amps, check the battery regularly during charging to make sure it doesn't overheat. If you're using a trickle charger, you can safely let the battery charge overnight after you've checked it regularly for the first couple of hours.
15   If the battery has removeable cell caps, measure the specific gravity with a hydrometer every hour during the last few hours of the charging cycle. Hydrometers are available inexpensively from auto parts stores – follow the instructions that come with the hydrometer. Consider the battery charged when there's no change in the specific gravity reading for two hours and the electrolyte in the cells is gassing (bubbling) freely. The specific gravity reading from each cell should be very close to the others. If not, the battery probably has a bad cell(s).
16   Some batteries with sealed tops have built-in hydrometers on the top that indicate the state of charge by the color displayed in the hydrometer window. Normally, a bright-colored hydrometer indicates a full charge and a dark hydrometer indicates the battery still needs charging. Check the battery manufacturer's instructions to be sure you know what the colors mean.
17   If the battery has a sealed top and no built-in hydrometer, you can hook up a digital voltmeter across the battery terminals to check the charge. A fully charged battery should read 12.6 volts or higher.
18   Further information on the battery and jump starting can be found in Chapter 5 and at the front of this manual.

13   Spark plug, plug wire, distributor cap and rotor check and replacement

Spark plugs

Refer to illustrations 13.2, 13.5a, 13.5b, 13.6 and 13.10
Note: Some 2.3L engines are equipped with two spark plugs per cylinder, for a total of eight plugs. There are four spark plugs on each side of the engine.

1   The spark plugs are located on the side(s) of the engine.
2   In most cases, the tools necessary for spark plug replacement include a spark plug socket which fits into a ratchet (spark plug sockets are padded inside to prevent damage to the porcelain insulators on the new

13.5a   Spark plug manufacturers recommend using a wire-type gauge when checking the gap – if the wire does not slide between the electrodes with a slight drag, adjustment is required

13.5b   To change the gap, bend the side electrode only, as indicated by the arrows, and be very careful not to crack or chip the porcelain insulator surrounding the center electrode

plugs and to hold the plugs in the socket during removal and installation), various extensions and a gap gauge to check and adjust the gaps on the new plugs (see illustration). A special plug wire removal tool is available for separating the wire boots from the spark plugs, but it isn't absolutely necessary. A torque wrench should be used to tighten the new plugs.
3   The best approach when replacing the spark plugs is to purchase the new ones in advance, adjust them to the proper gap and replace the plugs one at a time. When buying the new spark plugs, be sure to obtain the correct type for your particular engine. This information can be found on the Emission Control Information label located under the hood, in the factory owner's manual and in the Specifications Section in this Chapter. If differences exist between the plug specified on the emissions label and in the Specifications or owner's manual, assume the emissions label is correct.
4   Allow the engine to cool completely before attempting to remove any of the plugs. Some models have aluminum cylinder heads, which can be damaged if the spark plugs are removed when the engine is hot. While you are waiting for the engine to cool, check the new plugs for defects and adjust the gaps.
5   The gap is checked by inserting the proper thickness gauge between the electrodes at the tip of the plug (see illustration). The gap between the plugs should be the same as the one specified on the Emissions Control Information label. The gauge wire should just slide between the electrodes with a slight amount of drag. If the gap is incorrect,

Common spark plug conditions

NORMAL
Symptoms: Brown to grayish-tan color and slight electrode wear. Correct heat range for engine and operating conditions.
Recommendation: When new spark plugs are installed, replace with plugs of the same heat range.

WORN
Symptoms: Rounded electrodes with a small amount of deposits on the firing end. Normal color. Causes hard starting in damp or cold weather and poor fuel economy.
Recommendation: Plugs have been left in the engine too long. Replace with new plugs of the same heat range. Follow the recommended maintenance schedule.

CARBON DEPOSITS
Symptoms: Dry sooty deposits indicate a rich mixture or weak ignition. Causes misfiring, hard starting and hesitation.
Recommendation: Make sure the plug has the correct heat range. Check for a clogged air filter or problem in the fuel system or engine management system. Also check for ignition system problems.

ASH DEPOSITS
Symptoms: Light brown deposits encrusted on the side or center electrodes or both. Derived from oil and/or fuel additives. Excessive amounts may mask the spark, causing misfiring and hesitation during acceleration.
Recommendation: If excessive deposits accumulate over a short time or low mileage, install new valve guide seals to prevent seepage of oil into the combustion chambers. Also try changing gasoline brands.

OIL DEPOSITS
Symptoms: Oily coating caused by poor oil control. Oil is leaking past worn valve guides or piston rings into the combustion chamber. Causes hard starting, misfiring and hesitation.
Recommendation: Correct the mechanical condition with necessary repairs and install new plugs.

GAP BRIDGING
Symptoms: Combustion deposits lodge between the electrodes. Heavy deposits accumulate and bridge the electrode gap. The plug ceases to fire, resulting in a dead cylinder.
Recommendation: Locate the faulty plug and remove the deposits from between the electrodes.

TOO HOT
Symptoms: Blistered, white insulator, eroded electrode and absence of deposits. Results in shortened plug life.
Recommendation: Check for the correct plug heat range, over-advanced ignition timing, lean fuel mixture, intake manifold vacuum leaks, sticking valves and insufficient engine cooling.

PREIGNITION
Symptoms: Melted electrodes. Insulators are white, but may be dirty due to misfiring or flying debris in the combustion chamber. Can lead to engine damage.
Recommendation: Check for the correct plug heat range, over-advanced ignition timing, lean fuel mixture, insufficient engine cooling and lack of lubrication.

HIGH SPEED GLAZING
Symptoms: Insulator has yellowish, glazed appearance. Indicates that combustion chamber temperatures have risen suddenly during hard acceleration. Normal deposits melt to form a conductive coating. Causes misfiring at high speeds.
Recommendation: Install new plugs. Consider using a colder plug if driving habits warrant.

DETONATION
Symptoms: Insulators may be cracked or chipped. Improper gap setting techniques can also result in a fractured insulator tip. Can lead to piston damage.
Recommendation: Make sure the fuel anti-knock values meet engine requirements. Use care when setting the gaps on new plugs. Avoid lugging the engine.

MECHANICAL DAMAGE
Symptoms: May be caused by a foreign object in the combustion chamber or the piston striking an incorrect reach (too long) plug. Causes a dead cylinder and could result in piston damage.
Recommendation: Repair the mechanical damage. Remove the foreign object from the engine and/or install the correct reach plug.

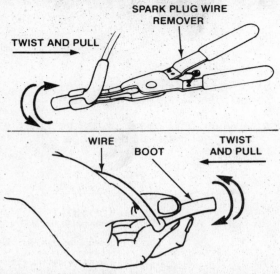

13.6   When removing the spark plug wires, pull only on the boot and twist it back-and-forth

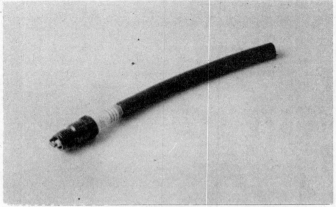

13.10   A length of 3/16-inch ID rubber hose will save time and prevent damaged threads when installing the spark plugs

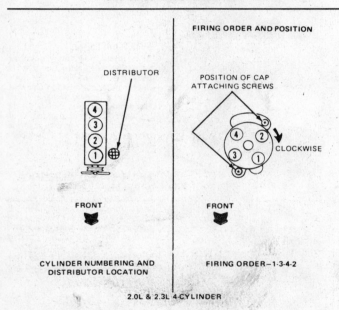

13.16a   Firing order and distributor cap terminals – 2.0L and 2.3L engines equipped with a distributor

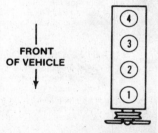

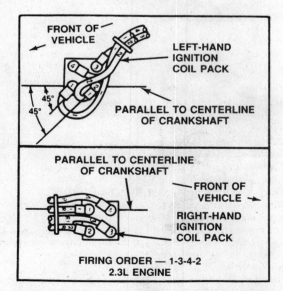

13.16b   Firing order and spark plug wire connection points – 2.3L engine with distributorless ignition

use the adjuster on the gauge body to bend the curved side electrode slightly until the specified gap is obtained (see illustration). If the side electrode is not exactly over the center electrode, bend it with the adjuster until it is. Check for cracks in the porcelain insulator (if any are found, the plug should not be used).

6   With the engine cool, remove the spark plug wire from one spark plug. Pull only on the boot at the end of the wire – do not pull on the wire. A plug wire removal tool should be used if available (see illustration).

7   If compressed air is available, use it to blow any dirt or foreign material away from the spark plug hole. A common bicycle pump will also work. The idea here is to eliminate the possibility of debris falling into the cylinder as the spark plug is removed.

8   Place the spark plug socket over the plug and remove it from the engine by turning in a counterclockwise direction.

9   Compare the spark plug to those shown in the accompanying photos to get an indication of the general running condition of the engine.

10   Thread one of the new plugs into the hole until you can no longer turn

it with your fingers, then tighten it with a torque wrench (if available) or the ratchet. It might be a good idea to slip a short length of rubber hose over the end of the plug to use as a tool to thread it into place, particularly if the cylinder head is made of aluminum (see illustration). The hose will grip the plug well enough to turn it, but will start to slip if the plug begins to cross-thread in the hole – this will prevent damaged threads and the accompanying repair costs.

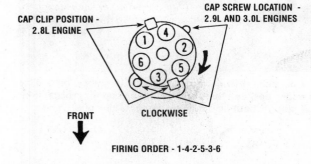

CYLINDER NUMBERING AND
DISTRIBUTOR LOCATION

DISTRIBUTOR

FRONT

FIRING ORDER AND ROTATION

CAP CLIP POSITION -
2.8L ENGINE

CAP SCREW LOCATION -
2.9L AND 3.0L ENGINES

FRONT

CLOCKWISE

FIRING ORDER - 1-4-2-5-3-6

13.16c Firing order and distributor cap terminals – 2.8L, 2.9L and 3.0L engines

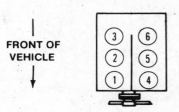

CYLINDER NUMBERING AND
FIRING ORDER

FRONT OF
VEHICLE

FIRING ORDER — 1-4-2-5-3-6
4.0L ENGINE

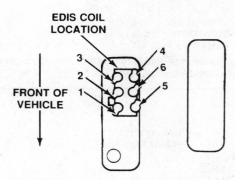

EDIS COIL
LOCATION

FRONT OF
VEHICLE

FIRING ORDER —.1-4-2-5-3-6
4.0L ENGINE

13.16d Firing order and spark plug wire connection points – 4.0L engine with distributorless ignition

11   Before pushing the spark plug wire onto the end of the plug, inspect it following the procedures outlined below.

12   Attach the plug wire to the new spark plug, again using a twisting motion on the boot until it is seated on the spark plug.

13   Repeat the procedure for the remaining spark plugs, replacing them one at a time to prevent mixing up the spark plug wires.

Spark plug wires

Refer to illustrations 13.16a, 13.16b, 13.16c and 13.16d

Note: *Every time a spark plug wire is detached from a spark plug, the distributor cap or the coil, silicone dielectric compound (a white grease available at auto parts stores) must be applied to the inside of each boot before reconnection. Use a small standard screwdriver to coat the entire inside surface of each boot with a thin layer of the compound.*

14   The spark plug wires should be checked and, if necessary, replaced at the same time new spark plugs are installed.

15   The easiest way to identify bad wires is to make a visual check while the engine is running. In a dark, well-ventilated garage, start the engine and look at each plug wire. Be careful not to come into contact with any moving engine parts. If there is a break in the wire, you will see arcing or a small spark at the damaged area. If arcing is noticed, make a note to obtain new wires.

16   The spark plug wires should be inspected one at a time, beginning with the spark plug for the number one cylinder (on four-cylinder engines, the number one cylinder is at the front of the engine; on V6 engines it's the cylinder closest to the radiator on the right bank), to prevent confusion. Clearly label each original plug wire with a piece of tape marked with the correct number. On 2.3L engines with a twin-plug ignition system, label the wires according to the side of the engine they attach to (intake or exhaust) as well as with the cylinder number. The plug wires must be reinstalled in the correct order to ensure proper engine operation **(see illustrations)**.

17   Disconnect the spark plug wire from the first spark plug. A removal tool can be used **(see illustration 13.6)**, or you can grab the wire boot, twist it slightly and pull the wire free. Do not pull on the wire itself, only on the rubber boot.

18   Push the wire and boot back onto the end of the spark plug. It should fit snugly. If it doesn't, detach the wire and boot once more and use a pair of pliers to carefully crimp the metal connector inside the wire boot until it does.

19   Using a clean rag, wipe the entire length of the wire to remove built-up dirt and grease.

20   Once the wire is clean, check for burns, cracks and other damage. Do not bend the wire sharply or you might break the conductor.

21   Disconnect the wire from the distributor or ignition coil pack. Again, pull only on the rubber boot. Check for corrosion and a tight fit. Replace the wire in the distributor or coil pack.

22   Inspect each of the remaining spark plug wires, making sure that each one is securely fastened at the distributor or coil pack and spark plug when the check is complete.

23   If new spark plug wires are required, purchase a set for your specific engine model. Pre-cut wire sets with the boots already installed are available. Remove and replace the wires one at a time to avoid mix-ups in the firing order.

Distributor cap and rotor

Refer to illustrations 13.24a, 13.24b, 13.25 and 13.26

Note 1: *It's common practice to install a new distributor cap and rotor each time new spark plug wires are installed. If you're planning to install new wires, install a new cap and rotor also. But if you're planning to reuse the existing wires, be sure to inspect the cap and rotor to make sure that they are in good condition.*

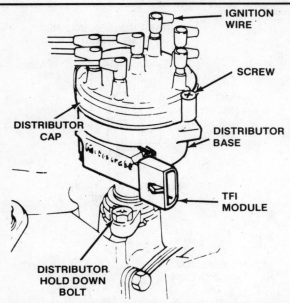

13.24a   To remove the distributor cap, loosen the retaining screws (shown) or pry back the retaining clips

13.24b   Check the distributor cap contacts for corrosion and for carbon tracks between them and check the cap for cracks (if in doubt about its condition, install a new one)

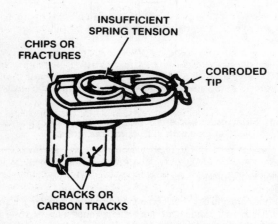

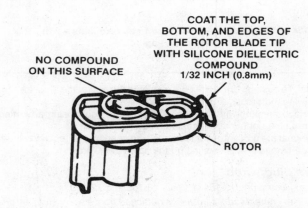

13.25   The ignition rotor should be checked for wear and corrosion as indicated here (if in doubt about its condition, buy a new one)

13.26   Apply silicone dielectric compound to single-point distributor rotors

Note 2: *Later 2.3L engines and all 4.0L engines use a distributorless ignition system – there isn't a cap or rotor.*

24   Pry back the cap clips or loosen the cap screws and detach the cap from the distributor **(see illustration)**. Check it for cracks, carbon tracks and worn, burned or loose terminals **(see illustration)**.

25   Check the rotor for cracks and carbon tracks. Make sure the center terminal spring tension is adequate and look for corrosion and wear on the rotor tip **(see illustration)**. **Note:** *The silicone dielectric compound used on single-point rotors darkens with age and may look like dirt or corrosion. Do not replace a rotor just because of the dielectric compound's appearance.*

26   Replace the cap and rotor if damage or defects are found. Note that the rotor is held on the shaft by two screws (some models) and on some models slides on and off and is indexed so it can only be installed one way. Before installing the cap, apply silicone dielectric compound to the rotor tip of single-point rotors **(see illustration)**.

27   When installing a new cap, remove the wires from the old cap one at a time and attach them to the new cap in the exact same location – do not

simultaneously remove all the wires from the old cap or firing order mix-ups may occur.

14   Automatic transmission shift linkage lubrication

Refer to illustration 14.3

1   Open the hood and locate the shift rod contact points.
2   Clean the linkage and pivot points.
3   Lubricate the shift linkage and pivot points with multi-purpose grease **(see illustration)**.

15   Chassis lubrication

Refer to illustrations 15.1, 15.2, 15.14a, 15.14b and 15.15

1   Refer to *Recommended_lubricants_and_fluids_*at the front of this Chapter to obtain the necessary grease, etc. You'll also need a grease

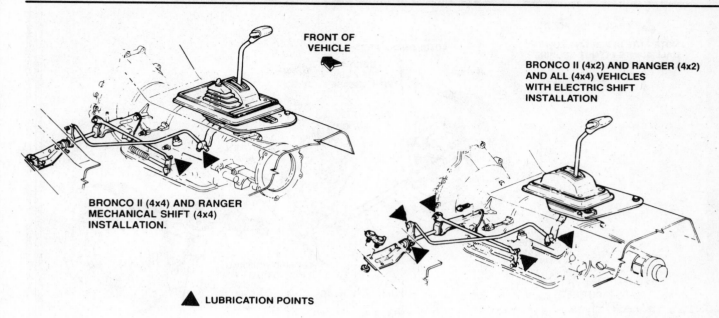

FRONT OF VEHICLE

BRONCO II (4x2) AND RANGER (4x2) AND ALL (4x4) VEHICLES WITH ELECTRIC SHIFT INSTALLATION

BRONCO II (4x4) AND RANGER MECHANICAL SHIFT (4x4) INSTALLATION.

▲ LUBRICATION POINTS

14.3 Automatic transmission shift lever and linkage (typical)

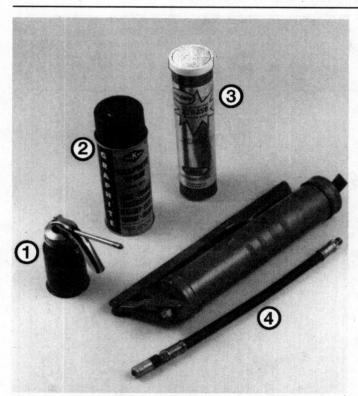

15.1 Materials required for chassis and body lubrication

1 *Engine oil* – Light engine oil in a can like this can be used for door and hood hinges
2 *Graphite spray* – Used to lubricate lock cylinders
3 *Grease* – Grease, in a variety of types and weights, is available for use in a grease gun. Check the Specifications for your requirements.
4 *Grease gun* – A common grease gun, shown here with a detachable hose and nozzle, is needed for chassis lubrication. After use, clean it thoroughly!

gun **(see illustration)**. Occasionally plugs will be installed rather than grease fittings. If so, grease fittings will have to be purchased and installed.

2   Look under the vehicle and see if grease fittings or plugs are installed in the tie-rod ends **(see illustration)**. If there are plugs, remove them and buy grease fittings, which will thread into the component. A dealer or auto parts store will be able to supply the correct fittings. Straight, as well as angled, fittings are available.

3   Also check the driveshaft universal joints for grease fittings. If the universal joints have grease fittings, they should be lubricated periodically. If not, they don't require periodic lubrication.

4   Constant velocity and double cardan joints (used at the front end of the rear driveshaft on 4WD models) are equipped with a flush-type fitting. This must be removed and an adapter installed to lubricate the joint.

5   For easier access under the vehicle, raise it with a jack and place jackstands under the frame. Make sure the vehicle is safely supported – DO NOT crawl under the vehicle when it is supported only by the jack! If the wheels are to be removed at this interval for tire rotation or brake inspection, loosen the lug nuts slightly while the vehicle is still on the ground.

6   Before beginning, force a little grease out of the nozzle to remove any dirt from the end of the gun. Wipe the nozzle clean with a rag.

7   With the grease gun and plenty of clean rags, crawl under the vehicle.

8   Wipe the tie-rod end grease fitting nipple clean and push the nozzle firmly over it. Squeeze the trigger on the grease gun to force grease into the component. They should be lubricated until the rubber seal is firm to the touch. Don't pump too much grease into the fitting as it could rupture the seal. If grease escapes around the grease-gun nozzle, the nipple is clogged or the nozzle is not completely seated on the fitting. Resecure the gun nozzle to the fitting and try again. If necessary, replace the fitting with a new one.

9   Wipe the excess grease from the components and the grease fitting. Repeat the procedure for the remaining fitting(s).

10   Open the hood and smear a little chassis grease on the hood latch mechanism. Have an assistant pull the hood release lever from inside the vehicle as you lubricate the cable at the latch.

11   Lubricate all the hinges (door, hood, etc.) with engine oil to keep them in proper working order.

12   The key lock cylinders can be lubricated with spray graphite or silicone lubricant, which is available at auto parts stores.

13   Lubricate the door weatherstripping with silicone spray. This will re-

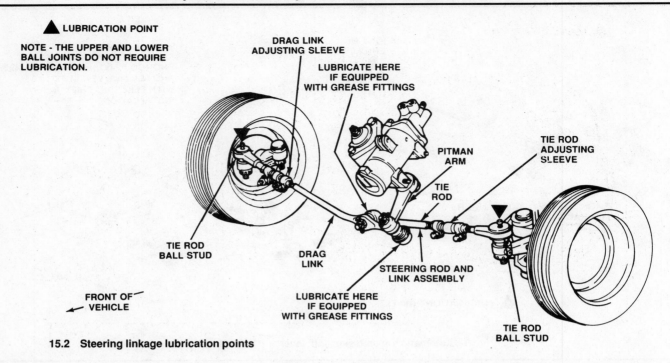

▲ **LUBRICATION POINT**

NOTE - THE UPPER AND LOWER BALL JOINTS DO NOT REQUIRE LUBRICATION.

DRAG LINK ADJUSTING SLEEVE

LUBRICATE HERE IF EQUIPPED WITH GREASE FITTINGS

PITMAN ARM

TIE ROD

TIE ROD ADJUSTING SLEEVE

TIE ROD BALL STUD

DRAG LINK

STEERING ROD AND LINK ASSEMBLY

LUBRICATE HERE IF EQUIPPED WITH GREASE FITTINGS

TIE ROD BALL STUD

FRONT OF VEHICLE

15.2   Steering linkage lubrication points

duce chafing and retard wear.
14   Lubricate the parking brake linkage **(see illustrations)**. Note that two different types of grease are required. Use multipurpose grease on the linkage, adjuster assembly and connectors; use speedometer cable lu-bricant on parts of the cable that touch other parts of the vehicle. Lubricate the cable twice, once with the parking brake set and once with it released.
15   On manual transmission-equipped models, lubricate the clutch link-age friction points **(see illustration)**.

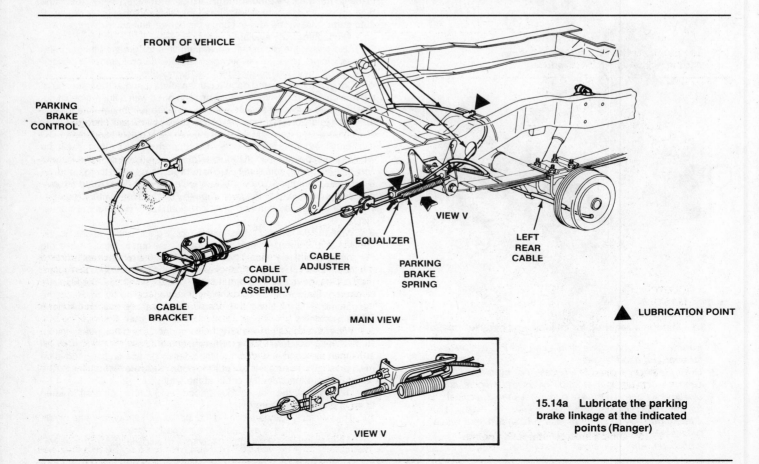

FRONT OF VEHICLE

PARKING BRAKE CONTROL

VIEW V

LEFT REAR CABLE

CABLE BRACKET

CABLE CONDUIT ASSEMBLY

CABLE ADJUSTER

EQUALIZER

PARKING BRAKE SPRING

MAIN VIEW

VIEW V

▲ **LUBRICATION POINT**

15.14a   Lubricate the parking brake linkage at the indicated points (Ranger)

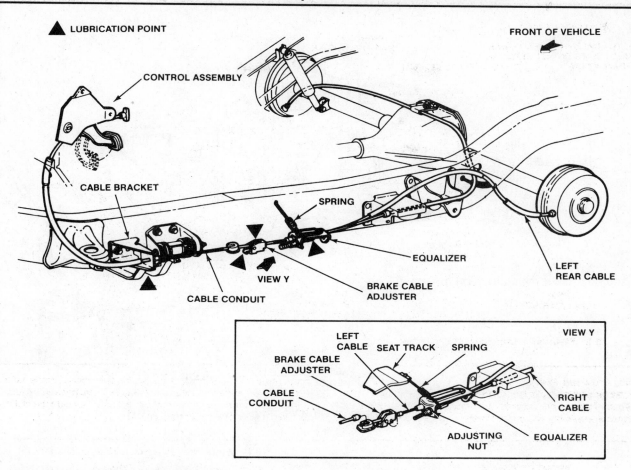

15.14b Lubricate the parking brake linkage at the indicated points (Bronco II)

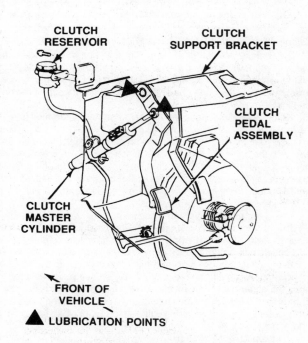

15.15 Clutch linkage lubrication points

16 Manual transmission lubricant level check and change

Note: *The transmission lubricant level and quality should not deteriorate under normal driving conditions. However, it's recommended that you check the level occasionally. The most convenient time would be when the vehicle is raised for another reason, such as an engine oil change.*

Lubricant level check

Refer to illustration 16.1

1   The transmission has a filler plug which must be removed to check the lubricant level (**see illustration**). If the vehicle is raised to gain access to the plug, be sure to support it safely on jackstands – DO NOT crawl under a vehicle which is supported only by a jack!

2   Remove the plug from the transmission and use your little finger to reach inside the housing and feel the lubricant level. It should be at or very near the bottom of the plug hole.

3   If it isn't, add the recommended lubricant through the plug hole with a syringe or squeeze bottle.

4   Install and tighten the plug securely and check for leaks after the first few miles of driving.

Lubricant change

Refer to illustration 16.5

5   Manual transmission lubricant does not normally need changing during the life of the vehicle, but if you wish to do so, place a drain pan

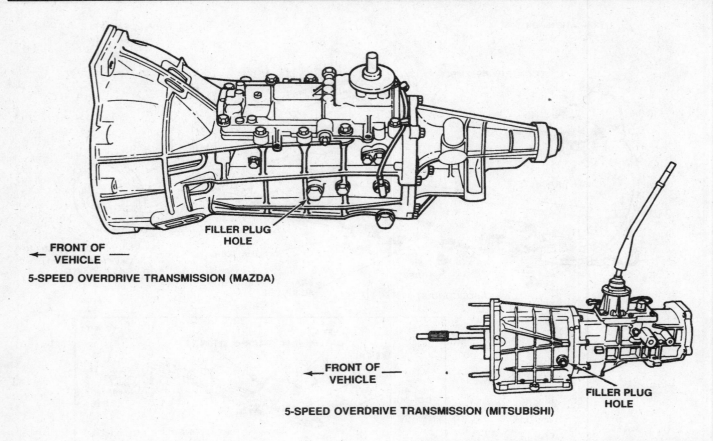

5-SPEED OVERDRIVE TRANSMISSION (MAZDA)

FILLER PLUG HOLE

← FRONT OF VEHICLE ——

← FRONT OF VEHICLE ——

5-SPEED OVERDRIVE TRANSMISSION (MITSUBISHI)

FILLER PLUG HOLE

16.1   Manual transmission filler plug locations – typical

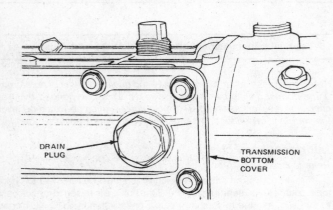

DRAIN PLUG

TRANSMISSION BOTTOM COVER

16.5   Manual transmission drain plug location – typical

beneath the drain plug. Remove the filler plug (**see illustration**), then remove the drain plug and let the lubricant drain into a pan. Let the lubricant drain for 10 minutes or more, then reinstall the filler plug and tighten securely. Check the fluid for metal chips that indicate transmission damage.

6   Fill the transmission to the bottom of the filler plug hole with recommended lubricant.

7   Install and tighten the filler plug securely and check for leaks after the first few miles of driving.

17   Differential (front and rear) lubricant level check and change

Refer to illustrations 17.2, 17.7 and 17.11

1   The rear differential (and front differential on 4WD models) has a check/fill plug which must be removed to check the lubricant level. If the vehicle is raised to gain access to the plug, be sure to support it safely on jackstands – DO NOT crawl under the vehicle when it's supported only by the jack!

2   Remove the lubricant check/fill plug from the differential (**see illustration**).

3   Use your little finger as a dipstick to make sure the lubricant level is even with the bottom of the plug hole. If not, use a syringe to add the recommended lubricant until it just starts to run out of the opening. On some models a tag is located in the area of the plug which gives information regarding lubricant type, particularly on models equipped with a limited slip differential.

4   Install the plug and tighten it securely.

5   If it is necessary to change the differential lubricant, remove the check/fill plug (**see illustration 17.2**), then drain the differential. Some differentials can be drained by removing the drain plug, while on some rear differentials it's necessary to remove the cover plate on the differential housing. As an alternative, a hand suction pump can be used to remove the differential lubricant through the filler hole. This is the only way to drain front axles which don't have a drain plug. If you remove the cover plate, obtain a tube of silicone sealant to be used when reinstalling the differential cover.

6   If equipped with a drain plug, remove the plug and allow the differential lubricant to drain completely. After the lubricant has drained, install the plug and tighten it securely.

17.2 The check/fill plug for the front differential on 4WD models (shown) is located in the axle housing – the check/fill plug for rear differentials is located in the differential housing, facing the front of the vehicle

17.7 A small hand pump can be used to remove the old lubricant from all differentials – it's the only method for front differentials which don't have a drain plug

7   If a suction pump is being used, insert the flexible hose (**see illustration**). Work the hose down to the bottom of the differential housing and pump the lubricant out.

8   If the differential is being drained by removing the cover plate, remove all of the bolts except the two near the top. Loosen the remaining two bolts and use them to keep the cover loosely attached. Allow the lubricant to drain into the pan, then completely remove the cover.

9   Using a lint-free rag, clean the inside of the cover and the accessible areas of the differential housing. As this is done, check for chipped gears and metal particles in the lubricant, indicating that the differential should be more thoroughly inspected and/or repaired.

10   Clean all old gasket material from the cover and differential housing.

11   Apply a bead of sealant to the cover mating surface. Run the bead inside the cover bolt holes (**see illustration**).

12   Place the cover on the differential housing and install the bolts. Tighten the bolts securely in a criss-cross pattern. Don't overtighten them or the cover may be distorted and leaks may develop.

13   On all models, use a hand pump, syringe or funnel to fill the differential housing with the specified lubricant until it's level with the bottom of the plug hole.

14   Install the check/fill plug and tighten it securely.

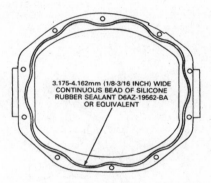

17.11 If you drain the differential by removing the cover, apply a bead of RTV sealant to the differential cover just before installation

3.175-4.162mm (1/8-3/16 INCH) WIDE CONTINUOUS BEAD OF SILICONE RUBBER SEALANT D6AZ-19562-BA OR EQUIVALENT

18   Transfer case lubricant level check and change

Refer to illustration 18.1

Lubricant level check

1   The transfer case has a check/fill plug which must be removed to check the lubricant level (**see illustration**). If the vehicle is raised to gain access to the plug, be sure to support it safely on jackstands – DO NOT crawl under a vehicle which is supported only by a jack!

2   Remove the plug from the transfer case and use your little finger to reach inside the housing and feel the lubricant level. It should be at or very near the bottom of the plug hole.

3   If it isn't, add the recommended lubricant through the plug hole with a syringe or squeeze bottle.

4   Install and tighten the plug securely and check for leaks after the first few miles of driving.

Lubricant change

5   To change the lubricant, remove the check/fill plug first. This will speed draining. Position a drain pan under the drain plug, remove the drain plug (**see illustration 18.1**) and let the lubricant drain.

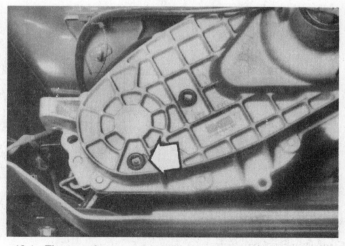

18.1 The transfer case check/fill plug (upper arrow) and drain plug (lower arrow)

6   Clean the drain plug threads, then reinstall the plug after the lubricant has finished draining.

7   Fill the transaxle to the bottom of the filler plug threads with the lubricant listed in this Chapter's Specifications.

8   Install the check/fill plug and tighten securely.

19.3   To remove the air filter on carbureted engines, remove the cover and lift the filter out

19   Air filter replacement

1   Purchase a new filter element for your specific engine type.

Carbureted engines

Refer to illustration 19.3

2   Remove the wing nut from the top of the housing and lift the cover off.

3   Remove the filter element **(see illustration)**.

4   Wipe the inside of the air cleaner housing with a clean cloth.

5   Place the new air filter element in the housing. If the element is marked TOP be sure the marked side faces up.

6   Install the cover and wing nut. Don't overtighten the nut!

EFI engines

Refer to illustrations 19.7a, 19.7b, 19.7c and 19.7d

7   Disconnect the vacuum hose(s) and outlet tube from the air cleaner cover **(see illustrations)**. Remove the cover retaining screws or disengage the clips and lift the cover off.

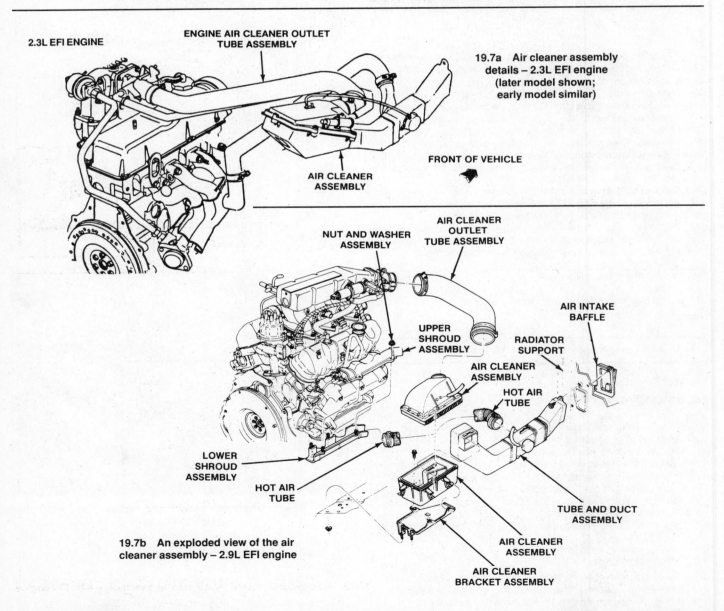

2.3L EFI ENGINE

ENGINE AIR CLEANER OUTLET TUBE ASSEMBLY

AIR CLEANER ASSEMBLY

19.7a   Air cleaner assembly details – 2.3L EFI engine (later model shown; early model similar)

FRONT OF VEHICLE

NUT AND WASHER ASSEMBLY

AIR CLEANER OUTLET TUBE ASSEMBLY

AIR INTAKE BAFFLE

UPPER SHROUD ASSEMBLY

RADIATOR SUPPORT

AIR CLEANER ASSEMBLY

HOT AIR TUBE

LOWER SHROUD ASSEMBLY

HOT AIR TUBE

TUBE AND DUCT ASSEMBLY

AIR CLEANER ASSEMBLY

AIR CLEANER BRACKET ASSEMBLY

19.7b   An exploded view of the air cleaner assembly – 2.9L EFI engine

8   Remove the filter element.

9   Wipe the inside of the air cleaner housing with a clean cloth.

10   Place the new air filter element in the housing. If the element is marked TOP be sure the marked side faces up.

11   Reinstall the cover and attach the clips or tighten the retaining screws. Don't overtighten the screws!

12   Reconnect the vacuum hose(s) and outlet tube.

20   Crankcase vent filter replacement

1   Obtain a new crankcase vent filter for your specific engine.

Filter in air cleaner

Refer to illustration 20.3

2   Remove the air cleaner cover to expose the crankcase vent filter.

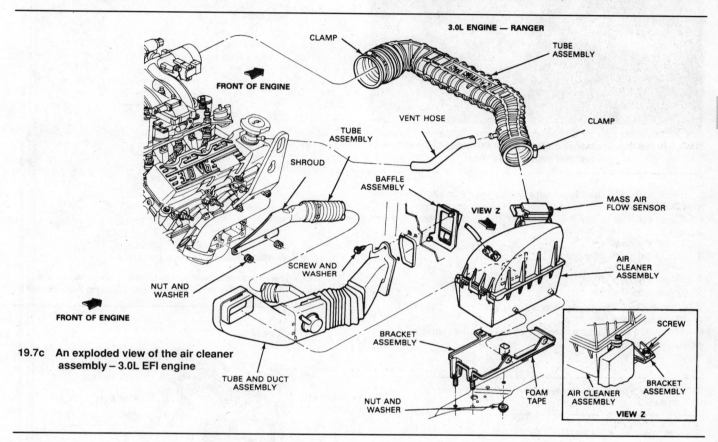

19.7c   An exploded view of the air cleaner assembly – 3.0L EFI engine

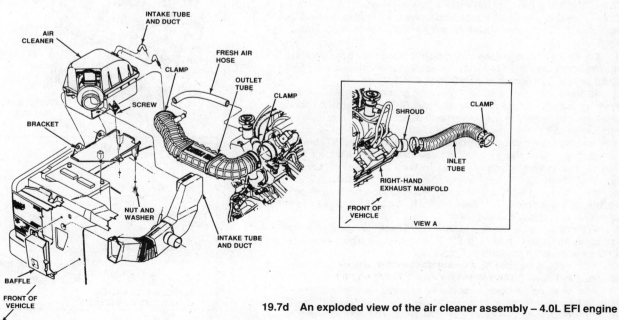

19.7d   An exploded view of the air cleaner assembly – 4.0L EFI engine

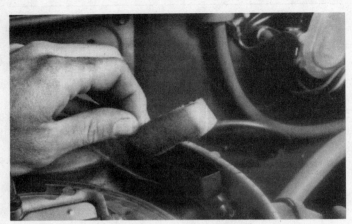

20.3   To replace an air cleaner-mounted crankcase ventilation filter, remove the air cleaner cover, lift out the filter, clean the filter pocket and install a new filter

3   Remove the filter from its pocket in the side of the air cleaner housing **(see illustration)**.
4   Clean the filter pocket with a cloth or paper towel moistened with solvent.
5   Install the new filter.
6   Install the air cleaner cover.

Filter in valve cover

Refer to illustration 20.9
7   The oil filler cap, filter and tube are replaced as an assembly.
8   Disconnect the filter tube.
9   Unscrew the oil filler cap from the valve cover **(see illustration)** and install a new one.

---

21   Positive Crankcase Ventilation (PCV) valve check and replacement

---

Refer to illustrations 21.1a, 21.1b, 21.1c and 21.1d
Note: *To maintain the efficiency of the PCV system, clean the hoses and check the PCV valve at the intervals recommended in the maintenance schedule. For additional information on the PCV system, refer to Chapter 6.*
1   Locate the PCV valve **(see illustration 20.9 and the accompanying illustrations).** On 2.3L EFI engines, the air cleaner must be removed (see Chapter 4) to gain access to the PCV valve.
2   To check the valve, first pull it out of the grommet in the rocker arm cover or manifold, or out of the lower hose. Shake the valve. It should rattle, indicating that it is not clogged with deposits. If the valve does not rattle, replace it with a new one. If it does rattle, reinstall it.
3   Start the engine and allow it to idle, then disconnect the PCV breather hose (from the air cleaner on most models). If vacuum is felt, the PCV valve system is working properly (see Chapter 6 for additional PCV system information).
4   If no vacuum is felt, the oil filler cap, hoses or rocker arm cover gasket may be leaking or the PCV valve may be bad. Check for vacuum leaks at the valve, filler cap and all hoses.
5   Pull straight up on the valve to remove it. Check the rubber grommet for cracks and distortion (on 2.3L EFI models, check the hose where the PCV valve seats). If it's damaged, replace it.
6   If the valve is clogged, the hose is also probably plugged. Remove the hose and clean it with solvent.
7   After cleaning the hose, inspect it for damage, wear and deterioration. Make sure it fits snugly on the fittings.
8   If necessary, install a new PCV valve. **Note:** *The elbow (models so equipped) is not part of the PCV valve. A new valve will not include the*

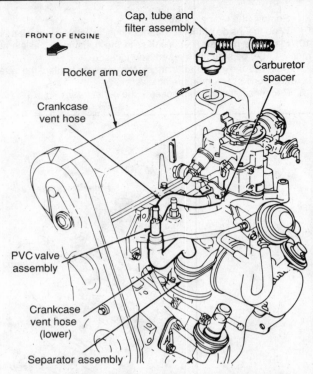

20.9   The crankcase ventilation filter on some models is mounted in the oil filler cap (2.0L shown, 2.3L and 2.8L similar)

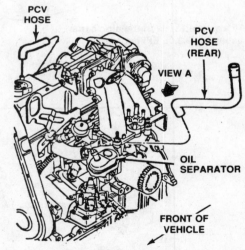

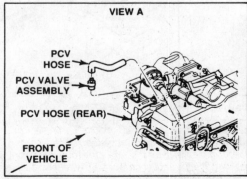

21.1a   PCV system (2.3L EFI engines)

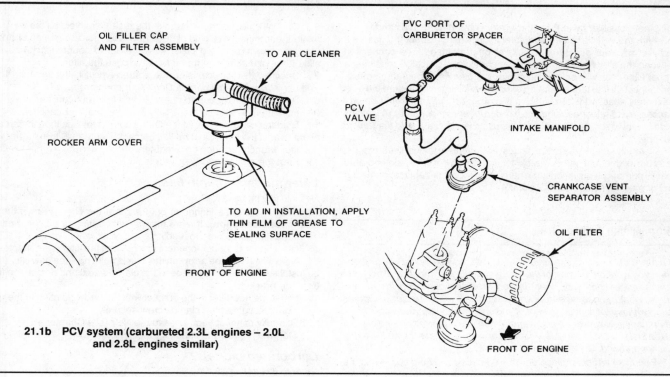

21.1b PCV system (carbureted 2.3L engines – 2.0L and 2.8L engines similar)

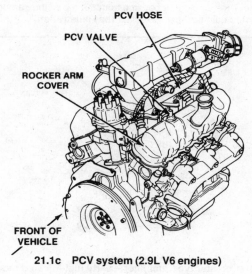

21.1c PCV system (2.9L V6 engines)

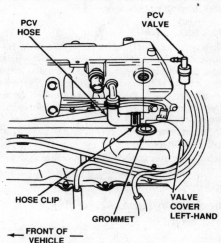

21.1d PCV system (4.0L V6 engine shown; 3.0L V6 engine similar)

elbow. The original must be transferred to the new valve. If a new elbow is purchased, it may be necessary to soak it in warm water for up to an hour to slip it onto the new valve. Do not attempt to force the elbow onto the valve or it will break.

9   Install the clean PCV system hose. Make sure that the PCV valve and hose are secure.

22 Fuel system check

Warning: *Gasoline is extremely flammable, so take extra precautions when you work on any part of the fuel system. Don't smoke or allow open flames or bare light bulbs near the work area, and don't work in a garage where a natural gas-type appliance (such as a water heater or clothes dryer) with a pilot light is present. If you spill any fuel on your skin, rinse it off immediately with soap and water. When you perform any kind of work on*

the fuel system, wear safety glasses and have a Class B type fire extinguisher on hand.

1   If you smell gasoline while driving or after the vehicle has been sitting in the sun, inspect the fuel system immediately.

2   Remove the gas filler cap and inspect it for damage and corrosion. The gasket should have an unbroken sealing imprint. If the gasket is damaged or corroded, install a new cap.

3   Inspect the fuel feed and return lines for cracks. Make sure that the connections between the fuel lines and the carburetor or fuel injection system and between the fuel lines and the in-line fuel filter are tight. **Warning:** *If your vehicle is fuel injected, you must relieve the fuel system pressure before servicing fuel system components. The fuel system pressure relief procedure is outlined in Chapter 4.*

4   Since some components of the fuel system – the fuel tank and part of the fuel feed and return lines, for example – are underneath the vehicle, they can be inspected more easily with the vehicle raised on a hoist. If

that's not possible, raise the vehicle and support it on jackstands.

5   With the vehicle raised and safely supported, inspect the gas tank and filler neck for punctures, cracks or other damage. The connection between the filler neck and the tank is particularly critical. Sometimes a rubber filler neck will leak because of loose clamps or deteriorated rubber. Inspect all fuel tank mounting brackets and straps to be sure the tank is securely attached to the vehicle. **Warning:** *Do not, under any circumstances, try to repair a fuel tank (except rubber components). A welding torch or any open flame can easily cause fuel vapors inside the tank to explode.*

6   Carefully check all rubber hoses and metal or nylon lines leading away from the fuel tank. Check for loose connections, deteriorated hoses, crimped lines and other damage. Repair or replace damaged sections as necessary (see Chapter 4).

23   Fuel filter – replacement

Warning: *Gasoline is extremely flammable, so take extra precautions when you work on any part of the fuel system. Don't smoke or allow open flames or bare light bulbs near the work area, and don't work in a garage where a natural gas-type appliance (such as a water heater or clothes dryer) with a pilot light is present. If you spill any fuel on your skin, rinse it off immediately with soap and water. When you perform any kind of work on the fuel system, wear safety glasses and have a Class B type fire extinguisher on hand.*

1   Periodic fuel filter replacement isn't required and Ford states that the inline filter used on fuel-injected models should last the life of the vehicle. Replace the filter if it becomes clogged.

Fuel-injected models

2   Obtain a new fuel filter before starting. **Warning:** *Be sure the new filter is specifically designed for your engine. Fuel injection system filters are built to withstand high pressure, and as a result, often cost more than filters meant for use in carbureted systems. Filters meant for carbureted systems may burst due to the high pressure. Also, be sure the new filter includes replacement hairpin clips (if used). Ford recommends against reusing the clips.*
Warning: *Before removing the fuel filter, the fuel system pressure must be relieved. See Chapter 4.*

3   Position the front end of the vehicle higher than the rear to prevent fuel siphoning. Remove the gas cap, then reinstall it after relieving the fuel system pressure.

Early models – reservoir-type filter

Refer to illustration 23.4

4   Locate the fuel filter on the left frame rail, near the fuel tank **(see illustration)**.

5   On 2WD models, remove three or four screws (depending on model) and take out the reservoir shield (if equipped).

6   On 4WD models, don't remove the reservoir shield all the way. Remove the transfer case skid plate (if necessary for access) and remove the three reservoir shield bolts. Turn the shield counterclockwise and slide it forward along the frame rail to expose the filter.

7   Unscrew the filter canister with a strap-type oil filter wrench. **Note:** *The canister will be full of fuel. Don't tilt it during removal.*

8   Remove the filter cartridge and O-ring from the canister.

9   Install a new filter cartridge and O-ring in the filter canister.

10   Hold the canister level so the O-ring doesn't fall out, then thread it on by hand until the O-ring just makes contact. Tighten 1/6 turn further with the filter wrench, but don't overtighten.

11   Start the engine and check for leaks.

Later models – inline filter

Refer to illustration 23.12

12   Inspect the hose fittings at both ends of the filter to see if they're clean **(see illustration)**. If more than a light coating of dust is present, clean the fittings before proceeding.

13   Disconnect the push-connect fittings from the filter (see Chapter 4).

14   Note which way the arrow on the filter is pointing – the new filter must be installed the same way. Loosen the clamp screw and detach the filter from the bracket.

15   Install the new filter in the bracket with the arrow pointing in the right direction and tighten the clamp screw securely.

16   Carefully connect each hose to the filter (see Chapter 4).

17   Start the engine and check for fuel leaks.

Carbureted models

Refer to illustration 23.18

18   Remove the air cleaner housing from the top of the carburetor (see Chapter 4) to gain access to the filter **(see illustration)**.

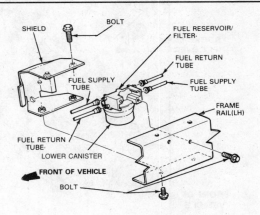

23.4   Canister type fuel filter – early fuel-injected models

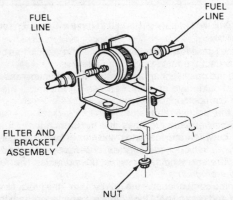

23.12   Inline fuel filter – later fuel-injected models

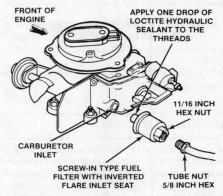

23.18   Screw-in fuel filter – carbureted models

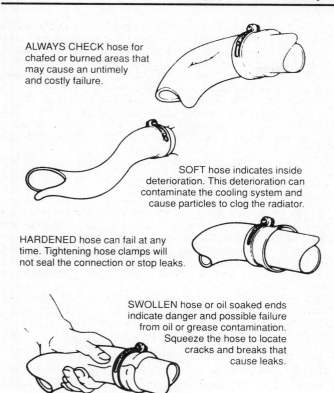

ALWAYS CHECK hose for chafed or burned areas that may cause an untimely and costly failure.

SOFT hose indicates inside deterioration. This deterioration can contaminate the cooling system and cause particles to clog the radiator.

HARDENED hose can fail at any time. Tightening hose clamps will not seal the connection or stop leaks.

SWOLLEN hose or oil soaked ends indicate danger and possible failure from oil or grease contamination. Squeeze the hose to locate cracks and breaks that cause leaks.

24.4 Hoses, like drivebelts, have a habit of failing at the worst possible time – to prevent the inconvenience of a blown radiator or heater hose, inspect them carefully as shown here

19 Place a rag under the filter, then remove the fuel line from the filter. Unscrew the fuel line from the filter while holding the filter hex with a back-up wrench. A flare-nut wrench should be used if available – it will prevent rounding off the fuel line fitting hex.
20 Unscrew the filter or fuel inlet fitting from the carburetor.
21 Apply a drop of Loctite hydraulic sealant No. 069 to the filter threads.
22 Apply one drop of Ford Threadlock and Sealer (part no. E0AZ-19554-AA) or equivalent to the flare-nut fitting threads. Thread the flare-nut into the filter by hand approximately two threads. Hold the filter with a back-up wrench and tighten the flare nut securely.
23 Reinstall the air cleaner housing.

24 Cooling system check

Refer to illustration 24.4

1 Many major engine failures can be attributed to a faulty cooling system. If the vehicle is equipped with an automatic transmission, the cooling system also plays an important role in prolonging transmission life because it cools the fluid.
2 The engine should be cold for the cooling system check, so perform the following procedure before the vehicle is driven for the day or after it has been shut off for at least three hours.
3 Remove the radiator cap and clean it thoroughly, inside and out, with clean water. Also clean the filler neck on the radiator. The presence of rust or corrosion in the filler neck means the coolant should be changed (see Section 32). The coolant inside the radiator should be relatively clean and transparent. If it's rust colored, drain the system and refill with new coolant.
4 Carefully check the radiator hoses and smaller diameter heater hoses (**see illustration**). Inspect each coolant hose along its entire

length, replacing any hose which is cracked, swollen or deteriorated. Cracks will show up better if the hose is squeezed. Pay close attention to hose clamps that secure the hoses to cooling system components, Hose clamps can pinch and puncture hoses, resulting in coolant leaks.
5 Make sure all hose connections are tight. A leak in the cooling system will usually show up as white or rust colored deposits on the area adjoining the leak. If wire-type clamps are used on the hoses, it may be a good idea to replace them with screw-type clamps.
6 Clean the front of the radiator and air conditioning condenser with compressed air, if available, or a soft brush. Remove all bugs, leaves, etc. embedded in the carburetor fins. Be extremely careful not to damage the cooling fins or cut your fingers on them.
7 If the coolant level has been dropping consistently and no leaks are detectable, have the radiator cap and cooling system pressure checked at a service station.

25 Exhaust system check

1 With the engine cold (at least three hours after the vehicle has been driven), check the complete exhaust system from the engine to end of the tailpipe. Ideally, the inspection should be done with the vehicle on a hoist to permit unrestricted access. If a hoist isn't available, raise the vehicle and support it securely on jackstands.
2 Check the exhaust pipes and connections for evidence of leaks, severe corrosion and damage. Make sure that all brackets and hangers are in good condition and are tight.
3 At the same time, inspect the underside of the body for holes, corrosion, open seams, etc. which may allow exhaust gases to enter the passenger compartment. Seal all body openings with silicone or body putty.
4 Rattles and other noises can often be traced to the exhaust system, especially the mounts and hangers. Try to move the pipes, muffler and catalytic converter. If the components can come in contact with the body or suspension parts, secure the exhaust system with new mounts.
5 Check the running condition of the engine by inspecting inside the end of the tailpipe. The exhaust deposits here are an indication of engine state-of-tune. If the pipe is black and sooty or coated with white deposits, the engine may need a tune-up, including a thorough fuel system inspection and adjustment.

26 Steering and suspension check

Refer to illustrations 26.10 and 26.11
Note: *The steering linkage and suspension components should be checked periodically. Worn or damaged suspension and steering linkage components can result in excessive and abnormal tire wear, poor ride quality and vehicle handling and reduced fuel economy. For detailed illustrations of the steering and suspension components, refer to Chapter 10.*

Shock absorber check

1 Park the vehicle on level ground, turn the engine off and set the parking brake. Check the tire pressures.
2 Push down at one corner of the vehicle, then release it while noting the movement of the body. It should stop moving and come to rest in a level position with one or two bounces.
3 If the vehicle continues to move up-and-down or if it fails to return to its original position, a worn or weak shock absorber is probably the reason.
4 Repeat the above check at each of the three remaining corners of the vehicle.
5 Raise the vehicle and support it on jackstands.
6 Check the shock absorbers for evidence of fluid leakage. A light film of fluid is no cause for concern. Make sure that any fluid noted is from the shocks and not from any other source. If leakage is noted, replace the shocks as a set.
7 Check the shock absorbers to be sure that they are securely mounted and undamaged. Check the upper mounts for damage and wear. If damage or wear is noted, replace the shock absorbers as a set.

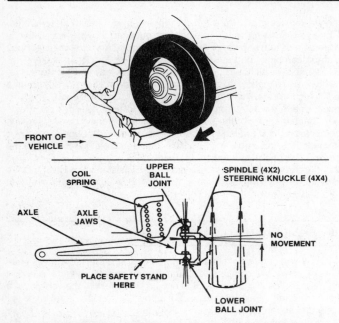

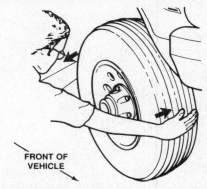

26.10   To check the suspension balljoints, try to move the lower edge of each front tire in-and-out while watching/feeling for movement at the top of the tire and balljoints

26.11   To check the steering gear and idler arm mounts and tie-rod connections for play, grasp each front tire like this and try to move it back-and-forth – if play is noted, check the steering gear mounts and make sure that they're tight; if either tie-rod is bent or worn, replace it

8   If the shock absorbers must be replaced, refer to Chapter 10 for the procedure.

Steering and suspension check

9   Visually inspect the steering system components for damage and distortion. Look for leaks and damaged seals, boots and fittings.

10 Clean the lower end of the steering knuckle. Have an assistant grasp the lower edge of the tire and move the wheel in-and-out **(see illustration)** while you look for movement at the steering knuckle-to-control arm joint. If there is any movement, the suspension balljoint must be replaced.

11 Grasp each front tire at the front and rear edges, push in at the front, pull out at the rear and feel for play in the steering system components **(see illustration)**. If any freeplay is noted, check the steering gear mounts and the tie-rod balljoints for looseness. If the steering gear mounts are loose, tighten them. If the tie-rods are loose, the balljoints may be worn (check to make sure the nuts are tight). Additional steering and suspension system illustrations can be found in Chapter 10.

Front wheel bearing check

12   Refer to Section 28 (2WD) or Section 29 (4WD) for the wheel bearing check, repack and adjustment procedure.

27   Brake system check

Refer to illustrations 27.7, 27.11 and 27.18

Note: *In addition to the specified intervals, the brake system should in-spected each time the wheels are removed or a malfunction is indicated. Because of the obvious safety considerations, the following brake sys-tem checks are some of the most important maintenance procedures you can perform on your vehicle.*

Symptoms of brake system problems

1   The disc brakes have built-in wear indicators which should make a high-pitched squealing or scraping noise when they're worn to the re-placement point. When you hear this noise, replace the pads immediate-ly or expensive damage to the rotors could result.

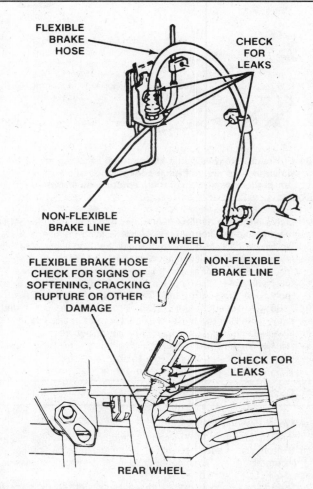

27.7   The brake hoses at front and rear of the vehicle should be inspected and replaced if they show any defects

2   Any of the following symptoms could indicate a potential brake sys-tem defect. The vehicle pulls to one side when the brake pedal is de-pressed, the brakes make squealing or dragging noises when applied, brake travel is excessive, the pedal pulsates and brake fluid leaks are noted (usually on the inner side of the tire or wheel). If any of these condi-tions are noted, inspect the brake system immediately.

27.11 **The lining thickness of the front disc brake pads (arrows) can be checked through the caliper inspection hole**

27.18 **Carefully peel back the rubber boot on each end of the wheel cylinder – if the exposed area is covered with brake fluid, or if fluid runs out, the wheel cylinder must be overhauled or replaced**

Brake lines and hoses

Note: *Steel tubing is used throughout the brake system, with the exception of flexible, reinforced hoses at the front wheels and as connectors at the rear axle. Periodic inspection of these lines is very important.*

3   Park the vehicle on level ground and turn the engine off.
4   Remove the wheel covers. Loosen, but do not remove, the lug nuts on all four wheels.
5   Raise the vehicle and support it securely on jackstands.
6   Remove the wheels (see *Jacking and towing* at the front of this book, or refer to your owner's manual, if necessary).
7   Check all brake lines and hoses for cracks, chafing of the outer cover, leaks, blisters and distortion. Check the brake hoses at the front and rear of the vehicle for softening, cracks, bulging, or wear from rubbing on other components **(see illustration)**. Check all threaded fittings for leaks and make sure the brake hose mounting bolts and clips are secure.
8   If leaks or damage are discovered, they must be fixed immediately. Refer to Chapter 9 for detailed brake system repair procedures.

Disc brakes

9   If it hasn't already been done, raise the vehicle and support it securely on jackstands. Remove the front wheels.
10   The disc brake calipers, which contain the pads, are now visible. Each caliper has an outer and an inner pad – all pads should be checked.
11   Note the pad thickness by looking through the inspection hole in the caliper **(see illustration)**. If the lining material is 1/8-inch thick or less, or if it is tapered from end-to-end, the pads should be replaced (see Chapter 9). Keep in mind that the lining material is riveted or bonded to a metal plate or shoe – the metal portion is not included in this measurement.
12   Check the condition of the brake disc. Look for score marks, deep scratches and overheated areas (they will appear blue or discolored). If damage or wear is noted, the disc can be removed and resurfaced by an automotive machine shop or replaced with a new one. Refer to Chapter 9 for more detailed inspection and repair procedures.
13   Remove the calipers without disconnecting the brake hoses (see Chapter 9). Lubricate the caliper slide rails with the special disc brake caliper slide grease listed in this Chapter's Specifications. On 1992 and later models, also lubricate the upper and lower inner pad slots on the knuckle.

Drum brakes

14   Refer to Chapter 9 and remove the rear brake drums.
15   **Warning:** *Dust produced by lining wear and deposited on brake components may contain asbestos, which is hazardous to your health. DO NOT blow it out with compressed air and DO NOT inhale it! DO NOT use gasoline or solvents to remove the dust. Brake system cleaner should be used to flush the dust into a drain pan. After the brake components are* wiped with a damp rag, dispose of the contaminated rag(s) and brake cleaner in a covered and labeled container. Try to use non-asbestos replacement parts whenever possible.

16   Note the thickness of the lining material on the rear brake shoes and look for signs of contamination by brake fluid or grease. If the lining material is within 1/16-inch of the recessed rivets or metal shoes, replace the brake shoes with new ones. The shoes should also be replaced if they are cracked, glazed (shiny lining surfaces), or contaminated with brake fluid or grease. See Chapter 9 for the replacement procedure.
17   Check the shoe return and hold-down springs and the adjusting mechanism to make sure they are installed correctly and in good condition. Deteriorated or distorted springs, if not replaced, could allow the linings to drag and wear prematurely.
18   Check the wheel cylinders for leakage by carefully peeling back the rubber boots **(see illustration)**. Slight moisture behind the boots is acceptable. If brake fluid is noted behind the boots or if it runs out of the wheel cylinder, the wheel cylinders must be overhauled or replaced (see Chapter 9).
19   Check the drums for cracks, score marks, deep scratches and hard spots, which will appear as small discolored areas. If imperfections cannot be removed with emery cloth, the drums must be resurfaced by an automotive machine shop (see Chapter 9 for more detailed information).
20   Refer to Chapter 9 and install the brake drums.
21   Install the wheels, but don't lower the vehicle yet.

Parking brake

Note: *The parking brake cable and linkage should be periodically lubricated (see Section 15). This maintenance procedure helps prevent the parking brake cable adjuster or the linkage from binding and adversely affecting the operation or adjustment of the parking brake.*

22   The easiest, and perhaps most obvious, method of checking the parking brake is to park the vehicle on a steep hill with the parking brake set and the transmission in Neutral. If the parking brake doesn't prevent the vehicle from rolling, refer to Chapter 9 and adjust it.

---

28   Front wheel bearing check, repack and adjustment – 2WD models

---

Check

Refer to illustrations 28.1 and 28.3

1   In most cases the front wheel bearings will not need servicing until the brake pads are changed. However, the bearings should be checked whenever the front of the vehicle is raised for any reason. Several items,

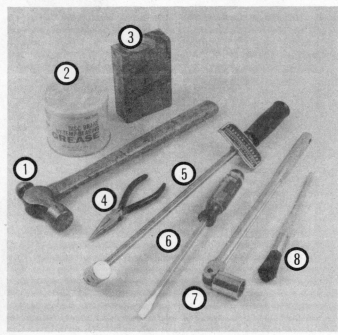

28.1   Tools and materials needed for front wheel bearing maintenance

1   *Hammer* – *A common hammer will do just fine*
2   *Grease* – *High-temperature grease that is formulated specially for front wheel bearings should be used*
3   *Wood block* – *If you have a scrap piece of 2x4, it can be used to drive the new seal into the hub*
4   *Needle-nose pliers* – *Used to straighten and remove the cotter pin in the spindle*
5   *Torque wrench* – *This is very important in this procedure; if the bearing is too tight, the wheel won't turn freely – if it's too loose, the wheel will "wobble" on the spindle. Either way, it could mean extensive damage.*
6   *Screwdriver* – *Used to remove the seal from the hub (a long screwdriver would be preferred)*
7   *Socket/breaker bar* – *Needed to loosen the nut on the spindle if it's extremely tight*
8   *Brush* – *Together with some clean solvent, this will be used to remove old grease from the hub and spindle*

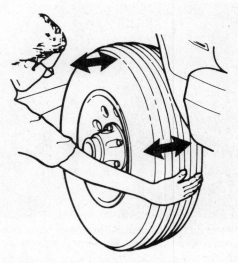

28.3   To check the wheel bearings, try to move the tire in-and-out – if any play is noted, or if the bearings feel rough or sound noisy when the tire is rotated, maintenance is required

including a torque wrench and special grease, are required for this procedure **(see illustration)**.

2   With the vehicle securely supported on jackstands, spin each wheel and check for noise, rolling resistance and freeplay. If any of these conditions are present, the bearings should be checked and then repacked with grease or replaced, if necessary.

3   Move the wheel in-and-out on the spindle **(see illustration)**. If there's any noticeable movement, the bearings should be checked and then repacked with grease or replaced, if necessary.

Repack

Refer to illustrations 28.7, 28.9, 28.15 and 28.16

4   Remove the wheel.

5   Remove the brake caliper (see Chapter 9) and hang it out of the way on a piece of wire. **Warning:** *DO NOT allow the brake caliper to hang by the rubber hose!*

6   Pry the grease cap out of the hub with a screwdriver or hammer and chisel.

7   Straighten the bent ends of the cotter pin, then pull the cotter pin out of the retaining nut and spindle **(see illustration)**. Discard the cotter pin and use a new one during reassembly.

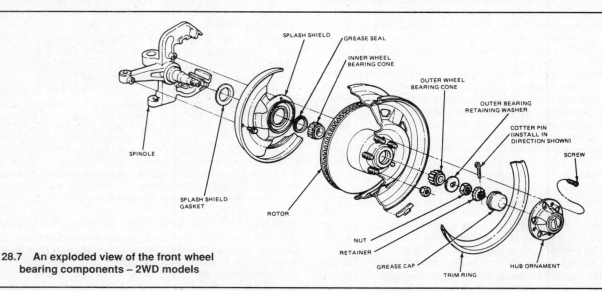

28.7   An exploded view of the front wheel bearing components – 2WD models

28.9 Pull out on the hub/rotor to dislodge the outer bearing

28.15 Pack each wheel bearing by working the grease into the rollers from the back side

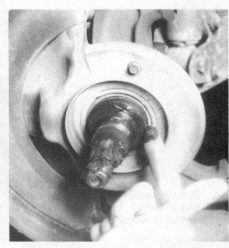

28.16 Apply a thin coat of grease to the spindle, particularly where the seal rides

8   Remove the adjusting nut and flat washer from the end of the spindle.

9   Pull the hub/rotor assembly out slightly, then push it back into its original position. This should force the outer bearing off the spindle enough so it can be removed **(see illustration)**.

10   Pull the hub/rotor assembly off the spindle.

11   Use a screwdriver to pry the grease seal out of the rear of the hub. As this is done, note how the seal is installed.

12   Remove the inner wheel bearing from the hub.

13   Use solvent to remove all traces of old grease from the bearings, hub and spindle. A small brush may prove helpful; however make sure no bristles from the brush embed themselves inside the bearing rollers. Allow the parts to air dry.

14   Carefully inspect the bearings for cracks, heat discoloration, worn rollers, etc. Check the bearing races inside the hub for wear and damage. If the bearing races are defective, the hub/rotor assemblies should be taken to a machine shop with the facilities to remove the old races and press new ones in. Note that the bearings and races come as matched sets and new bearings should never be installed on old races.

15   Use high-temperature front wheel bearing grease to pack the bearings. Work the grease completely into the bearings, forcing it between the rollers, cone and cage from the back side **(see illustration)**.

16   Apply a thin coat of grease to the spindle at the outer bearing seat, inner bearing seat, shoulder and seal seat **(see illustration)**.

17   Put a small quantity of grease inboard of each bearing race inside the hub. Using your finger, form a dam at these points to provide extra grease availability and to keep thinned grease from flowing out of the bearing.

18   Place the grease-packed inner bearing into the rear of the hub and put a little more grease outboard of the bearing.

19   Place a new seal over the inner bearing and tap the seal evenly into place with a hammer and block of wood until it's flush with the hub.

20   Carefully place the hub/rotor assembly onto the spindle and push the grease-packed outer bearing into position.

21   Install the flat washer and nut. Tighten the nut only slightly.

Adjustment

22   Spin the hub/rotor in a forward direction to seat the bearings and remove any grease or burrs which could cause excessive bearing play later.

23   While spinning the wheel, tighten the adjusting nut to the specified torque (Step 1 in this Chapter's Specifications).

24   Loosen the nut 1/2 turn, no more.

25   Tighten the nut to the specified torque (Step 3 in this Chapter's Specifications). Install the retainer, then install a new cotter pin through

the hole in the spindle and retainer. If the holes don't line up, don't turn the nut. Instead, remove the retainer and try it in a different position. The notches in the retainer are offset for this purpose. Keep trying the retainer in different positions until the holes line up.

26   Bend the ends of the cotter pin until they're flat against the nut. Cut off any extra length which could interfere with the grease cap.

27   Install the grease cap, tapping into place with a hammer.

28   Install the caliper (see Chapter 9).

29   Install the tire/wheel assembly on the hub/rotor and tighten the lug nuts snugly

30   Check the bearings in the manner described earlier in this Section.

31   Lower the vehicle and tighten the lug nuts to the torque listed in this Chapter's Specifications.

29   Front hub lock, spindle bearing and wheel bearing check and maintenance (4WD models)

1   In most cases the front wheel bearings will not need servicing until the brake pads are changed. However, the bearings should be checked whenever the front of the vehicle is raised for any reason. Several items, including a torque wrench and special grease, are required for this procedure **(see illustration 28.1)**. In addition to these tools you'll need a four-pronged spindle nut spanner wrench (Ford part no. T83T-1197-A or equivalent) for manual locking hubs or a 2 3/8-inch hex locknut wrench (Ford part no. T70T-4252-B or equivalent) for automatic locking hubs. These may be available at four-wheel drive shops. On both manual and automatic hubs, you'll also need a pair of snap-ring pliers.

Wheel bearing check

2   With the vehicle securely supported on jackstands, spin each wheel and check for noise, rolling resistance and freeplay. If any of these conditions are noted, the bearings should be checked and then repacked with grease or replaced, if necessary.

3   Move the wheel in-and-out on the spindle **(see illustration 28.3)**. If there's any noticeable movement, the bearings should be checked and then repacked with grease or replaced if necessary.

Hub lock, spindle and wheel bearing maintenance

4   The lubrication of hub locks, as well as spindle needle and thrust bearings on vehicles so equipped, should be checked at the intervals specified in the maintenance schedule.

5   Remove the wheel.

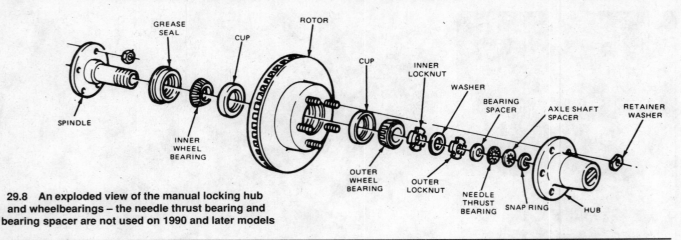

29.8   An exploded view of the manual locking hub and wheelbearings – the needle thrust bearing and bearing spacer are not used on 1990 and later models

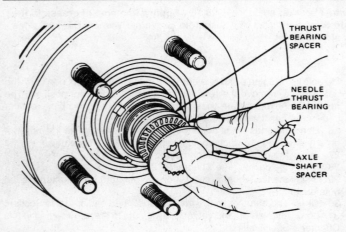

29.9   On all models, remove the snap-ring; on 1983 through 1989 models, remove the needle thrust bearing and bearing spacer as well

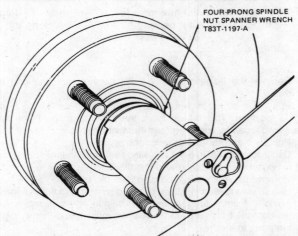

29.11   A four-pronged spanner wrench is required to remove the outer locknut; the nut is very tight, so don't use makeshift tools

6   Remove the brake caliper (see Chapter 9) and hang it out of the way on a piece of wire. **Warning:** *DO NOT allow the brake caliper to hang by the rubber hose!*
7   Remove the retainer washers from the wheel studs and take the locking hub off.

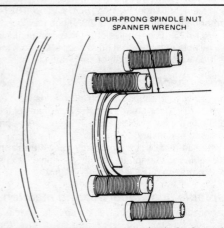

29.12   The same tool is used to remove the inner locknut; be sure the slot in the tool is positioned over the pin on the locknut

Manual locking hubs

Refer to illustrations 29.8, 29.9, 29.11, 29.12, 29.17 and 29.22

8   Using snap-ring pliers, carefully expand the snap-ring just enough to remove it from the end of the spindle shaft **(see illustration)**.
9   Remove the axle shaft spacer **(see illustration)**.
10   On 1983 through 1989 models, remove the needle thrust bearing and bearing spacer **(see illustration 29.9)**.
11   Remove the outer wheel bearing locknut with a four-prong spanner wrench (Ford part no. T83T-1197-A or equivalent) **(see illustration)**. **Note:** *This nut is very tight. Don't try to remove it with a makeshift tool.*
12   Remove the inner wheel bearing locknut with the spanner wrench **(see illustration)**. Be sure the notch in the wrench is positioned over the locknut pin as shown.
13   Perform Steps 9 through 20 of Section 28 to repack the wheel bearings. Be sure to use the type of grease listed in this Chapter's Specifications.
14   Install the inner locknut on the spindle and tighten it to the specified torque (Step 1 in this Chapter's Specifications).
15   Spin the brake rotor several turns in each direction to seat the bearings.
16   Loosen the inner locknut 1/4-turn, then retighten it to the specified torque (Step 3 in the Specifications).
17   Install the lockwasher and align the locknut pin with one of the holes in the lockwasher **(see illustration)**. If necessary, turn the inner locknut slightly to align the hole and pin.

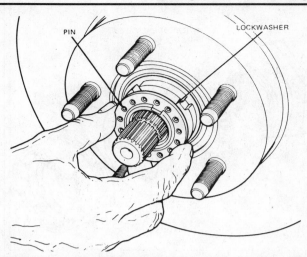

29.17   Align the pin in the locknut with one of the holes in the lockwasher; if necessary, adjust the locknut position slightly to align the pin with a hole

29.22   To remove the internal components from a manual locking hub, insert a small screwdriver behind the retaining ring and work it gently out of its groove – DO NOT remove the screw from the plastic dial

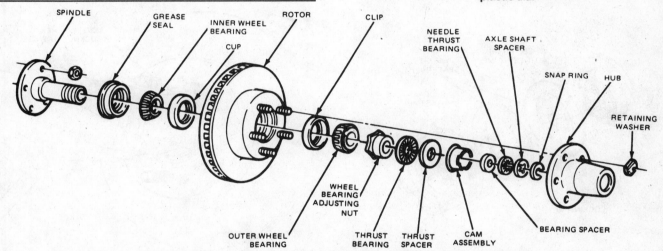

29.26   An exploded view of the automatic locking hub – on 1990 and later models, the needle thrust bearing and bearing spacer are not used and the thrust bearing is replaced by a plastic thrust washer

18   Install the outer locknut and tighten it to the specified torque (Step 4 in this Chapter's Specifications).

19   Lubricate the needle bearing spacer and needle bearing (if equipped) with the same grease used for the wheel bearings. Install them on the spindle.

20   Install the axle shaft spacer.

21   Install the snap-ring on the spindle.

22   Remove the lock ring that secures the inner components in the locking hub **(see illustration). Caution:** *Don't remove the screw from the plastic dial.*

23   Remove the internal assembly, spring and clutch gear. Lubricate the components with the specified grease.

24   Reassemble the hub and install the lock ring.

25   Install the locking hub on the wheel studs and secure it with the retainer washers.

Automatic locking hubs

Refer to illustrations 29.26, 29.27, 29.28, 29.29, 29.30, 29.31, 29.36 and 29.38

26   Using snap-ring pliers, carefully expand the snap-ring just enough to remove it from the end of the spindle shaft **(see illustration).**

27   Remove the axle shaft spacer **(see illustration).**

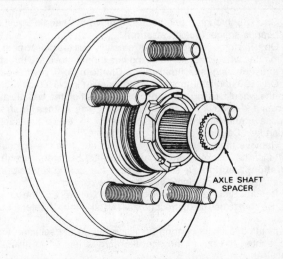

29.27   Remove the axle shaft spacer

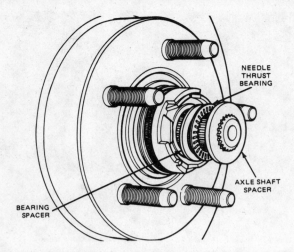

29.28   On 1983 through 1989 models, remove the needle thrust bearing and bearing spacer as well

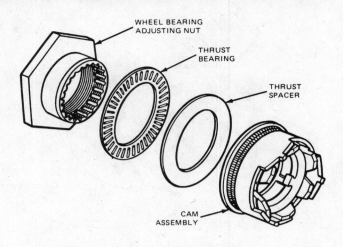

29.29   Wheel bearing adjusting nut assembly – 1983 through 1989 models with automatic locking hubs

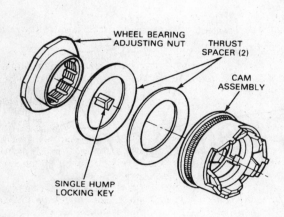

29.30   Wheel bearing adjusting nut assembly – 1990 and later models with automatic locking hubs

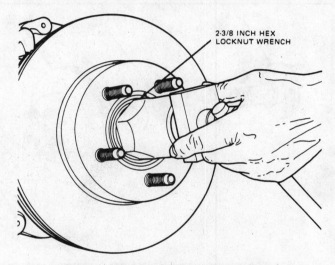

29.31   On automatic locking hubs, loosen the wheel bearing adjusting nut with a 2-3/8-inch hex locknut wrench

28   On 1983 through 1989 models, remove the needle thrust bearing and bearing spacer **(see illustration)**.

29   On 1983 through 1989 models, carefully pull the plastic cam assembly from the wheel bearing adjusting nut, then remove the thrust spacer and thrust bearing **(see illustration)**. **Caution:** *Don't pry the parts off.*

30   On 1990 and later models, carefully pull the plastic cam assembly from the wheel bearing adjusting nut, then pull off the two plastic thrust spacers and remove the locking key with a magnet **(see illustration)**. If necessary, rotate the adjusting nut slightly to relieve pressure on the locking key. **Caution:** *Don't pry the parts off.*

31   Remove the wheel bearing adjusting nut from the spindle with a 2-3/8-inch hex socket (Ford part on. T70T-4252-B or equivalent) **(see illustration)**. **Caution:** *Be sure to remove the locking key before you remove the nut or the spindle threads will be damaged.*

32   Perform Steps 9 through 20 of Section 28 to repack the wheel bearings. Be sure to use the correct grease (listed in this Chapter's Specifications).

33   Install the wheel bearing adjusting nut. While spinning the brake disc, tighten the nut to the specified torque (step 1 in this Chapter's Specifications).

34   Loosen the nut 1/4-turn.

35   Retighten the nut to the correct final torque (Step 3 in the Specifica-

tions).

36   On 1983 through 1989 models:
   a)   Line up the center of the spindle keyway slot with the closest hole in the wheel bearing adjusting nut. If necessary, tighten the adjusting nut so the next hole aligns with the keyway slot. It's important to align the hole and slot perfectly.
   b)   Lubricate the thrust bearing and thrust spacer with the specified grease (see this Chapter's Specifications). Install them on the spindle **(see illustration 29.29)**.
   c)   Line up the key in the fixed cam with the keyway slot in the spindle, then push the cam on over the adjusting nut **(see illustration)**.
   d)   Install the bearing spacer, needle thrust bearing and axle shaft spacer **(see illustration 29.28)**.
   e)   Install the snap-ring on the end of the spindle.

37   1990 and later models:
   a)   Line up the center of the spindle keyway slot with the closest lug in the wheel bearing adjusting nut. If necessary, tighten the adjusting nut so the next lug aligns with the keyway slot. Be sure the lug and slot line up exactly.
   b)   Install the locking key in the keyway slot, under the adjusting nut. Don't force the key in or it will be damaged. If it is difficult to insert, make sure the lug and slot are lined up exactly.

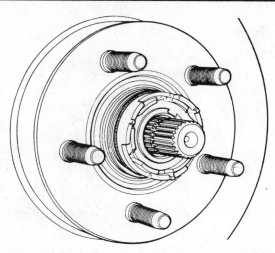

29.36 Position the cam over the wheel bearing adjusting nut – use extreme care to align the key accurately with the slot in the spindle

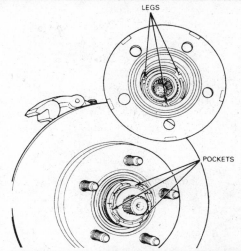

29.38 Align the legs in the automatic locking hub with the pockets on the cam when installing the hub

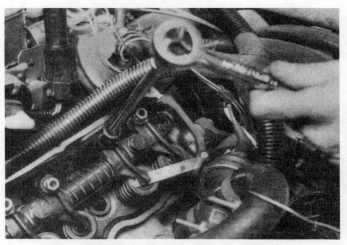

30.7 Adjusting valve clearance (2.8L V6 engine)

c) Install the two thrust spacers **(see illustration 29.30).**
d) Line up the key in the fixed cam with the keyway slot in the spindle, then push the cam on over the adjusting nut **(see illustration 29.36).**
e) Install the axle shaft spacer.
f) Install the snap-ring on the end of the spindle.

38 Line up the three legs on the automatic locking hub with the pockets in the cam **(see illustration)**, then install the locking hub and secure it with the retainer washers.

39 Install the wheel and tighten the wheel lug nuts to the torque listed in this Chapter's Specifications.

All models

40 Check that there's no endplay of the wheel. Measure the amount of torque required to turn the hub and compare it with this Chapter's Specifications.

---

30 Valve clearance check and adjustment (2.8L V6 engines only)

Refer to illustration 30.7

1 The valve stem-to-rocker arm clearance is adjusted manually on the 2.8L V6 engine. On all other models, it is adjusted automatically by hydraulic lifters.

2 The valve clearances are checked and adjusted with the engine cold.

3 Remove the valve covers (see Chapter 2).

4 Disconnect the coil (high-tension) wire from the distributor and ground it on the engine block.

5 Place your finger on the adjustment screw for the No. 5 cylinder intake valve **(see illustration 13.16c if you're not sure about cylinder locations).** Have an assistant operate the starter, a little at a time, until you can feel the rocker arm just start to move to open the valve.

6 With the engine in this position, you can adjust the valves for the number one cylinder.

7 Start with the intake valve clearance. Insert a feeler gauge of the thickness listed in this Chapter's Specifications between the intake valve stem and the rocker arm **(see illustration).** Withdraw it; you should feel a slight drag. If there's no drag or a heavy drag, loosen or tighten the adjuster screw until the correct clearance is obtained.

8 Adjust the number one exhaust valve using the same procedure you used for the intake valve(s). Be sure to use a feeler gauge of the thickness specified for exhaust valves.

9 Adjust the remaining valves by repeating the above procedure for the remaining cylinders. The following table shows which valves can be adjusted when a particular intake valve is just starting to open.

10 Reconnect the coil wire to the distributor and install the valve covers.

Intake valve opening on cylinder no.	Adjust the valves for cylinder no.
1	5
4	3
2	6
5	1
3	4
6	2

---

31 Windshield wiper blade check and replacement

Refer to illustrations 31.1a through 31.1e

1 Several wiper blade designs have been used for front and rear windshields. To determine which type you have, compare your vehicle's wip-

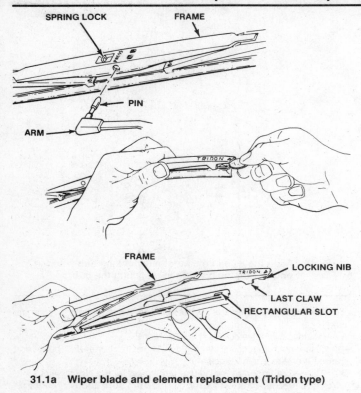

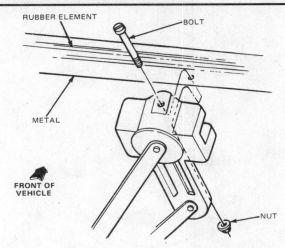

31.1a   **Wiper blade and element replacement (Tridon type)**

31.1b   **Rear wiper blade replacement (nut and bolt type)**

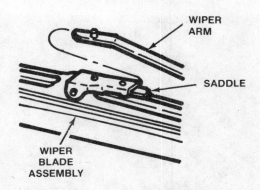

31.1c   **Rear wiper blade replacement (latch type)**

pers to the accompanying illustrations.

2   Road film can build up on the wiper blades and affect their efficiency, so they should be washed regularly with a mild detergent solution.

Check

3   The windshield wiper and blade assembly should be inspected periodically. Even if you don't use your wipers, the sun and elements will dry out the rubber portions, causing them to crack and break apart. If inspection reveals hardened or cracked rubber, replace the wiper blades. If inspection reveals nothing unusual, wet the windshield, turn the wipers on, allow them to cycle several times, then shut them off. An uneven wiper pattern across the glass or streaks over clean glass indicate that the blades should be replaced.

4   The operation of the wiper mechanism can loosen the fasteners, so they should be checked and tightened, as necessary, at the same time the wiper blades are checked (see Chapter 12 for further information regarding the wiper mechanism).

Blade assembly replacement (Tridon blades)

5   Park the wiper blades in a convenient position to be worked on. To do this, run the wipers, then turn the ignition key to Off when the wiper blades reach the desired position.

6   Lift the blade slightly from the windshield. Press on the spring lock to release the blade **(see illustration 31.1a)** and take the blade off. **Caution:** *Do not press too hard on the spring lock or it will be distorted.*

7   Push the new blade assembly onto the arm pivot pin. Make sure the spring lock secures the blade to the pin.

Blade element replacement (Tridon blades)

8   Remove the wiper blade from the arm (see Step 5).

9   Locate the name TRIDON stamped in the blade assembly **(see illustration 31.1a)**. Insert a coin or screwdriver at that point, pry the blade element downward from the blade frame and slide the blade element out.

10   Find the rectangular slot in one end of the new blade element. This end will be installed first.

11   At the end of the blade frame without the word TRIDON, find the first retaining claw.

12   Install the slotted end of the blade element into the first retaining claw, then through all the other claws. The element will snap into place when it's been pulled all the way in.

13   Check to make sure the element is securely retained in all of the claws and that the locking nib is positioned correctly.

Blade assembly replacement (early rear windshields)

14   Park the wiper blades in a convenient position to be worked on. To do this, run the wipers, then turn the ignition key to Off when the wiper blades reach the desired position.

15   If the rear wiper blade is secured by a nut and bolt, remove them **(see illustration 31.1b)**. Take the wiper blade off, install a new one and install the nut and bolt.

16   If the rear wiper blade is secured by a latch **(see illustration 31.1c)**, hold the arm and press down on the blade to release the latch. Slide the blade off, slide a new blade on and make sure the latch engages securely.

Blade assembly and element replacement (early Trico blades)

17   Park the wiper blades in a convenient position to be worked on. To do this, run the wipers, then turn the ignition key to Off when the wiper blades reach the desired position.

18   Lift the wiper arm off the windshield and pull the blade off the wiper arm pin **(see illustration 31.1d)**.

19   Find the wide point of the metal backing strip at one end of the element.

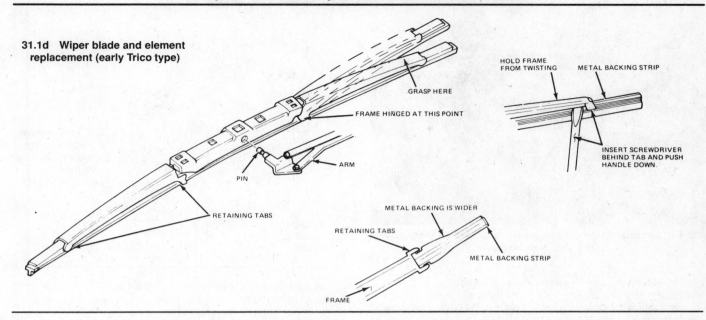

31.1d Wiper blade and element replacement (early Trico type)

31.1e Wiper blade and element replacement (later Trico type)

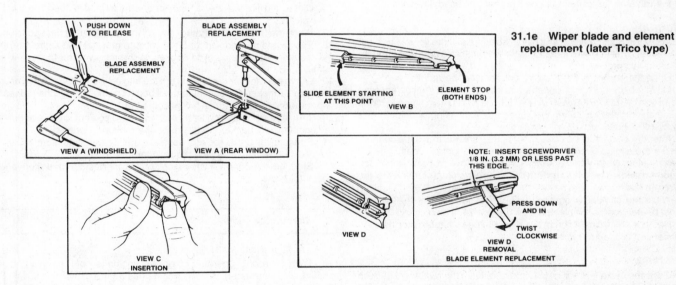

20   Pry one end of the element out of the blade with a screwdriver as shown in illustration 31.1d, then slide the element out of the rest of the retaining tabs.
21   Slide the new element into the four sets of retaining tabs. Make sure it is securely fastened.
22   Push the wiper blade firmly onto the wiper arm and make sure it is securely engaged.

Blade assembly and element replacement (later Trico blades)

23   Later design Trico blades are used for both front and rear windshields.
24   Park the wiper blades in a convenient position to be worked on. To do this, run the wipers, then turn the ignition key to Off when the wiper blades reach the desired position.
25   Let the blade assembly rest on the windshield and insert a small flat-bladed screwdriver into the release hole (see illustration 31.1e). Push down on the coil spring inside the hole and pull the wiper blade from the arm.

26   Insert a flat-bladed screwdriver 1/8-inch or less into the space between the element and rubber backing strip. While pressing the screwdriver down and inward, twist it clockwise to separate the element from the retaining tab.
27   Slide the element out of the other retaining tabs.
28   Slide the new element into four of the five retaining tabs. Twist the element into the fifth retaining tab to secure it.
29   Make sure the new element is secured by all five tabs, then push the blade onto the pivot pin until it locks.

32   Cooling system servicing (draining, flushing and refilling)

Refer to illustrations 32.4 and 32.5
Warning: *Antifreeze is a corrosive and poisonous solution, so be careful not to spill any of the coolant mixture on the vehicle's paint or on your skin. If this happens, rinse it off immediately with plenty of clean water. Consult local authorities regarding proper disposal procedures for antifreeze before draining the cooling system. In many areas, reclamation centers have been established to collect used oil and coolant mixtures.*

32.4   The radiator drain fitting (arrow) is located on the bottom right side of the radiator

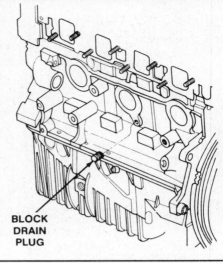

32.5   2.3L engine block drain plug – V6 engines have a drain plug on each side of the block

BLOCK
DRAIN
PLUG

1   Periodically, the cooling system should be drained, flushed and re-filled to replenish the antifreeze mixture and prevent formation of rust and corrosion, which can impair the performance of the cooling system and cause engine damage. When the cooling system is serviced, all hoses and the radiator cap should be checked and replaced if necessary.

Draining

2   Apply the parking brake and block the wheels. If the vehicle has just been driven, wait several hours to allow the engine to cool down before beginning this procedure.
3   Once the engine is completely cool, remove the radiator cap.
4   Move a large container under the radiator to catch the coolant **(see illustration)**. Attach a 3/8-inch diameter hose to the drain fitting to direct the coolant into the container, then open the drain fitting (a pair of pliers may be required to turn it).
5   After the coolant stops flowing out of the radiator, move the container under the engine block drain plug(s) – four-cylinder engines normally have one plug, while V6 engines generally have two plugs, one on each side of the engine **(see illustration)**. Remove the plug(s) and allow the coolant in the block to drain.
6   While the coolant is draining, check the condition of the radiator hoses, heater hoses and clamps (see Section 24, if necessary).
7   Replace any damaged clamps or hoses (see Chapter 3 for detailed replacement procedures).

Flushing

8   Once the system is completely drained, flush the radiator with fresh water from a garden hose until the water runs clear at the drain. The flushing action of the water will remove sediments from the radiator but will not remove rust and scale from the engine and cooling tube surfaces.
9   These deposits can be removed by the chemical action of a cleaner such as Ford Premium Cooling System Flush. Follow the procedure outlined in the manufacturer's instructions. If the radiator is severely corroded, damaged or leaking, it should be removed (see Chapter 3) and taken to a radiator repair shop.
10   The heater core should be backflushed whenever the cooling system is flushed. To do this, disconnect the heater return hose from the thermostat housing or engine. Slide a female garden hose fitting into the heater hose and secure it with a clamp. This will allow you to attach a garden hose securely.
11   Attach the end of a garden hose to the fitting you installed in the heater hose.
12   Disconnect the heater inlet hose and position it to act as a drain.
13   Turn the water on and off several times to create a surging action through the heater core. Then turn the water on full force and allow it to run for approximately five minutes.
14   Turn off the water and disconnect the garden hose from the female fitting. Remove the fitting from the heater return hose, then reconnect the hoses to the engine.

15   Remove the overflow hose from the coolant recovery reservoir. Drain the reservoir and flush it with clean water, then reconnect the hose.

Refilling

16   Close and tighten the radiator drain. Install and tighten the block drain plug(s).
17   Place the heater temperature control in the maximum heat position.
18   Slowly add new coolant (a 50/50 mixture of water and antifreeze) to the radiator until it is full. Add coolant to the reservoir up to the lower mark.
19   Leave the radiator cap off and run the engine in a well-ventilated area until the thermostat opens (coolant will begin flowing through the radiator and the upper radiator hose will become hot).
20   Turn the engine off and let it cool. Add more coolant mixture to bring the coolant level back up to the lip on the radiator filler neck.
21   Squeeze the upper radiator hose to expel air, then add more coolant mixture if necessary. Replace the radiator cap.
22   Start the engine, allow it to reach normal operating temperature and check for leaks.

---

33   Carburetor choke check

Refer to illustrations 33.3 and 33.8

1   The choke only operates when the engine is cold, so this check should be performed before the engine has been started for the day.
2   Open the hood and remove the air cleaner cover and filter from the top of the carburetor.
3   Locate the choke plate (the flat plate attached by small screws to a pivot shaft) in the carburetor throat **(see illustration)**.
4   Operate the throttle linkage and make sure the plate closes completely. Start the engine and watch the plate – when the engine starts, the choke plate should open slightly.
5   Allow the engine to continue running at idle speed. As the engine warms up to operating temperature, the plate should slowly open.
6   After several minutes, the choke plate should be fully open to the vertical position.
7   Note that the engine speed corresponds to the plate opening angle. With the plate closed, the engine should run at a fast idle speed. As the plate opens, the engine speed will decrease. The fast idle speed is controlled by the fast idle cam, and, even though the choke plate is open completely, the idle speed will remain high until the throttle plate is opened, releasing the fast idle cam. Check the drop in idle speed as the choke plate opens by occasionally tapping the accelerator.
8   If the choke doesn't work as described, shut off the engine and check the shaft and linkage for deposits which could cause binding **(see illustration)**. Use a spray-on choke cleaning solvent to remove the deposits as you operate the linkage. This should loosen up the linkage and

1

33.3 With the air cleaner cover removed, the choke plate can be checked

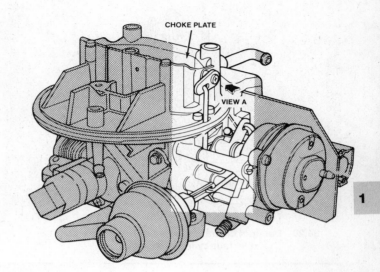

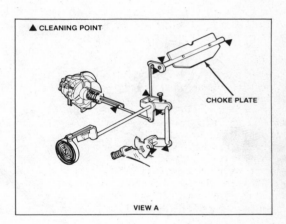

the shaft and allow the choke to work properly. If the choke still fails to function correctly, the choke bimetal assembly is malfunctioning and the carburetor may have to be overhauled. Refer to Chapter 4 for carburetor overhaul information.

9 At regular intervals, clean and lubricate the choke shaft, the fast idle cam and linkage and the vacuum diaphragm pulldown rod (if equipped) to ensure good choke performance.

34   Idle speed check and adjustment (carbureted models only)

1 This section covers fast idle and curb idle speed adjustments on carbureted models only. Idle speeds on fuel-injected models are computer controlled and don't normally require adjustment.

1983 and 1984 2.0L and 2.3L engines

Refer to illustrations 34.4, 34.7, 34.20 and 34.26

2 Warm the engine to normal operating temperature.

3 Place the transmission in Neutral or Park and turn the engine off.

4 Connect an accurate tune-up tachometer to the engine, following manufacturer's instructions. On models so equipped, connect the tachometer pickup to the TACH TEST terminal on the ignition coil **(see illustration)**.

5 Turn off the air conditioner (if equipped).

6 Disconnect and plug the EGR valve vacuum hose.

7 Move the choke linkage by hand and position the fast idle screw on the fast idle cam **(see illustration)**. The correct fast idle cam step is listed on the Vehicle Emission Control Information label under the hood.

8 Without touching the accelerator, start the engine.

33.8   Typical choke plate and linkage cleaning points

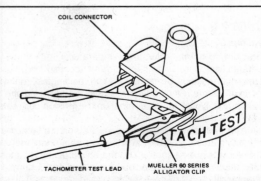

34.4   Some models are equipped with a tachometer connection terminal at the ignition coil

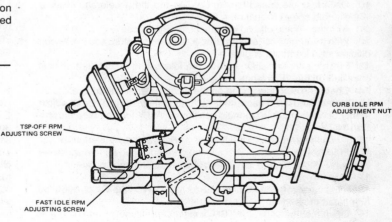

34.7   Carburetor adjustment points – 1983 and 1984 four-cylinder engines

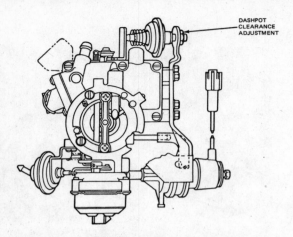

34.20   Dashpot clearance adjustment – 1983 and 1984 four-cylinder engines

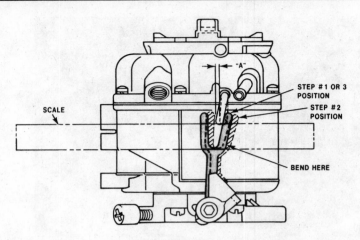

34.26   Bowl vent setting adjustment point – 1983 and 1984 four-cylinder engines

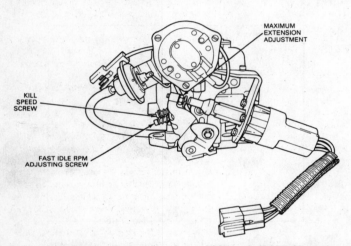

34.34   Carburetor adjustment points – 1985 and 1986 2.0L engines

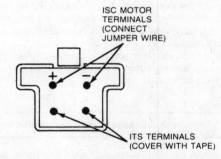

34.36   Idle speed control motor terminals – 1985 and 1986 2.0L engines

9   Compare the engine idle speed (fast idle) with the VECI label. Adjust it, if necessary, by turning the fast idle adjusting screw **(see illustration 34.7).**
10   Once fast idle speed is correctly set, tap the accelerator, then release it. Idle speed should drop to normal.
11   Turn the engine off and reconnect the EGR hose.
12   With the engine still at normal operating temperature and the air conditioner off, restart the engine.
13   Place the transmission in the curb idle speed adjustment position specified on the VECI label.
14   Check the curb idle speed on the tachometer and compare it to the VECI label. Adjust it, if necessary, by turning the curb idle speed adjustment nut on the throttle solenoid positioner (TSP) housing **(see illustration 34.7).**
15   Place the transmission in Neutral or Park and rev the engine.
16   Place the transmission back in the gear specified for idle speed adjustment. Recheck curb idle speed and readjust if necessary.
17   Turn the engine off.
18   If the carburetor has a dashpot, turn the key to the On position, but don't start the engine.
19   Open the throttle so the TSP plunger can extend.
20   Push the dashpot plunger as far in as it will go **(see illustration).** Measure the clearance between the tip of the plunger and its stop on the throttle vent lever. If not within the specifications on the VECI decal, loosen the dashpot locknut and turn the dashpot to adjust it.

21   Tighten the locknut and recheck the clearance to make sure it hasn't changed.
22   Turn the key off.
23   If the curb idle needed adjustment, adjust the bowl vent setting as described in the following Steps.
24   Turn the key to On, but don't start the engine. Open the throttle so the TSP plunger can extend.
25   Block the choke plate wide open.
26   Open the throttle and position the throttle vent lever so it isn't touching the bowl vent rod **(see illustration).**
27   Close the throttle to the idle position, measuring the travel of the fuel bowl vent rod from the wide open throttle position.
28   If the travel is not within this Chapter's Specifications, bend the throttle vent lever at the indicated notch **(see illustration 34.26)** to change it.

1985 and 1986 2.0L engines
Refer to illustrations 34.34 and 34.36
29   Warm the engine to normal operating temperature.
30   Place the transmission in Neutral and turn all accessories off.
31   Connect an accurate tune-up tachometer to the engine, following manufacturer's instructions. On models so equipped, connect the tachometer pickup to the TACH TEST terminal on the ignition coil **(see illustration 34.4).**
32   Start the engine and compare engine idle speed on the tachometer with the specifications on the VECI decal. If it is incorrect, there may be a fault in the electronic idle speed control system. This must be diagnosed by a Ford dealer service department or other qualified repair shop.
33   Turn the engine off.
34   Unplug the electrical connector for the idle speed control (ISC) motor **(see illustration).**

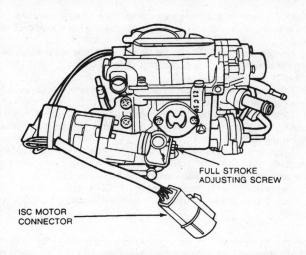

34.55   Idle speed control full-stroke adjustment point – 1987 and 1988 2.0L engine

35   On 1986 models, disconnect and plug the EGR valve vacuum hose.

36   Tape over the idle tracking switch (ITS) terminals (see illustration) to prevent accidental electrical contact and damage.

37   Use jumper leads to connect the battery directly to the idle speed control (ISC) motor terminals (see illustration 34.36). The motor shaft should retract. If it doesn't, switch the jumper wires at the ISC motor terminals so the shaft retracts. Once it does retract, disconnect the jumper leads from the motor and from the battery.

38   Start the engine and check idle speed (closed throttle rpm). If it isn't within the range listed in this Chapter's Specifications, adjust it by turning the kill speed screw (see illustration 34.34).

39   Place the fast idle screw on the cam step specified on the VECI label (see illustration 34.34). Don't touch the accelerator.

40   Compare fast idle speed with the VECI label. Adjust it, if necessary, by turning the fast idle screw (see illustration 34.34).

41   Tap the accelerator and let the engine return to idle speed.

42   Reconnect the jumper leads between the battery and the ISC motor terminals. The motor shaft should extend. If it retracts, switch the leads.

43   Once the motor shaft is extended, disconnect the jumper leads from the battery and terminals.

44   Check engine speed. If not within the ISC maximum extension range listed in this Chapter's Specifications, adjust it at the point shown in illus-

tration 34.34.

45   Remove the tape from the ITS terminals and reconnect the ISC motor electrical connector.

46   With all accessories off, make sure idle speed is at the rpm specified on the VECI label.

47   Turn the engine off.

48   Disconnect the engine coolant temperature switch.

49   Start the engine and check idle speed. It should be within the ISC function test rpm listed in this Chapter's Specifications. If not, the ISC system requires diagnosis by a Ford dealer or other qualified shop.

1987 and 1988 2.0L engines

Refer to illustrations 34.55, 34.56 and 34.57

50   Warm the engine to normal operating temperature.

51   Place the transmission in Neutral and turn all accessories off.

52   Connect an accurate tune-up tachometer to the engine, following manufacturer's instructions. On models so equipped, connect the tachometer pickup to the TACH TEST terminal on the ignition coil (see illustration 34.4).

53   Start the engine and compare engine idle speed on the tachometer with the specifications on the VECI label. If it is incorrect, there may be a fault in the electronic idle speed control system. This must be diagnosed by a Ford dealer service department or other qualified repair shop.

54   Turn the engine off.

55   Unplug the electrical connector for the idle speed control motor (see illustration).

56   Disconnect and plug the fast idle cam breaker vacuum hose (see illustration).

57   Tape over the idle tracking switch (ITS) terminals (see illustration) to prevent accidental electrical contact and damage.

58   Use jumper leads to connect the battery directly to the idle speed control (ISC) motor terminals (see illustration 34.57). The motor shaft should retract. If it doesn't, switch the jumper wires at the ISC motor terminals so the shaft retracts. Once it does retract, disconnect the jumper leads from the motor and from the battery.

59   Start the engine and check idle speed (closed throttle rpm). If it isn't within the range listed in this Chapter's Specifications, it must be adjusted by a Ford dealer service department or other qualified repair shop.

60   Place the fast idle screw on the cam step specified on the VECI label (see illustration 34.56). Don't touch the accelerator.

61   Compare fast idle speed with the VECI decal. Adjust it, if necessary, by turning the fast idle adjusting screw (see illustration 34.56).

62   Tap the accelerator and let the engine return to idle speed.

63   Reconnect the jumper leads between the battery and the ISC motor terminals. The motor shaft should extend. If it retracts, switch the leads.

64   Once the motor shaft is extended, disconnect the jumper leads from

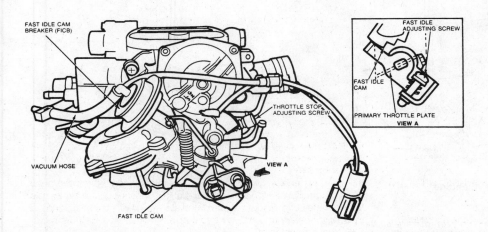

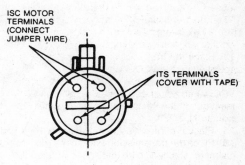

34.57   Idle speed control motor terminals – 1987 and 1988 2.0L engine

34.56   Fast idle and throttle stop adjustment points – 1987 and 1988 2.0L engine

the battery and terminals.

65   Check engine speed. If not within the ISC maximum extension range listed in this Chapter's Specifications, adjust it at the point shown in illustration 34.55 (full-stroke adjusting screw).

66   Remove the tape from the ITS terminals and reconnect the ISC motor electrical connector.

67   With all accessories off, make sure idle speed is at the rpm specified on the VECI label.

68   Turn the engine off.

69   Disconnect the engine coolant temperature switch.

70   Start the engine and check idle speed. It should be within the ISC function test rpm listed in this Chapter's Specifications. If not, the idle speed control system must be diagnosed by a Ford dealer or other qualified shop.

2.8L V6 engine

Refer to illustrations 34.77 and 34.81

71   Warm the engine to normal operating temperature.

72   Set the parking brake and block the wheels so the vehicle can't roll.

73   Turn all accessories off.

74   Connect an accurate tune-up tachometer to the engine, following manufacturer's instructions. On models so equipped, connect the tachometer pickup to the TACH TEST terminal on the ignition coil **(see illustration 34.4).**

75   Remove the air cleaner cover. Remove the clip inside the air cleaner tray that secures the temperature sensor. Detach the temperature sensor from the air cleaner, but leave it connected to the wiring harness.

76   Remove the air cleaner tray. Disconnect and plug the vacuum line at the bottom of the air cleaner.

77   Turn the engine off and watch the idle speed control (ISC) motor plunger **(see illustration)**. It should extend all the way within 10 seconds after the key is turned off.

78   Disconnect the electrical connector from the idle speed control motor.

79   Disconnect and plug the EGR vacuum hose.

80   Start the engine and let it idle.

81   Open the throttle by hand and position the fast idle adjusting screw on the high step of the fast idle cam **(see illustration)**.

82   Compare the tachometer reading with the fast idle specification on the VECI label. If it's incorrect, adjust by turning the fast idle screw **(see illustration 34.81).**

83   Open the throttle, release the fast idle screw from the fast idle cam and let the throttle lever rest against the plunger on the idle speed control motor.

84   Loosen the lock screw on the ISC bracket **(see illustration 34.77).** Turn the bracket adjusting screw to set engine speed at 2,000 rpm, then tighten the lock screw.

85   Connect the electrical connector to the idle speed control motor. Idle speed should return to normal automatically.

86   Move the throttle by hand to hold engine speed above 1,000 rpm. Push the ISC plunger all the way in, then quickly release the throttle and unplug the ISC connector.

87   Compare engine speed with the anti-dieseling speed listed in this Chapter's Specifications. Adjust it, if necessary, by turning the throttle stop adjustment screw **(see illustration 34.77).**

88   Reconnect the idle speed control and EGR vacuum hoses.

89   Turn the engine off, then start it again. Make sure curb idle speed is correct.

---

35   Driveshaft and driveaxle yoke lubrication (4WD models)

At the specified intervals, the slip yokes on the driveshafts and the right-front driveaxle should be lubricated (see this Chapter's Specifications for the correct lubricant). This requires removal of the driveshafts and driveaxle (see Chapter 8 for procedures).

---

36   Emission component inspection/replacement

1   Some emission control components on 1986 through 1988 models should be replaced at 60,000 miles or when the maintenance reminder light on the dashboard comes on, whichever occurs first. Ford specifies that replacement is required for Federal models and recommended for California and Canada models. The components and models are:
  a) EGR valve (1986 2.0 and 2.3L engines; 1987 2.3L and 2.9L engines; 1988 2.0L engines).
  b) EGR vacuum solenoid(s) (1986 2.3L engine).
  c) EGR vacuum solenoid filter (1987 and 1988 2.3L EFI engine).
  d) Exhaust gas oxygen sensor (1986 through 1988 models).
2   Component replacement is described in Chapter 6.

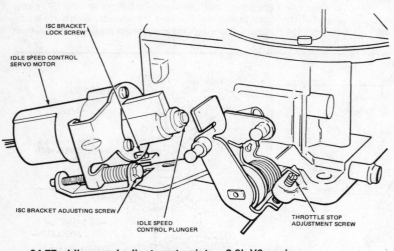

34.77   Idle speed adjustment points – 2.8L V6 engine

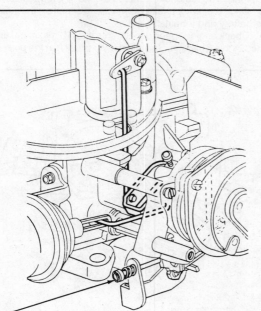

FAST IDLE RPM ADJUSTING SCREW
(SHOWN ON HIGH CAM/FAST IDLE STEP)

34.81   Fast idle adjustment point – 2.8L V6 engine

Chapter 2 Part A   Four-cylinder engines

Contents

2A

Specifications

General
Cylinder numbers (front-to-rear) 1–2–3–4
Firing order 1-3-4-2

Camshaft
Lobe lift (intake and exhaust) .... 0.2381 in
Endplay
  Standard .... 0.001 to 0.007 in
  Service limit .... 0.009 in
Journal diameter .... 1.7713 to 1.7720 in
Runout limit .... 0.005 in (total indicator reading)
Out-of-round limit .... 0.0005 in
Journal-to-bearing (oil) clearance
  Standard .... 0.001 to 0.003 in
  Service limit .... 0.006 in
Front bearing location .... 0.000 to 0.010 in below front face of bearing tower

Torque specifications   Ft-lbs (unless otherwise indicated)
Camshaft sprocket bolt .... 50 to 71
Crankshaft pulley/sprocket bolt
  1983 through 1986 .... 100 to 120
  1987 on .... 103 to 133
Camshaft retaining plate bolt .... 72 to 108 in-lbs
Auxiliary shaft sprocket bolt .... 28 to 40
Auxiliary shaft retaining plate screws .... 72 to 108 in-lbs
Timing belt outer cover bolt(s) .... 72 to 108 in-lbs
Timing belt tensioner adjustment bolt .... 14 to 21
Timing belt tensioner pivot bolt .... 28 to 40
Valve cover bolts
  1983 through 1986 .... 72 to 96 in-lbs
  1987 on .... 62 to 97 in-lbs
Cylinder head bolts
  Step 1 .... 50 to 60
  Step 2 .... 80 to 90
Flywheel/driveplate bolts .... 56 to 64
Intake manifold bolts
  1983 through 1986
    Step 1 .... 60 to 84 in-lbs
    Step 2 .... 14 to 21
  1987 on .... 15 to 22

POSITION OF CAP ATTACHING SCREWS

DISTRIBUTOR

CLOCKWISE

Firing order 1-3-4-2

Front

2.0L & 2.3L 4-cylinder engines with a distributor

FRONT OF VEHICLE

LEFT-HAND IGNITION COIL PACK

PARALLEL TO CENTERLINE OF CRANKSHAFT

PARALLEL TO CENTERLINE OF CRANKSHAFT

FRONT OF VEHICLE

RIGHT-HAND IGNITION COIL PACK

Distributorless 2.3L engines
Firing order 1-3-4-2

Cylinder location and distributor rotation

Torque specifications (continued)

Ft-lbs (unless otherwise indicated)

Exhaust manifold bolts	
1983 through 1986	
Step 1	60 to 84 in-lbs
Step 2	16 to 23
1987 on	
Step 1	178 to 204 in-lbs
Step 2	20 to 30
Oil pan-to-engine block bolts	
With four-piece gasket	
Small bolts	80 to 102 in-lbs
Large bolts	106 to 133 in-lbs
With one-piece gasket	
Pan to block	90 to 110 in-lbs
Pan to transmission	30 to 39
Oil pump bolts	15 to 21
Oil pump pick-up tube nut	30 to 41
Engine mount bracket-to-block bolts and studs	
1983 through 1985	
Passenger side (2.0L with A/C)	34 to 44
Passenger side (all others)	45 to 60
Driver side	45 to 60
1986 through 1988 2.0L engine	45 to 60
1986 and later 2.3L engine	
Passenger side	45 to 60
Driver side	
1986 through 1990	71 to 94
1991 on	45 to 65
Engine mount insulator-to-block bracket nuts	
1983 through 1985	65 to 85
1986 through 1988	
2.0L	65 to 85
2.3L	71 to 94
1989 on	65 to 85
Engine mount insulator-to-crossmember or frame bracket nuts	
1983 through 1988	71 to 94
1989 on	65 to 85

1   General information

This Part of Chapter 2 is devoted to in-vehicle repair procedures for the 2.0L and 2.3L Over Head Camshaft (OHC) four-cylinder engines.

Information concerning engine removal and installation, as well as engine block and cylinder head overhaul, is in Part E of this Chapter.

The following repair procedures are based on the assumption that the engine is installed in the vehicle. If the engine has been removed from the vehicle and mounted on a stand, many of the steps included in this Part of Chapter 2 will not apply.

The specifications included in this Part of Chapter 2 apply only to the engine and procedures in this Part. The specifications necessary for rebuilding the block and cylinder head are found in Part E.

2   Repair operations possible with the engine in the vehicle

Many major repair operations can be accomplished without removing the engine from the vehicle.

Clean the engine compartment and the exterior of the engine with some type of pressure washer before any work is done. A clean engine will make the job easier and will help keep dirt out of the internal areas of the engine.

Depending on the components involved, it may be a good idea to remove the hood to improve access to the engine as repairs are performed (refer to Chapter 11 if necessary).

If vacuum, exhaust, oil or coolant leaks develop, indicating a need for gasket or seal replacement, the repairs can generally be made with the engine in the vehicle. The intake and exhaust manifold gaskets, oil pan gasket, valve cover gasket and cylinder head gasket are all accessible with the engine in place. The crankshaft oil seals can also be replaced without removing the engine.

Engine components such as the intake and exhaust manifolds, the oil pan, the oil pump, the auxiliary shaft, the water pump, the starter motor, the alternator, the distributor and the fuel system components can be removed for repair with the engine in place.

Since the cylinder head can be removed without pulling the engine, camshaft and valve component servicing can also be accomplished with the engine in the vehicle.

In extreme cases caused by a lack of necessary equipment, repair or replacement of piston rings, pistons, connecting rods and rod bearings is possible with the engine in the vehicle. However, this practice is not recommended because of the cleaning and preparation work that must be done to the components involved.

3   Top Dead Center (TDC) for number one piston – locating

Refer to illustrations 3.6 and 3.7

1   Top Dead Center (TDC) is the highest point in the cylinder that each piston reaches as it travels up-and-down when the crankshaft turns. Each piston reaches TDC on the compression stroke and again on the exhaust stroke, but TDC generally refers to piston position on the compression stroke. The timing marks are referenced to the number one piston at TDC on the compression stroke.

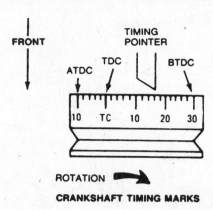

3.6 Turn the crankshaft until the TDC mark on the pulley is aligned with the pointer on the timing belt cover – note that in this illustration the crankshaft must be turned a few degrees more to align the mark with the pointer

4.6 Remove this screw (arrow) to detach the metal heater pipes from the valve cover

2   Positioning the piston(s) at TDC is an essential part of many procedures such as in-vehicle valve train service, timing belt replacement and distributor removal.

3   In order to bring any piston to TDC, the crankshaft must be turned using one of the methods outlined below. When looking at the front of the engine, normal crankshaft rotation is clockwise. **Caution:** *Turning the crankshaft backwards may cause the timing belt to jump teeth.*
  a) The preferred method is to turn the crankshaft with a large socket and breaker bar attached to the large bolt that's threaded into the front of the crankshaft.
  b) A remote starter switch, which may save some time, can also be used. Attach the switch leads to the switch and battery terminals on the solenoid. Once the piston is close to TDC, use a socket and breaker bar as described in the previous paragraph.
  c) If an assistant is available to turn the ignition switch to the Start position in short bursts, you can get the piston close to TDC without a remote starter switch. Use a socket and breaker bar as described in Paragraph a) to complete the procedure.

4   On all except 1989 and later 2.3L engines, locate the number one spark plug wire terminal in the distributor cap, then mark the distributor base directly under the terminal.

5   Remove the distributor cap as described in Chapter 1.

6   Turn the crankshaft (see Paragraph 3 above) until the ignition timing mark for TDC on the crankshaft pulley is aligned with the timing pointer on the belt cover **(see illustration).**

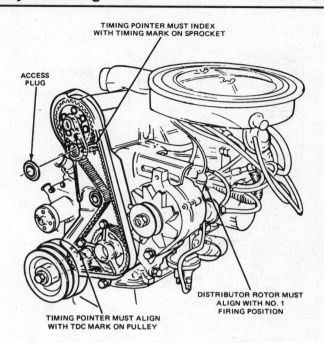

3.7 With number one piston at TDC on the compression stroke, the crankshaft TDC mark should align with the timing pointer and the camshaft index mark (visible though the timing belt cover hole) should align with the sprocket mark – on all except 1989 and later 2.3L engines, the distributor rotor should point to number one terminal in the cap

7   The camshaft index pointer and sprocket timing mark should be aligned when you look through the hole in the timing belt cover **(see illustration)**. On engines equipped with a distributor, the rotor should now be pointing directly at the mark you made earlier on the distributor. If it isn't, the piston is at TDC on the exhaust stroke.

8   To get the piston to TDC on the compression stroke, turn the crankshaft one complete turn (360-degrees) clockwise. The camshaft timing mark should now be aligned. On engines equipped with a distributor, the rotor should now be pointing at the mark. When the crankshaft an camshaft marks are aligned (and the distributor rotor points to number one terminal on engines equipped with a distributor), number one piston is at TDC on the compression stroke. **Note:** *If the crankshaft and camshaft timing marks won't align at the same time, the timing belt may be incorrectly installed.*

9   After the number one piston has been positioned at TDC on the compression stroke, TDC for any of the remaining cylinders can be located by turning the crankshaft and following the firing order (refer to the Specifications).

4   Valve cover – removal and installation

Refer to illustrations 4.6 and 4.7

1   Disconnect the negative cable from the battery.

2   If you're working on a carbureted model, remove the air cleaner (see Chapter 4).

3   Remove the PCV tube from the valve cover (see Chapter 6).

4   On fuel-injected models, remove the throttle body (see Chapter 4).

5   On fuel-injected models, remove the EGR supply tube (see Chapter 6).

6   Detach the wires from the spark plugs and detach the wire holder from the valve cover. Remove the screw that secures the heater tubes to the cover **(see illustration)**.

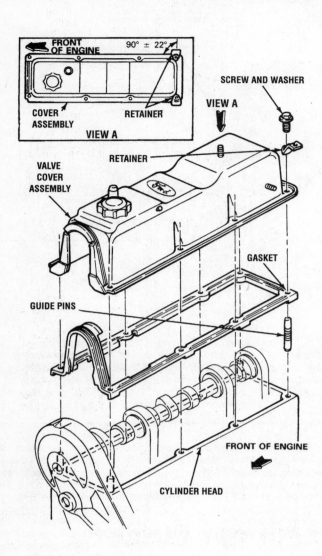

4.7   Exploded view of valve cover and related components (typical) – the retainers at the two rear corners are used on some 2.3L engines

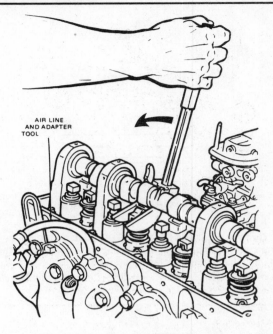

5.7   While compressed air holds the valve closed, a special tool is used to collapse the spring so the cam follower and lash adjuster can be removed

7   Remove the bolts and studs and separate the cover from the engine **(see illustration)**. It may be necessary to break the gasket seal by tapping the cover with a soft-face hammer. If it's really stuck, use a knife, gasket scraper or chisel to remove it, but be very careful not to damage the gasket sealing surfaces of the cover or head. Don't lose the sealing grommets.

8   Place clean rags in the camshaft gallery to keep foreign material out of the engine.

9   Remove all traces of gasket material from the cover and head. Be careful not to nick or gouge the surfaces. Clean the mating surfaces with lacquer thinner or acetone.

10   Reinstall the cover with a new gasket – apply Ford adhesive no. 7AZ-19B508-A (or an equivalent oil-resistant sealant) to the mating surfaces of the cover and head. The tabs on the gasket must fit into the slots in the cover. Install the bolts and tighten them in a criss-cross pattern to the torque listed in this Chapter's Specifications.

11   Reinstall the throttle body (see Chapter 4) and the remaining components previously removed or disconnected.

12   Run the engine and check for vacuum and oil leaks.

---

5   Valve seals and springs – replacement

Refer to illustrations 5.7, 5.8 and 5.17

Note: *Broken valve springs and defective valve stem seals can be replaced without removing the cylinder head. Two special tools and a compressed air source are normally required to perform this operation, so read through this Section carefully and rent or buy the tools before beginning the job. If compressed air isn't available, a length of nylon rope can be used to keep the valves from falling into the cylinder during this procedure.*

1   Refer to Section 4 and remove the valve cover.

2   Remove the spark plug from the cylinder which has the defective component. If all of the valve stem seals are being replaced, all of the spark plugs should be removed (see Chapter 1). **Note:** *On 1989 and later 2.3L engines (which have twin-plug ignition), remove only one spark plug from each cylinder.*

3   Turn the crankshaft until the piston in the affected cylinder is at top dead center on the compression stroke (refer to Section 3 for instructions). If you're replacing all of the valve stem seals, begin with cylinder number one and work on the valves for one cylinder at a time. Move from cylinder-to-cylinder following the firing order sequence (1-3-4-2).

4   Thread an adapter into the spark plug hole and connect an air hose from a compressed air source to it. Most auto parts stores can supply the air hose adapter. **Note:** *Many cylinder compression gauges utilize a screw-in fitting that may work with your air hose quick-disconnect fitting.*

5   Apply compressed air to the cylinder. The valves for that cylinder should be held in place by the air pressure. If the valve faces or seats are in poor condition, leaks may prevent the air pressure from retaining the valves – refer to the alternative procedure below.

6   If you don't have access to compressed air, an alternative method can be used. Position the piston at approximately 45-degrees before TDC on the compression stroke, then feed a long piece of nylon rope through the spark plug hole until it fills the combustion chamber. Be sure to leave the end of the rope hanging out of the engine so it can be removed easily. Use a large breaker bar and socket to rotate the crankshaft in the normal direction of rotation until slight resistance is felt.

7   Stuff shop rags into the cylinder head holes near the valves to prevent parts and tools from falling into the engine, then use a valve spring compressor to compress the spring **(see illustration)**.

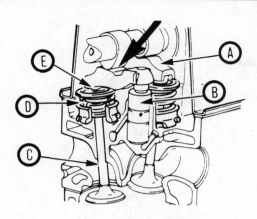

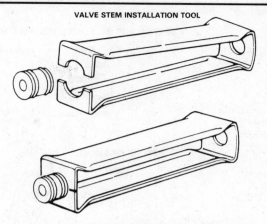

5.8   Valve components – note that in this view the camshaft
lobe is contacting the cam follower (arrow), which
compresses the valve spring and opens the valve – for work
described in Section 5 the valve should be closed, with the
cam lobe pointing up, away from the follower

5.17   Ford valve stem seal tool

8   With the spring compressed, slide the cam follower over the lash adjuster to remove it **(see illustration)**. Also remove the lash adjuster.
9   Still compressing the spring, remove the keepers. Release the valve
spring tool and remove the spring retainer, damper assembly and valve
spring.
10   Remove and discard the valve stem seal. **Note:** *If air pressure fails to
hold the valve in the closed position during this operation, the valve face
or seat is probably damaged. If so, the cylinder head will have to be removed for additional repair operations.*
11   Wrap a rubber band or tape around the top of the valve stem so the
valve will not fall into the cylinder, then release the air pressure.
12   Inspect the valve stem for damage. Rotate the valve in the guide and
check the end for eccentric movement, which would indicate that the
valve is bent.
13   Move the valve up-and-down in the guide and make sure it doesn't
bind. If the valve stem binds, either the valve is bent or the guide is damaged. In either case, the head will have to be removed for repair.
14   Reapply air pressure to the cylinder to retain the valve in the closed
position, then remove the tape or rubber band from the valve stem. Lubricate the valve stem with engine oil and install a new umbrella type guide
seal, if used.
15   Place the plastic installation cap over the end of the valve stem.
16   Start the valve stem seal carefully over the cap and push the seal
down until the jacket touches the top of the guide.
17   Remove the plastic cap and use the installation tool **(see illustration)** or two screwdrivers to bottom the seal on the valve guide.
18   Install the valve spring, damper and retainer, compress the spring
and install the keepers.
19   Install the lash adjuster and cam follower.
20   Disconnect the air hose and remove the adapter from the spark plug
hole. If a rope was used in place of air pressure, pull it out of the cylinder.
Caution: *Turn the crankshaft backwards only very slightly to release the
rope. Turning the crankshaft backwards excessively will cause the timing
belt to jump teeth.*
21   Reinstall the various components removed.
22   Start and run the engine, then check for oil leaks and unusual sounds
coming from the valve cover area.

6   **Timing belt – removal, installation and adjustment**

Refer to illustrations 6.13a, 6.13b, 6.14a, 6.14b and 6.28
Note: *On 1989 and later 2.3L engines, this procedure requires a special
tool (Ford part no. T89P-6316-A) to position the timing sensor correctly
during installation.*

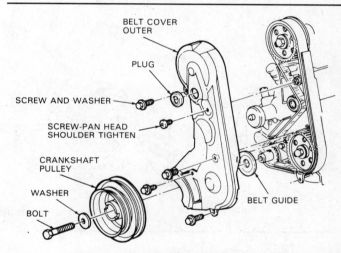

6.13a   Timing belt cover installation details (early models)

1   Disconnect the negative cable from the battery.
2   Remove the fan shroud (see Chapter 3).
3   Remove the fan and the water pump pulley (see Chapter 3).
4   Remove the drivebelts (see Chapter 1).
5   If the thermactor pump obstructs cover removal, remove it (see
Chapter 6).
6   Remove the power steering pump mounting bracket (see Chapter
10) and set the pump aside without disconnecting the hoses.
7   Drain the cooling system (see Chapter 1) and remove the upper radiator hose (see Chapter 3).
8   Remove the thermostat housing and gasket (see Chapter 3).
9   Position the number one piston at top dead center on the compression stroke (see Section 3). **Caution:** *Always turn the crankshaft in the
direction of normal rotation (clockwise, viewed from the front). Backward
rotation may cause the timing belt to jump teeth. DO NOT turn the crankshaft during this procedure, after the number one piston is at TDC, until
after the timing belt is reinstalled!*
10   On all except 1989 and later 2.3L engines, make sure the distributor
rotor is pointing at the number one plug wire terminal.
11   On 1989 and later 2.3L engines, remove the timing sensor (see
Chapter 5).
12   Remove the crankshaft drivebelt pulley and belt guide.
13   Remove the outer cover fasteners:
   a) On 1983 through 1988 models, remove four bolts and one screw
      and detach the outer timing belt cover **(see illustration)**.
   b) On 1989 and later models, remove one bolt and release eight in-
      terlocking tabs and detach the outer timing belt cover **(see il-
      lustration)**.

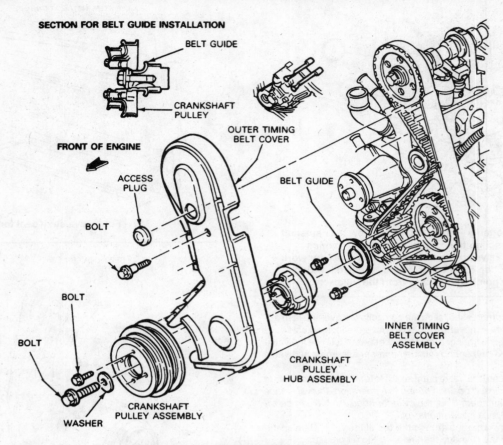

SECTION FOR BELT GUIDE INSTALLATION

BELT GUIDE

CRANKSHAFT PULLEY

FRONT OF ENGINE

OUTER TIMING BELT COVER

ACCESS PLUG

BELT GUIDE

BOLT

BOLT

BOLT

INNER TIMING BELT COVER ASSEMBLY

CRANKSHAFT PULLEY HUB ASSEMBLY

WASHER

CRANKSHAFT PULLEY ASSEMBLY

6.13b   Timing belt cover installation details (later models)

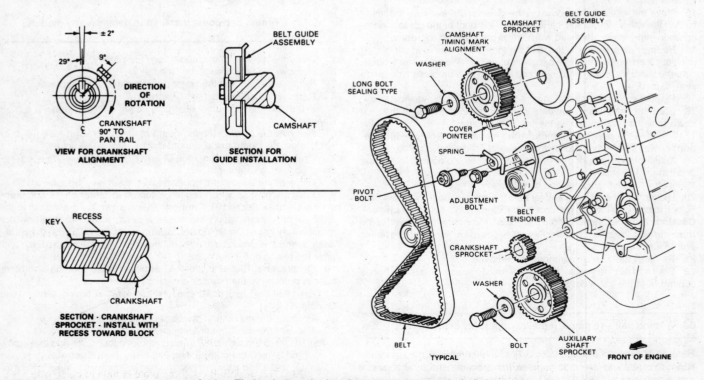

± 2°

29°   9°

DIRECTION OF ROTATION

CRANKSHAFT 90° TO PAN RAIL

VIEW FOR CRANKSHAFT ALIGNMENT

BELT GUIDE ASSEMBLY

CAMSHAFT

SECTION FOR GUIDE INSTALLATION

KEY   RECESS

CRANKSHAFT

SECTION · CRANKSHAFT SPROCKET · INSTALL WITH RECESS TOWARD BLOCK

CAMSHAFT SPROCKET

CAMSHAFT TIMING MARK ALIGNMENT

BELT GUIDE ASSEMBLY

WASHER

LONG BOLT SEALING TYPE

COVER POINTER

SPRING

PIVOT BOLT

ADJUSTMENT BOLT

BELT TENSIONER

CRANKSHAFT SPROCKET

WASHER

BELT

BOLT

AUXILIARY SHAFT SPROCKET

FRONT OF ENGINE

TYPICAL

6.14a   Timing belt and related components – exploded view

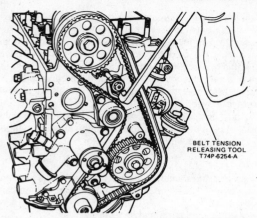

6.14b A special Ford tool or a prybar can be used to release the tension on the timing belt

14 Loosen the belt tensioner adjustment bolt, then position spreader tool no. T74P-6254-A on the tensioner pin and retract the belt tensioner **(see illustrations)**. If the special tool is not available, a prybar wedged between the roll pin and tensioner may work. Tighten the adjustment bolt to hold the tensioner in the retracted position.

15 Remove the timing belt and inspect it for wear and damage. If it's worn or damaged, replace the belt. **Caution:** *If in doubt about the belt condition, install a new one. If the belt breaks during engine operation, extensive damage may occur!*

16 Check the sprockets for wear, cracks and burrs on the teeth. If the sprockets are worn or damaged, they can be detached after removing the mounting bolts. Make sure the new sprockets are installed correctly **(see illustration 6.14a)**. Tighten the mounting bolts to the torque listed in this Chapter's Specifications. **Note:** *Install a new camshaft sprocket bolt or use Teflon sealing tape on the old bolt.*

17 Make sure the valve timing mark on the camshaft sprocket is aligned with the pointer on the engine case. Install the timing belt over the crankshaft sprocket, then over the auxiliary shaft sprocket.

18 Pull the belt up (pulling slack from between the auxiliary and camshaft sprockets) and install it on the camshaft sprocket in a counterclockwise direction so no slack will be between the two sprockets. Align the belt fore and aft on the sprockets.

19 Loosen the tensioner adjustment bolt to allow the tensioner to move against the belt. If the spring does not have enough tension to move the roller against the belt (the belt hangs loose), it may be necessary to insert tool no. T74P-6254-A or a prybar between the tensioner and pin and push the roller against the belt. Tighten the bolt to the torque listed in this Chapter's Specifications. **Note:** *The spring cannot be used to set belt tension. A wrench must be used on the tensioner assembly.*

20 Remove the spark plugs. Slowly rotate the crankshaft two complete turns in the direction of normal rotation to make sure the belt is seated and to remove any slack. While turning the crankshaft, feel and listen for valve-to-piston contact. Don't force the crankshaft – if binding is felt, recheck all work or seek professional advice!

21 Tighten the tensioner adjustment and pivot bolts to the torque listed in this Chapter's Specifications. Recheck the alignment of the valve timing marks.

22 On 1989 and later 2.3L engines, install and adjust the timing sensor (see Chapter 5).

23 Install the timing belt cover and tighten the mounting bolts securely.

24 The remaining installation steps are the reverse of removal. Be sure to tighten the crankshaft pulley/sprocket bolt to the torque listed in this Chapter's Specifications.

25 Bring the number one piston to top dead center on the compression stroke (see Section 3).

26 On all except 1989 and later 2.3L engines, remove the distributor cap and make sure the distributor rotor is pointing at the number one spark plug wire terminal.

27 Remove the access plug from the timing belt cover.

6.28 Before starting the engine, remove the plug from the belt cover and recheck the timing marks

28 Look through the access hole in the belt cover to be sure that the timing mark on the camshaft sprocket is lined up with the pointer **(see illustration)**.

29 Make sure the timing mark on the crankshaft pulley aligns with the TDC mark on the belt cover.

30 Reinstall the belt cover access plug.

31 If the marks don't align as described **(see illustration 3.7)**, recheck the timing belt installation.

---

7 Camshaft and followers – removal, inspection and installation

Refer to illustrations 7.9 and 7.12

Removal

1 Disconnect the negative cable from the battery.

2 Remove the valve cover, the timing belt cover and the timing belt (see Sections 4 and 6). Unbolt the alternator bracket from the cylinder head and push it aside.

3 Remove the spring clip from the hydraulic valve lash adjuster end of each cam follower.

4 Using a valve spring compressor, compress the valve spring and slide out the cam follower (see Section 5 if necessary). Keep the cam followers in order so they can be reinstalled in their original locations.

5 Lift out the hydraulic lash adjusters, keeping each one with its respective cam follower.

6 Remove the camshaft sprocket mounting bolt and washer. A long screwdriver placed through one of the holes in the sprocket will prevent the camshaft from turning.

7 Remove the sprocket with a puller, then remove the belt guide.

8 Remove the sprocket locating pin from the end of the camshaft.

9 Remove the camshaft retaining plate from the rear bearing pedestal **(see illustration)**.

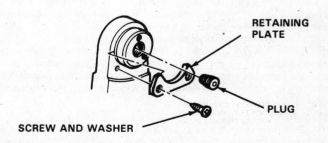

7.9 The camshaft retaining plate is held in place with two screws

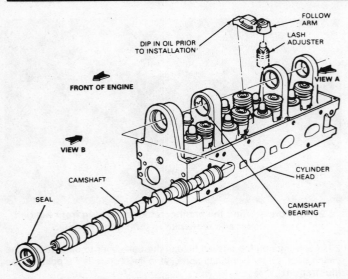

FOLLOW
ARM

LASH
ADJUSTER

DIP IN OIL PRIOR
TO INSTALLATION

VIEW A

FRONT OF ENGINE

VIEW B

CYLINDER
HEAD

CAMSHAFT

CAMSHAFT
BEARING

SEAL

7.12 Camshaft and related components – exploded view

10 Raise the vehicle and support it securely on jackstands.
11 Position a floor jack under the engine. Place a block of wood on the jack pad. Remove the left and right engine mount bolts and nuts. Raise the engine as high as it will go. Place blocks of wood between the engine mounts and frame brackets and remove the jack. **Warning:** *DO NOT place your hands under the engine where they would be crushed if the jack failed!*
12 Using a hammer and a brass or aluminum drift, drive the camshaft out toward the front of the engine, taking the front seal with it (**see illustration**). Be very careful not to damage the camshaft bearings and journals as it's pushed out.

Inspection
Camshaft and bearings
13 After the camshaft has been removed from the engine, cleaned with solvent and dried, inspect the bearing journals for uneven wear, pits and galling. If the journals are damaged, the bearing inserts in the head are probably damaged as well. Both the camshaft and bearings will have to be replaced with new ones. Measure the inside diameter of each camshaft bearing and record the results (take two measurements, 90-degrees apart, at each bearing).
14 Measure the camshaft bearing journals with a micrometer to determine if they're excessively worn or out-of-round. If they're more than 0.005-inch out-of-round, the camshaft should be replaced with a new one. Subtract the bearing journal diameters from the corresponding bearing inside diameter measurements to obtain the oil clearance. If it's excessive, new bearings must be installed. **Note:** *Camshaft bearing replacement requires special tools and expertise that place it outside the scope of the do-it-yourselfer. Take the head to an automotive machine shop to ensure that the job is done correctly.*
15 Check the camshaft lobes for heat discoloration, score marks, chipped areas, pitting and uneven wear. If the lobes are in good condition the camshaft can be reused.
16 Make sure the camshaft oil passages are clear and clean.
17 To check the thrust plate for wear, install the camshaft in the cylinder head and position the thrust plate at the rear. Using a dial indicator, check the total endplay by tapping the camshaft carefully back-and-forth. If the endplay is outside the specified limit, replace the thrust plate with a new one.

Cam followers
18 On early models, check the faces of the cam followers (which bear on the cam lobes) for signs of pitting, score marks and other forms of wear. They should fit snugly on the pivot bolt. On later models, check the rollers (which bear on the cam lobes) for signs of wear and for a loose fit in the follower. Replace followers that have these conditions.

19 Inspect the face which bears on the valve stem. If it's pitted, the cam follower must be replaced with a new one.
20 If excessive cam follower wear is evident (and possibly excessive cam lobe wear), it may be due to a malfunction of the valve drive lubrication tube. If this has occurred, replace the tube and the cam follower. If more than one cam follower is excessively worn, replace the camshaft, all the cam followers and the lubrication tube. This also applies where excessive cam lobe wear is found.
21 During any operation which requires removal of the valve cover, make sure that oil is being discharged from the lubrication tube nozzles by cranking the engine with the starter motor.

Installation
22 Liberally coat the camshaft journals and bearings with engine assembly lube or moly-base grease, then carefully install the camshaft in the cylinder head.
23 Install the retaining plate and screws.
24 Lubricate the new camshaft oil seal with engine oil and carefully tap it into place at the front of the cylinder head with a large socket and a hammer. Make sure it enters the bore squarely and seats completely.
25 Install the belt guide and pin at the front end of the camshaft, then carefully tap on the sprocket.
26 Install a new sprocket bolt or use Teflon sealing tape on the threads of the old one.
27 Coat the hydraulic lash adjusters with engine assembly lube or moly-base grease, then install them in their original locations.
28 Coat the camshaft lobes and cam followers with engine assembly lube or moly-base grease.
29 Install the timing belt (see Section 6).
30 Compress each valve spring and position each cam follower on its respective valve end and adjuster. Install the retaining spring clips.
31 Install the remaining components previously removed.

---

8   Auxiliary shaft – removal, inspection and installation

Refer to illustration 8.4
1 Detach the negative battery cable from the battery. Remove the large bolt from the front of the crankshaft and pull the drivebelt pulley off. Remove the bolts/screws and detach the outer timing belt cover (**see illustration 6.13a or 6.13b**).
2 Loosen the auxiliary shaft sprocket bolt (**see illustration 6.14a**). If the shaft turns, immobilize the sprocket by inserting a large screwdriver or 3/8-inch drive extension through one of the sprocket holes. Detach the timing belt (see Section 6).
3 Pull off the sprocket (a puller may be required) and remove the pin from the shaft.
4 Remove the three bolts and detach the auxiliary shaft cover (**see illustration**).
5 Remove the screws and detach the retaining plate.
6 Withdraw the shaft. If it's tight, reinstall the bolt and washer. Use a prybar and spacer block to pry out the shaft. Be extremely careful not to damage the bearings as you pull the shaft out of the block.
7 Examine the auxiliary shaft bearing for pits and score marks. Replacement must be done by a dealer service department or a repair shop (although it's easy to remove the old bearing, correct installation of the new one requires special tools). The auxiliary shaft may show signs of wear on the bearing journal or the eccentric. Score marks and damage to the bearing journals cannot be removed by grinding. If in doubt, ask a dealer service department to check the auxiliary shaft and offer advice on replacement. Examine the gear teeth for wear and damage. If either is evident, a replacement shaft must be obtained.
8 Dip the auxiliary shaft in engine oil before installing it in the block. Tap it in gently with a soft-face hammer to ensure that it's seated. Install the retaining plate and the auxiliary shaft cover.
9 The remainder of the procedure is the reverse of removal. Make sure that the auxiliary shaft pin is in place before installing the sprocket. Tighten the sprocket mounting bolt to the torque listed in this Chapter's Specifications.

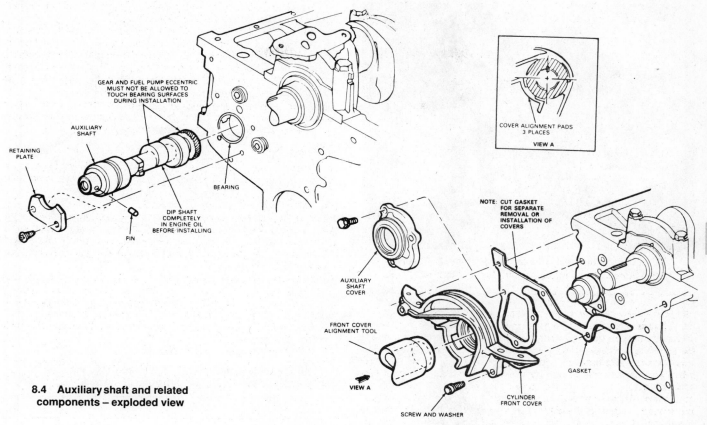

8.4 Auxiliary shaft and related components – exploded view

9 Front oil seals – replacement

Note: *The camshaft, crankshaft and auxiliary shaft oil seals are all replaced the same way, using the same tools, after the appropriate sprocket has been removed. When replacing the sprocket(s), always use a new Ford bolt or clean out the oil hole and use Teflon tape on the old bolt.*

1   Disconnect the negative battery cable from the battery.
2   To remove the camshaft or auxiliary shaft sprockets, refer to Section 7 or 8. Ford manufactures a special puller designed for this purpose.
3   To remove the crankshaft sprocket, use Ford tool no. T74P-6306-A or a gear puller.
4   Ford tool no. T74P-6700-B or equivalent may be used to remove all the seals. When using the tool, be sure the jaws are gripping the thin edge of the seal very tightly before operating the screw portion of the tool. If the tool isn't available, a hammer and chisel may be used to remove the seal(s) if care is exercised.
5   Clean the seal bore and shaft surface prior to installation of the new seal. Apply a thin layer of grease to the outer edge of the new seal(s).
6   Install the seal(s) with Ford tool no. T74P-6150A. If the special tool isn't available, you may be able to use a large deep socket and a hammer or a short piece of pipe, the sprocket bolt and a large flat washer.
7   Install the components removed to gain access to the seals.
8   If the front cover **(see illustration 8.4)** is removed for any reason, reinstall it without the seal. Before tightening the bolts, center the cover with Ford tool T74P-6019-B or equivalent, then install the seal as described previously.

10 Intake manifold – removal and installation

Carbureted models

Refer to illustrations 10.7, 10.11a and 10.11b

1   Drain the cooling system (see Chapter 1).
2   Remove the air cleaner (see Chapter 4).
3   Disconnect the throttle cable (see Chapter 4).
4   Label and disconnect all vacuum hoses that connect the intake manifold to the engine and vehicle.
5   Detach the coolant hose from the manifold.
6   Remove the engine oil dipstick and detach its tube from the manifold.
7   Disconnect the EGR heat tube **(see illustration)**.
8   Disconnect the PCV system (see Chapter 6).
9   Remove the distributor cap (see Chapter 1). Detach the spark plug loom from the valve cover and set the cap and wires out of the way.
10   Remove one bolt that secures the engine lifting "eye."
11   Remove the manifold bolts and the remaining bolt that secures the engine lifting "eye" **(see illustrations)**.
12   Clean the manifold and head mating surfaces and check the manifold for cracks. **Note:** *The mating surfaces of the head and manifold must be perfectly clean when the manifold is installed. Gasket removal solvents in aerosol cans are available at most auto parts stores and may be helpful when removing old gasket material that's stuck to the head and manifold. Be careful not to scrape or gouge the sealing surfaces.*
13   Clean and oil the manifold mounting bolts.
17   Reconnect the battery and refill the cooling system.
18   Start the engine and let it run while checking for coolant, fuel and vacuum leaks.
14   Position the new intake manifold gasket on the manifold.
15   Position the intake manifold and gasket, along with the lifting "eye", on the head, install the fasteners and tighten them in sequence, in two steps, to the torque listed in this Chapter's Specifications **(see illustrations 10.11a and 10.11b)**.
16   The remainder of installation is the reverse of removal.

10.7   Detach the heat tube (arrow) from the EGR valve

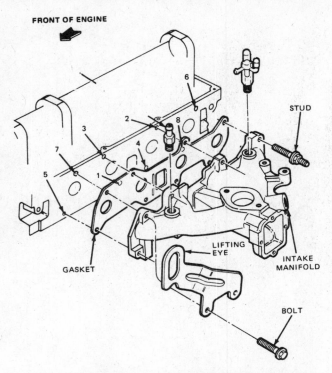

10.11a   Intake manifold (1983 through 1986 carbureted models) – be sure to tighten the bolts in the sequence shown

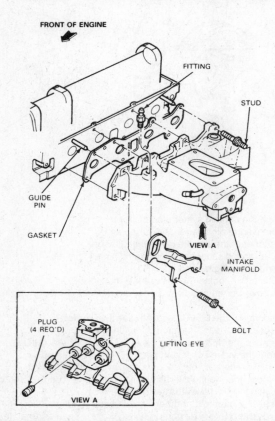

10.11b   Intake manifold (1987 and 1988 carbureted models) – use the bolt tighting sequence shown in illustration 10.11a

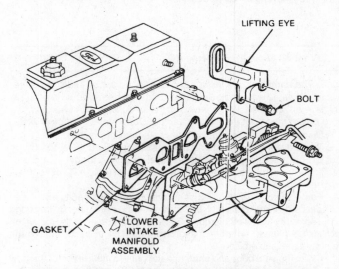

10.27   Intake manifold–typical (fuel-injected models)

Fuel-injected models

Refer to illustrations 10.27, 10.32a and 10.32b

19   Relieve the fuel system pressure (see Chapter 4).
20   Disconnect the negative battery cable from the battery.
21   Drain the cooling system (see Chapter 1).
22   Remove the engine cover (see Chapter 11).
23   Remove the air cleaner and ducts (see Chapter 4).
24   Label and disconnect the vacuum hoses from the throttle body and emissions devices attached to the intake manifold.

25   Remove the throttle body, fuel injection wiring harness, fuel rail and upper intake manifold (see Chapter 4).
26   Remove the four bottom mounting bolts from the intake manifold.
27   Remove the four upper mounting bolts from the manifold. Note that the front two bolts also secure the engine lifting "eye" **(see illustration)**.
28   Detach the manifold from the engine.
29   Clean the manifold and head mating surfaces and check the manifold for cracks. **Note:** *The mating surfaces of the head and manifold must be perfectly clean when the manifold is installed.* Gasket removal solvents in aerosol cans are available at most auto parts stores and may be helpful when removing old gasket material that's stuck to the head and manifold. Be careful not to scrape or gouge the sealing surfaces.

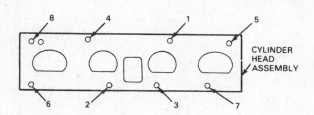

10.32a Intake manifold bolt tightening sequence – 1985 through 1988 fuel-injected models

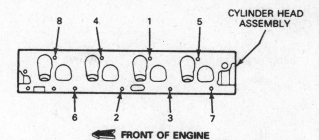

10.32b Intake manifold tightening sequence – 1989 and later models

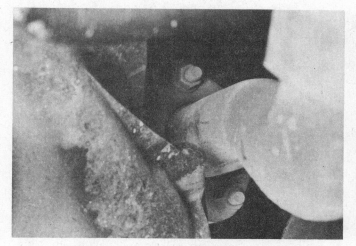

11.7 Remove the two exhaust pipe flange bolts

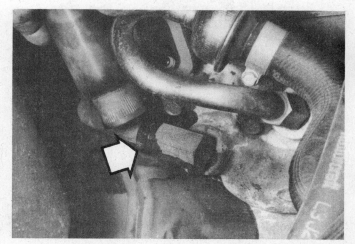

11.3 Remove the EGR line (arrow) at the exhaust manifold and loosen the EGR tube

30 Clean and oil the manifold mounting bolts.
31 Position the new intake manifold gasket on the manifold.
32 Position the intake manifold and gasket, along with the lifting "eye", on the head, install the fasteners and tighten them in sequence, in two steps, to the torque listed in this Chapter's Specifications **(see illustrations)**.
33 The remainder of installation is the reverse of removal.
34 Reconnect the battery and refill the cooling system.
35 Start the engine and let it run while checking for coolant, fuel and vacuum leaks.

11 Exhaust manifold – removal and installation

Refer to illustrations 11.3, 11.7, 11.8a and 11.8b

Removal

1 Disconnect the negative battery cable from the battery.
2 Remove the air cleaner and duct (see Chapter 4).
3 Disconnect the EGR tube from the exhaust manifold **(see illustration)** and loosen it at the EGR valve (see Chapter 6).
4 If you're working on a carbureted model, remove the thermactor check valve and detach the hose at the rear of the air by-pass valve (see Chapter 6).
5 Remove the screw that secures the heater hoses to the valve cover **(see illustration 4.6)**.
6 Disconnect the oxygen sensor wire (if equipped).
7 Detach the exhaust pipe from the manifold **(see illustration)**.
8 Remove the eight mounting bolts and detach the manifold from the engine **(see illustrations)**.
9 Clean the manifold and cylinder head mating surfaces with a gasket scraper, then wipe them off with a cloth saturated with lacquer thinner or acetone. Clean the bolt threads with a wire brush.

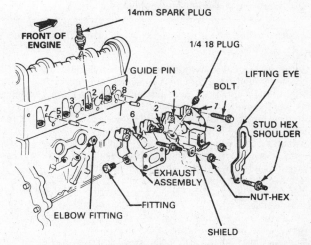

11.8a Exhaust manifold mounting details and bolt tightening sequence – 1983 through 1986 carbureted engines (typical)

Installation

10 Using a new gasket, install the manifold and the eight bolts attaching it to the cylinder head. Make sure the lifting "eye" is attached to the rear of the manifold. In the sequence shown, tighten the bolts (in two or three steps) to the torque listed in this Chapter's Specifications **(see illustrations 11.8a and 11.8b)**.
11 Reinstall all components removed for access to the manifold.
12 Reconnect the battery cable.
13 Run the engine and check for leaks.

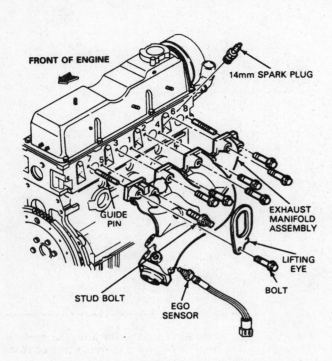

11.8b   Exhaust manifold mounting details and bolt tightening sequence (EFI engines shown; 1987 and 1988 carbureted engines similar)

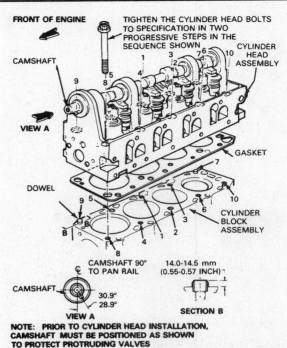

12.31   Be sure to turn the camshaft until the pin is in the five o'clock position as shown here before installing the head – also, tighten the head bolts in the sequence shown

12   Cylinder head – removal and installation

Refer to illustration 12.31

Removal

1   Begin the procedure by positioning the number one piston at top dead center (TDC) on the compression stroke (see Section 3).

2   Drain the cooling system (see Chapter 1). Remove the air cleaner assembly and the air duct.

3   Remove the screw retaining the heater hose to the valve cover **(see illustration 4.6)**.

4   Detach the distributor cap from the distributor (1983 through 1988 models). Label and detach the spark plug wires from the spark plugs and remove the distributor cap and wires as an assembly.

5   Remove the spark plugs.

6   Label and disconnect all vacuum hoses attached to the components on the head.

7   Remove the engine oil dipstick tube by pulling it straight out.

8   Remove the valve cover (see Section 4).

9   Remove the intake manifold bolts (see Section 10).

10   Loosen the alternator mounting bolts, remove the belt from the pulley and remove the bracket bolts.

11   Remove the upper radiator hose.

12   Remove the timing belt cover.

13   Make sure the valve timing is correct (see Section 6), then loosen the timing belt tensioner.

14   Remove the timing belt from the camshaft and auxiliary shaft sprockets.

15   Remove the exhaust manifold mounting bolts (see Section 11). The manifold itself can remain in place.

16   Remove the timing belt tensioner bolts.

17   Remove the timing belt tensioner spring stop from the cylinder head.

18   Disconnect the wire from the oil pressure sending unit at the left rear corner of the head.

19   Refer to Section 10 and remove the intake manifold.

20   Using a new head gasket, outline the cylinders and bolt pattern on a piece of cardboard. Be sure to indicate the front of the engine for reference. Punch holes at the bolt locations.

21   Loosen the cylinder head mounting bolts in 1/4-turn increments, working from the outside in, until they can be removed by hand.

22   Store the bolts in the cardboard holder as they're removed – this will ensure that they're reinstalled in their original locations.

23   Lift the head off the engine. If it's stuck, don't pry between the head and block. Instead, rap the head with a soft-face hammer or a block of wood and a hammer to break the gasket seal.

24   Place the head on a block of wood to prevent damage to the gasket surface. Refer to Part E for cylinder head disassembly and valve service procedures.

Installation

25   If a new cylinder head is being installed, transfer all external parts from the old cylinder head to the new one.

26   The mating surfaces of the cylinder head and block must be perfectly clean when the head is installed.

27   Use a gasket scraper to remove all traces of carbon and old gasket material, then clean the mating surfaces with lacquer thinner or acetone. If there's oil on the mating surfaces when the head is installed, the gasket may not seal correctly and leaks may develop. Use a vacuum cleaner to remove any debris that falls into the cylinders.

28   Check the block and head mating surfaces for nicks, deep scratches and other damage. If damage is slight, it can be removed with a file; if it's excessive, machining may be the only alternative.

29   Use a tap of the correct size to chase the threads in the head bolt holes. Mount each bolt in a vise and run a die down the threads to remove corrosion and restore the threads. Dirt, corrosion, sealant and damaged threads will affect critical head bolt torque readings.

30   Position the new gasket over the dowel pins in the block.

31   Make a mark on the cylinder head indicating the position of the pin in the end of the camshaft. Turn the camshaft until the pin is in the five o'clock position – this must be done to avoid damage to the valves when the head is installed **(see illustration)**.

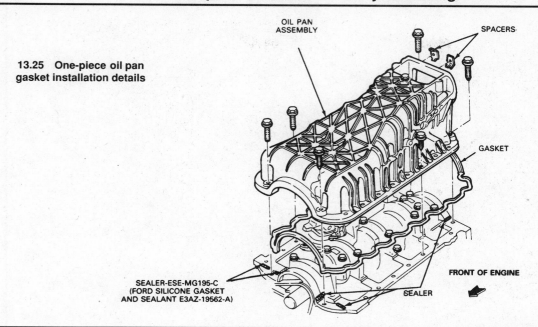

13.25 One-piece oil pan gasket installation details

OIL PAN ASSEMBLY

SPACERS

GASKET

FRONT OF ENGINE

SEALER

SEALER-ESE-MG195-C
(FORD SILICONE GASKET
AND SEALANT E3AZ-19562-A)

2A

32 Carefully position the head on the block without disturbing the gasket.

33 Install the cylinder head bolts and tighten them in sequence (see illustration 12.31) to the torque listed in this Chapter's Specifications.

34 Return the camshaft to its original position (with the pin aligned with the mark you made on the head).

35 The remainder of installation is the reverse of the removal procedure.

36 Change the engine oil and filter (see Chapter 1).

13 Oil pan – removal and installation

Note: *Some 1986 and later models have a one-piece oil pan gasket. Others have a four-piece gasket. Be sure to obtain the correct type for your engine.*

Removal

1 Position number one piston at Top Dead Center (see Section 3). This will also position the number four piston at the top of its travel, so the oil pan will clear the rear part of the crankshaft during removal.

2 Disconnect the negative battery cable from the battery.

3 On 1983 through 1988 models, remove the air cleaner (see Chapter 4). On 1989 and later models, detach the air cleaner outlet tube from the throttle body.

4 Refer to Section 17 and detach the engine mounts so the engine can be raised.

5 Remove the engine oil dipstick.

6 Drain the cooling system (see Chapter 1). Remove the fan and shroud and disconnect both hoses from the radiator (see Chapter 3).

7 On models equipped with an automatic transmission:
   a) Disconnect the transmission fluid cooler lines from the radiator.
   b) Remove the radiator mounting bolts.
   c) Lift the radiator up to provide removal clearance for the oil pan (it's removed toward the front on automatic transmission models), then wire it in the up position.

8 Raise the vehicle and support it securely on jackstands.

9 Drain the oil and remove the oil filter (see Chapter 1).

10 Disconnect the wire to the low oil level sensor (on the oil pan), if equipped.

11 Remove the starter motor (see Chapter 5).

12 Disconnect the exhaust manifold tube from the inlet pipe bracket at the thermactor check valve (see Chapter 4).

13 Detach the catalytic converter inlet pipe (if equipped).

14 Support the transmission with a jack. On automatic transmission-equipped models, use a block of wood to spread the load so the transmission oil pan won't be damaged.

15 Remove the transmission insulator and retainer (see Section 17). Remove the nuts that attach the transmission mount to the crossmember.

16 On models equipped with an automatic transmission:
   a) Detach the bellcrank from the converter housing (if equipped).
   b) Detach the fluid cooler lines from the retainer at the cylinder block.
   c) Remove the front crossmember.

17 On models equipped with a manual transmission, unbolt the right front shock absorber from the axle.

18 Using a block of wood to protect the oil pan, carefully raise the engine as far as it will safely go with a jack. Then place blocks of wood between the mounts and the subframe brackets. **Warning:** *Don't place any part of your body under the engine/transmission when it's supported only by a jack!*

19 On automatic transmission-equipped models, move the jack under the transmission and raise it slightly. Use a block of wood between the jack and transmission oil pan to protect the pan.

20 Remove the oil pan bolts and reinforcements.

21 Break the gasket seal by striking the pan with a rubber hammer, then detach the pan from the block and lower it to the crossmember.

22 Unbolt the pump and pick-up tube assembly from the engine and drop it into the pan (see Section 14).

23 Remove the oil pan toward the front (automatic) or rear (manual).

24 Remove all traces of old gasket material and sealant with a gasket scraper, then clean the pan and block mating surfaces with lacquer thinner or acetone. They must be perfectly clean to prevent oil leaks after the pan is installed. Remove and clean the oil pump pick-up screen.

Installation

Models with a one-piece gasket
Refer to illustration 13.25

25 Apply a dab of RTV sealant to the block at the six points indicated **(see illustration)**.

26 Place the oil pan gasket in the pan groove.

27 Position the oil pan on the crossmember. Install the oil pump and pickup tube and tighten the fasteners to the torque listed in this Chapter's Specifications.

28 Install and tighten the oil pan-to-block bolts just enough so the two oil-pan-to-transmission bolt holes are aligned. It should still be possible to shift the oil pan in relation to the engine.

**13.32   Four-piece oil pan gasket
installation details**

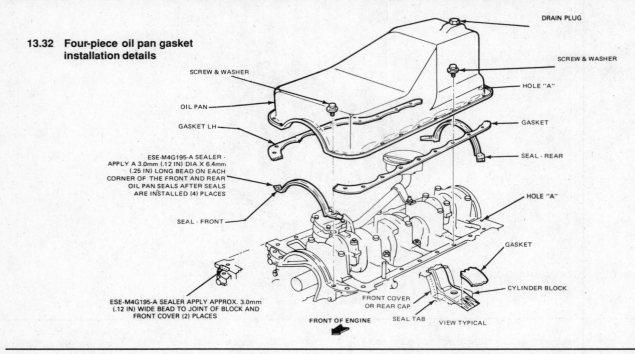

14.2   Oil pump mounting details

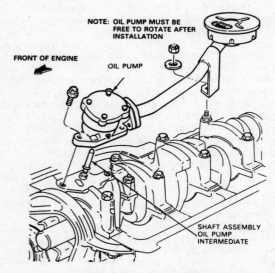

29   Install the two oil pan-to-transmission bolts. Tighten to the torque listed in this Chapter's Specifications, then loosen them 1/2-turn.
30   Tighten the oil pan-to-block bolts to the torque listed in this Chapter's Specifications.
31   Retighten the two oil pan-to-transmission bolts to the torque listed in this Chapter's Specifications.

Models with a four-piece gasket
Refer to illustration 13.32
32   Apply Ford sealer (ESE-M4G195-A or equivalent) to the block-to-front cover joints and to the corners of the front and rear seals. Position the end seals in place and press the tabs into the block **(see illustration)**.
33   Install guide pins in two of the pan-to-block bolt holes. These can be made by cutting the heads off a pair of extra bolts, grinding a taper and cutting a screwdriver slot in the ends.

34   Apply adhesive sealant (Ford specification ESE-M2G52-A or equivalent) evenly to the oil pan flange and to the side of the gasket that contacts the pan. Let the sealant dry past the wet stage, then stick the gaskets to the pan.
35   Position the pan on the crossmember. Install the oil pump and pick-up tube and tighten their fasteners to the torque listed in this Chapter's Specifications.
36   Place the oil pan on the block and install four bolts.
37   Remove the guide pins and install the remaining bolts.
38   Tighten all bolts to the torque listed in this Chapter's Specifications, starting from bolt A **(see illustration 13.32)**.

All models
39   The remaining steps are the reverse of removal, with the following additions:
   a)   Replace the oil filter, oil and coolant.
   b)   Use a new non-asbestos gasket at the catalytic converter connection.
   c)   Run the engine and check for leaks.
40   Remove the jackstands and lower the vehicle.

14   Oil pump – removal and installation

Refer to illustration 14.2
1   Remove the oil pan as described in Section 13.
2   Remove the nut securing the pick-up tube to the engine, then remove the bolts securing the pump to the engine. Remove the pump and pick-up tube as an assembly, then separate them when they're off the engine **(see illustration)**. The pump intermediate shaft should drop out as the pump is removed.
3   If there is any possibility that the pump is faulty or if an engine overhaul is being performed, replace the pump. **Caution:** *A faulty pump can ruin an otherwise good engine.*
4   Prime the pump before installation. Hold it with the pick-up tube up and pour a few ounces of clean oil into the inlet screen. Turn the pump driveshaft by hand until oil comes out the outlet.
5   Install the pump intermediate shaft with the collar end in the engine block. Be sure the intermediate shaft seats in the pump drive shaft or distributor. Hold the shaft in place and install the pump and oil pan (see Section 13). Be sure to tighten the bolts to the torque listed in this Chapter's Specifications.

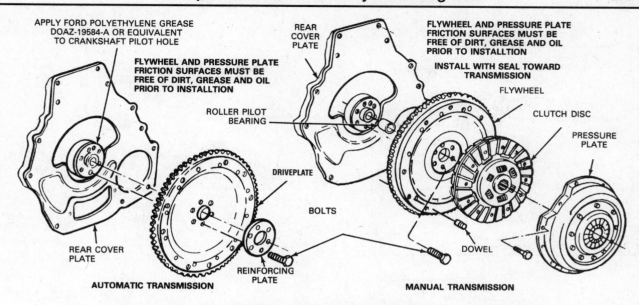

15.4 Driveplate (left) and flywheel (right) and related components – exploded view

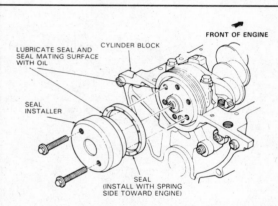

16.5 A special Ford tool is recommended to install the rear main oil seal

6   Add oil to the engine (see Chapter 1), then start it and be sure the oil pressure comes up. If it doesn't come up within 10 or 15 seconds, shut off the engine immediately and find the cause of the problem. **Caution:** *Continued running of the engine without oil pressure will severely damage the moving parts!*

7   Check for oil leaks.

15   Flywheel/driveplate – removal and installation

Refer to illustration 15.4

1   Raise the vehicle and support it securely on jackstands, then refer to Chapter 7 and remove the transmission. If it's leaking, now would be a very good time to replace the front pump seal/O-ring (automatic transmission only).

2   Remove the pressure plate and clutch disc (see Chapter 8) (manual transmission equipped vehicles). Now is a good time to check/replace the clutch components and pilot bearing.

3   Use a center-punch to make alignment marks on the flywheel/driveplate and crankshaft to ensure correct alignment during reinstallation.

4   Remove the bolts that secure the flywheel/driveplate to the crankshaft **(see illustration)**. If the crankshaft turns, wedge a screwdriver through the starter opening to jam the ring gear.

5   Remove the flywheel/driveplate from the crankshaft. Since the

flywheel is fairly heavy, be sure to support it while removing the last bolt.

6   Clean the flywheel to remove grease and oil. Inspect the surface for cracks, rivet grooves, burned areas and score marks. Light scoring can be removed with emery cloth. Check for cracked and broken ring gear teeth. Lay the flywheel on a flat surface and use a straightedge to check for warpage.

7   Clean and inspect the mating surfaces of the flywheel/driveplate and the crankshaft. If the crankshaft rear seal is leaking, replace it before reinstalling the flywheel/driveplate.

8   Position the flywheel/driveplate against the crankshaft. Be sure to align the marks made during removal. Note that some engines have an alignment dowel or staggered bolt holes to ensure correct installation. Before installing the bolts, apply thread locking compound to the threads.

9   Wedge a screwdriver through the starter motor opening to keep the flywheel/driveplate from turning as you tighten the bolts to the torque listed in this Chapter's Specifications.

10   The remainder of installation is the reverse of the removal procedure.

16   Rear main oil seal – replacement

Refer to illustration 16.5

1   Remove the transmission and all other components necessary, such as the clutch and pressure plate, to get at the oil seal in the back of the engine (see Chapters 7 and 8).

2   Remove the flywheel/driveplate (see Section 15).

3   Use a small punch to make two holes on opposite sides of the seal and install small sheet metal screws in the holes. Pry on the screws with two large screwdrivers until the seal is removed from the engine. It may be necessary to place small blocks of wood against the block to provide a fulcrum point for prying. **Caution:** *Be careful not to scratch or otherwise damage the crankshaft oil seal surface.*

4   Apply a thin film of engine oil to the outer edge of the new seal and the seal bore in the block, as well as the seal lips.

5   Position the seal on Ford special tool no. T82L-6701-A or its equivalent, then position the tool and seal at the rear of engine **(see illustration)**. Install the seal with the spring side toward the engine. Tighten the bolts alternately, a little at a time, to seat the seal in the block.

6   If the special seal installer is not available, work the seal into place and tap it gently into the bore with a soft-face hammer. Use the drive end of a socket extension, or other blunt, smooth object, to ease the lip of the seal over the end of the crankshaft.

7   The remainder of installation is the reverse of the removal procedure.

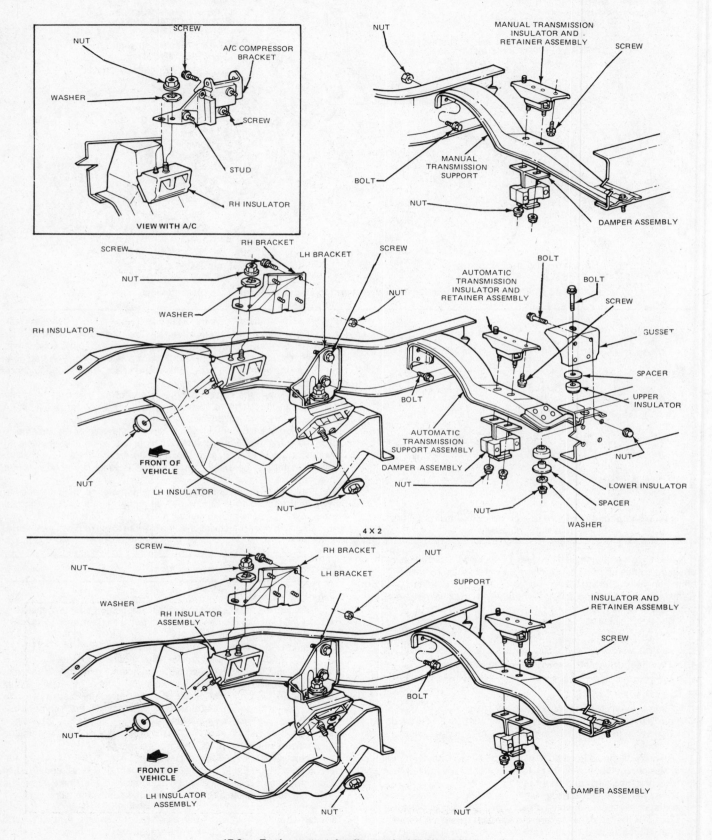

17.8a   Engine mount details – typical (2.0L engine)

2A

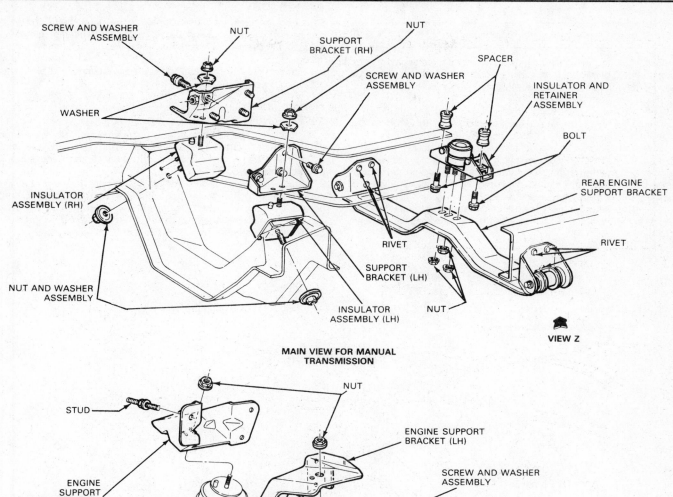

MAIN VIEW FOR MANUAL TRANSMISSION

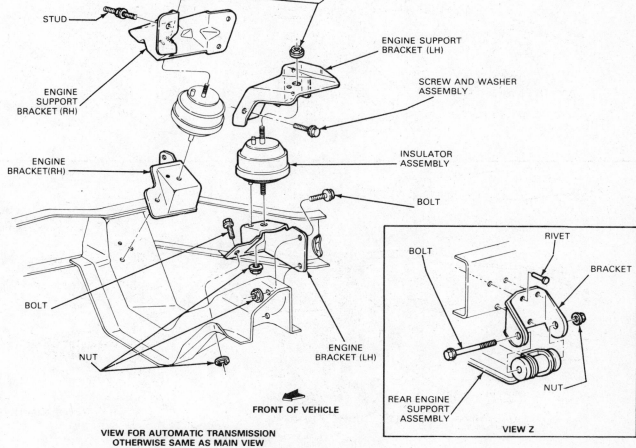

FRONT OF VEHICLE

VIEW FOR AUTOMATIC TRANSMISSION OTHERWISE SAME AS MAIN VIEW

17.8b   Engine mount details – typical (2.3L engine)

17   Engine mounts – check and replacement

1   Engine mounts seldom require attention, but broken or deteriorated mounts should be replaced immediately or the added strain placed on the driveline components may cause damage or wear.

Check

2   During the check, the engine must be raised slightly to remove the weight from the mounts.

3   Raise the vehicle and support it securely on jackstands, then position a jack under the engine oil pan. Place a large block of wood between the jack head and the oil pan, then carefully raise the engine just enough to take the weight off the mounts. **Warning:** *DO NOT place any part of your body under the engine when it's supported only by a jack!*

4   Check the mounts to see if the rubber is cracked, hardened or separated from the metal plates. Sometimes the rubber will split right down the center.

5   Check for relative movement between the mount plates and the engine or frame (use a large screwdriver or pry bar to attempt to move the mounts). If movement is noted, lower the engine and tighten the mount fasteners.

6   Rubber preservative should be applied to the mounts to slow deterioration.

Replacement

Refer to illustrations 17.8a and 17.8b

7   Disconnect the negative battery cable from the battery, then raise the vehicle and support it securely on jackstands (if not already done).

8   Remove the fasteners and detach the mount from the frame bracket **(see illustrations)**.

9   Raise the engine slightly with a jack or hoist (make sure the fan doesn't hit the radiator or shroud). Remove the mount-to-block nuts/bolts and detach the mount.

10   Installation is the reverse of removal. Use thread locking compound on the mount fasteners and be sure to tighten them securely.

Chapter 2 Part B
2.8L and 2.9L V6 engines

Contents

Specifications

General

Displacement
  1983 through 1985 models .... 2.8 liters
  1986 through 1991 models .... 2.9 liters
Cylinder numbers (front-to-rear)*
  Left (driver's side) 4–5–6
  Right side 1–2–3
Firing order 1-4-2-5-3-6

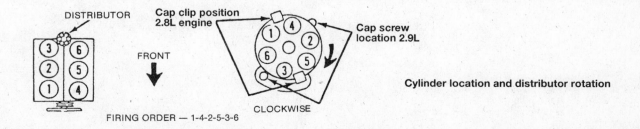

Cylinder location and distributor rotation

FIRING ORDER — 1-4-2-5-3-6

Camshaft

Lobe lift (intake and exhaust)	
2.8L	0.255 in
2.9L (approximate)	0.239 to 0.250 in
Allowable lobe lift loss	0.005 in
Theoretical valve lift @ zero lash	
2.8L (intake and exhaust)	0.3730 in
2.9L	
1986 and 1987 (intake and exhaust)	0.3730 in
1988-on (intake)	0.3588 in
1988-on (exhaust)	0.3703 in
Endplay	
Standard	0.0008 to 0.004 in
Service limit	
2.8L	0.006 in
2.9L	0.009 in
Journal-to-bearing (oil) clearance	
Standard	0.001 to 0.0026 in
Service limit	0.006 in
Journal diameter	
No. 1	1.7285 to 1.7293 in
No. 2	1.7135 to 1.7143 in
No. 3	1.6985 to 1.6992 in
No. 4	1.6835 to 1.6842 in
Runout, maximum (total indicator reading)	0.005 in
Out-of-round, maximum (total indicator reading)	0.0003 in
Bearing inside diameter	
No. 1	1.7302 to 1.7310 in
No. 2	1.7152 to 1.7160 in
No. 3	1.7002 to 1.7010 in
No. 4	1.6852 to 1.6860 in
Front bearing location	0.040 to 0.060 in below face of block
Camshaft gear backlash (2.8L only)	0.006 to 0.010 in
Timing chain tensioner face wear (2.9L only)	0.060 in

Torque specifications

	Ft-lbs (unless otherwise indicated)
Camshaft gear bolt (2.8L)	30 to 36
Camshaft sprocket bolt (2.9L)	19 to 28
Camshaft thrust plate bolts	13 to 16
Crankshaft damper bolt	85 to 96
Cylinder head bolts (2.8L)	
Step 1	29 to 40
Step 2	40 to 51
Step 3	70 to 85
Cylinder head bolts (2.9L)	
Step 1	22
Step 2	51 to 55
Step 3	Wait 5 minutes
Step 4	Turn 90-degrees
Exhaust manifold bolts	20 to 30
Exhaust pipe-to-manifold nuts	25 to 34
Flywheel bolts	47 to 52
Front cover plate bolts	10 to 13
Front cover bolts	13 to 16
Intake manifold bolts/nuts	
Step 1	Hand start and snug nuts at positions 3 and 4
Step 2	3 to 6
Step 3	6 to 11
Step 4	11 to 15
Step 5	15 to 18*
Intake manifold studs to block	10 to 12
Oil pump pick-up tube-to-pump bolt	6 to 10
Oil pump pick-up tube-to-main bearing cap bolt	12 to 15
Oil pan drain plug	15 to 21

Torque specifications (continued)

Ft-lbs (unless otherwise indicated)

Oil pan bolts
    1983 through 1987 .... 5 to 8
    1988-on .... 4 to 6
Rocker arm shaft support bolts .... 43 to 50
Valve cover bolts .... 3 to 5

Retighten in sequence to 15 to 18 ft-lbs after engine has been run.

1   General information

This Part of Chapter 2 is devoted to in-vehicle repair procedures for the 2.8L and 2.9L V6 engines. All information concerning engine removal and installation and engine block and cylinder head overhaul can be found in Part E of this Chapter.

The following repair procedures are based on the assumption that the engine is installed in the vehicle. If the engine has been removed from the vehicle and mounted on a stand, many of the steps outlined in this Part of Chapter 2 will not apply.

The Specifications included in this Part of Chapter 2 apply only to the procedures contained in this Part. Part E of Chapter 2 contains the Specifications necessary for cylinder head and engine block rebuilding.

2   Repair operations possible with the engine in the vehicle

Many major repair operations can be accomplished without removing the engine from the vehicle.

Clean the engine compartment and the exterior of the engine with some type of degreaser before any work is done. It will make the job easier and help keep dirt out of the internal areas of the engine.

Depending on the components involved, it may be helpful to remove the hood to improve access to the engine as repairs are performed (refer to Chapter 11 if necessary). Cover the fenders to prevent damage to the paint. Special pads are available, but an old bedspread or blanket will also work.

If vacuum, exhaust, oil or coolant leaks develop, indicating a need for gasket or seal replacement, the repairs can generally be made with the engine in the vehicle. The intake and exhaust manifold gaskets, timing cover gasket, oil pan gasket, crankshaft oil seals and cylinder head gaskets are all accessible with the engine in place.

Exterior engine components, such as the intake and exhaust manifolds, the oil pan (and the oil pump), the water pump, the starter motor, the alternator, the distributor and the fuel system components can be removed for repair with the engine in place.

Since the cylinder heads can be removed without pulling the engine, valve component servicing can also be accomplished with the engine in the vehicle. Replacement of the camshaft and timing gears or chain and sprockets is also possible with the engine in the vehicle.

In extreme cases caused by a lack of necessary equipment, repair or replacement of piston rings, pistons, connecting rods and rod bearings is possible with the engine in the vehicle. However, this practice is not recommended because of the cleaning and preparation work that must be done to the components involved.

3   Top Dead Center (TDC) for number one piston – locating

Refer to illustration 3.8

Note: *The following procedure is based on the assumption that the distributor is correctly installed. If you are trying to locate TDC to install the distributor correctly, piston position must be determined by feeling for compression at the number one spark plug hole, then aligning the ignition timing marks as described in Step 8.*

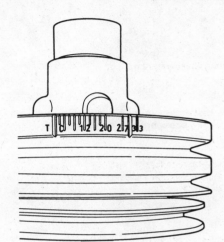

3.8   Typical 2.8L and 2.9L V6 timing marks

1   Top Dead Center (TDC) is the highest point in the cylinder that each piston reaches as it travels up-and-down when the crankshaft turns. Each piston reaches TDC on the compression stroke and again on the exhaust stroke, but TDC generally refers to piston position on the compression stroke.

2   Positioning the piston(s) at TDC is an essential part of many procedures such as rocker arm removal, camshaft and timing gear or chain/sprocket removal and distributor removal.

3   Before beginning this procedure, be sure to place the transmission in Neutral and apply the parking brake or block the rear wheels. Also, disable the ignition system by detaching the coil wire from the center terminal of the distributor cap and grounding it on the block with a jumper wire. Remove the spark plugs (see Chapter 1).

4   In order to bring any piston to TDC, the crankshaft must be turned using one of the methods outlined below. When looking at the front of the engine, normal crankshaft rotation is clockwise.

   a) The preferred method is to turn the crankshaft with a socket and ratchet attached to the bolt threaded into the front of the crankshaft.

   b) A remote starter switch, which may save some time, can also be used. Follow the instructions included with the switch. Once the piston is close to TDC, use a socket and ratchet as described in the previous paragraph.

   c) If an assistant is available to turn the ignition switch to the Start position in short bursts, you can get the piston close to TDC without a remote starter switch. Make sure your assistant is out of the vehicle, away from the ignition switch, then use a socket and ratchet as described in Paragraph a) to complete the procedure.

5   Note the position of the terminal for the number one spark plug wire on the distributor cap. If the terminal isn't marked, follow the plug wire from the number one cylinder spark plug to the cap.

6   Use a felt-tip pen or chalk to make a mark on the distributor body directly under the terminal.

4.3   Remove the choke air deflector plate to provide access to the passenger's side valve cover

4.5   Be sure to note the positions of the load-spreading washers (arrow) – if the valve cover screws are tightened down without the washers in place, the valve cover will be distorted and will leak oil

4.9   Disconnect the vacuum line at the canister purge solenoid to provide access to the driver's side valve cover

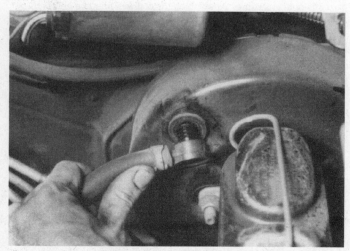

4.10   Disconnect the brake booster vacuum hose (if equipped)

7   Detach the cap from the distributor and set it aside (see Chapter 1 if necessary).

8   Turn the crankshaft (see Step 3 above) until the "TC" mark is aligned with the indicator on the engine front cover **(see illustration)**.

9   Look at the distributor rotor – it should be pointing directly at the mark you made on the distributor body.

10   If the rotor is 180-degrees off, the number one piston is at TDC on the exhaust stroke.

11   To get the piston to TDC on the compression stroke, turn the crankshaft one complete turn (360-degrees) clockwise. The rotor should now be pointing at the mark on the distributor. When the rotor is pointing at the number one spark plug wire terminal in the distributor cap and the ignition timing marks are aligned, the number one piston is at TDC on the compression stroke.

12   After the number one piston has been positioned at TDC on the compression stroke, TDC for any of the remaining pistons can be located by turning the crankshaft and following the firing order. Mark the remaining spark plug wire terminal locations on the distributor body just like you did for the number one terminal, then number the marks to correspond with the cylinder numbers. As you turn the crankshaft, the rotor will also turn. When it's pointing directly at one of the marks on the distributor, the piston for that particular cylinder is at TDC on the compression stroke.

4   Valve covers – removal and installation

2.8L engines

Refer to illustrations 4.3, 4.5, 4.9 and 4.10

1   Remove the air cleaner (see Chapter 4).

2   Disconnect the spark plug wires (see Chapter 1) and lay them out of the way.

3   If you're removing the passenger's side valve cover, remove the carburetor choke air deflector **(see illustration)**.

4   Remove the PCV valve and hose (see Chapter 1).

5   Remove the valve cover screws and load-spreading washers **(see illustration)**. Carefully note the locations of the washers so they can be reinstalled in their original positions.

6   On automatic transmission models:
   a) Remove the dipstick tube and bracket.
   b) Disconnect the kickdown linkage from the carburetor (see Chapter 7B).

7   If you're removing the right valve cover, place the thermactor hose and wiring harness out of the way.

4.17   Lift the valve cover out – tilt it as necessary to guide it past obstructions

8   Remove the oil filler cap.
9   Disconnect the canister purge solenoid vacuum line **(see illustration)**.
10   Disconnect the power brake booster vacuum hose (if equipped) **(see illustration)**.

2.9L engines

11   Disconnect the spark plug wires (see Chapter 1) and lay them back out of the way.
12   Disconnect the fuel inlet and return lines (see Chapter 4).
13   On air conditioned models, remove the dipstick tube and bracket, then remove the left-hand engine lifting bracket.
14   Remove the PCV valve, breather and hoses.
15   Remove the valve cover screws and load-spreading washers. Carefully note the locations of the washers so they can be reinstalled in their original positions.
16   Detach the three electrical connections from the right-hand valve cover.

All models

Refer to illustrations 4.17 and 4.20

17   Lift the cover off **(see illustration)**. If it won't come easily, don't pry it loose. Bump the end of the cover with a rubber mallet to break the gasket seal.
18   Clean all traces of gasket and sealant from the cover and cylinder head. Aerosol gasket removers, available from auto parts stores, can be used to ease gasket removal.
19   Coat the valve cover side of a new gasket with RTV sealant, then stick the gasket to the cover. Some gaskets are self-sticking and don't require RTV; simply peel off the plastic film and stick the gasket to the cover. On 1992 and later models, apply RTV to the left intake manifold-to-cylinder head parting seam; also apply RTV to each of the bolt holes on the exhaust side.
20   Install the cover and load-spreading washers **(see illustration)**. Tighten the screws evenly to the torque listed in this Chapter's Specifications.
21   The remainder of installation is the reverse of the removal Steps.
22   Run the engine and check for oil leaks.

---

5   Rocker arms and pushrods – removal, inspection and installation

Removal

Refer to illustrations 5.2 and 5.4

1   Refer to Section 4 and remove the valve cover(s).

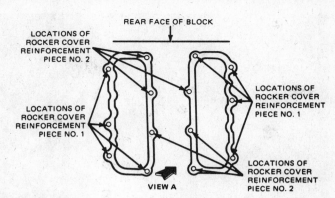

CAUTION:
IF ROCKER COVER IS TIGHTENED WITHOUT REINFORCEMENT PIECE, DEFORMATION OF THE ROCKER COVER WILL OCCUR. INSTALLING REINFORCEMENT PIECE AFTERWARD WILL NO LONGER PREVENT LEAKS.

4.20   Locations of the load-spreading washers – note that there are two different types; each type must go in the correct location

5.2   Loosen the three rocker arm shaft support bolts two turns at a time until they are completely loose, then lift the rocker arm assembly off the cylinder head

2   Loosen the rocker arm shaft support bolts two turns at a time, starting with the center bolt and working out, until the bolts can be removed by hand **(see illustration)**.
3   Lift the rocker shaft assembly and oil baffle off the cylinder head. The pins will hold the components together.
4   Lift the pushrods out of the engine. Place the pushrods in order in a

5.4   Keep the pushrods in order so they can be returned to their original positions – a holder such as this one is convenient to use and easy to make

holder **(see illustration)** so they can be returned to their original positions.

Inspection

Refer to illustration 5.5

5   Remove the pins and disassemble the rocker arm assembly **(see illustration)**. Place the parts in order on a clean workbench. Be sure you don't mix up the parts – they must be reassembled in exactly the same order they were in before disassembly.

6   Check each rocker arm for wear, cracks and other damage, especially where the pushrods and valve stems contact the rocker arm faces.

7   Make sure the hole at the pushrod end of each rocker arm is open. Plugging can be cleared with a piece of wire.

8   Check each rocker arm bore, and its corresponding position on the rocker shaft, for wear, cracks and galling. If the rocker arms or shaft are damaged, replace them with new ones.

9   Inspect the pushrods for cracks and excessive wear at the ends. Roll each pushrod across a piece of plate glass to see if it's bent (if it wobbles, it's bent).

10   If necessary, remove the plug from each end of the rocker shaft. Drill into one plug and insert a long steel rod through it to knock out the other

plug. Knock out the first plug in the same manner.

11   If the rocker shaft plugs were removed, tap in new ones with a hammer and suitable drift.

12   Assemble the rocker assembly **(see illustration 5.5)**. Lubricate all friction points with assembly lube.

13   Install new cotter pins in the ends of the rocker shaft. Be sure the rocker shaft notches **(see illustration 5.17)** will face down when the shaft is installed.

Installation

Refer to illustration 5.17

14   Coat each end of each pushrod with assembly lube, then install them in the engine. If you are reinstalling the original pushrods, be sure to return them to their original positions.

15   Coat the rocker arm pads with assembly lube.

16   Loosen the valve adjusting screws several turns.

17   Install the oil baffle and rocker arm assembly on the engine. The notch should face down **(see illustration)**.

18   Position the rocker arm ball ends in the pushrods.

19   Tighten the rocker shaft support bolts two turns at a time, working from the center bolt out, to the torque listed in this Chapter's Specifications.

20   The remainder of installation is the reverse of removal.

21   On 2.8L engines, adjust the valve clearances (see Chapter 1).

22   On 2.9L engines, adjust valve lash as follows:

a)   Place number one piston at top dead center on the compression stroke (see Section 3).

b)   Loosen the adjusting screws for the number one cylinder until there's a distinct gap between the rocker arm pad and the top end of the valve stem.

c)   Slowly tighten the adjusting screws until the rocker arm faces just touch the valve stems.

d)   Turn the adjusting screws in another 1-1/2 turns (equivalent to 0.070 in).

e)   Following the firing order (1-4-2-5-3-6), bring each piston to TDC on the compression stroke and repeat the adjustment procedure on that cylinder.

23   Run the engine and check for leaks.

---

6   Valve springs, retainers and seals – replacement

Refer to illustrations 6.4, 6.9a, 6.9b, 6.10a, 6.10b and 6.17

Note: *Broken valve springs and defective valve stem seals can be replaced without removing the cylinder heads. Two special tools and a*

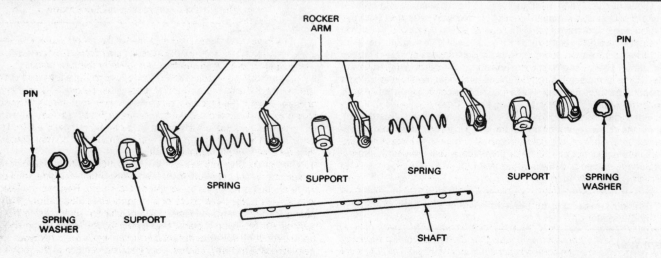

5.5   An exploded view of the rocker assembly

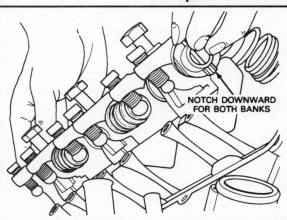

5.17 The notch in the rocker arm assembly must face down when installed

6.4 This is what the air hose adapter that threads into the spark plug hole looks like – they're commonly available from auto parts stores

6.9a Compress the valve spring then remove the keepers

compressed air source are normally required to perform this operation, so read through this Section carefully and rent or buy the tools before beginning the job. If compressed air isn't available, a length of nylon rope can be used to keep the valves from falling into the cylinder during this procedure.

1   Refer to Section 4 and remove the valve cover from the affected cylinder head. If all of the valve stem seals are being replaced, remove both valve covers.

2   Remove the spark plug from the cylinder which has the defective component. If all of the valve stem seals are being replaced, all of the spark plugs should be removed.

3   Turn the crankshaft until the piston in the affected cylinder is at top dead center on the compression stroke (refer to Section 3 for instructions). If you're replacing all of the valve stem seals, begin with cylinder number one and work on the valves for one cylinder at a time. Move from cylinder-to-cylinder following the firing order sequence (see this Chapter's Specifications).

4   Thread an adapter into the spark plug hole **(see illustration)** and connect an air hose from a compressed air source to it. Most auto parts stores can supply the air hose adapter. **Note:** *Many cylinder compression gauges utilize a screw-in fitting that may work with your air hose quick-disconnect fitting.*

5   Remove the rocker arm assembly on the affected side of the engine (see Section 5). If all of the valve stem seals are being replaced, remove both rocker assemblies.

6   Apply compressed air to the cylinder. **Warning:** *The piston may be forced down by compressed air, causing the crankshaft to turn suddenly. If the wrench used when positioning the number one piston at TDC is still attached to the bolt in the crankshaft nose, it could cause damage or injury when the crankshaft moves.*

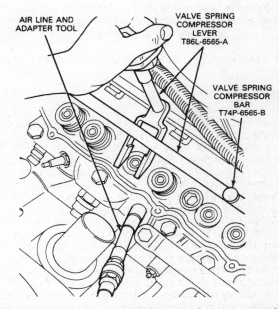

6.9b Here's the lever-type tool and bar used to compress the valve spring – these are special Ford tools, but equivalents may be available from automotive tool companies

7   The valves should be held in place by the air pressure. If the valve faces or seats are in poor condition, leaks may prevent air pressure from retaining the valves – refer to the alternative procedure below.

8   If you don't have access to compressed air, an alternative method can be used. Position the piston at a point just before TDC on the compression stroke, then feed a long piece of nylon rope through the spark plug hole until it fills the combustion chamber. Be sure to leave the end of the rope hanging out of the engine so it can be removed easily. Use a large ratchet and socket to rotate the crankshaft in the normal direction of rotation until slight resistance is felt.

9   Stuff shop rags into the cylinder head holes above and below the valves to prevent parts and tools from falling into the engine, then use a valve spring compressor to compress the spring. Remove the keepers with small needle-nose pliers or a magnet **(see illustration)**. **Note:** *A couple of different types of tools are available for compressing the valve springs with the head in place. One type grips the lower spring coils and presses on the retainer as the knob is turned, while the other type, shown here* **(see illustration)**, *utilizes a bar installed in place of the rocker arm shaft for leverage. Both types work very well, although the knob type is more readily available.*

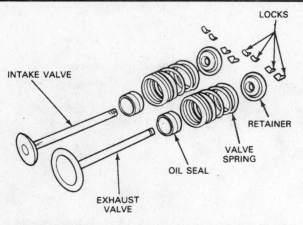

LOCKS

INTAKE VALVE

RETAINER

OIL SEAL

VALVE SPRING

EXHAUST VALVE

6.10a Valves and related components – exploded view

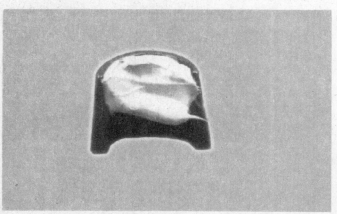

6.17 Apply a small dab of grease to each keeper as shown here before installation – it'll hold them in place on the valve stem as the spring is released

10　Remove the spring retainer and valve spring, then remove the guide oil seal **(see illustration)**. A special Ford tool is available for seal removal and installation **(see illustration)**. **Note:** *If air pressure fails to hold the valve in the closed position during this operation, the valve face or seat is probably damaged. If so, the cylinder head will have to be removed for additional repair operations.*

11　Wrap a rubber band or tape around the top of the valve stem so the valve won't fall into the combustion chamber, then release the air pressure. **Note:** *If a rope was used instead of air pressure, turn the crankshaft slightly in the direction opposite normal rotation.*

12　Inspect the valve stem for damage. Rotate the valve in the guide and check the end for eccentric movement, which would indicate that the valve is bent.

13　Move the valve up-and-down in the guide and make sure it doesn't bind. If the valve stem binds, either the valve is bent or the guide is damaged. In either case, the head will have to be removed for repair.

14　Reapply air pressure to the cylinder to retain the valve in the closed position, then remove the tape or rubber band from the valve stem. If a rope was used instead of air pressure, rotate the crankshaft in the normal direction of rotation until slight resistance is felt.

15　Lubricate the valve stem with engine oil and install a new guide seal.

16　Install the spring in position over the valve.

17　Install the valve spring retainer. Compress the valve spring and carefully position the keepers in the groove. Apply a small dab of grease to the inside of each keeper to hold it in place **(see illustration)**.

18　Remove the pressure from the spring tool and make sure the keepers are seated.

19　Disconnect the air hose and remove the adapter from the spark plug hole. If a rope was used in place of air pressure, pull it out of the cylinder.

20　Refer to Section 5 and install the rocker arm assembly.

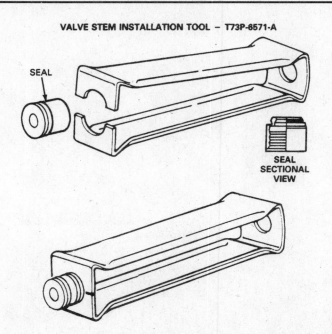

VALVE STEM INSTALLATION TOOL – T73P-6571-A

SEAL

SEAL SECTIONAL VIEW

6.10b The valve stem oil seals are removed and installed with this special Ford tool or equivalent

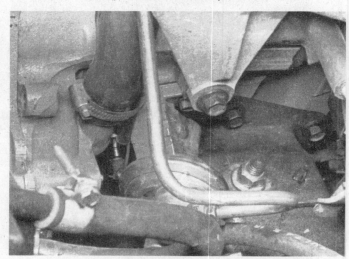

7.3 Disconnect the by-pass hose at the rear of the thermostat housing

21　Install the spark plug(s) and hook up the wire(s).

22　Refer to Section 4 and install the valve cover(s).

23　Start and run the engine, then check for oil leaks and unusual sounds coming from the rocker arm cover area.

7　Intake manifold – removal and installation

Removal

2.8L engines

Refer to illustrations 7.3 and 7.8

1　Disconnect the negative battery cable from the battery.

2　Remove the air cleaner (see Chapter 4) and disconnect the accelerator cable.

3　Drain the cooling system (see Chapter 1). Disconnect the radiator hose from the thermostat housing (see Chapter 3) and the by-pass hose from the intake manifold **(see illustration)**.

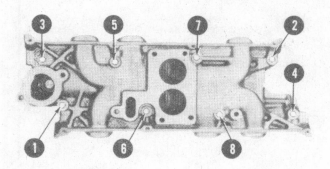

7.8   Intake manifold bolt locations and tightening sequence
(2.8L engine)

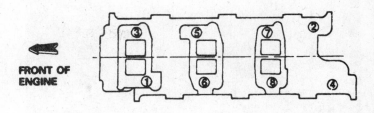

7.14   Intake manifold bolt locations and tightening sequence
(2.9L engine)

7.16   Be careful not to gouge the mating surfaces while scraping
and cover the lifter valley with clean shop rags to keep pieces of
gasket material out of the engine – gasket remover sprays are
available at auto parts stores and may be helpful

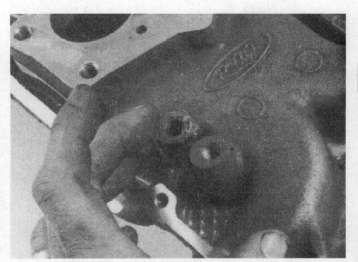

7.21   Apply sealant to the mounting bolt bosses before you
install the bolts

4   Remove the distributor (see Chapter 5).
5   Remove the fuel filter (see Chapter 1) and the fuel line to the carburetor.
6   On 1985 models, remove the carburetor and EGR spacer (see Chapter 4).
7   Remove the valve covers (see Section 4).
8   Remove the intake manifold bolts and nuts **(see illustration)**. Lift
the manifold off. If the manifold is stuck, tap it lightly with a plastic mallet
to break the gasket seal. If absolutely necessary, pry the manifold off, but
pry against a casting protrusion, not against any gasket mating surfaces,
or vacuum and oil leaks may occur.

2.9L engines
Refer to illustration 7.14

9   Disconnect the negative battery cable from the battery.
10   Remove the upper intake manifold assembly (see Chapter 4).
11   Drain the cooling system (see Chapter 1). Disconnect the radiator
hose from the thermostat housing (see Chapter 3).
12   Remove the distributor (see Chapter 5).
13   Remove the valve covers (see Section 4).
14   Remove the intake manifold bolts and nuts **(see illustration)**. The
bolts are different lengths. Label them so they can be returned to their
original locations.
15   Lift the manifold off. If the manifold is stuck, tap it lightly with a plastic
mallet to break the gasket seal. If absolutely necessary, pry the manifold
off, but pry against a casting protrusion, not against any gasket mating
surfaces, or vacuum and oil leaks may occur.

Installation
Refer to illustrations 7.16 and 7.21

16   Use a gasket scraper to remove all traces of sealant and old gasket
material, then clean the mating surfaces with lacquer thinner or acetone
(see illustration). If there's old sealant or oil on the mating surfaces
when the manifold is installed, oil or vacuum leaks may develop. When
working on the heads and block, cover the lifter valley with shop rags to
keep dirt out of the engine. Use a vacuum cleaner to remove any gasket
material that falls into the intake ports in the heads.
17   Use a tap of the correct size to chase the threads in the bolt holes,
then use compressed air (if available) to remove the debris from the
holes. **Warning:** *Wear safety glasses or a face shield to protect your eyes
when using compressed air! Remove excess carbon deposits and corrosion from the exhaust and coolant passages in the heads and manifold.*
18   Coat the gasket mating surfaces with a thin layer of sealant.
19   Install the gasket. Be sure to place the tab on the right head gasket
into the cutout in the intake manifold gasket.
20   Carefully set the manifold in place while the sealant is still wet. **Caution:** *Don't disturb the gasket and don't move the manifold fore-and-aft
after it contacts the gasket.*
21   Coat the manifold bolt bosses with sealant **(see illustration)**. Install
the bolts (and nuts, if equipped), then tighten them to the torque and in
the stages listed in this Chapter's Specifications.
    a) 2.8L engines: Follow the sequence in illustration 7.8.
    b) 2.9L engines: Follow the sequence in illustration 7.14.
22   The remainder of installation is the reverse of removal.
23   Start the engine and check carefully for leaks at the intake manifold
joints.
24   Recheck the mounting bolt and nut torque.

8.2　Remove the exhaust heat shield from the manifold (if equipped)

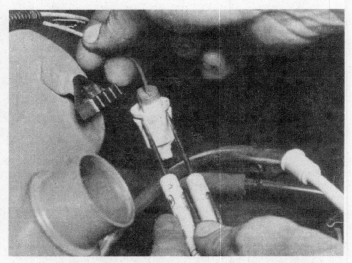

8.5　On single-wire EGO connectors, use two screwdrivers as shown to separate the connector halves

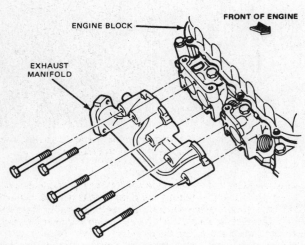

RIGHT SIDE

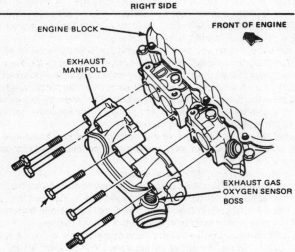

LEFT SIDE

8.7　Exhaust manifold bolt/stud locations (2.8L engine shown; 2.9L engine similar)

8　Exhaust manifolds – removal and installation

Removal

Refer to illustrations 8.2, 8.5 and 8.7

2.8L engines

1　Remove the air cleaner (see Chapter 4).
2　On the left manifold, remove the heat shroud **(see illustration)**.
3　Remove thermactor components as necessary to provide removal access (see Chapter 6).
4　Disconnect the choke heat tubes from the carburetor.

All models

5　On models with the exhaust gas oxygen sensor mounted directly in the exhaust manifold, disconnect its electrical connector **(see illustration)**.
6　Detach the exhaust pipe from the manifold. Apply penetrating oil to the nut threads if they are difficult to remove. Discard the exhaust pipe gasket.
7　Remove the manifold fasteners **(see illustration)**, then take the manifold off the engine.

Installation

8　Check the manifold for cracks and make sure the fastener threads are clean and undamaged. The manifold and cylinder head mating surfaces must be clean before the manifolds are installed – use a gasket scraper to remove all carbon deposits.
9　Position a new gasket (if available) and the manifold on the head and install the fasteners. Tighten evenly to the torque listed in this Chapter's Specifications, starting with the center bolt and working out.
10　Install a new exhaust pipe-to-manifold gasket, then tighten the pipe-to-manifold nuts to the torque listed in this Chapter's Specifications.
11　The remaining installation steps are the reverse of removal.
12　Start the engine and check for exhaust leaks.

9　Cylinder heads – removal and installation

Caution: *The engine must be completely cool when the heads are removed. Failure to allow the engine to cool off could result in head warpage.*
Note: *Ford recommends the use of guide studs to install the cylinder heads. These can be made by cutting the heads off of a pair of extra cylinder head bolts, grinding a taper and cutting a screwdriver slot in the cut ends.*

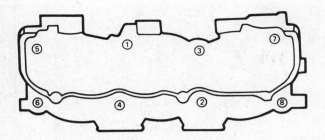

9.10a Cylinder head bolt loosening and tightening sequence (2.8L engines)

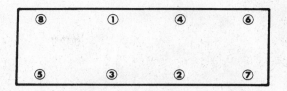

9.10b Cylinder head bolt loosening and tightening sequence (2.9L engines)

9.11 A back-up nut and two wrenches can be used to remove the studs

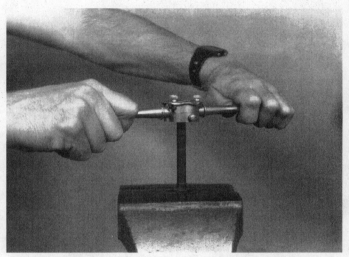

9.14 A die should be used to remove sealant and corrosion from the head bolt threads prior to installation

Removal

Refer to illustrations 9.10a, 9.10b, 9.11 and 9.14

1 Disconnect the negative battery cable from the battery.

2 On 2.8L models, remove the air cleaner (see Chapter 4) and disconnect the accelerator linkage.

3 Drain the cooling system (see Chapter 1).

4 Remove the distributor (see Chapter 5).

5 Disconnect the radiator hose from the thermostat housing and the coolant outlet hose from the intake manifold (see Chapter 3).

6 Remove the valve covers (see Section 4).

7 Remove the rocker arms and pushrods (see Section 5).

8 Remove the intake manifold (see Section 7).

9 Remove the exhaust manifold(s) (see Section 8).

10 Loosen the cylinder head bolts in several stages, following the specified sequence **(see illustrations)**.

11 Remove the head bolts and lift the head off. On 2.9L engines, discard the bolts; they must be replaced with new ones each time they're removed. If the head is stuck, try tapping lightly with a plastic mallet or hammer and wood block to break the gasket seal. If it won't come off, pry carefully, but do not pry against any gasket surfaces or leaks may occur. **Note:** *It may be necessary to remove the cylinder head studs in order to lift up and back on the cylinder heads to clear the front cover retainer. To remove the stud, run a nut down to the end of the threads. Tighten another nut securely against the first nut, then turn the first nut counterclockwise to unscrew the stud* **(see illustration)**.

Installation

12 The mating surfaces of the cylinder heads and block must be perfectly clean when the heads are installed. Use a gasket scraper to remove all traces of carbon and old gasket material, then clean the mating surfaces with lacquer thinner or acetone. If there's oil on the mating surfaces when the heads are installed, the gaskets may not seal correctly and leaks may develop. When working on the block, cover the lifter valley with shop rage to keep debris out of the engine. Use a vacuum cleaner to remove any debris that falls into the cylinders.

13 Check the block and head mating surfaces for nicks, deep scratches and other damage. If damage is slight, it can be removed with a file – if it's excessive, machining (must be done by an automotive machine shop) may be the only alternative.

14 Use a tap of the correct size to chase the threads in the head bolt holes. On 2.8L engines, mount each bolt in a vise and run a die down the threads to remove corrosion and restore the threads **(see illustration)**. Dirt, corrosion, sealant and damaged threads will affect torque readings.

15 Install the new gaskets on the block. The gaskets are marked FRONT and TOP to indicate correct position. Gaskets are not interchangeable between left and right sides.

16 Install guide studs in two of the cylinder head bolt holes (see the NOTE at the beginning of this Section for instructions on fabricating these studs).

17 Install the head over the guide studs.

18 Install head bolts (on 2.9L engines, use new head bolts) in the unoccupied holes and tighten them, using just your fingers. Remove the guide studs, then install bolts in their holes and tighten them with fingers.

19 Tighten the head bolts in stages to the correct torque.

  a) 2.8L engines: Tighten in the three stages listed in this Chapter's Specifications, following the sequence in illustration 9.10a.

  b) 2.9L engines: Tighten in the four stages listed in this Chapter's Specifications, following the sequence in illustration 9.10b.

20 The remaining installation steps are the reverse of removal.

21 On 2.8L engines, adjust the valves (see Chapter 1).

22 Run the engine and check for coolant and oil leaks.

10.9a   Remove the center retaining bolt to remove the pulley

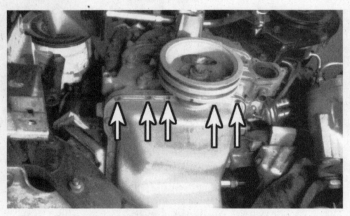

10.10   If removing the cover without removing the oil pan, be sure to remove the bolts that attach the oil pan to the cover (arrows)

10.9b   A puller may be necessary to remove the pulley

10.11a   Remove the guide sleeves from the front cover plate with your fingers – the sleeve chamfers face the front cover (2.8L engine)

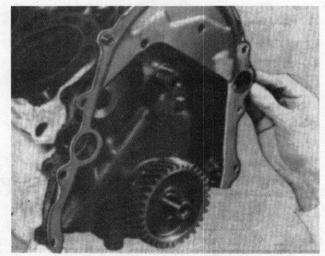

10.11b   Remove the attaching bolts and take the front cover plate off the engine (2.8L engine)

10   Engine front cover – removal and installation

Refer to illustrations 10.9a, 10.9b, 10.10, 10.11a, 10.11b, and 10.17

Note: *Ford recommends that the oil pan be removed before beginning this procedure. However, we found that the cover could be removed for gasket replacement or timing gear/chain inspection without removing the oil pan, as described in the Steps which follow. A new pan gasket will be required, however. If you're removing the cover to replace the timing gears or timing chain and sprockets, it will be necessary to remove the oil pan.*

Removal

1   If it's necessary to remove the timing gears or chain and sprockets, remove the oil pan (see Section 15).
2   Drain the cooling system (see Chapter 1).
3   Remove the fan and radiator (see Chapter 3).
4   Remove the air conditioning compressor bracket (if equipped) and set the compressor aside. DO NOT disconnect any refrigerant lines!
5   Remove the power steering pump bracket (if equipped) and set the pump aside. It isn't necessary to disconnect the hoses.
6   Remove the alternator (see Chapter 5).
7   Remove the thermactor pump (if equipped) (see Chapter 6).
8   Remove the water pump (see Chapter 3).
9   Remove the drivebelt pulley from the crankshaft **(see illustrations)**.
10   Remove the front cover bolts and take the front cover off the engine. If the oil pan is still on the engine, remove the bolts that secure the oil pan to the front cover **(see illustration)**. If the cover is stuck, tap it gently with a plastic mallet to break the gasket seal.

10.17   A special tool is used to align the front cover while the bolts are being tightened

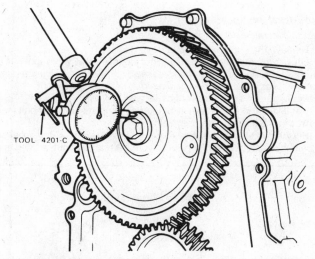

11.8   Camshaft endplay is checked with a dial indicator placed against the gear bolt boss

11   On 2.8L engines:
  a) Remove the front cover guide sleeves **(see illustration)**.
  b) Remove two bolts that secure the front cover plate. Remove the plate and gasket **(see illustration)**.

Installation

12   The mating surfaces of the cylinder block, front cover plate, front cover and oil pan must be perfectly clean when the plate and cover are installed. To prevent gasket scrapings from falling into the oil pan, place a few rags into the exposed area of the oil pan, being careful not to let them fall down into the pan. Then use a gasket scraper to remove all traces of carbon and old gasket material. Clean the mating surfaces with lacquer thinner or acetone. Use a razor blade to cut off the old oil pan gasket flush with the engine block.

13   Using a razor blade, cut the new oil pan gasket to fit the exposed oil pan rails, then stick the piece to the rails with an adhesive gasket sealant such as Fel-pro's High-tack. Put a 1/8-inch wide bead of RTV sealant into the corners where the oil pan rails and block meet. **Note:** *you must install the front cover plate (if equipped) and cover within ten minutes of applying the RTV sealant.*

14   On 2.8L engines, install the cover plate as follows:
  a) Apply a thin, even layer of RTV sealant to the mating surfaces on the engine and the rear side of the front cover plate.
  b) Place the cover plate gasket on the engine, then install the cover plate **(see illustration 10.11b).** Temporarily install four of the front cover bolts to position the cover plate accurately. Install both cover plate bolts, tighten the bolts to the torque listed in this Chapter's Specifications and remove the four bolts.
  c) Install new seal rings on the guide sleeves.
  d) Install the guide sleeves, without sealant, in the cylinder block. The sleeve chamfers face the front cover.

11.5   Timing gear backlash is checked with a dial indicator positioned against one of the camshaft gear teeth

15   Apply a thin, even coat of RTV sealant to the gasket on the oil pan rails.
16   Apply a thin, even coat of RTV sealant to the gasket surface on the front cover. Stick the gasket to the cover.
17   Place the front cover on the engine. Install all of the cover bolts and tighten them two or three turns. Place a centering tool in the front cover **(see illustration)**.
18   Tighten the front cover bolts to the torque listed in this Chapter's Specifications, then remove the centering tool.
19   The remaining installation steps are the reverse of removal.
20   Run the engine and check for coolant and oil leaks.

---

11   Timing gears (2.8L engine) – removal, inspection and installation

---

Backlash and endplay check
Refer to illustrations 11.5 and 11.8

1   Drain the cooling system (see Chapter 1).
2   Remove the oil pan (see Section 15).
3   Remove the front cover (see Section 10).
4   Remove the valve covers (see Section 4). Loosen the valve adjusting screws to relieve the valve spring tension.
5   Set up a dial indicator with its pointer against one of the camshaft gear teeth **(see illustration)**.
6   Hold the crankshaft gear from turning and rotate the camshaft gear against the dial indicator.
7   Note the indicator reading (gear backlash). If it is excessive (see this Chapter's Specifications), replace the camshaft and crankshaft gears as a set.
8   Set up the dial indicator to check camshaft endplay **(see illustration)**. Push the camshaft gear back against the thrust plate and zero the dial indicator.
9   Pry the camshaft gear forward against the dial indicator and note the reading (camshaft endplay). If it is excessive (see this Chapter's Specifications), replace the camshaft thrust plate or spacer ring (see Section 14). These are available in two thicknesses.

Removal
Refer to illustrations 11.11 and 11.12

10   Perform Steps 1 through 3 above, then remove the camshaft timing gear bolt. Tap the timing gear lightly with a plastic mallet to separate it from the camshaft.

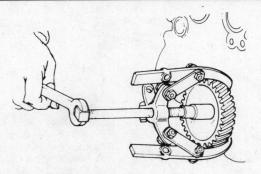

11.11   The timing gear is removed from the sprocket with a gear puller

11   Remove the crankshaft timing gear with a gear puller (see illustration).
12   If necessary, remove the timing gear Woodruff keys (see illustration).

Installation

Refer to illustrations 11.14, 11.15a and 11.15b

13   Install the Woodruff keys (if removed).
14   Install the camshaft gear and make sure it seats securely against the spacer. Tighten the camshaft gear bolt to the correct torque (see the torque listed in this Chapter's Specifications). Make sure the camshaft

gear alignment mark is positioned correctly (see illustration) so it will line up with the crankshaft gear mark after installation.
15   To install the crankshaft gear, align the keyway in the gear with the Woodruff key, then press the gear onto the shaft. Be sure the alignment marks on crankshaft and camshaft gears are positioned directly opposite each other (see illustration 11.14). Note: *To install the crankshaft gear, we fabricated an alignment tool by using a piece of 1-7/8-inch diameter pipe, 3-3/4 inches long and a bolt and washers* (see illustrations).
16   The remaining installation steps are the reverse of removal.
17   Run the engine and check for leaks.

12   Timing chain and sprockets (2.9L engine) – inspection, removal and installation

Camshaft endplay check

Refer to illustration 12.4

1   Remove the engine front cover (see Section 10).
2   Loosen the rocker arm adjusting nuts to release all valve spring tension. Caution: *Tension must be released to prevent breaking the camshaft sprocket when it's pried against in the following Steps.*
3   Push the camshaft rearward as far as it will go.
4   Install a dial indicator with its pointer on the camshaft gear bolt (see illustration). Set the indicator to zero.
5   Pry the camshaft forward with a large screwdriver or prybar between the camshaft sprocket and the block. Note the dial indicator reading and

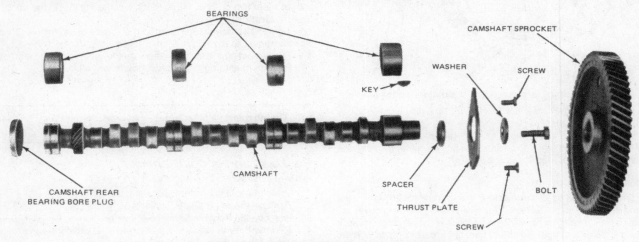

11.12   Camshaft components – exploded view

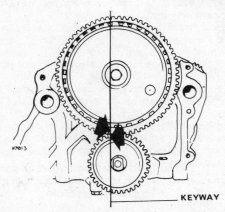

11.14   The timing marks on the gears must be directly opposite each other after the gears are installed

11.15a   The crankshaft timing gear can be installed with this fabricated installation tool

11.15b   The bolt threads into the crankshaft – tighten it against the washers and pipe to press the gear on

compare with the endplay listed in this Chapter's Specifications. Replace the camshaft thrust plate if endplay is excessive. The camshaft spacer ring and thrust plate are available in two thicknesses to adjust endplay.

Timing chain and tensioner inspection

Refer to illustration 12.7

6   Remove the engine front cover (see Section 10).

7   Remove the timing chain tensioner (**see illustration**).

8   Rotate the crankshaft counterclockwise (as viewed from the front of the engine) to take up the slack in the left side of the chain.

9   Mark a reference point on the block approximately halfway along the chain and measure from that point to the left side of the chain (**see illustration 12.7**).

10   Turn the crankshaft clockwise to take up slack on the right side of the chain.

11   Push the chain outward and measure from the reference point to the chain.

12   The difference between the two measurements is deflection. If deflection is excessive, replace the timing chain (see below).

13   Check the tensioner for wear and damage. If tensioner face wear exceeds the amount listed in this Chapter's Specifications, replace the tensioner.

2B

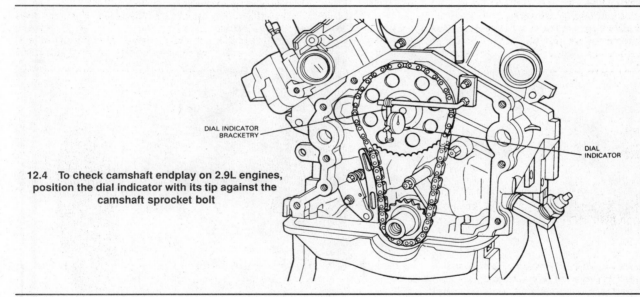

DIAL INDICATOR BRACKETRY

DIAL INDICATOR

12.4   To check camshaft endplay on 2.9L engines, position the dial indicator with its tip against the camshaft sprocket bolt

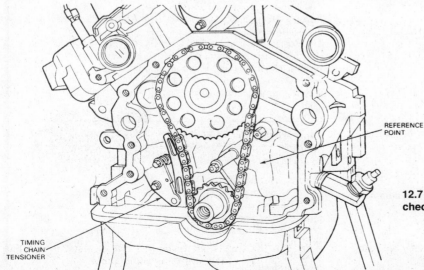

REFERENCE POINT

12.7   Timing chain deflection on 2.9L engines can be checked by measuring from a reference point on the block to the chain

TIMING CHAIN TENSIONER

13.2   If the lifters are not heavily coated with varnish, it may be possible to remove them with a magnet – store them in a marked box so they can be returned to their original positions if reused

13.7a   If the bottom of any lifter is worn concave, scratched or galled, replace the entire set with new ones

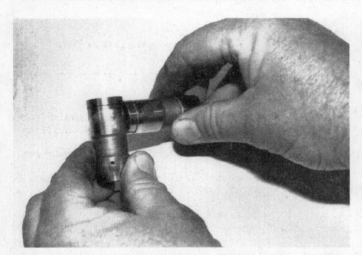

13.7b   The foot of each lifter should be slightly convex – the side of another lifter can be used as a straightedge to check it; if it seems flat, it's worn and must not be reused

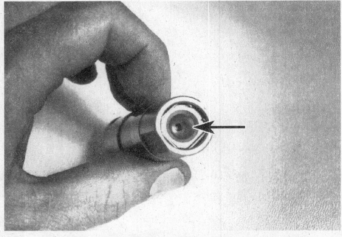

13.7c   Check the pushrod seat (arrow) in the top of each lifter for wear (hydraulic lifter shown; mechanical lifters similar)

Chain and sprocket removal

14   If you haven't already done so, remove the timing chain tensioner **(see illustration 12.7).**

15   Set the number one piston at top dead center on the compression stroke (see Section 3).

16   Remove the oil pan (see Section 15).

17   Remove the radiator (see Chapter 3).

18   Remove the front cover (see Section 10).

19   Make sure the crankshaft key slot and camshaft sprocket dowel hole are aligned with each other. Note their positions for installation.

20   Remove the camshaft sprocket bolt and washer, slide the sprocket off and remove it together with the chain. **Note:** *The camshaft sprocket may be secured with a Torx bolt. If so, use a Torx driver of the correct size. An Allen wrench will strip out the bolt head.*

21   Remove the crankshaft sprocket with a puller **(see illustration 11.11).**

Chain and sprocket installation

22   Align the crankshaft sprocket keyway with the key, then press the sprocket on. If it won't go easily, a puller can be fabricated **(see illustra-**

tions 11.15a and 11.15b). Make sure the timing mark (a small dot on the sprocket) faces up.

23   Position the chain on the crankshaft sprocket, then on the camshaft sprocket. Install the chain and camshaft sprocket together. Make sure the crankshaft key slot and camshaft sprocket dowel hole are aligned with each other.

24   The remainder of installation is the reverse of the removal steps.

***

13   Valve lifters – removal, inspection and installation

Removal

Refer to illustration 13.2

1   Remove the cylinder head(s) (see Section 9).

2   There are several ways to extract the lifters from their bores. Special tools designed to grip and remove lifters (Ford tool no. T70P-14151 or equivalent) are manufactured by many tool companies and are widely available, but may not be needed in every case. On engines without a lot of varnish buildup, the lifters can often be removed with a small magnet **(see illustration)** or even with your fingers. A machinist's scribe with a

14.17a   The camshaft thrust plate (2.8L engine)

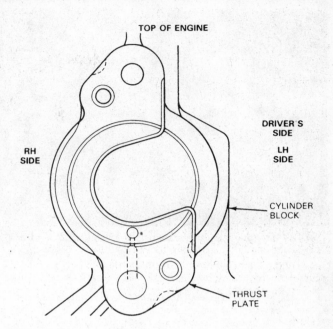

14.17b   The camshaft thrust plate (2.9L engine)

bent end can be used to pull the lifters out by positioning the point under the retainer ring in the top of each lifter. **Caution:** *Don't use pliers to remove the lifters unless you intend to replace them with new ones (along with the camshaft). The pliers may damage the precision machined and hardened lifters, rendering them useless. On engines with a lot of sludge and varnish, work the lifters up and down, using carburetor cleaner spray to loosen the deposits.*

3   Before removing the lifters, arrange to store them in a clearly labeled box to ensure that they're reinstalled in their original locations (**see illustration 13.2**).

4   Remove the lifters and store them where they won't get dirty.

Inspection

Refer to illustrations 13.7a, 13.7b and 13.7c

5   Parts for hydraulic valve lifters (used with 2.9L engines) are not available separately. The work required to remove them from the engine again if cleaning and overhaul is unsuccessful outweighs any potential savings from repairing them.

6   Clean the lifters with solvent and dry them thoroughly without mixing them up.

7   Check each lifter wall, pushrod seat and foot for scuffing, score marks and uneven wear (**see illustration**). Each lifter foot (the surface that rides on the cam lobe) must be slightly convex, although this can be difficult to determine by eye. If the base of the lifter is concave (**see illustration**), the lifters and camshaft must be replaced. If the lifter walls are damaged or worn (which isn't very likely), inspect the lifter bores in the engine block as well. If the pushrod seats (**see illustration**) are worn, check the pushrod ends.

8   If new lifters are being installed, a new camshaft must also be installed. If the camshaft is replaced, then use new lifters as well. Never install used lifters unless the original camshaft is used and the lifters can be reinstalled in their original locations!

Installation

9   The original lifters, if they're being reinstalled, must be returned to their original locations. Coat them with moly-base grease or engine assembly lube.

10   Install the lifters in the bores.

11   The remaining installation steps are the reverse of removal.

12   On 2.8L engines, adjust valve clearances (see Chapter 1).

14   Camshaft – removal, inspection and installation

Camshaft lobe lift check

1   In order to determine the extent of cam lobe wear, the lobe lift should

be checked prior to camshaft removal. Refer to Section 4 and remove the valve covers. The rocker arm assembly must also be removed (Section 5), but leave the pushrods in place.

2   Position the number one piston at TDC on the compression stroke (see Section 3).

3   Beginning with the number one cylinder, mount a dial indicator on the engine and position the plunger in-line with and resting on the first pushrod.

4   Zero the dial indicator, then very slowly turn the crankshaft in the normal direction of rotation until the indicator needle stops and begins to move in the opposite direction. The point at which it stops indicates maximum cam lobe lift.

5   Record this figure for future reference, then reposition the piston at TDC on the compression stroke.

6   Move the dial indicator to the remaining number one cylinder pushrod and repeat the check. Be sure to record the results for each valve.

7   Repeat the check for the remaining valves. Since each piston must be at TDC on the compression stroke for this procedure, work from cylinder-to-cylinder following the firing order sequence.

8   After the check is complete, compare the results to this Chapter's Specifications. If camshaft lobe lift is less than specified for any of the lobes, cam lobe wear has occurred and a new camshaft should be installed.

Removal

Refer to illustrations 14.17a, 14.17b and 14.18

9   Remove the valve covers (see Section 4).

10   Remove the rocker arms and pushrods (see Section 5).

11   Remove the intake manifold (see Section 7).

12   Remove the cylinder heads (see Section 9).

13   Remove the lifters (see Section 13).

14   Remove the oil pan (see Section 15).

15   Remove the engine front cover (see Section 10).

16   Remove the camshaft sprocket or gear bolt and remove the sprocket or gear.

17   Remove the camshaft thrust plate screws and take off the thrust plate (**see illustrations**).

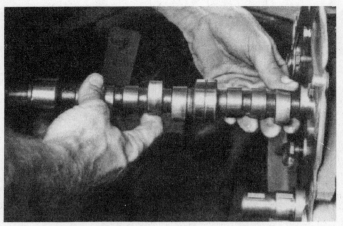

14.18   Carefully support the camshaft as you remove it from the block

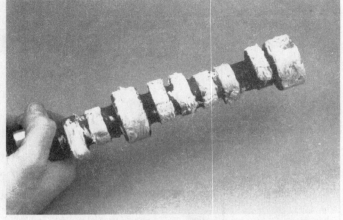

14.22   Apply moly-base grease or engine assembly lube to the lobes and journals on the camshaft prior to installation

18   Carefully pull the camshaft from the block, rotating it as you pull and supporting it with both hands **(see illustration)**. Take care not to damage camshaft bearing surfaces during removal.
19   Remove the Woodruff key and spacer ring from the camshaft.

Inspection

20   Refer to Part A, Section 7, for the camshaft and bearing inspection procedure. Lifter inspection procedures are covered in Section 13.

Bearing replacement

21   Camshaft bearing replacement requires special tools and expertise that place it outside the scope of the home mechanic. Take the block to an automotive machine shop to ensure that the job is done correctly.

Installation

Refer to illustration 14.22

22   Lubricate the camshaft bearing journals and cam lobes with moly-based grease or engine assembly lube **(see illustration)**.
23   Slide the camshaft into the engine. Support the cam near the block and be careful not to scrape or nick the bearings.
24   Install the spacer ring with its chamfered side toward the camshaft.
25   Install the camshaft Woodruff key.
26   Apply moly-based grease or engine assembly lube to the friction surfaces on both sides of the thrust plate. Install the thrust plate so it covers the oil gallery hole **(see illustrations 14.17a and 14.17b)**, then tighten the attaching bolts to the torque listed in this Chapter's Specifications.
27   The remaining installation steps are the reverse of removal.
28   Before starting the engine, change the oil and install a new oil filter (see Chapter 1).
29   On 2.8L engines, adjust the valves.

---

15   Oil pan and pump – removal and installation

Refer to illustrations 15.15 and 15.19

1   Disconnect the negative battery cable from the battery.
2   On 2.8L engines, remove the air cleaner (see Chapter 4).
3   On 2.9L engines, remove the air intake tube from the throttle body (see Chapter 4).
4   Remove the fan shroud bolts and place the shroud over the fan (see Chapter 3).
5   Remove the distributor (see Chapter 5). Stuff a clean shop rag into the distributor hole to keep dirt out of the engine.
6   Remove the transmission dipstick (automatic transmission models). Remove the transmission dipstick tube and plug the hole to keep dirt out

of the transmission.
7   If necessary for access, jack up the vehicle and place it securely on jackstands. DO NOT get under a vehicle that is supported only by a jack!
8   Drain the engine oil and remove the filter (see Chapter 1).
9   Remove the engine mount nuts (see Section 18).
10   On all except 2WD Ranger models, disconnect the muffler inlet pipes.
11   Detach the oil cooler bracket (if equipped) and lower it out of the way.
12   Remove the starter (see Chapter 5).
13   Position the transmission oil cooler lines out of the way (if equipped).
14   Detach the front stabilizer bar (if equipped) and move it forward out of the way (see Chapter 10).
15   Place a jack beneath the engine. Use a block of wood between the jack and engine to prevent damage. Raise the engine, place 2x4 wooden blocks between the engine mounts and brackets **(see illustration)** and lower the jack.
16   Disconnect the oil level sensor electrical connector (if equipped).
17   Remove the oil pan mounting bolts. Lower the pan to the frame. If it is stuck, tap it lightly with a rubber mallet to break the gasket seal.
18   On all except Ranger 2WD models, reach into the oil pan and remove the oil pump, crankcase baffle and pick-up tube attaching bolts. Lower the oil pump, crankcase baffle and pick-up tube into the oil pan.

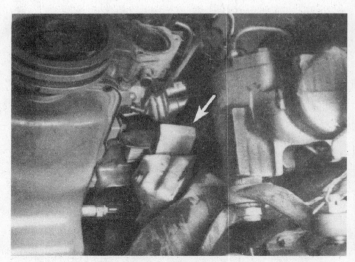

15.15   Install wooden blocks between the front engine mounts and brackets (arrow)

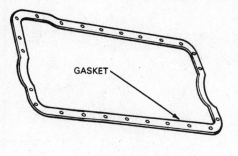

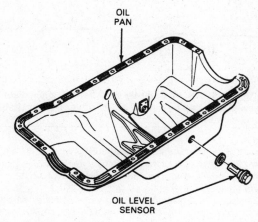

GASKET

OIL PAN

OIL LEVEL SENSOR

15.19   The oil pan and gasket – some models include an oil level sensor, which must be disconnected to remove the pan

19   Remove the oil pan and gasket **(see illustration)**. On 2WD Ranger models, remove the oil pump, crankcase baffle and pick-up tube attaching bolts and remove the pump and tube.

Installation

Refer to illustration 15.27

20   Use a gasket scraper or putty knife to remove all traces of gasket material and sealant from the pan, block and front cover.
21   Clean the mating surfaces with lacquer thinner or acetone. Make sure the block and front cover bolt holes are clean.
22   Check the oil pan flange for distortion, particularly around the bolt holes. If necessary, place the pan on a block of wood and use a hammer to flatten and restore the gasket surface.
23   Apply sealant to the joints where the timing cover meets the block. Also apply a small amount of sealant to the groove in the rear main bearing cap.
24   If the block doesn't have gasket alignment studs, stick the gasket to the block with gasket contact adhesive. If the block does have studs, carefully install a new gasket over them.
25   Fill either the inlet or outlet port of the oil pump with clean engine oil. Rotate the pump shaft to prime the pump.
26   On ranger 2WD models, position the oil pump (with a new gasket), baffle and inlet tube (with a new gasket) on the engine (see Caution below) and install the bolts, tightening them to the torques listed in this Chapter's Specifications. On all other models, put the components (with new gaskets) in the oil pan. **Caution:** *Be sure the intermediate shaft is installed in the oil pump, or the pump won't turn when the engine is run. Lift the pan into position below the engine and install the oil pump, baffle and inlet tube. Tighten the bolts and nut to the torques listed in this Chapter's Specifications.*
27   Install the oil pan bolts and tighten in two stages to the torque listed in this Chapter's Specifications. Start with bolt A **(see illustration)** and work around the oil pan; then start with bolt B and work around the oil pan again, tightening to the final torque.

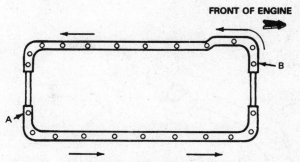

FRONT OF ENGINE

A

B

FIT THE OIL PAN BOLTS AND TIGHTEN IN TWO STEPS
STEP 1: START WITH BOLT A FOLLOW DIRECTION OF ARROWS
STEP 2: START WITH BOLT B FOLLOW DIRECTION OF ARROWS

15.27   Tighten the oil pan bolts in two stages, working your way around the pan in the direction of the arrows

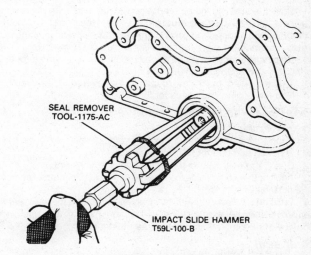

SEAL REMOVER TOOL-1175-AC

IMPACT SLIDE HAMMER T59L-100-B

16.4   Removing the front cover oil seal with a seal puller – cover installed on the engine

28   The remaining installation steps are the reverse of removal. Use a new oil filter and don't forget to fill the engine with oil.
29   Run the engine and check for leaks.

16 Crankshaft oil seals – replacement

Front seal – engine front cover in place

Refer to illustrations 16.4 and 16.7

1   Drain the cooling system and remove the drivebelts (see Chapter 1).
2   Remove the radiator (Chapter 3).
3   Remove the crankshaft pulley.
4   Remove the seal with a slide hammer and seal remover **(see illustration)**. Similar tools are available from rental outlets.
5   Check the seal bore and crankshaft, as well as the seal contact surface on the crankshaft pulley for nicks or burrs. Position the new seal in the bore with the open end of the seal facing IN.
6   A small amount of oil applied to the outer edge of the seal will make installation easier – don't overdo it! Also apply a small amount of oil to the seal lip

2B

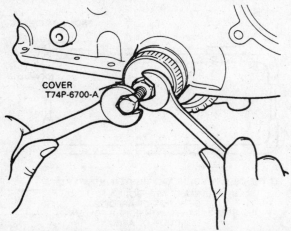

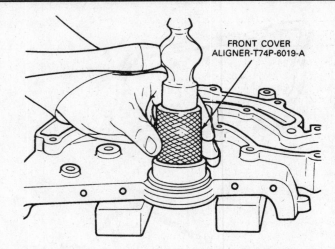

16.7   A Ford tool is available to install the front cover seal with the front cover on the engine – a large socket or piece of pipe the same diameter as the seal can also be used

16.14   Drive the seal in squarely and evenly – a large socket or piece of pipe can be used if a seal driver isn't available

7   Drive the seal into the bore until it seats against the front cover. Special tools are available **(see illustration)**, but if you don't have them, use a hammer and a socket the same diameter as the seal to drive the seal in. **Note:** *A piece of pipe can be used if a socket isn't available.*

8   Reinstall the crankshaft pulley and tighten its bolt to the torque listed in this Chapter's Specifications.

9   The remaining installation steps are the reverse of removal.

10   Run the engine and check for leaks.

Front seal – front cover removed

Refer to illustration 16.14

11   Support the front cover on wooden blocks, then drive out the seal with a punch and hammer.

12   Check the seal bore in the front cover for nicks or burrs.

13   Apply a thin coat of clean engine oil to the outer circumference of the seal and to the seal lip.

14   Position the new seal with its lip facing IN. Drive in the new seal with a seal driver **(see illustration)**. If a seal driver isn't available, use a socket or piece of pipe the same diameter as the seal.

Rear seal

Refer to illustrations 16.20 and 16.24

15   Remove the transmission (see Chapter 7).

16   Remove the clutch (if equipped) (see Chapter 8).

17   Remove the flywheel or driveplate (see Section 17).

18   Remove the engine rear plate.

19   With a sharp awl or similar tool, punch two holes in the seal on opposite sides just above the point where the main bearing cap meets the cylinder block.

20   Thread a sheet metal screw into each hole **(see illustration)**. Pry against the sheet metal screws with two large screwdrivers or small prybars to remove the seal. **Note:** *If you need a fulcrum to pry against, use small blocks of wood.* **Caution:** *Don't scratch or gouge the crankshaft seal surface.*

21   Clean the oil seal bore in the block and main bearing cap. Check the seal bore and crankshaft sealing surface for nicks or burrs.

22   Apply a thin coat of clean engine oil to the outer diameter of the seal. Apply a thin coat of Lubriplate or equivalent to the contact surfaces of the seal and crankshaft.

23   Position the seal in the bore with its open end facing IN.

24   Drive the seal in with a seal driver **(see illustration)** until it is securely seated. Use a socket or piece of pipe the same diameter as the seal if a seal driver isn't available.

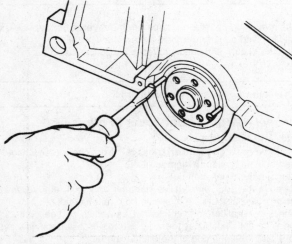

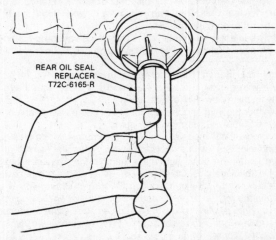

16.20   Thread two sheet metal screws into the crankshaft rear oil seal to pry it out

16.24   Install the crankshaft rear oil seal with the open end facing into the engine – use a socket or large piece of pipe if a seal driver isn't available

17 Flywheel/driveplate – removal and installation

1   Raise the vehicle and support it securely on jackstands, then refer to Chapter 7 and remove the transmission. If it's leaking, now would be a very good time to replace the front pump seal/O-ring (automatic transmission only).

2   Remove the pressure plate and clutch disc (see Chapter 8) (manual transmission equipped vehicles). Now is a good time to check/replace the clutch components and pilot bearing.

3   Use a center-punch to make alignment marks on the flywheel/driveplate and crankshaft to ensure correct alignment during reinstallation.

4   Remove the bolts that secure the flywheel/driveplate to the crankshaft. If the crankshaft turns, wedge a screwdriver through the starter opening to jam the flywheel.

5   Remove the flywheel/driveplate from the crankshaft. Since the flywheel is fairly heavy, be sure to support it while removing the last bolt.

6   Clean the flywheel to remove grease and oil. Inspect the surface for cracks, rivet grooves, burned areas and score marks. Light scoring can be removed with emery cloth. Check for cracked and broken ring gear teeth. Lay the flywheel on a flat surface and use a straightedge to check for warpage.

7   Clean and inspect the mating surfaces of the flywheel/driveplate and the crankshaft. If the crankshaft rear seal is leaking, replace it before reinstalling the flywheel/driveplate.

8   Position the flywheel/driveplate against the crankshaft. Be sure to align the marks made during removal. Note that some engines have an alignment dowel or staggered bolt holes to ensure correct installation. Before installing the bolts, apply thread locking compound to the threads.

9   Wedge a screwdriver through the starter motor opening to keep the flywheel/driveplate from turning as you tighten the bolts to the torque listed in this Chapter's Specifications.

10   The remainder of installation is the reverse of the removal procedure.

18 Engine mounts – check and replacement

Refer to illustration 18.8

1   Engine mounts seldom require attention, but broken or deteriorated mounts should be replaced immediately or the added strain placed on the driveline components may cause damage or wear.

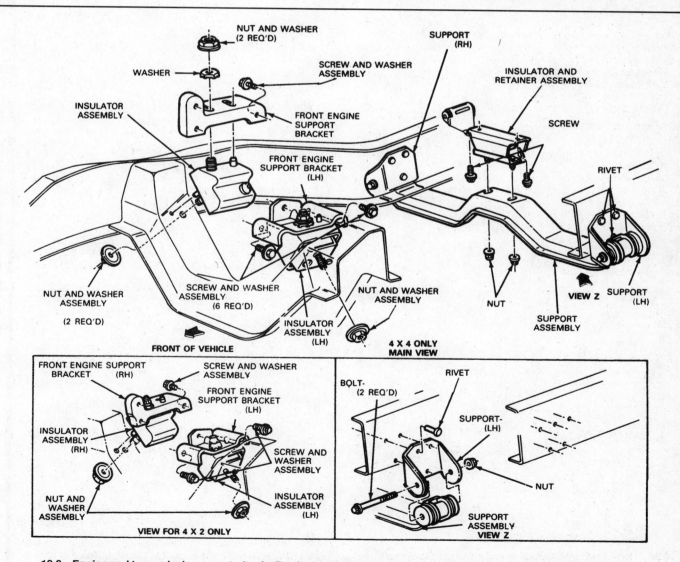

18.8   Engine and transmission mounts (typical) – the insulator shown in View Z is used on 1987 through 1990 models

Check

2   During the check, the engine must be raised slightly to remove the weight from the mounts.

3   Raise the vehicle and support it securely on jackstands, then position a jack under the engine oil pan. Place a large block of wood between the jack head and the oil pan, then carefully raise the engine just enough to take the weight off the mounts. **Warning:** *DO NOT place any part of your body under the engine when it's supported only by a jack!*

4   Check the mounts to see if the rubber is cracked, hardened or separated from the metal plates. Sometimes the rubber will split right down the center.

5   Check for relative movement between the mount plates and the engine or frame (use a large screwdriver or prybar to attempt to move the mounts). If movement is noted, lower the engine and tighten the mount fasteners.

6   Rubber preservative should be applied to the mounts to slow deterioration.

Replacement

7   Disconnect the negative battery cable from the battery, then raise the vehicle and support it securely on jackstands (if not already done).

8   Remove the fasteners and detach the mount (insulator) from the frame bracket **(see illustration)**.

9   Raise the engine slightly with a jack or hoist (make sure the fan doesn't hit the radiator or shroud). Remove the mount-to-block bolts and detach the mount.

10   Installation is the reverse of removal. Use thread locking compound on the mount bolts and be sure to tighten them securely.

Chapter 2 Part C 3.0L V6 engine

Contents

Specifications

General

Cylinder numbering (front-to-rear)	
Right bank	1–2–3
Left bank	4–5–6
Firing order	1-4-2-5-3-6
Timing chain deflection	Six degrees (see text)
Collapsed tappet gap (nominal)	0.088 to 0.189 inch
Camshaft endplay (maximum)	0.007 inch

Torque specifications

	Ft-lbs
Camshaft thrust plate bolts	7
Camshaft sprocket bolt	46
Cylinder head bolts	
Step one	59
Step two	Loosen one full turn
Step three	37
Step four	68
Exhaust manifold bolts	19
Flywheel/driveplate bolts	60
Intake manifold bolts	
Step one	11
Step two	19
Oil pump mounting bolt	35
Oil pan bolts	
Through 1991	7
1992 on	9
Rocker arm fulcrum bolts	
Step one	8
Step two	24
Rocker arm cover bolts/studs	9
Timing chain cover/water pump bolts	
6 mm	7
8 mm	19
Damper-to-crankshaft bolt	107

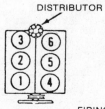

DISTRIBUTOR

FRONT

FIRING ORDER – 1-4-2-5-3-6

Cap screw location
3.0L engines

CLOCKWISE

Cylinder location and distributor rotation

1   General information

This Part of Chapter 2 is devoted to in-vehicle repair procedures for the 3.0L V6 engine. All information concerning engine removal and installation, repairs which require engine removal and engine block and cylinder head overhaul can be found in Part E of this Chapter.

The following repair procedures are based on the assumption that the engine is installed in the vehicle. If the engine has been removed from the vehicle and mounted on a stand, many of the steps outlined in this Part of Chapter 2 will not apply.

The Specifications included in this Part of Chapter 2 apply only to the procedures contained in this Part. Part E of Chapter 2 contains the Specifications necessary for cylinder head and engine block rebuilding.

2   Repair operations possible with the engine in the vehicle

Many major repair operations can be accomplished without removing the engine from the vehicle.

Clean the engine compartment and the exterior of the engine with some type of pressure washer before any work is done. A clean engine will make the job easier and will help keep dirt out of the internal areas of the engine.

Depending on the components involved, it may be a good idea to remove the hood to improve access to the engine as repairs are performed (refer to Chapter 11 if necessary).

If vacuum, exhaust, oil or coolant leaks develop, indicating a need for gasket or seal replacement, the repairs can generally be made with the engine in the vehicle. The intake and exhaust manifold gaskets, oil pan gasket and cylinder head gaskets are all accessible with the engine in place.

Exterior engine components such as the intake and exhaust manifolds, the oil pan (and the oil pump), the water pump, the starter motor, the alternator, the distributor and the fuel injection system components can be removed for repair with the engine in place.

Since the cylinder heads can be removed without pulling the engine, valve component servicing can also be accomplished with the engine in the vehicle.

In extreme cases caused by a lack of necessary equipment, repair or replacement of piston rings, pistons, connecting rods and rod bearings is possible with the engine in the vehicle. However, this practice is not recommended because of the cleaning and preparation work that must be done to the components involved.

3   Top Dead Center (TDC) for number one piston – locating

Refer to Chapter 2, Part B for this procedure.

4   Rocker arm covers – removal and installation

Removal
Refer to illustration 4.3
1   Disconnect the negative cable from the battery.
2   Disconnect the spark plug wires from the spark plugs on the side(s) you are disassembling. If they are not numbered, tag them so they won't get mixed up on reassembly.
3   Note the location of the wire routing clips and studs **(see illustration)** and pull the clips off the studs.

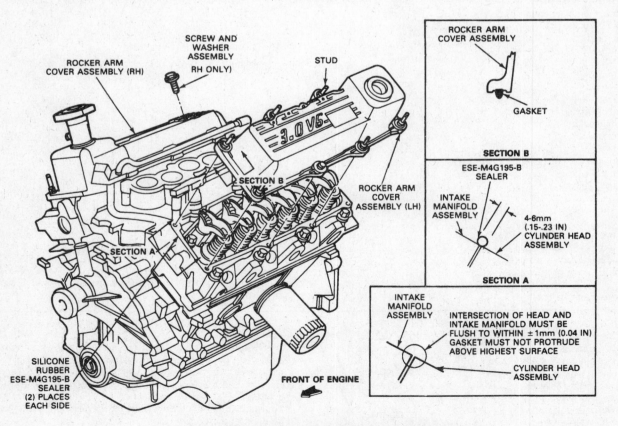

4.3   Rocker arm cover mounting details – exploded view

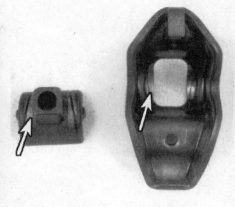

5.2 Loosen the bolt (arrow) and pivot the rocker arm to the side to remove the pushrod

5.3 A perforated cardboard box can be used to store the pushrods to ensure installation in their original locations

5.5 Check the rocker arm and fulcrum for wear and galling (arrows)

4 If the left-hand rocker arm cover is being removed, do the following:
   a) Remove the throttle body (see Chapter 4).
   b) Remove the PCV valve (see Chapters 1 and 6).
   c) Remove the fuel injector wiring harness stand-offs from the rocker arm cover studs on the side of the cover nearest the intake manifold. Move the harness aside so it won't obstruct removal of the cover.

5 If the right-hand rocker arm cover is being removed, do the following:
   a) Detach the electrical connectors at the cover.
   b) Detach the air cleaner closure hose from the oil filler neck.
   c) Perform Step 4c above.

6 Remove the rocker arm cover attaching bolts and studs, noting their locations. Use a deep socket to remove the studs.

7 Carefully remove the cover. Try bumping it with a rubber mallet to loosen it. If that doesn't work easily, use a sharp, thin-bladed knife to cut the sealant used at four points between the gasket and the cylinder head. Be careful to cut just the sealant, not the gasket.

Installation

8 Using a gasket scraper or putty knife, remove all traces of gasket material from the cylinder head. Clean off any oil or dirt with acetone or lacquer thinner and a cloth.

9 If the bolts and studs are held in the rocker arm cover by the gasket, note their locations and remove them. Carefully roll the gasket out of the rocker arm cover channel. Thoroughly clean the channel with a soft cloth.

10 Install a new gasket in the rocker arm cover channel with your fingers, aligning the stud and bolt holes. Install the fasteners in their holes. Hold each fastener in place with a nut driver or socket and roll the gasket collar around the fastener: The gasket should hold the fasteners in place when installed. **Note:** *Make sure the gasket lies flat in the rocker arm cover channel, with no bulges. If it isn't completely flat before installation, it will leak.*

11 Lightly oil all bolt and stud threads prior to installation.

12 Apply a bead of RTV sealant at the cylinder head-to-intake manifold rail step (two places per rail) **(see illustration 4.3)**.

13 Install the rocker arm cover straight onto the cylinder head. If it's shifted after contacting the sealant, the gasket could be pulled from its channel, causing leaks.

14 Tighten the studs and bolts to the torque listed in this Chapter's Specifications, working around the cover in several steps.

15 Reinstall the parts removed for access. Run the engine and check for oil or vacuum leaks.

5 Rocker arms and pushrods – removal, inspection, installation and adjustment

Removal, inspection and installation

Refer to illustrations 5.2, 5.3 and 5.5

1 Remove the rocker arm cover(s) (see Section 4).

2 Loosen the rocker arm fulcrum bolt until you can pivot the rocker arm to one side and pull the pushrod out of the valve lifter **(see illustration)**.

3 If you are removing more than one pushrod, store them in a holder made from a cardboard box **(see illustration)** so they can be returned to their original locations.

4 If you are going to remove all of the rocker arms, mark them so they can be returned to their original locations – don't mix them up!

5 Clean and examine all components for wear and damage. Pushrods may be rolled over a flat surface such as a piece of glass to check for straightness. Check the fulcrums and rockers for galling and wear. Wear frequently occurs at the points where the pushrods contact the rockers **(see illustration)**. Replace any parts showing evidence of wear.

6 Prior to installation, apply moly-base grease or engine assembly lube to the fulcrums and the ends of the rocker arms.

7 Check to be sure that the valve lifter is all the way down before installing the pushrod. Turn the crankshaft with a wrench until the lifter is down, if needed.

8 Install the pushrod and rocker arm and fulcrum. Tighten the rocker arm fulcrum bolt to the torque listed in this Chapter's Specifications.

9 If any parts have been replaced, check the collapsed tappet gap adjustment, as described below.

10 Reinstall the rocker arm cover(s) (see Section 4).

Collapsed tappet gap adjustment

Refer to illustration 5.12

Note: *Adjustment is only needed when valve train parts have been replaced or valves and/or seats have been ground a considerable amount.*

11 Set the number one cylinder at TDC (see Section 3). With the engine in this position you can check the tappet gap for the number one cylinder intake and exhaust valves. **Note:** *The arrangement of intake (I) and exhaust (E) valves, starting at the front (drivebelt) end of the engine, is as follows:*

Left cylinder bank
   I-E-I-E-I-E
Right cylinder bank
   E-I-E-I-E-I

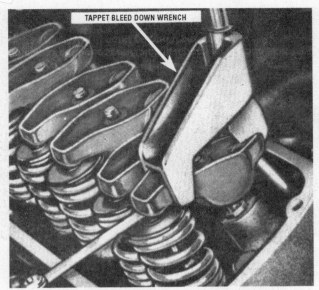

5.12   Checking valve clearance with a lifter bleed-down tool and a feeler gauge

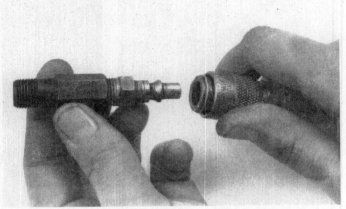

6.4   This is what the air hose adapter that threads into the spark plug hole looks like – they're commonly available from auto parts stores

12   Using Ford lifter bleed-down tool T70P-6513-A or equivalent **(see illustration)**, press on each rocker arm until the lifter leaks down. Check the clearance between the valve stem and rocker arm with a feeler gauge. Compare it to the collapsed tappet gap listed in this Chapter's Specifications and write it down.

13   Position each cylinder at TDC, following the firing order and adjusting each cylinder's valves when it's at TDC. If the clearances are within specification, install the rocker arm covers.

14   If there isn't enough clearance, use a shorter pushrod; too much clearance, use a longer one (available from your dealer). **Note:** *If one clearance is too large and another too small, try swapping the pushrods.*

6   Valve springs, retainers and seals – replacement

Refer to illustrations 6.4, 6.8, 6.9, 6.14 and 6.15

Note: *Broken valve springs and defective valve stem seals can be replaced without removing the cylinder head. Two special tools and a compressed air source are normally required to perform this operation, so read through this Section carefully and rent or buy the tools before beginning the job. If compressed air is not available, a length of nylon rope can be used to keep the valves from falling into the cylinder during this procedure.*

1   Refer to Section 4 and remove the rocker arm cover from the affected cylinder head. If all of the valve stem seals are being replaced, remove both rocker arm covers.

2   Remove the spark plug from the cylinder which has the defective component. If all of the valve stem seals are being replaced, all of the spark plugs should be removed.

3   Turn the crankshaft until the piston in the affected cylinder is at top dead center on the compression stroke (refer to Section 3 for instructions). If you are replacing all of the valve stem seals, begin with cylinder number one and work on the valves for one cylinder at a time. Move from cylinder-to-cylinder following the firing order sequence (1-4-2-5-3-6).

4   Thread an adapter into the spark plug hole and connect an air hose from a compressed air source to it **(see illustration)**. Most auto parts stores can supply the air hose adapter. **Note:** *Many cylinder compression gauges utilize a screw-in fitting that may work with your air hose quick-disconnect fitting.*

5   Remove the bolt, fulcrum and rocker arm for the valve with the defective part and pull out the pushrod. If all of the valve stem seals are being replaced, all of the rocker arms and pushrods should be removed (refer to Section 5).

6   Apply compressed air to the cylinder. The valves should be held in place by the air pressure. If the valve faces or seats are in poor condition, leaks may prevent the air pressure from retaining the valves – refer to the alternative procedure below.

7   If you do not have access to compressed air, an alternative method can be used. Position the piston at a point just before TDC on the compression stroke, then feed a long piece of nylon rope through the spark plug hole until it fills the combustion chamber. Be sure to leave the end of the rope hanging out of the engine so it can be removed easily. Use a large breaker bar and socket to rotate the crankshaft in the normal direction of rotation until slight resistance is felt.

8   Stuff shop rags into the cylinder head holes above and below the valves to prevent parts and tools from falling into the engine, then use a valve spring compressor to compress the spring/damper assembly. Remove the keepers with small needle-nose pliers or a magnet **(see illustration)**. **Note:** *A couple of different types of tools are available for compressing the valve springs with the head in place. One type grips the lower spring coils and presses on the retainer as the knob is turned, while the other type, shown here, utilizes the rocker arm bolt for leverage. Both types work very well, although the lever type is usually less expensive.*

9   Remove the spring retainer shield and valve spring assembly, then remove the valve stem seal **(see illustration)**. **Note:** *If air pressure fails to hold the valve in the closed position during this operation, the valve face or seat is probably damaged. If so, the cylinder head will have to be removed for additional repair operations.* **Note:** *If you remove more than one valve spring at a time, carefully label the parts according to cylinder number and whether they belong with the intake or exhaust valve.*

10   Wrap a rubber band around the top of the valve stem so the valve will not fall into the combustion chamber, then release the air pressure. **Note:** *If a rope was used instead of air pressure, turn the crankshaft slightly in the direction opposite normal rotation.*

11   Inspect the valve stem for damage. Rotate the valve in the guide and check the end for eccentric movement, which would indicate that the valve is bent.

12   Move the valve up-and-down in the guide and make sure it doesn't bind. If the valve stem binds, either the valve is bent or the guide is damaged. In either case, the head will have to be removed for repair.

13   Reapply air pressure to the cylinder to retain the valve in the closed position, then remove the tape or rubber band from the valve stem. If a rope was used instead of air pressure, rotate the crankshaft in the normal direction of rotation until slight resistance is felt.

14   Lubricate the valve stem with engine oil and install a new seal **(see illustration)**. Seal designs differ from cylinder to cylinder as well as between intake and exhaust valves.

15   Install the spring assembly and spring seat (where applicable) in position over the valve **(see illustration)**.

6.8 Compress the spring and remove the keepers with a magnet or needle-nose pliers

6.9 Once the valve spring assembly is removed, the seal (arrow) can be pulled off the valve guide boss

6.14 Carefully seat the new valve seal using a deep socket and a hammer

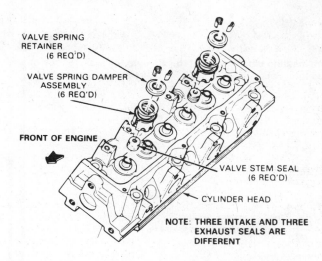

VALVE SPRING RETAINER (6 REQ'D)

VALVE SPRING DAMPER ASSEMBLY (6 REQ'D)

FRONT OF ENGINE

VALVE STEM SEAL (6 REQ'D)

CYLINDER HEAD

NOTE: THREE INTAKE AND THREE EXHAUST SEALS ARE DIFFERENT

6.15 An exploded view of the valve components

7.8 Use a scraper to remove the intake manifold gaskets

16 Install the valve spring retainer. Compress the valve spring assembly.

17 Position the keepers in the grooves. Apply a small dab of grease to the inside of each keeper to hold it in place if necessary. Remove the pressure from the spring tool and make sure the keepers are seated.

18 Disconnect the air hose and remove the adapter from the spark plug hole. If a rope was used in place of air pressure, pull it out of the cylinder.

19 Refer to Section 5 and install the rocker arm(s) and pushrod(s).

20 Install the spark plug(s) and hook up the wire(s).

21 Refer to Section 4 and install the rocker arm cover(s).

22 Start and run the engine, then check for oil leaks and unusual sounds coming from the rocker arm cover area.

7 Intake manifold – removal and installation

Refer to illustrations 7.8, 7.10, 7.11a, 7.11b and 7.13

Warning: Relieve the fuel system pressure before following this procedure (see Chapter 4).

Removal

1 Drain the coolant and disconnect the negative cable from the battery (see Chapter 1).

2 Disconnect the EGR tube nut from the EGR valve (if equipped). Loosen the tube nut and rotate the tube away from the valve. Remove the upper intake manifold (plenum) and throttle body (see Chapter 4).

3 Label and disconnect all wiring, vacuum and coolant hoses from the intake manifold. Disconnect the radiator top hose from the thermostat housing and position it out of the way.

4 Disconnect the fuel rails and lines and cap the fittings (see Chapter 4). **Note:** The injectors and fuel rails may be removed with the intake manifold as an assembly.

5 Remove the distributor and coil with the bracket as described in Chapter 5. Remove the pushrod from number three cylinder intake valve (see Section 5).

6 Remove the intake manifold mounting bolts/studs (this requires a Torx driver bit), noting the locations of the studs for reinstallation.

7 Remove the intake manifold. It may be necessary to pry between the manifold and the block, using the water pump lug as a fulcrum. Use care to avoid damaging the machined surfaces. **Caution:** Do not pry between the gasket surfaces or leaks will develop.

Installation

8 Clean away all traces of old gasket material (**see illustration**). Remove oil and dirt with a cloth and solvent, such as acetone or lacquer thinner.

9 Lightly oil all bolts and studs prior to assembly.

10   Apply a 1/8-inch bead of RTV sealant (Ford D6AZ-19562 or equivalent) at each corner where the head joins the engine block **(see illustration).**

11   Position the new gaskets and end seals on the engine with adhesive (Ford D7AZ-19B508-A or equivalent). Be sure the locating pins/tabs fit properly **(see illustrations).** **Note:** *Assembly must be completed within several minutes. Don't allow the RTV sealant to dry.*

12   Carefully set the lower manifold into place. Be sure the gaskets don't shift out of place. Install the bolts and studs in their original locations.

13   Tighten the bolts/studs in numerical sequence **(see illustration),** reaching the torque listed in this Chapter's Specifications in two steps.

14   Reinstall all parts removed for access in the reverse order of removal.

15   Refill the cooling system, run the engine and connect the negative battery cable. Check the ignition timing.

16   Run the engine and check for fuel, oil, vacuum and coolant leaks.

7.10   Put extra sealant in the four corners before installing the new gaskets

7.11a   The end seals have locating pins which must be pressed into place

7.11b   Be sure the locking tabs on the gaskets are engaged

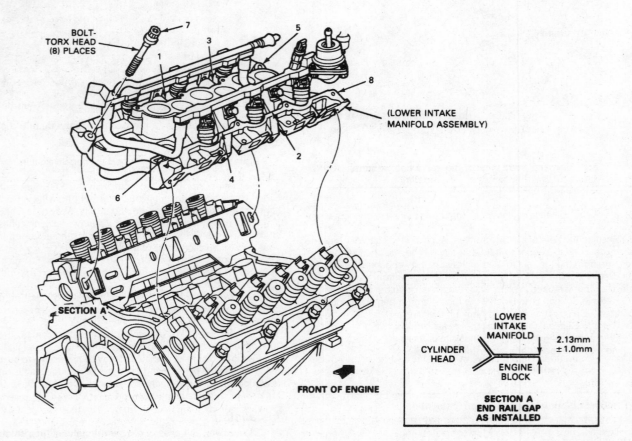

7.13   Intake manifold bolt tightening sequence

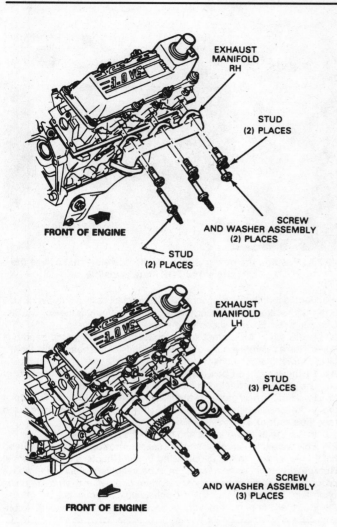

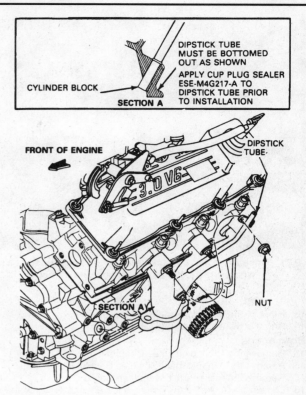

8.9   If the dipstick is removed from the engine, is must be coated with sealant and reinserted all the way

8   Install the bolts and studs finger tight in their correct locations, then tighten them to the torque listed in this Chapter's Specifications.
9   Reinstall the remaining parts in the reverse order of removal. If the dipstick tube was removed, apply sealant (Ford specification ESE-M4G217-A or equivalent) to the base of the dipstick tube **(see illustration)**. Be sure to insert the dipstick tube all the way.
10   Run the engine and check for exhaust leaks.

9   Cylinder heads – removal and installation

Refer to illustrations 9.21, 9.25 and 9.27

Removal

1   Drain the cooling system (see Chapter 1).
2   Disconnect the negative cable from the battery.
3   Remove the air cleaner duct tube.
4   Relieve fuel system pressure (see Chapter 4) and disconnect the fuel lines.
5   Label and disconnect the vacuum lines from the intake manifold and cylinder head(s).
6   Detach the top radiator hose and heater hoses from the engine and position them out of the way.
7   Remove the ignition coil (see Chapter 5).
8   Remove the throttle body (see Chapter 4).
9   Remove the distributor (see Chapter 5).

Left head

10   Remove the power steering pump belt (see Chapter 1). Unbolt the power steering pump bracket from the engine, then place the pump and bracket aside. Position the pump so it won't spill fluid.
11   Detach the dipstick tube from the exhaust manifold stud **(see illustration 8.9)**. Rotate the dipstick tube out of the way or remove it from the engine.
12   Remove the fuel line bracket bolt from the front of the head.

8.4   Exhaust manifolds – exploded view

8   Exhaust manifolds – removal and installation

Warning: *Allow the engine to cool completely before following this procedure.*

Removal

Refer to illustrations 8.4 and 8.9

1   Raise the vehicle and support it securely on jackstands. Disconnect the exhaust pipe(s) from the manifold(s) being removed. **Note:** *To ease removal of the manifold-to-pipe nuts, apply penetrating oil to the threads and allow it to soak in about 10 minutes.*
2   Remove the spark plugs from the side(s) being removed (see Chapter 1).
3   Left manifold: Remove the nut that secures the oil dipstick tube and bracket. Rotate the tube out of the way or remove it from the vehicle.
4   Unbolt and remove the exhaust manifold from the vehicle **(see illustration)**.

Installation

5   Clean all gasket surfaces thoroughly and inspect the manifold(s) for cracks and damage. Check the fasteners and bolt holes for stripped or damaged threads.
6   Lightly oil all bolts and studs prior to installation.
7   Position the manifold on the cylinder head.

9.21   Once the bolts are removed, pry the head loose at a point where the gasket surfaces won't be damaged

9.25   Position the new gasket over the dowels – make sure the UP (shown) or TOP mark is visible

Right head

13 Remove the alternator drivebelt (see Chapter 1).
14 Remove the alternator (see Chapter 5).

Both heads

15 Remove the spark plugs (see Chapter 1).
16 Remove the exhaust manifolds (see Section 8).
17 Remove the rocker arm covers (see Section 4).
18 Loosen the rocker arm fulcrum bolts enough to allow the rocker arms to be lifted off the pushrods and rotate them to one side (see Section 5).
19 Remove the pushrods (see Section 5). Store them so they can be re-installed in the same location.
20 Remove the intake manifold (see Section 7).
21 Remove the cylinder head bolts and lift the head off the engine **(see illustration)**. Lift the head clear of the locating dowels.

Installation

22 Thoroughly remove all traces of gasket material from the head and cylinder block with a gasket scraper and clean all parts with solvent. Use a rag and acetone or lacquer thinner to remove any traces of oil. See Chapter 2 Part E for cylinder head inspection procedures.

23 Use a tap of the correct size to chase the threads in the head bolt holes. Run a rethreading die along the threads of the head bolts. Lightly oil the threads of the bolts.

24 Recheck all head bolt holes and cylinder bores for any traces of coolant, oil or other foreign matter. Remove as needed.

25 Position the new gasket over the dowel pins on the block. The top of the gasket should be stamped TOP or UP to ensure correct installation **(see illustration)**. Don't use sealant on the gaskets.

26 Install the cylinder heads and head bolts finger tight.

27 Following the sequence shown **(see illustration)**, tighten the head bolts in four steps to the torque listed in this Chapter's Specifications. **Note:** *When cylinder head bolts have been tightened using the above procedure, it is not necessary to retighten bolts after extended engine operation. However, bolts may be rechecked for tightness if desired.*

28 Reinstall the parts removed in the reverse order of removal. Lubri-

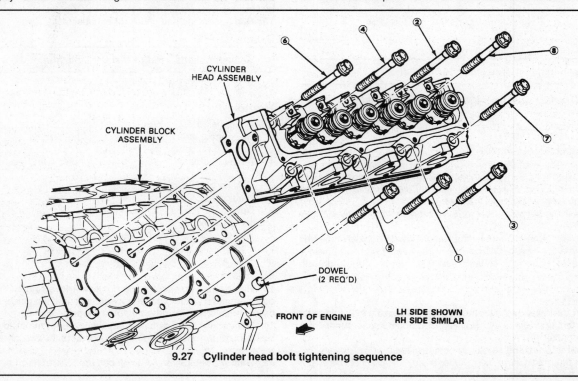

CYLINDER HEAD ASSEMBLY

CYLINDER BLOCK ASSEMBLY

DOWEL (2 REQ'D)

FRONT OF ENGINE

LH SIDE SHOWN
RH SIDE SIMILAR

9.27   Cylinder head bolt tightening sequence

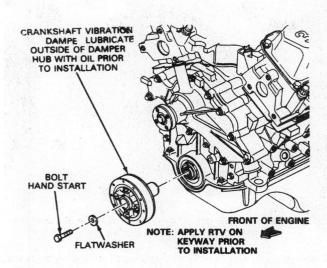

10.9 Press the crankshaft damper into place with an installation tool

10.4 Crankshaft damper mounting details – exploded view

icate the rocker arm components with oil conditioner (Ford D9AZ-19579-C or equivalent) or high-viscosity engine oil.
29 Install the pushrods in their original locations. For each valve, rotate the crankshaft until the valve lifter is at its lowest position. Install the rocker arms, fulcrums and bolts. Tighten them to the torque listed in this Chapter's Specifications.
30 Refill the cooling system, change the oil and filter (see Chapter 1) and run the engine. Check the ignition timing and inspect for any leaks.
31 If a component has been replaced or the valves ground, check collapsed tappet gap as described in Section 5.

10 Crankshaft front oil seal – replacement

Refer to illustrations 10.4 and 10.9

Removal

1 Disconnect the negative cable from the battery and remove the drivebelts (see Chapter 1).
2 Remove the four bolts that secure the drivebelt pulley to the crankshaft damper.
3 Remove the bolt and washer attaching the crankshaft damper to the crankshaft.
4 Remove the crankshaft damper with a bolt-type puller (Ford T58P-6316-D and T82L-6316-B or equivalent) **(see illustration)**. **Caution:** *Don't use a gear puller as it will damage the damper. Use a puller with bolts that thread into the hub. These are commonly available from auto parts stores*
5 Carefully pry out the old seal with a screwdriver or seal puller.

Installation

6 Clean and inspect the seal bore and crankshaft surfaces for damage, nicks, burrs or other roughness which may cause a new seal to fail. Correct as necessary.
7 Lubricate the new seal lip with moly-base grease and the outside edge of the seal with engine oil and install it with the special tools (Ford T82L-6316-A T70P-6B070-A) or equivalents.
8 If special tools are unavailable, carefully tap the seal into place using a large socket and a hammer.

9 Apply RTV sealant to the keyway in the damper, lubricate the outside of the damper hub with engine oil and position the damper on the crankshaft. Be sure the keyway is aligned with the crankshaft key. Install the damper using an installation tool (Ford T82L-6316-A) or equivalent **(see illustration)**. If unavailable, start the damper on with a soft-faced hammer and finish installation using the damper retaining bolt. Tighten the bolt to the torque listed in this Chapter's Specifications.
10 Reinstall the remaining parts in the reverse order of removal.
11 Run the engine and check for oil leaks.

11 Timing chain cover – removal and installation

Refer to illustrations 11.16, 11.17 and 11.18

Removal

1 Disconnect the negative cable from the battery.
2 Drain the oil and coolant and remove the drivebelts (see Chapter 1).
3 Remove the fan and water pump (see Chapter 3).
4 Remove the alternator belt tension adjusting bracket. Remove the stud that secures the alternator brace to the throttle body.
5 Remove the air cleaner hot air duct.
6 Remove the upper nuts from the motor mount insulators.
7 Models with air conditioning and automatic transmission: Remove the upper compressor mounting bolts and front cover front nuts.
8 Remove the distributor (see Chapter 5). **Caution:** *Be sure to remove the distributor or it will be broken when the engine is raised.*
9 Jack up the vehicle and position it securely on jackstands.
10 Models with air conditioning and automatic transmission: Remove the air conditioning compressor lower mounting bolts and tie the compressor out of the way. DO NOT disconnect any refrigerant lines! Once the compressor is secured, remove the compressor bracket.
11 Remove the crankshaft damper (see Section 10).
12 Remove the oil pan (see Section 14).
13 Remove the jackstands and lower the vehicle.
14 Remove the radiator bottom hose (see Chapter 3).
15 If necessary, remove the water pump (see Chapter 3). **Note:** *Water pump removal isn't normally necessary to remove the timing chain cover.*
16 Remove the ten timing cover attaching bolts **(see illustration)**. Bolts one through ten secure the timing cover; bolts 11 through 15 secure the water pump. **Note:** *The bolts are different lengths. Label them as they are removed so they can be reinstalled in the correct holes.*

FRONT COVER, WATER PUMP — FASTENER CHART

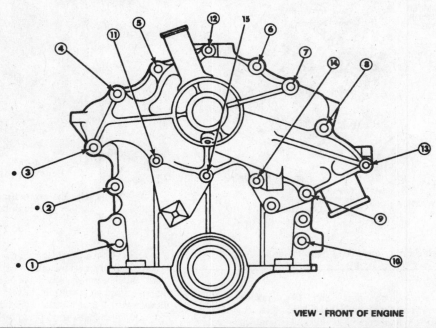

VIEW - FRONT OF ENGINE

Fastener and Hole No.	Fasteners			
	Part No.	Size	N•m	Ft-Lb
● 1	N804215	M8 x 1.25 x 72.25	25	19
● 2	N804215	M8 x 1.25 x 72.25	25	19
● 3	N606547-S8	M8 x 1.25 x 70.0	25	19
4	N606547-S8	M8 x 1.25 x 70.0	25	19
5	N605909-S8	M8 x 1.25 x 42.0	25	19
6	N804154-S8	M8 x 1.25 x 99.3	25	19
7	N606547-S8	M8 x 1.25 x 70.0	25	19
8	N606547-S8	M8 x 1.25 x 70.0	25	19
9	N606547-S8	M8 x 1.25 x 70.0	25	19
10	N605909-S8	M8 x 1.25 x 42.0	25	19
11	N804168-S8	M6 x 1.0 x 25.0	10	7
12	N804168-S8	M6 x 1.0 x 25.0	10	7
13	N804168-S8	M6 x 1.0 x 25.0	10	7
14	N804168-S8	M6 x 1.0 x 25.0	10	7
15	N804168-S8	M6 x 1.0 x 25.0	10	7

NOTE: ●Apply Pipe Sealant with Teflon D8AZ-19554-A (ESG-M4G194-A) Sealer to Fastener Threads

CA10182-E

11.16　The timing chain cover and water pump bolts – note that the bolts are different diameters and lengths – bolts one through ten secure the timing chain cover; bolts 11 through 15 secure the water pump

1*	M8x1.25x72.25	6	M8x1.25x99.3	11	M6x1.0x25.0
2*	M8x1.25x72.25	7	M8x1.25x70.0	12	M6x1.0x25.0
3*	M8x1.25x70.0	8	M8x1.25x70.0	13	M6x1.0x25.0
4	M8x1.25x70.0	9	M8x1.25x70.0	14	M6x1.0x25.0
5	M8x1.25x42.0	10	M8x1.25x42.0	15	M6x1.0x25.0

Apply pipe sealant (Ford part no. D6AZ-19558-A or equivalent) to the threads of these three bolts

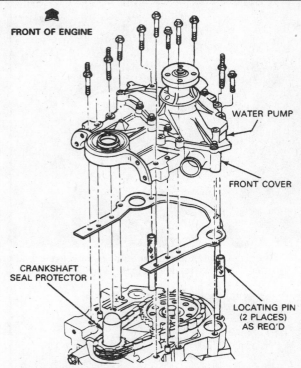

FRONT OF ENGINE

WATER PUMP

FRONT COVER

CRANKSHAFT
SEAL PROTECTOR

LOCATING PIN
(2 PLACES)
AS REQ'D

11.17   The timing chain cover and gasket – exploded view

17   Tap the cover loose with a soft-face hammer or carefully pry it loose with a flat-bladed screwdriver and remove it from the engine **(see illustration)**. **Caution:** *Do not use excessive force or you may crack the cover. If the cover is difficult to remove, recheck for remaining bolts. Also, don't pry between the gasket surfaces or they will be damaged, resulting in leaks.*
18   Thoroughly clean and inspect all parts and remove all traces of gasket material **(see illustration)**. Remove oil film with a solvent such as lacquer thinner or acetone.

Installation
19   Install the new gasket on the engine over the dowels. Use contact adhesive (Ford D7AZ-19B508-A or equivalent) to hold it in place. Position the cover on the engine.
20   Apply pipe sealant (Ford D6AZ-19558-A or equivalent) to the threads of bolts one, two and three **(see illustration 11.16)**. Install all bolts and tighten them evenly to the torque listed in this Chapter's Specifications.
21   Reinstall the remaining parts in the reverse order of removal.
22   Add oil and coolant as needed, run the engine and check for leaks.

---

12   Timing chain and sprockets – check, removal and installation

Refer to illustrations 12.4, 12.7, 12.11, 12.12, 12.15 and 12.18

Check
Note: *Timing chain deflection increases due to wear. If deflection becomes excessive, the timing chain and sprockets must be replaced. The following check is a method of measuring wear without disassembling the engine.*
1   Disconnect the negative cable from the battery.
2   Remove the left (driver's side) rocker arm cover (see Section 4).
3   Loosen the number five (center) cylinder exhaust rocker arm bolt. This is the fourth rocker arm from the drivebelt end of the engine. Rotate the rocker arm aside.

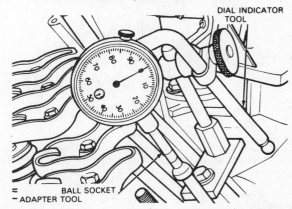

11.18   Scrape away all gasket material, then clean the mating surfaces with lacquer thinner or acetone

DIAL INDICATOR
TOOL

BALL SOCKET
ADAPTER TOOL

12.4   Mount a dial indicator on the pushrod to check valve lifter movement

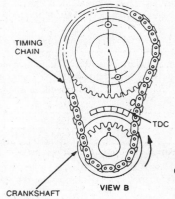

TIMING
CHAIN

TDC

CRANKSHAFT

VIEW B

12.7   Turn the crankshaft counterclockwise until the dial indicator registers movement

---

4   Install a dial indicator on the end of the pushrod **(see illustration)**.
5   Turn the crankshaft clockwise until the number one piston is at TDC on the compression stroke (see Section 3). This will take up the slack on the right side of the chain.
6   Zero the dial indicator.
7   Slowly turn the crankshaft counterclockwise until the first movement is seen on the dial indicator **(see illustration)**. Stop and observe the timing marks to determine the number of degrees from TDC.
8   If the reading exceeds six-degrees, replace the timing chain and sprockets.

2C

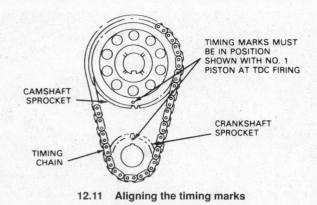

12.11   Aligning the timing marks

12.15   The crankshaft sprocket should have the keyway at the top (12 o'clock)

12.12   An exploded view of the timing chain components

Removal

9   Position the number one piston at Top Dead Center (see Section 3).
10   Remove the timing chain cover (see Section 11). Do not turn the crankshaft during damper removal.
11   Check that the upper and lower timing chain sprocket marks are aligned (**see illustration**). If they are not, temporarily install the crankshaft damper bolt and use it to turn the crankshaft clockwise until the two marks are adjacent to each other.
12   Remove the camshaft sprocket retaining bolt and washer (**see illustration**).
13   Pull the camshaft sprocket away from the engine and move it down slightly to release the chain from the crankshaft sprocket.
14   If the crankshaft sprocket won't come off by hand, carefully pry it off with two screwdrivers.

Installation

15   Reinstall the crankshaft sprocket (**see illustration**), making sure the keyway and timing mark are at the top (12 o'clock position).
16   If the sprocket is difficult to install, slip a length of pipe over the crankshaft and tap the sprocket into place with a small hammer. Make sure the key does not slip out of place.
17   Place the chain around the camshaft sprocket with the timing mark facing down (six o'clock position). Slip the chain over the crankshaft sprocket and position the camshaft sprocket on the camshaft. Tighten the bolt to the torque listed in this Chapter's Specifications.
18   At this point, the timing marks should be adjacent (camshaft sprocket mark at six o'clock and crankshaft sprocket mark at 12 o'clock) (**see illustration**). **Caution:** *Severe engine damage could result from improper timing. Rotate the engine very slowly clockwise, through two revolutions, using a wrench on the crankshaft bolt. If anything hits, do not force the engine to turn; back up and recheck the timing procedure.*
19   Reinstall the remaining parts in the reverse order of removal.
20   Add coolant and oil as needed, run the engine and check for leaks.

12.18   The timing marks (arrows) should be directly across from each other

13   Valve lifters – removal, inspection and installation

Refer to illustrations 13.3a, 13.3b, 13.4a, 13.4b, 13.6a, 13.6b, 13.6c and 13.6d

1   Remove the rocker arms and pushrods (see Section 5).
2   Remove the intake manifold (see Section 7). On engines equipped with roller lifters, unbolt the lifter guide plate retainer and lift off the guide plates.
3   There are several ways to extract the lifters from the bores. Special tools designed to grip and remove lifters (Ford T70L-6500-A or equivalent) are manufactured by several tool companies and are widely available (**see illustration**), but may not be needed in every case. On newer engines without a lot of varnish buildup, the lifters can often be removed with a small magnet (**see illustration**) or even with your fingers. A machinist's scribe with a bent end can be used to pull the lifters out by positioning the point under the retainer ring in the top of each lifter. **Caution:** *Do not use pliers to remove the lifters unless you intend to replace them with new ones (along with the camshaft). The pliers may damage the precision machined and hardened lifters, rendering them useless. On engines with considerable gum and varnish, work the lifters up and down, using carburetor cleaner spray to loosen the deposits.*
4   Before removing the lifters, arrange to store them in a clearly labelled box to ensure that they are reinstalled in their original locations. Remove the lifters and store them where they will not get dirty (**see illustrations**).

13.3a Stuck lifters can be removed with a special tool

13.3b You may be able to remove the lifters with a magnet

13.4a Be sure to store the lifters in an organized manner so they can be reinstalled in their original locations

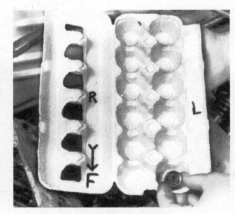

13.4b Old egg cartons work well for lifter storage

13.6a The foot of each lifter should be slightly convex – the side of another lifter can be used as a straightedge to check it; if it appears flat, it is worn and must not be reused (non-roller lifters only)

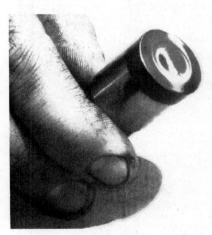

13.6b If the bottom of any lifter is concave, scratched or galled, replace the entire set with new lifters (non-roller lifters only)

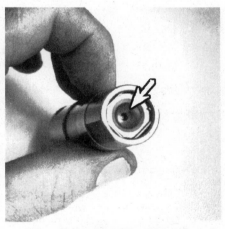

13.6c Check the pushrod seat (arrow) in the top of each lifter for wear

13.6d The roller on roller lifters must turn freely – check for wear and excessive play as well

Note: *If the engine is equipped with roller lifters, mark the front of each lifter (if it's not already marked) so it can be reinstalled in the same orientation (the roller must turn in the same direction).*

5   Clean the lifters with solvent and dry them thoroughly while still keeping them in order.

6   Check each lifter wall, pushrod seat and foot for scuffing, score marks and uneven wear. Each lifter foot (the surface that rides on the cam lobe) must be slightly convex, although this can be difficult to determine by eye. If the base of the lifter is concave **(see illustrations)**, the lifters and camshaft must be replaced. If the lifter walls are damaged or worn (which is not very likely), inspect the lifter bores in the engine block as well. If the pushrod seats **(see illustration)** are worn, check the pushrod ends. If the engine is equipped with roller lifters, make sure the rollers turn smoothly **(see illustration)**

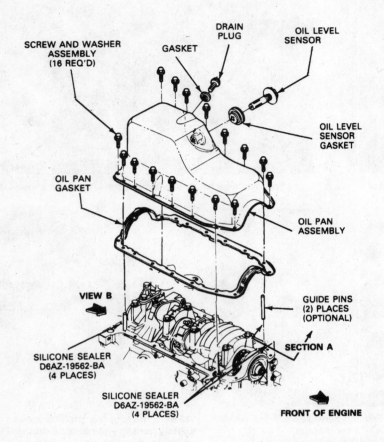

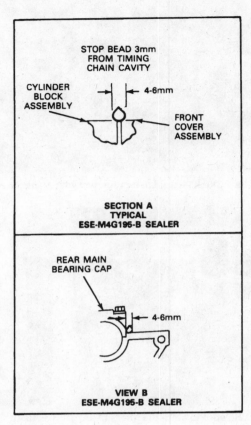

14.11   Oil pan mounting details

7   If new lifters are being installed, a new camshaft must also be installed. If a new camshaft is installed, then use new lifters as well. Never install used lifters unless the original camshaft is used and the lifters can be installed in their original locations.

8   Installation is the reverse of removal. Coat each lifter foot and pushrod seat with engine assembly lube.

14   Oil pan – removal and installation

Removal

Refer to illustration 14.11

1   Disconnect the negative cable from the battery.
2   Remove the oil dipstick.
3   Unbolt the fan shroud and lay it over the fan (see Chapter 3).
4   Remove the distributor (see Chapter 5).
5   Detach the motor mounts from the frame.
6   Raise the vehicle and support it securely on jackstands. Drain the oil and replace the oil filter (see Chapter 1).
7   Remove the retainer clip from the oil pan sensor and unplug the electrical connector from the sensor.
8   Remove the starter motor (see Chapter 5).
9   Remove the inspection cover from the front of the transmission.
10   On 2WD models, Remove the passenger's side axle beam (see Chapter 10). **Caution:** *Be sure to remove the brake caliper and tie it up out of the way.*
11   Unbolt the oil pan **(see illustration)**.
12   Use a hoist to raise the engine approximately two inches.
13   Detach the oil pan from the engine. If the pan is difficult to break loose, tap on it with a rubber mallet. **Caution:** *The oil pan is a tight fit between the*

transmission spacer plate and the oil pump pickup tube. Be careful not to damage the pickup tube when you remove the pan.

Installation

14   Remove all traces of old gasket material from the mating surfaces and clean the oil pan with solvent. Clean the block and pan mating surfaces with acetone or lacquer thinner to remove any traces of oil.

15   Install a new gasket on the oil pan **(see illustration 14.11)**, using contact adhesive (Ford D6AZ-19562-BA or equivalent).

16   Apply a 1/4-inch bead of RTV sealant (Ford D6AZ-19562-A or equivalent) to the junctions of the block and rear main bearing cap and also the junction points of the timing chain cover and block, for a total of four places. **Note:** *Follow the gasket manufacturer's instructions. Don't allow the sealant to dry before installing the pan.*

17   Position the oil pan on the engine block and install the bolts, tightening them to the torque listed in this Chapter's Specifications.

18   Reinstall the remaining parts in the reverse order of removal.

19   Add coolant and oil. Run the engine and check for oil and coolant leaks.

15   Oil pump and pickup – removal and installation

Refer to illustration 15.2

Removal

1   Remove the oil pan (see Section 14).
2   Remove the oil pump mounting bolt **(see illustration)**.
3   Lower the oil pump assembly and intermediate shaft from the block.

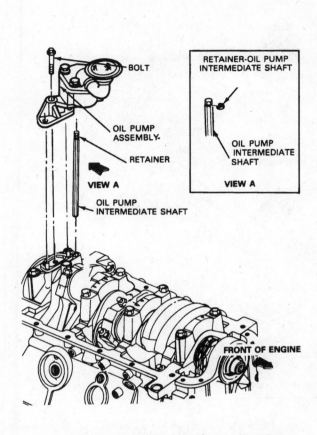

15.2   Oil pump mounting details – exploded view

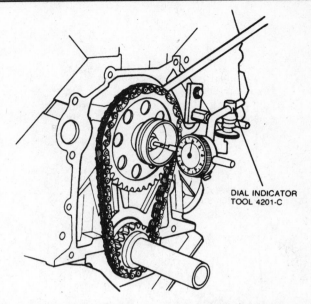

16.10   Check camshaft endplay with a dial indicator contacting the sprocket bolt

Installation

4   Prime the pump by pouring oil into the oil pickup and turning the pump shaft by hand.

5   Fit the oil pump intermediate shaft into the pump, taking care that the shaft seats completely in the pump. Do not try to force it. If it does not align, turn the pump slightly and try again.

6   Install the oil pump assembly, taking care to position the locating dowel and tighten the bolt to the torque listed in this Chapter's Specifications.

7   Reinstall the oil pan (see Section 14), add oil and a new filter. Run the engine and check for leaks.

---

16   Camshaft – removal and installation

Removal

Refer to illustrations 16.10 and 16.14

1   Disconnect the negative cable from the battery.

2   Remove the hoses that connect the air cleaner to the throttle body and rocker arm cover.

3   Drain the cooling system (see Chapter 1).

4   Remove the radiator, fan and air conditioning condenser (if equipped) (see Chapter 3).

5   Remove the distributor (see Chapter 5).

6   Remove the rocker arm covers (see Section 4).

7   Remove the rocker arms and pushrods (see Section 5).

8   Remove the intake manifold (see Section 7).

9   Remove the timing chain cover (see Section 11).

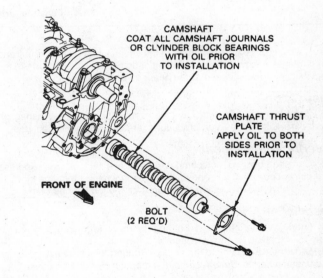

16.14   Camshaft installation details

10   Check camshaft endplay as follows:

   a)   Push the camshaft toward the rear of the engine.

   b)   Set up a dial indicator with its tip contacting the camshaft sprocket bolt **(see illustration)**. Set the dial indicator to zero.

   c)   Pry the camshaft forward and note the reading on the dial indicator. If it exceeds the maximum listed in this Chapter's Specifications, replace the thrust plate and inspect the thrust surface on the camshaft for wear, replacing the camshaft if it's worn excessively.

11   Remove the timing chain and camshaft sprocket (see Section 12).

12   Remove the starter (see Chapter 5).

13   Remove the oil pan (see Section 14).

14   Remove the camshaft thrust plate bolts **(see illustration)**.

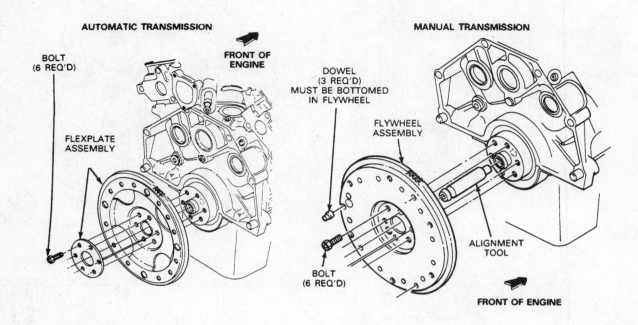

18.4   Flywheel/driveplate mounting details

15   Carefully pull the camshaft out of the engine, rotating as you pull and supporting it with two hands, one positioned near the block. Don't let the camshaft nick the surfaces of the bearings as it's removed.

Inspection

16   Refer to Part A, Section 7, for the camshaft and bearing inspection procedure. Lifter inspection procedures are covered in Section 13.

Bearing replacement

17   Camshaft bearing replacement requires special tools and expertise that place it outside the scope of the home mechanic. Take the block to an automotive machine shop to ensure that the job is done correctly.

Installation

18   Lubricate the camshaft bearing journals and cam lobes with moly-base grease or engine assembly lube.
19   Slide the camshaft into the engine. Support the cam near the block and use two hands. Be careful not to scrape or nick the bearings.
20   Coat both sides of the thrust plate with assembly lube or SAE 50 engine oil, then install it. Tighten its bolts to the torque listed in this Chapter's Specifications.
21   The remainder of installation is the reverse of the removal steps.

17   Engine mounts – check and replacement

1   Engine mounts seldom require attention, but broken or deteriorated mounts should be replaced immediately or the added strain placed on the driveline components may cause damage or wear.

Check

2   During the check, the engine must be raised slightly to remove the weight from the mounts.
3   Raise the vehicle and support it securely on jackstands, then posi-

tion a jack under the engine oil pan. Place a large block of wood between the jack head and the oil pan, then carefully raise the engine just enough to take the weight off the mounts. **Warning:** *DO NOT place any part of your body under the engine when it's supported only by a jack!*
4   Check the mounts to see if the rubber is cracked, hardened or separated from the metal plates. Sometimes the rubber will split right down the center.
5   Check for relative movement between the mount plates and the engine or frame (use a large screwdriver or prybar to attempt to move the mounts). If movement is noted, lower the engine and tighten the mount fasteners.
6   Rubber preservative should be applied to the mounts to slow deterioration.

Replacement

7   Disconnect the negative battery cable from the battery, then raise the vehicle and support it securely on jackstands (if not already done).
8   Remove the fasteners and detach the mount from the frame bracket.
9   Raise the engine slightly with a jack or hoist (make sure the fan doesn't hit the radiator or shroud). Remove the mount-to-block nuts/bolts and detach the mount.
10   Installation is the reverse of removal. Use thread locking compound on the mount bolts and be sure to tighten them securely.

18   Flywheel/driveplate – removal and installation

Refer to illustration 18.4

1   Raise the vehicle and support it securely on jackstands, then refer to Chapter 7 and remove the transmission. If it's leaking, now would be a very good time to replace the front pump seal/O-ring (automatic transmission only).
2   Remove the pressure plate and clutch disc (see Chapter 8 – manual transmission equipped vehicles). Now is a good time to check/replace the clutch components and pilot bearing.

19.3   Do not scratch the crankshaft when punching a hole in
the seal

19.5   You may be able to gently pry the seal out, but don't
scratch the sealing surfaces

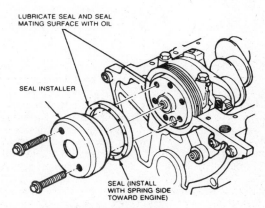

LUBRICATE SEAL AND SEAL
MATING SURFACE WITH OIL

SEAL INSTALLER

SEAL (INSTALL
WITH SPRING SIDE
TOWARD ENGINE)

NOTE: REAR FACE OF SEAL MUST BE WITHIN
0.127mm (0.005-INCH) OF THE REAR FACE OF THE BLOCK

19.7   A special Ford tool is used to install the seal

19.8   If the special tool isn't available, tap around the seal, slowly
working it into position

3   Use a center-punch to make alignment marks on the flywheel/drive-plate and crankshaft to ensure correct alignment during reinstallation.
4   Remove the bolts that secure the flywheel/driveplate to the crankshaft **(see illustration)**. If the crankshaft turns, wedge a screwdriver through the starter opening to jam the flywheel.
5   Remove the flywheel/driveplate from the crankshaft. Since the flywheel is fairly heavy, be sure to support it while removing the last bolt.
6   Clean the flywheel to remove grease and oil. Inspect the surface for cracks, rivet grooves, burned areas and score marks. Light scoring can be removed with emery cloth. Check for cracked and broken ring gear teeth. Lay the flywheel on a flat surface and use a straightedge to check for warpage.
7   Clean and inspect the mating surfaces of the flywheel/driveplate and the crankshaft. If the crankshaft rear oil seal is leaking, replace it before reinstalling the flywheel/driveplate (see Section 19).
8   Position the flywheel/driveplate against the crankshaft. Be sure to align the marks made during removal. Note that some engines have an alignment dowel or staggered bolt holes to ensure correct installation. Before installing the bolts, apply thread locking compound to the

threads. **Note**: *The flywheel is balanced separately from the engine. Don't use balance weights on a new flywheel.*
9   Wedge a screwdriver through the starter motor opening to keep the flywheel/driveplate from turning as you tighten the bolts to the torque listed in this Chapter's Specifications.
10   The remainder of installation is the reverse of the removal procedure.

19   Crankshaft rear oil seal – replacement

Refer to illustrations 19.3, 19.5, 19.7 and 19.8
1   Remove the transmission (see Chapter 7).
2   Remove the flywheel/driveplate (see Section 18).
3   Using a sharp awl, carefully punch one hole into the seal between the lip and the engine block **(see illustration)**.
4   Screw in the threaded end of Ford tool T77L-9533-B or equivalent. Use the tool to remove the seal.
5   If the special tool is unavailable, you may be able to pry the seal out with a screwdriver **(see illustration)**.

6   Thoroughly clean the seal bore and crankshaft sealing surface and lubricate the new seal with engine oil.

7   Place the new seal on Ford installer tool T82L-6701-A **(see illustration)** or equivalent. Position the tool and seal on the crankshaft. Alternate bolt tightening to properly seat the seal. **Note:** *Flywheel/driveplate bolts may be used if necessary.*

8   If the special tool is not available, carefully work the seal lip over the end of the crankshaft and tap the seal in with a hammer and blunt drift until it's properly seated in the bore **(see illustration)**. **Note:** *The rear face of this seal must be flush with the rear face of the block.*

9   Reinstall the remaining components in the reverse order of removal.

10   Start the engine and check for oil leaks.

Chapter 2 Part D 4.0L V6 engine

Contents

Specifications

General

Displacement . . . . 4.0 liters
Cylinder numbers (front-to-rear)
    Left (driver's) side 4–5–6
    Right side 1–2–3
Firing order 1-4-2-5-3-6

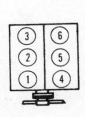
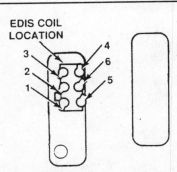

EDIS COIL
LOCATION

FIRING ORDER — 1-4-2-5-3-6
4.0L ENGINE

Front

Cylinder location and distributor rotation

Camshaft

Lobe lift (intake and exhaust)	0.2756 inch
Allowable lobe lift loss	0.005 inch
Endplay	
Standard	0.0008 to 0.004 inch
Service limit	0.009 inch
Thrust plate thickness	0.158 to 0.159 inch
Journal-to-bearing (oil) clearance	
Standard	0.001 to 0.0026 inch
Service limit	0.006 inch
Bearing inside diameter	
No. 1	1.954 to 1.955 inch
No. 2	1.939 to 1.940 inch
No. 3	1.919 to 1.920 inch
No. 4	1.924 to 1.925 inch
Runout, maximum (total indicator reading)	0.005 inch
Out-of-round, maximum (total indicator reading)	0.0003 inch
Journal diameter	
No. 1	1.951 to 1.952 inch
No. 2	1.937 to 1.938 inch
No. 3	1.922 to 1.923 inch
No. 4	1.907 to 1.908 inch
Front bearing location	0.040 to 0.060 inch below face of block

Oil pan-to-transmission spacer thicknesses

Coded yellow	0.010 inch
Coded blue	0.020 inch
Coded pink	0.030 inch

Crankshaft rear seal

Dimension from rear face of block	0.413 +0.008 -0.012 inch
Square to crankshaft centerline within	0.015 inch

Torque specifications

	Ft-lbs (unless otherwise indicated)
Camshaft sprocket bolt	44 to 50
Camshaft thrust plate bolts	84 to 120 in-lbs
Crankshaft pulley bolt	
Step 1	30 to 37
Step 2	Turn an additional 80- to 90-degrees
Cylinder head bolts	
Step 1	44
Step 2	Tighten intake manifold to 36 to 72 in-lbs
Step 3	59
Step 4	Tighten intake manifold to 72 to 132 in-lbs
Step 5	Turn an additional 80- to 85-degrees
Flywheel/driveplate bolts	59
Engine mount insulator-to-frame nuts	71 to 94
Exhaust manifold bolts	19
Exhaust pipe-to-manifold nuts	20
Timing chain cover bolts	13 to 15
Intake manifold bolts/nuts	
Step 1	36 to 72 in-lbs
Step 2	72 to 132 in-lbs
Step 3	132 to 180 in-lbs
Step 4	180 to 216 in-lbs*
Intake manifold studs to block	72 to 84 in-lbs
Oil pump pick-up tube to pump bolts	84 to 120 in-lbs
Oil pump-to-block bolts	156 to 180 in-lbs
Oil pan-to-block bolts	60 to 84 in-lbs
Valve cover bolts	
Step 1	36 to 60 in-lbs
Step 2	Wait 2 minutes
Step 3	Retighten to 36 to 60 in-lbs
Rocker arm shaft support bolts	
Step 1	24
Step 2	Tighten an additional 90-degrees

*Retighten in sequence to 180 to 216 in-lbs after the engine has been run.

1   General information

This Part of Chapter 2 is devoted to in-vehicle repair procedures for the 4.0L V6 engine, as well as procedures such as timing chain and sprocket and oil pan removal which require removal of the engine from the vehicle. All information concerning engine removal and installation and engine block and cylinder head overhaul can be found in Part E of this Chapter.

Most of the following repair procedures are based on the assumption that the engine is installed in the vehicle. If the engine has been removed from the vehicle and mounted on a stand, many of the steps outlined in this Part of Chapter 2 will not apply.

The Specifications included in this Part of Chapter 2 apply only to the procedures contained in this Part. Part E of Chapter 2 contains the Specifications necessary for cylinder head and engine block rebuilding.

2   Repair operations possible with the engine in the vehicle

Many major repair operations can be accomplished without removing the engine from the vehicle.

Clean the engine compartment and the exterior of the engine with some type of degreaser before any work is done. It will make the job easier and help keep dirt out of the internal areas of the engine.

Depending on the components involved, it may be helpful to remove the hood to improve access to the engine as repairs are performed (refer to Chapter 11 if necessary). Cover the fenders to prevent damage to the paint. Special pads are available, but an old bedspread or blanket will also work.

If vacuum, exhaust, oil or coolant leaks develop, indicating a need for gasket or seal replacement, the repairs can generally be made with the engine in the vehicle. The intake and exhaust manifold gaskets, timing cover gasket, crankshaft oil seals and cylinder head gasket are all accessible with the engine in place.

Exterior engine components, such as the intake and exhaust manifolds, the water pump, the starter motor, the alternator, the distributor and the fuel system components can be removed for repair with the engine in place. **Note:** *Removing the oil pan on a 4.0L engine requires removing the engine from the vehicle.*

Since the cylinder head can be removed without pulling the engine, valve component servicing can also be accomplished with the engine in the vehicle. Replacement of the timing chain and sprockets requires removal of the oil pan, so is not possible with the engine in the vehicle.

3   Top Dead Center (TDC) for number one piston – locating

Refer to illustration 3.5

Note: *The 4.0L engine is not equipped with a distributor. Piston position must be determined by feeling for compression at the number one spark plug hole as the crankshaft is rotated, then aligning the ignition timing marks as described in Step 5.*

1   Top Dead Center (TDC) is the highest point in the cylinder that each piston reaches as it travels up-and-down when the crankshaft turns. Each piston reaches TDC on the compression stroke and again on the exhaust stroke, but TDC generally refers to piston position on the compression stroke.

2   Positioning the piston(s) at TDC is an essential part of many procedures such as rocker arm removal, camshaft and timing chain/sprocket removal and distributor removal.

3   Before beginning this procedure, be sure to place the transmission in Neutral and apply the parking brake or block the rear wheels. Also, disable the ignition system by detaching the electrical connector from the coil pack above the left valve cover. Remove the spark plugs (see Chapter 1).

4   In order to bring any piston to TDC, the crankshaft must be turned in the normal direction of rotation using one of the methods outlined below.

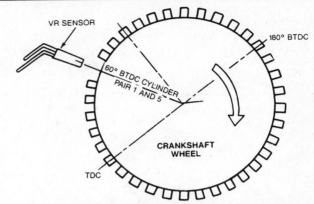

3.5   The crankshaft pulley has a gap at 60-degrees BTDC – TDC is located at the sixth tooth from the gap

When looking at the front of the engine, normal crankshaft rotation is clockwise.

   a) The preferred method is to turn the crankshaft with a socket and ratchet attached to the bolt threaded into the front of the crankshaft.

   b) A remote starter switch, which may save some time, can also be used. Follow the instructions included with the switch. Once the piston is close to TDC, use a socket and ratchet as described in the previous paragraph.

   c) If an assistant is available to turn the ignition switch to the Start position in short bursts, you can get the piston close to TDC without a remote starter switch. Make sure your assistant is out of the vehicle, away from the ignition switch, then use a socket and ratchet as described in Paragraph a) to complete the procedure.

5   The crankshaft pulley has 35 teeth, evenly spaced every 10-degrees around the pulley, and a gap where a 36th tooth would be. The gap is located at 60-degrees Before Top Dead Center (BTDC) **(see illustration)**. Turn the crankshaft (see Paragraph 4 above) until you feel compression at the number one spark plug hole, then turn it slowly until the sixth tooth after the missing tooth is aligned with the pointer on the variable reluctance sensor (located at the front of the engine).

6   After the number one piston has been positioned at TDC on the compression stroke, TDC for any of the remaining pistons can be located by turning the crankshaft and following the firing order.

4   Valve covers – removal and installation

Refer to illustration 4.13

Removal

1   Disconnect the negative cable from the battery. On 1992 and later models, remove the intake shield and air intake tube.

2   Disconnect the spark plug wires (see Chapter 1) and lay them aside.

3   If necessary, disconnect the fuel supply and return lines to provide removal access for the valve covers (see Chapter 4). **Warning:** *relieve fuel system pressure as described in Chapter 4 before disconnecting any fuel lines!*

Left valve cover

4   If necessary, remove the upper intake manifold to provide removal access for the valve cover (see Chapter 4). On 1992 and later models, remove the bolt from the air conditioning pipe over the upper intake manifold. Also remove the electrical connectors from the air conditioning compressor. Remove the compressor without disconnecting the lines and place it out of the way. (see Chapter 3)

Right valve cover

5   Remove the air cleaner inlet duct.

6   Disconnect the hose from the oil filler tube.

7   Remove the alternator (see Chapter 5).

8   Drain the cooling system and detach the radiator top hose from the engine (see Chapters 1 and 3).

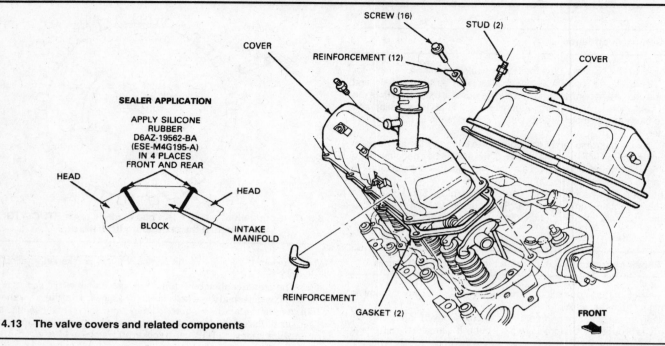

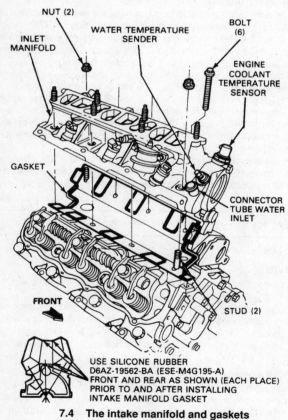

4.13   The valve covers and related components

7.4   The intake manifold and gaskets

um hose and disconnect the other five hoses from the vacuum tee on the plenum. Tag the hoses to aid installation.

13   Note the positions of the reinforcement pieces at the valve cover bolts, then remove the bolts (**see illustration**).

14   Lift the valve cover(s) off. If it's stuck, tap it lightly with a soft face mallet to break the gasket seal. Don't pry the cover off or the gasket surfaces will be distorted, causing a leak.

Installation

15   Using a gasket scraper, remove all all traces of gasket material from the valve cover and its mating surface on the cylinder head. Clean the surfaces with a solvent such as lacquer thinner or acetone.

16   Apply a dab of silicone sealer (Ford specification ESE-M4G195-A or equivalent) to the joints where the intake manifold meets the cylinder head.

17   Install the valve covers, using new gaskets. Install the valve cover bolts (be sure the reinforcing pieces are returned to their original locations). **Caution:** *Don't tighten the valve cover bolts without the reinforcing pieces in place, or the valve cover will be distorted, causing a leak.*

18   The remainder of installation is the reverse of the removal steps.

19   Run the engine and check for oil or fuel leaks.

---

5   Rocker arms and pushrods – removal, inspection, installation and adjustment

---

Refer to Chapter 2, Part B for this procedure. Follow the steps that apply to the 2.9L engine.

---

6   Valve springs, retainers and seals – replacement

Refer to Chapter 2, Part B for this procedure. Follow the steps that apply to the 2.9L engine.

---

7   Intake manifold – removal and installation

Refer to illustrations 7.4 and 7.9

1   Disconnect the negative cable from the battery.
2   Remove the upper intake manifold (see Chapter 4).
3   Remove the valve covers (See Section 4).

9   Remove the ignition coil pack and bracket (see Chapter 5).
10   Remove the low-pressure air conditioning hose bracket from the upper intake manifold. Don't disconnect any refrigerant lines!
11   Detach the vacuum hose from the air cleaner.

Both valve covers

12   Disconnect PCV hoses as needed to provide removal access for the valve cover(s). On 1992 and later models, remove the power brake vacu-

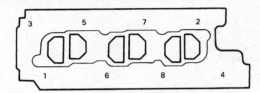

7.9   Intake manifold tightening sequence

4   Remove the intake manifold nuts and bolts and lift the manifold off **(see illustration)**. If it's stuck, tap it lightly with a soft face hammer to break the gasket seal. If necessary, pry the manifold off, but pry between a casting protrusion on the engine – don't pry against gasket surfaces.

5   Using a scraper, clean away all traces of old gasket material. Remove oil and dirt with a cloth and solvent, such as acetone or lacquer thinner.

6   Apply silicone sealant (Ford specification ESE-M4G195-C or equivalent) to the four corners where the manifold meets the engine block **(see illustration 7.4). Note:** *Install the manifold immediately after applying the sealant. If allowed to set up (approximately 15 minutes), the sealant won't work properly.*

7   Install the manifold gasket, then reapply sealant to the four corners.

8   Install the manifold over the studs. Install the nuts and bolts and tighten them finger-tight.

9   Tighten the nuts and bolts in the four stages listed in this Chapter's Specifications, following the sequence **(see illustration)**.

10   The remainder of installation is the reverse of the removal steps.

11   Run the engine and check for oil, coolant and vacuum leaks.

---

8   Exhaust manifolds – removal and installation

Removal

Left manifold

1   Remove the oil dipstick tube bracket from the engine.

2   If the power steering pump hoses obstruct manifold removal, disconnect them (see Chapter 10). Cap the hoses and fittings to keep out dirt and place the hose ends out of the way.

Right manifold

3   Drain the cooling system, detach the heater hose bracket and disconnect the heater hoses (see Chapter 3).

Both manifolds

4   Detach the exhaust pipe from the manifold. Apply some penetrating

oil to the threads of the nuts if they are difficult to remove.

5   Unbolt the manifold from the cylinder head and take it off.

Installation

6   Thoroughly clean the mating surfaces on cylinder head, manifold and exhaust pipe. Remove residue with a solvent such as acetone or lacquer thinner.

7   Place the manifold on the cylinder head. Tighten the bolts evenly, working from the center out, to the torque listed in this Chapter's Specifications.

8   Connect the exhaust pipe to the manifold and tighten the nuts evenly to the torque listed in this Chapter's Specifications.

9   The remainder of installation is the reverse of the removal steps. If the heater hoses were disconnected, fill the cooling system (see Chapter 1).

10   Run the engine and check for exhaust leaks.

---

9   Cylinder heads – removal and installation

Removal

Refer to illustration 9.14

1   Disconnect the negative cable from the battery.

2   Drain the cooling system (see Chapter 3).

3   Remove the valve covers (see Section 4).

4   Remove the rocker arms and pushrods (see Section 5).

5   Remove the intake manifold (see Section 7).

Left head

6   Remove the drivebelt (see Chapter 1).

7   Detach the air conditioning compressor from the engine (see Chapter 3) and place it out of the way. DO NOT disconnect any refrigerant lines!

8   Detach the power steering pump and bracket and set them out of the way (See Chapter 10). Don't disconnect the power steering hoses.

Right head

9   Remove the drivebelt (see Chapter 1).

10   Remove the alternator and bracket (see Chapter 5).

11   Remove the ignition coil pack and bracket (see Chapter 5).

Both heads

12   Remove the spark plugs (see Chapter 1).

13   Remove the exhaust manifolds (see Section 8).

14   Remove and discard the cylinder head bolts **(see illustration)**.

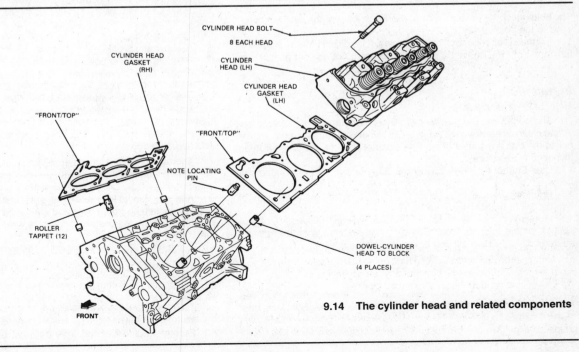

9.14   The cylinder head and related components

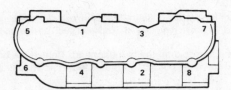

CYLINDER HEAD
BOLT TIGHTENING
SEQUENCE

9.22   Cylinder head tightening sequence

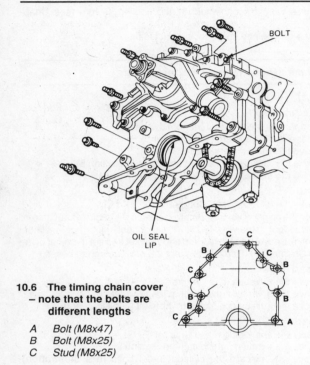

**10.6   The timing chain cover
– note that the bolts are
different lengths**

A   Bolt (M8x47)
B   Bolt (M8x25)
C   Stud (M8x25)

The bolts must be replaced with new ones whenever they are removed. Loosen the bolts in several stages.

15   Lift the cylinder head(s) off the engine. If it's difficult to remove, carefully pry it off. Pry against a casting protrusion, not against gasket surfaces.

Installation

Refer to illustration 9.22

16   Thoroughly remove all traces of gasket material with a gasket scraper and clean all parts with solvent. Use a rag and acetone or lacquer thinner to remove any traces of oil. See Chapter 2 Part E for cylinder head inspection procedures.

17   Use a tap of the correct size to chase the threads in the head bolt holes.

18   Recheck all head bolt holes and cylinder bores for any traces of coolant, oil or other foreign matter. Remove as needed.

19   Position the new gasket over the dowel pins on the block. Don't use sealant on the gaskets. Look closely for any markings on the gasket, such as "UP," that will tell you how to install the gasket.

20   Install new head bolts finger tight.

21   Position the intake manifold on the engine (see Section 7), but don't tighten the bolts yet.

22   Following the sequence shown **(see illustration)**, tighten the head bolts in three steps to the torque listed in this Chapter's Specifications.

Note: *The head bolts and intake manifold bolts are tightened in alternate stages to align the manifold with the heads. Be sure to refer to this Chap-*

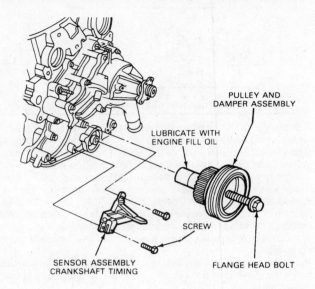

PULLEY AND
DAMPER ASSEMBLY

LUBRICATE WITH
ENGINE FILL OIL

SENSOR ASSEMBLY
CRANKSHAFT TIMING

SCREW

FLANGE HEAD BOLT

10.4   The crankshaft damper and timing sensor

ter's Specifications for the correct tightening stages. After the cylinder head torque steps are complete, follow Steps 3 and 4 for the intake manifold to tighten it fully to Specification.

23   The remainder of installation is the reverse of the removal steps.

24   Run the engine and check for oil, coolant and vacuum leaks.

---

10   Timing chain cover – removal and installation

Refer to illustrations 10.4 and 10.6

Removal

1   Remove the oil pan (see Section 14).

2   If not already done, remove the drivebelt (see Chapter 1).

3   Remove the water pump (see Chapter 3).

4   Remove the crankshaft pulley bolt **(see illustration)**. Remove the crankshaft pulley with a puller (Ford tool T74P-6316-A or equivalent). DO NOT pry the pulley off or use an impact puller!

5   Remove the crankshaft timing sensor.

6   Remove the cover bolts **(see illustration)**. **Note:** *The bolts are different lengths. Label them so they can be installed in the correct holes. Take the cover off. If it's stuck, tap it lightly with a soft-face hammer or pry it carefully to break the gasket seal. Don't use excessive force or you'll crack the cover. If it's difficult to remove, check to make sure you've removed all the bolts.*

Installation

7   Thoroughly clean and inspect all parts and remove all traces of gasket material. Remove oil film with a solvent such as lacquer thinner or acetone.

8   Apply sealant to the mating surfaces. Install the guide sleeves (if removed). Install the front cover and start the bolts two or three turns by hand. Note that the bolts are different lengths; be sure to install them in the correct holes.

9   Tighten the cover bolts evenly to the torque listed in this Chapter's Specifications.

10   Install the crankshaft timing sensor (see Chapter 5).

11   Install the crankshaft pulley with Ford tool T74P-6316-A or equivalent. Don't hammer the pulley on. Tighten the pulley bolt to the torque listed in this Chapter's Specifications.

12   The remainder of installation is the reverse of the removal steps.

13   Run the engine and check for oil or coolant leaks.

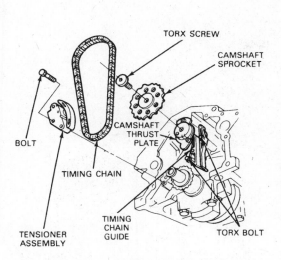

11.7   Timing chain and sprockets – exploded view

11   Timing chain and sprockets – inspection, removal and installation

Inspection
1   Refer to Chapter 2, Part B for this procedure.

Removal
Refer to illustrations 11.7 and 11.10

2   Set the number one cylinder to top dead center on the compression stroke (see Section 3).
3   Drain the cooling system and engine oil. Replace the oil filter (see Chapter 1).
4   Remove the oil pan (see Section 14).
5   Remove the drivebelt, if not already done (Chapter 1).
6   Remove the timing chain cover (see Section 10).
7   Remove the camshaft sprocket screw and the crankshaft sprocket key **(see illustration)**.
8   Remove the sprockets together with the chain.
9   Remove the chain tensioner and, if necessary, chain guide from the block.

Installation
10   Be sure the crankshaft and camshaft are positioned so the sprocket timing marks will align correctly after the sprockets are installed **(see illustration)**.
11   If the chain guide was removed, install it. Be sure its pin is inserted into the block oil hole, then tighten the bolts securely.
12   Place the sprockets in the chain with their timing marks aligned **(see illustration 11.10)**. Install the sprockets and chain together on the crankshaft and camshaft.
13   Use the tensioner clip to lock the tensioner in the retracted position, then install the tensioner.
14   Install the crankshaft key.
15   Make sure the sprocket timing marks are still aligned **(see illustration 11.10)**. The guide side of the chain must be straight, without any slack.
16   Install the camshaft sprocket bolt and tighten it to the torque listed in this Chapter's Specifications.
17   Remove the tensioner clip. The tensioner should take up any slack in the chain.
18   The remainer of installation is the reverse of the removal steps.
19   Run the engine and check for oil or coolant leaks.

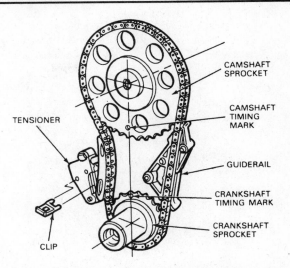

11.10   The timing marks on the camshaft and crankshaft must be directly opposite each other, as shown, after they are installed

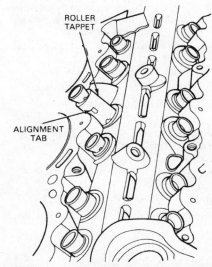

12.1   The alignment tab on each lifter must be positioned in its groove in the lifter bore

12   Valve lifters – removal, inspection and installation

Refer to illustration 12.1
   Refer to Chapter 2, Part C for these procedures. Note that when the lifters are installed, the alignment tab must fit in the groove in the lifter bore **(see illustration)**.

13   Camshaft – removal, inspection and installation

Endplay and lobe lift check
   Refer to Chapter 2, Part B for these procedures, but use the torques and tolerances listed in this Chapter's Specifications.

Removal
Refer to illustrations 13.8 and 13.16
1   Disconnect the negative cable from the battery.
2   Drain the cooling system and engine oil (see Chapter 1).

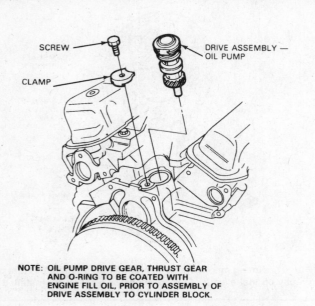

SCREW

CLAMP

DRIVE ASSEMBLY — OIL PUMP

NOTE: OIL PUMP DRIVE GEAR, THRUST GEAR AND O-RING TO BE COATED WITH ENGINE FILL OIL, PRIOR TO ASSEMBLY OF DRIVE ASSEMBLY TO CYLINDER BLOCK.

13.8   The 4.0L engine's oil pump drive is gear-driven by the camshaft and operates the oil pump through an intermediate shaft

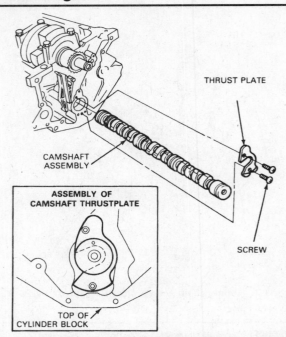

THRUST PLATE

CAMSHAFT ASSEMBLY

SCREW

ASSEMBLY OF CAMSHAFT THRUSTPLATE

TOP OF CYLINDER BLOCK

13.16   The camshaft and related components – the camshaft thrust plate must be installed with the correct side facing up

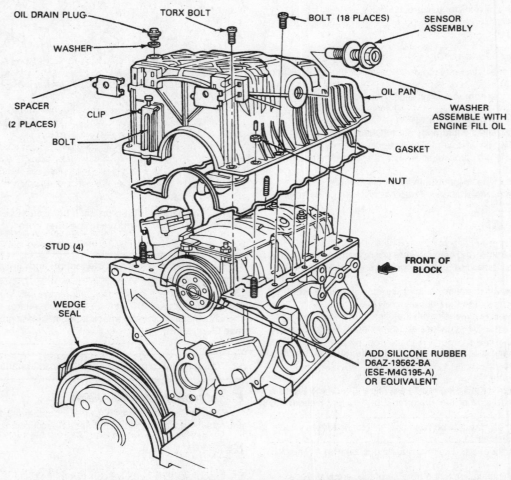

OIL DRAIN PLUG

TORX BOLT

BOLT (18 PLACES)

SENSOR ASSEMBLY

WASHER

SPACER (2 PLACES)

CLIP

BOLT

OIL PAN

WASHER ASSEMBLE WITH ENGINE FILL OIL

GASKET

NUT

STUD (4)

FRONT OF BLOCK

WEDGE SEAL

ADD SILICONE RUBBER D6AZ-19562-BA (ESE-M4G195-A) OR EQUIVALENT

14.2   The oil pan and related components – exploded view

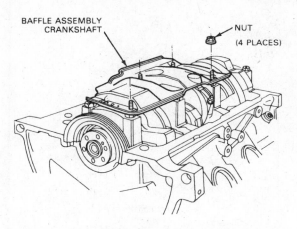

14.3 The oil baffle is secured to the main bearing caps

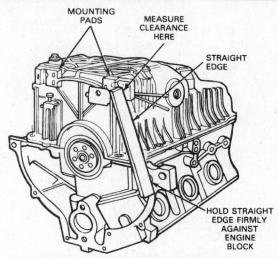

14.5 To select pan-to-transmission spacers, place a straightedge across the transmission mounting surface and each of the pan-to-transmission mounting pads in turn and measure the gap between the straightedge and the mounting pad

3   Remove the radiator and fan (see Chapter 3).
4   Remove the drivebelt (see Chapter 1).
5   Remove the spark plug wires (see Chapter 1).
6   Remove the ignition coil pack and bracket (see Chapter 5).
7   Remove the alternator (see Chapter 5).
8   Remove the oil pump drive gear from the block **(see illustration)**.
9   Remove the intake manifold (see Section 7). The upper intake manifold can be left attached to the lower manifold.
10 Remove the valve covers (see Section 4).
11 Remove the rocker arms and pushrods (see Section 5).
12 Remove the valve lifters (see Section 12).
13 Remove the oil pan (see Section 14).
14 Remove the timing chain cover (see Section 10).
15 Secure the timing chain tensioner in the retracted position with the clip (see Section 11). Align the camshaft sprocket timing marks. Remove the camshaft sprocket bolt, then take off the sprocket together with the chain.
16 Remove the camshaft thrust plate **(see illustration)**.
17 Carefully pull the camshaft out of the block, rotating it as you pull. Support the camshaft with both hands and be careful not let the camshaft lobes or journals nick the camshaft bearings.

Inspection

18 Refer to Chapter 2, Part A, for the camshaft and bearing inspection procedure. Lifter inspection procedures are covered in Part B. Use the Specifications in this Chapter.

Bearing replacement

19 Camshaft bearing replacement requires special tools and expertise that place it outside the scope of the home mechanic. Take the block to an automotive machine shop to ensure that the job is done correctly.

Installation

20 Lubricate the camshaft bearing journals and cam lobes with moly-base grease or engine assembly lube.
21 Slide the camshaft into the engine. Support the camshaft near the block and be careful not to scrape or nick the bearings.
22 Coat both sides of the thrust plate with assembly lube or SAE 50 engine oil, then install it. Tighten its bolts to the torque listed in this Chapter's Specifications.
23 The remainder of installation is the reverse of the removal steps.

---

14   Oil pan – removal and installation

Removal

Refer to illustrations 14.2 and 14.3

1   Remove the engine from the vehicle (see Part E of this Chapter).

2   Remove the oil pan fasteners **(see illustration)** and remove the pan from the engine.
3   If necessary, remove the baffle fasteners and remove the baffle **(see illustration)**.

Installation

Refer to illustration 14.5
Caution: *Since two of the oil pan bolts are attached to the transmission, spacers are used between the oil pan and transmission. Failure to select the spacers correctly can cause oil pan damage or oil leaks when the pan is installed.*

4   Using a gasket scraper, thoroughly clean all old gasket material from the oil pan and its mounting surface. Remove residue and oil film with a solvent such as acetone or lacquer thinner.
5   Place the pan on the engine. Place a straightedge across the transmission mounting surface on the cylinder block and one of the mounting pads for the oil pan-to-transmission bolts **(see illustration)**.
6   Measure the gap between the mounting pad and straightedge with a feeler gauge.
7   Move the straightedge to the other mounting pad and measure its gap.
8   Select spacers for the mounting pads to compensate for the gap. Spacers are available in three thicknesses (see this Chapter's Specifications).
9   Install a new pan gasket on the engine. Install the pan fasteners and tighten them evenly to the torque listed in this Chapter's Specifications.
10 Install the spacers on the mounting pads before bolting the engine to the transmission.
11 The remainder of installation is the reverse of removal.

---

15   Oil pump – removal and installation

Refer to illustration 15.7
1   Remove the oil pan (see Section 14).
2   Remove the oil pump bolts and take the pump off the engine.
3   Pull the oil pump intermediate drive shaft out of the engine.
4   Unbolt the inlet tube and screen from the pump.

Installation

5   Fill one of the pump ports with clean engine oil and rotate the pump by hand to prime it.
6   Install the oil pump inlet tube on the pump, using a new gasket.

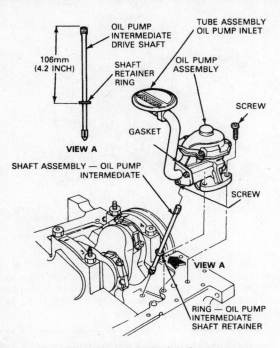

15.7   The oil pump and related components

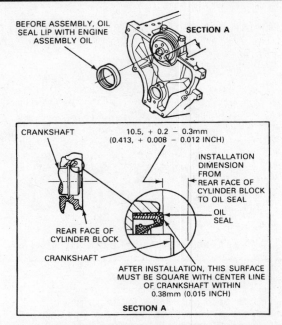

16.3   The crankshaft rear oil seal must be square with the crankshaft centerline and within the specified dimension from the rear face of the cylinder block

7   Insert the intermediate driveshaft into the engine, pointed end first. The pressed-on retaining ring on the shaft should be positioned as shown in the accompanying illustration.

8   Install the oil pump on the block, using a new gasket. Install the oil pump bolts and tighten them to the torque listed in this Chapter's Specifications.

9   The remainder of installation is the reverse of removal.

10   Run the engine and make sure oil pressure comes up to normal quickly. If it doesn't, stop the engine and find out the cause. Severe engine damage can result from running an engine with insufficient oil pressure!

16   Crankshaft oil seals – replacement

Refer to illustration 16.3

1   Refer to Chapter 2, Part B for this procedure. Note the following:

2   If a puller isn't available to remove the timing chain cover seal with

the cover on the engine, use a flat-bladed screwdriver and carefully pry the seal out.

3   After installation, squareness of the rear seal with the crankshaft centerline and the dimension from the seal to the rear face of the block must be within tolerances listed in this Chapter's Specifications (**see illustration**).

17   Flywheel/driveplate – removal and installation

Refer to Chapter 2, Part B for this procedure. Use the tightening torque listed in this Chapter's Specifications.

18   Engine mounts – check and replacement

Refer to Chapter 2, Part B for this procedure. Use the tightening torques listed in this Chapter's Specifications.

Chapter 2 Part E
General engine overhaul procedures

Contents

Specifications

Four-cylinder engines

General

Displacement	2.0 and 2.3 liters
Cylinder compression pressure	101 psi min
Oil pressure (engine warm at 2000 rpm	40 to 60 psi

Cylinder head

Warpage limit	0.003 in per 6 inches; 0.006 in overall

Valves and related components

Minimum valve margin width	1/32 in
Intake valve	
Seat angle	45-degrees
Seat width	0.060 to 0.080 in
Seat runout limit	0.0016 in
Stem diameter	0.3416 to 0.3423 in
Stem-to-guide clearance	0.0010 to 0.0027 in
Valve face runout limit	0.002 in
Valve face angle	44-degrees
Exhaust valve	
Seat angle	45-degrees
Seat width	0.070 to 0.090 in
Seat runout limit	0.0016 in
Stem diameter	0.3411 to 0.3418 in
Stem-to-guide clearance	0.0015 to 0.0032 in
Valve face runout limit	0.002 in
Valve face angle	44-degrees
Valve spring	
Pressure	
1983	
2.0L intake	71 to 79 lbs at 1.52 in
2.0L exhaust	142 to 156 lbs at 1.12 in
2.3L intake	71 to 79 lbs at 1.56 in
2.3L exhaust	159 to 175 lbs at 1.16 in
1984 on (intake and exhaust)	71 to 79 lbs at 1.52 in
Service limit	10% pressure loss at specified length
Free length (approximate)	
1983	
2.0L	1.922 in
2.3L	1.89 in
1984 on	1.877 in
Installed height	
1983	
2.0L	1.49 to 1.55 in
2.3L	1-17/32 to 1-19/32 in
1984 on	1.49 to 1.55 in
Valve lifter	
Diameter (standard)	0.8422 to 0.8427 in
Lifter-to-bore clearance	
Standard	0.0007 to 0.0027 in
Service limit	0.005 in
Collapsed tappet gap at camshaft	
Allowed	0.035 to 0.055 in
Desirable	0.040 to 0.050 in

Crankshaft and connecting rods

Connecting rod journal	
Diameter (standard)	2.0462 to 2.0472 in
Out-of-round limit	0.0006 in
Taper limit	0.0006 in per inch
Bearing oil clearance	
Desired	0.0008 to 0.0015 in
Allowable	0.0008 to 0.0026 in
Connecting rod side clearance (endplay)	
Standard	0.0035 to 0.0105 in
Service limit	0.014 in
Main bearing journal	
Diameter	
1983 through 1990	2.3982 to 2.399 in
1991 on	2.2051 to 2.2059 in
Out-of-round limit	0.0006 in
Taper limit	0.0006 in per inch
Bearing oil clearance	
Desired	0.0008 to 0.0015 in
Allowable	0.0008 to 0.0026 in
Crankshaft endplay	
Standard	0.004 to 0.008 in
Service limit	0.012 in

Cylinder bore

Diameter

2.0L .... 3.5165 to 3.5201 in

2.3L .... 3.7795 to 3.7831 in

Out-of-round limit .... 0.0015 in

Out-of-round service limit .... 0.005 in

Taper service limit .... 0.010 in

Pistons and rings

Piston diameter

2.0L

Coded red .... 3.5150 to 3.5156 in

Coded blue .... 3.5162 to 3.5168 in

0.003 in oversize .... 3.5174 to 3.5180 in

2.3L

1983 through 1990 .... 3.7780 to 3.7786 in

1991 on .... 3.7768 to 3.7779 in

Piston-to-bore clearance

1983 through 1991 .... 0.0014 to 0.0022 in

1991 on .... 0.0024 to 0.0034 in

Piston ring end gap

Compression rings .... 0.015 to 0.023 in

Oil ring rails

1983 through 1986 .... 0.015 to 0.055 in

1987 on .... 0.015 to 0.049 in

Piston ring side clearance

Compression rings

Standard

1983 through 1990 .... 0.0020 to 0.0040 in

1991 on .... 0.0016 to 0.0033 in

Service limit .... 0.006 in

Oil ring .... Snug fit

Torque specifications*   **Ft-lbs**

Main bearing cap bolts

1983 through 1986

Step 1 .... 50 to 60

Step 2 .... 80 to 90

1987 on

Step 1 .... 50 to 60

Step 2 .... 75 to 85

Connecting rod cap nuts

Step 1 .... 25 to 30

Step 2 .... 30 to 36

***Note**: Refer to Part A for additional torque specifications.*

2.8L, 2.9L and 4.0L V6 engines

General

Cylinder compression pressure .... 101 psi min

Oil pressure (engine warm at 2000 rpm) .... 40 to 60 psi

Cylinder head

Warpage limit .... 0.003 in per 6 inches; 0.006 in overall

Valves and related components

Minimum valve margin width .... 1/32 in

Intake valve

Seat angle 45-degrees

Seat width .... 0.060 to 0.079 in

Seat runout limit .... 0.0015 in

Stem diameter .... 0.3159 to 0.3167 in

Stem-to-guide clearance .... 0.0008 to 0.0025 in

Valve face runout limit .... 0.002 in

Valve face angle 44-degrees

Exhaust valve

Seat angle 45-degrees

Seat width .... 0.060 to 0.079 in

Seat runout limit .... 0.0015 in

Stem diameter .... 0.3149 to 0.3156 in

Stem-to-guide clearance .... 0.0018 to 0.0035 in

2E

Valves and related components (continued)

Valve face runout limit .... 0.002 in
Valve face angle 44-degrees
Valve spring
  Pressure .... 60.0 to 68.0 lbs at 1.585 in
  Service limit .... 10% pressure loss at specified length
  Free length (approximate) .... 1.91 in
  Installed height .... 1-37/64 to 1-39/64 in
  Maximum out of square .... 5/64 in
Valve lifter
  Diameter (standard)
    2.8L and 2.9L .... 0.8736 to 0.8741 in
    4.0L .... 0.8742 to 0.8755 in
  Lifter-to-bore clearance
  Standard
    2.8L and 2.9L .... 0.0009 to 0.0024 in
    4.0L .... 0.0005 to 0.0022 in
  Service limit .... 0.005 in

Crankshaft and connecting rods

Connecting rod journal
  Diameter (standard) .... 2.1252 to 2.1260 in
  Out-of-round limit .... 0.0006 in
  Taper limit .... 0.0006 in per inch
  Bearing oil clearance
  Desired
    2.8L and 2.9L .... 0.0006 to 0.0016 in
    4.0L .... 0.0003 to 0.0024 in
  Allowable .... 0.0005 to 0.0022 in
Connecting rod side clearance (endplay)
  Standard
    2.8L and 2.9L .... 0.004 to 0.011 in
    4.0L .... 0.0002 to 0.0025 in
  Service limit .... 0.014 in
Main bearing journal
  Diameter .... 2.2433 to 2.2441 in
  Out-of-round limit .... 0.0006 in
  Taper limit .... 0.0006 in per inch
  Bearing oil clearance
  Desired .... 0.0008 to 0.0015 in
  Allowable .... 0.0005 to 0.0019 in
Crankshaft endplay
  Standard
    2.8L and 2.9L .... 0.004 to 0.008 in
    4.0L .... 0.0016 to 0.0126 in
  Service limit .... 0.012 in

Cylinder bore

Diameter
  2.8L and 2.9L .... 3.6614 to 3.6630 in
  4.0L .... 3.9527 to 3.9543 in
Out-of-round limit .... 0.0015 in
Out-of-round service limit .... 0.005 in
Taper service limit .... 0.010 in

Pistons and rings

Piston diameter
  2.8L and 2.9L
    Coded red .... 3.6605 to 3.6615 in
    0.020 in oversize .... 3.6802 to 3.6812 in
  4.0L .... 3.9524 to 3.9531 in
Piston-to-bore clearance
  2.8L and 2.9L .... 0.0011 to 0.0019 in
  4.0L .... 0.0008 to 0.0019 in
Piston ring end gap
  Compression rings .... 0.015 to 0.023 in
  Oil ring rails .... 0.015 to 0.055 in
Piston ring side clearance
  Compression rings
    Standard .... 0.0020 to 0.0033 in
    Service limit .... 0.006 in
  Oil ring .... Snug fit

Torque specifications* | **Ft-lbs**

Main bearing cap bolts
   2.8L and 2.9L . . . . 65 to 75
   4.0L . . . . 66 to 77
Connecting rod cap nuts
   2.8L and 2.9L . . . . 19 to 24
   4.0L . . . . 18 to 24

*Note: *Refer to Parts B and D for additional torque specifications.*

3.0L V6 engine

General
Cylinder compression pressure . . . . 101 psi min
Oil pressure (engine warm at 2000 rpm) . . . . 40 to 60 psi

Cylinder head
Warpage limit . . . . 0.007 in

Valves and related components
Minimum valve margin width . . . . 1/32 in
Intake valve
   Seat angle 45-degrees
   Seat width . . . . 0.060 to 0.080 in
   Seat runout limit . . . . 0.003 in
   Stem diameter . . . . 0.3126 to 0.3134 in
   Stem-to-guide clearance . . . . 0.001 to 0.0027 in
   Valve face runout limit . . . . 0.002 in
   Valve face angle 44-degrees
Exhaust valve
   Seat angle 45-degrees
   Seat width . . . . 0.060 to 0.080 in
   Seat runout limit . . . . 0.003 in
   Stem diameter . . . . 0.3121 to 0.3129 in
   Stem-to-guide clearance . . . . 0.0015 to 0.0032 in
   Valve face runout limit . . . . 0.002 in
   Valve face angle 44-degrees
Valve spring
   Pressure . . . . 180 lbs at 1.16 in
   Service limit . . . . 10% pressure loss at specified length
   Free length (approximate) . . . . 1.84 in
   Installed height . . . . 1.58 in
Valve lifter
   Diameter (standard) . . . . 0.874 in
   Lifter-to-bore clearance
      Standard . . . . 0.0007 to 0.0027 in
      Service limit . . . . 0.005 in

Crankshaft and connecting rods
Connecting rod journal
   Diameter (standard) . . . . 2.1253 to 2.1261 in
   Out-of-round limit . . . . 0.0003 in
   Taper limit . . . . 0.0003 in per inch
   Bearing oil clearance
      Desired . . . . 0.001 to 0.0014 in
      Allowable . . . . 0.00086 to 0.0027 in
Connecting rod side clearance (endplay)
   Standard . . . . 0.006 to 0.014 in
   Service limit . . . . 0.014 in
Main bearing journal
   Diameter . . . . 2.5190 to 2.5198 in
   Out-of-round limit . . . . 0.0003 in
   Taper limit . . . . 0.0003 in per inch, 0.0006 in total
   Bearing oil clearance
      Desired . . . . 0.001 to 0.0014 in
      Allowable . . . . 0.0005 to 0.0023 in
Crankshaft endplay . . . . 0.004 to 0.008 in

Cylinder bore
Diameter . . . . 3.504 in
Out-of-round limit . . . . 0.001 in
Out-of-round service limit . . . . 0.002 in
Taper service limit . . . . 0.002 in

Pistons and rings

Piston diameter
  Coded red .... 3.5024 to 3.5031 in
  Coded blue .... 3.5035 to 3.5041 in
  Coded yellow .... 3.5045 to 3.5051 in
Piston-to-bore clearance .... 0.0012 to 0.0023 in
Piston ring end gap
  Compression rings .... 0.01 to 0.02 in
  Oil ring rails .... 0.010 to 0.049 in
Piston ring side clearance (compression rings) .... 0.0016 to 0.0037 in

Torque specifications*   **Ft-lbs**
Main bearing cap bolts 60
Connecting rod cap nuts 26
*Note: Refer to Part C for additional torque specifications.

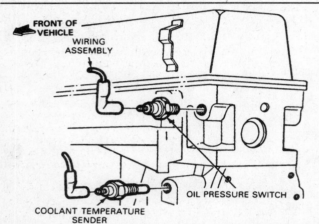

2.4a   Remove the oil pressure sending unit (switch) and install a pressure gauge in its place (four-cylinder engine shown, others similar)

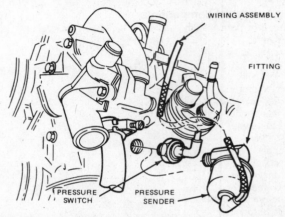

2.4b   On the V6 engine, the oil pressure sending unit (switch) is located on the left front of the engine (2.9L V6 shown, others similar)

1   General information

Included in this portion of Chapter 2 are the general overhaul procedures for the cylinder head(s) and internal engine components.

The information ranges from advice concerning preparation for an overhaul and the purchase of replacement parts to detailed, step-by-step procedures covering removal and installation of internal engine components and the inspection of parts.

The following Sections have been written based on the assumption that the engine has been removed from the vehicle. For information concerning in-vehicle engine repair, as well as removal and installation of the external components necessary for the overhaul, see Parts A through D of this Chapter and Section 7 of this Part.

The Specifications included in this Part are only those necessary for the inspection and overhaul procedures which follow. Refer to Parts A through D for additional Specifications.

2   Engine overhaul – general information

Refer to illustration 2.4

It's not always easy to determine when, or if, an engine should be completely overhauled, as a number of factors must be considered.

High mileage is not necessarily an indication that an overhaul is needed, while low mileage doesn't preclude the need for an overhaul. Frequency of servicing is probably the most important consideration. An engine that's had regular and frequent oil and filter changes, as well as other required maintenance, will most likely give many thousands of miles of reliable service. Conversely, a neglected engine may require an overhaul very early in its life.

Excessive oil consumption is an indication that piston rings, valve seals and/or valve guides are in need of attention. Make sure that oil leaks aren't responsible before deciding that the rings and/or guides are bad. Perform a cylinder compression check to determine the extent of the work required (see Section 2).

Check the oil pressure with a gauge installed in place of the oil pressure sending unit **(see illustration)** and compare it to this Chapter's Specifications. If it's extremely low, the bearings and/or oil pump are probably worn out.

Loss of power, rough running, knocking or metallic engine noises, excessive valve train noise and high fuel consumption rates may also point to the need for an overhaul, especially if they're all present at the same time. If a complete tune-up doesn't remedy the situation, major mechanical work is the only solution.

An engine overhaul involves restoring the internal parts to the specifications of a new engine. During an overhaul, the piston rings are replaced and the cylinder walls are reconditioned (rebored and/or honed). If a rebore is done by an automotive machine shop, new oversize pistons will also be installed. The main bearings, connecting rod bearings and camshaft bearings are generally replaced with new ones and, if necessary, the crankshaft may be reground to restore the journals. Generally, the valves are serviced as well, since they're usually in less-than-perfect condition at this point. While the engine is being overhauled, other components, such as the distributor, starter and alternator, can be rebuilt as well. The end result should be a like-new engine that will give many trouble-free miles. **Note:** *Critical cooling system components such as the hoses, drivebelts, thermostat and water pump MUST be replaced with new parts when an engine is overhauled. The radiator should be checked carefully to ensure that it isn't clogged or leaking (see Chapter 3). Also, we don't recommend overhauling the oil pump – always install a new one when an engine is rebuilt.*

Before beginning the engine overhaul, read through the entire procedure to familiarize yourself with the scope and requirements of the job. Overhauling an engine isn't difficult if you follow all of the instructions carefully, have the necessary tools and equipment and pay close attention to all specifications; however, it is time consuming. Plan on the vehicle being tied up for a minimum of two weeks, especially if parts must be taken to an automotive machine shop for repair or reconditioning. Check on availability of parts and make sure that any necessary special tools and equipment are obtained in advance. Most work can be done with typical hand tools, although a number of precision measuring tools are required for inspecting parts to determine if they must be replaced. Often an automotive machine shop will handle the inspection of parts and offer advice concerning reconditioning and replacement. **Note**: *Always wait until the engine has been completely disassembled and all components, especially the engine block, have been inspected before deciding what service and repair operations must be performed by an automotive machine shop. Since the block's condition will be the major factor to consider when determining whether to overhaul the original engine or buy a rebuilt one, never purchase parts or have machine work done on other components until the block has been thoroughly inspected. As a general rule, time is the primary cost of an overhaul, so it doesn't pay to install worn or substandard parts.*

As a final note, to ensure maximum life and minimum trouble from a rebuilt engine, everything must be assembled with care in a spotlessly clean environment.

3   Compression check

Refer to illustration 3.6

1   A compression check will tell you what mechanical condition the upper end (pistons, rings, valves, head gaskets) of your engine is in. Specifically, it can tell you if the compression is down due to leakage caused by worn piston rings, defective valves and seats or a blown head gasket. **Note:** *The engine must be at normal operating temperature and the battery must be fully charged for this check. Also, if the engine is equipped with a carburetor, the choke valve must be all the way open to get an accurate compression reading (if the engine's warm, the choke should be open).*

2   Begin by cleaning the area around the spark plugs before you remove them (compressed air should be used, if available, otherwise a small brush or even a bicycle tire pump will work). The idea is to prevent dirt from getting into the cylinders as the compression check is being done.

3   On all except 1989 and later 2.3L engines (which have twin plug ignition), remove all of the spark plugs from the engine (see Chapter 1). On models with twin plug ignition remove only one set of spark plugs (if you remove all eight plugs, the compression will escape out the open spark plug hole).

4   Block the throttle wide open.

5   Detach the coil wire from the center of the distributor cap and ground it on the engine block (if the vehicle has a distributor). Use a jumper wire with alligator clips on each end to ensure a good ground. On models with distributorless ignition, detach the primary (low voltage) electrical connectors from the coil packs (see Chapter 5). On fuel-injected models the fuel pump circuit should also be disabled (see Chapter 4).

6   Install the compression gauge in the number one spark plug hole (**see illustration**).

7   Crank the engine over at least seven compression strokes and watch the gauge. The compression should build up quickly in a healthy engine. Low compression on the first stroke, followed by gradually increasing pressure on successive strokes, indicates worn piston rings. A low compression reading on the first stroke, which doesn't build up during successive strokes, indicates leaking valves or a blown head gasket (a cracked head could also be the cause). Deposits on the undersides of the valve heads can also cause low compression. Record the highest gauge reading obtained.

8   Repeat the procedure for the remaining cylinders and compare the results to this Chapter's Specifications.

3.6   A gauge with a threaded fitting for the spark plug hole is preferred over the type that requires hand pressure to maintain the seal during the compression check

9   Add some engine oil (about three squirts from a plunger-type oil can) to each cylinder, through the spark plug hole, and repeat the test.

10   If the compression increases after the oil is added, the piston rings are definitely worn. If the compression doesn't increase significantly, the leakage is occurring at the valves or head gasket. Leakage past the valves may be caused by burned valve seats and/or faces or warped, cracked or bent valves.

11   If two adjacent cylinders have equally low compression, there's a strong possibility that the head gasket between them is blown. The appearance of coolant in the combustion chambers or the crankcase would verify this condition.

12   If one cylinder is 20-percent lower than the others, and the engine has a slightly rough idle, a worn exhaust lobe on the camshaft could be the cause.

13   If the compression is unusually high, the combustion chambers are probably coated with carbon deposits. If that's the case, the cylinder head(s) should be removed and decarbonized.

14   If compression is way down or varies greatly between cylinders, it would be a good idea to have a leak-down test performed by an automotive repair shop. This test will pinpoint exactly where the leakage is occurring and how severe it is.

4   Engine removal – methods and precautions

If you've decided that an engine must be removed for overhaul or major repair work, several preliminary steps should be taken.

Locating a suitable place to work is extremely important. Adequate work space, along with storage space for the vehicle, will be needed. If a shop or garage isn't available, at the very least a flat, level, clean work surface made of concrete or asphalt is required.

Cleaning the engine compartment and engine before beginning the removal procedure will help keep tools clean and organized.

An engine hoist or A-frame will also be necessary. Make sure the equipment is rated in excess of the combined weight of the engine and accessories. Safety is of primary importance, considering the potential hazards involved in lifting the engine out of the vehicle.

If the engine is being removed by a novice, a helper should be available. Advice and aid from someone more experienced would also be helpful. There are many instances when one person cannot simultaneously perform all of the operations required when lifting the engine out of the vehicle.

Plan the operation ahead of time. Arrange for or obtain all of the tools and equipment you'll need prior to beginning the job. Some of the equipment necessary to perform engine removal and installation safely and

2E

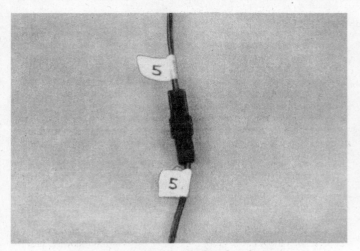

5.5   Label each wire before unplugging the connector

5.25   Use a hoist to lift the engine from the engine compartment

with relative ease are (in addition to an engine hoist) a heavy duty floor jack, complete sets of wrenches and sockets as described in the front of this manual, wooden blocks and plenty of rags and cleaning solvent for mopping up spilled oil, coolant and gasoline. If the hoist must be rented, make sure that you arrange for it in advance and perform all of the operations possible without it beforehand. This will save you money and time.

Plan for the vehicle to be out of use for quite a while. A machine shop will be required to perform some of the work which the do-it-yourselfer can't accomplish without special equipment. These shops often have a busy schedule, so it would be a good idea to consult them before removing the engine in order to accurately estimate the amount of time required to rebuild or repair components that may need work.

Always be extremely careful when removing and installing the engine. Serious injury can result from careless actions. Plan ahead, take your time and a job of this nature, although major, can be accomplished successfully.

5   Engine – removal and installation

Refer to illustrations 5.5 and 5.25
Warning: *The air conditioning system is under high pressure! Have a dealer service department or service station discharge the system before disconnecting any air conditioning system hoses or fittings.*

Removal

1   Refer to Chapter 4 and relieve the fuel system pressure (EFI equipped vehicles only), then disconnect the negative cable from the battery.
2   Cover the fenders and cowl and remove the hood (see Chapter 11). Special pads are available to protect the fenders, but an old bedspread or blanket will also work.
3   Remove the air cleaner assembly.
4   Drain the cooling system (see Chapter 1).
5   Label the vacuum lines, emissions system hoses, wiring connectors, ground straps and fuel lines to ensure correct reinstallation, then detach them. Pieces of masking tape with numbers or letters written on them work well **(see illustration)**. If there's any possibility of confusion, make a sketch of the engine compartment and clearly label the lines, hoses and wires.
6   Label and detach all coolant hoses from the engine.
7   Remove the cooling fan, shroud and radiator (see Chapter 3).
8   Remove the drivebelt(s) (see Chapter 1).
9   **Warning:** *Gasoline is extremely flammable, so extra precautions must be taken when working on any part of the fuel system. DO NOT smoke or allow open flames or bare light bulbs near the vehicle. Also, don't work in a garage if a natural gas appliance with a pilot light is pres-*

ent. Disconnect the fuel lines running from the engine to the chassis (see Chapter 4). Plug or cap all open fittings/lines.
10   Disconnect the throttle linkage (and TV linkage/speed control cable, if equipped) from the engine (see Chapter 4).
11   On power steering equipped vehicles, unbolt the power steering pump (see Chapter 10). Leave the lines/hoses attached and make sure the pump is kept in an upright position in the engine compartment (use wire or rope to restrain it out of the way).
12   On air conditioned models, unbolt the compressor (see Chapter 3) and set it aside. DO NOT disconnect the hoses!
13   Drain the engine oil (Chapter 1) and remove the filter.
14   Remove the starter motor (see Chapter 5).
15   Remove the alternator (see Chapter 5).
16   Unbolt the exhaust system from the engine (see Chapter 4).
17   If you're working on a vehicle with an automatic transmission, refer to Chapter 7 and remove the torque converter-to-driveplate fasteners.
18   Support the transmission with a jack. Position a block of wood between them to prevent damage to the transmission. Special transmission jacks with safety chains are available – use one if possible.
19   Attach an engine sling or a length of chain to the lifting brackets on the engine.
20   Roll the hoist into position and connect the sling to it. Take up the slack in the sling or chain, but don't lift the engine. **Warning:** *DO NOT place any part of your body under the engine when it's supported only by a hoist or other lifting device.*
21   Remove the transmission-to-engine block bolts. On engines so equipped, remove two bolts that secure the engine oil pan to the transmission.
22   Remove the engine mount-to-frame bolts.
23   Recheck to be sure nothing is still connecting the engine to the transmission or vehicle. Disconnect anything still remaining.
24   Raise the engine slightly. Carefully work it forward to separate it from the transmission. If you're working on a vehicle with an automatic transmission, be sure the torque converter stays in the transmission (clamp a pair of vise-grips to the housing to keep the converter from sliding out). If you're working on a vehicle with a manual transmission, the input shaft must be completely disengaged from the clutch. Slowly raise the engine out of the engine compartment **(see illustration)**. Check carefully to make sure nothing is hanging up.
25   Remove the flywheel/driveplate and mount the engine on an engine stand.

Installation

26   Check the engine and transmission mounts. If they're worn or damaged, replace them.
27   If you're working on a manual transmission equipped vehicle, install the clutch and pressure plate (see Chapter 7). Now is a good time to install a new clutch.

28 Carefully lower the engine into the engine compartment – make sure the engine mounts line up.

29 If you're working on an automatic transmission equipped vehicle, guide the torque converter into the crankshaft following the procedure outlined in Chapter 7.

30 If you're working on a manual transmission equipped vehicle, apply a dab of high-temperature grease to the input shaft and guide it into the crankshaft pilot bearing until the bellhousing is flush with the engine block.

31 Install the transmission-to-engine bolts and tighten them securely. **Caution:** *DO NOT use the bolts to force the transmission and engine together!*

32 Reinstall the remaining components in the reverse order of removal.

33 Add coolant, oil, power steering and transmission fluid as needed.

34 Run the engine and check for leaks and proper operation of all accessories, then install the hood and test drive the vehicle.

35 Have the air conditioning system recharged and leak tested.

6   Engine rebuilding alternatives

The do-it-yourselfer is faced with a number of options when performing an engine overhaul. The decision to replace the engine block, piston/connecting rod assemblies and crankshaft depends on a number of factors, with the number one consideration being the condition of the block. Other considerations are cost, access to machine shop facilities, parts availability, time required to complete the project and the extent of prior mechanical experience on the part of the do-it-yourselfer.

Some of the rebuilding alternatives include:

Individual parts – If the inspection procedures reveal that the engine block and most engine components are in reusable condition, purchasing individual parts may be the most economical alternative. The block, crankshaft and piston/connecting rod assemblies should all be inspected carefully. Even if the block shows little wear, the cylinder bores should be surface honed.

Short block – A short block consists of an engine block with a crankshaft and piston/connecting rod assemblies already installed. All new bearings are incorporated and all clearances will be correct. The existing camshaft, valve train components, cylinder head(s) and external parts can be bolted to the short block with little or no machine shop work necessary.

Long block – A long block consists of a short block plus an oil pump, oil pan, cylinder head(s), valve cover(s), camshaft and valve train components, timing sprockets and chain/belt or gears and timing cover. All components are installed with new bearings, seals and gaskets incorporated throughout. The installation of manifolds and external parts is all that's necessary.

Give careful thought to which alternative is best for you and discuss the situation with local automotive machine shops, auto parts dealers and experienced rebuilders before ordering or purchasing replacement parts.

7   Engine overhaul – disassembly sequence

1   It's much easier to disassemble and work on the engine if it's mounted on a portable engine stand. A stand can often be rented quite cheaply from an equipment rental yard. Before the engine is mounted on a stand, the flywheel/driveplate should be removed from the engine.

2   If a stand isn't available, it's possible to disassemble the engine with it blocked up on the floor. Be extra careful not to tip or drop the engine when working without a stand.

3   If you're going to obtain a rebuilt engine, all external components must come off first, to be transferred to the replacement engine, just as they will if you're doing a complete engine overhaul yourself. These include:

Alternator and brackets (if not removed during engine removal)
Emissions control components
Distributor (if equipped), spark plug wires and spark plugs

Thermostat and housing cover
Water pump
EFI components or carburetor
Intake/exhaust manifolds
Oil filter
Engine mounts
Clutch and flywheel/driveplate
Engine rear plate

Note: *When removing the external components from the engine, pay close attention to details that may be helpful or important during installation. Note the installed position of gaskets, seals, spacers, pins, brackets, washers, bolts and other small items.*

4   If you're obtaining a short block, which consists of the engine block, crankshaft, pistons and connecting rods all assembled, then the cylinder head(s), oil pan and oil pump will have to be removed as well. See Engine rebuilding alternatives for additional information regarding the different possibilities to be considered.

5   If you're planning a complete overhaul, the engine must be disassembled and the internal components removed in the following order:

Four-cylinder engines

Clutch and flywheel or driveplate
Valve cover
Intake and exhaust manifolds
Timing belt/sprockets and covers
Cylinder head
Camshaft and related components
Auxiliary shaft
Oil pan
Front cover (front oil seal housing)
Oil pump
Piston/connecting rod assemblies
Crankshaft and main bearings

V6 engines

Clutch and flywheel or driveplate
Valve covers
Rocker assemblies and pushrods
Intake and exhaust manifolds
Cylinder heads
Oil pan
Oil pump
Timing gear cover and cover plate (2.8L engine)
Timing chain cover and cover plate (2.9L, 3.0L and 4.0L engines)
Timing gears (2.8L engine)
Timing chain and sprockets (2.9L, 3.0L and 4.0L engines)
Valve lifters
Camshaft
Piston/connecting rod assemblies
Crankshaft and main bearings

6   Before beginning the disassembly and overhaul procedures, make sure the following items are available. Also, refer to *Engine overhaul – reassembly sequence* for a list of tools and materials needed for engine reassembly.

Common hand tools
Small cardboard boxes or plastic bags for storing parts
Gasket scraper
Ridge reamer
Vibration damper puller
Micrometers
Telescoping gauges
Dial indicator set
Valve spring compressor
Cylinder surfacing hone
Piston ring groove cleaning tool
Electric drill motor
Tap and die set
Wire brushes
Oil gallery brushes
Cleaning solvent

2E

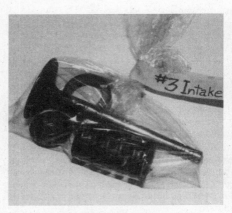

8.2   A small plastic bag, with an appropriate label, can be used to store the valve train components so they can be kept together and reinstalled in the original location

8.3   Use a valve spring compressor to compress the spring, then remove the keepers from the valve stem

8.4   If the valve won't pull through the guide, deburr the edge of the stem end and the area around the top of the keeper groove with a file or whetstone

---

8   Cylinder head – disassembly

Refer to illustrations 8.2, 8.3 and 8.4
Note: *New and rebuilt cylinder heads are commonly available for most engines at dealerships and auto parts stores. Due to the fact that some specialized tools are necessary for the disassembly and inspection procedures, and replacement parts may not be readily available, it may be more practical and economical for the home mechanic to purchase replacement head(s) rather than taking the time to disassemble, inspect and recondition the original(s).*

1   Cylinder head disassembly involves removal of the intake and exhaust valves and related components. If they're still in place, remove the rocker arm nuts, fulcrums and rocker arms from the cylinder head studs. Label the parts or store them separately so they can be reinstalled in their original locations.

2   Before the valves are removed, arrange to label and store them, along with their related components, so they can be kept separate and reinstalled in the same valve guides they are removed from **(see illustration)**.

3   Compress the springs on the first valve with a spring compressor and remove the keepers **(see illustration)**. Carefully release the valve spring compressor and remove the retainer, the spring and the spring seat (if used).

4   Pull the valve out of the head, then remove the oil seal from the guide. If the valve binds in the guide (won't pull through), push it back into the head and deburr the area around the keeper groove with a fine file or whetstone **(see illustration)**.

5   Repeat the procedure for the remaining valves. Remember to keep all the parts for each valve together so they can be reinstalled in the same locations.

6   Once the valves and related components have been removed and stored in an organized manner, the head should be thoroughly cleaned and inspected. If a complete engine overhaul is being done, finish the engine disassembly procedures before beginning the cylinder head cleaning and inspection process.

---

9   Cylinder head – cleaning and inspection

Refer to illustrations 9.12, 9.14, 9.15, 9.16, 9.17 and 9.18
1   Thorough cleaning of the cylinder head(s) and related valve train components, followed by a detailed inspection, will enable you to decide how much valve service work must be done during the engine overhaul. **Note:** *If the engine was severely overheated, the cylinder head is probably warped (see Step 12).*

Cleaning
2   Scrape all traces of old gasket material and sealing compound off the head gasket, intake manifold and exhaust manifold sealing surfaces. Be very careful not to gouge the cylinder head. Special gasket removal solvents that soften gaskets and make removal much easier are available at auto parts stores.
3   Remove all built up scale from the coolant passages.
4   Run a stiff wire brush through the various holes to remove deposits that may have formed in them.
5   Run an appropriate size tap into each of the threaded holes to remove corrosion and thread sealant that may be present. If compressed air is available, use it to clear the holes of debris produced by this operation. **Warning:** *Wear eye protection when using compressed air!*
6   Clean the rocker arm pivot stud threads with a wire brush.
7   Clean the cylinder head with solvent and dry it thoroughly. Compressed air will speed the drying process and ensure that all holes and recessed areas are clean. **Note:** *Decarbonizing chemicals are available and may prove very useful when cleaning cylinder heads and valve train components. They are very caustic and should be used with caution. Be sure to follow the instructions on the container.*
8   Clean the rocker arms, fulcrums or shafts, bolts and pushrods with solvent and dry them thoroughly (don't mix them up during the cleaning process). Compressed air will speed the drying process and can be used to clean out the oil passages.
9   Clean all the valve springs, spring seats, keepers and retainers with solvent and dry them thoroughly. Do the components from one valve at a time to avoid mixing up the parts.
10   Scrape off any heavy deposits that may have formed on the valves, then use a motorized wire brush to remove deposits from the valve heads and stems. Again, make sure the valves don't get mixed up.

Inspection
Note: *Be sure to perform all of the following inspection procedures before concluding that machine shop work is required. Make a list of the items that need attention.*

Cylinder head
11   Inspect the head very carefully for cracks, evidence of coolant leakage and other damage. If cracks are found, check with an automotive machine shop concerning repair. If repair isn't possible, a new cylinder head should be obtained.
12   Using a straightedge and feeler gauge, check the head gasket mating surface for warpage **(see illustration)**. If the warpage exceeds the limit listed in this Chapter's Specifications, it can be resurfaced at an automotive machine shop. **Note:** *If the V6 engine heads are resurfaced, the intake manifold flanges will also require machining.*

9.12   Check the cylinder head gasket surface for warpage by trying to slip a feeler gauge under the straightedge (see this Chapter's Specifications for the maximum warpage allowed and use a feeler gauge of that thickness)

9.14   A dial indicator can be used to determine the valve stem-to-guide clearance (move the valve stem as indicated by the arrows)

2E

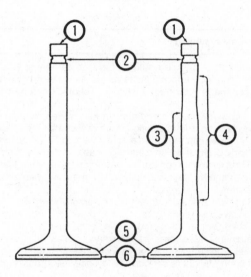

9.15   Check for valve wear at the points shown here

1	Valve tip	4	Stem (most worn area)
2	Keeper groove	5	Valve face
3	Stem (least worn area)	6	Margin

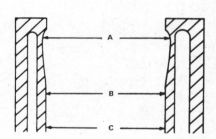

9.16   The margin width on each valve must be as specified (if no margin exists, the valve cannot be reused)

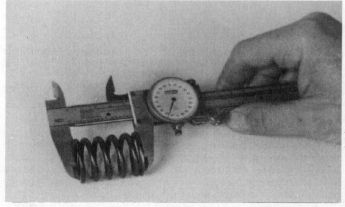

9.17   Measure the free length of each valve spring with a dial or vernier caliper

13   Examine the valve seats in each of the combustion chambers. If they're pitted, cracked or burned, the head will require valve service that's beyond the scope of the home mechanic.

14   Check the valve stem-to-guide clearance by measuring the lateral movement of the valve stem with a dial indicator attached securely to the head **(see illustration)**. The valve must be in the guide and approximately 1/16-inch off the seat. The total valve stem movement indicated by the gauge needle must be divided by two to obtain the actual clearance. After this is done, if there's still some doubt regarding the condition of the valve guides they should be checked by an automotive machine shop (the cost should be minimal).

Valves

15   Carefully inspect each valve face for uneven wear, deformation, cracks, pits and burned areas **(see illustration)**. Check the valve stem for scuffing and galling and the neck for cracks. Rotate the valve and check for any obvious indication that it's bent. Look for pits and excessive wear

on the end of the stem. The presence of any of these conditions indicates the need for valve service by an automotive machine shop.

16   Measure the margin width on each valve **(see illustration)**. Any valve with a margin narrower than specified will have to be replaced with a new one.

Valve components

17   Check each valve spring for wear (on the ends) and pits. Measure the free length and compare it to the Specifications **(see illustration)**.

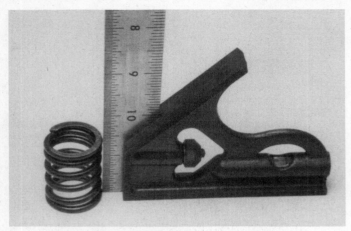

9.18   Check each valve spring for squareness

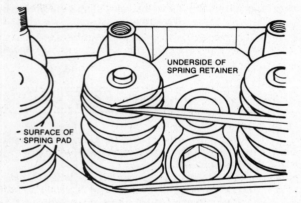

11.9   Be sure to check the valve spring installed height for each valve (the disatance from the top of the seat/shims to the underside of the retainer)

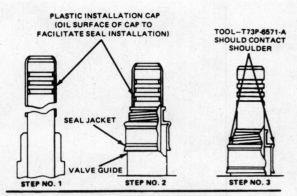

11.4   The plastic installation cap must be used to cover the valve stems on the four-cylinder engine when installing the new valve seals

Any springs that are shorter than specified have sagged and should not be reused. The tension of all springs should be checked with a special fixture before deciding that they're suitable for use in a rebuilt engine (take the springs to an automotive machine shop for this check).
18   Stand each spring on a flat surface and check it for squareness **(see illustration)**. If any of the springs are distorted or sagged, replace all of them with new parts.
19   Check the spring retainers and keepers for obvious wear and cracks. Any questionable parts should be replaced with new ones, as extensive damage will occur if they fail during engine operation.

Rocker arm components
20   Check the rocker arm faces (the areas that contact the pushrod ends and valve stems) for pits, wear, galling, score marks and rough spots. Check the rocker arm pivot contact areas and fulcrums (2.0L, 2.3L and 3.0L engines) or shafts (2.8L, 2.9L and 4.0L engines) as well. Look for cracks in each rocker arm and bolt (or shaft).
21   Inspect the pushrod ends for scuffing and excessive wear. Roll each pushrod on a flat surface, like a piece of plate glass, to determine if it's bent.
22   Check the rocker arm studs in the cylinder heads (3.0L engine) for damaged threads and secure installation.
23   Any damaged or excessively worn parts must be replaced with new ones.
24   If the inspection process indicates that the valve components are in generally poor condition and worn beyond the limits specified, which is usually the case in an engine that's being overhauled, reassemble the valves in the cylinder head and refer to Section 10 for valve servicing recommendations.

10   Valves – servicing

1   Because of the complex nature of the job and the special tools and equipment needed, servicing of the valves, the valve seats and the valve guides, commonly known as a valve job, should be done by a professional.
2   The home mechanic can remove and disassemble the head(s), do the initial cleaning and inspection, then reassemble and deliver it to a dealer service department or an automotive machine shop for the actual service work. Doing the inspection will enable you to see what condition the head and valvetrain components are in and will ensure that you know what work and new parts are required when dealing with an automotive machine shop.
3   The dealer service department, or automotive machine shop, will remove the valves and springs, recondition or replace the valves and valve seats, recondition the valve guides, check and replace the valve springs, spring retainers and keepers (as necessary), replace the valve seals with new ones, reassemble the valve components and make sure the installed spring height is correct. The cylinder head gasket surface will also be resurfaced if it's warped.
4   After the valve job has been performed by a professional, the head will be in like-new condition. When the head is returned, be sure to clean it again before installation on the engine to remove any metal particles and abrasive grit that may still be present from the valve service or head resurfacing operations. Use compressed air, if available, to blow out all the oil holes and passages.

11   Cylinder head – reassembly

Refer to illustrations 11.4 and 11.9
1   Regardless of whether or not the head was sent to an automotive repair shop for valve servicing, make sure it's clean before beginning reassembly.
2   If the head was sent out for valve servicing, the valves and related components will already be in place. Begin the reassembly procedure with Step 9.
3   On all except four-cylinder engines, lubricate and install the valve, then install new seals on each of the valve guides. Using a hammer and deep socket, gently tap each seal into place until it's seated on the guide. Don't twist or cock the seals during installation or they won't seat properly on the valve stems.

12.1 A ridge reamer is required to remove the ridge from the top of each cylinder – do this before removing the pistons!

12.3 Connecting rod side clearance is measured with feeler gauges inserted between the rod cap and crankshaft

12.6 Place short pieces of hose over the connecting rod studs to protect the crankshaft and cylinder walls

4   On four-cylinder engines, install the valve, then install the valve stem seals. Slip the plastic installation cap **(see illustration)** over the end of the valve stem to allow the seal to pass over the grooves in the valve stem. After installation, remove the platic cap and push the seal down until it's fully seated (if used) are installed over the valves after the valves are in place.
5   Beginning at one end of the head, lubricate and install the first valve. Apply moly-base grease or clean engine oil to the valve stem.
6   Drop the spring seat or shim(s) over the valve guide and set the valve spring and retainer in place.
7   Compress the springs with a valve spring compressor and carefully install the keepers in the upper groove, then slowly release the compressor and make sure the keepers seat properly. Apply a small dab of grease to each keeper to hold it in place if necessary **(see illustration)**.
8   Repeat the procedure for the remaining valves. Be sure to return the components to their original locations – don't mix them up!
9   Check the installed valve spring height with a ruler graduated in 1/32-inch increments or a dial caliper. If the head was sent out for service work, the installed height should be correct (but don't automatically assume that it is). The measurement is taken from the top of each spring seat or shim(s) to the bottom of the retainer **(see illustration)**. If the height is greater than the figure listed in this Chapter's Specifications, shims can be added under the springs to correct it. **Caution:** *Don't, under any circumstances, shim the springs to the point where the installed height is less than specified.*

10   On 3.0L V6 engines, apply moly-base grease to the rocker arm faces and the fulcrums, then install the rocker arms and pivots on the cylinder head studs.

---

12   Pistons/connecting rods – removal

Refer to illustrations 12.1, 12.3 and 12.6
Note: *Prior to removing the piston/connecting rod assemblies, remove the cylinder head(s), the oil pan and the oil pump by referring to the appropriate Sections in Chapter 2.*
1   Use your fingernail to feel if a ridge has formed at the upper limit of ring travel (about 1/4-inch down from the top of each cylinder). If carbon deposits or cylinder wear have produced ridges, they must be completely removed with a special tool **(see illustration)**. Follow the manufacturer's instructions provided with the tool. Failure to remove the ridges before attempting to remove the piston/connecting rod assemblies may result in piston breakage.
2   After the cylinder ridges have been removed, turn the engine upside-down so the crankshaft is facing up.
3   Before the connecting rods are removed, check the endplay with feeler gauges. Slide them between the first connecting rod and the crankshaft throw until the play is removed **(see illustration)**. The endplay is equal to the thickness of the feeler gauge(s). If the endplay exceeds the service limit, new connecting rods will be required. If new rods (or a new crankshaft) are installed, the endplay may fall under the specified minimum (if it does, the rods will have to be machined to restore it – consult an automotive machine shop for advice if necessary). Repeat the procedure for the remaining connecting rods.
4   Check the connecting rods and caps for identification marks. If they aren't plainly marked, use a small center-punch to make the appropriate number of indentations on each rod and cap (1, 2, 3, etc., depending on the engine type and cylinder they're associated with).
5   Loosen each of the connecting rod cap nuts 1/2-turn at a time until they can be removed by hand. Remove the number one connecting rod cap and bearing insert. Don't drop the bearing insert out of the cap.
6   Slip a short length of plastic or rubber hose over each connecting rod cap bolt to protect the crankshaft journal and cylinder wall as the piston is removed **(see illustration)**.
7   Remove the bearing insert and push the connecting rod/piston assembly out through the top of the engine. Use a wooden hammer handle to push on the upper bearing surface in the connecting rod. If resistance is felt, double-check to make sure that all of the ridge was removed from the cylinder.
8   Repeat the procedure for the remaining cylinders.
9   After removal, reassemble the connecting rod caps and bearing inserts in their respective connecting rods and install the cap nuts finger

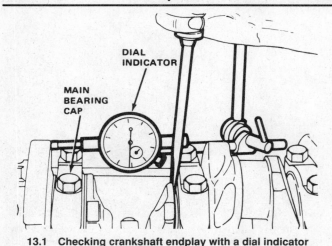

13.1   Checking crankshaft endplay with a dial indicator

13.3   Checking crankshaft endplay with a feeler gauge

tight. Leaving the old bearing inserts in place until reassembly will help prevent the connecting rod bearing surfaces from being accidentally nicked or gouged.

10   Don't separate the pistons from the connecting rods (see Section 17 for additional information).

13.4a   Use a center punch or number stamping dies to mark the main bearing caps to ensure installation in their original locations on the block (make the punch marks near one of the bolt heads)

13.4b   The arrow on the main bearing cap indicates the front of the engine

13   Crankshaft – removal

Refer to illustrations 13.1, 13.3 and 13.4

Note: *The crankshaft can be removed only after the engine has been removed from the vehicle. It's assumed that the flywheel or driveplate, vibration damper, timing gears or chain, oil pan, oil pump and piston/connecting rod assemblies have already been removed.*

1   Before the crankshaft is removed, check the endplay. Mount a dial indicator with the stem in line with the crankshaft and touching one of the crank throws **(see illustration)**.

2   Pry the crankshaft all the way to the rear and zero the dial indicator. Next, pry the crankshaft to the front as far as possible and check the reading on the dial indicator. The distance that it moves is the endplay. If it's greater than the limit listed in this Chapter's Specifications, check the crankshaft thrust surfaces for wear. If no wear is evident, new main bearings should correct the endplay.

3   If a dial indicator isn't available, feeler gauges can be used. Gently pry or push the crankshaft all the way to the front of the engine. Slip feeler gauges between the crankshaft and the front face of the thrust main bearing to determine the clearance **(see illustration)**.

4   Check the main bearing caps to see if they're marked to indicate their locations. They should be numbered consecutively from the front of the engine to the rear. If they aren't, mark them with number stamping dies or a center-punch **(see illustrations)**. Main bearing caps generally have a cast-in arrow, which points to the front of the engine **(see illustration)**. Loosen the main bearing cap bolts 1/4-turn at a time each, until they can be removed by hand. Note if any stud bolts are used and make sure they're returned to their original locations when the crankshaft is reinstalled.

5   Gently tap the caps with a soft-face hammer, then separate them from the engine block. If necessary, use the bolts as levers to remove the caps. Try not to drop the bearing inserts if they come out with the caps.

6   Carefully lift the crankshaft out of the engine. It may be a good idea to have an assistant available, since the crankshaft is quite heavy. With the bearing inserts in place in the engine block and main bearing caps, return the caps to their respective locations on the engine block and tighten the bolts finger tight.

14   Engine block – cleaning

Refer to illustrations 14.1, 14.8 and 14.10

Caution: *The core plugs (also known as freeze plugs or soft plugs) may be difficult or impossible to retrieve if they're driven into the block coolant passages.*

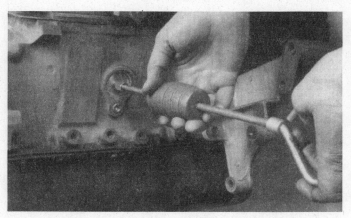

14.1   The core plugs should be removed with a puller – if they're driven into the block, they may be impossible to retrieve

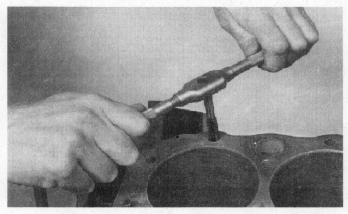

14.8   All bolt holes in the block – particularly the main bearing cap and head bolt holes – should be cleaned and restored with a tap (be sure to remove debris from the holes after this is done)

14.10   A large socket on an extension can be used to drive the new core plugs into the bores

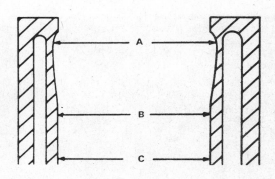

15.4a   Measure the diameter of each cylinder just under the wear ridge (A), at the center (B) and at the bottom (C)

2E

1   Drill a small hole in the center of each core plug and pull them out with an auto body type dent puller **(see illustration)**.
2   Using a gasket scraper, remove all traces of gasket material from the engine block. Be very careful not to nick or gouge the gasket sealing surfaces.
3   Remove the main bearing caps and separate the bearing inserts from the caps and the engine block. Tag the bearings, indicating which cylinder they were removed from and whether they were in the cap or the block, then set them aside.
4   Remove all of the threaded oil gallery plugs from the block. The plugs are usually very tight – they may have to be drilled out and the holes retapped. Use new plugs when the engine is reassembled.
5   If the engine is extremely dirty it should be taken to an automotive machine shop to be steam cleaned or hot tanked.
6   After the block is returned, clean all oil holes and oil galleries one more time. Brushes specifically designed for this purpose are available at most auto parts stores. Flush the passages with warm water until the water runs clear, dry the block thoroughly and wipe all machined surfaces with a light, rust preventive oil. If you have access to compressed air, use it to speed the drying process and to blow out all the oil holes and galleries. **Warning:** *Wear eye protection when using compressed air!*
7   If the block isn't extremely dirty or sludged up, you can do an adequate cleaning job with hot soapy water and a stiff brush. Take plenty of time and do a thorough job. Regardless of the cleaning method used, be sure to clean all oil holes and galleries very thoroughly, dry the block completely and coat all machined surfaces with light oil.
8   The threaded holes in the block must be clean to ensure accurate torque readings during reassembly. Run the proper size tap into each of the holes to remove rust, corrosion, thread sealant or sludge and restore damaged threads **(see illustration)**. If possible, use compressed air to

clear the holes of debris produced by this operation. Now is a good time to clean the threads on the head bolts and the main bearing cap bolts as well.
9   Reinstall the main bearing caps and tighten the bolts finger tight.
10   After coating the sealing surfaces of the new core plugs with Permatex no. 2 sealant, install them in the engine block **(see illustration)**. Make sure they're driven in straight and seated properly or leakage could result. Special tools are available for this purpose, but a large socket, with an outside diameter that will just slip into the core plug, a 1/2-inch drive extension and a hammer will work just as well.
11   Apply non-hardening sealant (such as Permatex no. 2 or Teflon pipe sealant) to the new oil gallery plugs and thread them into the holes in the block. Make sure they're tightened securely.
12   If the engine isn't going to be reassembled right away, cover it with a large plastic trash bag to keep it clean.

15   Engine block – inspection

Refer to illustrations 15.4a, 15.4b and 15.4c

1   Before the block is inspected, it should be cleaned as described in Section 14.
2   Visually check the block for cracks, rust and corrosion. Look for stripped threads in the threaded holes. It's also a good idea to have the block checked for hidden cracks by an automotive machine shop that has the special equipment to do this type of work. If defects are found, have the block repaired, if possible, or replaced.
3   Check the cylinder bores for scuffing and scoring.
4   Measure the diameter of each cylinder at the top (just under the ridge area), center and bottom of the cylinder bore, parallel to the crankshaft

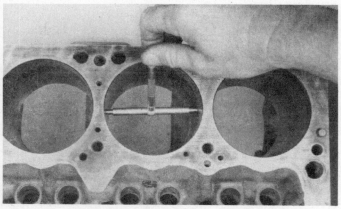

15.4b   The ability to "feel" when the telescoping gauge is at the correct point will be developed over time, so work slowly and repeat the check until you're satisfied the bore measurement is accurate

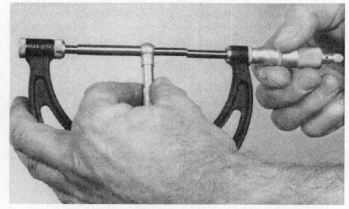

15.4c   The gauge is then measured with a micrometer to determine the bore size

7   To check the clearance, select a feeler gauge and slip it into the cylinder along with the matching piston. The piston must be positioned exactly as it normally would be. The feeler gauge must be between the piston and cylinder on one of the thrust faces (90-degrees to the piston pin bore).

8   The piston should slip through the cylinder (with the feeler gauge in place) with moderate pressure.

9   If it falls through or slides through easily, the clearance is excessive and a new piston will be required. If the piston binds at the lower end of the cylinder and is loose toward the top, the cylinder is tapered. If tight spots are encountered as the piston/feeler gauge is rotated in the cylinder, the cylinder is out-of-round.

10   Repeat the procedure for the remaining pistons and cylinders.

11   If the cylinder walls are badly scuffed or scored, or if they're out-of-round or tapered beyond the limits given in this Chapter's Specifications, have the engine block rebored and honed at an automotive machine shop. If a rebore is done, oversize pistons and rings will be required.

12   If the cylinders are in reasonably good condition and not worn to the outside of the limits, and if the piston-to-cylinder clearances can be maintained properly, then they don't have to be rebored. Honing is all that's necessary (see Section 16).

16.3a   A "bottle brush" hone will produce better results if you've never honed cylinders before

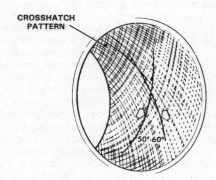

CROSSHATCH PATTERN

50°-60°

16.3b   The cylinder hone should leave a smooth, crosshatch pattern with the lines intersecting at approximately a 60-degree angle

16   Cylinder honing

Refer to illustrations 16.3a and 16.3b

1   Prior to engine reassembly, the cylinder bores must be honed so the new piston rings will seat correctly and provide the best possible combustion chamber seal. **Note:** *If you don't have the tools or don't want to tackle the honing operation, most automotive machine shops will do it for a reasonable fee.*

2   Before honing the cylinders, install the main bearing caps and tighten the bolts to the torque listed in this Chapter's Specifications.

3   Two types of cylinder hones are commonly available – the flex hone or "bottle brush" type and the more traditional surfacing hone with spring-loaded stones. Both will do the job, but for the less experienced mechanic the "bottle brush" hone will probably be easier to use. You'll also need some kerosene or honing oil, rags and an electric drill motor. Proceed as follows:

   a) Mount the hone in the drill motor, compress the stones and slip it into the first cylinder **(see illustration)**. Be sure to wear safety goggles or a face shield!

   b) Lubricate the cylinder with plenty of honing oil, turn on the drill and move the hone up-and-down in the cylinder at a pace that will produce a fine crosshatch pattern on the cylinder walls. Ideally, the crosshatch lines should intersect at approximately a 60-degree angle **(see illustration)**. Be sure to use plenty of lubricant and

axis **(see illustrations)**.

5   Next, measure each cylinder's diameter at the same three locations across the crankshaft axis. Compare the results to this Chapter's Specifications.

6   If the required precision measuring tools aren't available, the piston-to-cylinder clearances can be obtained, though not quite as accurately, using feeler gauge stock. Feeler gauge stock comes in 12-inch lengths and various thicknesses and is generally available at auto parts stores.

17.4a   The piston ring grooves can be cleaned with a special tool, as shown here, . . .

17.4b   . . . or a section of a broken ring

don't take off any more material than is absolutely necessary to produce the desired finish. **Note:** *Piston ring manufacturers may specify a smaller crosshatch angle than the traditional 60-degrees – read and follow any instructions included with the new rings.*

c) Don't withdraw the hone from the cylinder while it's running. Instead, shut off the drill and continue moving the hone up-and-down in the cylinder until it comes to a complete stop, then compress the stones and withdraw the hone. If you're using a "bottle brush" type hone, stop the drill motor, then turn the chuck in the normal direction of rotation while withdrawing the hone from the cylinder.

d) Wipe the oil out of the cylinder and repeat the procedure for the remaining cylinders.

4   After the honing job is complete, chamfer the top edges of the cylinder bores with a small file so the rings won't catch when the pistons are installed. Be very careful not to nick the cylinder walls with the end of the file.

5   The entire engine block must be washed again very thoroughly with warm, soapy water to remove all traces of the abrasive grit produced during the honing operation. **Note:** *The bores can be considered clean when a lint-free white cloth – dampened with clean engine oil- used to wipe them out doesn't pick up any more honing residue, which will show up as gray areas on the cloth. Be sure to run a brush through all oil holes and galleries and flush them with running water.*

6   After rinsing, dry the block and apply a coat of light rust preventive oil to all machined surfaces. Wrap the block in a plastic trash bag to keep it clean and set it aside until reassembly.

17   Pistons/connecting rods – inspection

Refer to illustrations 17.4a, 17.4b, 17.10 and 17.11

1   Before the inspection process can be carried out, the piston/connecting rod assemblies must be cleaned and the original piston rings removed from the pistons. **Note:** *Always use new piston rings when the engine is reassembled.*

2   Using a piston ring installation tool, carefully remove the rings from the pistons. Be careful not to nick or gouge the pistons in the process.

3   Scrape all traces of carbon from the top of the piston. A handheld wire brush or a piece of fine emery cloth can be used once the majority of the deposits have been scraped away. Do not, under any circumstances, use a wire brush mounted in a drill motor to remove deposits from the pistons. The piston material is soft and may be eroded away by the wire brush.

4   Use a piston ring groove cleaning tool to remove carbon deposits from the ring grooves. If a tool isn't available, a piece broken off the old ring will do the job. Be very careful to remove only the carbon deposits – don't remove any metal and do not nick or scratch the sides of the ring grooves **(see illustrations)**.

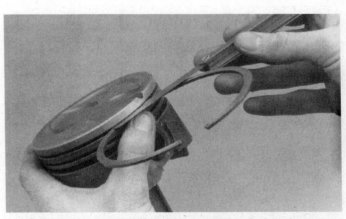

17.10   Check the ring side clearance with a feeler gauge at several points around the groove

5   Once the deposits have been removed, clean the piston/rod assemblies with solvent and dry them with compressed air (if available). Make sure the oil return holes in the back sides of the ring grooves are clear.

6   If the pistons and cylinder walls aren't damaged or worn excessively, and if the engine block is not rebored, new pistons won't be necessary. Normal piston wear appears as even vertical wear on the piston thrust surfaces and slight looseness of the top ring in its groove. New piston rings, however, should always be used when an engine is rebuilt.

7   Carefully inspect each piston for cracks around the skirt, at the pin bosses and at the ring lands.

8   Look for scoring and scuffing on the thrust faces of the skirt, holes in the piston crown and burned areas at the edge of the crown. If the skirt is scored or scuffed, the engine may have been suffering from overheating and/or abnormal combustion, which caused excessively high operating temperatures. The cooling and lubrication systems should be checked thoroughly. A hole in the piston crown is an indication that abnormal combustion (preignition) was occurring. Burned areas at the edge of the piston crown are usually evidence of spark knock (detonation). If any of the above problems exist, the causes must be corrected or the damage will occur again. The causes may include intake air leaks, incorrect fuel/air mixture, incorrect ignition timing and EGR system malfunctions.

9   Corrosion of the piston, in the form of small pits, indicates that coolant is leaking into the combustion chamber and/or the crankcase. Again, the cause must be corrected or the problem may persist in the rebuilt engine.

10   Measure the piston ring side clearance by laying a new piston ring in each ring groove and slipping a feeler gauge in beside it **(see illustration)**. Check the clearance at three or four locations around each groove. Be sure to use the correct ring for each groove – they are different. If the side clearance is greater than the figure listed in this Chapter's Specifications, new pistons will have to be used.

2E

17.11   Measure the piston diameter at a 90-degree angle to the piston pin and in line with it

18.1   The oil holes should be chamfered so sharp edges don't gouge or scratch the new bearings

18.3   Rubbing a penny lengthwise on each journal will reveal its condition – if copper rubs off and is embedded in the crankshaft, the journals should be reground

18.4   Use a wire or stiff plastic bristle brush to clean the oil passages in the crankshaft

11   Check the piston-to-bore clearance by measuring the bore (see Section 15) and the piston diameter. Make sure the pistons and bores are correctly matched. Measure the piston across the skirt, at a 90-degree angle to and in line with the piston pin **(see illustration)**. Subtract the piston diameter from the bore diameter to obtain the clearance. If it's greater than specified, the block will have to be rebored and new pistons and rings installed.

12   Check the piston-to-rod clearance by twisting the piston and rod in opposite directions. Any noticeable play indicates excessive wear, which must be corrected. The piston/connecting rod assemblies should be taken to an automotive machine shop to have the pistons and rods resized and new pins installed.

13   If the pistons must be removed from the connecting rods for any reason, they should be taken to an automotive machine shop. While they are there have the connecting rods checked for bend and twist, since automotive machine shops have special equipment for this purpose. **Note:** *Unless new pistons and/or connecting rods must be installed, do not disassemble the pistons and connecting rods.*

14   Check the connecting rods for cracks and other damage. Temporarily remove the rod caps, lift out the old bearing inserts, wipe the rod and cap bearing surfaces clean and inspect them for nicks, gouges and scratches. After checking the rods, replace the old bearings, slip the caps into place and tighten the nuts finger tight. **Note:** *If the engine is being rebuilt because of a connecting rod knock, be sure to install new rods.*

18   Crankshaft – inspection

Refer to illustrations 18.1, 18.3, 18.4, 18.6 and 18.8

1   Remove all burrs from the crankshaft oil holes with a stone, file or scraper **(see illustration)**.

2   Check the main and connecting rod bearing journals for uneven wear, scoring, pits and cracks.

3   Rub a penny accross each journal several times **(see illustration)**. If a journal picks up copper from the penny, it's too rough and must be reground.

4   Clean the crankshaft with solvent and dry it with compressed air (if available). Be sure to clean the oil holes with a stiff brush **(see illustration)** and flush them with solvent.

5   Check the rest of the crankshaft for cracks and other damage. It should be magnafluxed to reveal hidden cracks – an automotive machine shop will handle the procedure.

6   Using a micrometer, measure the diameter of the main and connecting rod journals and compare the results to this Chapter's Specifications **(see illustration)**. By measuring the diameter at a number of points around each journal's circumference, you'll be able to determine whether or not the journal is out-of-round. Take the measurement at each end of the journal, near the crank throws, to determine if the journal is tapered.

18.6   Measure the diameter of each crankshaft journal at several points to detect taper and out-of-round conditions

18.8   If the seals have worn grooves in the crankshaft journals, or if the seal contact surfaces are nicked or scratched, the new seals will leak

2E

7   If the crankshaft journals are damaged, tapered, out-of-round or worn beyond the limits given in the Specifications, have the crankshaft reground by an automotive machine shop. Be sure to use the correct size bearing inserts if the crankshaft is reconditioned.

8   Check the oil seal journals at each end of the crankshaft for wear and damage. If the seal has worn a groove in the journal, or if it's nicked or scratched **(see illustration)**, the new seal may leak when the engine is reassembled. In some cases, an automotive machine shop may be able to repair the journal by pressing on a thin sleeve. If repair isn't feasible, a new or different crankshaft should be installed.

9   Refer to Section 19 and examine the main and rod bearing inserts.

19   Main and connecting rod bearings – inspection

Refer to illustration 19.1

1   Even though the main and connecting rod bearings should be replaced with new ones during the engine overhaul, the old bearings should be retained for close examination, as they may reveal valuable information about the condition of the engine **(see illustration)**.

2   Bearing failure occurs because of lack of lubrication, the presence of dirt or other foreign particles, overloading the engine and corrosion. Regardless of the cause of bearing failure, it must be corrected before the engine is reassembled to prevent it from happening again.

3   When examining the bearings, remove them from the engine block, the main bearing caps, the connecting rods and the rod caps and lay them out on a clean surface in the same general position as their location in the engine. This will enable you to match any bearing problems with the corresponding crankshaft journal.

4   Dirt and other foreign particles get into the engine in a variety of ways. It may be left in the engine during assembly, or it may pass through filters or the PCV system. It may get into the oil, and from there into the bearings. Metal chips from machining operations and normal engine wear are often present. Abrasives are sometimes left in engine components after reconditioning, especially when parts are not thoroughly cleaned using the proper cleaning methods. Whatever the source, these foreign objects often end up embedded in the soft bearing material and are easily recognized. Large particles will not embed in the bearing and will score or gouge the bearing and journal. The best prevention for this cause of bearing failure is to clean all parts thoroughly and keep everything spotlessly clean during engine assembly. Frequent and regular engine oil and filter changes are also recommended.

5   Lack of lubrication (or lubrication breakdown) has a number of interrelated causes. Excessive heat (which thins the oil), overloading (which squeezes the oil from the bearing face) and oil leakage or throw off (from excessive bearing clearances, worn oil pump or high engine speeds) all contribute to lubrication breakdown. Blocked oil passages, which usually are the result of misaligned oil holes in a bearing shell, will also oil starve a bearing and destroy it. When lack of lubrication is the cause of bearing failure, the bearing material is wiped or extruded from the steel backing

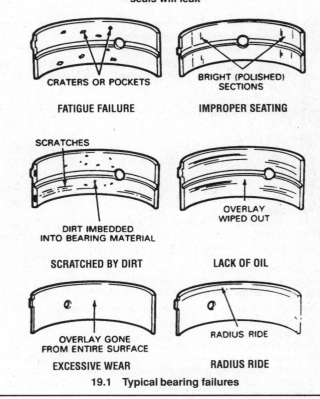

FATIGUE FAILURE — CRATERS OR POCKETS

IMPROPER SEATING — BRIGHT (POLISHED) SECTIONS

SCRATCHED BY DIRT — SCRATCHES, DIRT IMBEDDED INTO BEARING MATERIAL

LACK OF OIL — OVERLAY WIPED OUT

EXCESSIVE WEAR — OVERLAY GONE FROM ENTIRE SURFACE

RADIUS RIDE — RADIUS RIDE

19.1   Typical bearing failures

of the bearing. Temperatures may increase to the point where the steel backing turns blue from overheating.

6   Driving habits can have a definite effect on bearing life. Full throttle, low speed operation (lugging the engine) puts very high loads on bearings, which tends to squeeze out the oil film. These loads cause the bearings to flex, which produces fine cracks in the bearing face (fatigue failure). Eventually the bearing material will loosen in pieces and tear away from the steel backing. Short trip driving leads to corrosion of bearings because insufficient engine heat is produced to drive off the condensed water and corrosive gases. These products collect in the engine oil, forming acid and sludge. As the oil is carried to the engine bearings, the acid attacks and corrodes the bearing material.

7   Incorrect bearing installation during engine assembly will lead to bearing failure as well. Tight fitting bearings leave insufficient bearing oil clearance and will result in oil starvation. Dirt or foreign particles trapped behind a bearing insert result in high spots on the bearing which lead to failure.

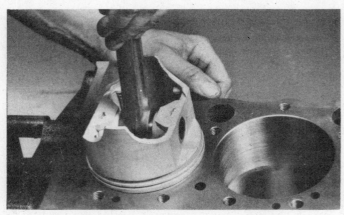

21.3   When checking piston ring end gap, the ring must be square in the cylinder bore (this is done by pushing the ring down with the top of a piston as shown)

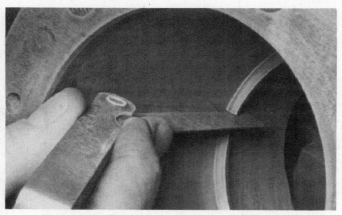

21.4   With the ring square in the cylinder, measure the end gap with a feeler gauge

20   Engine overhaul – reassembly sequence

1   Before beginning engine reassembly, make sure you have all the necessary new parts, gaskets and seals as well as the following items on hand:

Common hand tools
A 1/2-inch drive torque wrench
Piston ring installation tool
Piston ring compressor
Vibration damper installation tool
Short lengths of rubber or plastic hose to fit over connecting rod bolts
Plastigage
Feeler gauges
A fine-tooth file
New engine oil
Engine assembly lube or moly-base grease
Gasket sealant
Thread locking compound

2   In order to save time and avoid problems, engine reassembly must be done in the following general order:

Four-cylinder engines

New camshaft bearings (must be done by automotive machine shop)
Piston rings
Crankshaft and main bearings
Piston/connecting rod assemblies
Oil pump
Cylinder front cover (front crankshaft oil seal housing)
Oil pan
Auxiliary shaft
Camshaft and related components
Cylinder head
Timing belt/sprockets and covers
Intake and exhaust manifolds
Valve cover
Flywheel/driveplate

V6 engines

New camshaft bearings (must be done by automotive machine shop)
Piston rings
Crankshaft and main bearings
Piston/connecting rod assemblies
Camshaft
Valve lifters
Timing gears (2.8L engine)
Timing gear cover plate and cover (2.8L engine)
Timing chain and sprockets (2.9L, 3.0L and 4.0L engines)
Timing chain cover (2.9L, 3.0L and 4.0L engines)

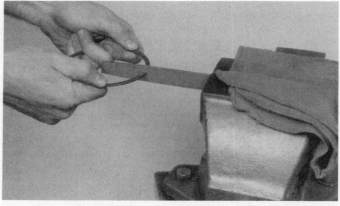

21.5   If the end gap is too small, clamp a file in a vise and file the ring ends (from the outside in only) to enlarge the gap slightly

Oil pump
Oil pan
Cylinder heads
Intake and exhaust manifolds
Rocker assemblies and pushrds
Valve covers
Flywheel/driveplate

21   Piston rings – installation

Refer to illustrations 21.3, 21.4, 21.5, 21.9a, 21.9b and 21.12

1   Before installing the new piston rings, the ring end gaps must be checked. It's assumed that the piston ring side clearance has been checked and verified correct (see Section 17).

2   Lay out the piston/connecting rod assemblies and the new ring sets so the ring sets will be matched with the same piston and cylinder during the end gap measurement and engine assembly.

3   Insert the top (number one) ring into the first cylinder and square it up with the cylinder walls by pushing it in with the top of the piston (**see illustration**). The ring should be near the bottom of the cylinder, at the lower limit of ring travel.

4   To measure the end gap, slip feeler gauges between the ends of the ring until a gauge equal to the gap width is found (**see illustration**). The feeler gauge should slide between the ring ends with a slight amount of drag. Compare the measurement to this Chapter's Specifications. If the gap is larger or smaller than specified, double-check to make sure you have the correct rings before proceeding.

5   If the gap is too small, it must be enlarged or the ring ends may come in contact with each other during engine operation, which can cause se-

21.9a Installing the spacer/expander in the oil control ring groove

21.9b DO NOT use a piston ring installation tool when installing the oil ring side rails

21.12 Installing the compression rings with a ring expander – the mark (arrow) must face up

22.5 Upper main bearing in position (flanged thrust bearing shown) – the oil hole in the bearing must align with the oil hole(s) in the block

rious damage to the engine. The end gap can be increased by filing the ring ends very carefully with a fine file. Mount the file in a vise equipped with soft jaws, slip the ring over the file with the ends contacting the file face and slowly move the ring to remove material from the ends. When performing this operation, file only from the outside in (see illustration).

6   Excess end gap isn't critical unless it's greater than 0.040-inch. Again, double-check to make sure you have the correct rings for your engine.

7   Repeat the procedure for each ring that will be installed in the first cylinder and for each ring in the remaining cylinders. Remember to keep rings, pistons and cylinders matched up.

8   Once the ring end gaps have been checked/corrected, the rings can be installed on the pistons.

9   The oil control ring (lowest one on the piston) is usually installed first. It's composed of three separate components. Slip the spacer/expander into the groove (see illustration). If an anti-rotation tang is used, make sure it's inserted into the drilled hole in the ring groove. Next, install the lower side rail. Don't use a piston ring installation tool on the oil ring side rails, as they may be damaged. Instead, place one end of the side rail into the groove between the spacer/expander and the ring land, hold it firmly in place and slide a finger around the piston while pushing the rail into the groove (see illustration). Next, install the upper side rail in the same manner.

10 After the three oil ring components have been installed, check to make sure that both the upper and lower side rails can be turned smoothly in the ring groove.

11 The number two (middle) ring is installed next. It's usually stamped with a mark which must face up, toward the top of the piston. **Note:** Always follow the instructions printed on the ring package or box – different

manufacturers may require different approaches. Do not mix up the top and middle rings, as they have different cross sections.

12 Use a piston ring installation tool and make sure the identification mark is facing the top of the piston, then slip the ring into the middle groove on the piston (see illustration). Don't expand the ring any more than necessary to slide it over the piston.

13 Install the number one (top) ring in the same manner. Make sure the mark is facing up. Be careful not to confuse the number one and number two rings.

14 Repeat the procedure for the remaining pistons and rings.

---

22   Crankshaft – installation and main bearing oil clearance check

---

Refer to illustrations 22.5, 22.11, 22.15 and 22.31

1   Crankshaft installation is the first step in engine reassembly. It's assumed at this point that the engine block and crankshaft have been cleaned, inspected and repaired or reconditioned.

2   Position the engine with the bottom facing up.

3   Remove the main bearing cap bolts and lift out the caps. Lay them out in the proper order to ensure correct installation.

4   If they're still in place, remove the original bearing inserts from the block and the main bearing caps. Wipe the bearing surfaces of the block and caps with a clean, lint-free cloth. They must be kept spotlessly clean.

Main bearing oil clearance check

5   Clean the back sides of the new main bearing inserts and lay one in each main bearing saddle in the block. If one of the bearing inserts from each set has a large groove in it, make sure the grooved insert is installed in the block. Lay the other bearing from each set in the corresponding main bearing cap. Make sure the tab on the bearing insert fits into the recess in the block or cap. **Caution:** *The oil holes in the block must line up with the oil holes in the bearing insert* (see illustration). *Do not hammer the bearing into place and don't nick or gouge the bearing faces. No lubrication should be used at this time.*

6   The flanged thrust bearing must be installed in the number three main bearing cap and saddle.

7   Clean the faces of the bearings in the block and the crankshaft main bearing journals with a clean, lint-free cloth.

8   Check or clean the oil holes in the crankshaft, as any dirt here can go only one way – straight through the new bearings.

9   Once you're certain the crankshaft is clean, carefully lay it in position in the main bearings.

10 Before the crankshaft can be permanently installed, the main bearing oil clearance must be checked.

11 Cut several pieces of the appropriate size Plastigage (they must be slightly shorter than the width of the main bearings) and place one piece

2E

22.11 Lay the Plastigage strips (arrow) on the main bearing journals, parallel to the crankshaft centerline

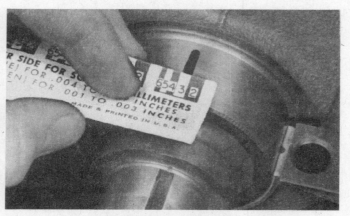

22.15 Compare the width of the crushed Plastigage to the scale on the envelope to determine the main bearing oil clearance (always take the measurement at the widest point of the Plastigage); be sure to use the correct scale – standard and metric ones are included

22.31 Use a screwdriver to tap new wedge seals into the groove on each side of the rear main bearing cap

on each crankshaft main bearing journal, parallel with the journal axis **(see illustration)**.

12   Clean the faces of the bearings in the caps and install the caps in their respective positions (don't mix them up) with the arrows pointing toward the front of the engine. Don't disturb the Plastigage.

13   Starting with the center main and working out toward the ends, tighten the main bearing cap bolts, in three steps, to the torque listed in this Chapter's Specifications. Don't rotate the crankshaft at any time during this operation.

14   Remove the bolts and carefully lift off the main bearing caps. Keep them in order. Don't disturb the Plastigage or rotate the crankshaft. If any of the main bearing caps are difficult to remove, tap them gently from side-to-side with a soft-face hammer to loosen them.

15   Compare the width of the crushed Plastigage on each journal to the scale printed on the Plastigage envelope to obtain the main bearing oil clearance **(see illustration)**. Check the Specifications to make sure it's correct.

16   If the clearance is not as specified, the bearing inserts may be the wrong size (which means different ones will be required). Before deciding that different inserts are needed, make sure that no dirt or oil was between the bearing inserts and the caps or block when the clearance was measured. If the Plastigage was wider at one end than the other, the journal may be tapered (refer to Section 18).

17   Carefully scrape all traces of the Plastigage material off the main bearing journals and/or the bearing faces. Use your fingernail or the edge of a credit card – don't nick or scratch the bearing faces.

Final crankshaft installation

18   Carefully lift the crankshaft out of the engine.

19   Clean the bearing faces in the block, then apply a thin, uniform layer of moly-base grease or engine assembly lube to each of the bearing surfaces. Be sure to coat the thrust faces as well as the journal face of the thrust bearing.

20   Make sure the crankshaft journals are clean, then lay the crankshaft back in place in the block.

21   Clean the faces of the bearings in the caps, then apply lubricant to them.

22   Install the caps in their respective positions with the arrows pointing toward the front of the engine.

23   Install the bolts.

24   Tighten all except the thrust bearing cap bolts to the specified torque (work from the center out and approach the final torque in three steps).

25   Tighten the thrust bearing cap bolts to 10-to-12 ft-lbs.

26   Tap the ends of the crankshaft forward and backward with a lead or brass hammer to line up the main bearing and crankshaft thrust surfaces.

27   Retighten all main bearing cap bolts to the specified torque, starting with the center main and working out toward the ends.

28   On manual transmission equipped models, install a new pilot bearing in the end of the crankshaft (see Chapter 8).

29   Rotate the crankshaft a number of times by hand to check for any obvious binding.

30   The final step is to check the crankshaft endplay with a feeler gauge or a dial indicator as described in Section 13. The endplay should be correct if the crankshaft thrust faces aren't worn or damaged and new bearings have been installed.

31   If you are working on a 2.8L V6 engine, install new wedge seals at the sides of the rear main bearing cap **(see illustration)**.

---

23   Pistons/connecting rods – installation and rod bearing oil clearance check

---

Refer to illustrations 23.5a, 23.5b, 23.9, 23.11, 23.13 and 23.17

1   Before installing the piston/connecting rod assemblies, the cylinder walls must be perfectly clean, the top edge of each cylinder must be chamfered, and the crankshaft must be in place.

2   Remove the cap from the end of the number one connecting rod (refer to the marks made during removal). Remove the original bearing inserts and wipe the bearing surfaces of the connecting rod and cap with a clean, lint-free cloth. They must be kept spotlessly clean.

Connecting rod bearing oil clearance check

3   Clean the back side of the new upper bearing insert, then lay it in place in the connecting rod. Make sure the tab on the bearing fits into the

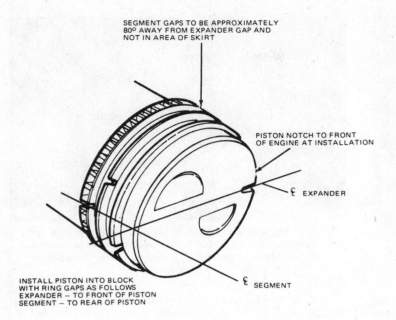

SEGMENT GAPS TO BE APPROXIMATELY 80° AWAY FROM EXPANDER GAP AND NOT IN AREA OF SKIRT

PISTON NOTCH TO FRONT OF ENGINE AT INSTALLATION

EXPANDER

SEGMENT

INSTALL PISTON INTO BLOCK WITH RING GAPS AS FOLLOWS
EXPANDER – TO FRONT OF PISTON
SEGMENT – TO REAR OF PISTON

23.5a Ring gap positioning (four-cylinder engines)

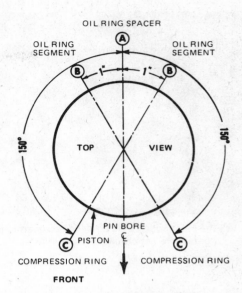

OIL RING SPACER

OIL RING SEGMENT

OIL RING SEGMENT

150°

150°

TOP   VIEW

PIN BORE

PISTON

COMPRESSION RING

COMPRESSION RING

FRONT

23.5b Ring gap positioning (V6 engines)

A) *Oil ring spacer butt connection*

B) *Oil ring side rail gaps*

C) *Compression ring gaps*

2E

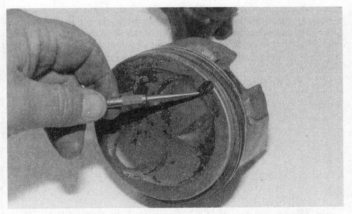

23.9 The notch or arrow in the top of each piston must face the FRONT of the engine as the pistons are installed

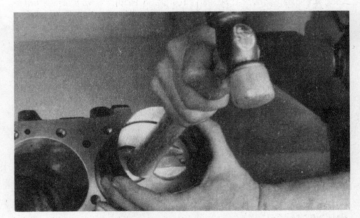

23.11 Drive the piston gently into the cylinder bore with the end of a wooden or plastic hammer handle

recess in the rod. Don't hammer the bearing insert into place and be very careful not to nick or gouge the bearing face. Don't lubricate the bearing at this time.

4   Clean the back side of the other bearing insert and install it in the rod cap. Again, make sure the tab on the bearing fits into the recess in the cap, and don't apply any lubricant. It's critically important that the mating surfaces of the bearing and connecting rod are perfectly clean and oil free when they're assembled.

5   Position the piston ring gaps at intervals around the piston **(see illustrations)**.

6   Slip a section of plastic or rubber hose over each connecting rod cap bolt.

7   Lubricate the piston and rings with clean engine oil and attach a piston ring compressor to the piston. Leave the skirt protruding about 1/4-inch to guide the piston into the cylinder. The rings must be compressed until they're flush with the piston.

8   Rotate the crankshaft until the number one connecting rod journal is at BDC (bottom dead center) and apply a coat of engine oil to the cylinder walls.

9   With the mark or notch on top of the piston **(see illustrations)** facing the front of the engine, gently insert the piston/connecting rod assembly

into the number one cylinder bore and rest the bottom edge of the ring compressor on the engine block.

10   Tap the top edge of the ring compressor to make sure it's contacting the block around its entire circumference.

11   Gently tap on the top of the piston with the end of a wooden hammer handle **(see illustration)** while guiding the end of the connecting rod into place on the crankshaft journal. The piston rings may try to pop out of the ring compressor just before entering the cylinder bore, so keep some downward pressure on the ring compressor. Work slowly, and if any resistance is felt as the piston enters the cylinder, stop immediately. Find out what's hanging up and fix it before proceeding. Do not, for any reason, force the piston into the cylinder – you might break a ring and/or the piston.

12   Once the piston/connecting rod assembly is installed, the connecting rod bearing oil clearance must be checked before the rod cap is permanently bolted in place.

13   Cut a piece of the appropriate size Plastigage slightly shorter than the width of the connecting rod bearing and lay it in place on the number one connecting rod journal, parallel with the journal axis **(see illustration)**.

14   Clean the connecting rod cap bearing face, remove the protective

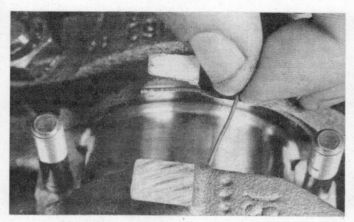

23.13   Lay the Plastigage strips on each rod bearing journal, parallel to the crankshaft centerline

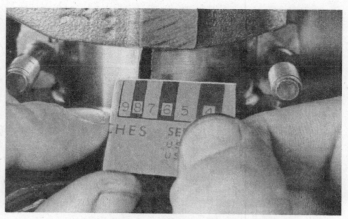

23.17   Measuring the width of the crushed Plastigage to determine the rod bearing oil clearance (be sure to use the correct scale – standard and metric ones are included)

hoses from the connecting rod bolts and install the rod cap. Make sure the mating mark on the cap is on the same side as the mark on the connecting rod.

15   Install the nuts and tighten them to the torque listed in this Chapter's Specifications, working up to it in three steps. **Note:** *Use a thin-wall socket to avoid erroneous torque readings that can result if the socket is wedged between the rod cap and nut. If the socket tends to wedge itself between the nut and the cap, lift up on it slighty until it no longer contacts the cap. Do not rotate the crankshaft at any time during this operation.*

16   Remove the nuts and detach the rod cap, being very careful not to disturb the Plastigage.

17   Compare the width of the crushed Plastigage to the scale printed on the Plastigage envelope to obtain the oil clearance (**see illustration**). Compare it to the Specifications to make sure the clearance is correct.

18   If the clearance is not as specified, the bearing inserts may be the wrong size (which means different ones will be required). Before deciding that different inserts are needed, make sure that no dirt or oil was between the bearing inserts and the connecting rod or cap when the clearance was measured. Also, recheck the journal diameter. If the Plastigage was wider at one end than the other, the journal may be tapered (refer to Section 18).

Final connecting rod installation

19   Carefully scrape all traces of the Plastigage material off the rod journal and/or bearing face. Be very careful not to scratch the bearing – use your fingernail or the edge of a credit card.

20   Make sure the bearing faces are perfectly clean, then apply a uniform layer of clean moly-base grease or engine assembly lube to both of them. You'll have to push the piston into the cylinder to expose the face of the bearing insert in the connecting rod – be sure to slip the protective hoses over the rod bolts first.

21   Slide the connecting rod back into place on the journal, remove the protective hoses from the rod cap bolts, install the rod cap and tighten the nuts to the specified torque. Again, work up to the torque in three steps.

22   Repeat the entire procedure for the remaining pistons/connecting rods.

23   The important points to remember are:
   a) Keep the back sides of the bearing inserts and the insides of the connecting rods and caps perfectly clean when assembling them.
   b) Make sure you have the correct piston/rod assembly for each cylinder.
   c) The notch or mark on the piston must face the front of the engine.
   d) Lubricate the cylinder walls with clean oil.
   e) Lubricate the bearing faces when installing the rod caps after the oil clearance has been checked.

24   After all the piston/connecting rod assemblies have been properly installed, rotate the crankshaft a number of times by hand to check for any obvious binding.

25   As a final step, the connecting rod endplay must be checked. Refer to Section 12 for this procedure.

26   Compare the measured endplay to the Specifications to make sure it's correct. If it was correct before disassembly and the original crankshaft and rods were reinstalled, it should still be right. If new rods or a new crankshaft were installed, the endplay may be inadequate. If so, the rods will have to be removed and taken to an automotive machine shop for resizing.

24   Initial start-up and break-in after overhaul

Warning: *Have a fire extinguisher handy when starting the engine for the first time.*

1   Once the engine has been installed in the vehicle, double-check the engine oil and coolant levels.

2   With the spark plugs out of the engine and the ignition system disabled (see Section 3), crank the engine until oil pressure registers on the gauge or the light goes out.

3   Install the spark plugs, hook up the plug wires and restore the ignition system functions (see Section 3).

4   Start the engine. It may take a few moments for the fuel system to build up pressure, but the engine should start without a great deal of effort. **Note:** *If backfiring occurs through the carburetor or throttle body, recheck the valve timing and ignition timing.*

5   After the engine starts, it should be allowed to warm up to normal operating temperature. While the engine is warming up, make a thorough check for fuel, oil and coolant leaks.

6   Shut the engine off and recheck the engine oil and coolant levels.

7   Drive the vehicle to an area with minimum traffic, accelerate at full throttle from 30 to 50 mph, then allow the vehicle to slow to 30 mph with the throttle closed. Repeat the procedure 10 or 12 times. This will load the piston rings and cause them to seat properly against the cylinder walls. Check again for oil and coolant leaks.

8   Drive the vehicle gently for the first 500 miles (no sustained high speeds) and keep a constant check on the oil level. It is not unusual for an engine to use oil during the break-in period.

9   At approximately 500 to 600 miles, change the oil and filter.

10   For the next few hundred miles, drive the vehicle normally. Do not pamper it or abuse it.

11   After 2000 miles, change the oil and filter again and consider the engine broken in.

Chapter 3   Cooling, heating and air conditioning systems

Contents

Specifications

General

Thermostat
   Type .... Wax pellet
   Opening temperature
      Four-cylinder engines .... 188 to 195-degrees F
      2.8L, 2.9L and 4.0L V6 engines .... 192 to 199-degrees F
   Fully open
      Four-cylinder engines .... 212-degrees F
      2.8L, 2.9L and 4.0L V6 engines .... 226-degrees F
Coolant temperature sending unit switched
   (lamp on) .... 249-degrees F

Torque specifications

Ft-lbs (unless otherwise indicated)

Cooling fan-to-clutch bolts .... 50 to 70 in-lbs
Fan clutch-to-water pump
   Four-cylinder engines (bolts) .... 12 to 18
   V6 engine (nut) 30
Thermostat housing bolt .... 12 to 15
Water pump bolts
   Four-cylinder engines .... 13 to 21
   2.8L, 2.9L and 4.0L V6 engines .... 84 to 108 in-lbs
   3.0L V6 engine* .... 84 in-lbs

*The water pump and timing chain cover share bolts on the 3.0L V6 engine. See Chapter 2C for additional information.

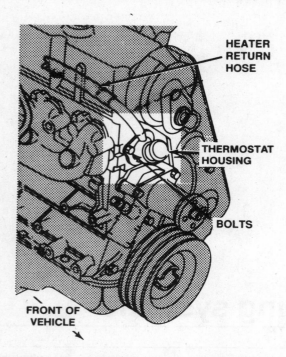

3.7a   **The location of the thermostat on four-cylinder engines**

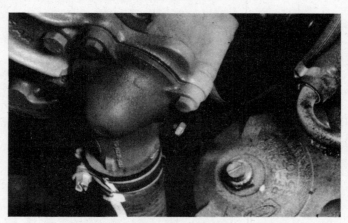

3.7b   **The thermostat on some 2.8L V6 engines is mounted low on the front of the engine**

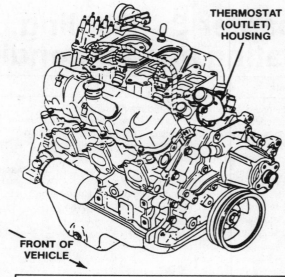

3.7c   **The thermostat on some 2.8L V6 engines, as well as all 2.9L and 4.0L V6 engines, is mounted at the front of the intake manifold**

1   General information

Engine cooling system

All vehicles covered by this manual employ a pressurized engine cooling system with thermostatically controlled coolant circulation. An impeller type water pump mounted on the front of the block pumps coolant through the engine. The coolant flows around each cylinder and toward the rear of the engine. Cast-in coolant passages direct coolant around the intake and exhaust ports, near the spark plug areas and in close proximity to the exhaust valve guides.

A wax pellet type thermostat is located in a housing near the front of the engine. During warm up, the closed thermostat prevents coolant from circulating through the radiator. As the engine nears normal operating temperature, the thermostat opens and allows hot coolant to travel through the radiator, where it's cooled before returning to the engine.

The cooling system is sealed by a pressure type radiator cap, which raises the boiling point of the coolant and increases the cooling efficiency of the radiator. If the system pressure exceeds the cap pressure relief value, the excess pressure in the system forces the spring-loaded valve inside the cap off its seat and allows the coolant to escape through the overflow tube into a coolant reservoir. When the system cools the excess coolant is automatically drawn from the reservoir back into the radiator.

The coolant reservoir does double duty as both the point at which fresh coolant is added to the cooling system to maintain the proper fluid level and as a holding tank for overheated coolant.

This type of cooling system is known as a closed design because coolant that escapes past the pressure cap is saved and reused.

Heating system

The heating system consists of a blower fan and heater core located in the heater box, the hoses connecting the heater core to the engine cooling system and the heater/air conditioning control head on the dashboard. Hot engine coolant is circulated through the heater core. When the heater mode is activated, a flap door opens to expose the heater box to the passenger compartment. A fan switch on the control head activates the blower motor, which forces air through the core, heating the air.

Air conditioning system

The air conditioning system consists of a condenser mounted in front of the radiator, an evaporator mounted adjacent to the heater core, a compressor mounted on the engine, a filter-drier (accumulator) which contains a high pressure relief valve and the plumbing connecting all of the above components.

A blower fan forces the warmer air of the passenger compartment through the evaporator core (sort of a radiator-in-reverse), transferring the heat from the air to the refrigerant. The liquid refrigerant boils off into low pressure vapor, taking the heat with it when it leaves the evaporator.

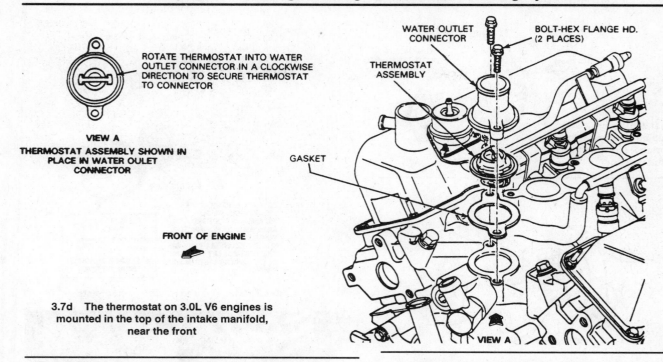

ROTATE THERMOSTAT INTO WATER
OUTLET CONNECTOR IN A CLOCKWISE
DIRECTION TO SECURE THERMOSTAT
TO CONNECTOR

VIEW A
THERMOSTAT ASSEMBLY SHOWN IN
PLACE IN WATER OULET
CONNECTOR

FRONT OF ENGINE

WATER OUTLET
CONNECTOR

BOLT-HEX FLANGE HD.
(2 PLACES)

THERMOSTAT
ASSEMBLY

GASKET

VIEW A

**3.7d   The thermostat on 3.0L V6 engines is
mounted in the top of the intake manifold,
near the front**

2   Antifreeze – general information

Warning: *Do not allow antifreeze to come in contact with your skin or
painted surfaces of the vehicle. Rinse off spills immediately with plenty of
water. If consumed, antifreeze can be fatal; children and pets are attracted by its sweet taste, so wipe up garage floor and drip pan coolant
spills immediately. Keep antifreeze containers covered and repair leaks in
your cooling system as soon as they are noticed.*

The cooling system should be filled with a water/ethylene glycol based
antifreeze solution, which will prevent freezing down to at least -20-de-
grees F, or lower if local climate requires it. It also provides protection
against corrosion and increases the coolant boiling point.

The cooling system should be drained, flushed and refilled at the specified intervals (see Chapter 1). Old or contaminated antifreeze solutions
are likely to cause damage and encourage the formation of rust and scale
in the system. Use distilled water with the antifreeze.

Before adding antifreeze, check all hose connections, because antifreeze tends to search out and leak through very minute openings. Engines don't normally consume coolant, so if the level goes down, find the
cause and correct it.

The exact mixture of antifreeze-to-water which you should use depends on the relative weather conditions. The mixture should contain at
least 50 percent antifreeze, but should never contain more than 70 percent antifreeze. Consult the mixture ratio chart on the antifreeze
container before adding coolant. Hydrometers are available at most auto parts
stores to test the coolant. Use antifreeze which meets specification ESE-
M97B44-A (Ford part No. E2FZ-19549-A) or equivalent.

3   Thermostat – check and replacement

Warning: *Do not remove the radiator cap, drain the coolant or replace the
thermostat until the engine has cooled completely.*

Check

1   Before assuming the thermostat is to blame for a cooling system
problem, check the coolant level, drivebelt tension (see Chapter 1) and
temperature gauge (or light) operation.
2   If the engine seems to be taking a long time to warm up (based on
heater output or temperature gauge operation), the thermostat is probably stuck open. Replace the thermostat with a new one.

3   If the engine runs hot, use your hand to check the temperature of the
upper radiator hose. If the hose isn't hot, but the engine is, the thermostat
is probably stuck closed, preventing the coolant inside the engine from es-
caping to the radiator. Replace the thermostat. **Caution:** *Don't drive the
vehicle without a thermostat. The computer may stay in open loop and
emissions and fuel economy will suffer.*
4   If the upper radiator hose is hot, it means that the coolant is flowing
and the thermostat is open. Consult the Troubleshooting Section at the
front of this manual for cooling system diagnosis.

Replacement

Refer to illustrations 3.7a, 3.7b, 3.7c, 3.7d, 3.14a, 3.14b and 3.15
5   Disconnect the negative battery cable from the battery.
6   Drain the cooling system (see Chapter 1). If the coolant is relatively
new or in good condition (see Chapter 1), save it and reuse it.
7   Follow the upper radiator hose to the engine to locate the thermostat
housing. The housing is located as follows:
   a) Four-cylinder engines: on the right side of the cylinder head **(see
       illustration)**.
   b) 2.8L, 2.9L and 4.0L V6 engines: either low on the left side of the
       engine next to the water pump **(see illustration)** or at the front of
       the intake manifold **(see illustration)**.
   c) 3.0L V6 engine: in the top of the intake manifold near the front **(see
       illustration)**.
8   On four-cylinder engines, disconnect the heater return hose from the
thermostat housing cover.
9   Loosen the hose clamp, then detach the hose from the fitting. If it's
stuck, grasp it near the end with a pair of adjustable pliers and twist it to
break the seal, then pull it off. If the hose is old or deteriorated, cut it off and
install a new one.
10   If the outer surface of the large fitting that mates with the hose is deteriorated (corroded, pitted, etc.) it may be damaged further by hose removal. If it is, the thermostat housing cover will have to be replaced.
11   Remove the bolts and detach the housing cover. If the cover is stuck,
tap it with a soft-face hammer to jar it loose. Be prepared for some coolant
to spill out as the gasket seal is broken.
12   Note how it's installed (which end is facing up), then turn the thermostat counterclockwise and remove it and the gasket.
13   Stuff a rag into the engine opening, then remove all traces of old gasket material and sealant from the housing and cover with a gasket scraper. Remove the rag from the opening and clean the gasket mating
surfaces with lacquer thinner or acetone.

3

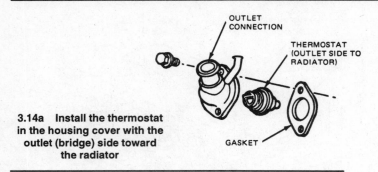

3.14a   Install the thermostat in the housing cover with the outlet (bridge) side toward the radiator

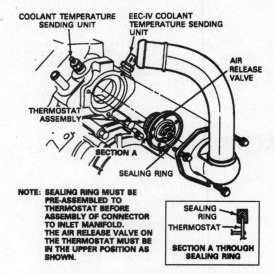

NOTE: SEALING RING MUST BE PRE-ASSEMBLED TO THERMOSTAT BEFORE ASSEMBLY OF CONNECTOR TO INLET MANIFOLD. THE AIR RELEASE VALVE ON THE THERMOSTAT MUST BE IN THE UPPER POSITION AS SHOWN.

3.14b   Thermostat and related components

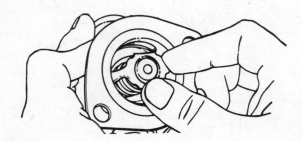

3.15   On four-cylinder engines, the port alignment of the thermostat to the housing cover is necessary to allow maximum coolant flow to the heater

4.3a   Most hose clamps can be loosened with a socket (arrow) . . .

4.3b   . . . or a screwdriver (arrow)

14   Install the new thermostat in the housing cover with the bridge section in the outlet housing **(see illustration)**. On all except the 4.0L engine, turn the thermostat clockwise to lock it in place on the flats cast into the housing. On 4.0L engines, make sure the sealing ring is correctly positioned and the air release valve is positioned up **(see illustration)**.

15   On four-cylinder models, make sure the thermostat is aligned properly to allow full flow to the heater **(see illustration)**.

16   Separate gaskets are used on all engines except the 4.0L engine. Gaskets may be plain or precoated with adhesive. On precoated gaskets, peel the protective paper away from the adhesive. Coat the plain gasket on both sides with a thin, even layer of gasket sealant. Place the gasket on the housing cover.

17   Install the housing cover and bolts. Tighten the bolts to the torque listed in this Chapter's Specifications.

18   Reattach the hose to the fitting and tighten the hose clamp securely.

19   On four-cylinder engines, connect the heater return hose to the thermostat housing cover.

20   Refill the cooling system (see Chapter 1).

21   Start the engine and allow it to reach normal operating temperature, then check for leaks and proper thermostat operation (as described in Steps 2 through 4).

4   Radiator – removal and installation

Refer to illustrations 4.3a, 4.3b, 4.5 and 4.8

Warning: Wait until the engine is completely cool before beginning this procedure.

1   Disconnect the negative battery cable from the battery.

2   Drain the cooling system (see Chapter 1). If the coolant is relatively new or in good condition, save it and reuse it.

3   Loosen the hose clamps, then detach the radiator hoses from the fittings **(see illustrations)**. If they're stuck, grasp each hose near the end with a pair of adjustable pliers and twist it to break the seal, then pull it off – be careful not to distort the radiator fittings! If the hoses are old or deteriorated, cut them off and install new ones.

4   Disconnect the reservoir hose from the radiator filler neck.

5   If the radiator is equipped with a finger guard, remove it. If it has a shroud, remove the screws that attach the shroud to the radiator and slide the shroud toward the engine **(see illustration)**.

6   If the vehicle is equipped with an automatic transmission, disconnect the cooler lines from the radiator. Use a drip pan to catch spilled fluid.

7   Plug the lines and fittings to avoid spillage and contamination.

8   Remove the radiator mounting bolts and brackets (models so equipped) **(see illustration)**.

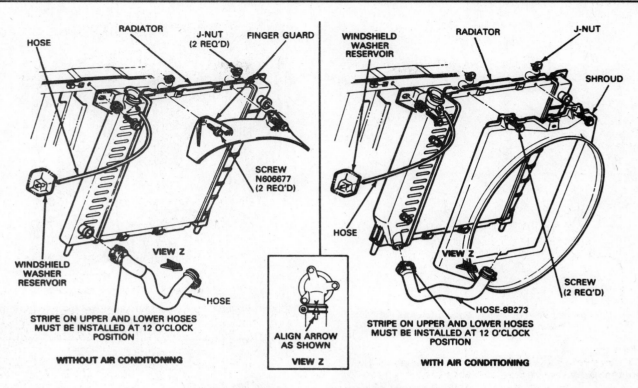

4.5   The radiator and shroud or finger guard (typical)

4.8   Some radiators have brackets like this at the top to secure them – others have bolts securing the top of the radiator to the vehicle (1983 through 1985 models shown)

9   Carefully lift the radiator up and out of its lower mounting pads or grommets. Remove the radiator and be careful not to spill coolant on the vehicle or scratch the paint.

10   With the radiator removed, it can be inspected for leaks and damage. If it needs repair, have a radiator shop or dealer service department perform the work as special techniques are required.

11   Bugs and dirt can be removed from the radiator with compressed air and a soft brush. Don't bend the cooling fins as this is done.

12   Check the radiator mounts for deterioration and make sure there's nothing in them when the radiator is installed.

13   Installation is the reverse of the removal procedure with the following additions:

a)   After installation, fill the cooling system with the proper mixture of antifreeze and water (see Chapter 1).

b)   Start the engine and check for leaks. Allow the engine to reach normal operating temperature, indicated by the upper radiator hose becoming hot. Recheck the coolant level and add more if required.

c)   If you're working on an automatic transmission equipped vehicle, check and add transmission fluid as needed.

---

5   Cooling fan and viscous clutch – inspection, removal and installation

---

Warning: *To avoid possible injury or damage, DO NOT operate the engine with a damaged fan. Do not attempt to repair fan blades – replace a damaged fan with a new one.*

Viscous clutch inspection

1   Disconnect the negative cable from the battery.

2   Rock the fan back and forth by hand to check for excessive bearing play.

3   With the engine cold, turn the fan blades by hand. The fan should turn freely.

4   Visually inspect for substantial fluid leakage from the clutch assembly. If problems are noted, replace the clutch assembly.

5   Reconnect the battery cable and warm up the engine. With the engine completely warmed up, turn off the ignition switch and disconnect the negative battery cable from the battery. Turn the fan by hand. Some drag should be evident. If the fan turns easily, replace the fan clutch.

Removal and installation
Four-cylinder engines
Refer to illustration 5.9

6   Disconnect the negative cable from the battery.

7   Disconnect the reservoir hose from the radiator filler neck.

8   Remove the screws securing the shroud to the radiator and slide the shroud toward the engine (see Section 4).

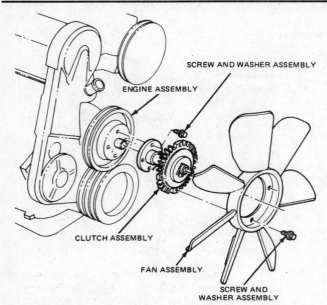

5.9   An exploded view of the fan and clutch assembly (four-cylinder engines)

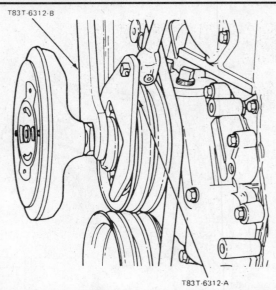

5.16a   The large nut that secures the fan/clutch assembly has left-hand threads; the special tool numbers shown are for all models except 4.0L

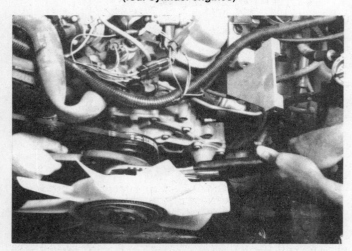

5.16b   Use a strap wrench and large adjustable pliers to remove the nut if the special tools are not available

9   Remove the four screws and washers attaching the fan/clutch assembly to the water pump drive belt hub **(see illustration)**.
10   Lift the fan/clutch assembly out of the engine compartment.
11   Inspect the fan blades for damage and defects. Replace it if necessary by removing the screws securing the fan to the clutch assembly. **Caution:** *If the fan clutch is stored, position it with the radiator side facing down. Otherwise the fluid may leak out.*
12   Installation is the reverse of removal. Be sure to tighten the fan and clutch mounting bolts evenly and securely.

V6 engines
Refer to illustrations 5.16a, 5.16b and 5.18

13   Disconnect the negative cable from the battery.
14   Disconnect the reservoir hose from the radiator filler neck.
15   Remove the screws securing the shroud to the radiator and slide the shroud toward the engine (see Section 4).
16   Perform the following:
   a)   Remove the large nut securing the clutch hub assembly to the water pump drivebelt hub. **Caution:** *On all engines except the 1991 and later 4.0L, this nut has left-hand threads and must be rotated clockwise for removal. 1991 and later 4.0L models have standard right-hand threads.*

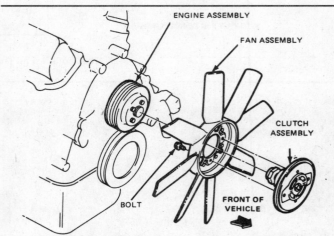

5.18   An exploded view of the fan and clutch assembly (typical V6 engine)

   b)   To remove the nut, use special tools: Fan Clutch Pulley Holder (Ford part No. T84T-6312-C [4.0L] or T83T-6312-A [all others]) and Fan Clutch Nut Wrench (Ford part No. T84T-6312-D [4.0L] or T83T-6312-B [all others]), or equivalents **(see illustration)**.
   c)   If the special tools are not available, use a strap wrench to hold the assembly from rotating and use large adjustable pliers to remove the large nut **(see illustration)**.
17   Lift the fan/clutch assembly out of the engine compartment.
18   Inspect the fan blades for damage and defects. Replace it if necessary by removing the bolts securing the fan to the clutch assembly **(see illustration)**. If the fan clutch is stored, position it with the radiator side facing down.
19   Installation is the reverse of the removal steps. Be sure to tighten the fan and clutch mounting nut to the torque listed in this Chapter's Specifications.

---

6   Coolant reservoir – removal and installation

1   Disconnect the radiator overflow hose from the base of the coolant reservoir (see Chapter 1). If the washer fluid reservoir is part of the cool-

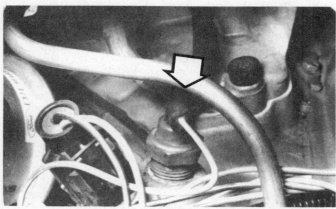

7.2a   The temperature sending unit (arrow) is located on the intake manifold on 2.8L V6 engines (2.9L and 4.0L similar)

ant reservoir, disconnect the hose from the washer fluid reservoir side also.

2   Connect a hose to the fitting on the coolant reservoir and drain the coolant from the reservoir. If the washer fluid reservoir is part of the coolant reservoir, drain the washer fluid reservoir in a similar manner.

3   Remove the reservoir attachment to the inner fender panel.

4   Lift the reservoir out of the engine compartment.

5   Installation is the reverse of removal. Refill the reservoir with coolant (see Chapter 1).

7   Coolant temperature sending unit – removal and installation

Refer to illustrations 7.2a and 7.2b

1   Allow the cooling system to completely cool down (five hours minimum), then open the radiator filler cap to relieve any pressure in the cooling system. Install the cap. This will minimize coolant loss during this procedure.

2   Disconnect the electrical connector from the top of the sending unit (see illustration 2.4 in Chapter 2, Part E and the accompanying illustrations).

3   Apply sealant D8AZ-19554-A, or equivalent, to the threads of the new sending unit.

4   Remove the old sending unit from the engine. Place your finger over the hole in the engine to minimize coolant loss.

5   Immediately install the new sending unit and tighten securely.

6   Connect the sending unit electrical connector.

7   Refill the cooling system (see Chapter 1).

8   Start the engine and check for leaks.

8   Water pump – check and replacement

Check

1   A failure in the water pump can cause serious engine damage due to overheating.

2   There are three ways to check the operation of the water pump while it's installed on the engine. If the pump is defective, it should be replaced with a new or rebuilt unit.

3   With the engine running at normal operating temperature, squeeze the upper radiator hose. If the water pump is working properly, a pressure surge should be felt as the hose is released. **Warning:** *Keep your hands away from the fan blades!*

4   Water pumps are equipped with weep or vent holes. If a failure occurs in the pump seal, coolant will leak from the hole. In most cases you'll need a flashlight to find the hole on the water pump from underneath to check for leaks.

5   If the water pump shaft bearings fail there may be a howling sound at the front of the engine while it's running. Shaft wear can be felt if the water

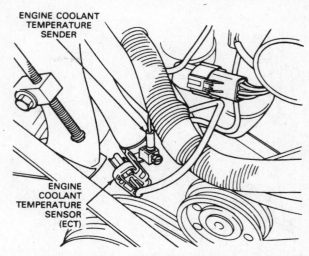

7.2b   The temperature sending unit (sender) is located near the thermostat housing on 3.0L engines – follow the electrical wiring from the connector back to the sending unit

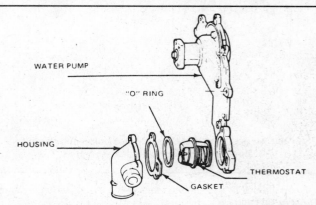

8.13a   The 2.8L, 2.9L and 4.0L engine water pump is bolted to the front of the engine; some 2.8L engines include the thermostat housing in the water pump

pump pulley is rocked up and down (while the engine's off). Don't mistake drivebelt slippage, which causes a squealing sound, for water pump bearing failure.

Replacement

Refer to illustrations 8.13a, 8.13b and 8.13c

Warning: *Wait until the engine is completely cool before beginning this procedure.*

6   Disconnect the negative battery cable from the battery.

7   Drain the cooling system (see Chapter 1). If the coolant is relatively new or in good condition, save it and reuse it.

8   Remove the cooling fan and shroud (see Section 4).

9   Remove the drivebelts (see Chapter 1) and the pulley at the end of the water pump shaft.

10   Loosen the clamps and detach the hoses from the water pump. If they're stuck, grasp each hose near the end with a pair of adjustable pliers and twist it to break the seal, then pull it off. If the hoses are deteriorated, cut them off and install new ones.

11   V6 engines: If necessary, remove the alternator and its mounting bracket from the water pump.

12   Four-cylinder engine: Remove the outer timing belt cover (see Chapter 2A).

13   Remove the bolts and detach the water pump from the engine **(see illustrations)**. Note the locations of the various lengths and different types of bolts as they're removed to ensure correct installation.

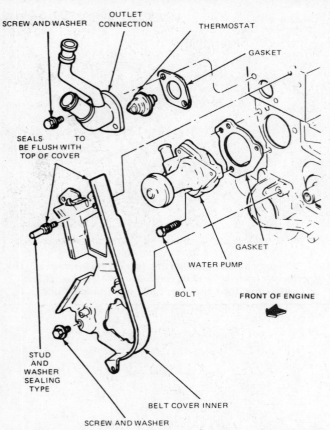

8.13b   **An exploded view of the water pump and related components (four-cylinder engine)**

14   Clean the bolt threads and the threaded holes in the engine to remove corrosion and sealant.
15   Compare the new pump to the old one to make sure they're identical.

16   Remove all traces of old gasket material from the engine gasket surface with a gasket scraper.
17   Clean the engine and new water pump gasket mating surfaces with lacquer thinner or acetone.
18   Apply a thin coat of RTV sealant to the engine side of the new gasket.
19   Apply a thin layer of RTV sealant to the gasket mating surface of the new pump, then carefully mate the gasket and the pump. Slip a couple of bolts through the pump mounting holes to hold the gasket in place.
20   Carefully attach the pump and gasket to the engine and thread the bolts into the holes finger tight.
21   Install the remaining bolts (if they also hold the alternator bracket in place, be sure to reposition the bracket at this time). Tighten them evenly to the torque listed in this Chapter's Specifications in 1/4-turn increments. Don't overtighten them or the pump may be distorted. **Note:** *Some of the water pump bolts on the 3.0L V6 also secure the timing chain cover to the block. Refer to Chapter 2C for additional information.*
22   Reinstall all parts removed for access to the pump.
23   Refill the cooling system and check the drivebelt tension (see Chapter 1). Run the engine and check for leaks.

9   Heater – general information

The heater circulates engine coolant through a small radiator (heater core) in the passenger compartment. Air is drawn in through an opening in the cowl, then blown (by the blower motor) through the heater core to pick up heat. The heated air is blended with varying amounts of unheated air to regulate the temperature. The heated air is then blown into the passenger compartment. Various doors in the heater control the flow of air to the floor and through the instrument panel louvers and defroster outlets.

10   Heater control assembly – removal and installation

1983 through 1988 models
Refer to illustrations 10.3, 10.10, 10.11 and 10.13
Removal
1   Disconnect the negative cable from the battery.
2   On models so equipped, pull the control knobs from the radio shafts.

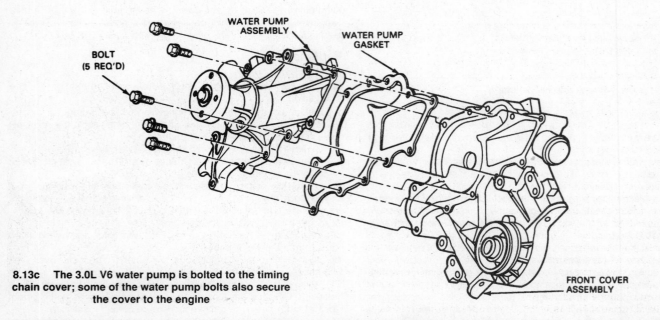

8.13c   **The 3.0L V6 water pump is bolted to the timing chain cover; some of the water pump bolts also secure the cover to the engine**

10.3   The bottom trim panel is held in place with spring-type clips

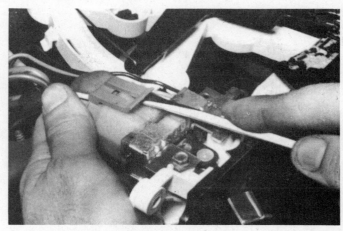

10.10   Spread the clips and pull the electrical connector from the function control

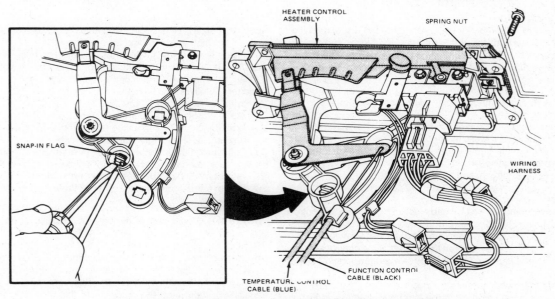

10.11   Remove the function cable snap-in flag with a screwdriver

3   Pry the bottom trim panel(s) from the instrument panel. They are held in place by spring-type clips **(see illustration)**.

4   Remove the four screws securing the top cluster trim panel to the upper finish panel pad.

5   Remove the four bolts securing the bottom of the cluster finish panel.

6   Remove the cigar lighter.

7   Pull the headlight switch to the ON position to allow room for trim panel removal.

8   Remove the cluster trim panel.

9   Remove the four screws securing the control assembly to the instrument panel.

10   Pull the control assembly through the opening in the instrument panel far enough to allow removal of the electrical connections. Carefully spread the clips on the electrical connectors and disconnect the connectors for the blower switch and illumination light **(see illustration)**.

11   On the bottom side of the control assembly, use a screwdriver or needle-nose pliers to release the function cable (black) snap-in flag from the control bracket **(see illustration)**.

12   Pull enough cable through the instrument opening until the function cable (black) can be held vertical to the control assembly, then remove the cable end from the function lever.

13   On the top of the control assembly, use needle-nose pliers to release

the temperature cable (blue) and the outside air door cable snap-in flags (white) **(see illustration)**.

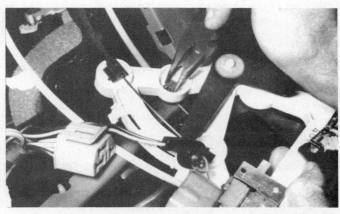

10.13   Use needle-nose pliers to release the temperature cable (blue) and air door cable (white) snap-in flags

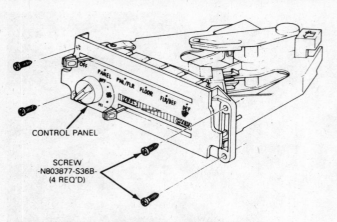

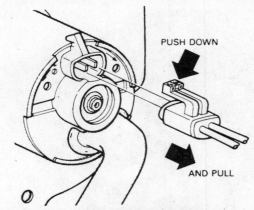

10.28   Control assembly mounting screws

12.3   Push down on the electrical connector locking tab and disconnect the connector

14 Rotate the control assembly down 90-degrees and disconnect the temperature cable wire from the temperature control lever and the air door cable wire from the air door control lever. Remove the control assembly from the instrument panel.

Installation

15 Pull the control cables through the instrument panel opening by approximately eight inches.

16 Hold the control assembly up to the instrument panel with the control assembly face pointed toward the floor.

17 Attach the temperature cable (blue) and the air door (white) to the control levers. Rotate the assembly back to the normal position and snap the cable flags into the control assembly bracket. **Note:** *The letters BL on the bottom of the control assembly bracket indicate the location for the blue temperature control cable snap-in flag.*

18 Gently bend the function control cable (black) down to the control assembly (end of cable pointing toward the floor) and attach the cable wire to the function control lever. Snap the cable flag into the control assembly racket. **Note:** *The letters BK on the bottom of the control assembly bracket indicate the location for the black temperature control cable snap-in flag.*

19 Install the electrical wire harness connectors.

20 Position the control assembly into the instrument panel and install the four mounting screws.

21 Complete the installation by installing the various trim panels and instrument panel items previously removed. Check for proper operation and adjust the cables if necessary (see Section 11).

1989 and later models

Refer to illustration 10.28

Removal

22 Disconnect the negative cable from the battery.

23 Remove the ashtray. Disconnect the electrical connector from the cigar lighter.

24 Remove the two screws securing the ashtray retainer to the instrument panel.

25 Remove the ashtray bracket from the instrument panel and disconnect the electrical connector from the illumination bulb socket.

26 On 4WD models, disconnect the electrical connector from the electronic shift-on-the-fly transfer switch.

27 Carefully pull the finish panel away from the instrument panel and instrument cluster. The finish panel pops straight back for approximately one-inch, the pull up and remove it.

28 Remove the four screws securing the control panel to the instrument panel **(see illustration)**.

29 Pull the control assembly through the opening in the instrument panel far enough to allow removal of the electrical connections. Carefully

spread the clips on the electrical connectors and disconnect the connectors for the blower switch and illumination light.

30 Use a small screwdriver to remove the two-hose vacuum harness from the vacuum switch on the side of the control assembly.

31 At the back of the control assembly, use a screwdriver or needle-nose pliers to release the temperature and function cable snap-in flag from the white control bracket.

32 At the bottom of the control assembly, remove the temperature control cable (black cable with a blue snap-in flag) from the control by rotating the cable until the T-pin releases the cable.

33 Pull enough cable through the instrument opening until the function cable (white cable with black snap-in flag) can be held vertical to the control assembly, then remove the cable end from the function lever.

34 Remove the control assembly from the instrument panel.

Installation

35 Pull the control cables through the instrument panel opening by approximately eight inches.

36 Hold the control assembly up to the instrument panel with the control assembly face pointed toward the floor.

37 Carefully bend and attach the function cable (white) to the white plastic lever. Rotate the control assembly back to its normal position for installation, then snap the black cable flag into the control assembly bracket.

38 On the opposite side of the control assembly, attach the black temperature control cable with the blue snap-in flag to the blue plastic lever on the control assembly. Be sure that the end of the cable is seated securely with the T-top pin on the control assembly. Rotate the cable to its operating position and snap the blue cable flag into the control assembly bracket.

39 Install the electrical wire harness connectors.

40 Connect the dual terminal on the vacuum hose to the vacuum switch on the control assembly.

41 Position the control assembly into the instrument panel and install the four mounting screws.

42 Complete the installation by installing the various trim panels and instrument panel items previously removed. Check for proper operation and adjust the cables if necessary (see Section 11).

---

11   Heater control cables – check and adjustment

Check

1   Move the control lever all the way from left to right.

2   If the control lever stops before the end and bounces back, the cables should be considered misadjusted and heater output may be substandard.

12.6   Remove the three screws securing the heater blower motor

12.7   Carefully pull the blower assembly from the heater assembly

Adjustment

3   Disengage the glove box door and let it hang down to provide access to the control cables.

4   Working through the glove box opening, remove the cable jacket from its metal attaching clip on top of the heater assembly. The cable ends should remain attached to the door cams and/or crank arms at this time.

5   To adjust the temperature control cable, set the temperature lever to cool and hold it in this position.

6   Push gently on the cable jacket (blue) to seat the blend door (push until you feel resistance).

7   Reinstall the cable to the clip by pushing the jacket into the clip from the top until it snaps in.

8   To adjust the function control cable, set the function control lever to defrost and hold it in this position.

9   Pull on the cam jacket until the cam travel stops.

10   Reinstall the cable to the clip by pushing the jacket into the clip from the top until it snaps in.

11   To adjust the outside air control cable, set the lever to the Off position and hold it in this position.

12   Set the outside air door crank arm (white) in the down position (door closed to shut off air flow).

13   Reinstall the cable to the clip by pushing the jacket into the clip from the top until it snaps in.

14   Run the system on high and actuate the levers, check for proper operation. Readjust if necessary.

15   Install the glove box door.

12   Heater blower motor – replacement

Refer to illustrations 12.3, 12.6, 12.7 and 12.8

Note: *The blower motor is located in the right side of the engine compartment.*

1   Disconnect the negative cable from the battery.

2   Depending on engine type, the air cleaner and/or solenoid cover box may have to be removed to gain access to the blower motor.

3   Working in the engine compartment, push down on the electrical connector locking tab and disconnect the connector from the blower motor **(see illustration)**.

4   On 1989 and later models, perform the following:

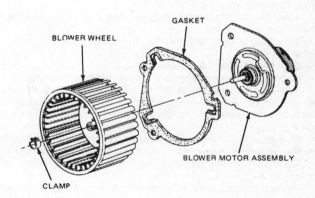

12.8   An exploded view of the blower motor and wheel assembly

a)   Disconnect the vacuum hose from the vacuum check valve.

b)   Disconnect the vacuum line attached to the heater blower assembly from the vacuum source on the engine intake manifold and remove it from the routing channel.

5   Disconnect the small rubber cooling tube from the blower motor.

6   Remove the three screws securing the blower motor to the heater blower assembly **(see illustration)**.

7   Being very careful not to damage the gasket, pull the blower motor assembly out of the heater assembly **(see illustration)**.

8   If necessary, remove the clamp on the motor shaft and remove the blower wheel from the motor **(see illustration)**.

9   Installation is the reverse of the removal procedures with the addition of the following:

a)   Replace the gasket between the blower motor and heater assembly if its condition is in doubt. This gasket must be good to prevent moisture from entering the assembly.

b)   Make sure the electrical connector is fully seated and that it "clicks" into place.

13.5   Disconnect the heater hoses from the fittings at the firewall

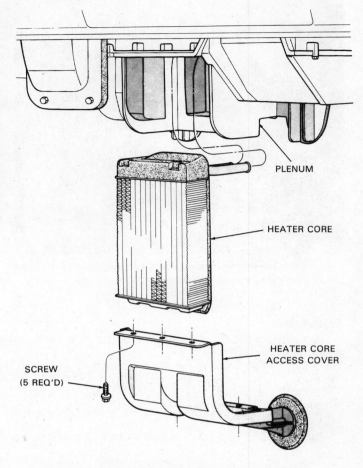

13.8   An exploded view of the heater core assembly

PLENUM

HEATER CORE

HEATER CORE ACCESS COVER

SCREW (5 REQ'D)

13   Heater core – replacement

Refer to illustrations 13.5, 13.8 and 13.9

1   Allow the cooling system to completely cool down (at least five hours).
2   Using a thick cloth for protection, turn the radiator filler cap to the first stop.
3   Step back and let the pressure release.
4   Once the pressure has been released, tighten the radiator cap.
5   Working within the engine compartment, loosen the clamps on the heater hoses at the engine compartment side of the firewall **(see illustration)**. Twist the hoses and carefully separate them from the heater core tubes.
6   Plug or cap the heater core tubes to prevent coolant from spilling into the passenger compartment when the heater core is removed.
7   Place a plastic sheet on the vehicle floor to prevent stains in case the coolant spills.
8   Working in the passenger compartment, remove the screws securing the heater core access cover to the plenum assembly **(see illustration)**.
9   Carefully pull the heater core rearward and down and remove it from the plenum assembly **(see illustration)**.
10   Installation is the reverse of the removal procedure with the following additions:
    a)   Fill the cooling system (see Chapter 1).
    b)   Run the engine and check for leaks and test the heater.

14   Air conditioning system – check and maintenance

Warning: *The air conditioning system is under high pressure. Do not loosen any hose fittings or remove any components until after the system has been discharged by a dealer service department or service station. Always wear eye protection when disconnecting air conditioning system fittings.*

1   The following maintenance checks should be performed on a regular basis to ensure that the air conditioner continues to operate at peak efficiency.
    a)   Check the compressor drivebelt. If it's worn or deteriorated, replace it (see Chapter 1).
    b)   Check the drivebelt tension and, if necessary, adjust it (see Chapter 1).

    c)   Check the system hoses. Look for cracks, bubbles, hard spots and deterioration. Inspect the hoses and all fittings for oil bubbles and seepage. If there's any evidence of wear, damage or leaks, replace the hose(s).
    d)   Inspect the condenser fins for leaves, bugs and other debris. Use a "fin comb" or compressed air to clean the condenser.
    e)   Make sure the system has the correct refrigerant charge.
2   It's a good idea to operate the system for about 10 minutes at least once a month, particularly during the winter. Long term non-use can cause hardening, and subsequent failure, of the seals.
3   Because of the complexity of the air conditioning system and the special equipment necessary to service it, in-depth troubleshooting and repairs are not included in this manual. However, simple checks and component replacement procedures are provided in this Chapter. For more complete information on the air conditioning system, refer to the Haynes automotive heating and air conditioning manual.
4   The most common cause of poor cooling is simply a low system refrigerant charge. If a noticeable drop in cool air output occurs, the following quick check will help you determine if the refrigerant level is low.

Checking the refrigerant charge

5   Warm the engine up to normal operating temperature.
6   Place the air conditioning temperature selector at the coldest setting and put the blower at the highest setting. Open the doors (to make sure the air conditioning system doesn't cycle off as soon as it cools the passenger compartment).

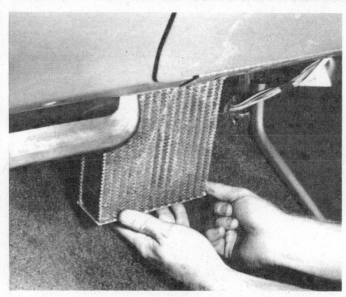

13.9   Pull the heater core rearward and down and remove the heater core

7   With the compressor engaged – the clutch will make an audible click and the center of the clutch will rotate – feel the evaporator inlet pipe between the orifice and the accumulator with one hand while placing your other hand on the surface of the accumulator housing.

8   If both surfaces feel about the same temperature and if both feel a little cooler than the surrounding air, the refrigerant level is probably okay. Further inspection of the system is beyond the scope of the home mechanic and should be left to a professional.

9   If the inlet pipe has frost accumulation or feels cooler than the accumulator surface, the refrigerant charge is low. Add refrigerant.

Adding refrigerant

10   Buy an automotive charging kit at an auto parts store. A charging kit includes a 14-ounce can of refrigerant, a tap valve and a short section of hose that can be attached between the tap valve and the system low side service valve. Because one can of refrigerant may not be sufficient to bring the system charge up to the proper level, it's a good idea to buy a few additional cans. Make sure that one of the cans contains red refrigerant dye. If the system is leaking, the red dye will leak out with the refrigerant and help you pinpoint the location of the leak. **Warning:** *Never add more than three cans of refrigerant to the system.*

11   Hook up the charging kit by following the manufacturer's instructions. **Warning:** *DO NOT hook the charging kit hose to the system high side!*

12   Warm up the engine and turn on the air conditioner. Keep the charging kit hose away from the fan and other moving parts.

13   If the system in your vehicle is an accumulator type:
 a) Add refrigerant to the low side of the system until both the accumulator surface and the evaporator inlet pipe feel about the same temperature. Allow stabilization time between each addition.
 b) Once the accumulator surface and the evaporator inlet pipe feel about the same temperature, add the contents remaining in the can.

---

15   Air conditioning system compressor – removal and installation

---

Warning: *The air conditioning system is under high pressure. DO NOT disassemble any part of the system (hoses, compressor, line fittings, etc.) until after the system has been depressurized by a dealer service depart-*

ment or service station. Always wear eye protection when working on the air conditioning system.

Note: *The accumulator (see Section 17) should be replaced whenever the compressor is replaced.*

1   Have the air conditioning system discharged (see Warning above).
2   Disconnect the negative cable from the battery.
3   Disconnect the compressor clutch wiring harness.
4   Remove the drivebelt (see Chapter 1).
5   Disconnect the refrigerant lines from the rear of the compressor. Plug the open fittings to prevent entry of dirt and moisture.
6   Unbolt the compressor from the mounting brackets and lift it out of the vehicle.
7   If a new compressor is being installed, follow the directions with the compressor regarding the draining of excess oil prior to installation.
8   The clutch may have to be transferred from the original to the new compressor; special tools may be required – consult the shop that sold you the replacement compressor.
9   Installation is the reverse of removal with the following additions:
 a) Replace all O-rings with new ones specifically made for air conditioning system use and lubricate them with refrigerant oil.
 b) Have the system evacuated, recharged and leak tested by the shop that discharged it.

---

16   Air conditioning system condenser – removal and installation

---

Warning: *The air conditioning system is under high pressure. DO NOT disassemble any part of the system (hoses, compressor, line fittings, etc.) until after the system has been depressurized by a dealer service department or service station. Always wear eye protection when working on the air conditioning system.* **Note:** *The accumulator (see Section 17) should be replaced whenever the condenser is replaced.*

1   Have the air conditioning system discharged (see Warning above).
2   Remove the battery (see Chapter 5).
3   Drain the cooling system (see Chapter 1).
4   Remove the radiator (see Section 4).
5   Disconnect the refrigerant lines from the condenser.
6   Remove the mounting bolts from the condenser brackets.
7   Lift the condenser out of the vehicle and plug the lines to keep dirt and moisture out.
8   If the original condenser will be reinstalled, store it with the line fittings on top to prevent oil from draining out.
9   If a new condenser is being installed, pour one ounce of refrigerant oil into it prior to installation.
10   Reinstall the components in the reverse order of removal. Be sure the rubber pads are in place under the condenser.
11   Have the system evacuated, recharged and leak tested by the shop that discharged it.

---

17   Air conditioning system accumulator – removal and installation

---

Warning: *The air conditioning system is under high pressure. DO NOT disassemble any part of the system (hoses, compressor, line fittings, etc.) until after the system has been depressurized by a dealer service department or service station. Always wear eye protection when working on the air conditioning system.*

1   Have the air conditioning system discharged (see Warning above).
2   Disconnect the negative cable from the battery.
3   Unplug the electrical connector from the pressure switch near the top of the accumulator.
4   Disconnect the refrigerant lines from the accumulator. Use a back-up wrench to prevent twisting the tubing.
5   Plug the open fittings to prevent entry of dirt and moisture.
6   Loosen the mounting bracket bolts and lift the accumulator out.
7   If a new accumulator is being installed, remove the Schrader valve and pour the oil out into a measuring cup, noting the amount. Add fresh

3

refrigerant oil to the new accumulator equal to the amount removed from the old unit plus one ounce.

8   Installation is the reverse of removal. Take the vehicle back to the shop that discharged it. Have the air conditioning system evacuated, charged and leak tested.

Chapter 4   Fuel and exhaust systems

Contents

Specifications

Fuel pump

Carbureted models
Flow volume (minimum)
Four-cylinder engines .... 1 pint in 25 seconds
V6 engine .... 1 pint in 30 seconds
Fuel pressure
Four-cylinder engines .... 5 to 7 psi
V6 engine .... 4.5 to 6.5 psi
Fuel-injected models
Fuel pressure (ignition On, engine off – all models) .... 40 psi

Torque specifications

	Ft-lbs (unless otherwise indicated)
Mechanical fuel pump-to-engine bolts	14 to 21
Carburetor-to-intake manifold nuts	
Model YFA-1V	13 to 14
Model 2150-2V	14 to 16
Asian Model Y	13 to 14
Fuel injection system (2.3L 4-cylinder engine)	
Fuel rail mounting bolts	15 to 22
Upper intake manifold mounting bolts	
1985 and 1986 models	14 to 21
1987 and later models	15 to 22
Throttle body bolts and nuts	12 to 15
Fuel injection system (2.9L V6 engine)	
Upper intake manifold mounting bolts	12 to 15
Throttle body-to-upper intake manifold bolts	71 to 106 in-lbs
Fuel rail mounting bolts	71 to 102 in-lbs
Fuel injection system (3.0L V6 engine)	
Upper intake manifold bolts	19
Fuel rail mounting bolts	72 to 96 in-lbs
Fuel injection system (4.0L engine)	
Upper intake manifold bolts/nuts	15 to 18
Throttle body bolts	76 to 106 in-lbs
Fuel rail mounting bolts	72 to 96 in-lbs

4

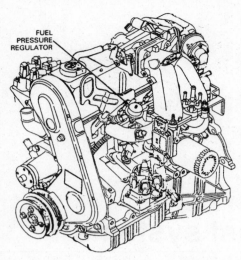

2.2   Fuel pressure regulator location on the 2.3L four-cylinder engine

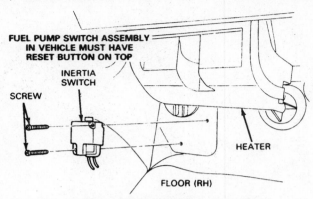

2.5   The inertia switch is located under the dash on the passenger side of the firewall

1   General information

Fuel system

The fuel system consists of the fuel tank(s), the fuel pump(s), an air cleaner assembly, either a carburetor or a fuel injection system and the various steel, plastic and/or nylon lines and fittings connecting all components together.

The fuel pump on carbureted models is a mechanical type mounted on the engine block and driven off the camshaft. 1985 through 1988 fuel-injected models have a low pressure pump mounted inside the fuel tank and a high pressure pump mounted on the chassis. 1989 and later fuel-injected models are equipped with only a single high pressure pump located within the fuel tank.

Exhaust system

All models are equipped with one (four-cylinder) or two (V6) exhaust manifold(s), a catalytic converter, an exhaust pipe and a muffler. Any component of the exhaust system can be replaced. See Chapter 6 for further details regarding the catalytic converter.

2   Fuel pressure relief procedure (fuel-injected models)

Warning: *The fuel system pressure must be relieved before disconnecting fuel lines and fittings on fuel-injected models. Gasoline is extremely flammable, so take extra precautions when you work on any part of the fuel system. Don't smoke or allow open flames or bare light bulbs near the work area, and don't work in a garage where a natural gas-type appliance (such as a water heater or clothes dryer) with a pilot light is present. If you spill any fuel on your skin, rinse it off immediately with soap and water. When you perform any kind of work on the fuel system, wear safety glasses and have a Class B type fire extinguisher on hand.*

Four-cylinder engine

Refer to illustration 2.2

1   Remove the fuel tank cap.
2   Disconnect the vacuum line from the fuel pressure regulator **(see illustration)**.
3   Connect a hand-operated vacuum pump to the fitting on the fuel pressure regulator and apply 25 in. Hg of vacuum. The fuel pressure will be released and the fuel will exit to the fuel tank through the fuel return hose.

4   Disconnect the vacuum pump and reconnect the vacuum line to the fuel pressure regulator.

V6 engines

Refer to illustration 2.5

5   The fuel pump switch – sometimes called the "inertia switch"- shuts off fuel to the engine in the event of a collision. This switch affords a simple and convenient means by which fuel pressure can be relieved before servicing any fuel injection component. The switch is located in the passenger compartment under the dash **(see illustration)**.
6   Unplug the electrical connector from the inertia switch.
7   Crank the engine with the starter for 15 to 20 seconds.
8   The fuel system pressure is now relieved. When you're finished working on the fuel system, reconnect the electrical connector back onto the switch and push the reset button on the top of the switch.

3   Fuel lines and fittings – general information

Refer to illustrations 3.1, 3.5, 3.9, 3.10, 3.13, 3.14 and 3.26
Warning: *The fuel system pressure must be relieved before disconnecting fuel lines and fittings on fuel-injected models (see Section 2). Gasoline is extremely flammable, so take extra precautions when you work on any part of the fuel system. Don't smoke or allow open flames or bare light bulbs near the work area, and don't work in a garage where a natural gas-type appliance (such as a water heater or clothes dryer) with a pilot light is present. If you spill any fuel on your skin, rinse it off immediately with soap and water. When you perform any kind of work on the fuel system, wear safety glasses and have a Class B type fire extinguisher on hand.*

Push connect fittings – disassembly and reassembly

Refer to illustrations 3.1, 3.5 and 3.9
1   Ford uses two different push connect fitting designs. Fittings used with 3/8 and 5/16-inch diameter lines have a "hairpin" type clip; fittings used with 1/4-inch diameter lines have a "duck bill" type clip **(see illustration)**. The procedure used for releasing each type of fitting is different. The clips should be replaced whenever a connector is disassembled.
2   Disconnect all push connect fittings from fuel system components such as the fuel filter, the carburetor/fuel charging assembly, the fuel tank, etc. before removing the assembly.

3/8 and 5/16-inch fittings (hairpin clip)

3   Inspect the internal portion of the fitting for accumulations of dirt. If more than a light coating of dust is present, clean the fitting before disassembly.
4   Some adhesion between the seals in the fitting and the line will occur over a period of time. Twist the fitting on the line, then push and pull the fitting until it moves freely.

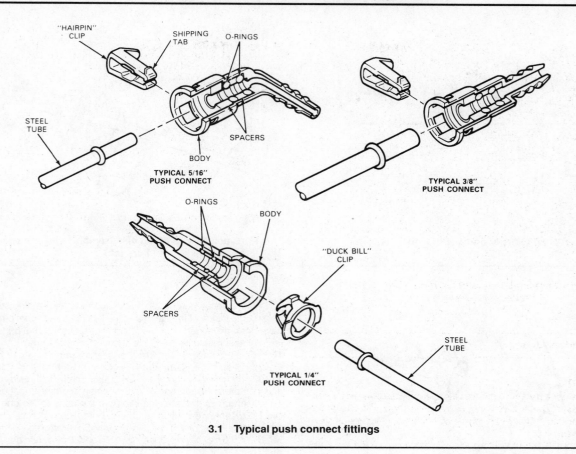

3.1   Typical push connect fittings

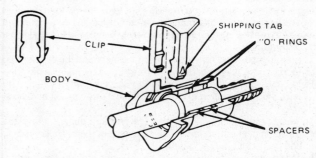

3.5   An exploded view of the hairpin clip type push connect fitting

5   Remove the hairpin clip from the fitting by bending the shipping tab down until it clears the body (**see illustration**). Then, using nothing but your hands, spread each leg about 1/8-inch to disengage the body and push the legs through the fitting. Finally, pull lightly on the triangular end of the clip and work it clear of the line and fitting. Remember, don't use any tools to perform this part of the procedure.

6   Grasp the fitting and hose and pull it straight off the line.

7   Do not reuse the original clip in the fitting. A new clip must be used.

8   Before reinstalling the fitting on the line, wipe the line end with a clean cloth. Inspect the inside of the fitting to ensure that it's free of dirt and/or obstructions.

9   To reinstall the fitting on the line, align them and push the fitting into place. When the fitting is engaged, a definite click will be heard. Pull on the fitting to ensure that it's completely engaged (**see illustration**). To install the new clip, insert it into any two adjacent openings in the fitting with the triangular portion of the clip pointing away from the fitting opening. Using your index finger, push the clip in until the legs are locked on the outside of the fitting. Pull on the fitting to ensure that its fully engaged.

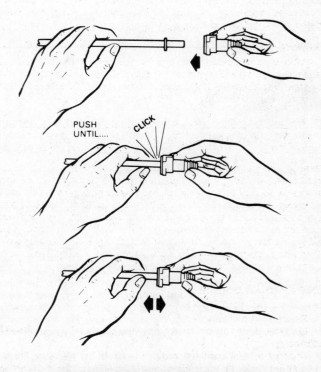

3.9   Reassembling a push connect fitting

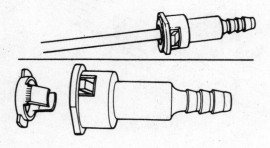

3.10   A push connect fitting with a duck bill clip

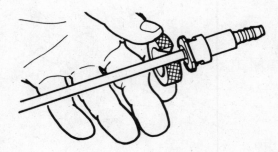

3.13   Duck bill clip fitting disassembly using the special Ford tool

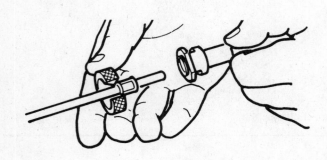

3.14   Pulling off the duck bill clip type push connect fitting

1/4-inch fittings (duck bill clip)

Refer to illustrations 3.10, 3.13 and 3.14

10   The duck bill clip type fitting consists of a body, spacers, O-rings and the retaining clip **(see illustration)**. The clip holds the fitting securely in place on the line. One of the two following methods must be used to disconnect this type of fitting.

11   Before attempting to disconnect the fitting, check the visible internal portion of the fitting for accumulations of dirt. If more than a light coating of dust is evident, clean the fitting before disassembly.

12   Some adhesion between the seals in the fitting and line will occur over a period of time. Twist the fitting on the line, then push and pull the fitting until it moves freely.

13   The preferred method used to disconnect the fitting requires a special tool. To disengage the line from the fitting, align the slot in the push connect disassembly tool (Ford Part no. T82L-9500-AH or equivalent tool) with either tab on the clip (90-degrees from the slots on the side of the fitting) and insert the tool **(see illustration)**. This disengages the duck bill from the line. **Note:** *Some fuel lines have a secondary bead which aligns with the outer surface of the clip. The bead can make tool insertion difficult. If necessary, use the alternative disassembly method described in Step 16.*

14   Holding the tool and the line with one hand, pull the fitting off **(see illustration)**. **Note:** *Only moderate effort is necessary if the clip is properly disengaged. The use of anything other than your hands should not be required.*

15   After disassembly, inspect and clean the line sealing surface. Also inspect the inside of the fitting and the line for any internal parts that may have been dislodged from the fitting. Any loose internal parts should be immediately reinstalled (use the line to insert the parts).

16   The alternative disassembly procedure requires a pair of small adjustable pliers. The pliers must have a jaw width of 3/16-inch or less.

17   Align the jaws of the pliers with the openings in the side of the fitting and compress the portion of the retaining clip that engages the body. This disengages the retaining clip from the body (often one side of the clip will disengage before the other – both sides must be disengaged).

18   Pull the fitting off the line. **Note:** *Only moderate effort is required if the retaining clip has been properly disengaged. Do not use any tools for this procedure.*

19   Once the fitting is removed from the line end, check the fitting and line for any internal parts that may have been dislodged from the fitting. Any loose internal parts should be immediately reinstalled (use the line to insert the parts).

20   The retaining clip will remain on the line. Disengage the clip from the line bead to remove it. Do not reuse the retaining clip – install a new one!

21   Before reinstalling the fitting, wipe the line end with a clean cloth. Check the inside of the fitting to make sure that it's free of dirt and/or obstructions.

22   To reinstall the fitting, align it with the line and push it into place. When the fitting is engaged, a definite click will be heard. Pull on the fitting to ensure that it's fully engaged.

23   Install the new replacement clip by inserting one of the serrated edges on the duck bill portion into one of the openings. Push on the other side until the clip snaps into place.

Spring lock couplings (1988 and later models) – disassembly and reassembly

Refer to illustration 3.26

24   The fuel supply and return lines used on EFI engines utilize spring lock couplings at the engine fuel rail end instead of plastic push connect fittings. The male end of the spring lock coupling, which is girded by two O-rings, is inserted into a female flared end engine fitting. The coupling is secured by a garter spring which prevents disengagement by gripping the flared end of the female fitting. On 1989 and later models, a cup-tether assembly provides additional security.

25   To disconnect the spring lock coupling supply fitting, you will need to obtain a spring lock coupling tool or its equivalent, as follows:

   a) 3/8-inch return fitting, tool D87L-9280-A.
   b) 1/2-inch return fitting, tool D87L-9280-B.
   c) 5/8-inch return fitting, tool T83P-19623-C.

26   Study the accompanying illustrations carefully before detaching any spring lock coupling fitting **(see illustration)**.

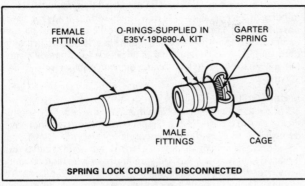

FEMALE FITTING

O-RINGS-SUPPLIED IN E35Y-19D690-A KIT

GARTER SPRING

MALE FITTINGS

CAGE

SPRING LOCK COUPLING DISCONNECTED

TO CONNECT COUPLING

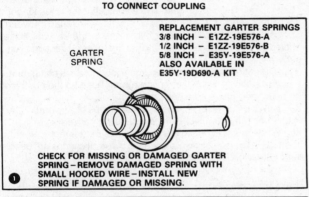

GARTER SPRING

REPLACEMENT GARTER SPRINGS
3/8 INCH – E1ZZ-19E576-A
1/2 INCH – E1ZZ-19E576-B
5/8 INCH – E35Y-19E576-A
ALSO AVAILABLE IN
E35Y-19D690-A KIT

❶ CHECK FOR MISSING OR DAMAGED GARTER SPRING – REMOVE DAMAGED SPRING WITH SMALL HOOKED WIRE – INSTALL NEW SPRING IF DAMAGED OR MISSING.

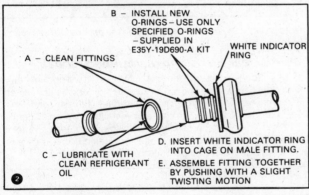

A – CLEAN FITTINGS

B – INSTALL NEW O-RINGS – USE ONLY SPECIFIED O-RINGS – SUPPLIED IN E35Y-19D690-A KIT

WHITE INDICATOR RING

C – LUBRICATE WITH CLEAN REFRIGERANT OIL

D. INSERT WHITE INDICATOR RING INTO CAGE ON MALE FITTING.

E. ASSEMBLE FITTING TOGETHER BY PUSHING WITH A SLIGHT TWISTING MOTION

❷

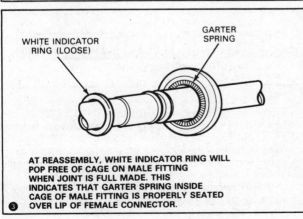

WHITE INDICATOR RING (LOOSE)

GARTER SPRING

❸ AT REASSEMBLY, WHITE INDICATOR RING WILL POP FREE OF CAGE ON MALE FITTING WHEN JOINT IS FULL MADE. THIS INDICATES THAT GARTER SPRING INSIDE CAGE OF MALE FITTING IS PROPERLY SEATED OVER LIP OF FEMALE CONNECTOR.

TO DISCONNECT COUPLING
CAUTION – DISCHARGE SYSTEM BEFORE DISCONNECTING COUPLING

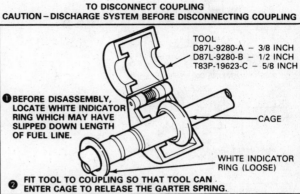

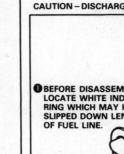

TOOL
D87L-9280-A – 3/8 INCH
D87L-9280-B – 1/2 INCH
T83P-19623-C – 5/8 INCH

CAGE

WHITE INDICATOR RING (LOOSE)

❶ BEFORE DISASSEMBLY, LOCATE WHITE INDICATOR RING WHICH MAY HAVE SLIPPED DOWN LENGTH OF FUEL LINE.

❷ FIT TOOL TO COUPLING SO THAT TOOL CAN ENTER CAGE TO RELEASE THE GARTER SPRING.

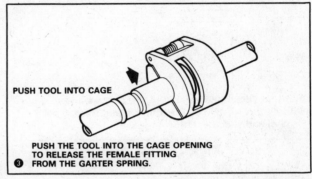

PUSH TOOL INTO CAGE

❸ PUSH THE TOOL INTO THE CAGE OPENING TO RELEASE THE FEMALE FITTING FROM THE GARTER SPRING.

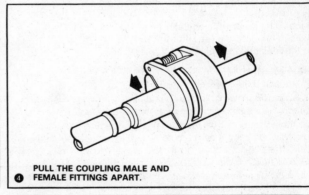

❹ PULL THE COUPLING MALE AND FEMALE FITTINGS APART.

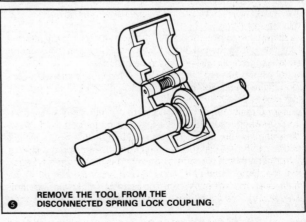

❺ REMOVE THE TOOL FROM THE DISCONNECTED SPRING LOCK COUPLING.

3.26 Connecting and disconnecting spring lock coupling fittings

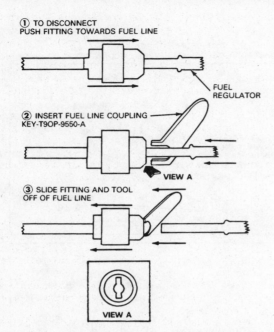

3.27 To detach the fuel return line-to-pressure regulator fitting, push in on the fitting, insert the special tool and slide the fitting off the regulator

Refer to illustration 3.27

27 Disengage the locking tabs on the connector retainer and separate the halves of the retainer.

28 Push the fitting toward the regulator, insert Ford tool no. T90-9550-A into the slots in the coupling **(see illustration)**.

29 Using the tool, pull the fitting from the regulator.

Fuel lines – plastic

Refer to illustration 3.30

Warning: *Avoid using alternative tubing materials with nylon fuel tubing. Use of nonapproved tubing could pose a hazard in service.*

30 Plastic tubing must not be repaired using hose and hose clamps. Push connect fittings cannot be repaired except to replace the retaining clips. Should the plastic tubing, push connect fittings or steel tubing ends become damaged, approved service parts must be used to service the lines **(see illustration)**.

31 The plastic fuel lines can be damaged by torches, welding sparks, grinding and other operations which involve heat. If any repairs or service operations are performed which involve heat relocate all fuel system components, especially the plastic fuel lines, to be certain they will not be damaged. It is recommended that all plastic fuel lines be removed from the vehicle if a torch or high heat producing equipment is to be used for service.

Metal fuel lines

32 If a section of metal fuel line must be replaced, only seamless steel tubing should be used, since copper or aluminum does not have enough durability to withstand normal operating vibration.

33 If only one section of metal fuel line is damaged, it can be cut out and replaced with rubber hose. Be sure to use only reinforced fuel resistant hose, identified by the word "fluoroelastomer" on the hose. The inside diameter of the rubber hose should match the outside diameter of the steel tubing. The rubber hose should be cut four inches longer than the section it's replacing, so there is two inches of overlap between the rubber hose and the metal line at either end of the section. Hose clamps should be used to secure both ends of the repaired section and tightened securely.

34 If a section of metal line longer than six inches is being removed, use a combination of metal tubing and rubber hose so the hose lengths will be no longer than ten inches.

35 Never use rubber hose within four inches of any part of the exhaust system or within ten inches of the catalytic converter.

36 When replacing hose clamps, make sure the replacement clamp is identical to the one being replaced, as different clamps are used depending on location within the fuel line system.

---

4   Fuel pump/fuel pressure – check

Note: *Always make sure there is fuel in the tank before assuming the fuel pump is defective.*

Mechanical fuel pump (carbureted models)

1 If a problem occurs in the fuel pump itself, it will normally either deliver no fuel at all or not enough to sustain high engine speeds or loads.

2 When an engine develops a lean (fuel starved) condition, the fuel pump is often to blame, but the same symptoms will be evident if the fuel filter is clogged. A lean condition will also occur if the carburetor is malfunctioning, the fuel lines and hoses are leaking, kinked or restricted or the electrical system is shorting out or malfunctioning.

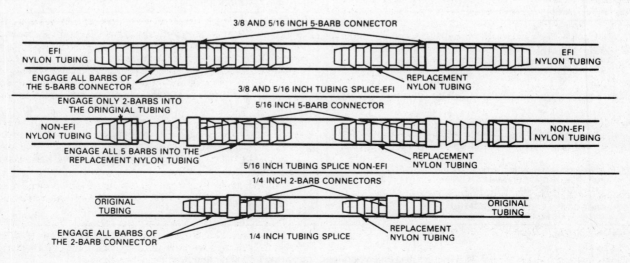

3.30   Plastic fuel line splicing combinations

General check

3   If the fuel pump is noisy:
   a)   Check for loose fuel pump mounting bolts and, if necessary, tighten them to the torque listed in this Chapter's Specifications. Replace the gasket if necessary.
   b)   Check for loose or missing fuel line mounting clips. Loose or missing clips will sound louder when you are sitting inside the vehicle than when standing outside of it. Tighten the clips on the fuel lines if necessary.
   c)   Check for a worn, or sticking fuel pump pushrod.

4   Before assuming a fuel pump is defective:
   a)   Be sure the tank has fuel in it.
   b)   Be sure the fuel filter is not plugged. If it hasn't been changed recently, install a new one.
   c)   Inspect all rubber hoses from the fuel pump to the fuel tank for kinks and cracks. With the engine idling, check all fuel lines and rubber hoses and connections from the fuel pump to the fuel tank for fuel leaks. Tighten any loose connections and replace kinked, cracked or leaking fuel lines or hoses as required. Leaking or kinked lines or hoses will severely affect fuel pump performance.
   d)   Inspect the fuel pump inlet and outlet connections for fuel leaks. Tighten them if necessary.
   e)   Inspect the fuel pump diaphragm crimp (the area where the stamped steel section is attached to the casting) and the breather hole(s) in the casting for evidence of fuel or oil leakage. Replace the pump if it's leaking.

Output (capacity) test

Warning: Gasoline is extremely flammable, so take extra precautions when you work on any part of the fuel system. Don't smoke or allow open flames or bare light bulbs near the work area, and don't work in a garage where a natural gas-type appliance (such as a water heater or clothes dryer) with a pilot light is present. If you spill any fuel on your skin, rinse it off immediately with soap and water. When you perform any kind of work on the fuel system, wear safety glasses and have a Class B type fire extinguisher on hand.

5   Remove the air cleaner assembly (see Section 8).
6   Carefully disconnect the fuel line at the fuel filter inlet (see Chapter 1).
7   Attach a section of rubber fuel hose to the end of the disconnected line with hose clamps and route the end of the hose into an approved gasoline container (1/2-liter or 1 pint minimum). **Note:** *It may be necessary to attach a section of hose to the disconnected fuel line in order to reach the container. Disconnect the high tension wire from the coil and ground it on the engine with a jumper wire. Crank the engine over about 10 revolutions. The fuel pump should deliver at least 1/3-pint of fuel.*
8   If the output is adequate, perform the pressure test below.
9   If the output is less than specified, repeat the test with a remote fuel supply. Detach the hose from the fuel pump inlet line and attach a separate section of fuel hose to the line with a hose clamp. Route the end of the hose into the remote fuel supply (an approved gasoline container at least half full of fuel) and repeat the procedure in Step 7. If the output is now as specified, the problem is either a plugged in-tank filter or a kinked or leaking fuel hose. Make the necessary repairs.

Pressure test

10   Connect a fuel pressure gauge (0 to 15 psi) to the fuel filter end of the line.
11   Start the engine – it should be able to run for over 30 seconds on the fuel in the carburetor bowl – and read the pressure after ten seconds. Compare your reading to the pressure listed in this Chapter's Specifications.
12   If pump pressure is not as specified, install a new fuel pump (see Section 7).
13   Reconnect the fuel lines and install the air cleaner.

Electric fuel pump (fuel-injected models)

General check

14   Verify the fuel pump actually runs. Remove the fuel filler cap and have an assistant turn the ignition switch to On – you should hear a brief whirring noise as the pump comes on and pressurizes the system. Have the assistant start the engine (if possible). This time you should hear a constant whirring sound from the pump (but it's more difficult to hear with the engine running).
15   If the pump doesn't run (makes no sound), check the fuel pump fuse (see Chapter 12). If the fuse is okay, proceed to the next step. If the fuse is blown, replace it and see if the pump works. If it still doesn't run, go to the next step.
16   With the ignition Off, unplug the fuel pump electrical connector. Using a jumper wire, ground the negative terminal of the fuel pump. Using a fused jumper wire, apply 12-volts to the other terminal.
17   If the fuel pump doesn't run, replace it (see Section 7). If it does run, the problem lies somewhere in the electrical circuit to the fuel pump (refer to the wiring diagrams at the back of this manual).

Pressure check

18   Relieve the fuel pressure (see Section 2).
19   Connect a fuel pressure gauge to the Schrader valve on the fuel rail.
20   Turn the ignition switch to the On position. The fuel pump should run for about two seconds, then the pressure should hold steady. Note the reading on the gauge and compare it to the pressure listed in this Chapter's Specifications.
21   Start the engine and allow it to idle. The pressure should be lower by 3 to 10 psi. If all the pressure readings are within specifications, the system is operating properly.
22   If the pressure did not drop by 3 to 10 psi after starting the engine, apply 10-inches Hg of vacuum to the pressure regulator. If the pressure drops, repair the vacuum source to the regulator. If the pressure doesn't drop, replace the regulator.
23   If the pressure is higher than specified, check for a faulty regulator or a pinched or clogged fuel return hose or pipe.
24   If the pressure is lower than specified:
   a)   Inspect the fuel filter – make sure it's not clogged.
   b)   Look for a pinched or clogged fuel hose or line between the fuel tank and the fuel rail.
   c)   Check the pressure regulator for a malfunction. With the engine running, pinch the fuel return line. If the pressure rises, replace the fuel pressure regulator.
   d)   Look for leaks in the fuel feed line.
   e)   Check for leaking injectors.
25   After the testing is done, relieve the fuel system pressure (see Section 2) and remove the fuel pressure gauge.

4

5   Fuel tank – removal and installation

Refer to illustrations 5.9a and 5.9b

Warning: *Gasoline is extremely flammable, so take extra precautions when you work on any part of the fuel system. Don't smoke or allow open flames or bare light bulbs near the work area, and don't work in a garage where a natural gas-type appliance (such as a water heater or clothes dryer) where a pilot light is present. If you spill any fuel on your skin, rinse it off immediately with soap and water. When you perform any kind of work on the fuel tank, wear safety glasses and have a Class B type fire extinguisher on hand.*

Note: *The following procedure is much easier to perform if the fuel tank is empty. Some tanks have a drain plug for this purpose. If the tank does not have a drain plug, siphon the fuel into an approved gasoline container using a siphoning kit, available at most auto parts stores. Never start the siphoning action by mouth!*

1   Remove the fuel tank filler cap to relieve pressure in the fuel tank.
2   If the vehicle is fuel-injected, relieve the fuel system pressure (see Section 2).
3   Detach the negative cable from the battery.
4   If the tank still has fuel in it, you can drain it at the fuel feed line after raising the vehicle. If the tank has a drain plug, remove it and allow the fuel to collect in an approved gasoline container.
5   Raise the vehicle and support it securely on jackstands.

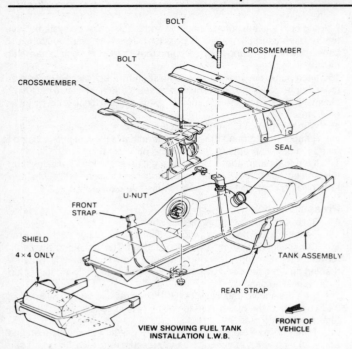

5.9a   Typical center mounted fuel tank (Ranger models)

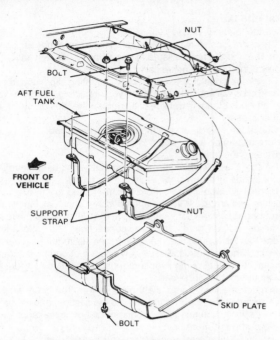

5.9b   Typical rear mounted fuel tank (Bronco II models – 4WD model shown, 2WD similar)

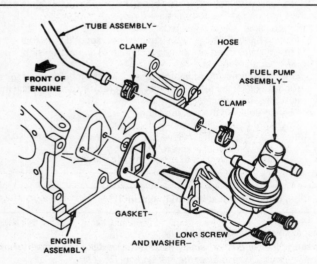

7.2   Fuel pump mounting details (four-cylinder engine)

6   Disconnect the fuel lines, the vapor return line and the fuel filler neck. **Note:** *The fuel feed and return lines and the vapor return line are three different diameters, so reattachment is simplified. If you have any doubts, however, clearly label the three lines and the fittings. Be sure to plug the hoses to prevent leakage and contamination of the fuel system.*

7   Siphon the fuel from the tank at the fuel feed – not the return – line (use a siphoning kit, available at most auto parts stores).

8   If the vehicle is equipped with a skid plate under the tank, remove it. Support the fuel tank with a floor jack or jackstands. Position a piece of wood between the jack head and the fuel tank to protect the tank.

9   Disconnect both fuel tank retaining straps and pivot them down until they are hanging out of the way **(see illustrations)**.

10   Lower the tank enough to disconnect the wires and ground strap from the fuel pump/fuel gauge sending unit.

11   Remove the tank from the vehicle.

12   Installation is the reverse of removal.

6   Fuel tank cleaning and repair – general information

1   All repairs to the fuel tank or filler neck should be carried out by a professional who has experience in this critical and potentially dangerous work. Even after cleaning and flushing of the fuel system, explosive fumes can remain and ignite during repair of the tank.

2   If the fuel tank is removed from the vehicle, it should not be placed in an area where sparks or open flames could ignite the fumes coming out of the tank. Be especially careful inside garages where a natural gas-type appliance is located, because the pilot light could cause an explosion.

7   Fuel pump – removal, installation and inertia switch resetting

Warning: *Gasoline is extremely flammable, so take extra precautions when you work on any part of the fuel system. Don't smoke or allow open flames or bare light bulbs near the work area, and don't work in a garage where a natural gas-type appliance (such as a water heater or clothes dryer) with a pilot light is present. If you spill any fuel on your skin, rinse it off immediately with soap and water. When you perform any kind of work on the fuel system, wear safety glasses and have a Class B type fire extinguisher on hand.*

Removal and installation

Mechanical fuel pump (carbureted models)
Refer to illustration 7.2

1   Unscrew the fuel filler cap to release any pressure within the fuel tank. If the lines to the fuel pump use threaded ,fittings loosen them (at the pump) with the proper size wrench (a flare nut wrench is recommended), then retighten them until they're just snug. Don't disconnect the lines at this time.

2   Loosen the mounting bolts two turns **(see illustration)**. Use your hands to loosen the fuel pump if it's stuck to the block (do not use a tool – you could damage the pump). If you cannot loosen the pump by hand, have an assistant operate the starter while you keep one hand on the pump. As the camshaft turns, it will operate the pump – when the pump feels loose, stop turning the engine over.

3   Disconnect the fuel lines from the pump. Be sure to use a backup wrench (if threaded fittings are used). The outlet line may be pressurized,

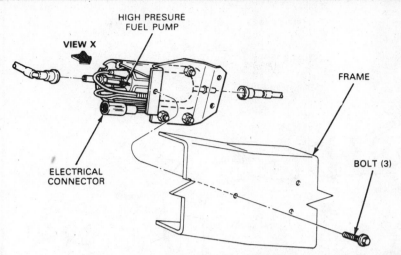

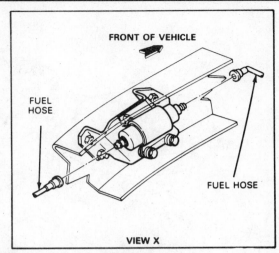

7.13   Details of the frame-mounted high pressure fuel pump (1985 through 1988 models)

so protect your eyes with safety goggles and wrap the fitting with a shop rag, then loosen it carefully.

4   Remove the fuel pump bolts and detach the pump and gasket. Discard the old gasket. On V6 engines, remove the pushrod from the block.

5   Remove all old gasket material and sealant from the engine block. If you're installing the original pump, remove all the old gasket material from the pump mating surface as well. Wipe the mating surfaces of the block and pump with a cloth saturated with lacquer thinner.

6   On V6 engines, install the pushrod into the block.

7   Insert the bolts through the pump (to use as a guides for the new gasket) and place the gasket in position on the fuel pump mounting flange. Position the fuel pump on the block (make sure the pump arm engages the camshaft properly). Tighten the bolts a little at a time to the torque listed in this Chapter's Specifications.

8   Attach the fuel lines to the pump. Start the threaded fitting (where applicable) by hand to avoid cross-threading it. Tighten the outlet nut securely. If any of the hoses are cracked, hardened or otherwise deteriorated, replace them at this time.

9   Start the engine and check for fuel leaks.

10   Stop the engine and check the fuel line connections for leaks by running a finger under each fitting. Check for oil leaks at the fuel pump mounting gasket.

Electric fuel pump (fuel-injected models)

Refer to illustrations 7.13 and 7.17

Note: *1985 through 1988 models are equipped with two fuel pumps. The high pressure pump is frame mounted and is accessible from under the vehicle. The low pressure pump is located within the fuel tank and requires removal of the fuel tank for replacement. On 1989 and later models there is only one fuel pump and it is located within the fuel tank.*

High pressure pump (1985 through 1988 models)

11   Relieve the fuel system pressure (refer to Section 2).

12   Remove the push connectors on the fuel lines and disconnect them from the fuel pump. Disconnect the electrical connector from the fuel pump.

13   Remove the bolts securing the fuel pump to the frame and remove it **(see illustration)**.

14   Installation is the reverse of the removal procedure.

In-tank pump (1985 through 1988 models) and single fuel pump (1989 and later models)

15   Remove the fuel tank (see Section 5).

16   Remove any dirt that has accumulated where the fuel sender/pump is attached to the fuel tank. Do not allow the dirt to enter the fuel tank.

17   Using a brass punch or wood dowel only, tap the lock ring counterclockwise until it's loose **(see illustration)**.

18   Carefully pull the fuel pump/sending unit assembly from the tank.

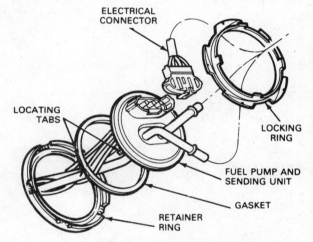

7.17   Details of the in-tank fuel pump

19   Remove the old lock ring gasket and discard it.

20   Clean the fuel pump mounting flange and the tank mounting surface and seal ring groove.

21   Installation is the reverse of the removal procedure with the following additions:

   a) Apply a thin coat of heavy grease to the new lock ring gasket to hold it in place during assembly.

   b) Clean the fuel sender/pump mounting surface of the fuel tank.

   c) Install the fuel sender/pump unit into the fuel tank so the tabs of the unit are positioned into the slots in the fuel tank. Make sure to keep the gasket in place during installation until the lock ring has been tightened.

   d) Hold the fuel sender/pump unit in place, install and tighten the locking ring clockwise until the stop is against the retainer ring tab.

Inertia switch resetting (fuel-injected models)

22   The inertia switch shuts off fuel to the engine in the event of a collision. Once the switch has shut off the fuel, it must be manually reset before the engine can be started.

23   The switch is located on the toe-board to the right of the transmission hump.

24   Turn the ignition switch to Off.

25   Check for leaking fuel in the engine compartment, fuel lines and tank (s). **Warning:** *If you see or smell gasoline, do not reset the switch.*

26   If no fuel leak is apparent, reset the switch by pushing the reset button on the top of the switch.

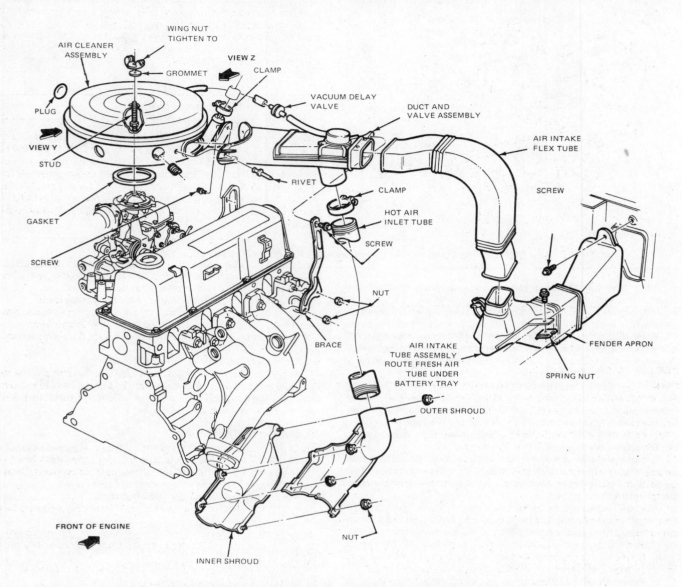

8.2   Air cleaner details (four-cylinder carbureted model shown, others similar)

27   Turn the ignition switch to Start for a few seconds, then to Off.
28   Again, check for leaking fuel.

8   Air cleaner housing – removal and installation

Carbureted models

Refer to illustration 8.2

1   Disconnect the negative cable from the battery.
2   Detach the fresh air inlet tube from the mouth of the snorkel **(see illustration)**.
3   Clearly label and detach all vacuum hoses, lines and electrical connectors as necessary from the air cleaner housing.
4   On 4-cylinder engines, perform the following:
  a) Remove the bolt and disconnect the air cleaner support bracket from the engine lifting eye.
  b) Remove the screw and disconnect the duct and valve assembly from the support bracket.

5   Loosen the hose clamp and disconnect the hot air inlet tube.
6   Remove the wing nut and grommet (if equipped) from the air cleaner housing and remove the cover.
7   Lift the air cleaner housing off of the carburetor. Cover the carburetor inlet to prevent the entry of foreign matter.
8   Remove the air cleaner filter element. Inspect it for signs of dust or dirt leaking through holes in the filter material or past the end seals (see Chapter 1).
9   On 4-cylinder models, to remove the remainder of the intake assembly, perform the following:
  a) Remove the air intake flex tube from the air intake tube assembly.
  b) Remove the two bolts securing the air intake tube assembly to the radiator support panel and to the inner fender apron. Remove the air intake tube.
10 On V6 models, perform the following:
  a) To remove the remainder of the intake assembly, remove the bolt securing the fresh air tube to the brace.
  b) Disconnect the fresh air tube from the radiator support panel and remove the fresh air tube.

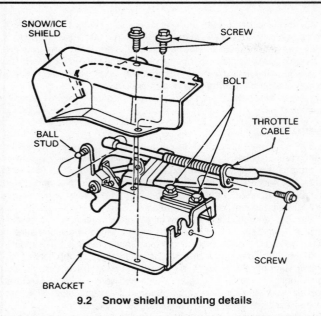

9.2 Snow shield mounting details

Labels: SNOW/ICE SHIELD, SCREW, BOLT, THROTTLE CABLE, BALL STUD, SCREW, BRACKET

11 Installation is the reverse of removal. Inspect the gasket between the air cleaner body and the carburetor and replace it if necessary.

Fuel-injected models

Note: *The air cleaner housing assemblies vary slightly between the various models and years, and the following procedure applies to all of them. However, it is a general guideline and small differences may be noted. Carefully study the illustrations in Section 19 of Chapter 1 that apply to your vehicle before removing the air cleaner housing.*

12 Disconnect the negative cable from the battery.
13 Loosen the hose clamps on the engine air cleaner outlet tube assembly. Remove the tube assembly from the throttle body and the air filter case assembly. Cover the throttle body inlet to prevent the entry of foreign matter.
14 Remove the screws securing the air cleaner assembly upper half. Disconnect the small hose from the upper case half and remove the upper half and the air cleaner filter.
15 To remove the remainder of the assembly, perform the following:
   a) On models so equipped, loosen the hose clamp on the engine hot air tube and disconnect the tube from the air cleaner intake.
   b) Remove the bolt securing the air cleaner intake tube to the air cleaner intake deflector next to the radiator support. Remove the intake tube from the lower half of the air cleaner assembly.
   c) Remove the fasteners securing the lower half of the air cleaner assembly to the mounting bracket on the inner fender apron. Remove the lower half of the air cleaner assembly.
16 Installation is the reverse of the removal procedure. Tighten all hose clamps and fittings securely.

9 Accelerator cable – replacement

Refer to illustration 9.2
1 Disconnect the cable from the negative terminal of the battery.
2 Remove the air cleaner housing if you're working on a carbureted model (see Section 8). If you're working on a fuel-injected model, remove the snow shield from the accelerator cable bracket **(see illustration)**.
3 Disconnect the accelerator cable from the ballstud on the throttle lever. It may be necessary to pry it off with a screwdriver.
4 Unbolt the cable from the bracket at the intake manifold.
5 Working under the dash, detach the end of the cable from the top of the accelerator pedal. Compress the retaining tangs on cable casing and push the cable through the firewall.

6 Note how the cable is routed, then remove it from the vehicle.
7 Installation is the reverse of removal. Before starting the engine, make sure the accelerator pedal operates freely and the throttle lever on the carburetor or throttle body returns to the fully closed position when you take your foot off the pedal.

10 Carburetor – removal and installation

Warning: *Gasoline is extremely flammable, so take extra precautions when you work on any part of the fuel system. Don't smoke or allow open flames or bare light bulbs near the work area, and don't work in a garage where a natural gas-type appliance (such as a water heater or clothes dryer) where a pilot light is present. If you spill any fuel on your skin, rinse it off immediately with soap and water. When you perform any kind of work on the fuel tank, wear safety glasses and have a Class B type fire extinguisher on hand.*

Removal

1 Remove the fuel filler cap to relieve fuel tank pressure.
2 Remove the air cleaner from the carburetor. Be sure to label all vacuum hoses attached to the air cleaner housing.
3 Disconnect the accelerator cable from the throttle lever.
4 If the vehicle is equipped with an automatic transmission, disconnect the TV (kickdown) cable or linkage from the throttle lever.
5 Clearly label all vacuum hoses and fittings, then disconnect the hoses.
6 Disconnect the fuel line from the carburetor.
7 Label the wires and terminals, then unplug all electrical connectors.
8 Remove the mounting fasteners and detach the carburetor from the intake manifold. Remove the carburetor mounting gasket. Stuff a shop rag into the intake manifold openings.

Installation

9 Use a gasket scraper to remove all traces of gasket material and sealant from the intake manifold (and the carburetor, if it's being reinstalled), then remove the shop rag from the manifold openings. Clean the mating surfaces with lacquer thinner or acetone.
10 Place a new gasket on the intake manifold.
11 Lower the carburetor into position and install the mounting fasteners.
12 To prevent carburetor distortion or damage, tighten the fasteners to the torque listed in this Chapter's Specifications in a criss-cross pattern, 1/4-turn at a time.
13 The remaining installation steps are the reverse of removal.
14 Check and, if necessary, adjust the idle speed.
15 If the vehicle is equipped with an automatic transmission, refer to Chapter 7B for the TV cable adjustment procedure.
16 Start the engine and check carefully for fuel leaks.

11 Carburetor – diagnosis and overhaul

Warning: *Gasoline is extremely flammable, so take extra precautions when you work on any part of the fuel system. Don't smoke or allow open flames or bare light bulbs near the work area, and don't work in a garage where a natural gas-type appliance (such as a water heater or clothes dryer) where a pilot light is present. If you spill any fuel on your skin, rinse it off immediately with soap and water. When you perform any kind of work on the fuel tank, wear safety glasses and have a Class B type fire extinguisher on hand.*

Diagnosis

1 A thorough road test and check of carburetor adjustments should be done before any major carburetor service work. Specifications for some adjustments are listed on the Vehicle Emissions Control Information (VECI) label found in the engine compartment.

4

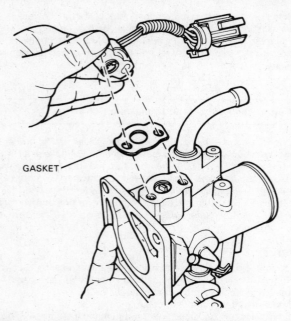

GASKET

12.4　Throttle Position Sensor (TPS) details

2　Carburetor problems usually show up as flooding, hard starting, stalling, severe backfiring and poor acceleration. A carburetor that's leaking fuel and/or covered with wet looking deposits definitely needs attention.

3　Some performance complaints directed at the carburetor are actually a result of loose, out-of-adjustment or malfunctioning engine or electrical components. Others develop when vacuum hoses leak, are disconnected or are incorrectly routed. The proper approach to analyzing carburetor problems should include the following items:

　a) Inspect all vacuum hoses and actuators for leaks and correct installation (see Chapters 1 and 6).
　b) Tighten the intake manifold and carburetor mounting nuts/bolts evenly and securely.
　c) Perform a cylinder compression test (see Chapter 2, Part E).
　d) Clean or replace the spark plugs as necessary (see Chapter 1).
　e) Check the spark plug wires (see Chapter 1).
　f) Inspect the ignition primary wires.
　g) Check the ignition timing (follow the instructions printed on the Emissions Control Information label).
　h) Check the fuel pump pressure/volume (see Section 4).
　i) Check the heat control valve in the air cleaner for proper operation (see Chapter 1).
　j) Check/replace the air filter element (see Chapter 1).
　k) Check the PCV system (see Chapter 6).
　l) Check/replace the fuel filter (see Chapter 1). Also, the strainer in the tank could be restricted.
　m) Check for a plugged exhaust system.
　n) Check EGR valve operation (see Chapter 6).
　o) Check the choke-it should be completely open at normal engine operating temperature (see Chapter 1).
　p) Check for fuel leaks and kinked or dented fuel lines (see Chapters 1 and 4).
　q) Check accelerator pump operation with the engine off (remove the air cleaner cover and operate the throttle as you look into the carburetor throat – you should see a stream of gasoline enter the carburetor).
　r) Check for incorrect fuel or bad gasoline.
　s) Check the valve clearances (if applicable) and camshaft lobe lift (see Chapters 1 and 2)
　t) Have a dealer service department or repair shop check the electronic engine and carburetor controls.

4　Diagnosing carburetor problems may require that the engine be started and run with the air cleaner off. While running the engine without the air cleaner, backfires are possible. This situation is likely to occur if the carburetor is malfunctioning, but just the removal of the air cleaner can lean the fuel/air mixture enough to produce an engine backfire. **Warning:** *Do not position any part of your body, especially your face, directly over the carburetor during inspection and servicing procedures. Wear eye protection!*

Overhaul

5　Once it's determined that the carburetor needs an overhaul, several options are available. If you're going to attempt to overhaul the carburetor yourself, first obtain a good quality carburetor rebuild kit (which will include all necessary gaskets, internal parts, instructions and a parts list). You'll also need some special solvent and a means of blowing out the internal passages of the carburetor with air.

6　An alternative is to obtain a new or rebuilt carburetor. They are readily available from dealers and auto parts stores. Make absolutely sure the exchange carburetor is identical to the original. A tag is usually attached to the top of the carburetor or a number is stamped on the float bowl. It will help determine the exact type of carburetor you have. When obtaining a rebuilt carburetor or a rebuild kit, make sure the kit or carburetor matches your application exactly. Seemingly insignificant differences can make a large difference in engine performance.

7　If you choose to overhaul your own carburetor, allow enough time to disassemble it carefully, soak the necessary parts in the cleaning solvent (usually for at least one-half day or according to the instructions listed on the carburetor cleaner) and reassemble it, which will usually take much longer than disassembly. When disassembling the carburetor, match each part with the illustration in the carburetor kit and lay the parts out in order on a clean work surface. Overhauls by inexperienced mechanics can result in an engine which runs poorly or not at all. To avoid this, use care and patience when disassembling the carburetor so you can reassemble it correctly.

8　Because carburetor designs are constantly modified by the manufacturer in order to meet increasingly more stringent emissions regulations, it isn't feasible to include a step-by-step overhaul of each type. You'll receive a detailed, well illustrated set of instructions with any carburetor overhaul kit; they will apply in a more specific manner to the carburetor on your vehicle.

12　Electronic fuel injection (2.3L four-cylinder engine) – component removal and installation

---

Warning: *Gasoline is extremely flammable, so take extra precautions when you work on any part of the fuel system. Don't smoke or allow open flames or bare light bulbs near the work area, and don't work in a garage where a natural gas-type appliance (such as a water heater or clothes dryer) where a pilot light is present. If you spill any fuel on your skin, rinse it off immediately with soap and water. When you perform any kind of work on the fuel tank, wear safety glasses and have a Class B type fire extinguisher on hand.*

Throttle Position Sensor (TPS)

Refer to illustration 12.4

1　Disconnect the electrical connector to the TPS.
2　Make alignment marks from the throttle body to the TPS to aid in installation (if the same sensor is to be used).
3　Remove the two screws securing the TPS to the throttle body.
4　Detach the sensor from the throttle body **(see illustration)**.
5　Remove the gasket and all traces of old gasket material from the throttle body (and the TPS, if the same one is to be reinstalled).
6　Position a new gasket on the throttle body, followed by the sensor. Make sure the tangs on the sensor are in alignment with the blade on the throttle shaft.
7　If a new switch has been installed, adjust it as closely as possible to the position the old switch was in. Install the screws and tighten them securely, making sure the marks are aligned (if the old switch is being used).
8　Plug in the electrical connector.

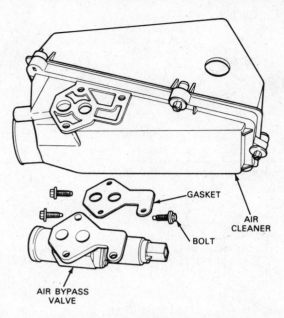

12.12 Air bypass valve mounting details (typical)

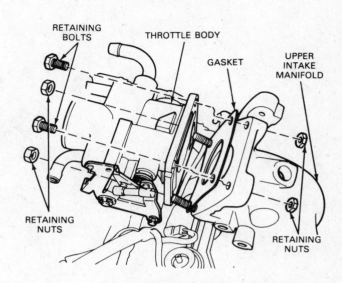

12.17 Throttle body installation details

9   Take the vehicle to a dealer service department or other repair shop to have the TPS adjusted properly, since special tools are required.

Air bypass valve

Refer to illustration 12.12

10   Unplug the electrical connector from the air bypass valve (it's located under the air cleaner housing).
11   Remove the air cleaner housing (see Section 8).
12   Remove the bolts and detach the valve from the air cleaner housing **(see illustration)**. Remove all traces of gasket material from the valve and the housing.
13   Installation is the reverse of removal. Be sure to use a new gasket.

Throttle body

Refer to illustration 12.17

14   Disconnect the cable from the negative terminal of the battery. Remove the snow shield and detach the accelerator cable from the throttle lever **(see illustration 9.2)**.
15   Unplug the electrical connector for the throttle position sensor.
16   Detach the air intake hose, crankcase vent hose and the air bypass hose from the throttle body.
17   Remove the nuts and bolts retaining the throttle body to the upper intake manifold **(see illustration)**. Remove the throttle body and gasket.
18   Remove all traces of old gasket material from the throttle body and upper intake manifold. Place a new gasket on the upper intake manifold and install the throttle body, tightening the fasteners to the torque listed in this Chapter's Specifications.
19   The remainder of installation is the reverse of the removal procedure.

Upper intake manifold

20   If desired, remove the throttle body following Steps 14 through 17. (It isn't necessary unless you're replacing the upper intake manifold.) If you don't remove the throttle body, be sure to detach the hoses, TPS electrical connector and accelerator cable from it.
21   Label and detach the vacuum hoses from the vacuum tree on the top of the upper intake manifold.
22   Unscrew the flange nut on the EGR pipe from the EGR valve (see Chapter 6). Detach the PCV hose from the underside of the upper intake manifold.

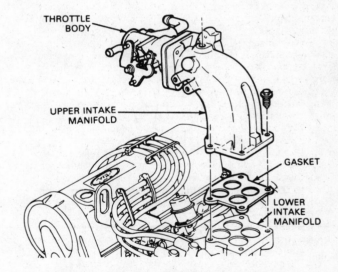

12.22 Upper intake manifold mounting details

23   Remove the bolts securing the upper intake manifold to the lower intake manifold **(see illustration)**. Remove the upper intake manifold.
24   Remove all traces of old gasket material from the upper and lower intake manifolds. Place a new gasket on the lower intake manifold, install the upper intake manifold and install the bolts. Tighten the bolts to the torque listed in this Chapter's Specifications, in a criss-cross pattern.
25   The remainder of installation is the reverse of the removal procedure.

Fuel rail and injectors

Refer to illustrations 12.31 and 12.32

26   Relieve the fuel system pressure (see Section 2), then disconnect the cable from the negative terminal of the battery.
27   Remove the upper intake manifold (see Steps 20 through 23).
28   Detach the fuel fittings from the fuel rail (see Section 3).

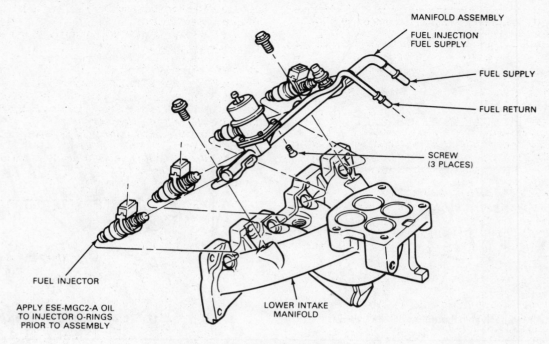

MANIFOLD ASSEMBLY
FUEL INJECTION FUEL SUPPLY
FUEL SUPPLY
FUEL RETURN
SCREW (3 PLACES)
FUEL INJECTOR
APPLY ESE-MGC2-A OIL TO INJECTOR O-RINGS PRIOR TO ASSEMBLY
LOWER INTAKE MANIFOLD

12.31   Fuel rail installation details

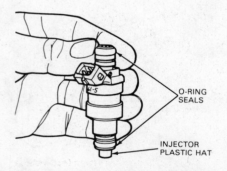

O-RING SEALS

INJECTOR PLASTIC HAT

12.32   Lubricate the injector O-rings with engine oil before installation

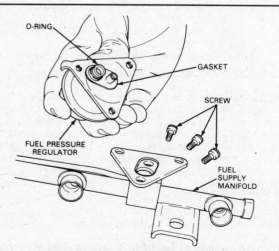

O-RING

GASKET

SCREW

FUEL PRESSURE REGULATOR

FUEL SUPPLY MANIFOLD

12.38   Fuel pressure regulator details

29   Unplug the electrical connectors from the fuel injectors and reposition the harness out of the way.

30   Detach the vacuum hose from the top of the fuel pressure regulator.

31   Remove the two bolts securing the fuel rail to the lower intake manifold **(see illustration)**. Carefully pull the fuel rail and injectors from the intake manifold.

32   To remove an injector, twist the injector back and forth while pulling it from the fuel rail. Remove the O-ring seals from each end of the injectors **(see illustration)**. Whenever the fuel rail is removed it's a good idea to replace all of the O-ring seals.

33   Check the plastic hat on the end of each injector. If one is missing, look for it in the injector port in the lower intake manifold. If a hat appears to be damaged, replace it.

34   Install new O-ring seals on the injectors. Lightly lubricate the O-rings with engine oil and push them into their ports on the fuel rail, using a twisting and pushing motion. **Caution:** *Don't use silicone grease to lubricate the O-rings – it will clog the injectors.*

35   Install the fuel rail and injector assembly to the lower intake manifold, guiding the injectors into their ports. Install the fuel rail bolts and tighten them to the torque listed in this Chapter's Specifications.

36   The remainder of installation is the reverse of removal. Be sure to check for fuel leaks.

Fuel pressure regulator

Refer to illustration 12.38

37   If you're working on a 1988 or earlier model, remove the fuel rail by following Steps 26 through 31. On 1989 and later models it isn't necessary to remove the fuel rail for access to the regulator.

38   Remove the three screws and detach the regulator from the fuel rail **(see illustration)**.

39   If the same regulator will be installed, remove the O-ring and install a new one. Also, remove the old gasket and all traces of gasket material from the regulator and fuel rail.

40   Install a new gasket on the regulator. Apply a light film of engine oil to the O-ring, then position the regulator on the fuel rail. **Caution:** *Don't use silicone grease on the O-ring – it may clog the injectors.* Install the screws and tighten them securely.

41   The remainder of installation is the revers of the removal procedure.

13   Electronic fuel injection (V6 engines) – component removal and installation

Upper intake manifold and throttle body

Refer to illustration 13.10

Removal

1   Disconnect the negative cable from the battery.
2   Detach the air intake tube from the throttle body.
3   Remove the snow shield and detach the accelerator cable from the throttle lever. Also disconnect the cruise control cable, if equipped.
4   Label and disconnect the vacuum hoses from the upper intake manifold and the throttle body.
5   Disconnect the PCV hose (see Chapter 6).
6   Detach the spark plug wires from the clip at the rear of the upper intake manifold (4.0L engine only).
7   Remove the bolt that secures the air conditioning refrigerant line at the upper rear part of the manifold. DO NOT disconnect any refrigerant lines.
8   Remove the alternator brace (3.0L engine only).
9   Label and disconnect any electrical connectors attached to the throttle body or upper intake manifold.
10   Remove the bolts and nuts that secure the upper intake manifold/throttle body to the lower intake manifold. Remove the upper intake manifold and gasket **(see illustration)**.

Installation

11   Thoroughly clean all traces of old gasket from the mating surfaces of the upper and lower intake manifolds. Remove residue with a solvent such as acetone or lacquer thinner.
12   Chase the bolt threads in the lower manifold with a tap of the correct size. Run a die over the threads of the upper manifold bolts and studs.
13   Lightly oil bolt and stud threads before installation.
14   Install a new gasket on the lower manifold.
15   Install the upper intake manifold. Install the bolts and nuts, tightening them finger tight.

16   Tighten the bolts and nuts, a little at a time, to the torque listed in this Chapter's Specifications.
17   The remainder of installation is the reverse of the removal steps. Run the engine and check for fuel leaks.

Air bypass valve

Refer to illustrations 13.19a, 13.19b and 13.19c

18   Disconnect the air bypass valve electrical connector.
19   Remove the two screws that secure the air bypass valve **(see illustrations)**. Take off the valve and gasket.
20   Make sure the gasket surfaces on the valve and throttle body are completely clean.
21   Install the air bypass valve and tighten its screws to the torque listed in this Chapter's Specifications.
22   Connect the electrical connector.

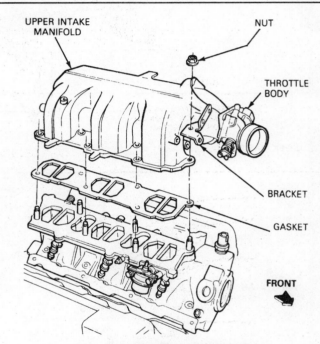

13.10   Upper intake manifold details (4.0L engine shown, others similar)

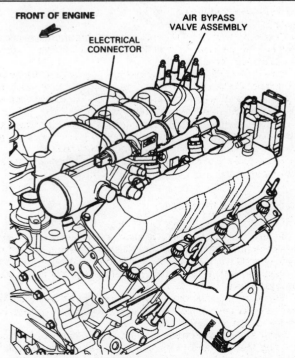

13.19a   The air bypass valve on the 3.0L engine is mounted on top of the throttle body

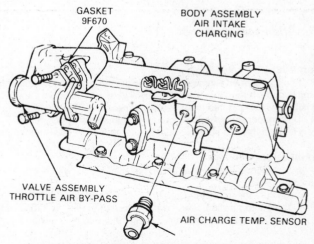

13.19b   Details of the upper intake manifold and related components – 4.0L engine

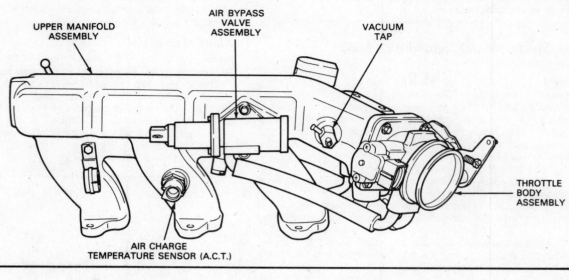

UPPER MANIFOLD ASSEMBLY

AIR BYPASS VALVE ASSEMBLY

VACUUM TAP

THROTTLE BODY ASSEMBLY

AIR CHARGE TEMPERATURE SENSOR (A.C.T.)

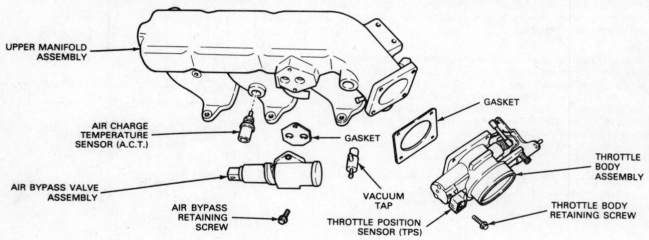

UPPER MANIFOLD ASSEMBLY

AIR CHARGE TEMPERATURE SENSOR (A.C.T.)

AIR BYPASS VALVE ASSEMBLY

AIR BYPASS RETAINING SCREW

GASKET

VACUUM TAP

THROTTLE POSITION SENSOR (TPS)

GASKET

THROTTLE BODY ASSEMBLY

THROTTLE BODY RETAINING SCREW

13.19c   Details of the upper intake manifold and related components – 2.9L engine

Throttle Position Sensor (TPS)

Refer to illustration 13.25

Removal

23 Look for scribed alignment marks on the throttle position sensor and throttle body. If they aren't visible, make your own (this only applies to switches with elongated holes for adjustment).

24 Disconnect the electrical connector from the sensor.

25 Remove the two screws and take the sensor off (**see illustration**).

Installation

26 Installation is the reverse of the removal steps, with the following additions:

  a) Be sure the rotary tangs on the sensor are aligned properly. Slide them into position over the throttle shaft blade, then (on models with elongated holes only) rotate the throttle position sensor clockwise only to align the scribe marks. Rotating the sensor counterclockwise may cause excessive idle speeds.

  b) Be sure the red seal is inside the connector housing.

  c) Tighten the screws securely.

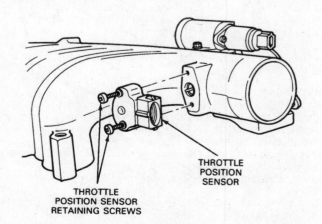

THROTTLE POSITION SENSOR

THROTTLE POSITION SENSOR RETAINING SCREWS

13.25   The Throttle Position Sensor (TPS) is mounted on the side of the throttle body (3.0L engine shown, others similar)

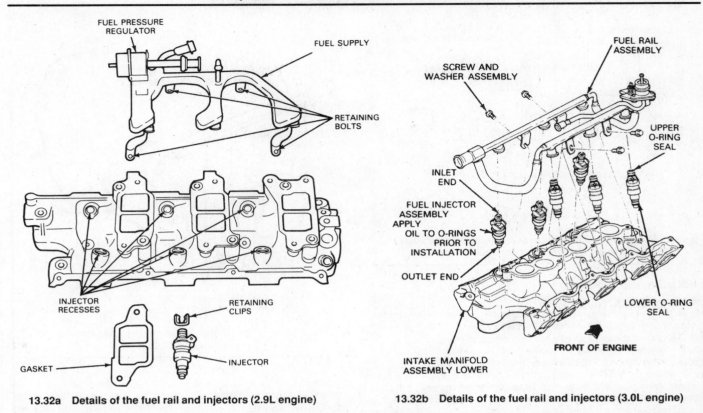

13.32a   Details of the fuel rail and injectors (2.9L engine)

13.32b   Details of the fuel rail and injectors (3.0L engine)

Fuel rail and injectors

Refer to illustrations 13.32a, 13.32b and 13.32c

Removal

27 Disconnect the negative cable from the battery.
28 Remove the upper intake manifold (see Steps 1 through 10).
29 Relieve fuel system pressure (see Section 2) and disconnect the fuel lines from the fuel rail (see Section 3).
30 Carefully unplug the electrical connectors from the fuel injectors.
31 Disconnect the fuel pressure regulator vacuum line.
32 Remove the bolts that secure the fuel rail to the lower intake manifold **(see illustrations)**.
33 Carefully lift the fuel rail and rock it from side to side to separate it from the injectors. **Caution:** *The fuel rail and injectors are delicate. Protect the sealing areas and fuel orifices from dirt or rough handling.*
34 To remove the injectors, pull and gently rock the injector from side to side. The injectors on 2.9L engines are also retained by a clip that must be pried off.
35 If you're working on a 4.0L engine, remove the gasket on the lower intake manifold and clean off all traces of old gasket material from the manifold and fuel rail.

Installation

36 Make sure the injector caps are clean and undamaged.
37 Check O-rings for deterioration or damage and replace as needed **(see illustration 12.32)**. Each injector has two O-rings – it's a good idea to replace all of them whenever the fuel rail is removed.
38 Lubricate the O-rings with clean engine oil. **Note:** *Don't lubricate the O-rings with silicone grease – it may clog the injectors.*
39 If the injectors were removed, gently push and twist them into the fuel rail.
40 If you're working on a 4.0L engine, place a new gasket on the lower intake manifold.
41 Lower the fuel rail into place, with the injectors positioned over their holes in the lower intake manifold. Push the fuel rail down to ensure the injectors are securely seated in the manifold and fuel rail.

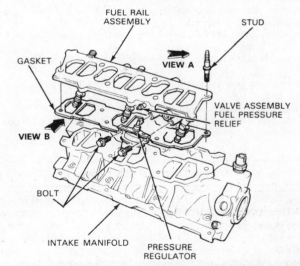

13.32c   Details of the fuel rail and injectors (4.0L engine)

42 Hold the fuel rail in position, install the bolts and tighten them to the torque listed in this Chapter's Specifications.
43 Connect the fuel lines (see Section 3).
44 Temporarily reconnect the battery cable. Turn the key to On, but don't start the engine. Leave the key On for two to three seconds to pressurize the fuel system.
45 Check for leaks around the injectors with a clean paper towel. If leaks are found, fix the problem before continuing. Disconnect the negative battery cable one again.
46 The remainder of installation is the reverse of removal.
47 Start the engine and let it idle for two minutes. Turn the engine off and check again for fuel leaks. Repair any leaks.

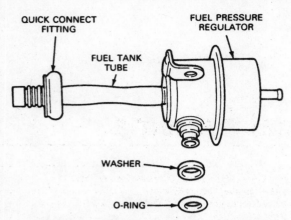

13.52a   Details of the fuel pressure regulator (regulator for the 2.9L engine shown, 4.0L regulator similar)

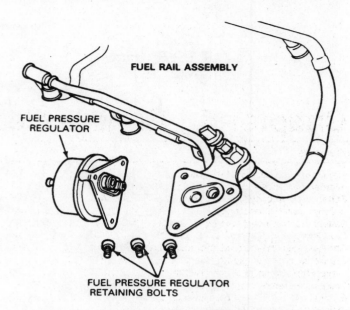

13.52b   Installation details of the fuel pressure regulator – 3.0L engine

Fuel pressure regulator

Refer to illustration 13.52a and 13.52b

48   Relieve fuel system pressure (see Section 2), then disconnect the cable from the negative terminal of the battery.

49   Disconnect the vacuum line from the pressure regulator.

50   If you're working on a 2.9L engine or a 4.0L engine, disconnect the fuel return line from the regulator (see Section 3).

51   Remove the two (2.9L engine) or three (all others) bolts that secure the pressure regulator to the fuel rail. **Note:** *To reach the pressure regulator bolts on some models, it may be necessary to loosen or remove the fuel rail bolts on the pressure regulator side of the fuel rail. Lift the fuel rail just enough to reach the pressure regulator bolts.*

52   Remove the pressure regulator, gasket or washer and O-ring **(see illustration)**.

53   Clean the mating surfaces on the pressure regulator and fuel rail. Be careful not to scratch the surfaces.

54   Installation is the reverse of the removal steps, with the following additions:

   a) Use a new gasket or washer, new O-ring and new pressure regulator bolts.
   b) Tighten the bolts securely.
   c) Reconnect the battery cable, turn the ignition key to the On position and check for leaks.

14   Exhaust system service – general information

Warning: *Inspection and repair of exhaust system components should be done only after enough time has elapsed after driving the vehicle to allow the system components to cool completely. Also, when working under the vehicle, make sure it is securely supported on jackstands.*

1   The exhaust system consists of the exhaust manifold(s), the catalytic converter, the muffler, the tailpipe and all connecting pipes, brackets, hangers and clamps. The exhaust system is attached to the body with mounting brackets and rubber hangers. If any of these components are improperly installed, excessive noise and vibration will be transmitted to the body.

2   Conduct regular inspections of the exhaust system to keep it safe and quiet. Look for any damaged or bent parts, open seams, holes, loose connections, excessive corrosion or other defects which could allow exhaust fumes to enter the vehicle. Deteriorated exhaust system components should not be repaired; they should be replaced with new parts.

3   If the exhaust system components are extremely corroded or rusted together, welding equipment will probably be required to remove them. The convenient way to accomplish this is to have a muffler repair shop remove the corroded sections with a cutting torch. If, however, you want to save money by doing it yourself (and you don't have a welding outfit with a cutting torch), simply cut off the old components with a hacksaw. If you have compressed air, special pneumatic cutting chisels can also be used. If you do decide to tackle the job at home, be sure to wear safety goggles to protect your eyes from metal chips and work gloves to protect your hands.

4   Here are some simple guidelines to follow when repairing the exhaust system:

   a) Work from the back to the front when removing exhaust system components.
   b) Apply penetrating oil to the exhaust system component fasteners to make them easier to remove.
   c) Use new gaskets, hangers and clamps when installing exhaust systems components.
   d) Apply anti-seize compound to the threads of all exhaust system fasteners during reassembly.
   e) Be sure to allow sufficient clearance between newly installed parts and all points on the underbody to avoid overheating the floor pan and possibly damaging the interior carpet and insulation. Pay particularly close attention to the catalytic converter and heat shield.

Chapter 5   Engine electrical systems

Contents

Specifications

General

Alternator brush length	
New	0.48 in
Minimum	0.25 in
Ignition coil resistance	
Dura-Spark II	
Primary resistance	0.8 to 1.6 ohms
Secondary resistance	5,700 to 10,500 ohms
TFI-IV	
Primary resistance	
1983	Not available
1984 through 1988	0.3 to 1.0 ohms
1989 on	Not available
Secondary resistance	
1983	Not available
1984 and 1985	8,000 to 11,500 ohms
1986 through 1988	6,500 to 11,500 ohms
1989 on	Not available
Ignition timing*	
2.0L four-cylinder	
1983	6 degrees BTDC
1984	8 degrees BTDC
1985 and later	6 degrees BTDC
2.3L four-cylinder	
1983	
High altitude	10 degrees BTDC
All others	
Manual	6 degrees BTDC
Automatic	8 degrees BTDC
1984	
High altitude	10 degrees BTDC
All others	6 degrees BTDC
1985 and later	10 degrees BTDC
V6 engines	10 degrees BTDC

*The information on the Vehicle Emission Control Information label supersedes this information, if different.

Torque specifications

	Ft-lbs (unless otherwise indicated)
Distributor hold-down bolt	17 to 25
Starter mounting bolts	15 to 20

1   General information and precautions

The engine electrical systems include all ignition, charging and starting components. Because of their engine-related functions, these components are considered separately from chassis electrical devices like the lights, instruments, etc.

Be very careful when working on the engine electrical components. They are easily damaged if checked, connected or handled improperly. The alternator is driven by an engine drivebelt which could cause serious injury if your hands, hair or clothes become entangled in it with the engine running. Both the starter and alternator are connected directly to the battery and could arc or even cause a fire if mishandled, overloaded or shorted out.

Never leave the ignition switch on for long periods of time with the engine off. Don't disconnect the battery cables while the engine is running. Correct polarity must be maintained when connecting battery cables from another source, such as another vehicle, during jump starting. Always disconnect the negative cable first and hook it up last or the battery may be shorted by the tool being used to loosen the cable clamps.

Additional safety related information on the engine electrical systems can be found in *Safety first* near the front of this manual. It should be referred to before beginning any operation included in this Chapter.

2   Battery – removal and installation

Refer to illustration 2.1

1   Disconnect both cables from the battery terminals **(see illustration)**. **Caution:** *Always disconnect the negative cable first and hook it up last or the battery may be shorted by the tool being used to loosen the cable clamps.* **Note:** *On 1992 and later models, when the battery is disconnected and reconnected, the Electronic Control Assembly (computer) may require ten miles or more of driving to relearn strategies. This may cause temporary abnormal running.*
2   Locate the battery hold-down clamp at the top of the battery. Remove the bolts and nut and the hold-down clamp.
3   Lift out the battery. Special straps that attach to the battery posts are available – lifting and moving the battery is much easier if you use one.
4   Installation is the reverse of removal. Make sure the battery cables and battery post are free of corrosion. Clean if necessary (see Section 4).

3   Battery – emergency jump starting

Refer to the *Booster battery (jump) starting* procedure at the front of this manual.

4   Battery cables – check and replacement

1   Periodically inspect the entire length of each battery cable for damage, cracked or burned insulation and corrosion. Poor battery cable connections can cause starting problems and decreased engine performance.
2   Check the cable-to-terminal connections at the ends of the cables for cracks, loose wire strands and corrosion. The presence of white, fluffy deposits under the insulation at the cable terminal connection is a sign that the cable is corroded and should be replaced. Check the terminals for distortion, missing mounting bolts and corrosion.
3   When replacing the cables, always disconnect the negative cable first and hook it up last or the battery may be shorted by the tool used to loosen the cable clamps. Even if only the positive cable is being replaced, be sure to disconnect the negative cable from the battery first.
4   Disconnect and remove the cable. Make sure the replacement cable is the same length and wire size (diameter).
5   Clean the threads of the starter relay or ground connection with a wire brush to remove rust and corrosion. Apply a light coat of petroleum jelly to the threads to prevent future corrosion.

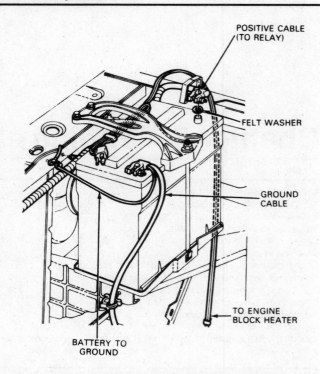

POSITIVE CABLE
(TO RELAY)

FELT WASHER

GROUND
CABLE

TO ENGINE
BLOCK HEATER

BATTERY TO
GROUND

2.1   To remove the battery, disconnect both cables (negative [ground] first) and remove the battery hold down bolts, nut and clamp

6   Attach the cable to the starter relay or ground connection and tighten the mounting nut/bolt to the torque listed in this Chapter's Specifications.
7   Before connecting the new cable to the battery, make sure that it reaches the battery post without having to be stretched. Clean the battery posts and cable ends thoroughly and apply a light coat of petroleum jelly to prevent corrosion.
8   Connect the positive cable first, followed by the negative cable.

5   Ignition systems – general information

Distributor type (Dura Spark II and TFI-IV)

The 1983 and 1984 2.3L four-cylinder and 1983 through 1988 2.0L four-cylinder models are equipped with the Dura-Spark II ignition system. All other models with a distributor type ignition use the Thick Film Integrated IV (TFI-IV) ignition module.

These types of ignition systems have solid state electronic designs consisting of an ignition module, coil, distributor, spark plug wires and spark plugs. Mechanically, these systems are similar to a breaker point system, except that the distributor cam and ignition points are replaced by an armature and magnetic pickup unit. The coil primary circuit is controlled by an amplifier module.

When the ignition is switched on, the ignition primary circuit is energized. When the distributor armature "teeth" or "spokes" approach the magnetic coil assembly, a voltage is induced which signals the amplifier to turn off the coil primary current. A timing circuit in the amplifier module turns the coil current back on after the coil field has collapsed.

When it's on, current flows from the battery through the ignition switch, the coil primary winding, the amplifier module and then to ground. When the current is interrupted, the magnetic field in the ignition coil collapses, inducing a high voltage in the coil secondary windings. The voltage is conducted to the distributor where the rotor directs it to the appropriate spark plug. This process is repeated continuously.

6.2 To use a calibrated ignition tester (available at most auto parts stores), simply disconnect a spark plug wire, attach the wire to the tester, clip the tester to a convenient ground (like a rocker arm cover bolt) and operate the starter – if there's enough power to fire the plug, sparks will be visible between the electrode tip and the tester body

The distributor on models with the Dura Spark II system is equipped with centrifugal and vacuum advance mechanisms which control the actual point of ignition based on engine speed and load. As engine speed increases, two weights move out and alter the position of the armature in relation to the distributor shaft, advancing the ignition timing. As engine load increases (when climbing hills or accelerating, for example), a drop in intake manifold vacuum causes the base plate to move slightly in the opposite direction (clockwise) under the action of the spring in the vacuum unit, retarding the timing and counteracting the centrifugal advance. Under light loads (moderate steady speeds, for example), the comparatively high intake manifold vacuum acting on the vacuum advance diaphragm causes the base plate assembly to move in a counterclockwise direction to provide a greater amount of timing advance.

The Thick Film Integrated IV (TFI-IV) ignition module is housed in a molded thermoplastic box mounted on the base of the distributor. The important difference between the Dura-Spark II and TFI-IV modules is that the TFI-IV module is controlled by the Electronic Engine Control IV (EEC-IV),while the Dura-Spark II module is not. The TFI-IV/EEC-IV type distributor is similar to the Dura-Spark II model but has neither a centrifugal nor a vacuum advance mechanism (advance is handled by the computer instead). The TFI-IV module does, however, include a "push start" mode that allows push starting of the vehicle if necessary.

Distributorless (DIS) type

The 1989 and later 2.3L four-cylinder and 1990 and later 4.0L V6 engines are equipped with the Distributorless Ignition System (DIS) that is a solid state electronic design. It consists of a crankshaft timing sensor, DIS module (four-cylinder) or EDIS module (V6), two ignition coil packs (four-cylinder) or one ignition coil pack (V6), the spark angle portion of the EECIV, the spark plug wires and the spark plugs. The four-cylinder models feature a twin spark plug cylinder head and are equipped with an ignition coil for each pair of spark plugs.

This ignition system does not have any moving parts (no distributor) and all engine timing and spark distribution is handled electronically. This system has fewer parts that require replacement and provides more accurate spark timing. During engine operation, the DIS ignition module and the EEC IV module calculates spark angle and determines the turn on and firing time of the ignition coil.

On four-cylinder models, the crankshaft timing sensor is a dual Hall effect magnetic switch, which is actuated by the dual vane cup on the end of the crankshaft pulley hub. This sensor generates two separate signals, one for base timing and engine RPM information and the other for the ignition coils. On V6 models, the crankshaft timing sensor is a variable reluctance-type consisting of a 36-tooth trigger wheel with one missing tooth that is incorporated into the crankshaft front damper. The

signal generated by this sensor is called a Variable Reluctance Sensor signal(VRS)and it provides the base timing and engine RPM information to the DIS or EDIS ignition modules. The main function of the DIS (four-cylinder) or EDIS (V6) module is to synchronize the ignition coils so they are turned on an off in the proper sequence for accurate spark control.

6 Ignition system – check

Refer to illustration 6.2
Warning: *Because of the very high secondary (spark plug) voltage generated by the ignition system, extreme care should be taken when this check is done.*

Distributor type ignition system (Dura-Spark II and TFI-IV)

Calibrated ignition tester method

1 If the engine turns over but won't start, disconnect the spark plug lead from any spark plug and attach it to a calibrated ignition tester (available at most auto parts stores). Make sure the tester is designed for Ford ignition systems if a universal tester isn't available.

2 Connect the clip on the tester to a bolt or metal bracket on the engine **(seeillustration)**, crank the engine and watch the end of the tester to see if bright blue, well-defined sparks occur.

3 If sparks occur, sufficient voltage is reaching the plug to fire it (repeat the check at the remaining plug wires to verify that the distributor cap and rotor are OK). However, the plugs themselves may be fouled, so remove and check them as described in Chapter 1 or install new ones.

4 If no sparks or intermittent sparks occur, remove the distributor cap and check the cap and rotor as described in Chapter 1. If moisture is present, dry out the cap and rotor, then reinstall the cap and repeat the spark test.

5 If there's still no spark, detach the secondary coil wire from the distributor cap and hook it up to the tester (reattach the plug wire to the spark plug), then repeat the spark check.

   a) If no sparks occur, check the primary (small) wire connections at the coil to make sure they're clean and tight. Refer to Section 7 and check the ignition coil. Make any necessary repairs, then repeat the check again. If there's still no spark, the coil-to-cap wire may be bad. If a known good wire doesn't make any difference in the test results, the ignition module or other internal components may be defective.

   b) If sparks now occur, the distributor cap, rotor or plug wire(s) (or all of them) may be defective.

Alternative method

Note: *If you're unable to obtain a calibrated ignition tester, the following method will allow you to determine if the ignition system has spark, but it won't tell you if there's enough voltage produced to actually initiate combustion in the cylinders.*

6 Remove the wire from one of the spark plugs. Using an insulated tool, hold the wire about 1/4-inch from a good ground and have an assistant crank the engine.

7 If bright blue, well-defined sparks occur, sufficient voltage is reaching the plug to fire it (repeat the check on the remaining spark plug wires to verify the cap and rotor are OK). However, the plug(s) may be fouled, so remove and check them as described in Chapter 1 or install new ones.

8 If there's no spark, check the remaining wires in the same manner. A few sparks followed by no spark is the same condition as no spark at all.

9 If no sparks occur, remove the distributor cap and check the cap and rotor as described in Chapter 1. If moisture is present, dry out the cap and rotor, then reinstall the cap and repeat the spark test.

10 If there's still no spark, disconnect the secondary coil wire from the distributor cap, hold it about 1/4-inch from a good engine ground and crank the engine again.

   a) If no sparks occur, check the primary (small) wire connections at the coil to make sure they're clean and tight. Check the coil (see Section 7). Make any necessary repairs, then repeat the check. If there's still no spark, the coil-to-cap wire may be bad. If a known

5

good wire doesn't make any difference in the test results, the ignition module or other internal components may be defective. Refer further testing to a Ford dealer or qualified electrical specialist.

b) If sparks now occur, the distributor cap, rotor or plug wire(s) (or all of them) may be defective.

Distributorless (DIS) ignition system

Calibrated ignition tester method

Note: *On 2.3L four-cylinder models (dual-plug ignition), disconnect the spark plugs for this test from the exhaust side only.*

11   If the engine turns over but won't start, disconnect the spark plug lead from any spark plug and attach it to a calibrated ignition tester (available at most auto parts stores). Make sure the tester is designed for Ford ignition systems if a universal tester isn't available.

12   Connect the clip on the tester to a bolt or metal bracket on the engine **(see illustration 6.2)**, crank the engine and watch the end of the tester to see if bright blue, well-defined sparks occur.

13   If sparks occur, sufficient voltage is reaching the spark plug to fire it (repeat the check at the remaining plug wires to verify that all the ignition coils and wires are functioning). However, the plugs themselves may be fouled, so remove and check them as described in Chapter 1 or install new ones.

14   If no sparks or intermittent sparks occur, there's a problem in the ignition system. Check for a bad spark plug wire by swapping wires. Refer further testing to a Ford dealer or qualified electrical specialist.

Alternative method

Note: *If you're unable to obtain a calibrated ignition tester, the following method will allow you to determine if the ignition system has spark, but it won't tell you if there's enough voltage produced to actually initiate combustion in the cylinders.*

Note: *On 2.3L four-cylinder models (dual-plug ignition), disconnect the spark plugs for this test from the exhaust side only.*

15   Remove the wire from one of the spark plugs. Using an insulated tool, hold the wire about 1/4-inch from a good ground and have an assistant crank the engine.

16   If bright blue, well-defined sparks occur, sufficient voltage is reaching the plug to fire it. However, the plug(s) may be fouled, so remove and check them as described in Chapter 1 or install new ones.

17   If there's no spark, check the remaining wires in the same manner. A few sparks followed by no spark is the same condition as no spark at all. If there's spark at some wires but not at others, bad spark plug wires may be the problem. Swap the wires and re-test to see if the wires are the problem.

18   If there's still no sparks or intermittent sparks, there's a problem in the ignition system. Refer further testing to a Ford dealer or qualified electrical specialist.

---

7   Ignition coil – check and replacement

Check (distributor-type ignition systems only)

Note: *Checking the ignition coils on distributorless ignition systems is beyond the scope of the home mechanic. Take the vehicle to a dealer service department for testing.*

1   With the engine off, disconnect the wires from the coil. Connect an ohmmeter across the coil primary (small wire) terminals. The resistance should be as listed in this Chapter's Specifications. If not, replace the coil.

2   Connect an ohmmeter between the negative primary terminal and the secondary terminal (the one the distributor cap wire connects to). The resistance should be as listed in this Chapter's Specifications. If not, replace the coil.

Replacement

Distributor type ignition system (Dura Spark II and TFI-IV)

3   Disconnect the negative cable from the battery.

4   Detach the wires from the primary terminals on the coil (some coils have a single electrical connector for the primary wires).

5   Unplug the coil secondary lead.

6   Remove both bracket bolts and detach the coil.

7   Installation is the reverse of the removal procedure.

Distributorless (DIS) ignition system

Refer to illustrations 7.9, 7.11a and 7.11b

8   Disconnect the negative cable from the battery.

9   Squeeze the locking tabs of the ignition coil wire retainer by hand and remove the spark plug wires from the ignition coil pack with a twisting and pulling motion **(see illustration)**. DO NOT just pull on the wires to disconnect them. **Note:** *Label each wire so it can be returned to its original location.* Disconnect all spark plug wires.

10   Disconnect the engine wiring harness from the ignition coil assembly(ies). On 1992 and later models, remove the air conditioning line-to-plenum bolt and reposition the line for access to the coil pack screws.

11   Remove the three (V6) or four (four-cylinder) screws securing the ignition coil pack to the mounting bracket on the engine **(see illustrations)**. On four-cylinder models, repeat for the other coil pack. **Note:** *1992 and later V6 models may have Torx screws.*

12   Installation is the reverse of the removal procedure with the following additions:

a) Prior to installing the spark plug lead into the ignition coil, coat the entire interior of the rubber boot with Silicone Dielectric Compound (Ford part No. D7AZ-19A133-A) or equivalent.

b) Insert each spark plug wire into the proper terminal of the ignition coil. Push the wire into the terminal and make sure the boots are fully seated and both locking tabs are engaged properly.

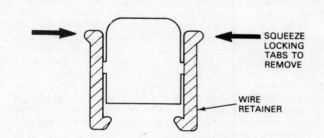

SQUEEZE
LOCKING
TABS TO
REMOVE

WIRE RETAINER

7.9   Squeeze the locking tabs to release the spark plug wire

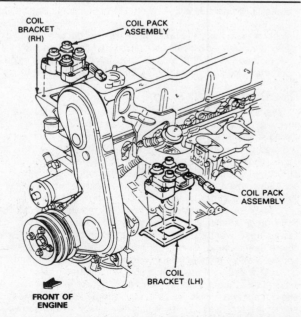

COIL BRACKET (RH)

COIL PACK ASSEMBLY

COIL PACK ASSEMBLY

COIL BRACKET (LH)

FRONT OF ENGINE

7.11a   The ignition coil packs and their mounting brackets (1991 and earlier four-cylinder models – on later models the packs are both on the right side)

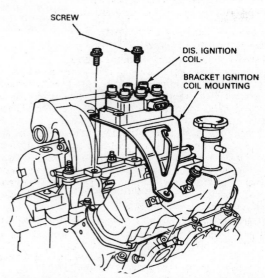

7.11b   The ignition coil pack and its mounting bracket
(V6 models)

8   Crankshaft timing sensor (distributorless ignition systems) – removal and installation

Four-cylinder models

Removal

Refer to illustrations 8.3 and 8.6

1   Disconnect the negative cable from the battery.
2   Disconnect the crankshaft timing sensor electrical connector from the engine main wiring harness.
3   Pry out the red retaining clip and remove the four wires, then remove the large electrical connector from the crankshaft timing sensor assembly (see illustration).

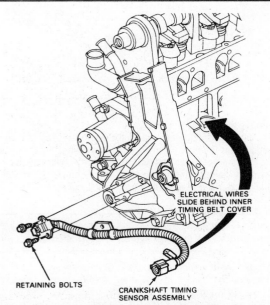

8.6   The crankshaft timing sensor assembly and wiring harness
(four-cylinder models)

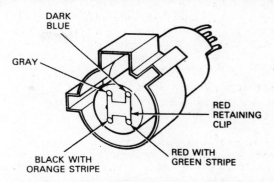

8.3   Pry out the red retaining clip and remove the four wires from the large electrical connector (four-cylinder models)

4   Remove the accessory drivebelts, the crankshaft pulley assembly and the timing belt outer cover (see Chapter 2A).
5   Rotate the crankshaft so the keyway is at the ten o'clock position. This will locate the vane window of both the inner and outer vane cups (part of the crankshaft pulley hub assembly) over the crankshaft timing sensor assembly.
6   Remove the two bolts securing the crankshaft timing sensor assembly to the cylinder block (see illustration).
7   Remove the bolt securing the wiring harness plastic retainer to the mounting bracket. Carefully slide the wiring harness out from behind the timing belt inner cover and remove the crankshaft timing sensor assembly.

Installation

Refer to illustration 8.13

8   If a new crankshaft timing sensor assembly is being installed, remove the large electrical connector from it. If installing the old assembly, the connector is already removed.
9   Slide the electrical wire harness behind the timing belt inner cover.
10   Install the crankshaft timing sensor assembly into place and install the two bolts finger tight at this time.
11   Install the large electrical connector onto the harness. **Caution:** *Ensure the four wires are installed in the proper location within the connector* (see illustration 8.3). *If installed incorrectly the sensor will NOT operate correctly.*
12   Connect the electrical connector to the engine main wiring harness.
13   Rotate the crankshaft so the outer vane on the crankshaft pulley hub assembly engages both sides of the Crankshaft Hall-Effect Sensor Positioner (Ford part No. T89P-6316-A), or equivalent (see illustration).

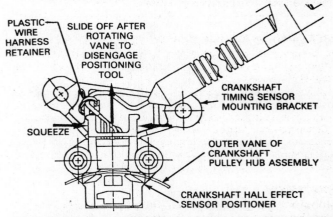

8.13   Rotate the crankshaft so the outer vane on the crankshaft pulley hub assembly engages both sides of the Crankshaft Hall Effect Sensor Positioner

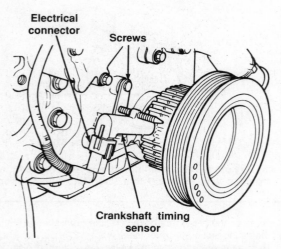

8.20   The crankshaft timing sensor assembly and wiring harness (V6 models)

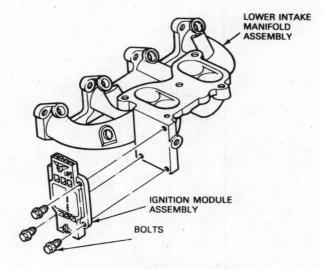

9.3   DIS ignition module mounting bolts

Tighten the crankshaft timing sensor assembly mounting bolts.
14   Rotate the crankshaft so the outer vane on the crankshaft pulley hub assembly no longer engages the positioner tool, then remove the tool.
15   Install the wire harness plastic retainer, install the bolt and tighten securely. If a new retainer was installed, trim off the excess.
16   Install the timing belt outer cover, the crankshaft pulley assembly and the accessory drive belts (see Chapter 2A).
17   Attach the negative cable to the battery.

V6 models

Refer to illustration 8.20

18   Disconnect the negative cable from the battery.
19   Disconnect the crankshaft timing sensor electrical connector from the engine main wiring harness.
20   Remove the two bolts securing the crankshaft timing sensor assembly to the cylinder block **(see illustration)**. Remove the assembly.
21   Installation is the reverse of the removal procedure.

**9   Ignition module – DIS or EDIS
(distributorless ignition systems) – removal and installation**

Note: *Diagnosing the ignition module requires special equipment, placing it out of the scope of the home mechanic. However, you can replace the module if it has been diagnosed defective.*

DIS (four-cylinder models)

Refer to illustration 9.3

1   Disconnect the negative cable from the battery.
2   Disconnect each electrical connector at the DIS ignition module. Push down on the connector locking tab where it is stamped PUSH and then pull it away from the DIS module.
3   Remove the three bolts securing the DIS module to the lower intake manifold **(see illustration)**.
4   Installation is the reverse of the removal procedure with the following additions:
   a)   Apply an even coat (approximately 1/32-inch) of Silicone Dielectric Compound (Ford part No. D7AZ-19A331-A), or equivalent, to the mounting surface of the DIS ignition module.
   b)   Mount the module and bolts and tighten the bolts securely.

EDIS (V6 models)

Refer to illustration 9.8

5   Disconnect the negative cable from the battery.

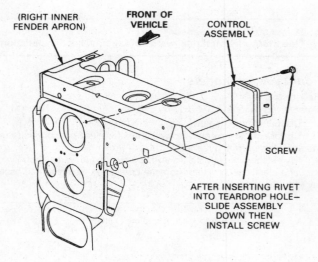

9.8   EDIS ignition module installation details

6   Remove the battery (see Section 2).
7   Disconnect the electrical connector from the EDIS ignition module.
8   Remove the screw securing the EDIS module to the lower panel adjacent to the radiator **(see illustration)**. Slide the assembly up to remove the positioning rivet from the teardrop hole in the panel and remove it.
9   Installation is the reverse of the removal procedure.

**10   Ignition module
(distributor type ignition systems) – replacement**

Caution: *The ignition module is a delicate and relatively expensive electronic component. Failure to follow the step-by-step procedures could result in damage to the module and/or other electronic devices, including the EEC-IV microprocessor itself. Additionally, all devices under computer control are protected by a Federally mandated extended warranty. Check with your dealer before attempting to replace them yourself.*

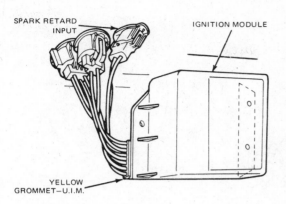

10.2 Duraspark II ignition systems will be equipped with one of two ignition modules: the Universal Ignition Module (UIM), has three electrical connectors; the standard Duraspark II module has two connectors

10.6 To remove the TFI-IV ignition module from the distributor base, remove the two screws (arrows), . . .

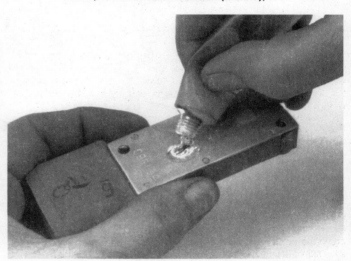

10.7 . . . then pull the module straight down to detach the spade terminals from the stator connector

10.8 Be sure to wipe the back side of the module clean and apply a film of dielectric grease (essential for cool operation of the module) – DO NOT use any other type of grease!

Note: *Diagnosing the ignition module requires special equipment, placing it out of the scope of the home mechanic. However, you can replace the module if it has been diagnosed defective.*

Duraspark II ignition module

Refer to illustration 10.2

1   Disconnect the negative cable from the battery.
2   Vehicles equipped with a Duraspark II system may have either the standard Duraspark II module or the universal ignition module (UIM) **(see illustration)**. If your vehicle is equipped with the standard module, unplug both connectors; if your vehicle is equipped with the UIM module, unplug all three connectors.
3   Remove the mounting screws and detach the module.
4   Installation is the reverse of the removal procedure.

TFI-IV ignition module

Refer to illustrations 10.6, 10.7 and 10.8

5   Remove the distributor from the engine (refer to Section 11) if access to the module is blocked.
6   Remove the two module mounting screws **(see illustration)**.
7   Pull straight down on the module to disconnect the spade connectors from the stator connector **(see illustration)**.

8   Whether you are installing the old module or a new one, wipe the back side of the module clean with a soft, clean rag and apply a film of silicone dielectric grease to the back side of the module **(see illustration)**. DO NOT use any other type of grease!
9   Installation is the reverse of removal. When plugging in the module, make sure that the three terminals are inserted all the way into the stator connector.

---

11   Distributor – removal and installation

1983 and 1984 2.3L and all 2.0L four-cylinder models (Dura-Spark II)

Refer to illustration 11.5, 11.6 and 11.8

Removal

1   Disconnect the negative cable from the battery.
2   Remove the alternator drivebelt and pivot the alternator to one side (see Chapter 1).
3   Remove the distributor cap (see Chapter 1). Move the cap and spark plug wires out of the way.
4   Disconnect the vacuum advance hose from the distributor and plug it.

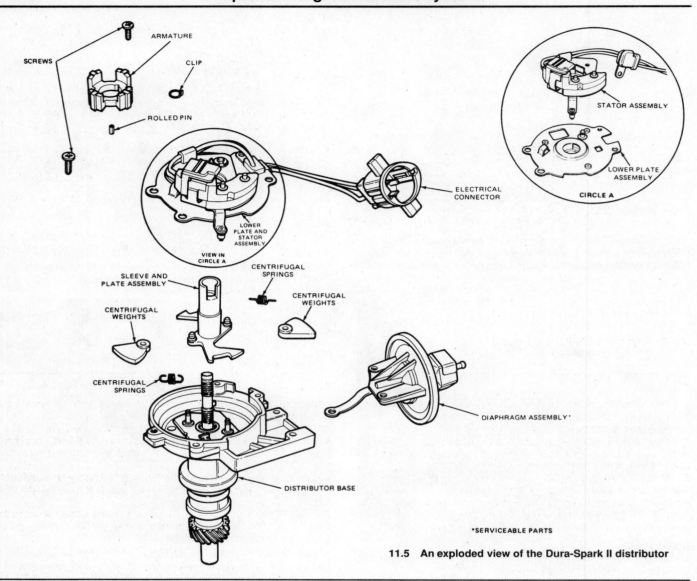

11.5   An exploded view of the Dura-Spark II distributor

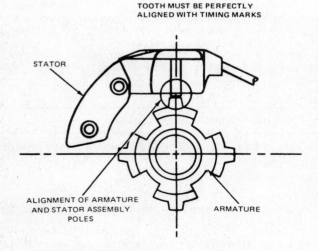

11.6   Alignment of the stator assembly pole and any armature pole

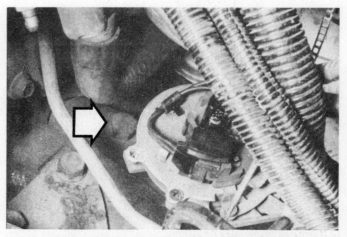

11.8   Arrow points to a typical distributor hold-down bolt and clamp location (2.3L four-cylinder engine shown)

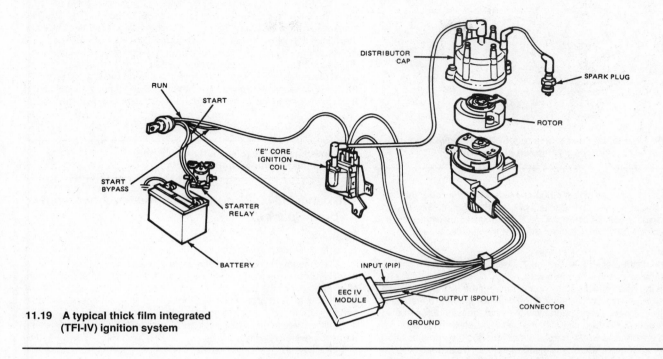

11.19 A typical thick film integrated (TFI-IV) ignition system

5   Disconnect the distributor electrical connector **(see illustration)**.
6   Rotate the engine to align the stator assembly pole and any armature pole **(see illustration)**.
7   Make a mark on the edge of the distributor base directly below the rotor tip and in line with it. Also, mark the distributor base and the engine block to ensure that the distributor is installed correctly.
8   Remove the distributor hold-down bolt and clamp **(see illustration)**, then pull the distributor straight up to remove it (note that the rotor will rotate slightly as the helical gear disengages from the camshaft). **Caution:** *DO NOT turn the engine while the distributor is removed, or the alignment marks will be useless.*

Installation
9   Insert the distributor into the engine in exactly the same relationship to the block that it was in when removed.
10   To mesh the helical gears on the camshaft and the distributor, it may be necessary to turn the rotor slightly. If the distributor doesn't seat completely, the hex-shaped recess in the lower end of the distributor shaft is not mating properly. Recheck the alignment marks between the distributor base and the block to verify that the distributor is in the same position it was in before removal. Also check the rotor to see if it's aligned with the mark you made on the edge of the distributor base. **Note:** *If the crankshaft has been moved while the distributor is out, locate Top Dead Center (TDC) for the number one piston (see Chapter 2) and position the distributor and rotor accordingly.*
11   Place the hold-down clamp in position and loosely install the bolt.
12   Connect the vacuum advance hose to the distributor.
13   Install the distributor cap (see Chapter 1).
14   Reconnect the distributor electrical connector.
15   Move the alternator back into position, reinstall the drivebelt and adjust it (see Chapter 1).
16   Connect the negative cable onto the battery.
17   Check the ignition timing (see Section 13) and tighten the distributor hold-down bolt to the torque value listed in this Chapter's Specifications.

All other models (TFI-IV)
Refer to illustrations 11.19, 11.24a and 11.24b

Removal
18   Disconnect the negative cable from the battery.

19   Disconnect the primary lead wire connector from the ignition coil **(see illustration)**.
20   Prior to removing the distributor cap, mark the position of the No. 1 spark plug wire tower on the distributor base for future reference. Also, mark the distributor base and the engine block to ensure that the distributor is installed correctly.
21   Remove the distributor cap (see Chapter 1) and turn the engine over until the rotor is pointing toward the number one spark plug terminal (see locating TDC procedure in Chapter 2).
22   On 1983 through 1985 models, remove the two screws securing the rotor and remove the rotor. On all other models, pull the rotor straight up and off the distributor shaft.
23   Disconnect the electrical connector from the module on the distributor.
24   Remove the distributor hold-down bolt and clamp, then pull the distributor straight up to remove it **(see illustration)**. Some engines may be

11.24a Remove the distributor hold-down bolt and clamp (arrow)

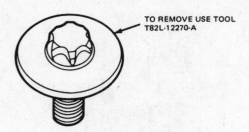

TO REMOVE USE TOOL
T82L-12270-A

**11.24b   A special Ford tool is required to remove the
security-type hold-down clamp bolt**

equipped with a security type distributor hold-down bolt **(see illustration)**. If so equipped, use Ford special tool (part No. T82L-12270-A) and
remove the special bolt. **Caution:** *DO NOT turn the engine while the distributor is removed, or the alignment marks will be useless.*

Installation

25   Insert the distributor into the engine in exactly the same relationship
to the block that it was in when removed.

26   To mesh the helical gears on the camshaft and the distributor, it may
be necessary to turn the rotor slightly. If the distributor doesn't seat completely, the hex-shaped recess in the lower end of the distributor shaft is
not mating properly. Recheck the alignment marks between the distributor base and the block to verify that the distributor is in the same position
it was in before removal. Also check the rotor to see if it's aligned with the
mark you made on the edge of the distributor base. **Note:** *If the crankshaft has been moved while the distributor is out, locate Top Dead Center
(TDC) for the number one piston (see Chapter 2) and position the distributor and rotor accordingly.*

27   Place the hold-down clamp in position and loosely install the bolt.

28   Install the rotor. On 1983 through 1985 models, install the two
screws securing the rotor. On all other models, align the rotor correctly,
then push the rotor straight down onto the distributor shaft.

29   Install the distributor cap and tighten the cap screws securely.

30   Plug in the module electrical connector.

31   Connect the cable to the negative terminal of the battery.

32   Check the ignition timing (see Section 13) and tighten the distributor
hold-down bolt to the torque listed in this Chapter's Specifications.

**12   Stator assembly (distributor type ignition
systems) – removal and installation**

*1983 and 1984 2.3L and all 2.0L four-cylinder models
(Dura-Spark II)*

Removal

Refer to illustration 12.4

1   Disconnect the negative cable from the battery.

2   Remove the distributor cap (see Chapter 1). Move the cap and spark
plug wires out of the way.

3   Remove the rotor from the distributor shaft (see Chapter 1, if necessary).

4   Disconnect the distributor electrical connector from the main wiring
harness **(see illustration)**.

5   Use a small gear puller or two screwdrivers, lever the armature off
the distributor shaft.

6   Remove the two screws securing the lower plate assembly and stator assembly to the distributor base. Note that there are two different size
screws used.

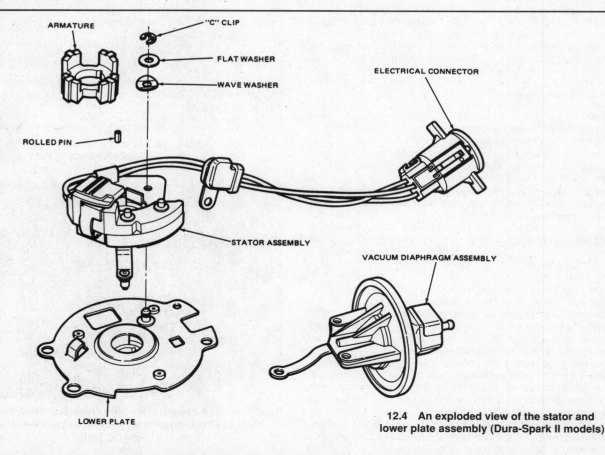

ARMATURE

"C" CLIP

FLAT WASHER

WAVE WASHER

ROLLED PIN

ELECTRICAL CONNECTOR

STATOR ASSEMBLY

VACUUM DIAPHRAGM ASSEMBLY

LOWER PLATE

**12.4   An exploded view of the stator and
lower plate assembly (Dura-Spark II models)**

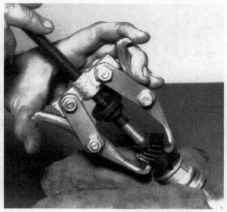

12.25 With the distributor shaft housing locked securely in a vise lined with several shop rags to prevent damage to the housing, drive out the roll pin with a 5/32-inch pin punch

12.27 With the distributor shaft pointing up like this, use a small puller to separate the drive gear from the shaft

12.28 Inspect the distributor shaft for burrs and residue buildup in the vicinity of the hole for the drive gear roll pin (remove it with emery cloth to prevent damage to the distributor shaft bushing when removing and installing the shaft)

7 To remove the stator from the lower plate, remove the E-clip, flat washer and wave washer and remove the stator assembly.

Installation
8 Before installing the stator, remove and dirt or grease from parts that are to be reused.
9 Install the stator onto the lower plate. Position the wave washer with the outer edges facing up and install it followed by the flat washer and the E-clip. Make sure the E-clip is properly seated in the lower plate post.
10 Install the lower plate/stator assembly into the distributor base. Correctly engage the stator arm pin with the hole in the vacuum diaphragm arm. This is necessary for proper ignition advance operation.
11 Attach the lower plate/stator assembly to the distributor base. Be sure to install the two different size mounting screws in their correct locations. Tighten the screws securely.
12 There are two notches in the armature. Position the armature so the unused notch is installed onto the new roll pin. Push the armature down on the distributor shaft until it is properly seated.
13 Connect the distributor electrical connector to the main wiring harness.
14 Align the rotor correctly, then push the rotor straight down onto the distributor shaft.
15 Install the distributor cap (see Chapter 1).
16 Connect the negative cable onto the battery and adjust the ignition timing (see Section 13).

All other models (TFI-IV)
Refer to illustrations 12.25, 12.27, 12.28, 12.29, 12.30, 12.31, 12.35, 12.44a and 12.44b

Removal
17 Disconnect the distributor cap from the distributor (see Chapter 1, if necessary).
18 Position the distributor cap out of the way with the wires attached.
19 Disconnect the TFI module from the wire harness.
20 Remove the distributor (refer to Section 11).
21 Remove the rotor (refer to Chapter 1 if necessary).
22 Although not absolutely necessary, it's a good idea to remove the ignition module (Section 10) to prevent possible damage to the module while the distributor is being disassembled.
23 Clamp the lower end of the distributor housing in a vise. Place shop rags in the vise jaws to prevent damage to the distributor and don't over-tighten the vise.

24 Before removing the drive gear, note that the roll pin is slightly offset. When the distributor is reassembled, the roll pin cannot be reinstalled through the drive gear and distributor shaft holes unless the holes are perfectly lined up.
25 With an assistant holding the distributor steady in the vise, use a 5/32-inch diameter pin punch to hammer the roll pin out of the shaft **(see illustration)**.
26 Loosen the vise and reposition the distributor with the drive gear facing up.
27 Remove the drive gear with a small puller **(see illustration)**.
28 Before removing it from the distributor, check the shaft for burrs or built up residue, particularly around the drive gear roll pin hole **(see illustration)**. If burrs or residue are evident, polish the shaft with emery paper and wipe it clean to prevent damage to the lip seal and bushing in the distributor base.
29 After removing any burrs/residue, remove the shaft assembly by gently pulling on the plate. Note the relationship of the spacer washer to the distributor base before removing the washer **(see illustration)**.

12.29 As soon as you remove the distributor shaft, note how the washer is installed before removing it (it could easily fall out and get lost)

5

12.30   To detach the octane rod (if equipped) from the distributor, remove the retaining screw (arrow) – note the condition of the small square rubber grommet that seals the octane rod hole when you pull the rod out (it seals the interior of the distributor to prevent moisture from damaging the electronics)

12.31   To remove the octane rod, lift the inner end of the rod off the stator assembly post (arrow) – to remove the stator assembly, remove both mounting screws (arrows) and lift the stator straight up off the posts

12.35   If the O-ring at the base of the distributor is worn or damaged, replace it with a new one

12.44a   After securing the distributor assembly upside down in a vise, note the roll pin holes in the drive gear and the shaft, then tap the drive gear onto the shaft with a deep socket and hammer

30   If equipped with an octane rod, remove the octane rod retaining screw **(see illustration)**.

31   If equipped with an octane rod, lift the inner end of the rod off the stator retaining post **(see illustration)** and pull the octane rod from the distributor base. **Note:** *Don't lose the grommet installed in the octane rod hole. The grommet protects the electronic components of the distributor from moisture.*

32   Remove the two stator screws **(see illustration 12.31)**.

33   Gently lift it straight up and remove the stator assembly from the distributor.

Installation

34   Check the shaft bushing in the distributor base for wear or signs of excessive heat buildup. If signs of wear and/or damage are evident, replace the complete distributor assembly.

35   Inspect the O-ring at the base of the distributor. If it's damaged or worn, remove it and install a new one **(see illustration)**.

36   Inspect the base casting for cracks and wear. If any damage is evident, replace the distributor assembly.

37   Place the stator assembly in position over the shaft bushing and

press it down onto the distributor base until it's completely seated on the posts.

38   Install the stator screws and tighten them securely.

39   Insert the octane rod through the hole in the distributor base and push the inner end of the rod onto the post. **Note:** *Make sure that the octane rod hole is proper sealed by the grommet.*

40   Reinstall the octane rod screw and tighten it securely.

41   Apply a light coat of engine oil to the distributor shaft and insert the shaft through the bushing.

42   Mount the distributor in the vise with the lower end up. Be sure to line the vise jaws with a few clean shop rags to protect the distributor base. Place a block of wood under the distributor shaft to support it and prevent it from falling out while the drive gear is being installed.

43   Align the hole in the distributor shaft with the drive gear hole. Remember that the hole is offset so the gear can only go on one way.

44   Using a deep socket and hammer, carefully tap the drive gear back onto the distributor shaft **(see illustration)**. Make sure the hole in the drive gear and the hole in the shaft are lined up. Because the holes were drilled off center by the factory, they must be perfectly aligned or the roll pin cannot be installed **(see illustration)**.

12.44b If the drive gear and shaft roll pin holes are misaligned, the roll pin cannot be driven through the drive gear and shaft holes – this drive gear must now be pulled off the shaft and realigned

45 Once the drive gear is seated and the holes are lined up, turn the distributor sideways in the vise and, with an assistant steadying it, drive a new roll pin into the drive gear with a 5/32-inch pin punch. Make sure that neither end of the roll pin protrudes from the drive gear.

46 Check the distributor shaft for smooth rotation, then remove the distributor assembly from the vise.

47 Install the TFI-IV module (refer to Section 10).

48 Install the rotor (refer to Chapter 1 if necessary).

49 Install the distributor (refer to Section 11).

13 Ignition timing

Note: *This procedure applies to all models equipped with distributors. However, check the Vehicle Emission Control Information label on your vehicle to see if it specifies additional steps or a different procedure. If it does, follow the label instructions. No timing adjustments are possible on vehicles equipped with distributorless ignition systems (1989 and later 2.3L engines and all 4.0L engines).*

1 Apply the parking brake and block the wheels. Place the transmission in Park (automatic) or Neutral (manual). Turn off all accessories (heater, air conditioner, etc.).

2 Start the engine and warm it up. Once it has reached normal operating temperature, turn it off.

3 If the distributor has a vacuum advance line, disconnect and plug the hose (not the fitting on the distributor).

4 Disconnect the single white or black wire at the connector near the distributor or remove the shorting bar from the double connector (if equipped).

5 If the vehicle is equipped with Dura-Spark II and has a barometric pressure switch, disconnect it from the ignition module. Install a jumper wire across the pins at the ignition module connector (yellow and black wires).

6 Connect an inductive timing light and a tachometer in accordance with the manufacturer's instructions. **Caution:** *Make sure that the timing light and tach wires don't hang anywhere near the fan or they may become entangled in the fan blades when the engine runs.*

7 Locate the timing notch in the crankshaft pulley and the timing scale on the front of the engine (see the locating TDC procedure in Chapter 2).

8 Start the engine again.

9 Point the timing light at the timing marks and note whether the timing notch is aligned with the correct mark on the scale (refer to the VECI label or this Chapter's Specifications).

10 If the proper mark isn't aligned with the stationary pointer, loosen the distributor hold-down bolt. Turn the distributor to change timing until the correct timing mark is aligned with the stationary pointer. Tighten the dis-

tributor hold-down bolt securely when the timing is correct and recheck it to make sure it didn't change when the bolt was tightened.

11 Turn off the engine.

12 Plug in the single wire connector or install the shorting bar and attach the vacuum hoses (if applicable).

13 Remove the jumper wire and re-connect the barometric pressure switch (if applicable).

14 Restart the engine and check the idle speed. If it's incorrect on carbureted models, adjust it (refer to Chapter 1). Because fuel injected models are equipped with automatic idle speed control, idle rpm is not adjustable. If the idle rpm is not within the specified range, take the vehicle to a dealer service department or repair shop. Adjustment requires specialized test equipment and procedures that are beyond the scope of the home mechanic.

15 Turn off the engine.

16 Remove the timing light and tachometer.

14 Charging system – general information and precautions

The charging system includes the alternator, either an internal or an external voltage regulator, an ammeter or charge indicator light, the battery, a fusible link and the wiring between all the components. The charging system supplies electrical power for the ignition system, the lights, the radio, etc. The alternator is driven by a drivebelt at the front of the engine.

The purpose of the voltage regulator is to limit the alternator's voltage to a preset value. This prevents power surges, circuit overloads, etc., during peak voltage output. On EVR (external voltage regulator) systems, the regulator is mounted on the right fender apron of the vehicle. On IAR (integral alternator/regulator) systems, a solid-state regulator is housed inside the alternator itself.

The fusible link is a short length of insulated wire integral with the engine compartment wiring harness. The link is four wire gauges smaller in diameter than the circuit it protects. Production fusible links and their identification flags are identified by the flag color. Refer to Chapter 12 for detailed information regarding the identification colors of both production and service fusible links.

The charging system doesn't ordinarily require periodic maintenance. However, the drivebelt, battery and wires and connections should be inspected at the intervals outlined in Chapter 1.

Be very careful when making electrical circuit connections to the vehicle and note the following:
  a) When reconnecting wires to the alternator from the battery, be sure to note the polarity.
  b) Before using arc welding equipment to repair any part of the vehicle, disconnect the wires from the alternator and the battery terminals.
  c) Never start the engine with a battery charger connected.
  d) Always disconnect both battery leads before using a battery charger.
  e) The alternator is turned by the engine drivebelt which could cause serious injury if your hands or clothes become entangled in it with the engine running.
  f) Because the alternator is connected directly to the battery, it could arc or cause a fire if overloaded or shorted out.
  g) Wrap a plastic bag over the alternator and secure it with rubber bands before steam cleaning the engine.

15 Charging system – check

General test

Refer to illustrations 15.2 and 15.3

1 If a malfunction occurs in the charging circuit, don't automatically assume that the alternator is causing the problem.

First check the following items:
  a) Check the drivebelt tension and condition (see Chapter 1).

5

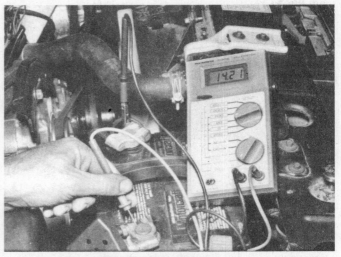

15.2   Connect a voltmeter between the battery terminals and check the battery voltage with the engine off

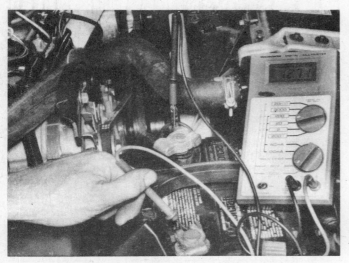

15.3   With the engine running at a fast idle the voltage should be between 14 and 15 volts

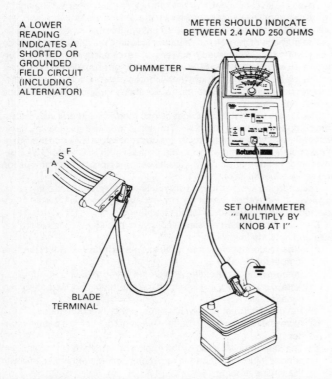

15.7   Temporarily install a blade terminal in the wiring harness F terminal, then measure resistance between the F terminal and ground with an ohmmeter

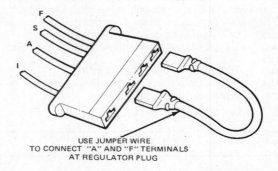

15.8   Remove the blade terminal. Connect a jumper wire between terminals A and F

e) Start the engine and check the alternator for abnormal noises (a shrieking or squealing sound indicates a bad bearing).
f) Check the specific gravity of the battery electrolyte. If it's low, charge the battery (doesn't apply to maintenance free batteries).
g) Make sure the battery is fully charged (one bad cell in a battery can cause overcharging by the alternator).
h) Disconnect the battery cables (negative first, then positive). Inspect the battery posts and the cable clamps for corrosion. Clean them thoroughly if necessary (see Chapter 1). Reconnect the cable to the positive terminal.
i) With the key off, connect a test light between the negative battery post and the disconnected negative cable clamp.
  1) If the test light does not come on, reattach the clamp and proceed to the next Step.
  2) If the test light comes on, there is a short (drain) in the electrical system of the vehicle. The short must be repaired before the charging system can be checked.
  3) Disconnect the alternator wiring harness.
    (a) If the light goes out, the alternator is bad.
    (b) If the light stays on, pull each fuse until the light goes out (this will tell you which component is shorted).

2   Using a voltmeter, check the battery voltage with the engine off. It should be approximately 12-volts **(see illustration)**.

3   Run the engine at a fast idle (approximately 1500 rpm) and check the battery voltage again after the voltage stops rising **(see illustration)**. This may take a few minutes. It should now be higher than battery voltage, but not more than 2 volts higher (external voltage regulator) or 2.5 volts higher (integral voltage regulator).

Replace it if it's worn or deteriorated.
b) Make sure the alternator mounting and adjustment bolts are tight.
c) Inspect the alternator wiring harness and the electrical connectors at the alternator and voltage regulator (if external). They must be in good condition and tight.
d) Check the fusible link (if equipped) located between the starter relay and the alternator. If it's burned, determine the cause, repair the circuit and replace the link (the vehicle won't start and/or the accessories won't work if the fusible link blows). Sometimes a fusible link may look good, but still be bad. If in doubt, remove it and check for continuity.

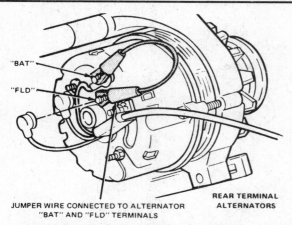

15.11 Pull back the cover from the BAT terminal and connect a jumper wire between the FLD and BAT terminals

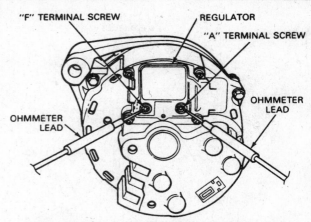

15.26 Connect an ohmmeter between the A and F terminal screws

4   If the voltage reading is less than the specified charging voltage, perform the Under-voltage test in this Section. If it is higher, perform the Over-voltage test.

5   Turn on the high beam headlights and turn the heater or air conditioner blower to its highest setting. Run the engine at 2,000 rpm and check the voltage reading. It should now be at least 0.5 volt higher than battery voltage. If not, perform the appropriate Under-voltage test.

6   If the voltage readings are correct in the preceding Steps, the charging system is working properly.

Under-voltage test – external voltage regulator

Refer to illustrations 15.7, 15.8 and 15.11

7   Unplug the electrical connector from the regulator. Temporarily install a blade terminal in the wiring harness F terminal, then measure resistance between the F terminal and ground with an ohmmeter **(see illustration)**. It should read 2.4 ohms or more.
  a) If it is less than specified, repair the shorted or grounded field circuit in the alternator or wiring harness, then repeat the load test (Step 5).
  b) If the ohmmeter reading is correct, proceed with Step 8.

8   Remove the blade terminal. Connect a jumper wire between terminals A and F **(see illustration)**.

9   Repeat the load test (Step 5) with the jumper wire connected.
  a) If the reading is more than 0.5-volt above battery voltage, the problem is in the wiring or regulator. Perform the S circuit test (ammeter equipped models) or S and I circuit tests (indicator light equipped models) to isolate the problem.
  b) If the reading is still too low, continue with Step 10.

10   Remove the jumper wire from the electrical connector, but leave the connector unplugged for now.

11   Disconnect the FLD terminal wire at the back of the alternator. Pull back the cover from the BAT terminal and connect a jumper wire between the FLD and BAT terminals **(see illustration)**.

12   Repeat the load test (Step 5).
  a) If voltage is now 0.5 volt or more above battery voltage, perform the S or S and I circuit test below.
  b) If voltage is still too low, proceed to Step 13.

13   Turn off the engine and move the positive voltmeter lead to the BAT terminal on the alternator.
  a) If the voltmeter now indicates battery voltage, replace the alternator.
  b) If the voltmeter indicates zero, check the wire between the alternator and starter relay for breaks or bad connections and repair as needed.

Over-voltage test – external voltage regulator

14   Start this test with the regulator electrical connector plugged in.

15   Connect a jumper wire between the base of the voltage regulator and the alternator frame casting.

16   Repeat the no-load test (Step 3).
  a) If the voltage reading drops to within the specified range, check for a poor ground at the alternator, at the regulator, between the engine and firewall, or at either end of the negative battery cable.
  b) If the voltage is still too high, perform Step 17.

17   Unplug the electrical connector from the voltage regulator and repeat the no-load test (Step 3).
  a) If the voltage reading is now correct, replace the voltage regulator.
  b) If the voltage reading is still too high, check for a short between the A and F circuits.

S circuit test (ammeter-equipped vehicles) – external voltage regulator

18   Unplug the electrical connector from the voltage regulator. Connect the voltmeter positive lead to the S terminal in the connector. Connect the negative lead to the battery negative terminal.

19   Check the voltmeter reading with the engine off. It should be zero.

20   Turn the ignition key to the On position, but don't start the engine. The voltmeter should indicate battery voltage.
  a) If there is no voltage with the key On, check the S wire between the ignition switch and electrical connector for a break or bad connection.
  b) If the voltage readings are as specified, replace the voltage regulator.

21   Repeat the load test (Step 5).

S and I circuit test (indicator light-equipped vehicles) – external voltage regulator

22   Unplug the electrical connector from the regulator, then connect a jumper wire between the A and F terminals **(see illustration 15.8)**.

23   Connect the voltmeter negative lead to battery negative terminal.

24   Start the engine and let it idle.

25   Connect the voltmeter positive lead to the S terminal, then the I terminal in the regulator connector. The I terminal voltage reading should be approximately twice as high as the S terminal voltage reading.
  a) If the voltage readings are correct, replace the voltage regulator.
  b) If there is no voltage, check the S and I circuit wiring for breaks or bad connections). Remove the jumper wire.

Under-voltage test – integral voltage regulator

Refer to illustrations 15.26, 15.27, 15.29 and 15.31

26   Unplug the electrical connector from the regulator. Connect an ohmmeter between the A and F terminal screws **(see illustration)**. The ohmmeter should indicate at least 2.4 ohms.
  a) If the ohmmeter reading is too low, the regulator is defective. **Caution:** *The regulator failure may have been caused by a shorted rotor or field circuit. These must be checked before replacing the regulator or the new regulator may fail as well. Checking the rotor*

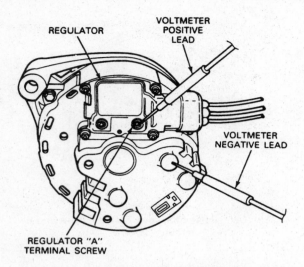

15.27   Connect the voltmeter negative lead to the alternator rear housing and the positive lead to the regulator A terminal screw

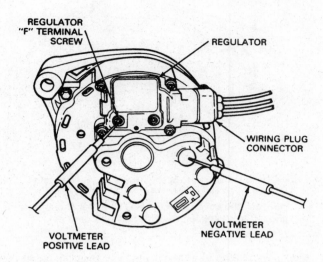

15.29   Connect the voltmeter negative lead to the alternator frame and the positive lead to the F terminal screw

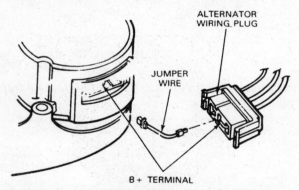

15.31   Connect a 12-gauge jumper wire between the alternator B+ terminal and its corresponding terminal in the electrical connector

and field circuit requires disassembly of the alternator and should be done by a dealer or electrical shop. It may be less expensive to replace the alternator with a rebuilt unit.

b) If the ohmmeter reading is within specifications, reconnect the electrical connector to the regulator and perform Step 27.

27   Connect the voltmeter negative lead to the alternator rear housing and the positive lead to the regulator A terminal screw **(see illustration)**. The voltmeter should indicate battery voltage. If not, check the A circuit for breaks or bad connections.

28   If the voltmeter indicates battery voltage in Step 27, place the ignition key in the Off position.

29   Connect the voltmeter negative lead to the alternator frame and the positive lead to the F terminal screw **(see illustration)**.

a) If the voltmeter indicates no voltage, replace the alternator.

b) If the voltmeter indicates battery voltage, proceed to Step 30.

30   Turn the ignition key to the Run position, but don't start the engine. Touch the voltmeter negative lead to the rear of the alternator and the positive lead to the F terminal screw on the regulator.

a) If the voltmeter indicates more than 1.5 volts, perform the S and I circuit test – integral regulator in this Section.

b) If the voltmeter indicates 1.5 volts or less, proceed to Step 31.

31   Disconnect the alternator electrical connector. Connect a 12-gauge jumper wire between the alternator B+ terminal and its corresponding terminal in the electrical connector **(see illustration)**. Perform the load

test (Step 5) with the voltmeter positive terminal connected to one of the B+ jumper wire terminals.

a) If voltage increases to more than 0.5-volt above battery voltage, check the wiring from alternator to starter relay for breaks or bad connections.

b) If the voltage does not increase to more than 0.5 volt above battery voltage, perform Step 32.

32   Connect a jumper wire between the alternator rear housing and the regulator F terminal screw **(see illustration 15.29)**. Repeat the load test (Step 5) with the voltmeter positive lead connected to one of the B+ jumper wire terminals.

a) If voltage increases by more than 0.5 volt, replace the regulator.

b) If voltage doesn't increase by more than 0.5 volt, replace the alternator.

Over-voltage test – integral voltage regulator

33   Turn the key to the On position but leave the engine off.

34   Connect the voltmeter negative lead to the alternator rear housing, then connect the positive lead to the A terminal screw and a regulator grounding screw in turn **(see illustration 15.27)**. If the voltage readings differ by more than 0.5 volt, check the A circuit for breaks or bad connections.

35   Check for loose regulator grounding screws and tighten as needed.

36   If the voltage reading is still too high, place the ignition key in the Off position. Connect the voltmeter negative lead to the alternator frame. Connect the voltmeter positive lead to the A terminal screw, then to the F terminal screw **(see illustration 15.27)**.

a) If the voltage readings at the two screw heads are different, replace the alternator.

b) If the voltage readings at the two screw heads are the same, replace the regulator.

S and I circuit test – integral voltage regulator

Refer to illustration 15.38

37   Disconnect the alternator electrical connector.

38   Connect one jumper wire from the alternator A terminal to its corresponding terminal in the electrical connector. Connect another jumper wire from the regulator F screw to the alternator housing **(see illustration)**.

39   Start the engine and let it idle.

40   Connect the voltmeter negative lead to the alternator housing. Connect the positive lead to the connector S terminal and I terminal in turn **(see illustration 15.38)**. Voltage at the I terminal should be approximately double the reading at the S terminal.

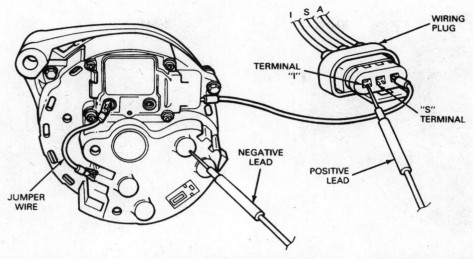

15.38 Connect one jumper wire from the alternator A terminal to its corresponding terminal in the electrical connector, then connect another jumper wire from the regulator F screw to the alternator housing

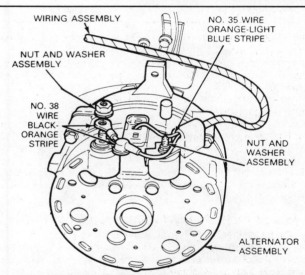

16.2a Depress the lock tab and pull up to disconnect the push-on type connector, then remove the nuts and washers securing the remaining connectors (early side-terminal alternator)

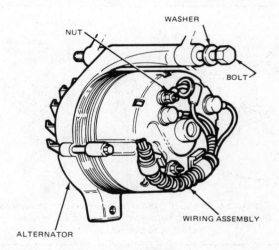

16.2b Pull straight out and disconnect the push-on type connector, then remove the nut securing the remaining connector and the nut securing the wiring assembly (early rear-terminal alternator)

a) If the readings are as specified, replace the regulator.
b) If there is no voltage, check the wiring for breaks or bad connections. If the wiring is good, replace the alternator.

16 Alternator – removal and installation

Refer to illustrations 16.2a and 16.2b

1 Disconnect the negative cable from the battery.
2 On 1983 through 1988 models, perform the following:
  a) On side-terminal alternators, depress the lock tab and pull up and disconnect the push-on type connector for the stator and field terminals on top of the alternator (**see illustration**). Remove the nuts and washers securing the remaining connectors to the rear of the alternator.
  b) On rear-terminal alternators, pull straight out and disconnect the push-on type connectors for both the stator and field terminals

(**see illustration**). Remove the nut securing the remaining connector to the rear of the alternator and the nut securing the wiring assembly.
3 On 1989 and later models, pull straight out and disconnect the push-on type connectors for both the stator and field terminals.
4 Loosen the alternator adjustment and pivot bolts, pivot the alternator up to release tension and detach the drivebelt.
5 Remove the adjustment and pivot bolts and remove the alternator from the engine.
6 Installation is the reverse of removal. After the alternator is installed, adjust the drivebelt tension (refer to Chapter 1).

17 Alternator brushes – replacement

Note: *Internal replacement parts for alternators may not be readily available in your area. Check into availability before starting this procedure.*

17.2   Scribe a line across the housing that can be used for alignment during installation

17.3a   Remove the three through bolts (arrows) and separate the housing

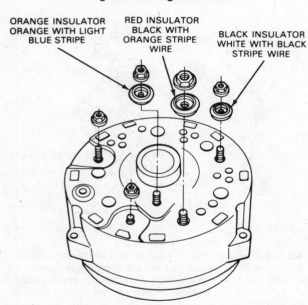

ORANGE INSULATOR
ORANGE WITH LIGHT
BLUE STRIPE

RED INSULATOR
BLACK WITH
ORANGE STRIPE
WIRE

BLACK INSULATOR
WHITE WITH BLACK
STRIPE WIRE

17.3b   Note the locations of the insulators as they must be installed correctly

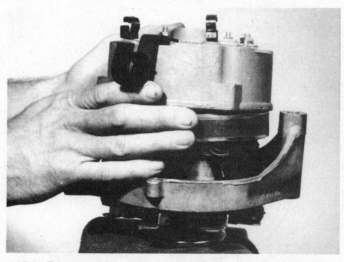

17.4   Separate the front housing and rotor assembly from the rear housing

1983 through 1988 models with external regulator

Rear-terminal alternator

Refer to illustrations 17.2, 17.3a, 17.3b, 17.4, 17.5a, 17.5b, 17.7a, 17.7b and 17.7c

Note: *Some 1986 and later models are equipped with an internal regulator. Carefully inspect the alternator to identify what type you are working on.*

1   Remove the alternator as described in Section 16.

2   Scribe a line across the length of the alternator housing to ensure correct reassembly **(see illustration)**.

3   Remove the housing through bolts and the nuts and insulators from the rear housing **(see illustration)**. Make a careful note of all insulator locations **(see illustration)**.

4   Withdraw the rear housing section from the stator, rotor and front housing assembly **(see illustration)**.

17.5a   Remove the nuts securing the brush holder and remove the holder and the one brush within it

17.5b   Remove the rear field housing nut (orange) securing the remaining brush

17.7b   Use a screwdriver to hold the brush in place

17.7c   Insert a paper clip through the hole in the back to retain the bottom brush

5   Remove the brushes and springs from the brush holder assembly, which is located inside the rear housing **(see illustrations)**.

6   Check the length of the brushes against the wear dimensions given in the Specifications and replace the brushes with new ones if necessary.

7   Install the springs and brushes in the holder assembly **(see illustrations)** and retain them in place by inserting a piece of stiff wire through

17.7a   Install the bottom brush in the rear field housing

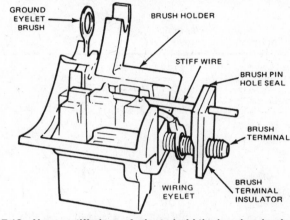

17.18   Use as stiff piece of wire to hold the brushes in place

the rear housing and brush terminal insulator **(see illustration)**. Make sure enough wire protrudes through the rear housing so it can be withdrawn later in this procedure.

8   Attach the rear housing, rotor and front housing assembly to the stator, making sure the scribe marks are aligned.

9   Install the housing through bolts and rear end insulators and nuts but do not tighten the nuts at this time.

10   Carefully extract the piece of wire from the rear housing and make sure that the brushes are seated on the slip ring. Tighten the through bolts and rear housing nuts.

11   Install the alternator as described in Section 16.

Side-terminal alternator
Refer to illustration 17.18

12   Remove the alternator as described in Section 16 and scribe a mark on both end housings and the stator for ease of reassembly.

13   Remove the through bolts and separate the front housing and rotor from the rear housing and stator. Be careful that you do not separate the rear housing and stator.

14   Use a soldering iron to unsolder and disengage the brush holder from the rear housing. Remove the brushes and springs from the brush holders.

15   Remove the two brush holder attaching screws and lift the brush holder from the rear housing.

16   Remove any sealing compound from the brush holder and rear housing.

17   Inspect the brushes for damage and check their dimensions against the specifications. If they are worn, replace them with new ones.

18   To reassemble, install the springs and brushes in the brush holders, inserting a piece of stiff wire to hold them in place **(see illustration)**.

5

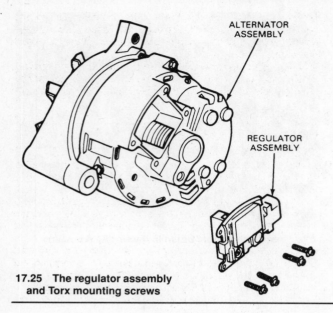

17.25 The regulator assembly and Torx mounting screws

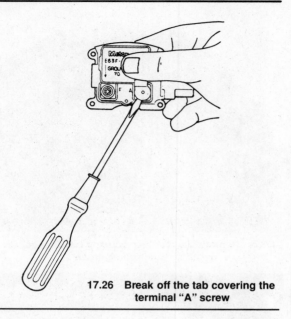

17.26 Break off the tab covering the terminal "A" screw

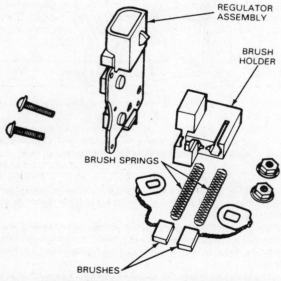

17.27 An exploded view of the brush holder assembly

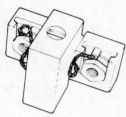

17.30 Tip the holder back slightly so the nuts and washers fall toward the nut side of the slot, then insert the brush terminals past the washers into the slot

19   Place the brush holder in position in the rear housing, using the wire to retract the brushes through the hole in the rear housing.
20   Install the brush holder attaching screws and push the holder toward the shaft opening as you tighten the screws. **Caution:** *The rectifier can be overheated and damaged if the soldering is not done quickly. Press the brush holder lead onto the rectifier lead and solder them in place.*
21   Place the rotor and front housing in position in the stator and rear housing. After aligning the scribe marks, install the through bolts.
22   Turn the fan and pulley to check for binding in the alternator.
23   Withdraw the wire which is retracting the brushes and seal the hole with waterproof cement. **Caution:** *Do not use RTV-type sealer on the hole.*

1986 and later models with internal regulator

Refer to illustrations 17.25, 17.26, 17.27, 17.30, 17.31 and 17.33
Note: *Some 1986 through 1988 models are equipped with an external regulator. Carefully inspect the alternator to determine which type you are working on.*

24   Remove the alternator (see Section 16).
25   Remove the four Torx screws (No. T20 head) securing the regulator/brush holder assembly to the rear housing **(see illustration)**. Remove the regulator/brush holder assembly.
26   Hold the regulator/brush holder assembly in one hand and using a screwdriver break off the tab covering the terminal "A' screw **(see illustration)**.
27   Remove the two Torx screws (No. T20 head) securing the regulator to the brush holder **(see illustration)**. Remove the regulator from the brush holder assembly.
28   Remove the springs from the holder. Slide the nuts, washers and brush terminals from the brush holder.

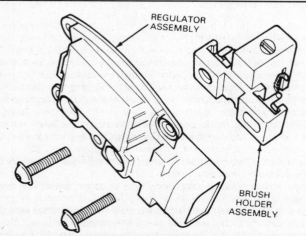

17.31 Position the brush holder onto the regulator

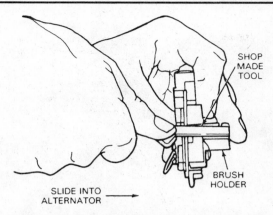

17.33   Hold the brushes and springs in place with a bent piece of flat steel

29   Inspect the brushes for damage and check their dimensions against the specifications. If they are worn, replace them with new ones.
30   Position the nuts and washers into the brush holder. Tip the holder back slightly so the nuts and washers fall toward the nut side of the slot. Insert the brush terminals past the washers into the slot **(see illustration)**.
31   Wipe the regulator base plate clean and position the brush holder onto it **(see illustration)**. Install the Torx screws and tighten securely.
32   Cover the head of the terminal "A" screw with electrical tape. Press it on so it will stick and stay in place.
33   Install the springs into the brush holder. Locate and hold the brushes and springs in place with a bent piece of flat steel **(see illustration)**. Loop brush leads toward the brush end of the brush holder.
34   Wipe the alternator base plate clean and position the regulator/brush holder onto it. Remove the bent piece of steel holding the springs in place. Install the Torx screws and tighten securely.

18   Voltage regulator – removal and installation

1983 through 1988 models with external regulator

Note: *Some 1986 and later models are equipped with an integral regulator. Carefully inspect the alternator to determine which type of regulator you are working on.*
1   Disconnect the negative cable from the battery.
2   Within the engine compartment, locate the voltage regulator. It is usually positioned near the front of the vehicle.
3   Push the two tabs on either side of the quick-release electrical connector securing the wiring harness to the regulator. Pull the quick-release connector straight out of the regulator.
4   Remove bolts securing the regulator to the body panel and remove the regulator.
5   Installation is the reverse of the removal procedure. Make sure the electrical connector clips are positioned firmly into the regulator terminals. The clips will "click" into place when attached properly.

1986 and later models with integral regulator

Note: *Some 1986 through 1988 models are equipped with an external regulator. Carefully inspect the alternator to identify what type of regulator you are working on.*
6   Remove the alternator as described in Section 16.
7   Remove the four Torx screws (No. T20 head) securing the regulator/brush holder assembly to the rear housing **(see illustration 17.25)**. Remove the regulator/brush holder assembly.
8   Installation is the reverse of the removal procedure with the following:

a)   If removed, install the springs into the brush holder. Locate and hold the brushes and springs in place with a bent piece of flat steel **(see illustration 17.33)**. Loop brush leads toward the brush end of the brush holder.
b)   Wipe the alternator base plate clean and position the regulator/brush holder onto it. Remove the bent piece of steel holding the springs in place. Install the Torx screws and tighten securely.

19   Starting system – general information

The function of the starting system is to crank the engine to start it. The system is composed of the starter motor, starter relay, battery, ignition switch, safety switch and connecting wires.
Turning the ignition key to the Start position actuates the starter relay through the starter control circuit. The starter relay then connects the battery to the starter. The battery supplies the electrical energy to the starter motor, which does the actual work of cranking the engine.
Vehicles equipped with an automatic transmission have a Neutral start switch in the starter control circuit, which prevents operation of the starter unless the shift lever is in Neutral or Park.
The circuit on vehicles with a manual transmission incorporates a starter/clutch interlock switch that prevents operation of the starter motor unless the clutch pedal is depressed.
Never operate the starter motor for more than 30 seconds at a time without pausing to allow it to cool for at least two minutes. Excessive cranking can cause overheating, which can seriously damage the starter.

20   Starter motor and circuit – in-vehicle check

Note: *Before diagnosing starter problems, make sure the battery is fully charged (see Chapter 1).*
1   If the starter motor doesn't turn at all when the switch is operated, make sure the shift lever is in Neutral or Park (automatic transmission) or the clutch pedal is depressed (manual transmission).
2   Make sure the battery is fully charged and that all cables at the battery and starter relay terminals are not corroded and that they are secure.
3   If the starter motor spins but the engine doesn't turn over, then the drive assembly in the starter motor is slipping and the starter motor must be replaced (see Section 21).
4   If, when the switch is actuated, the starter motor doesn't operate at all, but the starter relay operates (clicks), then the problem lies with either the battery, the starter relay contacts or the starter motor electrical connections.
5   If the starter relay doesn't click when the ignition switch is actuated, the battery could be discharged, or either the starter relay circuit is open or the relay itself is defective. Check the starter relay circuit (see the next Step).
6   To check the starter relay circuit, remove the push-on electrical connector from the relay (red with blue stripe). Make sure that the connection is clean and secure and the relay bracket is grounded. If the connections are good, check the operation of the relay with a jumper wire. To do this, place the transmission in Park (automatic) or Neutral (manual). Remove the push-on connector from the relay (if not already done). Connect a jumper wire between the battery positive terminal and the relay push-on connector terminal. If the starter motor now operates, the starter relay is okay. The problem is in the ignition switch, Neutral start switch, starter/clutch interlock switch, or in the starting circuit wiring (look for open or loose connections). Reconnect the push-on electrical connector.
7   If the starter motor still doesn't operate, and the relay does not click, replace the starter relay (see Section 22).
8   If the starter motor cranks the engine at an abnormally slow speed, first make sure the battery is fully charged and that all terminal connections are tight. If the engine is partially seized or has the wrong viscosity oil in it (in cold weather), it will crank slowly. Also, verify the battery's Cold Cranking Amp (CCA) rating is sufficient for the engine (an auto parts store can usually tell you what the minimum should be).

5

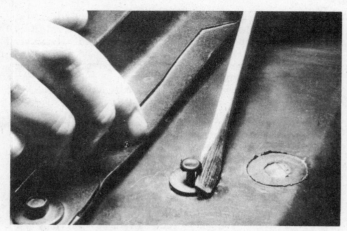

22.1 Pry up on tab securing the plastic box to gain access to the relay, then loosen the bolt securing the unit and remove it

22.4 Disconnect the neutral start (automatic transmission) or clutch interlock (manual transmission) switch wire from the starter relay (arrow) – some models also have an ignition wire connected to the relay

9   Run the engine until normal operating temperature is reached, then disconnect the coil wire from the distributor cap and ground it on the engine.

10   Connect a voltmeter positive lead to the positive battery post and connect the negative lead to the negative post. A fully charged battery should read about 12.6 volts. If the reading is lower, charge the battery before proceeding.

11   Crank the engine and take the voltmeter readings as soon as a steady figure is indicated. Do not allow the starter motor to turn for more than 15 seconds at a time. A reading of 9 volts or more, with the starter motor turning at normal cranking speed, is normal. If the reading is 9 volts or more but the cranking speed is slow, the relay contacts are burned, there is a bad connection or the starter motor is faulty. If the reading is less than 9 volts and the cranking speed is slow, the starter motor is bad or the battery is discharged.

---

21   Starter motor – removal and installation

---

1   Disconnect the negative cable from the battery.
2   Raise the vehicle and support it securely on jackstands.
3   Disconnect the large cable from the terminal on the starter motor.
4   Remove four bolts or nuts securing the starter motor and remove the starter from the engine.
5   Installation is the reverse of the removal procedure. Tighten the mounting bolts to the torque listed in this Chapter's Specifications.

---

22   Starter relay – removal and installation

Refer to illustrations 22.1 and 22.4

1   The starter relay on some models is located in the engine compartment on the fenderwell inside a black plastic box **(see illustration)**.
2   Disconnect the negative cable from the battery.
3   Label the wires and the terminals on the relay to prevent mix-up during installation.
4   Disconnect the ignition and neutral start (automatic transmission) or clutch interlock (manual transmission) switch wires from the starter relay **(see illustration)**.
5   Disconnect the positive battery cable and the feed cable from the starter relay.
6   Disconnect the starter feed cable from the other terminal on the starter relay.
7   Remove the mounting bolts and detach the relay.
8   Installation is the reverse of the removal procedure with the following additions:
   a) Prior to installing the relay, clean the fender panel surface with a wire brush or sandpaper to provide a good grounding surface.
   b) Attach the relay to the fender panel and tighten the bolts. **Caution:** *Do not overtighten the bolts as they are self-threading and can easily strip out the holes in the sheet metal.*
   c) Be sure to connect the cables to the correct terminals on the relay. Refer to the labels made in Step 3.

Chapter 6 Emissions control systems

Contents

Specifications

Torque specifications

Ft-lbs (unless otherwise indicated)

Thermactor (air pump) pulley bolts	120 to 300 in-lbs
Thermactor (air pump) mounting bolts	25
EGR valve bolts	120 to 240 in-lbs
Exhaust Gas Oxygen (EGO) sensor	30

1 General information

Refer to illustration 1.7

To prevent pollution of the atmosphere from incompletely burned and evaporating gases, and to maintain good driveability and fuel economy, a number of emission control systems are incorporated. They include the:

Electronic Engine Control system
Exhaust Gas Recirculation (EGR) system
Managed air thermactor system
Fuel evaporative emissions control system
Positive Crankcase Ventilation (PCV) system
Inlet air temperature control system
Catalytic converter
Spark control system

All of these systems are linked, directly or indirectly, to the emissions control system.

The Sections in this Chapter include general descriptions, checking procedures within the scope of the home mechanic and component replacement procedures (when possible) for each of the systems listed above.

Before assuming that an emissions control system is malfunctioning, check the fuel and ignition systems carefully. The diagnosis of some emission control devices requires specialized tools, equipment and training. If checking and servicing become too difficult or if a procedure is beyond your ability, consult a dealer service department. Remember, the most frequent cause of emissions problems is simply a loose or broken vacuum hose or wire, so always check the hose and wiring connections first.

This doesn't mean, however, that emission control systems are partic-

ularly difficult to maintain and repair. You can quickly and easily perform many checks and do most of the regular maintenance at home with common tune-up and hand tools. **Note:** *Because of a Federally mandated extended warranty which covers the emission control system components, check with your dealer about warranty coverage before working on any emissions-related systems. Once the warranty has expired, you may wish to perform some of the component checks and/or replacement procedures in this Chapter to save money.*

Pay close attention to any special precautions outlined in this Chapter. It should be noted that the illustrations of the various systems may not exactly match the system installed on the vehicle you're working on because of changes made by the manufacturer during production or from year-to-year.

A Vehicle Emissions Control Information label is located in the engine compartment **(see illustration)**. This label contains important emissions specifications and adjustment information, as well as a vacuum hose schematic with emissions components identified. When servicing the engine or emissions systems, the VECI label in your particular vehicle should always be checked for up-to-date information.

2 Electronic Engine Control (EEC-IV) system

General description

1   All vehicles equipped with TFI-IV electronic ignition systems (see Chapter 5) are also equipped with the Electronic Engine Control (EEC-IV) system. The EEC-IV system consists of an onboard computer, known as the Electronic Control Assembly (ECA), and the information sensors, which monitor various functions of the engine and send data to the ECA.

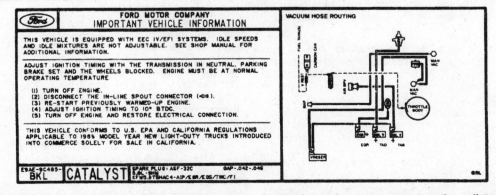

1.7   The Vehicle Emissions Control Information (VECI) label is located in the engine compartment on the radiator support, and it contains important emissions specifications and adjustment information, as well as a vacuum hose schematic with emissions components that applies to the emission-related devices on the vehicle you're working on

Based on the data and the information programmed into the computer's memory, the ECA generates output signals to control various engine functions via control relays, solenoids and other actuators.

2   The ECA, which is located under the instrument panel, either under the right or left kick panel (depending on year and model) is the "brain" of the EEC-IV system. It receives data from a number of sensors and other electronic components (switches, relays, etc.). Based on the information it receives, the ECA generates output signals to control various relays, solenoids and other actuators (see the following Sections). The ECA is specifically calibrated to optimize the emissions, fuel economy and driveability of the vehicle.

3   Because of a Federally-mandated extended warranty which covers the ECA, the information sensors and all components under its control, and because any owner-induced damage to the ECA, the sensors and/or the control devices may void the warranty, it isn't a good idea to attempt diagnosis or replacement of the ECA at home. Take the vehicle to a dealer service department if the ECA or a system component malfunctions.

Information input sensors

Note: *Not all of the following devices will be on the vehicle. The VECI label is the most specific and accurate source of information for determining what sensors are on the vehicle.*

4   When battery voltage is applied to the compressor clutch, a signal is sent to the ECA, which interprets the signal as an added load created by the air conditioning compressor and increases engine idle speed accordingly to compensate.

5   The Air Charge Temperature sensor (ACT), threaded into a runner of the intake manifold, provides the ECA with fuel/air mixture temperature information. The ECA uses this information to correct fuel flow and control fuel flow during cold enrichment (cold starts).

6   The EGR Valve Position Sensor (EVP), located on the EGR valve, tells the ECA the position of the EGR valve.

7   The Engine Coolant Temperature (ECT) sensor, which is threaded into a coolant passage in the intake manifold monitors engine coolant temperature. The ECT sends the ECA a constantly varying voltage signal which influences ECA control of the fuel mixture, ignition timing and EGR operation.

8   The Manifold Absolute Pressure (MAP) sensor measures the absolute pressure of the mixture in the intake manifold and sends a signal to the ECA that is proportional to absolute pressure.

9   The exhaust gas oxygen sensors (EGO), which are threaded into the exhaust manifolds, constantly monitor the oxygen content of the exhaust gases. A voltage signal which varies in accordance with the difference between the oxygen content of the exhaust gases and the surrounding atmosphere is sent to the ECA. The ECA converts this exhaust gas oxygen content signal to the fuel/air ratio, compares it to the ideal ratio for current engine operating conditions and alters the signal to the injectors accordingly.

10   The Throttle Position Sensor (TPS), which is mounted on the side of the carburetor or throttle body (see Chapter 4) and connected directly to the throttle shaft, senses throttle movement and position, then transmits an electrical signal to the ECA. This signal enables the ECA to determine when the throttle is closed, in its normal cruise condition or wide open.

Output devices

Note: *Not all of the following devices will be on the vehicle. Also, the location and appearance of the following devices may differ somewhat on the vehicle from those illustrated and/or described below. The VECI label is the most specific and accurate source of information for determining what devices are on the vehicle.*

11   The air conditioning and cooling fan controller module is operated by the ECA, the coolant temperature switch and the brake light switch. The controller module provides an output signal which controls operation of the A/C compressor clutch and the engine cooling fan.

12   The EEC power relay, which is activated by the ignition switch, supplies battery voltage to the ECA when the switch is on.

13   The canister purge solenoid (CANP) switches manifold vacuum to operate the canister purge valve when a signal is received from the ECA. Vacuum opens the purge valve when the solenoid is energized, allowing fuel vapor to flow from the canister to the intake manifold.

14   The EGR control solenoid switches manifold vacuum to operate the EGR valve on command from the ECA. Vacuum opens the EGR valve when the solenoid is energized.

15   The EGR shut-off solenoid is an electrically operated vacuum valve located between the manifold vacuum source and the EGR valve. A controlled vacuum bleed is located between the solenoid and the EGR valve. This vacuum bleed is a Backpressure Variable Transducer (BVT). These two devices operate the EGR valve for optimum performance. Solenoid switch vacuum is also supplied to the canister purge valve.

16   The EGR vent solenoid opens the EGR control solenoid vacuum line. When the vent solenoid is energized, the control solenoid opens the EGR valve.

17   The feedback control solenoid regulates the idle, off idle and main system fuel/air ratios in accordance with signals from the ECA.

18   The solenoid-operated fuel injectors are located in the throttle body or in the intake ports of vehicles equipped with fuel injection. The ECA controls the length of time the injector is open. The "open" time of the injector determines the amount of fuel delivered. For information regarding injector replacement, refer to Chapter 4.

19   The fuel pump relay (used on fuel-injected models) is activated by the ECA with the ignition switch in the On position. When the ignition switch is turned to the On position, the relay is activated to supply initial line pressure to the system. For information regarding fuel pump check and replacement, refer to Chapter 4.

20   The Idle Speed Control (ISC) motor changes idle speed in accordance with signals from the ECA. For information regarding ISC replacement, refer to Chapter 4.

21   The Thermactor Air By-Pass (TAB) solenoid provides a vacuum signal to the by-pass valve in response to signals from the ECA. the TAB valve then by-passes the thermactor air pump to the atmosphere. For information regarding the thermactor system, refer to Section 5 in this Chapter.

22   The Thermactor Air Diverter (TAD) solenoid provides a vacuum signal to the diverter valve in response to signals from the ECA. The TAD valve then diverts thermactor pump air to either the exhaust manifold or the catalytic converter. For more information regarding the thermactor system, refer to Section 5 in this Chapter.

23   The TFI-IV ignition module (see Chapter 5), mounted on the side of the distributor base, triggers the ignition coil and determines dwell. The ECA uses a signal from the Profile Ignition Pick-Up to determine crankshaft position. Ignition timing is determined by the ECA, which then signals the module to fire the coil. For further information regarding the TFI-IV module, refer to the appropriate Section in Chapter 5.

EEC-IV system trouble codes

Refer to illustration 2.26

24   The EEC-IV engine management system has a self-diagnosis capability that stores trouble codes in the PCM (computer) that identify problem areas in the system. You can retrieve these codes and use them as an aid to diagnosing problems in the engine management system. Often, when a code is stored in the PCM, the "SERVICE ENGINE SOON" light on the instrument panel will illuminate.

25   In the engine compartment, find the "Self-Test" connector. Usually, the connector has two parts: a large one with six output terminals and a single input terminal. The connector is located on the right (passenger's) side of the firewall, near the strut tower.

26   With the engine off, connect the positive probe of an analog voltmeter to the battery positive post. Unplug the "Self-Test" connector. Connect a jumper wire between the input to pin 2 on the larger connector and connect the voltmeter negative probe to pin 4 **(see illustration)**. Set the voltmeter on a 15 or 20-volt scale, then connect a timing light to the engine. The three types of codes this test will provide are:

    O - **Key On Engine Off (KOEO)** (on-demand codes with the engine off)

    C - **Continuous Memory** (codes stored when the engine was running)

    R - **Engine Running (ER)** (codes produced as the engine is running)

O (KOEO)

27   Turn on the ignition and watch the voltmeter needle. It will display the

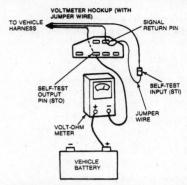

2.26 To output the trouble codes, connect a voltmeter as shown and, using a jumper wire, bridge the self-test input connector to the signal return pin (terminal number 2)

codes as sweeps of the needle. For example, two sweeps followed by three sweeps is code 23, with a four-second delay between codes. Write the codes down for reference. The codes will appear in numerical order, repeating once.

C (Continuous Memory)

28   After the KOEO codes are reported, there will be a short pause and any stored Continuous Memory codes will appear in order. Remember that the "Pass" code is 11, or sweep, two-second pause, sweep.

R (Engine Running)

29   Start the engine. The first part of this test makes sure the system can advance the ignition timing. Check the ignition timing. It should be advanced about 20-degrees above base timing (check the VECI label for the base timing specification).

30   Shut off the engine, restart it and run it for two minutes, then turn it off for ten seconds before restarting it. The voltmeter needle should make some quick sweeps, then show an engine code (two sweeps for a four-cylinder engine, three for a V6). After another pause will be one sweep, the signal to tap the accelerator so the system can check throttle component operation (this is called the "throttle goose test"). After this there will be a pause, followed by the Engine Running codes, which will appear in the same manner as before, repeating twice.

CODE	Test condition	Probable cause
11	o,r,c	System Pass
12	r	Cannot control rpm during Self-Test high rpm check
13	r	Cannot control rpm during Self-Test low rpm check
14	c	PIP circuit failure
15	o	EEC processor Read Only Memory (ROM) test failed
15	c	EEC processor Keep Alive Memory (KAM) test failed
16	o	Ignition Diagnostic Monitor (IDM) signal not received
18	r	SPOUT circuit open
18	r	Erratic IDM input to processor/SPOUT circuit grounded
19	o	Failure in EEC processor internal voltage
21	o,r	Engine Coolant Temp (ECT) out of Self-Test range
22	o,r,c	Manifold Absolute Pressure (MAP) out of Self-Test range
23	o,r	Throttle Position (TP) out of Self-Test range
24	o,r	Air Charge Temp (ACT) out of Self-Test range
26	o,r	Mass Air Flow (MAF) out of Self-Test range
28	c	Loss of IDM--right side
29	c	Insufficient input from Vehicle Speed Sensor (VSS)
31	o,r,c	EVP circuit below minimum voltage
32	o,r,c	EVP voltage below closed limit
33	r,c	EGR valve opening not detected
34	o,r,c	EVP voltage above closed limit
35	o,r,c	EVP circuit above maximum voltage
41	r	HEGO sensor circuit indicates system lean
41	c	No HEGO switch detected
42	r	HEGO sensor circuit indicates system rich
45	c	Coil 1, 2, or 3 failure
48	c	Loss of IDM--left side
51	o,c	ECT indicated -40 F/circuit open
52	o	Power Steering Pressure Switch (PSPS) circuit open
52	r	PSPS circuit did not change states
53	o,c	TP circuit above maximum voltage
54	o,c	ACT indicated -40 F/circuit open
56	o,c	MAF circuit above maximum voltage
57	o	Octane adjust service pin in use/circuit grounded
61	o,c	ECT indicated 254 F/circuit grounded
63	o,c	TP circuit below minimum voltage

CODE	Test condition	Probable cause
64	o,c	ACT indicated 254 F/circuit grounded
66	c	MAF circuit below minimum voltage
67	o	Neutral Drive Switch (NDS) circuit open/A/C on
67	c	Clutch Switch circuit failure
72	r	Insufficient MAP/MAF change during Dynamic Response Test
73	r	Insufficient TP change during Dynamic Response Test
74	r	Brake On/Off (BOO) circuit failure/not actuated during Self-Test
77	r	Operator error (Dynamic Response/Cylinder Balance Tests)
79	o	A/C on/Defrost on during Self-Test
84	o	EGR Vacuum Regulator (EVR) circuit failure
85	o	Canister Purge (CANP) circuit failure
86	o	Shift Solenoid (SS) circuit failure
87	o,c	Primary Fuel Pump circuit failure
88	c	Loss of Dual Plug Input control
89	o	Clutch Converter Override (CCO) circuit failure
95	o,c	Fuel Pump circuit open – EEC processor to motor ground
96	o,c	Fuel Pump circuit open – battery to EEC processor
98	r	Hard fault present
111	O,R,C	System Pass
112	O,C	Air Charge Temp ACT [IAT*] Sensor circuit below minimum voltage/ 254 F indicated
113	O,C	Air Charge Temp ACT [IAT*] Sensor circuit above maximum voltage/ -40 F indicated
114	O,O,R	Air Charge Temp ACT [IAT*] higher or lower than expected during KOEO, ER
116	O,R	Engine Coolant Temp (ECT) higher or lower than expected during KOEO, ER
117	O,C	Engine Coolant Temp (ECT) Sensor circuit below minimum voltage/ 254 F indicated
118	O,C	Engine Coolant Temp (ECT) Sensor circuit above maximum voltage/ -40 F indicated
121	O,R,C	Closed Throttle Voltage higher or lower than expected
122	O,C	Throttle Position (TP) Sensor circuit below minimum voltage
123	O,C	Throttle Position (TP) Sensor circuit above maximum voltage
124	C	Throttle Position (TP) Sensor voltage higher than expected
125	C	Throttle Position (TP) Sensor voltage lower than expected
126	O,R,C	MAP or BP [BARO*] Sensor higher or lower than expected
128	R	MAP vacuum circuit failure
129	R	Insufficient Mass Air Flow (MAF) change during Dynamic Response Test
136	R	HEGO [HO2S-2*] sensor circuit indicates system always lean
137	R	HEGO [HO2S-2*] sensor circuit indicates system always rich
139	C	No Oxygen Sensor (HEGO) [HO2S-2*] Switches detected
144	C	No Oxygen Sensor (HEGO) [HO2S-1*] Switches detected
157	C	Mass Air Flow (MAF) Sensor circuit below minimum voltage
158	O,C	Mass Air Flow (MAF) Sensor circuit above maximum voltage
159	O,R	Mass Air Flow (MAF), higher or lower than expected during KOEO, ER
167	R	Insufficient Throttle Position change during Dynamic Response Test
171	C	Fuel system at adaptive limits, Oxygen Sensor (HEGO) [HO2S-1*] unable to switch
172	R,C	Lack of Oxygen Sensor (HEGO) [HO2S-1*] Switches, indicates lean
173	R,C	Lack of Oxygen Sensor (HEGO) [HO2S-1*] Switches, indicates rich
174	C	HEGO switching time is slow
175	C	Lack of Oxygen Sensor (HEGO) [HO2S-2*] switching, fuel system at adaptive limit
176	C	HEGO [HO2S-2*] sensor circuit indicates system always lean (Front side)
177	C	HEGO [HO2S-2*] sensor circuit indicates system always rich (Front side)
178	C	HEGO switching time is slow
179	C	Fuel system at lean adaptive limit at part throttle, system rich
181	C	Fuel system at rich adaptive limit at part throttle, system lean
182	C	Fuel system at lean adaptive limit at idle, system rich
183	C	Fuel system at rich adaptive limit at idle, system lean
184	C	Mass Air Flow (MAF) higher than expected
185	C	Mass Air Flow (MAF) lower than expected
186	C	Injector pulse width higher than expected
187	C	Injector pulse width lower than expected
188	C	Fuel system at part throttle lean adaptive limit, system rich
189	C	Fuel system at part throttle rich adaptive limit, system lean
191	C	Fuel system at idle lean adaptive limit, system rich
192	C	Fuel system at idle rich adaptive limit, system lean
211	C	Profile Ignition Pickup (PIP) circuit failure
212	C	Loss of Ignition Diagnostic Monitor (IDM) input to ECA/ SPOUT circuit grounded
213	R	SPOUT circuit open
214	C	Cylinder Identification (CID) circuit failure
215	C	EEC [PCM*] Processor detected Coil 1 primary circuit failure
216	C	EEC [PCM*] Processor detected Coil 2 primary circuit failure
217	C	EEC [PCM*] Processor detected Coil 3 primary circuit failure
218	C	Loss of Ignition Diagnostic Monitor (IDM) signal-left side
219	C	SPOUT signal defaulted to 10 degrees BTDC/SPOUT circuit open
222	C	Loss of Ignition Diagnostic Monitor (IDM) signal-right side
223	C	Loss of Dual Plug Inhibit (DPI) control

6

CODE	Test condition	Probable cause
224	C	Erratic Ignition Diagnostic Monitor (IDM) input to processor
225	R	Knock not sensed during Dynamic Response Test
226	O	Ignition Diagnostic Monitor (IDM) signal not received
311	R	Thermactor [AIR*] air system inoperative(right side)
312	R	Thermactor [AIR*] air upstream during Self-Test
313	R	Thermactor [AIR*] air not bypassedduring Self-Test
314	R	Thermactor [AIR*] air system inoperative (left side)
326	R,C	PFE/DPFE [EGR*] sensor circuit voltage lower than expected
327	O,R,C	PFE/DPFE [EGR*] circuit below minimum voltage
328	O,R,C	EGR closed valve voltage lower than expected
332	R,C	Insufficient EGR flow detected
334	O,R,C	EGR closed-valve voltage higher than expected
335	O	PFE/DPFE [EGR*] sensor voltage out of Self-Test range
336	R,C	PFE [EGR*] sensor circuit voltage higher than expected
337	O,R,C	PFE/DPFE [EGR*] circuit above maximum voltage
338	C	Engine coolant temperature [ECT*] lowerthan normal
339	C	Engine coolant temperature [ECT*] higher than normal
341	O	Octane Adjust Service Pin in use or circuit open
411	R	Cannot control rpm during ER low rpm check
412	R	Cannot control rpm during ER high rpm check
452	C	Insufficient input from Vehicle Speed Sensor (VSS)
511	O	EEC [PCM*] Processor Read Only Memory (ROM) test failure
512	C	EEC [PCM*] Processor Keep Alive Memory (KAM) test failure
513	C	Failure in EEC [PCM^] processor internal voltage
519	O	Power Steering Pressure Switch PSPS [PSP*] circuit open
521	R	Power Steering Pressure Switch PSPS [PSP*] circuit did not change states
522	O	Vehicle not in PARK or NEUTRAL [PNP*]during KOEO
524	O,C	Low speed fuel pump circuit open (battery to ECA)
525	O	Vehicle was either in gear or AC was on during Self-Test
526	O	Neutral Pressure Switch NPS [PNP*] circuit closed; A/C on
527	O	Neutral Drive Switch NDS [PNP*] circuitopen/A/C on
528	C	Clutch Switch Circuit failure
529	C	Data Communications Link DCL or EEC [PCM*] processor circuit failure
533	C	Data Communications Link DCL or Electronics Instrument Cluster (EIC) circuit failure
536	R,C	Brake On/Off (BOO) circuit failure / not actuated during ER
538	R	Insufficient RPM change during ER Dynamic Response Test or operator error
539	O	AC On/Defrost ON during KOEO
542	O,C	Fuel Pump secondary circuit failure
543	O,C	Fuel Pump secondary circuit failure
551	O	IAS [IAC*] circuit failure
552	O	Air management 1 AM1 [AIRB*] circuit failure
553	O	Air management 2 AM2 [AIRB*] circuit failure
554	O	Fuel Pressure Regulator Control (FPRC) solenoid circuit failure
556	O,C	Fuel Pump Relay primary circuit failure
557	O,C	Fuel Pump primary circuit failure
558	O	EGR Vacuum Regulator (EVR) circuit failure
559	O	Air Conditioning ON (ACON) relay circuit failure
563	O	High Speed Electro-Drive Fan HEDF [HFC*] circuit failure
564	O	Electro-Drive Fan EDF [FC*] circuit failure
565	O	Canister Purge (CANP) circuit failure
566	O	3-4 Shift Solenoid circuit failure
617	C	1-2 shift error (E40D)
618	C	2-3 shift error (E40D)
619	C	3-4 shift error (E40D)
621	O	Shift Solenoid #1 (SS1) circuit failure
622	O	Shift Solenoid #2 (SS2) circuit failure
624	O,C	Electronic Pressure Control (EPC) solenoid or driver circuit failure
625	O	Electronic Pressure Control (EPC) driver open in ECA
626	O	Coast Clutch Solenoid (CCS) circuit failure (E40D)
627	O,C	Converter Clutch Control solenoid circuit failure
628	O,C	Lock-Up Solenoid (LUS) failure, excessive clutch slippage
629	O	Converter Clutch Control circuit failure or Lock-Up Solenoid (LUS) circuit failure
631	O	Overdrive Cancel Indicator Light (OCIL) circuit failure
632	R	Overdrive Cancel Switch (OCS) not changing state (E40D)
633	O	4 x 4 switch is closed (E40D)
634	C	Manual Lever Position (MLP) sensor voltage out of Self-Test range or A/C on (E40D)
636	O,R	Transmission Oil Temperature (TOT) sensor voltage out of Self-Test range
637	O,C	Transmission Oil Temperature (TOT) sensor voltage out of Self-Test maximum
638	O,C	Transmission Oil Temperature (TOT) sensor voltage below Self-Test minimum
639	R,C	Insufficient input from the Transmission Speed Sensor (TSS)
641	O	Shift solenoid #3 (SS3) circuit failure
643	O,C	Converter Clutch Control (CCC) circuit failure
645	C	Incorrect gear ratio obtained for first gear
646	C	Incorrect gear ratio obtained for second gear
647	C	Incorrect gear ratio obtained for third gear
648	C	Incorrect gear ratio obtained for fourth gear
649	C	Electronic Pressure Control (EPC) range failure
651	C	Electronic Pressure Control (EPC) circuit failure
652	O	Modulated Converter Clutch Control (MCCC) solenoid output circuit error
654		MLP sensor not in Park position
656		Converter Clutch Control (CCC) continuous slip error detected
998	R	Hard fault present (FMEM mode)

KEY: O -Key On Engine Off (KOEO) (ER)   C = Continuous Memory   R = Engine Running

Component replacement

Note: *Because of the Federally-mandated extended warranty which covers the ECA, the information sensors and the devices it controls, check with your dealer about warranty coverage.*

Air Charge Temperature (ACT) sensor

31   Disconnect the negative cable from the battery.
32   Locate the ACT sensor in the intake manifold.
33   Unplug the electrical connector from the sensor.
34   Remove the sensor with a wrench.
35   Wrap the threads of the new sensor with thread-sealing tape to prevent air leaks.
36   Installation is the reverse of removal.

EGR Valve Position (EVP) sensor

37   Disconnect the negative cable from the battery.
38   Locate the EVP sensor on top of the EGR valve.
39   Unplug the electrical connector from the sensor.
40   Remove the three mounting bolts and detach the sensor.
41   Installation is the reverse of removal.

Engine Coolant Temperature (ECT) sensor

42   Disconnect the negative cable from the battery.
43   Locate the ECT sensor on the intake manifold.
44   Unplug the electrical connector from the sensor.
45   Remove the sensor with a wrench.
46   Wrap the threads of the new sensor with thread-sealing tape to prevent coolant leakage.
47   Installation is the reverse of removal.

Manifold Absolute Pressure (MAP) sensor

48   Disconnect the negative cable from the battery.
49   Locate the MAP sensor on the firewall or inner fender panel.
50   Unplug the electrical connector from the sensor.
51   Detach the vacuum line from the sensor.
52   Remove the mounting screws and detach the sensor.
53   Installation is the reverse of removal.

Exhaust Gas Oxygen (EGO) sensor

54   Disconnect the negative cable from the battery.
55   Locate the EGO sensor on the exhaust manifold.
56   If it's more convenient, raise the vehicle and support it securely on jackstands.
57   Unplug the electrical connector from the sensor.
58   Remove the sensor with a wrench.
59   Coat the threads of the new sensor with anti-seize compound to prevent the threads from welding themselves to the manifold.
60   Installation is the reverse of removal.

Throttle Position (TP) sensor

61   Don't attempt to replace the TP sensor! Specialized calibration equipment is necessary to adjust the switch once it's installed, making adjustment beyond the scope of the home mechanic.

Canister Purge Solenoid

62   Disconnect the negative cable from the battery.
63   Locate the canister purge solenoid in the engine compartment.
64   Unplug the electrical connector from the solenoid.
65   Label the vacuum hoses and ports, then detach the hoses.
66   Remove the solenoid.
67   Installation is the reverse of removal.

Vacuum control solenoids

68   Disconnect the negative cable from the battery.
69   If necessary, remove the coolant reservoir (see Chapter 3).
70   Locate the vacuum control solenoids to be replaced (refer to the VECI label).
71   Unplug the electrical connector from the solenoid.

3.2　Loosen the bolt securing the MCU electrical connector retainer, then carefully pull the connector straight up from the unit

72　Label the vacuum hoses and ports, then detach the hoses.
73　Remove the solenoid/bracket screws and detach the solenoid.
74　Installation is the reverse of removal.

Mass Air Flow (MAF) sensor

75　The mass air flow sensor is mounted in the air intake duct.
76　Disconnect the negative cable from the battery.
77　Disconnect the MAF sensor electrical connector.
78　Detach the air cleaner duct and MAF sensor from the air cleaner and from the throttle body. Remove the mounting screws and take the MAF sensor out of the engine compartment.
79　Installation is the reverse of removal.

3　Microprocessor Control Unit (MCU) (1983 and 1984 2.0L and 2.3L four-cylinder engines)

　　The MCU is the heart of the electronic engine fuel control system used on 1983 and 1984 2.0L and 2.3L four-cylinder engines. Its function is to keep the air/fuel ratio at a proper balance to obtain maximum catalyst efficiency. The MCU is the master of the fuel control "loop" which consists of the microprocessor, exhaust gas oxygen (EGO) sensor and the carburetor with a feedback carburetor actuator (FBCA).
　　The EGO sensor senses whether the mixture is rich or lean, and a signal is sent to the MCU module, which sends a signal to the FBCA to alter the fuel/air ratio. This operation is called "closed loop" operation. During the "open loop" operation, the input from the EGO sensor is ignored. During this mode the MCU sends out a fixed signal to the FBCA.
　　The determining factor when the system goes into open loop is based upon information from the switch input, which senses parameters such as coolant temperature, manifold vacuum and engine rpm. Generally, the vehicle will be in closed loop when the vehicle is at operating temperature and at a steady part-throttle cruise.
　　Other functions controlled by the MCU are Canister Purge (CANP), Thermactor Air Diverter (TAD), Thermactor Air Bypass (TAB), Throttle Kicker (TK), and Spark Retard System, or spark retard through the knock sensor.
　　The MCU is located inside the black box on the right side of the engine compartment.

Component replacement

Refer to illustration 3.2

1　Disconnect the negative cable from the battery.
2　Carefully pry up and remove the plastic black box top. Loosen the bolt securing the MCU electrical connector retainer, then carefully pull the connector straight up from the unit and disconnect it **(see illustration)**.
3　Working under the inside fender well, remove the two screws securing the black box and MCU unit. Remove the MCU unit.
4　Installation is the reverse of the removal procedure.

4　Exhaust Gas Recirculation (EGR) system

Note: 1988 and later 2.9L V6 engines and 1990 and later 3.0L and 4.0L V6 engines are not equipped with an EGR system.

General description

Refer to illustrations 4.2 and 4.4

1　The EGR system is designed to reintroduce small amounts of exhaust gas into the combustion cycle, thus reducing the generation of oxides of nitrogen (NOx) emissions. The amount of exhaust gas reintroduced and the timing of the cycle is controlled by various factors such as engine speed, altitude, manifold vacuum, exhaust system backpressure, coolant temperature and throttle angle. All EGR valves are vacuum actuated (the vacuum diagram for that particular vehicle is shown on the Vehicle Emissions Control Information [VECI] label in the engine compartment). Three types of EGR valves are used on these vehicles: the integral backpressure transducer valve, the ported valve and the electronic type.

Ported valve (1985 through 1988 2.0L four-cylinder engines and 1986 and 1987 2.9L V6 engines

2　The ported EGR valve is operated by a vacuum signal from the EGR port, which actuates the valve diaphragm **(see illustration on page 6-6)**. As the vacuum increases sufficiently to overcome the spring, the valve is opened, allowing EGR flow. The amount of flow is contingent upon the tapered pintle or the poppet position, which is affected by the vacuum signal.

Integral backpressure transducer valve (1983 and 1984 2.0L and 1984 2.3L four-cylinder engines)

3　The integral backpressure transducer EGR valve combines backpressure and EGR ported vacuum into one unit. The valve won't operate on vacuum alone it requires both inputs to operate. There are two basic types of backpressure valves: poppet and tapered pintle.

Electronic valve (1985 and later 2.3L four-cylinder engines and 1984 and 1985 2.8L V6 engines)

4　The electronic EGR valve used in EEC-IV systems controls EGR flow with an EGR valve position (EVP) sensor attached to the top of the valve **(see illustration on page 6-6)**. The valve is operated by a vacuum signal from the dual EGR solenoid valves or the electronic vacuum regulator which actuates the valve diaphragm. As supply vacuum overcomes the spring load, the diaphragm is actuated, lifting the pintle off the seat and allowing exhaust gas to recirculate. The amount of flow is proportional to the pintle position. The EVP sensor sends an electrical signal indicating its position to the ECA.

Checking

Ported valve (1985 2.0L four-cylinder engine)

5　Make sure that all vacuum lines are properly routed (see the VECI label in the engine compartment), secure and in good condition (not cracked, kinked or broken off).
6　When the engine is cold, unplug the hose to the EGR valve. There should be no vacuum to operate the EGR valve. If there is vacuum, check the ported vacuum switch (PVS) or temperature vacuum switch (TVS) and replace them as required.
7　There should be no vacuum to the valve at curb idle (engine warm). If there is vacuum, check that the vacuum is coming from the correct source.
8　There should be vacuum to the valve at 3000 rpm. If there is no vacuum, check the hoses and hose routing, the TVS and PVS and replace them as required.
9　With the engine at idle, apply 8 in-Hg vacuum to the valve.
10　With the engine at idle, use a hand vacuum pump to trap 4 in-Hg vacuum in the valve. Vacuum shouldn't drop more than 1 in-Hg in 30 seconds. If it does, replace the valve.
11　When the valve is suspected of leaking (indicated by a rough idle or stalling) perform the following simple check:
　　a)　Insert a blocking gasket (no flow holes) between the valve and base and reinstall the valve.
　　b)　If the engine idle improves, replace the valve and remove the blocking gasket. If the idle doesn't improve, the rough idling problem is not related to the valve.

6

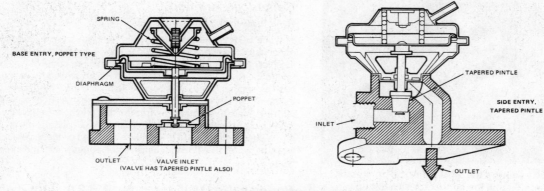

4.2   A typical ported EGR valve

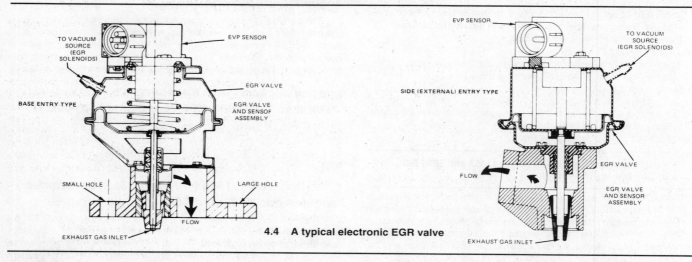

4.4   A typical electronic EGR valve

Ported valve (1986 through 1988 2.0L four-cylinder engine and 1986 and 1987 2.9L V6 engines)

12   Make sure that all vacuum lines are properly routed (see the VECI label in the engine compartment), secure and in good condition (not cracked, kinked or broken off).

13   There should be no vacuum to the valve at curb idle with the engine at normal operating temperature.

14   Install a portable tachometer following manufacturer's instructions.

15   On fuel-injected models, disconnect the idle bypass valve electrical connector.

16   Remove the vacuum supply hose from the EGR valve nipple and plug the hose.

17   Start the engine and let it idle in neutral. Check idle speed and adjust if necessary (see Chapter 1).

18   Using a hand vacuum pump, slowly apply 5-10 in-Hg vacuum to the EGR valve vacuum nipple. When vacuum is applied, if any of the following occur, replace the valve:

   a)   Engine does not stall or run roughly.
   b)   Idle speed does not drop by more than 100 rpm.
   c)   Idle speed does not return to normal (+/- 25 rpm) after vacuum is removed.

19   Disconnect the portable tachometer.

20   On models so equipped, reconnect the electrical connector to the idle air bypass valve.

21   Unplug and reconnect the vacuum hose to the EGR valve.

Integral backpressure transducer valve (1983 and 1984 2.0L and 1984 2.3L four-cylinder engines)

22   Make sure that all vacuum lines are properly routed (see the VECI label in the engine compartment), all connections are secure and no vacuum hoses are cracked, crimped or broken.

23   Detach the vacuum line to the EGR valve and plug it. Connect a vacuum pump to the EGR valve. Start the engine and let it idle. Apply 6 in-Hg vacuum to the valve. It should bleed off and the valve should not operate. If the vacuum holds and the valve opens and stays open, i.e. the valve does not bleed off the vacuum, replace the valve.

24   There should be no vacuum to the valve at idle under any conditions. If there is, check the hose routing.

25   There should be no vacuum to the valve nor should the valve operate when the engine is cold. If there is vacuum at the valve when the engine is cold, check the ported vacuum switch (PVS) or the thermal vacuum switch (TVS) and replace as required. (The PVS is a temperature actuated switch that changes vacuum connections when the coolant temperature changes; the TVS, which is used with some systems instead of the PVS, controls vacuum to the EGR valve by responding to the temperature of the inlet air heated by the exhaust manifold. Most PVS switches are mounted somewhere on the intake manifold; most TVS switches are located in the air cleaner housing (refer to the VECI label to determine which kind of switch it is and where it is located).

26   There should be vacuum to the valve at 3000 rpm with a normally warm engine. If there isn't, check back through the vacuum line from the EGR to the vacuum source; for example, the TVS and/or the PVS may not be opening. Check and replace as required.

27   If a valve is suspected of sticking, remove it from the engine and cycle the valve by pressing carefully with your fingers against the lower transducer plate. If the valve sticks open when you release your fingers, replace it.

Electronic valve (1985 and later 2.3L engines and 1984 and 1985 2.8L V6 engines)

Note: *Aside from the following check and maintenance steps, the electronic EGR valve cannot be diagnosed or serviced by the home mechanic. Additional checks must be done by a dealer service department.*

4.38   Remove the two nuts (arrows) securing the EGR valve (typical)

4.40   The EGR spacer is secured with five bolts (arrows) (typical)

28   Make sure the vacuum hoses are in good condition and hooked up correctly.

29   Clean the inlet and outlet ports with a wire brush or scraper. Do not sandblast the valve or clean it with gasoline or solvents, as they will damage the valve.

30   To perform a leakage test, connect a vacuum pump to the EGR valve.

31   Using a hand vacuum pump, apply five to six in-Hg of vacuum to the valve.

32   Trap the vacuum it should not drop more than 1 in-Hg in 30 seconds.

33   If the specified conditions are not met, the EGR valve, O-ring or EVP must be replaced.

Component replacement

Refer to illustrations 4.38 and 4.40

34   Disconnect the negative cable from the battery.

35   When replacing any vacuum hoses, remove only one hose at a time and make sure that the replacement hose is of the same quality and size as the hose being replaced.

36   On engines with an electronic valve, unplug the electrical connector from the EGR valve position sensor.

37   If the vehicle is powered by a four-cylinder engine, unscrew the threaded fitting that attaches the EGR pipe to the EGR valve.

38   Remove the EGR valve mounting nuts and detach the valve **(see illustration)** and discard the gasket.

39   Remove the old gasket. Be sure to thoroughly clean the gasket surfaces of the valve and the intake manifold. Use a new gasket when installing the valve and check for leaks when the job is completed.

40   Remove the bolts securing the EGR spacer and remove the spacer **(see illustration)**.

41   If you're replacing an electronic type EGR valve but not the position sensor, remove the sensor from the old valve (see Section 2) and install it on the new valve.

42   Installation is the reverse of the removal procedure.

5   Thermactor system

Note: *Thermactor systems are not used on 1989 through 1991 models.*

General description

1   The thermactor (air injection) exhaust emission control system reduces carbon monoxide and hydrocarbon content in the exhaust gases by injecting fresh air into the hot exhaust gases leaving the exhaust ports. When fresh air is mixed with hot exhaust gases, oxidation is increased, reducing the concentration of hydrocarbons and carbon monoxide and converting them into harmless carbon dioxide and water.

2   All of these models utilize either a conventional thermactor system or a "managed air" thermactor system (some 1984 and 1985 2.8L engines). The two systems are basically the same. The managed air thermactor system diverts thermactor air either upstream to the exhaust manifold check valve or downstream to the rear section check valve and dual bed catalyst. An extended idle air bypass system in carburetor equipped vehicles also vents thermactor air to the atmosphere during extended idling.

3   On managed air systems, an air control valve directs the air upstream or downstream. An air bypass valve is used to dump air to the atmosphere. In some applications, the two valves are combined into a single air bypass/control valve.

Checking

Air supply pump

4   Check and adjust the drivebelt tension (see Chapter 1).

5   Disconnect the air supply hose at the air bypass valve inlet.

6   The pump is operating satisfactorily if air flow is felt at the pump outlet with the engine running at idle, increasing as the engine speed is increased.

7   If the air pump doesn't pass the above tests, replace it with a new or rebuilt unit.

Air bypass valve

8   With the engine running at idle, disconnect the hose from the valve outlet.

9   Remove the vacuum hose from the port and remove or bypass any restrictors or delay valves in the vacuum hose.

10   Verify that vacuum is present in the vacuum hose by putting your finger over the end.

11   Reconnect the vacuum hose to the port.

12   With the engine running at 1500 rpm, the air pump supply air should be felt or heard at the air bypass valve outlet.

13   With the engine running at 1500 rpm, disconnect the vacuum hose. Air at the valve outlet should be decreased or shut off and air pump supply air should be felt or heard at the silencer ports.

14   Reconnect all hoses.

15   If the normally closed air bypass valve doesn't successfully pass the above tests, check the air pump (refer to Steps 5 through 7).

16   If the air pump is operating satisfactorily, replace the air bypass valve with a new one.

Check valve

17   Disconnect the hoses from both ends of the check valve, carefully noting the installed position of the valve and the hoses.

18   Blow through both ends of the check valve, verifying that air flows in one direction only.

19   If air flows in both directions or not at all, replace the check valve with a new one.

20   When reconnecting the valve, make sure it is installed in the proper direction.

6

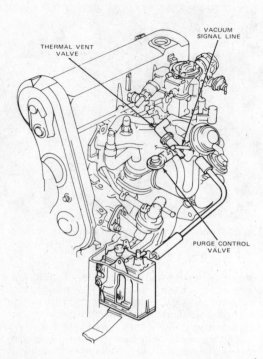

THERMAL VENT VALVE

VACUUM SIGNAL LINE

PURGE CONTROL VALVE

6.2a   Typical 2.0L and 2.3L carbureted evaporative emissions control system

Thermactor system noise test

21   The thermactor system is not completely noiseless. Under normal conditions, noise rises in pitch as the engine speed increases. To determine if noise is the fault of the air injection system, detach the drivebelt (after verifying that the belt tension is correct) and operate the engine. If the noise disappears, proceed with the following diagnosis. **Caution:** *The pump must accumulate 500 miles (vehicle miles) before the following check is valid.*

22   If the belt noise is excessive:
   a) Check for a loose belt and tighten as necessary (refer to Chapter 1).
   b) Check for a seized pump and replace it if necessary.
   c) Check for a loose pulley. Tighten the mounting bolts as required.
   d) Check for loose, broken or missing mounting brackets or bolts. Tighten or replace as necessary.

23   If there is excessive mechanical noise:
   a) Check for an overtightened mounting bolt.
   b) Check for an overtightened drivebelt (refer to Chapter 1).
   c) Check for excessive flash on the air pump adjusting arm boss and remove as necessary.
   d) Check for a distorted adjusting arm and, if necessary, replace the arm.

24   If there is excessive thermactor system noise (whirring or hissing sounds):
   a) Check for a leak in the hoses (use a soap and water solution to find the leaks) and replace the hose(s) as necessary.
   b) Check for a loose, pinched or kinked hose and reassemble, straighten or replace the hose and/or clamps as required.
   c) Check for a hose touching other engine parts and adjust or reroute the hose to prevent further contact.
   d) Check for an inoperative bypass valve (refer to Step 8) and replace if necessary.
   e) Check for an inoperative check valve (refer to Step 17) and replace if necessary.
   f) Check for loose pump or pulley mounting fasteners and tighten as necessary.

   g) Check for a restricted or bent pump outlet fitting. Inspect the fitting and remove any casting flash blocking the air passageway. Replace bent fittings.
   h) Check for air dumping through the bypass valve (only at idle). On many vehicles, the thermactor system has been designed to dump air at idle to prevent overheating the catalytic converter. This condition is normal. Determine that the noise persists at higher speeds before proceeding.
   i) Check for air dumping through the bypass valve (the decel and idle dump). On many vehicles, the thermactor air is dumped into the air cleaner or the remote silencer. Make sure that the hoses are connected properly and not cracked.

25   If there is excessive pump noise, make sure the pump has had sufficient break-in time (at least 500 miles). Check for a worn or damaged pump and replace as necessary.

Component replacement

26   To replace the air bypass valve, air supply control valve, check valve, combination air bypass/air control valve or the silencer, clearly label, then disconnect, the hoses leading to them, replace the faulty component and reattach the hoses to the proper ports. Make sure the hoses are in good condition. If not, replace them with new ones.

27   To replace the air supply pump, first loosen the engine drivebelt (see Chapter 1), then remove the pump mounting bolts from the mounting bracket. Label all wires and hoses as they're removed to facilitate installation of the new unit.

28   After the new pump is installed, adjust the drivebelts to the specified tension (see Chapter 1).

6   Fuel evaporative emissions control system

Refer to illustrations 6.2a, 6.2b and 6.2c

General description

1   This system is designed to prevent hydrocarbons from being released into the atmosphere by trapping and storing fuel vapor from the fuel tank, the carburetor or the fuel injection system.

2   The serviceable parts of the system include a charcoal filled canister and the connecting lines between the fuel tank, fuel tank filler cap and the carburetor or fuel injection system **(see illustrations)**.

3   Vapor trapped in the gas tank is vented through a valve in the top of the tank. From the valve, the vapor is routed through a single line to a charcoal canister located in the engine compartment near the radiator, where it's stored until the next time the engine is started. When the engine's started, the vapors are routed to the carburetor or fuel injection system to be burned in the engine.

Checking

4   There are no moving parts and nothing to wear in the canister. Check for loose, missing, cracked or broken fittings and inspect the canister for cracks and other damage. If the canister is damaged, replace it (see following). Check all hoses, particularly at their connections, for cracks and other damage.

5   Check for fuel smells around the vehicle. Make sure the gas cap gasket is in good condition and properly installed (there should be a sealing imprint on the gasket where it mates with the filler neck).

Component replacement
Charcoal canister

6   Locate the canister in the engine compartment.

7   Reach up above the canister, remove the single mounting bolt and remove the canister.

8   Clearly label the hoses and detach them from the canister.

9   Installation is the reverse of the removal procedure.

All other components

10   Referring to the VECI label of the vehicle, locate the component you intend to replace.

11   Label the hoses, then detach them and remove the component.

12   Installation is the reverse of removal.

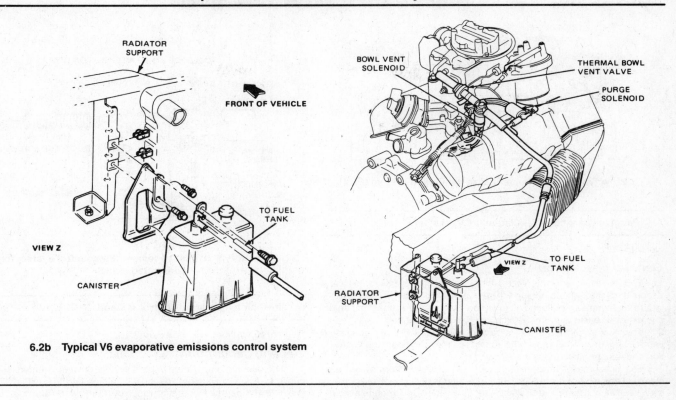

RADIATOR
SUPPORT

FRONT OF VEHICLE

VIEW Z

CANISTER

TO FUEL
TANK

BOWL VENT
SOLENOID

THERMAL BOWL
VENT VALVE

PURGE
SOLENOID

VIEW Z

TO FUEL
TANK

RADIATOR
SUPPORT

CANISTER

6.2b Typical V6 evaporative emissions control system

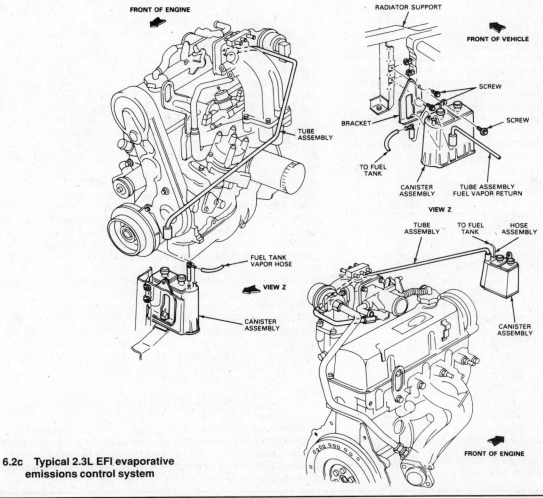

FRONT OF ENGINE

TUBE
ASSEMBLY

FUEL TANK
VAPOR HOSE

VIEW Z

CANISTER
ASSEMBLY

RADIATOR SUPPORT

FRONT OF VEHICLE

SCREW

BRACKET

SCREW

TO FUEL
TANK

CANISTER
ASSEMBLY

TUBE ASSEMBLY
FUEL VAPOR RETURN

VIEW Z

TUBE
ASSEMBLY

TO FUEL
TANK

HOSE
ASSEMBLY

CANISTER
ASSEMBLY

FRONT OF ENGINE

**6.2c Typical 2.3L EFI evaporative
emissions control system**

6

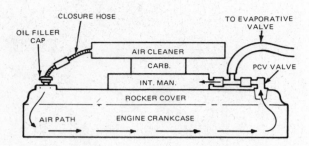

7.2   A typical positive crankcase ventilation system (PCV)

7   Positive Crankcase Ventilation (PCV) system

Refer to illustration 7.2

General description

1   The Positive Crankcase Ventilation (PCV) system cycles crankcase vapors back through the engine where they are burned. The valve regulates the amount of ventilating air and blow-by gas to the intake manifold and prevents backfire from traveling into the crankcase.

2   The PCV system consists of a replaceable PCV valve, a crankcase ventilation filter and the connecting hoses (see the accompanying illustration and various illustrations in Chapter 1).

3   The air source for the crankcase ventilation (PCV) system is in the air cleaner. Drawn by intake manifold vacuum, air passes through the crankcase ventilation filter (in the oil filler cap or air cleaner) and through a hose connected to the air cleaner housing. On models with a crankcase ventilation filter integrated into the oil filler cap, the cap is sealed at the opening to prevent the entrance of outside air. From the crankcase ventilation filter, the air flows into the rocker arm chamber and the crankcase, from which it circulates up into another section of the rocker arm chamber and finally enters a spring-loaded regulator valve (PCV valve) that controls the amount of flow as operating conditions vary. The vapors are routed to the intake manifold through the crankcase vent hose tube and fittings. This process goes on continuously while the engine is running.

Checking

4   Checking procedures for the PCV system components are included in Chapter 1.

Component replacement

5   See Chapter 1.

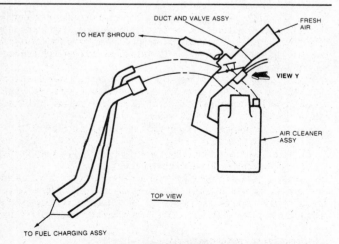

8.3b   A typical inlet air temperature control system for EFI models

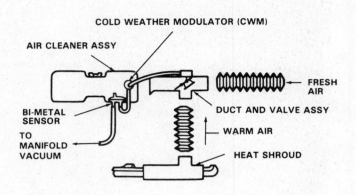

8.3a   A typical inlet air temperature control system for carbureted models

8   Inlet air temperature control system

Refer to illustrations 8.3a and 8.3b

General description

1   The inlet air temperature control system provides heated intake air during warmup, then maintains the inlet air temperature within a 70-degree F to 105-degree F operating range by mixing warm and cool air. This allows leaner fuel/air mixture settings for the carburetor or EFI system, which reduces emissions and improves driveability.

2   Two fresh air inlets one warm and one cold are used. The balance between the two is controlled by intake manifold vacuum, a cold weather modulator (CWM) and a bimetal sensor. A vacuum motor, which operates a heat duct valve in the air cleaner, is operated by intake manifold vacuum.

3   When the underhood temperature is cold, warm air radiating off the exhaust manifold is routed by a shroud which fits over the manifold up through a hot air inlet tube and into the air cleaner **(see illustrations)**. This provides warm air for the carburetor or EFI, resulting in better driveability and faster warmup. As the underhood temperature rises, a heat duct valve is gradually closed by a vacuum motor and the air cleaner draws air through a cold (fresh) air duct instead. The result is a consistent intake air temperature.

4   A temperature vacuum switch mounted on the air cleaner housing monitors the temperature of the inlet air heated by the exhaust manifold. A bimetal disc in the temperature vacuum switch orients itself in one of two positions, depending on the temperature. One position allows vacuum through a hose to the motor; the other position blocks vacuum.

5   The vacuum motor itself is regulated by a cold weather modulator (CWM), mounted in the side of the air cleaner housing assembly, between the temperature vacuum switch and the motor, which provides the motor with a range of graduated positions between fully open and fully closed.

Checking

Note: *Make sure that the engine is cold before beginning this test.*

6   Always check the vacuum source and the integrity of all vacuum hoses between the source and the vacuum motor before beginning the following test. Do not proceed until they're okay.

7   Apply the parking brake and block the wheels.

8   On carbureted models, detach, but do not remove, the air cleaner housing and element (see Chapter 4). On EFI models, remove components as necessary from the air intake duct in order to see the vacuum motor door (see Chapter 4).

9   Observe the heat duct valve position; it should be open. If it isn't, it may be binding or sticking. Make sure that it's not rusted in an open or closed position by attempting to move it by hand. If it's rusted, it can usually be freed by cleaning and oiling the hinge. If it fails to work properly after servicing, replace it.

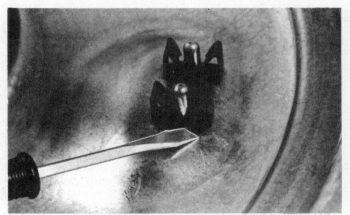

8.20 To remove the bimetal sensor, detach the hoses, then pry off the retaining clip with a small screwdriver (carbureted model shown)

8.28 To remove the vacuum motor, label and detach the hoses, then drill out the rivet (arrow) and slide out the retaining strap (carbureted model shown)

10   If the heat duct valve is okay but the motor still fails to operate correctly, check carefully for a leak in the hose leading to it. Check the vacuum source to and from the bimetal sensor and the cold weather modulator as well. If no leak is found, replace the vacuum motor (see Step 26).

11   Start the engine. If the heat duct valve has moved or moves to the "heat on" (closed to fresh air) position, go to Step 15.

12   If the door stays in the "heat off" (closed to warm air) position, place a finger over the bimetal sensor bleed. The duct door must move rapidly to the "heat on" position. If it does, the bimetal sensor is probably faulty. If the door doesn't move to the "heat on" position, remove the vacuum hose from the vacuum motor and check to see if there's vacuum (finger still over the bleed). If there's no vacuum, stop the engine and replace the vacuum motor (see Step 26). Repeat this Step with the new vacuum motor.

13   With the engine off, allow the bimetal sensor and the cold weather modulator to cool completely. If outside temperature is high, ice may speed this process.

14   Restart the engine. The duct door should move to the "heat on" position. If the door doesn't move or moves only partially, replace the bimetal sensor (see Step 18).

15   Start and run the engine briefly (less than 15 seconds). The duct door should move to the "heat on" position.

16   Shut off the engine and watch the duct door. It should stay in the "heat on" position for at least two minutes.

17   If it doesn't stay in the "heat on" position for at least two minutes, replace the CWM (see Step 23).

Component replacement

Refer to illustrations 8.20 and 8.28

Bimetal sensor

18   Clearly label, then detach both vacuum hoses from the bimetal sensor (one is coming from the vacuum source at the manifold and the other is going to the vacuum motor).

19   Remove the air cleaner housing cover assembly (see Chapter 4).

20   Pry the sensor retaining clip off with a screwdriver **(see illustration)**.

21   Remove the bimetal sensor.

22   Installation is the reverse of removal procedure.

Cold weather modulator (CWM)

23   Locate the CWM, then detach both vacuum hoses and remove the CWM.

24   Slide the CWM retaining clip off and remove the CWM.

25   Installation is the reverse of removal procedure.

Vacuum motor

26   On carbureted models, remove the air cleaner housing assembly (see Chapter 4). On EFI models, remove the air intake duct (see Chapter 4). Place the assembly on a workbench.

27   Detach the vacuum hose from the motor.

28   Drill out the vacuum motor retaining strap rivet **(see illustration)**.

29   Remove the motor.

30   Installation is the reverse of removal. Use a sheet metal screw of the appropriate size to replace the rivet.

9   Catalytic converter

Note: *Because of a Federally mandated extended warranty which covers emissions-related components such as the catalytic converter, check with a dealer service department before replacing the converter at your own expense.*

General description

1   The catalytic converter is an emission control device added to the exhaust system to reduce pollutants from the exhaust gas stream. There are two types of converters. The conventional oxidation catalyst reduces the levels of hydrocarbon (HC) and carbon monoxide (CO). The three-way catalyst lowers the levels of oxides of nitrogen (NOx) as well as hydrocarbons (HC) and carbon monoxide (CO).

Checking

2   The test equipment for a catalytic converter is expensive and highly sophisticated. If you suspect that the converter on your vehicle is malfunctioning, take it to a dealer or authorized emissions inspection facility for diagnosis and repair.

3   Whenever the vehicle is raised for servicing of underbody components, check the converter for leaks, corrosion, dents and other damage. Check the welds/flange bolts that attach the front and rear ends of the converter to the exhaust system. If damage is discovered, the converter should be replaced.

4   Although catalytic converters don't break too often, they do become plugged. The easiest way to check for a restricted converter is to use a vacuum gauge to diagnose the effect of a blocked exhaust on intake vacuum.

   a) Open the throttle until the engine speed is about 2000 RPM.
   b) Release the throttle quickly.
   c) If there is no restriction, the gauge will quickly drop to not more than 2 in Hg or more above its normal reading.
   d) If the gauge does not show 5 in Hg or more above its normal reading, or seems to momentarily hover around its highest reading for a moment before it returns, the exhaust system, or the converter, is plugged (or an exhaust pipe is bent or dented, or the core inside the muffler has shifted).

Component replacement

5   The converter is bolted to the exhaust system, refer to the exhaust system removal and installation section in Chapter 4.

6

10   Spark control system (Dura-Spark II models)

Note: *The information in this Section is applicable only to models equipped with the Dura-Spark II ignition system (see Chapter 5). On EEC-IV ignition system equipped models, the spark advance and retard functions are controlled by the Electronic Engine Control (EEC) microprocessor; checks and tests involving the spark control system on these vehicles must be performed by a Ford dealer service department.*

General description

1   The spark control system is designed to reduce hydrocarbon and oxides of nitrogen emissions by advancing the ignition timing when the engine is cold.
2   These systems are fairly complex and have many valves, relays, amplifiers and other components built into them. Each vehicle will have a system peculiar to the model year, geographic region and gross vehicle weight rating. A schematic diagram located under the hood will give the exact details of the components and vacuum line routing of the specific system equipped on the vehicle.
3   Various vacuum switches are used in the emissions systems for modifying the spark timing and engine idle. These vacuum switches have varying number of ports, from two to four, depending on their function.

Ported Vacuum Switches (PVS)

4   A ported vacuum switch is situated in the cooling system to increase engine idle rpm when the engine overheats. When the coolant is at normal temperature, the vacuum goes through the top and center ports of the PVS, providing the distributor with vacuum advance suitable for normal driving. When hot, the PVS center and bottom ports are connected so that engine manifold vacuum allows the distributor to advance and increase idle.

Distributor vacuum vent valve

5   Some engines use a distributor vacuum vent valve both to prevent fuel from migrating into the distributor advance diaphragm and to act as a spark advance delay valve. During light acceleration, deceleration and idle, the vent dumps vacuum through a check valve. This keeps the distributor from advancing excessively for the load and evacuates the fuel in the spark port line.

Cold Start Spark Advance (CSSA)

6   The CSSA system is located in the distributor spark advance system. When coolant temperature is below 128-degrees F, it momentarily traps the spark port vacuum at the distributor advance diaphragm. The vacuum follows a path through the carburetor vacuum tap, the Distributor Retard Control Valve (DRCV), the CSSA port vacuum switch and then the cooling vacuum switch to the distributor. At coolant temperatures above 128-degrees F, the CSSA PVS operates and the vacuum follows a path from the carburetor spark port through the cooling PVS to the distributor.

Cold Start Hold Spark (CSSH)

7   When the engine is cold, the CSSH momentarily provides spark advance for improved cold engine acceleration. Below 128-degrees F, the CSSH ported vacuum switch is closed and the distributor vacuum is routed through a restrictor. Under cold starting conditions, the high vacuum present advances the distributor. During cold acceleration, the vacuum is slowly bled off through the restrictor, slowing the vacuum advance during initial acceleration.

Spark Delay Valve (SDV)

8   SDV's are designed to slow the air flow in one direction while a check valve allows free flow in the opposite direction. This allows closer control of vacuum operated emission devises.

Checking

9   Visually check all vacuum hoses for cracks, splits or hardening. Remove the distributor cap and rotor and apply a vacuum to the distributor advance port (and retard port, if so equipped) to see if the breaker or relay plate inside of the distributor moves. The plate should move opposite the distributor direction of rotation when vacuum is applied to the advance port and should move in the direction of rotation if vacuum is applied to the retard port (if so equipped).
10   Checking of the temperature relays, delay valves or other modifiers of the spark timing system is beyond the scope of the home mechanic. Consult an expert if you suspect that you have other problems within the spark advance system.

Component replacement

11   When replacing any vacuum hoses, remove only one hose at a time and make sure the replacement hose is of the same quality and same size as the hose being replaced.
12   If it is determined that a malfunction in the spark control system is due to a faulty distributor, refer to Chapter 5 for the replacement procedure.

11   Emissions maintenance reminder light resetting

1   Some models are equipped with an emissions maintenance reminder light on the dashboard (usually labelled EGR or EMISS) that comes on at approximately 60,000 miles to remind you to service your emissions system when scheduled (see Chapter 1).
2   The timer for the light measures the amount of time the ignition key is on, not actual mileage, so the actual mileage at which the light comes on will vary from vehicle to vehicle.
3   After servicing is completed, the light must be re-set to come on again in 60,000 miles. To reset the light, proceed as follows.
4   Turn the ignition switch to the Off position.
5   Working under the dash, lightly push a Phillips screwdriver through the 0.2 inch hole with the sticker labelled RESET and lightly press down and hold.
6   Still pressing the screwdriver down, turn the ignition switch to the Run position. The maintenance reminder light will come on and should remain lighted for as long as the screwdriver is pressed down. Hold the screwdriver down for approximately five seconds.
7   Remove the screwdriver. The light should go out within approximately 2 to 5 seconds, indicating a reset has occurred (if the light does not go out, return to Step 4 and repeat the procedure). Turn the ignition switch to Off.
8   Turn the ignition switch to Run. The maintenance reminder light should light for approximately 2 to 5 seconds and then go out. This verifies that a proper reset of the module has been accomplished. If the light remains on, return to Step 4 and repeat the procedure
9   Turn the ignition switch to Off.

Chapter 7 Part A   Manual transmission

Contents

Specifications

Transmission types	Four-speed synchromesh and five-speed synchromesh
Lubricant type	See Chapter 1

Torque specifications

	Ft-lbs
Access cover-to-case screw (Mazda)	23 to 34
Crossmember-to-frame nuts	65 to 85
Damper-to-crossmember nuts	71 to 94
Transmission (clutch housing)-to-engine bolt or nut	28 to 38
Transmission-to-clutch housing bolts or nuts	30 to 40

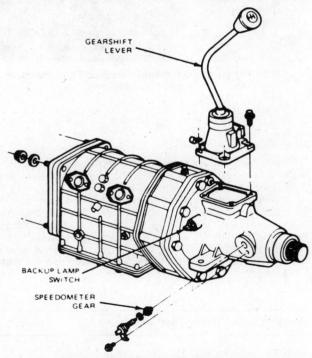

1.1a   A typical 2WD five-speed manual transmission (Mazda) (1983 through 1992 models)

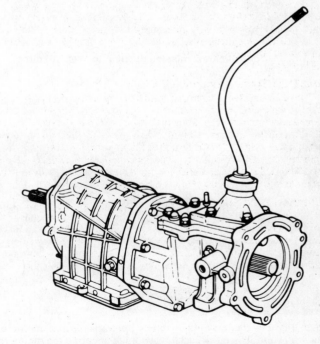

1.1b   A typical 4WD five-speed manual transmission (Mitsubishi)

7A

---

1   General information

Refer to illustrations 1.1a and 1.1b

All vehicles covered in this manual come equipped with either a four-speed or five-speed manual transmission **(see illustrations)** or an automatic transmission. All information on the manual transmission is included in this Part of Chapter 7. Information on the automatic transmission can be found in Part B of this Chapter.

2.2   Hold back the carpet and remove the shifter boot retaining bolts or screws

2.3   After the shifter boot is removed, remove the four retaining bolts and lift the shift lever assembly straight up and out

2.5   Cover the transmission opening to keep out dirt

3.2   Pry up on the transmission mount and check for excessive looseness

3.3   Remove the two nuts attaching the transmission mount to the frame crossmember and the two bolts securing the mount to the transmission extension housing

Due to the complexity, unavailability of replacement parts and the special tools necessary, internal transmission repair procedures are not recommended for the home mechanic.

Depending on the expense involved in having a faulty transmission overhauled, it may be an advantage to consider replacing the unit with either a new or rebuilt one. Your local dealer or transmission shop should be able to supply you with information concerning cost, availability and exchange policy. Regardless of how you decide to remedy a transmission problem, you can still save a lot of money by removing and installing the unit yourself.

2   Shift lever – removal and installation

Refer to illustrations 2.2, 2.3 and 2.5
1   Place the transmission in Neutral.
2   Carefully pull up the carpeting and remove the shifter boot retaining bolts **(see illustration)**.
3   Remove the bolts securing the retainer cover to the gearshift lever retainer on the transmission extension housing **(see illustration)**.
4   Pull the gearshift lever assembly, shim and bushing straight up and out from the gearshift lever retainer on the transmission extension housing.

5   Cover the opening in the top of the transmission extension housing with a clean rag to avoid the entry of foreign matter **(see illustration)**.
6   Installation is the reverse of the removal Steps.

3   Transmission mount – check and replacement

Refer to illustrations 3.2 and 3.3

Check

1   Insert a large screwdriver or prybar into the space between the transmission extension housing and the frame crossmember and pry up.
2   The transmission should not move significantly away from the mount insulator **(see illustration)**. If it does, the mount should be replaced.

Replacement

3   To replace the mount, remove the two nuts securing the mount to the frame crossmember and the two bolts securing the mount to the transmission extension housing **(see illustration)**.
4   To replace the damper (models so equipped), remove the two nuts securing the damper to the frame crossmember.
5   Place a jack under the transmission with a piece of wood on top of it to protect the transmission case. Apply a slight amount of jack pressure and raise the transmission. Remove the mount or damper and install a new one.
6   Installation is the reverse of the removal Steps.

4   Manual transmission – removal and installation

Refer to illustrations 4.7a, 4.7b, 4.8 and 4.15

1   Disconnect the negative cable from the battery. Place the cable out of the way so it cannot accidentally come in contact with the negative-terminal of the battery, as this would once again allow power into the electrical system of the vehicle.
2   From inside the vehicle, remove the shift lever (see Section 2).
3   From inside the vehicle, disconnect the barbed end of the clutch/starter interlock switch rod from the clutch pedal. Remove the lockpin and remove the master cylinder pushrod from the clutch pedal. Remove the plastic bushing.
4   From under the hood, remove the top two transmission-to-engine bolts.
5   Raise the vehicle and support it securely on jackstands.
6   Remove the driveshaft(s) (see Chapter 8) and install a plug in the transmission rear extension housing or transfer case to prevent lubricant leakage. On 1992 and later V6 models, remove the exhaust system (see Chapter 4).
7   On vehicles with an internal slave cylinder, disconnect the hydraulic fluid line from the clutch slave cylinder (see Chapter 8) and plug the line to prevent fluid spillage. On external slave cylinder models, remove the two mounting bolts **(see illustration)**. Move the slave cylinder out of the way and secure it with wire **(see illustration)**.
8   Remove the bolt securing the speedometer cable retaining bracket and remove the bracket and bolt as an assembly. Disconnect the speedometer cable from the transmission or transfer case **(see illustration)**.
9   Remove the starter motor (see Chapter 5).
10   Disconnect the electrical connections from the back-up light and shift indicator switch.
11   Place a jack under the engine and protect the oil pan with a wood block. Apply a slight amount of jack pressure to support the rear of the engine.
12   On 4WD models, remove the transfer case (see Chapter 7 Part C).
13   Disconnect the catalytic converter, then disconnect the crossover pipe on models so equipped (see Chapter 4). On V6 models, remove the exhaust system.
14   Place a transmission jack under the transmission, apply a slight amount of jack pressure to support the transmission. Remove the remaining bolts securing the transmission.

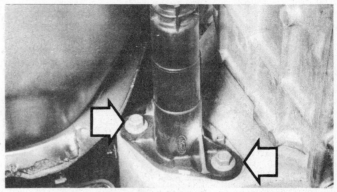

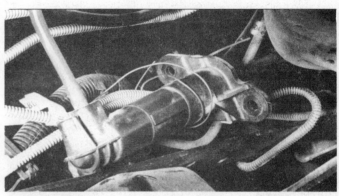

4.7a   **Remove the slave cylinder mounting bolts (arrows)**

4.7b   **Once the slave cylinder is removed, wire the unit to the frame, out of the way**

4.8   **Remove the bolt and retainer securing the speedometer cable and disconnect the speedometer cable from the transmission**

15   Remove the bolts and nuts securing the transmission mount to the frame crossmember **(see illustration)**.
16   Remove the nuts and bolts securing the frame crossmember to the frame side rails. **Note:** *If you do not remove the mount from the transmission, it will be necessary to raise the transmission enough to clear the mount studs, then slide the crossmember toward the rear.*
17   Slowly lower the jack supporting the engine and carefully pull the transmission toward the rear and work it free from the locating dowels. Pull the transmission straight back until the input shaft clears the clutch assembly.
18   Lower the transmission jack and remove the transmission.
19   Installation is the reverse of the removal Steps with the following additions:
   a) Mount the transmission in a transmission jack and position it under the vehicle.

7A

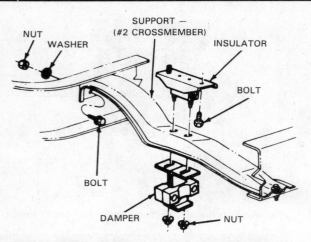

4.15 An exploded view of a typical transmission mount

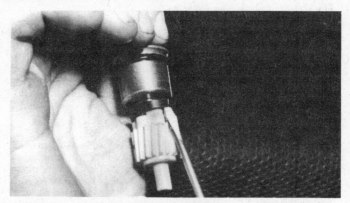

5.3 Pry the retaining clip from the pinion gear and slide the gear off of the cable

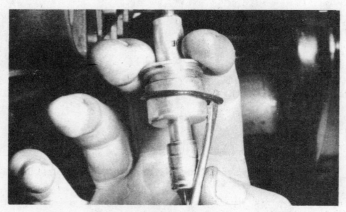

5.4 Pry off the old O-ring with a small screwdriver

b) Start the transmission input shaft into the clutch disc. Align the shaft splines with the clutch disc splines and move the transmission forward.
c) Tighten the bolts and nuts to the torque listed in this Chapter's Specifications.
d) On models with internal slave cylinders, bleed the clutch hydraulic system (see Chapter 8).

5   Speedometer pinion gear and seal – replacement

Refer to illustrations 5.3 and 5.4

1   Remove the bolt securing the speedometer cable retaining bracket and remove the bracket and bolt as an assembly **(see illustration 4.8).**
2   Pull the speedometer cable and pinion gear straight out of the transmission or transfer case.
3   Use a small screwdriver to remove the retaining clip from the pinion gear, then slide the gear off the cable **(see illustration)**.
4   If necessary, use a small screwdriver to remove the O-ring from the retaining groove **(see illustration)**. Discard the O-ring.
5   Lubricate the new O-ring with transmission lubricant and install it in the retaining groove. Make sure it's seated correctly and not twisted.
6   Install the pinion gear on the cable and install the retaining clip. Make sure the clip is properly seated in the groove.
7   Install the speedometer pinion gear and cable in the transfer case or transmission and secure it with the bolt and bracket.

6   Extension housing oil seal – replacement

Note: *This procedure applies only to 2WD models that are not equipped with a transfer case.*

1   Raise the vehicle and support it securely on jackstands.
2   Remove the driveshaft (see Chapter 8). Some transmission lubricant may drain out when the driveshaft slip joint is withdrawn from the extension housing.
3   Pry the oil seal out with a seal removal tool or screwdriver.
4   Inspect the oil seal sealing surface on the driveshaft slip joint for scoring or burrs that may damage the new oil seal. If the yoke is damaged in any way, replace it.
5   Inspect the extension housing counterbore for burrs. If found, remove them with emery cloth or medium-grit wet-and-dry sandpaper. Use a clean cloth dipped in solvent and remove any sanding residue from the counterbore.
6   Apply silicone sealant to the outside diameter of the new seal and apply transmission lubricant to the seal lip and end of the rubber boot portion.
7   Install the new seal and make sure it is completely seated in the counterbore.
8   Install the driveshaft (see Chapter 8).
9   Lower the vehicle and check the transmission lubricant level, topping it up, if necessary (see Chapter 1).

7   Manual transmission overhaul – general information

Overhauling a manual transmission is a difficult job for the do-it-yourselfer. It involves the disassembly and reassembly of many small parts. Numerous clearances must be precisely measured and, if necessary, changed with select fit spacers and snap-rings. As a result, if transmission problems arise, it can be removed and installed by a competent do-it-yourselfer, but overhaul should be left to a transmission repair shop. Rebuilt transmissions may be available – check with your dealer parts department and auto parts stores. At any rate, the time and money involved in an overhaul is almost sure to exceed the cost of a rebuilt unit.

Nevertheless, it's not impossible for an inexperienced mechanic to rebuild a transmission if the special tools are available and the job is done in a deliberate step-by-step manner so nothing is overlooked.

The tools necessary for an overhaul include internal and external snap-ring pliers, bearing puller, slide hammer, set of pin punches, dial indicator and possibly a hydraulic press. In addition, a large, sturdy workbench and a large vise or transmission stand will be required.

During disassembly of the transmission, make careful notes of how each piece comes off, where it fits in relation to other pieces and what holds it in place.

Before taking the transmission apart for repair, it will help if you have some idea what area of the transmission is malfunctioning. Certain problems can be closely tied to specific areas in the transmission, which can make component examination and replacement easier. Refer to the Troubleshooting section at the front of this manual for information regarding possible sources of trouble.

Chapter 7 Part B   Automatic transmission

Contents

Specifications

Transmission types	C3, C5 and A4LD
Fluid type and capacity	See Chapter 1

Torque specifications   **Ft-lbs** (unless otherwise indicated)

C3 transmission

Shifter trunnion bolt	13 to 23
Bellcrank bracket bolts	20 to 30
Shifter bezel screws	12 to 36 in-lbs
Transmission mount-to-crossmember nuts	71 to 94
Transmission mount-to-transmission bolts	60 to 80
Driveplate-to-torque converter nuts	27 to 49
Transmission-to-engine bolts	28 to 38
Torque converter-to-driveplate nuts	20 to 34
Outer downshift lever nut	84 to 132 in-lbs
Inner manual lever nut	30 to 40
Neutral start switch	84 to 120 in-lbs
Oil cooler line-to-connector	84 to 120 in-lbs
Connector-to-case	120 to 180 in-lbs
Filler tube-to-engine clip bolt	28 to 38
Trunnion bolt	156 to 276 in-lbs
Front band adjusting screw locknut	35 to 45

C5 transmission

Shifter trunnion bolt	13 to 23
Bellcrank bracket bolts	20 to 30
Shifter bezel screws	12 to 36 in-lbs
Transmission mount-to-crossmember nuts	71 to 94
Transmission mount-to-transmission bolts	60 to 80
Driveplate-to-torque converter nuts	20 to 34
Torque converter housing-to-engine rear cover plate	24 to 36 in-lbs
Torque converter-to-driveplate nuts	20 to 34
Transmission-to-engine bolts	28 to 38
Oil cooler line-to-transmission case	18 to 23
Oil cooler line nut	144 to 216 in-lbs
Intermediate band adjusting screw locknut	40
Low-reverse band adjusting screw locknut	40

A4LD transmission

Shifter trunnion bolt	156 to 276 in-lbs
Bellcrank bracket bolts	20 to 30
Shifter bezel screws	12 to 36 in-lbs
Transmission mount-to-transmission bolts	60 to 80
Transmission mount-to-crossmember nuts	71 to 94
Transmission-to-engine bolts	28 to 38
Torque converter housing cover-to-converter housing	144 to 192 in-lbs
Inner manual lever nut	30 to 40
Torque converter-to-driveplate nut	20 to 34
Neutral start switch	84 to 120 in-lbs
Oil cooler line-to-transmission case connector	18 to 23
Oil cooler line-to-connector tube nut	144 to 216 in-lbs

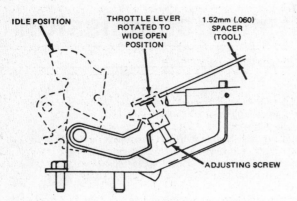

IDLE POSITION — THROTTLE LEVER ROTATED TO WIDE OPEN POSITION — 1.52mm (.060) SPACER (TOOL) — ADJUSTING SCREW

3.3 With the throttle wide open, insert the spacer tool and adjust the screw until contact is made

1 General information

All vehicles covered in this manual come equipped with either a four-speed or five-speed manual transmission or an automatic transmission. All information on the automatic transmission is included in this Part of Chapter 7. Information on the manual transmission can be found in Part A of this Chapter.

Due to the complexity of the automatic transmissions covered in this manual and the need for specialized equipment to perform most service operations, this Chapter contains only general diagnosis, routine maintenance, adjustment and removal and installation procedures.

If the transmission requires major repair work, it should be taken to a dealer service department or an automotive or transmission repair shop. You can, however, remove and install the transmission yourself and save the expense, even if the repair work is done by a transmission shop.

2 Diagnosis – general

Note: *Automatic transmission malfunctions may be caused by five general conditions: poor engine performance, improper adjustments, hydraulic malfunctions, mechanical malfunctions or malfunctions in the computer or its signal network. Diagnosis of these problems should always begin with a check of the easily repaired items: fluid level and condition (see Chapter 1), shift linkage adjustment and throttle linkage adjustment. Next, perform a road test to determine if the problem has been corrected or if more diagnosis is necessary. If the problem persists after the preliminary tests and corrections are completed, additional diagnosis should be done by a dealer service department or transmission repair shop. Refer to the Troubleshooting Section at the front of this manual for information on symptoms of transmission problems.*

Preliminary checks

1   Drive the vehicle to warm the transmission to normal operating temperature.
2   Check the fluid level as described in Chapter 1:
   a) If the fluid level is unusually low, add enough fluid to bring the level within the designated area of the dipstick, then check for external leaks (see below).
   b) If the fluid level is abnormally high, drain off the excess, then check the drained fluid for contamination by coolant. The presence of engine coolant in the automatic transmission fluid indicates that a failure has occurred in the internal radiator walls that separate the coolant from the transmission fluid (see Chapter 3).

   c) If the fluid is foaming, drain it and refill the transmission, then check for coolant in the fluid or a high fluid level.
3   Check the engine idle speed. **Note:** *If the engine is malfunctioning, do not proceed with the preliminary checks until it has been repaired and runs normally.*
4   Check the throttle valve cable for freedom of movement. Adjust it if necessary (see Section 3). **Note:** *The throttle cable may function properly when the engine is shut off and cold, but it may malfunction once the engine is hot. Check it cold and at normal engine operating temperature.*
5   Inspect the shift control linkage (see Section 4). Make sure that it's properly adjusted and that the linkage operates smoothly.

Fluid leak diagnosis

6   Most fluid leaks are easy to locate visually. Repair usually consists of replacing a seal or gasket. If a leak is difficult to find, the following procedure may help.
7   Identify the fluid. Make sure it's transmission fluid and not engine oil or brake fluid (automatic transmission fluid is a deep red color).
8   Try to pinpoint the source of the leak. Drive the vehicle several miles, then park it over a large sheet of cardboard. After a minute or two, you should be able to locate the leak by determining the source of the fluid dripping onto the cardboard.
9   Make a careful visual inspection of the suspected component and the area immediately around it. Pay particular attention to gasket mating surfaces. A mirror is often helpful for finding leaks in areas that are hard to see.
10   If the leak still cannot be found, clean the suspected area thoroughly with a degreaser or solvent, then dry it.
11   Drive the vehicle for several miles at normal operating temperature and varying speeds. After driving the vehicle, visually inspect the suspected component again.
12   Once the leak has been located, the cause must be determined before it can be properly repaired. If a gasket is replaced but the sealing flange is bent, the new gasket will not stop the leak. The bent flange must be straightened.
13   Before attempting to repair a leak, check to make sure that the following conditions are corrected or they may cause another leak. **Note:** *Some of the following conditions cannot be fixed without highly specialized tools and expertise. Such problems must be referred to a transmission repair shop or a dealer service department.*

Gasket leaks

14   Check the pan periodically. Make sure the bolts are tight, no bolts are missing, the gasket is in good condition and the pan is flat (dents in the pan may indicate damage to the valve body inside).
15   If the pan gasket is leaking, the fluid level or the fluid pressure may be too high, the vent may be plugged, the pan bolts may be too tight, the pan sealing flange may be warped, the sealing surface of the transmission housing may be damaged, the gasket may be damaged or the transmission casting may be cracked or porous. If sealant instead of gasket material has been used to form a seal between the pan and the transmission housing, it may be the wrong sealant.

Seal leaks

16   If a transmission seal is leaking, the fluid level or pressure may be too high, the vent may be plugged, the seal bore may be damaged, the seal itself may be damaged or improperly installed, the surface of the shaft protruding through the seal may be damaged or a loose bearing may be causing excessive shaft movement.
17   Make sure the dipstick tube seal is in good condition and the tube is properly seated. Periodically check the area around the speedometer gear or sensor for leakage. If transmission fluid is evident, check the O-ring for damage.

Case leaks

18   If the case itself appears to be leaking, the casting is porous and will have to be repaired or replaced.
19   Make sure the oil cooler hose fittings are tight and in good condition.

Fluid comes out vent pipe or fill tube

20   If this condition occurs, the transmission is overfilled, there is coolant in the fluid, the case is porous, the dipstick is incorrect, the vent is plugged or the drain back holes are plugged.

---

3   Kickdown rod (1983 through 1985 models) – adjustment

Refer to illustration 3.3

Note 1: *1985 2.3L EFI models and all other models except 1983 through 1985 are equipped with a kickdown cable instead of a rod. The cable requires no adjustment unless it is replaced, and then the only adjustment necessary is to depress the accelerator all the way to the floor after the cable has been installed.*

Note 2: *Whenever possible, run the engine until it reaches normal operating temperature prior to adjusting the kickdown rod.*

1   Have an assistant hold the accelerator in the wide-open position.
2   Open the hood and check that the throttle is in the wide-open position.
3   Insert a 1.52 mm (0.06 inch) spacer between the throttle lever and the adjusting screw **(see illustration)**.
4   Slowly turn the adjusting screw until contact is made between the screw and the spacer.
5   Remove the spacer.

6   Have the assistant release the accelerator. **Warning:** *After adjustment, check to insure the accelerator returns to idle on slow release of foot pressure without binding or dragging.*

---

4   Shift linkage – adjustment

1983 through 1988 models (floor shift)

Refer to illustrations 4.2a, 4.2b, 4.2c and 4.2d

1   Raise the vehicle and support it securely on jackstands.
2   Have an assistant position the shift selector in the Drive position and hold it in place during adjustment **(see illustrations)**. On A4LD models, do not use Overdrive. Loosen the trunnion bolt. **Note:** *Make sure the shift lever detent pawl is held against the rearward Drive detent stop during adjustment.*
3   Position the transmission manual shift lever in the Drive position by moving the bellcrank lever all the way rearward, then forward the specified number of detentes (three detent positions on C3 and C5 transmissions; four detentes on A4LD transmissions).
4   With the floor shift lever in the Drive position, apply light forward pressure (toward front of vehicle) to the shifter control lower arm while tightening the trunnion bolt to the torque listed in this Chapter's Specifications. The forward pressure will ensure correct positioning within the drive detent.

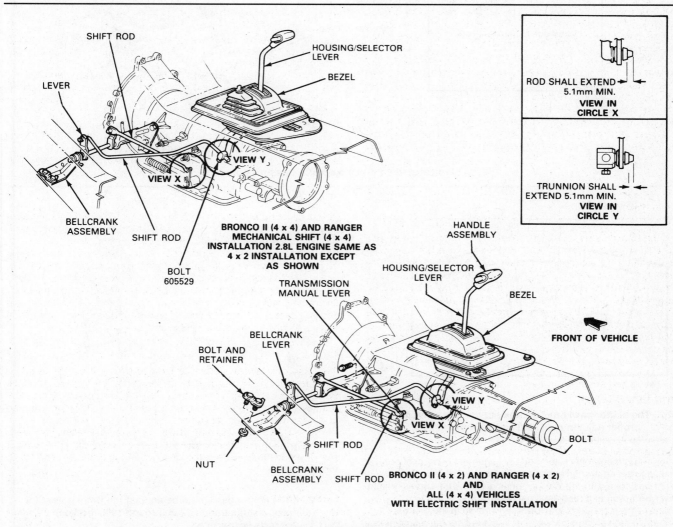

4.2a   Typical shift control linkage (C3 and A4LD transmissions)

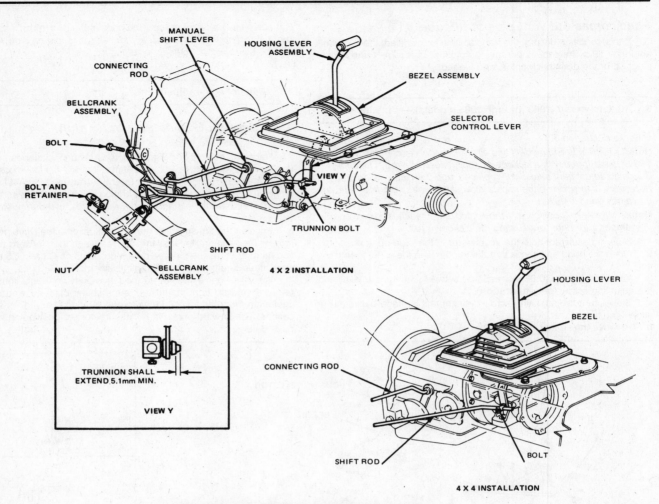

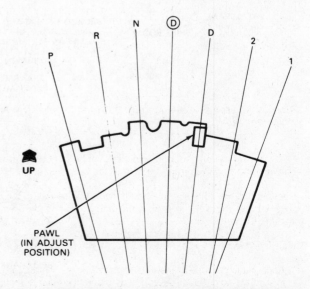

4.2b   Typical shift control linkage (C5 transmissions)

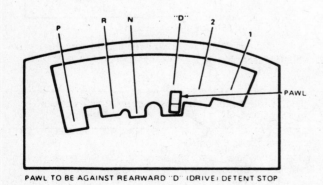

PAWL TO BE AGAINST REARWARD "D" (DRIVE) DETENT STOP

**4.2c   The shifter pawl must be against the Drive detent for
proper adjustment (1983 and 1984 models)**

**4.2d   The shifter pawl must be against the Drive detent for
proper adjustment (1985 through 1988 models)**

5   After adjustment, check for Park engagement. The control lever
must move to the right when engaged in Park. Check the control lever in
all detent positions with the engine running to ensure correct detent/
transmission action and readjust if necessary.

6   Remove the jackstands and lower the vehicle to the ground.

7   Test drive the vehicle slowly at first to make sure the adjustment is
correct.

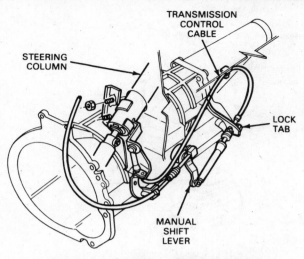

4.10   Shift control cable (1989 and later models)

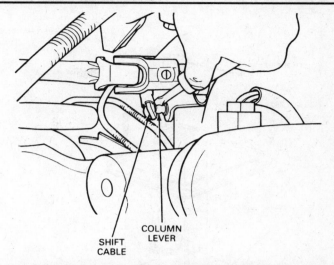

6.1   Carefully pry the end fitting from the steering column lever ball stud

1989 and later models (column shift)

Refer to illustration 4.10

8   Raise the vehicle and support it securely on jackstands.

9   Have an assistant position the column shift selector lever in the Drive (Overdrive) position and hold in place during adjustment. If working by yourself, hang an eight-pound weight on the gear selector lever.

10   Working under the vehicle, pull down on the lock tab on the shift cable and remove the fitting from the manual shift lever ball stud with a screwdriver **(see illustration)**.

11   Position the transmission manual shift lever in the Drive (Overdrive) position by moving the bellcrank lever all the way rearward (counter-clockwise), then forward three detentes (clockwise).

12   Connect the cable end fitting to the manual lever ball stud.

13   Push up on the lock tab and lock the cable in the correctly adjusted position.

14   If used, remove the weight from the gear selector lever.

15   After adjustment, check for Park engagement. The control lever must move to the right when engaged in Park. Check the control lever in all detent positions with the engine running to ensure correct detent/transmission action and adjust and readjust if necessary.

16   Remove the jackstands and lower the vehicle to the ground.

17   Test drive the vehicle slowly at first to make sure the adjustment is correct.

6.2   Remove the nuts securing the shift cable bracket to the steering column bracket and remove the bracket

7B

5   Bellcrank assembly (1983 through 1988 models) – removal and installation

1   Raise the vehicle and support it securely on jackstands.

2   Disconnect the two shift rod ends from the bellcrank assembly levers.

3   Remove the two bolts securing the bellcrank assembly to the bellhousing. Remove the bolt and retainer assembly securing the bellcrank assembly to the frame rail.

4   Remove the bellcrank assembly from the vehicle.

5   Installation is the reverse of the removal Steps with the following additions.

  a) Apply multi-purpose grease to the bellcrank assembly shaft prior to insertion and grease the rod ends before inserting the rod into the assembly. **Note:** *Install new grommets in the bellcrank lever arms prior installing the rods.*

  b) Adjust the shift linkage (see Section 4).

  c) Remove the jackstands and lower the vehicle to the ground.

6   Shift control cable (1989 and later models) – removal and installation

Refer to illustrations 6.1 and 6.2

1   Use a screwdriver to pry the end fitting from the steering column lever ball stud **(see illustration)**.

2   Remove the nuts securing the shift cable bracket to the steering column bracket and remove the bracket **(see illustration)**.

3   Raise the vehicle and support it securely on jackstands.

4   Working under the vehicle, pull down on the lock tab on the shift cable and remove the fitting from the manual lever ball stud with a screwdriver **(see illustration 4.10)**.

5   Bend back the retaining tab and disengage the cable from the transmission bracket. Slide the cable downward from the transmission bracket and remove the cable.

6   Installation is the reverse of the removal procedure with the following additions:

  a) Adjust the shift linkage (see Section 4).

  b) Remove the jackstands and lower the vehicle to the ground.

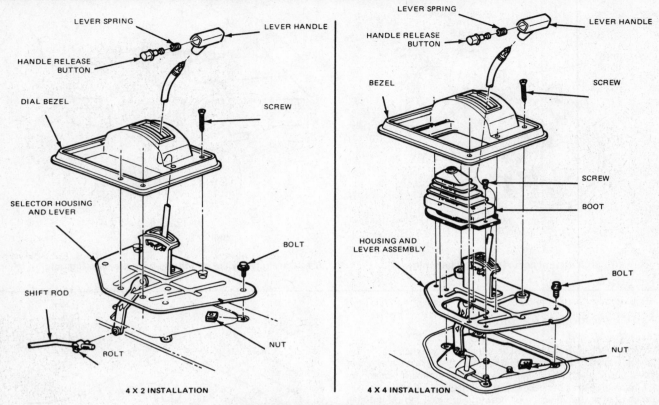

7.3 An exploded view of the shift lever housing assembly

---

7 Shift lever housing (1983 through 1988 models) – removal and installation

Refer to illustration 7.3

Removal

1 Working under the vehicle, loosen the trunnion bolt and remove the trunnion and shift rod from the shift control arm grommet. **Caution:** *Be careful when removing the trunnion to avoid damage to the shifter lower arm.*

2 Working inside the vehicle, move the shift lever to the Drive position.

3 Grab the lever handle firmly, pull straight up and remove the handle/button assembly from the lever **(see illustration)**.

4 Remove the screws securing the trim bezel. On 4WD models, remove the bolts securing the transfer case shift lever boot to the housing. Partially pull the bezel up and disconnect the indicator light electrical connector. Remove the trim bezel.

5 Remove the four bolts (2WD models) or six bolts (4WD models) securing the selector housing to the floor pan and remove the selector housing from the vehicle.

Installation

6 Install the selector housing onto the floor pan and install the four or six mounting bolts.

7 On 4WD models, install the transfer case shift lever boot and bolts.

8 Working under the vehicle, apply grease to the trunnion prior to installing it onto the grommet. Connect the shift rod and trunnion onto the shift control arm. Adjust the shift linkage (see Section 4).

9 Connect the indicator light electrical connector and install the trim bezel and mounting screws.

10 Move the shift lever to the Drive position.

11 Place the shift handle/button on the shift lever. Use a rubber mallet to carefully tap the center of the handle until it is completely seated. **Note:** *If*

the handle's chrome trim ring is not lined up with the shift lever lower character groove, the handle is not completely seated onto the shift lever. Remove the handle and repeat this step until the handle is seated correctly.

---

8 Extension housing oil seal – replacement

Refer to illustrations 8.3, 8.6 and 8.7
Note: *This procedure applies only to 2WD models that are not equipped with a transfer case.*

1 Raise the vehicle and support it securely on jackstands.

2 Remove the driveshaft (see Chapter 8). Some transmission fluid may drain out when the driveshaft universal joint is withdrawn from the extension housing.

3 To remove the oil seal from the end of the extension housing use Ford special tool (part No. T71P-7657-A) to withdraw the seal. If the special tool is not available, and there is access, use a thin-bladed screwdriver or chisel to pry out the oil seal **(see illustration)**.

4 Inspect the oil seal contact surface on the universal joint yoke for scoring or burrs that may damage the new oil seal. If the yoke is damaged in any way, replace it.

5 Inspect the extension housing counterbore for burrs. If found, remove them with emery cloth or medium grit wet-or-dry sandpaper. Use a clean cloth dipped in solvent and remove any sanding residue from the counterbore.

6 Apply silicone sealant to the outside (case) diameter of the new oil seal **(see illustration)**.

7 Install the new extension housing oil seal and make sure it is completely seated in the counterbore **(see illustration)**.

8 Install the driveshaft (see Chapter 8).

9 Lower the vehicle and check the transmission fluid level. Top it up, if necessary (see Chapter 1).

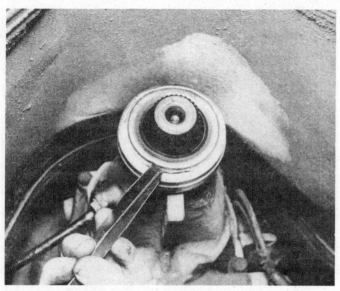

8.3   Be extremely careful not to damage the sealing surface on the housing when prying out the extension housing seal

8.6   Apply a generous bead of silicone sealant to the outside perimeter of the new seal

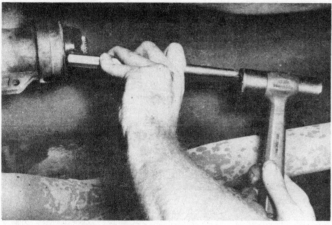

8.7   Installing the new extension housing oil seal with a punch and hammer – a large socket or length of pipe of the proper diameter may also be used to install the oil seal

9.5   Paint across one of the converter studs and the driveplate – this assures correct alignment on reassembly

7B

7   Remove the driveshaft(s) (see Chapter 8). Tie a plastic bag over the end of the extension housing to prevent the entry of dirt and to catch any residual transmission fluid.

8   If equipped, remove the transfer case (see Chapter 7C).

9   Remove the bolt securing the speedometer cable retaining bracket and remove the bracket and bolt as an assembly. Disconnect the speedometer cable from the transmission.

10   Disconnect the shift rod or cable from the transmission manual shift lever (see Sections 4 and 6) and the kickdown rod or cable from the transmission downshift lever.

11   On 1983 through 1988 models, remove the two bolts securing the bellcrank bracket to the torque converter housing.

12   Remove the bolts securing the starter motor, move it out of the way and secure it with wire.

13   Detach the electrical connectors from the transmission.

14   Disconnect the vacuum hose from the transmission vacuum modulator.

15   Place a transmission jack beneath the transmission and apply jack pressure to slightly raise the transmission. Use safety chains to help steady the transmission on the jack.

16   Remove the nuts and bolts securing the rear mount and insulator to the crossmember.

9   Automatic transmission – removal and installation

Refer to illustrations 9.5, 9.21 and 9.23

1   Disconnect the negative cable from the battery. Place the cable out of the way so it cannot accidentally come in contact with the negative terminal of the battery, as this would allow power into the electrical system of the vehicle.

2   Raise the vehicle and support it securely on jackstands.

3   Drain the transmission fluid (see Chapter 1), then reinstall the pan.

4   Remove the torque converter cover.

5   Mark the driveplate and one of the torque converter studs with white paint so they can be installed in the same position **(see illustration)**.

6   Remove the torque converter-to-driveplate nuts. Rotate the crankshaft for access to each nut. Rotate the crankshaft in a clockwise direction only (as viewed from the front). **Caution:** *Do not rotate four-cylinder engines in the opposite direction as the timing belt will jump a tooth and disrupt timing.*

9.21   The oil cooler lines should be removed with the aid of a flare-nut wrench

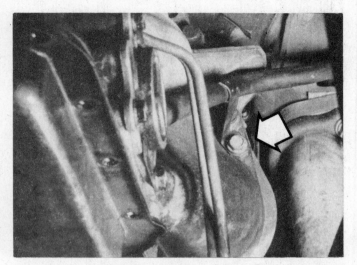

9.23   The location of the transmission filler tube bolt (arrow) (C5 transmission shown)

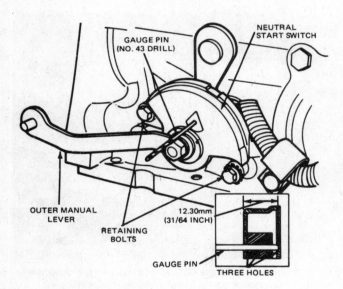

10.4   On the C5 transmission, remove the two bolts, then remove the neutral start switch

17   Remove the crossmember-to-frame side support attaching bolts and remove the crossmember insulator and support and damper (if equipped).

18   Remove the nuts and bolts securing the crossmember to the frame rails, raise the transmission slightly and remove the crossmember.

19   Support the engine with a jack. Use a block of wood under the oil pan to spread the load.

20   Slightly lower the transmission.

21   Disconnect the transmission oil cooler lines from the transmission and plug them to prevent the entry of dirt. Use a flare-nut wrench to avoid rounding off the nuts (see illustration).

22   Remove the lower transmission-to-engine bolts.

23   Remove the bolt securing the filler tube and remove the filler tube (see illustration).

24   Make sure the transmission is securely mounted in the transmission jack. Remove the two upper transmission-to-engine bolts.

25   With all the transmission-to-engine bolts removed, carefully move the transmission to the rear to disengage it from the engine block dowel

pins and make sure the torque converter is detached from the driveplate. Secure the torque converter to the transmission so it won't fall out during removal.

26   Installation is the reverse of the removal Steps with the following additions:

a)   Position the converter in the transmission, making sure the converter hub is fully seated in the pump gear. You'll have to rotate the converter while pushing firmly in. You should hear a number of clicks as you're rotating and pushing it. When there are no more clicks and the converter feels secure in the pump gear, the converter is fully seated.

b)   Rotate the converter to align the studs and the drain plug with the holes in the driveplate.

c)   With the transmission secured to the jack, raise it into position. Be sure to keep it level so the torque converter does not slide forward and disengage from the pump gear.

d)   Move the transmission forward, carefully aligning the dowel pins on the engine with their holes in the transmission.

e)   Guide the torque converter studs through their holes in the driveplate. The white paint mark on the driveplate and the stud made in Step 5 must line up. When the transmission is squarely against the engine, install two transmission-to-engine bolts and tighten them carefully, being sure you're not forcing the engine and transmission together with the bolts. If so, stop and check that there's nothing between the engine and transmission and that the torque converter is fully seated.

f)   When installing the driveplate-to-torque converter nuts, position the driveplate so the pilot hole is in the six o'clock position. First, install one nut through the pilot hole and tighten it, followed by the remaining nuts. Do not attempt to install it in any other way.

g)   After installation, adjust the kickdown rod and gear selector linkage.

h)   Lower the vehicle.

i)   Fill the transmission with the specified fluid (see Chapter 1), run the engine and check for fluid leaks.

---

10   Neutral start switch – removal, installation and adjustment

C5 transmission

Refer to illustration 10.4

1   Raise the vehicle and place it securely on jackstands.

2   Disconnect the downshift linkage rod from the transmission downshift lever.

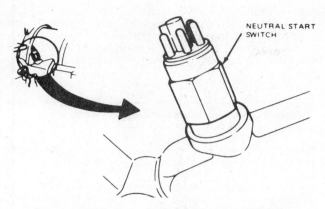

10.13   The neutral start switch for the C3 and A4LD transmissions – the switch is very fragile and a special Ford tool is recommended for removal and installation

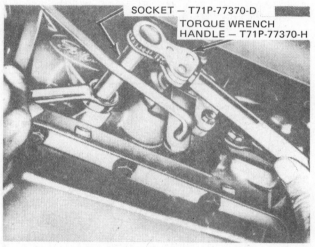

12.3   Adjusting the intermediate band on a C5 transmission

3   Apply penetrating oil to the downshift lever shaft and nut and allow it to soak for a few minutes. Remove the transmission downshift lever retaining nut and lift off the lever.
4   Remove the two bolts securing the neutral start switch **(see illustration)**.
5   Disconnect the electrical connector from the switch and remove the switch.
6   To install, place the switch on the transmission and install the mounting bolts finger tight.
7   Move the shift selector to Neutral.
8   Rotate the switch and insert a No. 43 drill bit into the gauge pin hole. The drill bit must be inserted a full 1/2 inch **(see illustration 10.4)**. Tighten the mounting bolts securely and remove the drill bit.
9   Check that the engine will start only when the shift selector is in the Neutral or Park positions.

C3 and A4LD transmissions

Refer to illustration 10.13
10   Disconnect the negative cable from the battery.
11   Disconnect the electrical connector from the switch.
12   Ford tool (part No. T74P-77247-A) is designed to remove the switch without damaging it.
13   Carefully remove the switch **(see illustration)**. **Caution:** *It is easy to crush or puncture the walls of the switch.*
14   Install the switch and tighten it to the torque listed in this Chapter's Specifications. Use the same special tool used for removal to avoid damaging the switch.

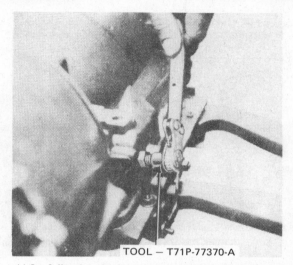

11.3   Adjusting the front band on a C3 transmission

15   Install the electrical connector.
16   Connect the negative cable to the battery.
17   Check that the engine will start only when the shift selector is in the Neutral or Park positions.

11   Front band – adjustment (1983 and 1984 C3 transmissions)

Refer to illustration 11.3
1   Remove the downshift rod from the transmission downshift lever.
2   Clean off all dirt from around the band adjusting screw area located on the left side of the transmission. Remove and discard the locknut.
3   Install a new locknut on the adjusting screw a few turns – don't thread it all the way down. Tighten the adjusting screw using Ford special tool (part No. T71P-77370-A) or a preset torque wrench and socket. If using a preset torque wrench, set it at 120 in-lbs. Tighten the adjusting screw until the tool handle clicks **(see illustration)**.
4   Back off the adjusting screw exactly two turns.
5   Hold the adjusting screw to keep it from turning and tighten the locknut to the torque listed in this Chapter's Specifications.
6   Install the downshift rod on the transmission downshift lever.

12   Intermediate band – adjustment (1983 and 1984 C5 models)

Refer to illustration 12.3
1   Clean off all dirt from around the band adjusting screw area located on the left side of the transmission next to the shift linkage. Remove and discard the locknut.
2   Install a new locknut on the adjusting screw a few turns – don't thread it all the way down.
3   Use the Ford special tool (part No. T71P-77370-H) and socket (part No. T71P-77370-D) or a preset torque wrench and socket. If using a preset torque wrench, set it at 120 in-lbs. Tighten the adjusting screw until the tool handle clicks **(see illustration)**.
4   Back off the adjusting screw exactly 4 1/4 turns.
5   Hold the adjusting screw to keep it from turning and tighten the locknut to the torque listed in this Chapter's Specifications.

13   Low-reverse band – adjustment (1983 and 1984 C5 models)

Refer to illustration 13.3
1   Clean off all dirt from around the band adjusting screw area. Remove the locknut and discard it.
2   Install a new locknut on the adjusting screw a few turns – don't thread it all the way down.

7B

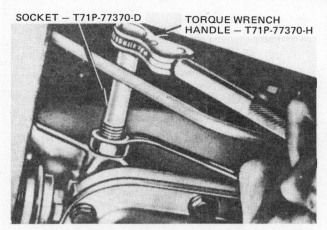

SOCKET — T71P-77370-D   TORQUE WRENCH
HANDLE — T71P-77370-H

13.3 Adjusting the low-reverse band on a C5 transmission

3   Use the Ford special tool (part No. T71P-77370-H) and socket (part No. T71P-77370-D) or a preset torque wrench and socket to tighten the adjusting screw. If using a preset torque wrench, set it at 120 in-lbs. Tighten the adjusting screw until the tool handle clicks (see illustration).

4   Back off the adjusting screw exactly 3 turns.

5   Hold the adjusting screw to keep it from turning and tighten the locknut to the torque listed in this Chapter's Specifications.

14   Transmission mount – check and replacement

1   Insert a large screwdriver or prybar into the space between the transmission extension housing and the crossmember and try to pry the transmission up slightly.

2   The transmission should not move away from the mount much at all.

3   To replace the mount, remove the nuts attaching the mount to the crossmember and the bolts attaching the mount to the transmission.

4   Raise the transmission slightly with a jack and remove the mount, noting which holes are used in the crossmember for proper alignment during installation.

5   Installation is the reverse of the removal procedure. Be sure to tighten the nuts/bolts securely.

Chapter 7 Part C   Transfer case

Contents

7C

Specifications

Lubricant type .... See Chapter 1

Torque specifications   **Ft-lbs** (unless otherwise indicated)
Breather vent .... 72 to 168 in-lbs
Shifter bolts
   Large .... 70 to 90
   Small .... 31 to 42
Heat shield bolts .... 27 to 37
Transfer case-to-transmission bolts
   Manual control .... 25 to 35
   Electronic control .... 25 to 43
Yoke or flange nut
   1983 through 1985 models .... 120 to 150
   1986 and later models .... 150 to 180
   Skid plate-to-frame bolt .... 22 to 30
   Wire connection bracket .... 60 to 84 in-lbs

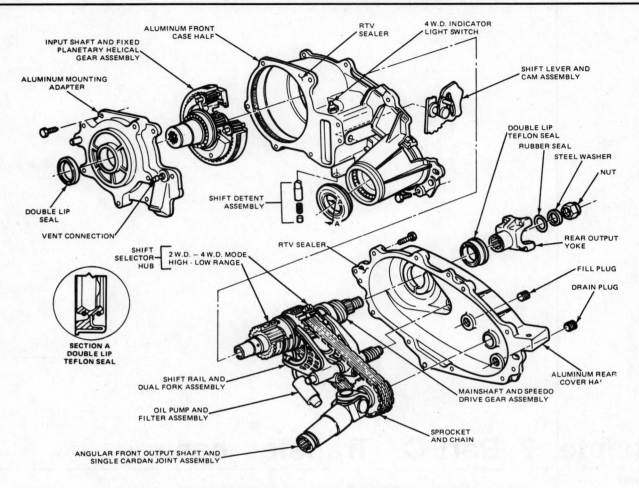

1.1a   An exploded view of the three-piece Borg-Warner 13-50 transfer case

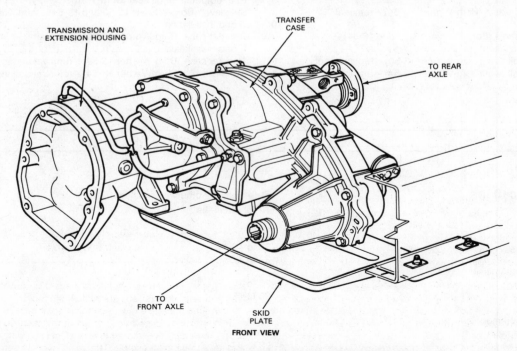

1.1b   The electronically controlled Borg-Warner 13-50 transfer case

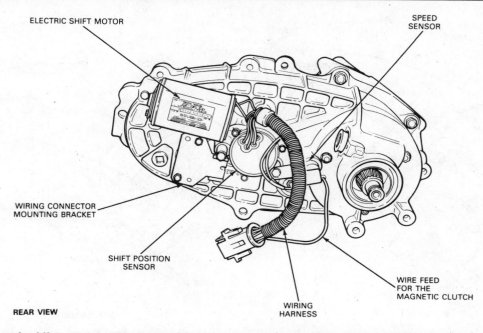

1.1c   The electric shift motor controls the operation of the electronically controlled Borg-Warner 13-50 transfer case

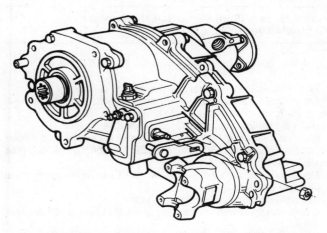

1.1d   The three-piece Borg-Warner 13-54 transfer case

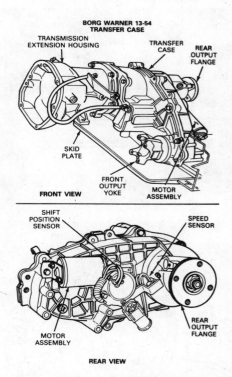

1.1e   The electronically controlled Borg-Warner 13-54 transfer case

1   General information

Refer to illustrations 1.1a, 1.1b, 1.1c, 1.1d, 1.1e and 1.2

Four-wheel drive (4WD) models are equipped with either the Borg-Warner 13-50 or 13-54 transfer case. These are three-piece part-time transfer cases **(see illustrations)**. The units transfer power from the transmission to the rear axle and, when actuated, also to the front driveaxle. The units are lubricated by a positive-displacement oil pump that channels oil flow through drilled holes in the rear output shaft. The pump turns with the rear output shaft and allows towing of the vehicle at maximum legal road speeds for extended distances without disconnecting the front or rear driveshafts.

Beginning in 1987, all Bronco II vehicles equipped with two-wheel drive (2WD) have a Borg-Warner 13-59 transfer case, even though no power is transmitted to the front wheels. The transfer port for the front driveshaft is plugged **(see illustration)**. This transfer case runs dry (does not contain any lubricant).

Due to the complexity of the transfer cases covered in this manual and the need for specialized equipment to perform most service operations, this Chapter contains only general diagnosis, routine maintenance, adjustment and removal and installation procedures.

If the transfer case requires major repair work, it should be taken to a dealer service department or an automotive or transmission repair shop. You can, however, remove and install the transfer case yourself and save the expense, even if the repair work is done by a transmission shop.

7C

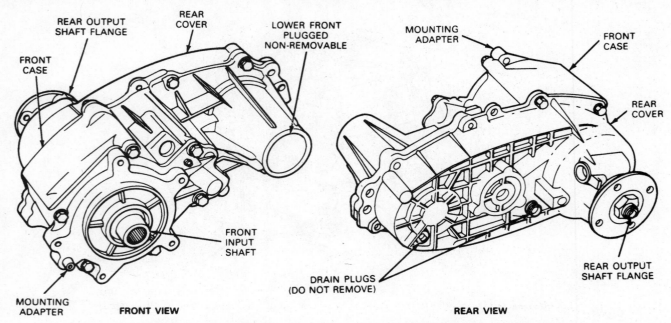

FRONT VIEW   REAR VIEW

1.2   A non-functioning transfer case is used on all 1987 and later 2WD Bronco II models

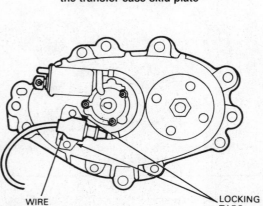

2.2   On models so equipped, remove the four bolts and remove the transfer case skid plate

2   Transfer case (Borg-Warner 13-50) – removal and installation

Refer to illustrations 2.2, 2.4, 2.5, 2.8, 2.9, 2.10, 2.12, 2.13a, 2.13b and 2.15

1   Raise the vehicle and support it securely on jackstands.

2   On models so equipped, remove the four bolts securing the skid plate to the frame and remove it **(see illustration)**.

3   Drain the lubricant from the transfer case (see Chapter 1).

4   Squeeze the locking tabs together then pull the electrical connector apart and disconnect the electrical connector from the transfer case **(see illustration)**.

5   Disconnect the 4WD indicator switch electrical connector from the transfer case **(see illustration)**.

6   Disconnect both driveshafts (see Chapter 8).

7   Disconnect the speedometer cable assembly from the transfer case rear cover.

8   On electronically controlled models, disconnect the vent hose from the mounting bracket **(see illustration)**.

2.4   Squeeze the locking tabs together and disconnect the electrical connector

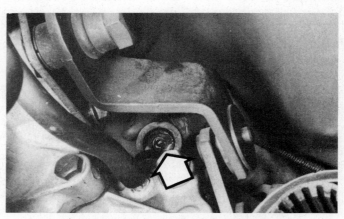

2.5   The arrow points to the 4WD indicator plug

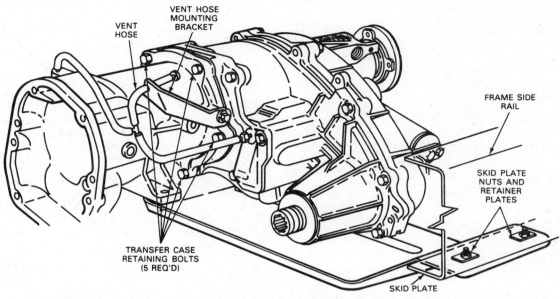

2.8   Disconnect the vent hose from the mounting bracket on electronically controlled models

9   On manually controlled models, disconnect the vent hose from nipple on the housing **(see illustration)**.

10   On manually controlled models, remove the large bolt and the small bolt retaining the shifter to the extension housing **(see illustration)**. Pull on the control lever unit until the bushing slides off the transfer case shift lever pin. If necessary, unscrew the shift lever from the control lever.

11   On models so equipped, remove the bolts securing the heat shield to the transfer case and remove it **(see illustration)**. **Warning:** *The cata-lytic converter is located next to the heat shield and is extremely hot after the engine has been run. Be careful when working around the converter and, if possible, allow the converter to cool down several hours prior to working around it.*

12   Place a transmission jack beneath the transfer case and apply jack pressure to slightly raise the transfer case **(see illustration)**. Use safety chains to help steady the transfer case on the jack.

13   Remove the five bolts securing the transfer case to the transmission and extension housing **(see illustrations)**.

14   Slide the transfer case rearward and off the transmission output shaft, then lower the transfer case from the vehicle. Remove and discard the gasket between the transfer case and the extension housing.

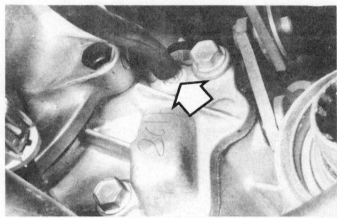

2.9   The vent hose slips over a nipple on the housing (arrow)

7C

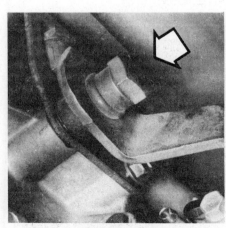

2.10   Disconnect the large bolt securing the shifter to the extension housing

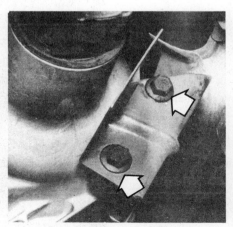

2.11   Two bolts secure the heat shield to the transfer case (arrows)

2.12   Use a block of wood between the jack and transfer case when supporting the transfer case

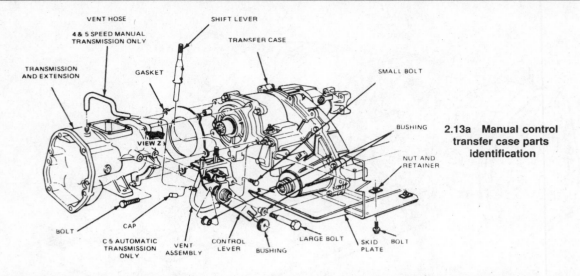

2.13a   Manual control transfer case parts identification

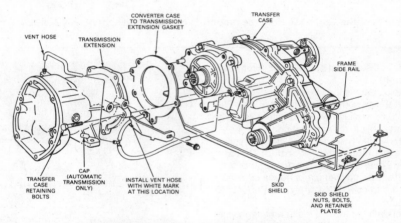

2.13b   Electronic control transfer case mounting

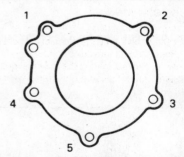

2.15   Transfer case mounting bolt tightening sequence

15   Installation is the reverse of the removal Steps with the following additions:

a) Install a new gasket between the transfer case and the extension housing.

b) Position the transfer case on a jack, raise the transfer case into position, then slide the transfer case onto the transmission output shaft, making sure the splines align, until the transfer case seats over the dowel pin.

c) Install the five bolts securing the transfer case and tighten to the torque listed in this Chapter's Specifications and in the torque sequence shown **(see illustration)**. **Note:** *On manually controlled*

models, always tighten the large bolt securing the shifter to the extension housing before tightening the small bolt.

d) On models so equipped, install the vent assembly so the white marking on the hose is positioned in the notch in the shifter or the mounting bracket (electronically controlled models). **Note:** *The upper end of the vent hose should be two inches above the top of the shifter on manually controlled models.*

e) Refill the transfer case lubricant (see Chapter 1).

3   Shift lever (Borg-Warner 13-50 and 13-54) – removal and installation

Refer to illustration 3.3

Removal

Note: *Remove the shift ball only if the shift ball, boot or lever is to be replaced. If the ball, boot or lever are not being replaced, remove the ball, boot and lever as an assembly.*

1   Remove the plastic insert from the shift ball. Warm the ball with a heat gun or portable hair dryer to 140 to 180-degrees F and knock the ball off the lever with a piece of wood and a hammer. Be careful not to damage the finish on the shift lever.

2   Remove the rubber boot and the floor pan cover.

3   Disconnect the vent hose from the control lever **(see illustration)**.

4   Unscrew the shift lever from the control lever.

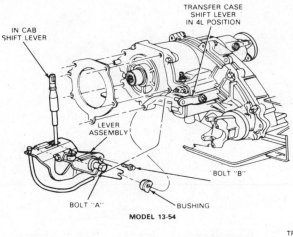

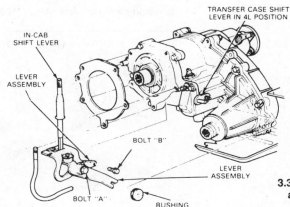

3.3 Manual control transfer case shift lever assembly (Borg-Warner 13-50 and 13-54)

5   Remove the large and small housing bolts securing the shifter to the extension housing. Remove the control lever and bushings.

Installation

6   Prior to installing the shift assembly, move the transfer case lever to the "4L" position (lever down) **(see illustration 3.3).**
7   Install the large and small bolts finger tight and move the cam plate rearward until the bottom chamfered corner of the neutral lug just contacts the forward right edge of the shift lever.
8   Hold the cam plate in position and tighten the large bolt first, then the smaller one. Tighten the bolts to the torque listed in this Chapter's Specifications.
9   Attach the shift lever to the control lever and move the in-cab shift lever to all positions and check for positive engagement. There should be clearance between the shift lever and the cam plate in the "2H" front, "4H" rear (clearance not to exceed 0.13-in) and "4L" shift positions.
10   Tighten the shift lever-to-control lever bolts securely.
11   Install the vent assembly so the white mark on the housing is indexed into the notch in the shifter, if applicable. **Note:** *The upper end of the vent hose should be two inches above the top of the shifter and positioned inside of the shift lever boot.*
12   Install the floor pan cover and the rubber boot.
13   Warm the shift ball with a heat gun or portable hair dryer to 140 to 180-degrees F and carefully tap the ball onto the lever with a piece of wood and a hammer. Install the plastic insert into the shift ball. **Note:** *The shift ball must be tapped onto the lever until all of the knurled portion of the shaft is covered.*
14   Check the transfer case for proper operation.

4   Electronic shift controls (Borg-Warner 13-50 and 13-54) - removal and installation

1983 through 1988 models
Refer to illustrations 4.2 and 4.3
1   Insert a small screwdriver into the notch in the light lens and carefully pry off the lens. Remove both lenses.
2   Remove the two screws securing the console, pull down on the rear of it, then push it forward and disengage it from the front mounting clips **(see illustration).**

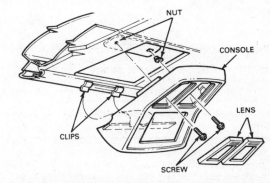

4.2 Two screws and a pair of mounting clips hold the overhead console in place

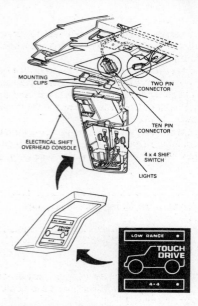

4.3   Disconnect the electrical connectors and remove the console

3   Disconnect the two electrical connectors and remove the console **(see illustration)**.
4   Installation is the reverse of the removal Steps.

1989 and later models

Refer to illustration 4.9
5   Disconnect the negative cable from the battery.
6   Open the ashtray and remove the two screws securing the ashtray and the instrument cluster trim panel. Remove the ashtray.
7   Pull rearward around the perimeter of the instrument cluster trim panel and unsnap it. Depress the hazard warning switch on the steering column and remove the instrument cluster trim panel.
8   Remove the screws securing the shift control assembly and partially pull the assembly out from the instrument panel.
9   Disconnect the electrical connector from the control assembly and remove the assembly **(see illustration)**.
10   Installation is the reverse of the removal Steps.

5   Electronic control module (Borg-Warner 13-50) – removal and installation

Refer to illustration 5.3
1   Disconnect the negative cable from the battery.
2   Remove the instrument panel pad.
3   Remove the two screws securing the module to the instrument panel **(see illustration)**.
4   Pull the module partially up and disconnect the three electrical connectors from it, then remove the module assembly.
5   Installation is the reverse of the removal Steps.

6   Front output shaft oil seal (Borg-Warner 13-50) – replacement

Removal

1   Raise the vehicle and support it securely on jackstands.
2   Remove the front driveshaft from the axle input yoke. Loosen the clamp securing the driveshaft boot to the transfer case. Pull the driveshaft and boot assembly out of the transfer case front output shaft.

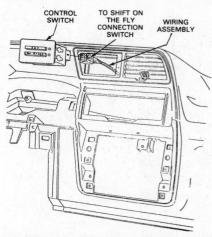

4.9   Electronic shift control switch (1989 and later models)

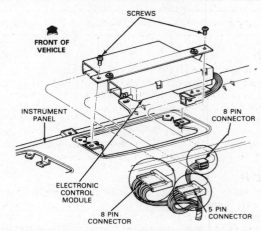

5.3   Remove the screws, disconnect the electrical connectors and remove the module from the instrument panel

3   Drain the transfer case lubricant (see Chapter 1).
4   To remove the front oil seal from the output housing bore use Ford special tool (part No. 1175-AC) and slide hammer (part No. T50T-100-A), or equivalent and withdraw the oil seal.

Installation

5   Inspect the oil seal contact surface on the housing for scoring or burrs that may damage the new oil seal. If found, remove them with emery cloth or medium grit wet-and-dry sandpaper. Use a clean cloth dipped in solvent and remove any sanding residue from the counterbore.
6   Apply multi-purpose grease to the oil seal. Position the seal into the front output shaft housing bore and make sure the seal is not cocked in the bore.
7   To drive the front oil seal into the output housing bore use Ford special tool (part No. T83T-7065-B) and driver (part No. T80T-4000-W), or carefully drive the seal into the bore with a hammer and a large socket or piece of pipe of the appropriate size.
8   Clean the transfer case front output female splines and apply multi-purpose grease to them. Insert the front driveshaft splined shaft into the female splines.
9   Connect the front driveshaft to the axle input yoke and tighten the bolts to the torque listed in the Chapter 8 Specifications.
10   Install the driveshaft boot over the external groove on the transfer case front input shaft and secure the boot with the clamp.
11   Refill the transfer case lubricant (refer to Chapter 1).
12   Remove the jackstands and lower the vehicle.

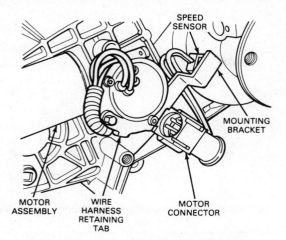

9.5 Shift motor electrical connector location

---

7 Rear output shaft oil seal (Borg-Warner 13-50) – replacement

Removal

1 Raise the vehicle and support it securely on jackstands.
2 Remove the rear driveshaft from the transfer case output shaft yoke or flange (see Chapter 8) and wire the driveshaft out of the way.
3 Remove the nut, steel washer and rubber seal securing the output shaft flange or yoke. Remove the flange or yoke from the output shaft.
4 To remove the rear output shaft oil seal from the transfer case use Ford special tool (part No. 1175-AC) and slide hammer (part No. T50T-100-A), or equivalent and withdraw the oil seal.

Installation

5 Inspect the oil seal contact surface on the housing for scoring or burrs that may damage the new oil seal. If found, remove them with emery cloth or medium-grit wet-and-dry sandpaper. Use a clean cloth dipped in solvent to remove any sanding residue from the counterbore.
6 Apply multipurpose grease to the oil seal lips and circumference. Position the seal into the rear output shaft housing bore and make sure the seal is not cocked in the bore.
7 To drive the rear oil seal into the output housing bore use Ford special tool (part No. T83T-7065-B) and driver (part No. T80T-4000-W), or carefully drive the seal into the bore with a hammer and a large socket or piece of pipe of the appropriate size.
8 Install the flange (or yoke), rubber seal, steel washer and nut. Tighten the nut to the torque listed in this Chapter's Specifications.
9 Connect the rear driveshaft to the transfer case output shaft flange or yoke (see Chapter 8).
10 Remove the jackstands and lower the vehicle.

---

8 Transfer case (Borg-Warner 13-59) – removal and installation

Removal

1 Raise the vehicle and support it securely on jackstands.
2 Disconnect the rear driveshaft from the transfer case output flange (see Chapter 8).
3 Disconnect the speedometer cable assembly from the transfer case rear cover.
4 Place a transmission jack beneath the transfer case and apply jack pressure to slightly raise the transfer case. Use safety chains to steady the transfer case on the jack.
5 Remove the five bolts securing the transfer case to the transmission extension housing, slide the transfer case to the rear, off the output shaft and lower it from the vehicle. Discard the gasket.

Installation

6 Clean off all old gasket residue from both sealing surfaces with lacquer thinner. Install a new gasket between the transmission extension housing and the transfer case.
7 Slide the transfer case onto the transmission output shaft, making sure the splines align, until the transfer case seats over the dowel pin.
8 Install the five bolts securing the transfer case and tighten to the torque listed in this Chapter's Specifications and in the torque sequence shown (see illustration 2.15).
9 Connect the speedometer cable assembly to the transfer case and tighten the bolt to the torque listed in this Chapter's Specifications.
10 Connect the rear driveshaft to the transfer case output flange (see Chapter 8).

---

9 Transfer case (Borg-Warner 13-54) – removal and installation

Removal and installation

Refer to illustration 9.5

1 Raise the vehicle and support it securely on jackstands.
2 On models so equipped, remove the four bolts securing the skid plate to the frame and remove it.
3 Drain the lubricant from the transfer case (see Chapter 1).
4 On models so equipped, remove the damper from the transfer case.
5 On electronically controlled models, squeeze the locking tabs together, then pull the electrical connector apart. Disconnect the electrical connector from the transfer case motor and from the mounting bracket (see illustration).
6 Disconnect the 4WD indicator switch wire connector from the transfer case.
7 Disconnect both driveshafts (see Chapter 8).
8 Disconnect the speedometer cable assembly from the transfer case rear cover.
9 Disconnect the vent hose from the mounting bracket. **Warning:** *The catalytic converter is located adjacent to the vent hose and is extremely hot after the engine has been run. Be careful when working around the converter and, if possible, allow the converter to cool down several hours prior to working around it.*
10 On manually controlled models, remove the nut from the shift lever and remove the shift lever.
11 On manually controlled models, remove the large bolt and the small bolt retaining the shifter to the extension housing. Pull on the control lever unit until the bushing slides off the transfer case shift lever pin.
12 Place a transmission jack beneath the transfer case and apply jack pressure to slightly raise the transfer case. Use safety chains to steady the transfer case on the jack.
13 Remove the five bolts securing the transfer case to the transmission extension housing.
14 Slide the transfer case rearward and off the transmission output shaft, then lower the transfer case from the vehicle. Remove and discard the gasket between the transfer case and the extension housing.
15 Installation is the reverse of the removal procedure with the following additions:
  a) Install a new gasket between the transfer case and the extension housing.
  b) Slide the transfer case onto the transmission output shaft until the transfer case seats over the dowel pin.
  c) Install the five bolts securing the transfer case and tighten to the torque listed in this Chapter's Specifications and in the torque sequence shown (see illustration 2.15). **Note:** *On manually controlled models, always tighten the large bolt securing the shifter to the extension housing before tightening the small bolt.*
  d) Install the vent assembly so the white marking on the hose is positioned in the notch in the shifter or the mounting bracket (electrically controlled models). **Note:** *The upper end of the vent hose should be 3/4-inch above the top of the shifter on manually controlled models.*
  e) Refill the lubricant in the transfer case (see Chapter 1).

7C

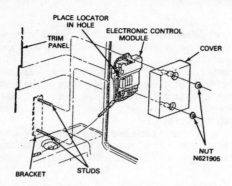

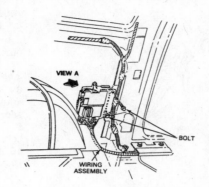

10.2   Electronic control module mounting nuts and cover (Ranger models)

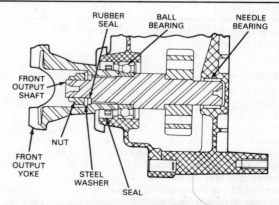

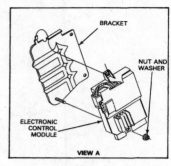

10.3 Electronic control module mounting bolts (Bronco II models)

10   Electronic control module (Borg-Warner 13-54) – removal and installation

Refer to illustrations 10.2 and 10.3

1   Disconnect the negative cable from the battery.
2   On Ranger models, working inside the cab, remove the two nuts securing the control module and cover to the trim panel behind the driver's seat **(see illustration)**. Remove the cover.
3   On Bronco II models, working inside the cab, remove the access panel cover on the side trim panel behind the driver's seat. Remove the two bolts securing the control module and bracket **(see illustration)**.
4   Pull the control module part way out and disconnect the electrical connector(s) from the module. Remove the control module.
5   Installation is the reverse of the removal steps.

11   Front output shaft oil seal (Borg-Warner 13-54) – replacement

Refer to illustration 11.6

Removal

1   Raise the vehicle and support it securely on jackstands.
2   On models so equipped, remove the damper from the transfer case.
3   Remove the skid plate from the frame.
4   Drain the transfer case lubricant (see Chapter 1).
5   Remove the front driveshaft from the transfer case output shaft (see Chapter 8). Tie it up out of the way.
6   Use a 30 mm thin-walled socket to remove the front output shaft nut, washer, rubber seal and yoke **(see illustration)**.
7   Remove the dust seal from the yoke opening of the transfer case.
8   Carefully pry out the oil seal with a large screwdriver.

Installation

9   Inspect the oil seal contact surface on the housing for scoring or burrs that may damage the new oil seal. If found, remove them with emery cloth or medium-grit wet-and-dry sandpaper. Use a clean cloth dipped in solvent and remove any sanding residue from the counterbore.
10   Apply multi-purpose grease to the oil seal. Position the seal into the front output shaft housing bore and make sure the oil seal is not cocked in the bore.
11   To drive the front oil seal into the output housing bore use Ford special tool (part No. T83T-7065-B) and driver (part No. T80T-4000-W), or carefully drive the seal into the bore with a hammer and a large socket or piece of pipe of the appropriate size.
12   Install the front yoke onto the splines, then install the rubber seal, steel washer and nut. Tighten the nut to the torque listed in this Chapter's Specifications.
13   Connect the front driveshaft (see Chapter 8).
14   Refill the transfer case with lubricant (see Chapter 1).
15   Remove the jackstands and lower the vehicle.

12   Rear output shaft oil seal (Borg-Warner 13-54 and 13-59) – replacement

Removal

1   Raise the vehicle and support it securely on jackstands.
2   Remove the rear driveshaft from the transfer case output shaft flange or yoke and wire the driveshaft out of the way (see Chapter 8).
3   Use a 30 mm thin-walled socket to remove the nut securing the flange or yoke.
4   Remove the steel washer and rubber seal, then remove the flange or yoke.
5   Carefully pry and pull on the outer curved lip of the oil seal and remove it from the transfer case.

Installation

6   Inspect the oil seal contact surface on the housing for scoring or burrs that may damage the new oil seal. If found, remove them with emery cloth or medium grit wet-and-dry sandpaper. Use a clean cloth dipped in solvent and remove any sanding residue from the counterbore.
7   Apply multi-purpose grease to the oil seal lips and circumference. On 13-59 models, also fill the speedometer gear cavity with multi-purpose grease. On all models, position the seal into the front output shaft housing bore and make sure the oil seal is not cocked in the bore.
8   To drive the front oil seal into the output housing bore use Ford special tool (part No. T83T-7065-B) and driver (part No. T80T-4000-W), or carefully drive the seal into the bore with a hammer and a large socket or piece of pipe of the appropriate size.
9   Install the output flange or yoke onto the output shaft splines.
10   Install the rubber seal, steel washer and nut. Tighten the nut to the torque listed in this Chapter's Specifications.
11   Connect the rear driveshaft to the transfer case output shaft flange (see Chapter 8).
12   Remove the jackstands and lower the vehicle.

11.6   Front output shaft oil seal components

Chapter 8 Clutch and drivetrain

Contents

Specifications

Clutch

Type	Single dry plate, diaphragm spring
Actuation	Hydraulic
Driveshaft type	One or two-piece with CV, single or double cardan type joints

Rear axle

Type	Integral carrier
Ring gear size	6.75 in, 7.5 in or 8.8 in. See identification tag
Lubricant type	See Chapter 1

Front driveaxle

Type	Dana Model 28
Hubs	Manual or optional automatic locking hubs
Lubricant type	See Chapter 1

Torque specifications   Ft-lbs (unless otherwise indicated)

Clutch

Clutch housing-to-engine block bolt	28 to 38
Clutch housing-to-transmission bolt or nut	30 to 40
Pressure plate-to-flywheel bolt	15 to 24
Clutch master cylinder-to-firewall bolt	15 to 20
Dust cover-to-clutch housing bolt	60 to 120 in-lbs
Slave cylinder-to-clutch housing bolt	15 to 20
Slave cylinder-to-transmission nut	156 to 240 in-lbs

8

Torque specifications (conrinued)

Ft-lbs (unless otherwise indicated)

Driveshaft

Double cardan type driveshaft	
Flange-to-transfer case bolts	
1983 and 1984	12 to 15
1985 on	12 to 16
Flange-to-rear axle bolts	
1983 and 1984	12 to 15
1985 through 1989	61 to 87
1990 on	70 to 95
Driveshaft-to-companion flange bolt	70 to 95
Front driveshaft U-bolt nuts	8 to 15
Front driveshaft-to-front yoke bolt	10 to 15

Rear axle

Cover bolts (with metal cover)	25 to 35
Cover bolts (with plastic cover)	15 to 20
Oil filler plug	15 to 30
Pinion shaft lock bolt	15 to 30
Leaf spring U-bolt nuts	55 to 75
Rear shock absorber-to-axle bracket bolt or nut	40 to 60

Front axle

Pivot bolt	120 to 150
Pivot bracket-to-frame nut	70 to 92
Axle stud	155 to 205
Lower balljoint nut	
1983 through 1985	80
1986 on	95 to 110
Upper balljoint nut	
1983 through 1985	110
1986 on	85 to 110
Bearing cap bolts	35 to 40
Carrier shear bolt	75 to 95
Front shock absorber-to-radius arm nut	42 to 72
Front spring seat nut	70 to 100
Front radius arm bracket bolt	
Front	27 to 37
Lower	160 to 220
Differential pinion shaft lock bolt	15 to 30
Differential cover bolt	15 to 20

1   General information

The information in this Chapter deals with the components from the rear of the engine to the rear wheels, except for the transmission (and transfer case, if equipped), which are dealt with in the previous Chapter. For the purposes of this Chapter, these components are grouped into three categories; clutch, driveshaft and rear axle. Separate Sections within this Chapter offer general descriptions and checking procedures for components in each of the three groups.

Since nearly all the procedures covered in this Chapter involve working under the vehicle, make sure it's securely supported on sturdy jackstands or on a hoist where the vehicle can be easily raised and lowered.

2   Clutch – description and check

Refer to illustration 2.6

1   All vehicles with a manual transmission use a single dry plate, diaphragm spring type clutch. The clutch disc has a splined hub which allows it to slide along the splines of the transmission input shaft. The clutch and pressure plate are held in contact by spring pressure exerted by the diaphragm in the pressure plate.

2   The clutch release system is operated by hydraulic pressure. The hydraulic release system consists of the clutch pedal, a master cylinder and fluid reservoir, the hydraulic line, a release cylinder and release lever (1983 and 1984 models), or internal slave cylinder (1985 and later mod-

els) and the clutch release (or throwout) bearing.

3   When pressure is applied to the clutch pedal to release the clutch on 1983 and 1984 models, hydraulic pressure is exerted against the outer end of the clutch release lever. As the lever pivots, it pushes against the release bearing. This pressure pushes against the diaphragm spring of the pressure plate assembly, which in turn releases the clutch plate.

4   On 1985 and later models, an internal slave cylinder mounted concentrically on the transmission input shaft pushes directly on the release bearing. This eliminates the need for a release lever.

5   Terminology can be a problem when discussing the clutch components because common names are in some cases different from those used by the manufacturer. For example, the driven plate is also called the clutch plate or disc, the clutch release bearing is sometimes called a throwout bearing, the release cylinder is sometimes called the operating or slave cylinder.

6   Other than to replace components with obvious damage, some preliminary checks should be performed to diagnose clutch problems.

   a) The first check should be of the fluid level in the clutch master cylinder. If the fluid level is low, add fluid as necessary and inspect the hydraulic system for leaks. If the master cylinder reservoir has run dry, bleed the system as described in Section 9 and retest the clutch operation.

   b) To check "clutch spin down time," run the engine at normal idle speed with the transmission in Neutral (clutch pedal up – engaged). Disengage the clutch (pedal down), wait several seconds and shift the transmission into Reverse. No grinding noise should be heard. A grinding noise would most likely indicate a problem in the pressure plate or the clutch disc.

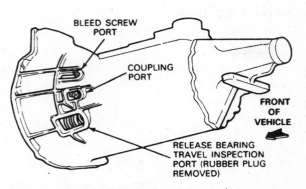

2.6   **On later models, release cylinder and bearing travel can be checked through the inspection port**

c) To check for complete clutch release, run the engine (with the parking brake applied to prevent movement) and hold the clutch pedal   approximately 1/2-inch from the floor. Shift the transmission between 1st gear and Reverse several times. If the shift is hard or the transmission grinds, component failure is indicated. Check the release cylinder pushrod travel (1983 and 1984 models) or the release bearing travel (later models equipped with an inspection port) **(see illustration)**. With the clutch pedal depressed completely, the release cylinder pushrod (or cylinder) should extend substantially. If it doesn't, check the fluid level in the clutch master cylinder (see Chapter 1). On 1985 and later models, bleed the system (see Section 9).
d) Visually inspect the pivot bushing at the top of the clutch pedal to make sure there is no binding or excessive play.
e) On 1983 and 1984 models, crawl under the vehicle and make sure the clutch release lever is solidly mounted on the ball stud.

3.5a   **Loosen the pressure plate bolts (arrows) a little at a time in a criss-cross pattern**

3   Clutch components – removal, inspection and installation

Warning: *Dust produced by clutch wear and deposited on clutch components may contain asbestos, which is hazardous to your health. DO NOT blow it out with compressed air and DO NOT inhale it. DO NOT use gasoline or petroleum-based solvents to remove the dust. Brake system cleaner should be used to flush the dust into a drain pan. After the clutch components are wiped clean with a rag, dispose of the contaminated rags and cleaner in a covered, marked container.*

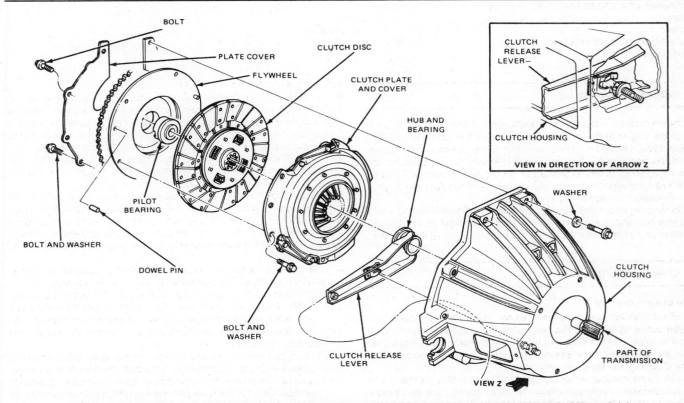

3.5b   **An exploded view of the typical clutch assembly used on 2.0L and 2.3L engines (1983 and 1984 models)**

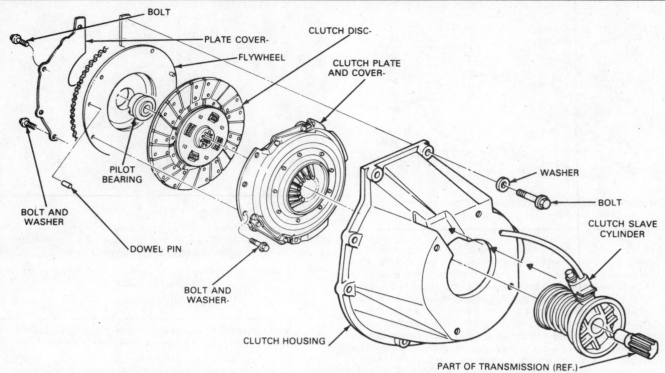

3.5c An exploded view of the clutch assembly for 1985 through 1987 4-cylinder engines – note the elimination of the release lever (V6 engines similar)

Note: *The 1985 and later models are equipped with a hydraulic clutch release system that eliminates the clutch release lever. The differences are noted in the following procedure.*

Removal

Refer to illustrations 3.5a, 3.5b and 3.5c

1   Access to the clutch components is normally accomplished by removing the transmission (and transfer case on 4x4 models), leaving the engine in the vehicle. If, of course, the engine is being removed for major overhaul, then check the clutch for wear and replace worn components as necessary. However, the relatively low cost of the clutch components compared to the time and trouble spent gaining access to them warrants their replacement anytime the engine or transmission is removed, unless they are new or in near perfect condition. The following procedures are based on the assumption the engine will stay in place.

2   Referring to Chapter 7 Part A and Part C, remove the transmission and transfer case (if equipped) from the vehicle. Support the engine while the transmission is out. Preferably, an engine hoist should be used to support it from above. However, if a jack is used underneath the engine, make sure a piece of wood is positioned between the jack and oil pan to spread the load. **Caution:** *The pickup for the oil pump is very close to the bottom of the oil pan. If the pan is bent or distorted in any way, engine oil starvation could occur.*

3   To support the clutch disc during removal, install a clutch alignment tool through the clutch disc hub.

4   Carefully inspect the flywheel and pressure plate for indexing marks. The marks are usually an X, an O or a white letter. If they cannot be found, scribe marks yourself so the pressure plate and the flywheel will be in the same alignment during installation.

5   Turning each bolt only 1/4-turn at a time, loosen the pressure plate-to-flywheel bolts **(see illustration)**. Work in a criss-cross pattern until all spring pressure is relieved evenly. Then hold the pressure plate securely and completely remove the bolts, followed by the pressure plate and clutch disc **(see illustrations)**.

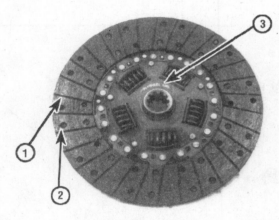

3.9 The clutch disc

1   *Lining – this will wear down in use*
2   *Rivets – these secure the lining and will damage the flywheel or pressure plate if allowed to contact the surfaces*
3   *Marks – "Flywheel side" or similar*

Inspection

Refer to illustrations 3.9 and 3.11

6   Ordinarily, when a problem occurs in the clutch, it can be attributed to wear of the clutch driven plate assembly (clutch disc). However, all components should be inspected at this time.

7   Inspect the flywheel for cracks, heat checking, grooves and other obvious defects. If the imperfections are slight, a machine shop can machine the surface flat and smooth, which is highly recommended regardless of the surface appearance. Refer to Chapter 2 for the flywheel removal and installation procedure.

8   Inspect the pilot bearing (see Section 5).

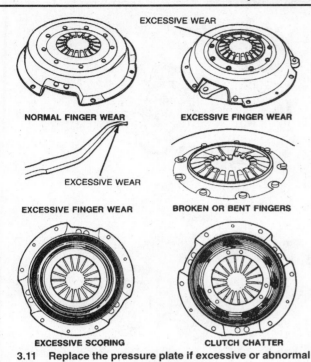

EXCESSIVE WEAR

NORMAL FINGER WEAR   EXCESSIVE FINGER WEAR

EXCESSIVE WEAR

EXCESSIVE FINGER WEAR   BROKEN OR BENT FINGERS

EXCESSIVE SCORING   CLUTCH CHATTER

3.11   Replace the pressure plate if excessive or abnormal wear is noted

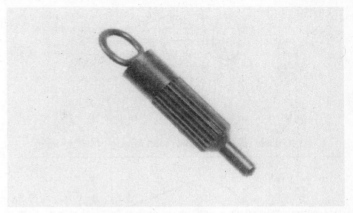

3.13   A clutch alignment tool can be purchased at most auto parts stores and eliminates all guesswork when centering the clutch disc in the pressure plate

place grease on the release lever contact areas and the transmission input shaft bearing retainer.

17   If removed, install the clutch release bearing as described in Section 4.

18   Install the transmission, slave cylinder and all components removed previously. Tighten all fasteners to the torque values listed in this Chapter's Specifications.

9   Inspect the lining on the clutch disc. There should be at least 1/16-inch of lining above the rivet heads. Check for loose rivets, distortion, cracks, broken springs and other obvious damage **(see illustration)**. As mentioned above, ordinarily the clutch disc is routinely replaced, so if in doubt about the condition, replace it with a new one.

10   The release bearing should also be replaced along with the clutch disc (see Section 4).

11   Check the machined surfaces and the diaphragm spring fingers of the pressure plate **(see illustration)**. If the surface is grooved or otherwise damaged, replace the pressure plate. Also check for obvious damage, distortion, cracking, etc. Light glazing can be removed with sandpaper or emery cloth. If a new pressure plate is required, new and factory-rebuilt units are available.

Installation

Refer to illustration 3.13

12   Before installation, clean the flywheel and pressure plate machined surfaces with lacquer thinner, acetone or brake system cleaner. It's important that no oil or grease is on these surfaces or the lining of the clutch disc. Handle the parts only with clean hands.

13   Position the clutch disc and pressure plate against the flywheel with the clutch held in place with an alignment tool **(see illustration)**. Make sure it's installed properly (most replacement clutch plates will be marked "flywheel side" or something similar – if not marked, install the clutch disc with the flat side of the hub toward the flywheel).

14   Tighten the pressure plate-to-flywheel bolts only finger tight, working around the pressure plate.

15   Center the clutch disc by ensuring the alignment tool extends through the splined hub and into the pilot bearing in the crankshaft. Wiggle the tool up, down or side-to-side as needed to bottom the tool in the pilot bearing. Tighten the pressure plate-to-flywheel bolts a little at a time, working in a criss-cross pattern to prevent distorting the cover. After all of the bolts are snug, tighten them to the torque listed in this Chapter's Specifications. Remove the alignment tool.

16   On 1983 and 1984 models, using high-temperature grease, lubricate the inner groove of the release bearing (see Section 4). On all models, also

4   Clutch release bearing – removal, inspection and installation

Warning: *Dust produced by clutch wear and deposited on clutch components may contain asbestos, which is hazardous to your health. DO NOT blow it out with compressed air and DO NOT inhale it. DO NOT use gasoline or petroleum-based solvents to remove the dust. Brake system cleaner should be used to flush the dust into a drain pan. After the clutch components are wiped clean with a rag, dispose of the contaminated rags and cleaner in a covered, marked container.*

1983 and 1984 models
Removal

1   Disconnect the negative cable from the battery.

2   Remove the transmission and clutch housing (see Chapter 7 Part A).

3   Remove the clutch release lever from the ball stud, then remove the bearing from the lever **(see illustration 3.5b)**.

Inspection

4   Hold the center of the bearing and rotate the outer portion while applying pressure. If the bearing doesn't turn smoothly or if it's noisy, replace it with a new one. Wipe the bearing with a clean rag and inspect it for damage, wear and cracks. Don't immerse the bearing in solvent – it's sealed for life and to do so would ruin it. Also check the release lever for cracks and other damage.

Installation

5   Lightly lubricate the clutch lever crown and spring retention crown where they contact the bearing with high-temperature grease. Fill the inner groove of the bearing with the same grease.

6   Attach the release bearing to the clutch lever.

7   Lubricate the clutch release lever ball socket with high-temperature grease and push the lever onto the ball stud until it's firmly seated.

8   Apply a light coat of high-temperature grease to the face of the release bearing where it contacts the pressure plate diaphragm fingers.

9   Prior to installing the transmission, apply a light coat of grease to the transmission front bearing retainer.

10   The remainder of installation is the reverse of the removal Steps. Tighten all bolts to the torque values listed in this Chapter's Specifications.

8

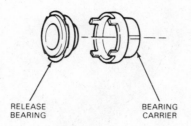

4.12   Release bearing details (1985 through 1987 models)

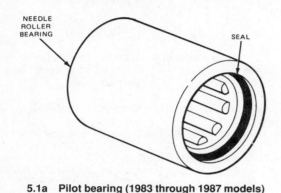

5.1a   Pilot bearing (1983 through 1987 models)

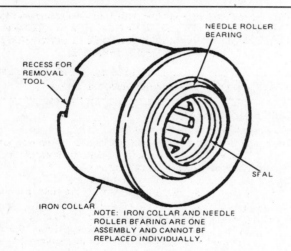

NOTE: IRON COLLAR AND NEEDLE ROLLER BEARING ARE ONE ASSEMBLY AND CANNOT BE REPLACED INDIVIDUALLY.

5.1b   Pilot bearing (1988 and later models)

1985 through 1987 models
Removal and inspection
Refer to illustration 4.12

11   Remove the slave cylinder (see Section 7).

12   Carefully pull back on the four retainers of the release bearing carrier and remove the release bearing from it **(see illustration)**.

13   Inspect the bearing (see Step 4 above) and replace if necessary.

Installation
14   Apply a light coat of high-temperature lithium-based grease to the face of the release bearing where it contacts the pressure plate diaphragm fingers.

15   Fill the inner groove and the inside diameter of the bearing with the same grease.

16   Align the outer grooves in the bearing with the bearing carrier retainers and press the release bearing into the carrier until it bottoms out.

17   Install the slave cylinder (see Section 7).

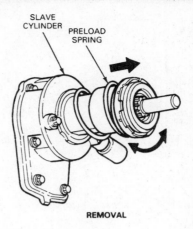

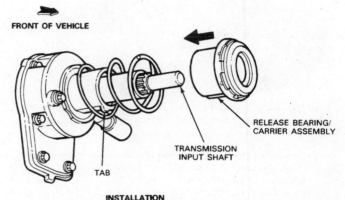

4.19   Release bearing details (1988 and later models)

1988 and later models
Removal and inspection
Refer to illustration 4.19

18   Remove the transmission and clutch housing (see Chapter 7).

19   Within the clutch housing, twist the release bearing and carrier assembly until resistance is felt. Continue to turn the assembly further and the preload spring will push the release bearing off the slave cylinder **(see illustration)**.

20   Inspect the bearing (see Step 4 above) and replace if necessary.

Installation
21   Apply a light coat of high-temperature lithium-based grease to the face of the release bearing, where it contacts the pressure plate diaphragm fingers.

22   Lubricate the inner bore of the bearing and bearing carrier with the same grease.

23   Push the release bearing and carrier onto the slave cylinder until it bottoms out **(see illustration 4.19)**.

24   Install the transmission (see Chapter 7 Part A).

---

5   Pilot bearing – inspection and replacement

Refer to illustrations 5.1a. 5.1b and 5.5

1   The clutch pilot bearing is a needle roller type bearing which is pressed into the rear of the crankshaft **(see illustrations)**. It is greased at the factory and does not require additional lubrication. Its primary purpose is to support the front of the transmission input shaft. The pilot bearing should be inspected whenever the clutch components are removed from the engine. Due to its inaccessibility, if you are in doubt as to its condition, replace it with a new one. **Note:** *If the engine has been removed from the vehicle, disregard the following steps which do not apply.*

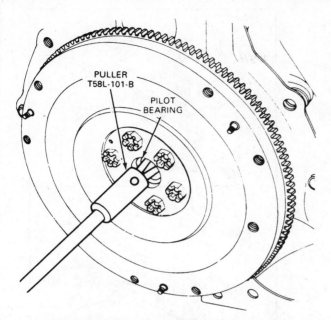

5.5   One method of removing the pilot bearing requires an internal puller connected to a slide hammer

2   Remove the transmission (refer to Chapter 7 Part A).
3   Remove the clutch components (see Section 3).
4   Inspect for any excessive wear, scoring, lack of grease, dryness or obvious damage. If any of these conditions are noted, the bearing should be replaced. A flashlight will be helpful to direct light into the recess.
5   Removal can be accomplished with a special puller and slide hammer **(see illustration)**, but an alternative method also works very well.
6   Find a solid steel bar which is slightly smaller in diameter than the bearing. Alternatives to a solid bar would be a wood dowel or a socket with a bolt fixed in place to make it solid.
7   Check the bar for fit – it should just slip into the bearing with very little clearance.
8   Pack the bearing and the area behind it (in the crankshaft recess) with heavy grease. Pack it tightly to eliminate as much air as possible.
9   Insert the bar into the bearing bore and strike the bar sharply with a hammer which will force the grease to the back side of the bearing and push it out. Remove the bearing and clean all grease from the crankshaft recess.
10   To install the new bearing, lightly lubricate the outside surface with lithium-based grease, then drive it into the recess with a soft-face hammer. The seal must face out **(see illustrations 5.1a and 5.1b)**.
11   Install the clutch components, transmission and all other components removed previously, tightening all fasteners properly.

---

6   Clutch hydraulic line quick-disconnect fittings (1988 and later models) – general information

Refer to illustration 6.2
1   The hydraulic lines on 1988 and later models are equipped with quick-disconnect fittings and a special tool is required for separation (Ford part No. T88T-70522-A).
2   Depress the white retainer within the quick-disconnect fitting with the special tool while pulling on the hydraulic line, then disconnect the male connector **(see illustration)**. To install, push the male connector into the female connector until it locks into place.
3   There should be no loss of hydraulic fluid during separation of the fittings so there is no need to bleed the system after a fitting has been disconnected, unless shifting is hard or there's a lack of clutch reserve travel.

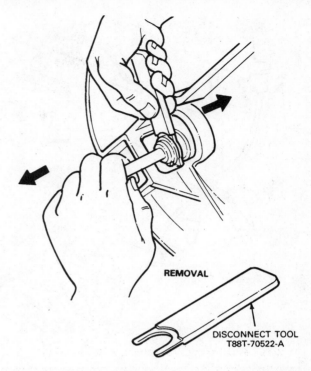

REMOVAL

DISCONNECT TOOL
T88T-70522-A

6.2   To detach the hydraulic line with a quick-disconnect fitting from the slave cylinder, use the tool shown (or an equivalent substitute) to push the white plastic collar back while pulling on the line (1988 and later models)

---

7   Clutch slave cylinder – removal and installation

1983 and 1984 models

Refer to illustrations 7.5 and 7.6
1   The slave cylinder on 1983 and 1984 models is removed and installed as a complete unit with the master cylinder and hydraulic line. The slave cylinder itself is not available separately.
2   Disconnect the negative cable from the battery.
3   Inside the passenger compartment, remove the cotter pin and detach the master cylinder pushrod from the clutch pedal.
4   Raise the vehicle and support it securely on jackstands.
5   On four cylinder engines, unbolt the dust shield from the clutch housing. Push the release cylinder to the rear to separate it from the housing, then slide it out of its mount **(see illustration)**.
6   On V6 engines, unbolt the release cylinder from the clutch housing **(see illustration)**. Pull the release cylinder out, disengaging the pushrod. Set the pushrod-to-cylinder plastic bearing inserts aside for later use.
7   Unbolt the master cylinder from the firewall and the reservoir from the cowl. Lift the master cylinder up and remove it, together with the hydraulic line and release cylinder.
8   Installation is the reverse of the removal Steps with the following additions:
a)   New systems are equipped with a shipping strap. The strap places the cylinder pushrod in the correct position for installation and provides a bearing insert. Don't remove the strap; the first pedal stroke after installation will break it and let the system operate normally.
b)   Route the hydraulic line above the brake tubes and below the steering column. On 2.8L engines, the tube must rest on top of the clutch housing.
c)   Clean the master cylinder pushrod bushing and coat lightly with SAE 30 engine oil.
d)   After installation, press the clutch pedal at least 10 times to make sure the system works properly.

8

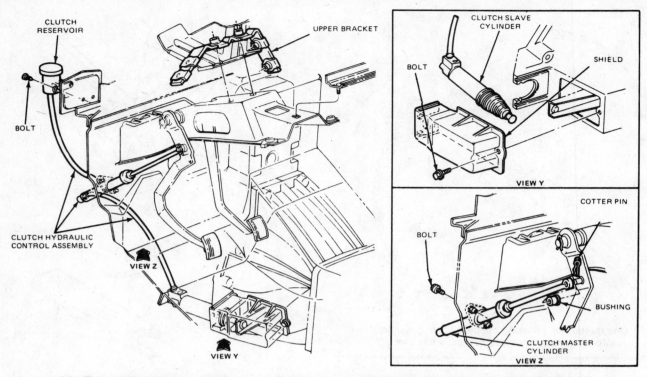

7.5   Remove the bolt securing the slave cylinder dust cover and remove the cover (four-cylinder engines)

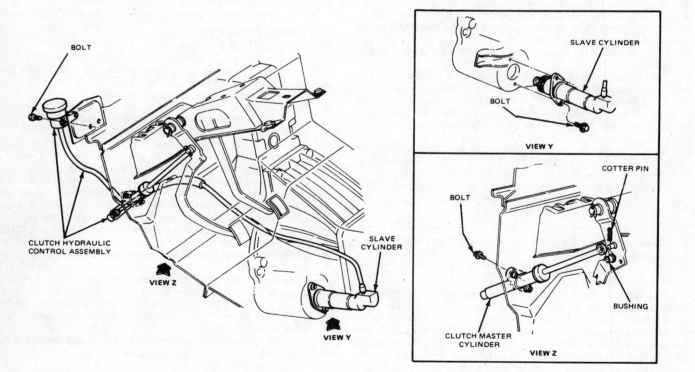

7.6   On 2.8L V-6 models, remove the bolts securing the slave cylinder to the clutch housing

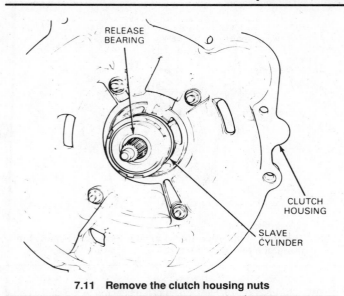

7.11   **Remove the clutch housing nuts**

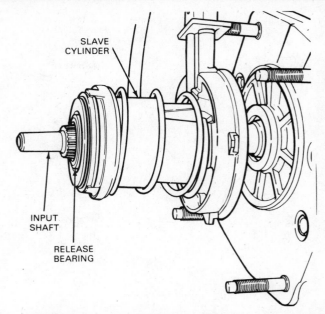

7.12   **Clutch slave cylinder removal (1985 through 1987 models)**

1985 through 1987 models

Refer to illustrations 7.11 and 7.12

9   Remove the clip securing the hydraulic hose to the slave cylinder. Disconnect the hose from the slave cylinder. Have rags handy as some fluid will be lost as the line is removed. **Caution:** *Don't allow brake fluid to come into contact with paint as it will damage the finish.*

10   Remove the transmission (see Chapter 7 Part A).

11   Remove the nuts securing the clutch housing and remove the clutch housing **(see illustration).**

12   Slide the slave cylinder assembly off the transmission input shaft **(see illustration).**

13   Installation is the reverse of the removal Steps with the following additions:
   a) Install the slave cylinder onto the input shaft with the tower portion facing the transmission.
   b) Install the clutch housing onto the transmission and make sure the slave cylinder is properly located in the notches of the clutch housing.
   c) Connect the hydraulic line to the release cylinder and install the clip.
   d) Bleed the clutch hydraulic system (see Section 9).

1988 and later models

Refer to illustration 7.18

Note: *Prior to removing the slave cylinder, disconnect the master cylinder pushrod from the clutch pedal. If not disconnected, permanent damage to the master cylinder will occur if the clutch pedal is depressed while the slave cylinder is disconnected.*

14   Pry off the retainer bushing and disconnect the master cylinder pushrod from the clutch pedal.

15   Disconnect the hydraulic quick disconnect fitting from the slave cylinder (see Section 6).

16   Remove the transmission (see Chapter 7 Part A).

17   On 2.9L 4x4 models remove the bolts securing the clutch housing to the transmission and remove the clutch housing.

18   Remove the bolts securing the slave cylinder to the transmission and slide the slave cylinder assembly off the transmission input shaft **(see illustration).**

19   Installation is the reverse of the removal Steps with the following additions:
   a) Install the slave cylinder onto the input shaft with the hydraulic line facing toward the left side of the transmission.
   b) Install the slave cylinder mounting bolts and tighten to the torque listed in this Chapter's Specifications.
   c) If necessary, bleed the clutch hydraulic system (see Section 9).

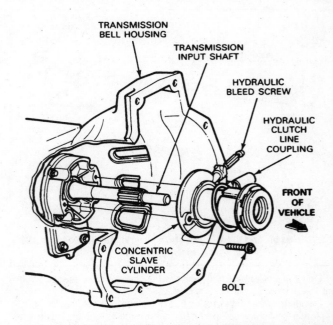

7.18   **Clutch slave cylinder removal (1988 and later models)**

8   Clutch master cylinder and reservoir – removal and installation

Removal

1983 and 1984 models

1   The clutch master cylinder is removed a a unit with the complete hydraulic system, including the hydraulic line and release cylinder (see Section 7).

1985 and later models

Refer to illustration 8.6

2   Disconnect the negative cable from the battery.

3   Working inside the vehicle, remove the spring clip or retainer bushing and disconnect the pushrod from the top of the clutch pedal.

8

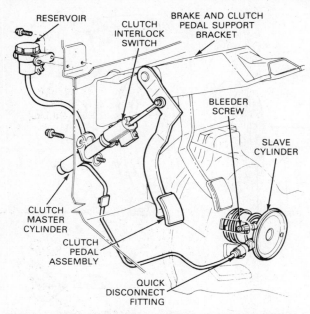

8.6   Typical clutch master cylinder layout (1988 and later models shown)

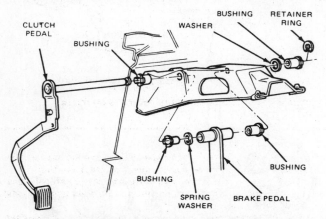

10.2   An exploded view of the clutch pedal (1983, 1984 and 1988 and later models)

4   On 1988 and later models, remove the clutch/starter interlock switch from the pushrod.
5   Disconnect the hydraulic line from the slave cylinder (see Section 7).
6   Within the engine compartment, remove the bolts securing the master cylinder reservoir to the firewall (see illustration). Be careful not to spill any of the fluid.
7   Working in the same area, remove the bolts securing the master cylinder to the firewall. Be careful not to spill any of the fluid.
8   Remove the master cylinder and reservoir from the engine compartment.

Installation

9   Install the master cylinder through the firewall and make sure the pushrod is positioned on the correct side of the clutch pedal so it can be installed onto the pedal's pivot pin.
10   Attach the master cylinder to the firewall and install the mounting bolts. Tighten the bolts to the torque listed in this Chapter's Specifications.
11   Attach the master cylinder reservoir to the firewall and install the mounting bolts, tightening them securely.
12   Connect the hydraulic line to the slave cylinder (see Section 7).

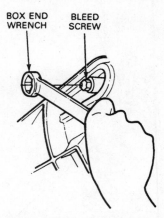

9.6   The bleeder valve on 1985 and later models is accessible through a port on the left side of the clutch housing

13   Working inside the vehicle, connect the pushrod to the clutch pedal and install the clip or retainer bushing.
14   On 1988 and later models, install the clutch/starter interlock switch.
15   Connect the negative cable onto the battery.
16   Fill the clutch master cylinder reservoir with brake fluid conforming to DOT 3 specifications and bleed the clutch system (see Section 9).

9   Clutch hydraulic system – bleeding

Refer to illustration 9.6

1   The hydraulic system on 1983 and 1984 models is bled and sealed at the factory and can't be bled in service.
2   On 1985 and later models, the hydraulic system should be bled to remove all air whenever air enters the system. This occurs when any part of the system has been removed (except on 1988 and later models, which use quick-disconnect fittings designed to prevent fluid loss or air leakage when opened) or if the fluid level has been allowed to fall so low that air has been drawn into the master cylinder. The procedure is very similar to bleeding a brake system, but depends mainly on gravity, rather than the pumping action of the pedal, for the bleeding effect.
3   Fill the master cylinder to the top with new brake fluid conforming to DOT 3 specifications. **Caution:** *Do not re-use any of the fluid coming from the system during the bleeding operation or use fluid which has been inside an open container for an extended period of time.*
4   Raise the vehicle and place it securely on jackstands to gain access to the bleed fitting, which is located on the left side of the clutch housing.
5   Remove the dust cap which fits over the bleeder valve and push a length of clear plastic hose over the valve. Place the other end of the hose into a clear container partially filled with brake fluid.
6   Open the bleeder valve (see illustration). Fluid will run from the master cylinder, down the hydraulic line, into the release cylinder and out through the clear plastic tube. Let the fluid run out until it is free of bubbles. **Note:** *Don't let the fluid level drop too low in the master cylinder, or air will be drawn into the hydraulic line and the whole process will have to be started over.*
7   Close the bleed valve.
8   Have an assistant slowly depress the clutch pedal and hold it. Open the bleed valve on the release cylinder, allowing fluid to flow through the clear plastic hose. Close the bleed valve when the flow stops. Once closed, have your assistant release the pedal.
9   Continue this process until all air is evacuated from the system, indicated by a solid stream of fluid being ejected from the bleed valve each time with no air bubbles in the hose or container.
10   Install the dust cap and lower the vehicle. Check carefully for proper operation before placing the vehicle in normal service.

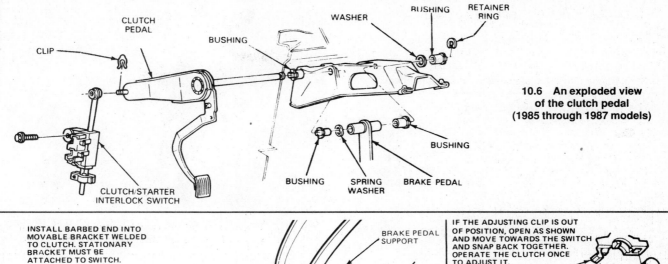

**10.6   An exploded view
of the clutch pedal
(1985 through 1987 models)**

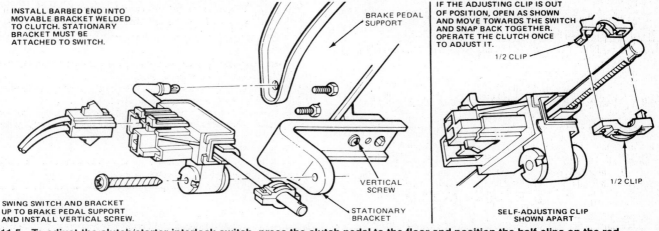

11.5   To adjust the clutch/starter interlock switch, press the clutch pedal to the floor and position the half-clips on the rod closer to the switch (1985 through 1987 models only)

---

10   Clutch pedal – removal and installation

1   Disconnect the negative cable from the battery.

1983 and 1984 models

Refer to illustration 10.2

2   Remove the lockpin from the master cylinder pushrod. Separate the pushrod from the clutch pedal and remove the bushing **(see illustration)**.

3   Remove the retainer ring from the end of the clutch shaft. Remove the bushings and spring washers and remove the clutch pedal from the shaft.

4   Installation is the reverse of the removal Steps. Clean, inspect and lubricate the clutch shaft bushings with engine oil prior to installation.

1985 through 1987 models

Refer to illustration 10.6

5   Remove the clip securing the clutch/starter switch pushrod to the clutch pedal. Using a screwdriver, pry the pushrod and bushing from the clutch pedal pivot pin.

6   Remove the retainer ring from the end of the clutch shaft **(see illustration)**.

7   Slide the clutch pedal assembly from the pedal support bracket and catch the brake pedal assembly that pivots on the clutch shaft. Let the brake pedal rest on the floor.

8   Installation is the reverse of the removal Steps. Clean, inspect and lubricate the clutch shaft bushings with engine oil prior to installation.

1988 and later models

9   Disconnect the barbed end of the clutch/starter interlock switch rod from the clutch pedal. Remove the lockpin and remove the master cylinder pushrod from the clutch pedal. Remove the plastic bushing.

10   On 1989 and later models, remove the plastic side panel on the driver's sidewall. Remove the bolts securing the parking brake assembly and move it out of the way to one side.

11   Pry the retainer from the clip on the pedal support bracket **(see illustration 10.2)**.

12   Perform Steps 7 and 8 to complete removal and installation.

---

11   Clutch/starter interlock switch (1985 through 1987 models) - check and adjustment

Refer to illustration 11.5

1   1985 and later manual transmission models are equipped with a clutch/starter interlock switch, which requires that the clutch pedal be fully depressed in order to start the engine. The interlock switch on 1988 and later models is not adjustable.

2   Disconnect the negative cable from the battery.

3   Working inside the vehicle, disconnect the electrical connector at the switch located under the instrument panel.

4   Use a test light or ohmmeter and test the switch continuity. With the pedal up (clutch engaged), the switch contacts should be open. The test light should not illuminate or the ohmmeter should indicate no continuity. With the clutch pedal pressed to the floor, the switch contacts should be closed (the test light should come on or the ohmmeter should indicate continuity).

5   If the switch doesn't work, remove the clip and reposition the clip closer to the switch **(see illustration)**.

8

6   Depress the clutch pedal to the floor and reset the adjustment of the switch.

7   If the switch still does not operate properly, replace it.

12   Driveshaft and universal joints – description and check

1   The driveshaft(s) is a tube running between the transfer case and the rear axle or front axle. Universal joints are located at either end of the driveshaft(s) and permit power to be transmitted to the rear and/or front wheels at varying angles.

2   The driveshaft(s) features a splined yoke at one end, which slips into the transmission extension housing or the transfer case. This arrangement allows the driveshaft(s) to slide back-and-forth within the transmission or transfer case as the vehicle is in operation.

3   An oil seal is used to prevent leakage of fluid at this point and to keep dirt and contaminants from entering the transmission or transfer case. If leakage is evident at the front of the driveshaft, replace the oil seal referring to the procedures in Chapter 7.

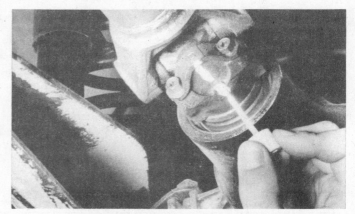

13.3   Index the driveshaft U-joint assembly for reinstallation

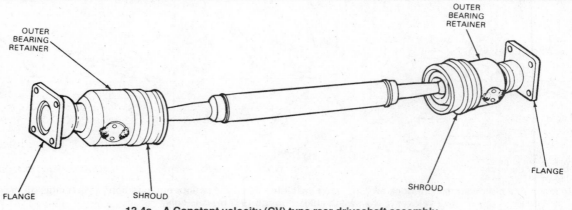

13.4a   A Constant velocity (CV) type rear driveshaft assembly

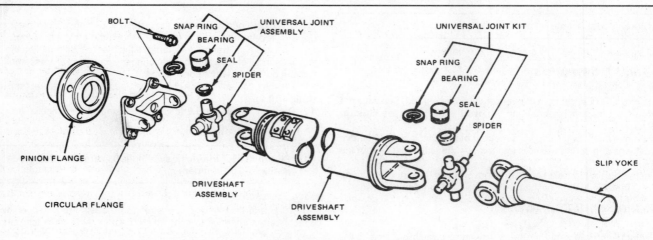

CIRCULAR FLANGE APPLICATION–TYPICAL

13.4b   An exploded view of front and rear driveshaft assembly with single cardan U-joint

4   The driveshaft assembly(ies) requires very little service. The universal joints on models not equipped with grease fittings are lubricated for life and must be replaced if problems develop. The driveshaft(s) must be removed from the vehicle for this procedure.

5   Since the driveshaft(s) is a balanced unit, it's important that no undercoating, mud, etc. be allowed to stay on it. When the vehicle is raised for service it's a good idea to clean the driveshaft(s) and inspect it for any obvious damage. Also check that the small weights used to originally balance the driveshaft(s) are in place and securely attached. Whenever the driveshaft(s) is removed it's important that it be reinstalled in the same relative position to preserve the balance.

6   Problems with the driveshaft(s) are usually indicated by a noise or vibration while driving the vehicle. A road test should verify if the problem is the driveshaft(s) or another vehicle component:

a)   On an open road, free of traffic, drive the vehicle and note the engine speed (rpm) at which the problem is most evident.

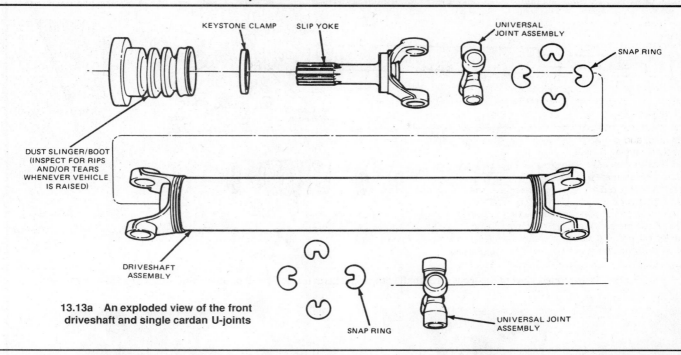

13.13a   An exploded view of the front driveshaft and single cardan U-joints

b) With this noted, drive the vehicle again, this time manually keeping the transmission in 1st, then 2nd, then 3rd gear ranges and running the engine up to the engine speed noted.

c) If the noise or vibration occurs at the same engine speed regardless of which gear the transmission is in, the driveshaft(s) is not at fault because the speed of the driveshaft(s) varies in each gear.

d) If the noise or vibration decreased or was eliminated, visually inspect the driveshaft(s) for damage, material on the shaft which would effect balance, missing weights and damaged universal joints. Another possibility for this condition would be tires which are out-of-balance or a bent or damaged wheel(s).

7   To check for worn universal joints:

a) On an open road, free of traffic, drive the vehicle slowly until the transmission is in High gear. Let off on the accelerator, allowing the vehicle to coast, then accelerate. A clunking or knocking noise will indicate worn universal joints.

b) Drive the vehicle at a speed of about 10 to 15 mph and then place the transmission in Neutral, allowing the vehicle to coast. Listen for abnormal driveline noises.

c) Raise the vehicle and support it securely on jackstands. With the transmission in Neutral, manually turn the driveshaft(s), watching the universal joints for excessive play.

---

13   Driveshaft(s) – removal and installation

Note: *Whenever two-piece driveshafts are involved, first remove the rear driveshaft and then the front driveshaft.*

Rear driveshaft

Refer to illustrations 13.3, 13.4a and 13.4b

1   Disconnect the negative cable from the battery.

2   Raise the vehicle and support it securely on jackstands. Place the transmission in Neutral with the parking brake off.

3   Using a scribe, white paint or a hammer and punch, place marks on the driveshaft and the differential flange in line with each other **(see illustration)**. This is to make sure the driveshaft is reinstalled in the same position to preserve the balance.

4   On CV joint driveshafts, remove the bolts securing the outer bearing flange to the transfer case. On all other types, remove the rear universal joint bolts and straps. Turn the driveshaft (or tires) as necessary to bring the bolts into the most accessible position **(see illustrations)**. If the dri-

veshaft has a spline on one end be sure to scribe an index mark on the two parts to ensure proper position during installation. **Caution:** *Do not allow the driveshaft to hang free. Support it during the removal procedure.*

5   Repeat this procedure for the opposite end if it is equipped with a universal joint coupled to a flange.

6   If the opposite end is equipped with a sliding joint (spline), simply slide the yoke off the splined shaft.

7   On all types other than CV joints, tape the bearing caps to the spider to prevent the caps from coming off during removal.

8   Lower the rear of the driveshaft and then slide the front out of the transmission or transfer case.

9   If the shaft being removed is the front shaft of a two-piece unit, remove the bolts securing the center bearing assembly. Make sure both ends of the shafts are marked for installation purposes.

10   To prevent loss of fluid and protect against contamination while the driveshaft is out, wrap a plastic bag over the transmission or transfer case housing and hold it in place with a rubber band.

11   Installation is the reverse of the removal Steps with the following additions:

a) Remove the plastic bag from the transmission or transfer case and wipe the area clean. Inspect the oil seal carefully. Procedures for replacement of this seal can be found in Chapter 7.

b) Slide the front of the driveshaft into the transfer case.

c) Raise the rear of the driveshaft into position, checking to be sure the marks are in alignment. If not, make sure the transmission is still in Neutral, then turn the rear wheels to match the pinion flange and the driveshaft.

d) On all types other than CV joints, remove the tape securing the bearing caps and install the straps and bolts. Tighten the bolts to the torque listed in this Chapter's Specification.

Front driveshaft – 4x4 models

Refer to illustrations 13.13a and 13.13b

Note: *This procedure requires a number 30 Torx bit to remove the mounting bolts securing the front driveshaft U-joint.*

12   Using a scribe, white paint or a hammer and punch, place marks on the driveshaft and the differential flange in line with each other **(see illustration 13.3)**. This is to make sure the driveshaft is reinstalled in the same position to preserve the balance.

13   Remove the rear universal joint bolts and straps **(see illustrations)**. Turn the driveshaft (or tires) as necessary to bring the bolts into the most

8

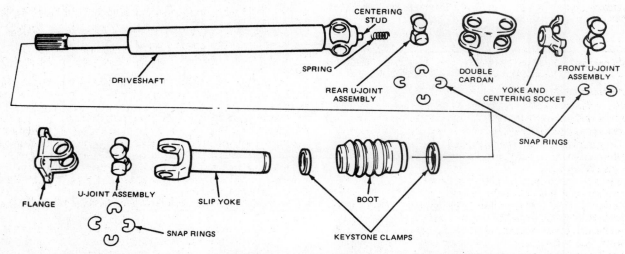

13.13b   An exploded view of the front driveshaft with single cardan U-joint and double cardan U-joint at transfer case

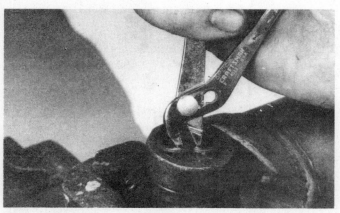

14.2   Remove the universal joint snap rings with small pliers

14.4a   The universal joint bearing caps can be pressed out with a vise and sockets

accessible position.

14   Pry back the protective boot from the transfer case.

15   Slide the splined yoke out of the transfer case and remove the front driveshaft assembly.

16   To prevent loss of fluid and protect against contamination while the driveshaft is out, wrap a plastic bag over the transfer case housing and hold it in place with a rubber band.

17   Installation is the reverse of the removal Steps with the following additions:

   a)   Remove the plastic bag from the transfer case and wipe the area clean. Inspect the oil seal carefully. Procedures for replacement of this seal can be found in Chapter 7.

   b)   Slide the rear of the driveshaft into the transfer case.

   c)   Raise the front of the driveshaft into position, checking to be sure the marks are in alignment. If not, make sure the transmission is still in Neutral, then turn the front wheels to match the pinion flange and the driveshaft.

   d)   Remove the tape securing the bearing caps and install the straps and bolts. Tighten the bolts to the torque listed in this Chapter's Specifications.

Constant Velocity (CV) driveshaft – Bronco II models with A4LD automatic transmission

18   Removal is basically the same as with regular universal joint driveshafts except the driveshaft is attached to the transfer case and rear axle flange by the flanges on the outer bearing retainer.

14.4b   The bearing cap can be extracted with locking pliers

19   Using a scribe, white paint or a hammer and punch, place marks on the driveshaft and the flanges in line with each other (see illustration 13.3). This is to make sure the driveshaft is reinstalled in the same position to preserve the balance. **Note:** *The CV joint components are matched dur-*

ing manufacture and cannot be interchanged with components from another CV joint.

14 Single cardan type U-joint – overhaul

Refer to illustrations 14.2, 14.4a and 14.4b
Note: *A press or large vise will be required for this procedure. It may be a good idea to take the driveshaft to a repair or machine shop where the universal joints can be replaced for you, normally at a reasonable charge.*
1 Remove the driveshaft (see Section 13).
2 Place the driveshaft in a sturdy vise and remove the snap-rings from the spider **(see illustration)**.
3 Supporting the driveshaft, place it in position on either an arbor press or on a workbench equipped with a vise.
4 Place a piece of pipe or a large socket with the same inside diameter over one of the bearing caps. Position a socket with a slightly smaller diameter than the cap on the opposite bearing cap **(see illustration)** and use the vise or press to force the cap out (inside the pipe or large socket), stopping just before it comes completely out of the yoke. Use the vise or large pliers to work the cap the rest of the way out **(see illustration)**.
5 Transfer the sockets to the other side and press the opposite bearing cap out in the same manner.
6 After the bearings have been removed, lift the spider from the yoke and thoroughly clean all dirt and debris from the yokes on both ends of the driveshaft.
7 Pack the new universal joint bearings with grease. Ordinarily, specific instructions for lubrication will be included with the universal joint servicing kit and should be followed carefully.
8 Position the spider in the yoke and partially install one bearing cap in the yoke.
9 Start the spider into the bearing cap and then partially install the other cap. Align the spider and press the bearing caps into position, being careful not to damage the dust seals.
10 Install the snap-rings. If difficulty is encountered in seating the snap-rings, strike the driveshaft yoke sharply with a hammer. This will spring the yoke ears slightly and allow the snap-rings to seat in the groove.
11 Install the driveshaft (see Section 13).

15 Double cardan type U-joint – overhaul

Note: *A press or large vise will be required for this procedure. It may be a good idea to take the driveshaft to a repair or machine shop where the universal joints can be replaced for you, normally at a reasonable charge.*
1 Remove the driveshaft (see Section 13).
2 Place the driveshaft in a sturdy vise, being careful not to dent the driveshaft.
3 Use paint or small punch and hammer and mark the positions of the spiders, the center yoke and the centering socket as related to the stud yoke which is welded to the front of the driveshaft tube. The spiders must be assembled with the bosses in their original position to provide proper clearance.
4 Use a small screwdriver and pry out the snap-rings that attach the bearings in the front of the center yoke.
5 Supporting the driveshaft, place it in position on either an arbor press or on a workbench equipped with a vise.
6 Place a piece of pipe or a large socket with the same inside diameter over one of the bearing caps. Position a socket which is of slightly smaller diameter than the cap on the opposite bearing cap and use the vise or press to force the cap out (inside the pipe or large socket), stopping just before it comes completely out of the yoke **(see illustration 14.4a).** Use the vise or large pliers to work the cap the rest of the way out **(see illustration 14.4b).**
7 Transfer the sockets to the other side and press the opposite bearing cap out in the same manner.
8 Repeat Steps 6 and 7 and remove all bearings from the universal joints.

9 With the front bearing cups removed, remove the spider from the center yoke.
10 Pull the centering socket yoke off the center stud and remove the rubber seal from the centering ball stud.
11 Remove the snap rings from the center yoke and from the driveshaft yoke.
12 Press or drive the bearing out as previously described.
13 With the bearing cups removed, remove the center yoke from the spider.
14 Remove the spider from the driveshaft yoke.
15 After the bearings have been removed, lift the spider from the yoke and thoroughly clean all dirt and debris from the yokes on both ends of the driveshaft. If using a repair kit, install all of the parts supplied.
16 Pack the new universal joint bearings with grease. Ordinarily, specific instructions for lubrication will be included with the universal joint servicing kit and should be followed carefully.
17 Remove the clamps on the driveshaft dust boot seal and discard the clamps.
18 Note the orientation of the slip yoke to the driveshaft tube for installation during assembly. Mark the relationship of the slip yoke to the driveshaft tube.
19 Carefully pull the slip joint from the driveshaft, be careful not to damage the boot seal.
20 Inspect the spline area and thoroughly clean all foreign matter from the splines with solvent.
21 Lubricate the splines with multi-purpose grease.
22 Install the dust boot seal loosely on the driveshaft tube, then install the yoke into the driveshaft in its original position. Refer to the marks made prior to removal.
23 Install new clamps on the dust boot seal and tighten securely.
24 To assemble the double cardan joints, position the spider in the driveshaft yoke. Make sure the spider bosses (or lubricating plugs) are in their original positions.
25 Start the spider into the bearing cap and then partially install the other cap. Align the spider and press the bearing caps into position, being careful not to damage the dust seals.
26 Install new snap-rings. If difficulty is encountered in seating the snap-rings, strike the driveshaft yoke sharply with a hammer. This will spring the yoke ears slightly and allow the snap-rings to seat in the groove.
27 Repeat Step 25 and 26 for the remaining bearings.
28 Pack the socket relief and the ball with multi-purpose grease, then position the center yoke over the spider ends and press in the bearing.
29 Install new snap-rings.
30 Install a new seal on the centering ball stud and position the centering socket yoke on the stud.
31 Place the front spider in the center yoke and make sure the spider bosses (or lubricating plugs) are in their original positions.
32 Start the spider into the bearing cap and then partially install the other cap. Align the spider and press the bearing caps into position, being careful not to damage the dust seals.
33 Install new snap-rings. If difficulty is encountered in seating the snap-rings, strike the driveshaft yoke sharply with a hammer. This will spring the yoke ears slightly and allow the snap-rings to seat in the groove.
34 If so equipped, lubricate the U-joints through the grease fittings with multi-purpose grease.
35 Install the driveshaft (see Section 13).

16 Constant velocity (CV) U-joint – removal and installation

Note: *The CV joints are matched assemblies and should not be interchanged with components from another CV joint. The CV joint cannot be serviced and if faulty the entire assembly must be replaced as a unit.*

Removal
Refer to illustrations 16.2, 16.3, 16.5, 16.6, 16.7, 16.9, 16.11 and 16.12
1 Remove the driveshaft (see Section 13).
2 Remove the clamp securing the shroud to the outer bearing race and

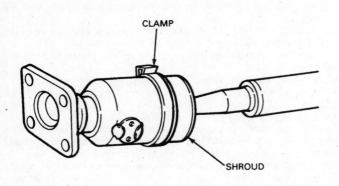

16.2   Remove the clamp securing the shroud to the outer bearing race and flange assembly

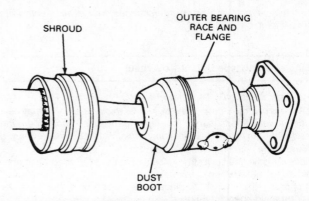

16.3   Pull back the shroud and remove the rubber boot or outer bearing race and flange assembly

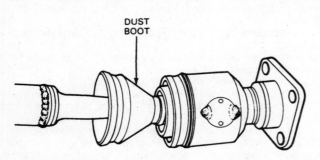

16.5   Carefully peel the rubber boot away from the outer bearing race and flange assembly

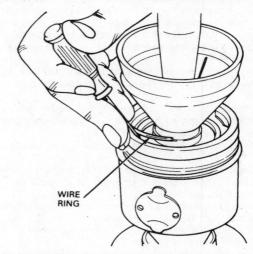

16.6   Use a small screwdriver and remove the wire ring securing the inner race to the outer race

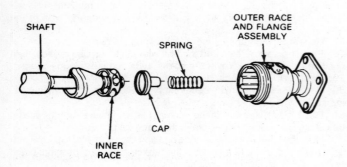

16.7   An exploded view of the CV joint

10   If necessary, remove the clamp securing the boot to the shaft and remove the boot.
11   Carefully pry the ball bearings from the cage with a screwdriver **(see illustration)**. Do not damage or scratch the cage, race or ball bearings during removal. **Caution:** *Remove any sharp edges on the screwdriver to guard against damage to the finished surfaces of the components during removal.*
12   Rotate the inner race to align with the cage window and remove the inner race through the wider end of the bearing cage **(see illustration)**.

Installation

Refer to illustrations 16.13 and 16.15

13   Position the inner bearing race with the circlip counterbore facing the large end of the cage **(see illustration)**. Install the inner bearing race into the bearing cage through the large end of the cage.
14   Push the race to the top of the cage and rotate the race until all the ball slots are aligned with the windows. This will lock the race to the top of the cage.
15   Once alignment is achieved, install the ball bearings **(see illustration)**. Press the ball bearings through the bearing cage with the heel of your hand. Repeat this procedure until all bearings are installed.
16   If removed, install a new rubber dust boot on the shaft and secure it with a new clamp. Make sure the boot is seated in the groove correctly. **Note:** *The clamp is a fixed-diameter push-on type metal ring.*
17   Install the inner bearing assembly onto the shaft. Make sure the circlip groove is exposed.

flange assembly **(see illustration)**.
3   Remove the shroud (don't tear it) and remove the rubber boot or outer bearing race and flange assembly **(see illustration)**.
4   Lightly tap the end of the shroud with a blunt instrument and remove the shroud from the dust boot.
5   Carefully peel the rubber boot away from the outer bearing race and flange assembly **(see illustration)**.
6   Remove the wire ring securing the inner race to the outer race **(see illustration)**.
7   Remove the inner race and shaft assembly from the outer race and flange assembly **(see illustration)**.
8   Remove the cap and spring from inside the outer retainer.
9   Use snap-ring pliers and remove the circlip that secures the inner race assembly to the shaft **(see illustration)**. Discard the circlip and remove the inner race assembly.

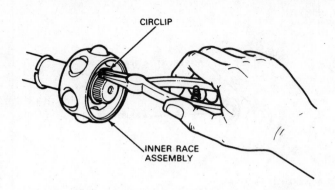

16.9   Use snap-ring pliers and remove the clip securing the inner race assembly to the shaft

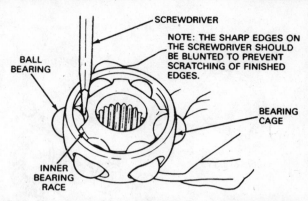

16.11   Use a screwdriver and carefully pry the ball bearings from the cage

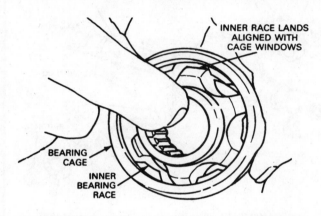

16.12   Align the inner race lands with the cage windows and remove the inner race through the wider end of the bearing cage

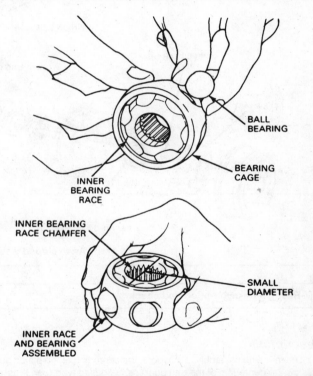

16.15   Install the ball bearings through the bearing cage with the heel of your hand

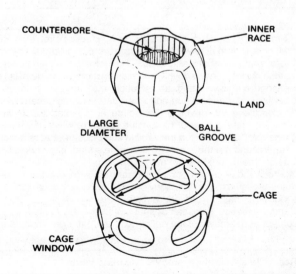

16.13   Position the inner bearing race with the circlip counterbore facing the same direction as the large end of the cage

18   Install a new circlip onto the shaft and make sure it is properly seated in the shaft groove. Do not bend or twist the circlip during installation.
19   Install the spring and cap in the outer bearing retainer and flange.

20   Fill the outer bearing retainer with constant velocity joint grease, Ford part No. D8RZ-19590-A or equivalent multi-purpose bearing grease.
21   Insert the inner race and shaft assembly into the outer bearing retainer flange.
22   Push the inner race down until the wire spring groove is exposed and install the wire ring.
23   Fill the top of the outer bearing retainer with constant velocity joint grease, Ford part No. D8RZ-19590-A or equivalent multi-purpose bearing grease. Clean off excessive grease from the outside of the bearing retainer.
24   Pull the rubber dust boot over the retainer and make sure the boot is fully seated in its groove.
25   Insert a dull screwdriver blade between the boot and outer bearing retainer and allow the trapped air to escape from the boot.
26   Install the shroud over the boot and retainer and install the clamp.
27   Install the driveshaft (see Section 13).

8

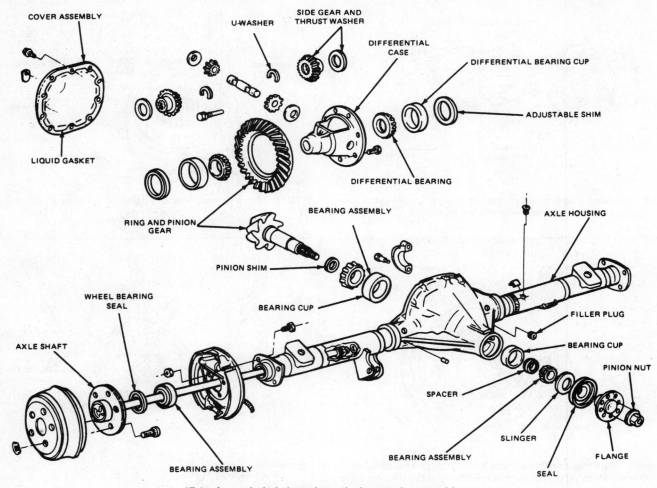

17.1 An exploded view of a typical rear axle assembly

17 Rear axle – description and check

Refer to illustration 17.1

Description

1   The rear axle assembly is a hypoid (the centerline of the pinion gear is below the centerline of the ring gear) semi-floating type **(see illustration)**. The differential carrier is a casting with a pressed steel cover and the axle tubes are made of steel, pressed and welded into the carrier.
2   An optional Traction-Lok limited slip rear axle is also available. This differential allows for normal operation until one wheel loses traction. The unit utilizes multi-disc clutch packs and a speed sensitive engagement mechanism which locks both axleshafts together, applying equal rotational power to both wheels.
3   In order to undertake certain operations, particularly replacement of the axleshafts, it's important to know the axle identification number. It's located on a small metal tag near one of the cover bolts.

Check

4   Many times a problem is suspected in the rear axle area when, in fact, it lies elsewhere. For this reason, a thorough check should be performed before assuming a rear axle problem.
5   The following noises are those commonly associated with rear axle diagnosis procedures:
   a) Road noise is often mistaken for mechanical faults. Driving the vehicle on different surfaces will show whether the road surface is the cause of the noise. Road noise will remain the same if the ve-

hicle is under power or coasting.
   b) Tire noise is sometimes mistaken for mechanical problems. Tires which are worn or low on air pressure are particularly susceptible to emitting vibrations and noises. Tire noise will remain about the same during varying driving situations, where rear axle noise will change during coasting, acceleration, etc.
   c) Engine and transmission noise can be deceiving because it will travel along the driveline. To isolate engine and transmission noises, make a note of the engine speed at which the noise is most pronounced. Stop the vehicle and place the transmission in Neutral and run the engine to the same speed. If the noise is the same, the rear axle is not at fault.
6   Overhaul and general repair of the rear axle is beyond the scope of the home mechanic due to the many special tools and critical measurements required. Thus, the procedures listed here will involve axleshaft removal and installation, axleshaft oil seal replacement, axleshaft bearing replacement and removal of the entire unit for repair or replacement.

18 Rear axle assembly – removal and installation

1   Loosen the lug nuts on the rear wheels.
2   Raise the rear of the vehicle, support it securely and remove the rear wheels.
3   Disconnect the brake lines from the rear axle housing and wheel cylinders (see Chapter 9).
4   Remove the rear brake drums and disconnect the emergency brake cable from each side (see Chapter 9).

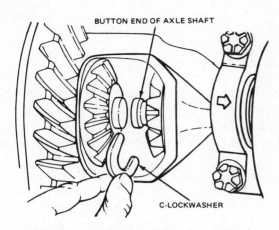

BUTTON END OF AXLE SHAFT

C-LOCKWASHER

19.9 With the pinion shaft removed and the axleshafts pushed inward, the C-locks can be removed

5   Disconnect the rear axle housing vent tube from the frame rail.
6   Position a floor jack under the rear axle and raise it slightly to take the strain off the mounting U-bolts.
7   Remove the nuts from all U-bolts securing the rear axle to the leaf spring.
8   Lower and remove the rear axle housing from under the vehicle.
9   Installation is the reverse of the removal Steps with the following additions:
   a) Adjust the emergency brake cable tension (see Chapter 9).
   b) Bleed the brake system (see Chapter 9).
   c) Install the rear wheels and lug nuts.
   d) Lower the vehicle and tighten the lug nuts to the torque listed in Chapter 1.

19   Axleshafts, bearings and oil seals – removal and installation

Refer to illustration 19.9

Axleshaft removal

1   Loosen the lug nuts on the rear wheels.
2   Raise the rear of the vehicle, support it securely on jack stands and remove the rear wheels.
3   Remove the rear brake drums (see Chapter 9).
4   Clean all dirt from the area surrounding the carrier cover.
5   Remove the cover from the differential carrier and allow the oil to drain into a container.
6   On all axles except 3.73:1 and 4.10:1 proceed to Step 8.
7   On 3.73:1 and 4.10:1 axles the pinion shaft nut must be rotated to place the side gear to provide clearance for C-lock removal and installation.
8   Remove the pinion shaft lock bolt and slide the shaft out. **Note:** *The pinion gears may be left in place. Once the axleshafts are removed, reinstall the pinion shaft and lock bolt.*
9   *Push the flanged end of the axleshafts toward the center of the vehicle and remove the C-locks from the button end of the axleshafts* (**see illustration**).
10   Carefully remove the axleshafts from the housing. Do not damage the oil seal at the end of the housing.

Oil seal and bearing

11   Insert a rear axle bearing remover, Ford part No. T77F-1102-A and slide hammer, Ford part No. T50T-0100-A or equivalent axle bearing remover with a slide hammer, into the bore of the bearing and position it behind the bearing outer race. Using the slide hammer withdraw the bearing and oil seal as a unit.
12   Thoroughly clean the rear axle housing bore with a rag and solvent.

13   Lubricate the new bearing with rear axle lubricant and install the bearing into the housing bore. Use an axle tube bearing driver tool, Ford part No. T78P-1225-A, or large socket that matches the outer bearing race. Tap the bearing in until it's into the full depth of its recess. **Caution:** *Do not tap on the inner bearing race while installing the bearing as it will be damaged.*
14   Apply multi-purpose grease between the lips of the axleshaft seal.
15   Install a new axleshaft seal using the axle tube seal installation tool, Ford part No. Y4T78P-1177-A, or a large socket that matches the seal diameter. **Caution:** *If the seal is installed incorrectly or gets cocked during installation it will be damaged leading to component failure and an oil leak.*

Axleshaft Installation

16   On all axles except 3.73:1 and 4.10:1, carefully insert the axle into the housing and install the C-lock on the button end of the axleshaft splines. Push the shaft outboard until the shaft splines engage and the C-lock seats in the counterbore of the differential side gear.
17   Position the differential pinion shaft through the case and pinion gears, aligning the hole in the shaft with the lock bolt hole. Apply thread locking compound to the lock bolt and install the bolt in the lock bolt hole.
18   On 3.73:1 and 4.10:1 axles, rotate the pinion shaft so the relief in the shaft faces the side gear and install the C-lock on the axle shaft button end.
19   Rotate the pinion shaft 180-degrees so the relief faces the opposite side gear. Install the C-lock on the axle shaft button end.
20   Rotate the pinion shaft 90-degrees to align the hole in the case and shaft and install the lock bolt. Tighten the lock bolt to the torque listed in this Chapter's Specifications.
21   Clean the gasket mounting surface on the rear axle housing and cover of all old gasket material residue with lacquer thinner or gasket remover. Apply a continuous bead of silicone sealant, Ford part No. D6AZ-19562-B, or equivalent. Run the bead inside the bolt holes and install the cover and bolts.
22   Tighten the bolts in a crisscross pattern to the torque listed in this Chapter's Specifications.
23   Refill the axle with the correct quantity and grade of lubricant (see Chapter 1).

20   Front axle (4x4 models) – removal and installation

1   Raise the front of the vehicle and install jackstands under the radius arm brackets.
2   Disconnect the driveshaft from the front axle yoke (see Section 13).
3   Remove the front brake caliper (see Chapter 9). **Caution:** *Tie the caliper assembly up with a piece of wire to keep any strain off the flexible brake lines.*
4   Remove the tie rod ends from the steering linkage (see Chapter 10).
5   Position a floor jack under the axle arm assembly and slightly compress the front coil spring. Remove the nut securing the lower portion of the spring to the axle beam.
6   Carefully lower the jack and remove the coil spring, spacer, seat and stud. **Caution:** *The axle arm assembly must be supported on the jack throughout spring removal and installation. Do not let the arm assembly hang suspended by the brake hose.*
7   Remove the shock absorber from the radius arm bracket.
8   Remove the stud and bolts securing the radius arm bracket and radius arm to the axle beam. Remove the bracket and radius arm.
9   Remove the pivot bolt securing the right axle arm assembly to he frame crossmember. Remove the clamps securing the axleshaft boot to the axleshaft slip yoke and axleshaft. Slide the rubber boot over the stub shaft.
10   Once the right driveshaft is disconnected from the slip yoke, lower the floor jack and remove the right axle arm assembly.
11   Position the jack under the differential housing and remove the bolt securing the left axle to the frame crossmember. Lower and remove the left axle arm assembly.
12   Installation is the reverse of the removal procedure with the following addition.

8

13 Tighten all fasteners to the torque listed in this Chapter's Specifications and related Chapters.

21   Shaft and joint assembly – removal and installation

Removal

1 Loosen the lug nuts on the front wheels.
2 Raise the front of the vehicle, support it securely on jackstands and remove the front wheels.
3 Remove the front brake calipers (see Chapter 9).
4 Remove the locking hubs, wheel bearings and locknuts (see Chapter 1).
5 Remove the nuts securing the spindle to the steering knuckle. Tap the spindle with a plastic or soft faced hammer to jar the spindle free. Remove the spindle.
6 Remove the splash shield.
7 On the right side of the vehicle, pull the shaft and joint assembly out of the carrier.
8 Working on the right side, remove the metal clamps from the shaft and joint assembly and the stub shaft. Slide the rubber boot onto the stub shaft and pull the shaft and joint assembly from the splines of the stub shaft.

Installation

9 On the right side of the carrier, install the rubber boot and new metal clamps on the stub shaft slip yoke. The spline will fit only one way. Be sure it is fully seated and crimp the metal clamp.
10 On the left side of the carrier, slide the shaft and joint assembly through the knuckle and engage the splines on the shaft in the carrier.
11 Install the splash shield. Install the spindle on the steering knuckle, then install and tighten the spindle nuts to the torque listed in Chapter 10.
12 Use the bearing cup replacer, Ford part No. T73T-4222-B and driver handle part No. T80T-4000-W or equivalent, drive the bearing cups into the rotor.
13 Pack the inner liner and outer wheel bearings with wheel bearing grease.
14 Place the inner wheel bearing into the inner cup and drive the grease seal into the bore with the special tools used in Step 12. Coat the bearing seal lip with wheel bearing grease.
15 Install the rotor on the spindle and install the outer wheel bearing into the cup.
16 Install the locknut, thrust bearing, snap-ring and locking hubs.
17 Install the brake caliper (see Chapter 9).
18 Install the front wheels and lower the vehicle.
19 Tighten the lug nuts to the torque listed in the Chapter 1 Specifications.

22   Right slip yoke and stub shaft assembly, carrier, carrier oil seal and bearing – removal and installation

Removal

1 Loosen the lug nuts on the front wheels.
2 Raise the front of the vehicle, support it securely on jackstands and remove the front wheels.
3 Remove the nuts and U-bolts connecting the driveshaft to the yoke (see Section 13).
4 Remove the spindles and the left and right shaft and U-joint assemblies (see Section 21).
5 Place a transmission jack under the carrier and remove both bolts securing the carrier to the support arm. Separate the carrier from the support arm and drain the lubricant from the carrier. Remove the carrier.
6 Rotate the slip yoke and shaft assembly so the open side of the snap ring is exposed. Remove the snap ring.
7 Remove the slip yoke and shaft assembly from the carrier.
8 Remove the oil seal and caged needle bearing.

Installation

9 Clean and inspect the bearing bore or nicks and burrs before installing a new caged bearing. Drive the bearing in until it is fully seated in the bore.
10 Coat the oil seal with multi-purpose grease and drive it into the carrier housing.
11 Install the slip yoke and shaft assembly into the carrier so the snapping groove in the shaft is visible.
12 Install the snap ring in the groove and make sure it is completely seated in the groove.
13 Clean all traces of gasket sealant from the mating surfaces with lacquer thinner or gasket remover. Apply RTV sealant in a 1/4-inch wide bead. The bead should be continuous and should not pass through or outside the holes.
14 Position the carrier on the transmission jack and install it in position on the support arm. Use the guide pins for alignment. Install and tighten the bolts in a clockwise pattern.
15 Install the shear bolt securing the carrier to the axle arm and tighten securely.
16 Install both spindles and the left and right shaft and joint assemblies.
17 Connect the driveshaft to the yoke (see Section 13).
18 Fill the carrier with lubricant (see Chapter 1).
19 Install the front wheels and lower the vehicle.
20 Tighten the lug nuts to the torque listed in the Chapter 1 Specifications.

Chapter 9   Brakes

Contents

Specifications

General

Brake fluid type .... See Chapter 1

Disc brakes

Minimum pad lining thickness .... See Chapter 1
Brake disc
   Disc thickness
      Standard .... 0.870 in
      Minimum* .... 0.810 in
   Maximum runout .... 0.003 in

*Refer to marks stamped into the disc (they supersede information printed here).

Drum brakes

Drum wear limit .... Refer to marks cast into drum
Minimum lining thickness .... See Chapter 1

Torque specifications   **Ft-lbs** (unless otherwise indicated)
Wheel cylinder bolts .... 120 to 240 in-lbs
Drum brake backing plate-to-axle housing bolt .... 20 to 40
Brake booster-to-firewall bolt .... 13 to 25
Master cylinder-to-firewall bolt .... 13 to 25
Master cylinder-to-brake booster nut .... 13 to 25
RABS valve
   Mounting bolts (1987 and 1988) .... 144 to 204 in-lbs
   Mounting screw (1988 and later) .... 15 to 20
RABS sensor mounting bolt .... 25 to 30

9

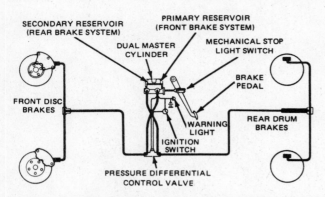

1.2a   Dual master cylinder brake system (1983 through 1985 models shown, others similar)

1   General information

Refer to illustrations 1.2a and 1.2b

The vehicles covered by this manual are equipped with hydraulically operated front and rear brake systems. The front brakes are disc type and the rear brakes are drum type. Both the front and rear brakes are self adjusting. The front disc brakes automatically compensate for pad wear, while the rear drum brakes incorporate an adjustment mechanism which is activated as the brakes are applied when the vehicle is driven in reverse. On 1987 and later models, a Rear Anti-lock Brake System (RABS) is optional.

Hydraulic system

The hydraulic system consists of two separate circuits **(see illustration)**. The master cylinder has separate reservoirs for the two circuits and in the event of a leak or failure in one hydraulic circuit, the other circuit will remain operative **(see illustration)**. If one circuit fails, the other will remain functional and a warning indicator will light up on the instrument panel, showing that a failure has occurred.

Combination valve (1983 through 1985 models)

A combination valve, located in the engine compartment below the master cylinder, consists of three sections providing the following func-tions. The metering section limits pressure to the front brakes until a pre-determined input pressure is reached and until the rear brakes are activated. There is no restriction at inlet pressures below 3 psi, allowing pressure equalization during non-braking periods. The proportioning section proportions outlet pressure to the rear brakes after a predetermined rear input pressure has been reached, preventing early rear wheel lock-up under heavy brake loads. The valve is also designed to assure full pressure to one brake system should the other system fail. The pressure differential warning switch incorporated into the combination valve is designed to continuously compare the front and rear brake pressure from the master cylinder and energize the dash warning light in the event of either a front or rear brake system failure. The design of the switch and valve are such that the switch will stay in the "warning" position once a failure has occurred. The only way to turn the light off is to repair the cause of the failure and apply brake pedal pressure.

Power brake booster

The optional power brake booster, utilizing engine manifold vacuum and atmospheric pressure to provide assistance to the hydraulically op-erated brakes, is mounted on the firewall in the engine compartment.

Parking brake

The parking brake operates the rear brakes only, through cable ac-tuation. It's activated by a pedal mounted on the left side kick panel.

Precautions

There are some general precautions involving the brake system on this vehicle:

a) Use only brake fluid conforming to DOT 3 specifications.

b) The brake pads and linings may contain asbestos fibers which are hazardous to your health if inhaled. Whenever you work on the brake system components, clean all parts with brake system cleaner or denatured alcohol. Do not allow the fine to become air-borne.

c) Safety should be paramount whenever any servicing of the brake components is performed. Do not use parts or fasteners which are not in perfect condition, and be sure that all clearances and torque specifications are adhered to. If you are at all unsure about a certain procedure, seek professional advice. Upon completion of brake system work, test the brakes carefully in a controlled area before putting the vehicle into normal service. If a problem is sus-pected in the brake system, don't drive the vehicle until it's fixed.

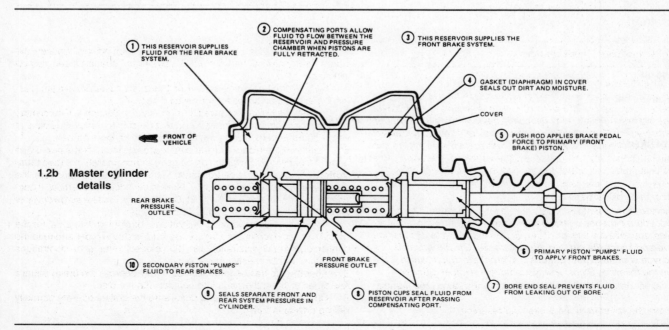

1.2b   Master cylinder details

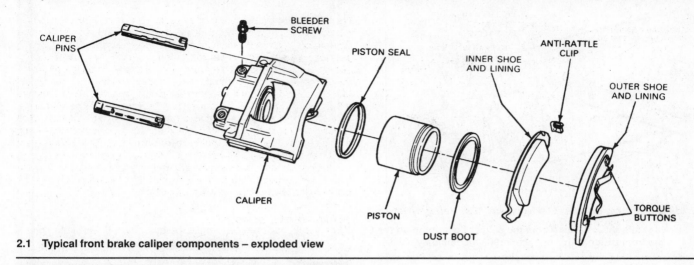

2.1   Typical front brake caliper components – exploded view

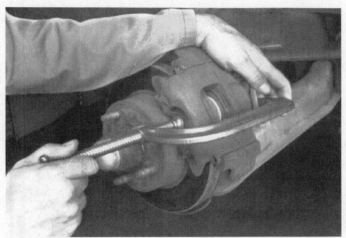

2.6   Using a large C-clamp, push the piston back into the bore just enough to allow the caliper to slide off the brake disc easily – note that one end of the C-clamp is on the flat area of the inboard side of the caliper and the other end (screw end) is pressing on the outer pad

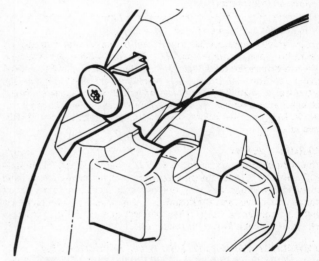

2.7a   Bolt head style pin sticks outside the caliper and must be cut off for removal (1983 models only)

2   Front brake pads – replacement

Refer to illustrations 2.1, 2.6 and 2.7a through 2.7p

Warning: *Disc brake pads must be replaced on both front wheels at the same time – never replace the pads on only one wheel. Also, the dust created by the brake system may contain asbestos, which is harmful to your health. Never blow it out with compressed air and don't inhale any of it. An approved filtering mask should be worn when working on the brakes. Do not, under any circumstances, use petroleum-based solvents to clean brake parts. Use brake cleaner or denatured alcohol only!*

Note: *When servicing the disc brakes, use only high quality, nationally recognized name brand pads.*

Note: *There are several types of caliper retaining pins used. The pin removal procedure depends on how the pin is installed. To remove the retaining pins, squeeze the outside of the pin until the tabs (stops) enter the pin groove and knock the pin through the groove. On 1983 models, the bolt head type is different and requires a different procedure which is described in the following Steps. Always remove the upper pin first.*

1   The caliper design for all models is basically the same **(see illustration).**

2   Remove the cover from the brake fluid reservoir.

3   Apply the parking brake and block the rear wheels. Loosen the wheel lug nuts, raise the front of the vehicle and support it securely on jackstands.

4   Remove the front wheels. Work on one brake assembly at a time, using the assembled brake for reference if necessary.

5   Inspect the brake disc carefully as outlined in Section 4. If machining is necessary, follow the information in that Section to remove the disc, at which time the pads can be removed from the calipers as well.

6   Push the piston back into the bore to provide room for the new brake pads. An eight inch C-clamp can be used to accomplish this **(see illustration).** As the piston is depressed to the bottom of the caliper bore, the fluid in the master cylinder will rise. Make sure it doesn't overflow. If necessary, siphon off some of the fluid. **Caution:** *Don't use a screwdriver or similar tool to pry the piston away from the disc.*

7   Follow the accompanying illustrations, beginning with 2.7a, for the actual pad replacement procedure. Be sure to stay in order and read the caption under each illustration. On 1983 models, refer to the illustrations that relate to that specific model only.

8   After the job has been completed, firmly depress the brake pedal a few times to bring the pads into contact with the disc.

9   Check for fluid leakage and make sure the brakes operate normally before driving in traffic.

9

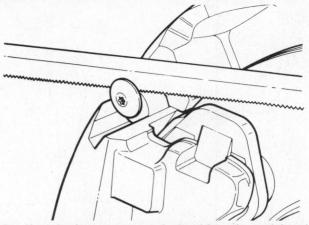

2.7b Separate the bolt head from the caliper by tapping on the pin from inside with a hammer (1983 models only)

2.7c Use a hacksaw to remove the head from the retaining pin (1983 models only)

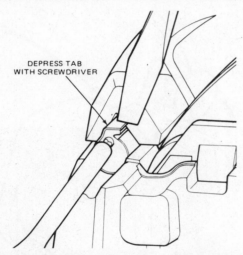

2.7d Depress the retaining tab on the pin with a screwdriver while tapping on the pin with a hammer and punch until the tab is depressed into the V-slot (1983 models only)

2.7e Use pliers and squeeze the caliper retaining pin while prying the other end until the tabs on the pin enter the groove (1984 and later models)

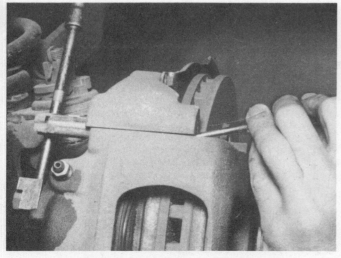

2.7f Drive out the pin with a punch and hammer

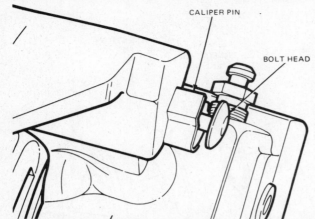

2.7g If the caliper isn't going to be removed for service, suspend it with a length of wire to relieve any strain on the brake hose

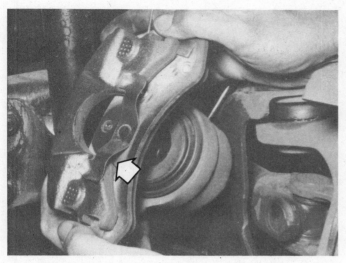

2.7h   This spring clip (arrow) holds the outside brake pad to the caliper – push down on the pad, releasing the locking tabs and slide the pad out of the caliper, then remove the inner pad and the anti-rattle clips from the spindle

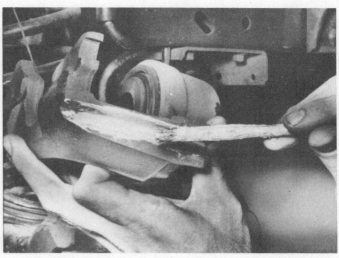

2.7i   Prior to installing the caliper, lightly lubricate the V-grooves where the caliper slides into the anchor plate with disc brake caliper grease

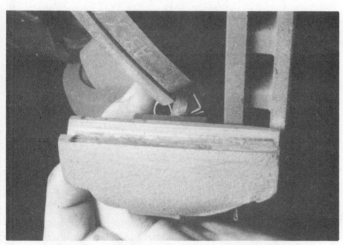

2.7j   Make sure the tabs on the spring clip are positioned correctly and the clip is fully seated on the inner pad

2.7k   Insert a new anti-rattle clip on the lower end of the inner pad

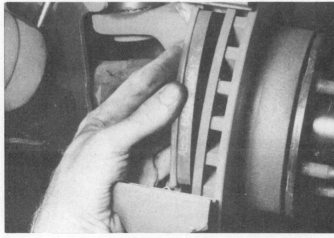

2.7l   Compress the anti-rattle clip and slide the upper end of the inner pad into position

2.7m   Use a C-clamp to depress the piston into the caliper until it bottoms out

9

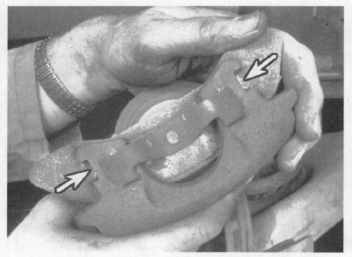

2.7n Push the outer pad into position on the caliper ears, making sure the torque buttons seat fully into the retention notches (arrows)

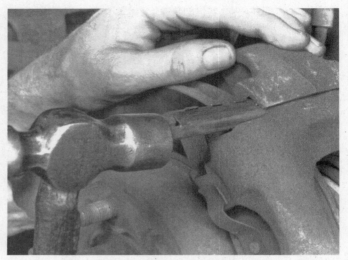

2.7o Place the caliper and outer pad assembly over the disc and inner pad, then drive the caliper pins into their grooves

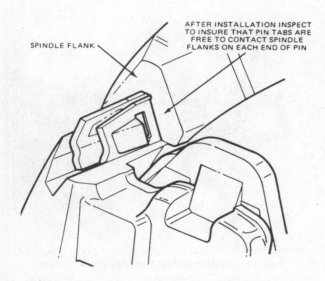

2.7p When both pins have been installed, check to be sure the pin tabs on each side of the spindle flank are exposed

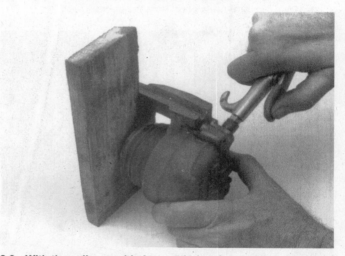

3.6 With the caliper padded to catch the piston, use compressed air to force the piston out of its bore – make sure your hands or fingers are not between the piston and caliper

---

3　Front brake caliper – removal, overhaul and installation

Refer to illustrations 3.6, 3.7, 3.8, 3.13, 3.14, 3.15a, 3.15b and 3.16

Warning: *Dust created by the brake system may contain asbestos, which is harmful to your health. Never blow it out with compressed air and don't inhale any of it. An approved filtering mask should be worn when working on the brakes. Do not, under any circumstances, use petroleum-based solvents to clean brake parts. Use brake cleaner or denatured alcohol only!*

Note: *If an overhaul is indicated (usually because of fluid leakage) explore all options before beginning the job. New and factory rebuilt calipers are available on an exchange basis, which makes this job quite easy. If it's decided to rebuild the calipers, make sure a rebuild kit is available before proceeding. Always rebuild the calipers in pairs – never rebuild just one of them.*

Removal

1　Apply the parking brake and block the rear wheels. Loosen the wheel lug nuts, raise the front of the vehicle and support it securely on jackstands.

2　Remove the front wheels.

3　Remove the brake hose inlet fitting bolt and detach the hose from the caliper. Have a rag handy to catch spilled fluid and wrap a plastic bag tightly around the end of the hose to prevent fluid loss and contamination. **Note:** *If the caliper will not be completely removed from the vehicle – as for pad inspection or disc removal – leave the hose connected and suspend the caliper with a length of wire. This will save the trouble of bleeding the system.*

4　Refer to the first few Steps in Section 2 to separate the caliper from the spindle – it's part of the brake pad replacement procedure.

Overhaul

5　Clean the exterior of the caliper with brake cleaner or denatured alcohol. Never use gasoline, kerosene or petroleum-based cleaning solvents. Place the caliper on a clean workbench.

6　Position a wood block or several shop rags in the caliper as a cushion, then use compressed air to remove the piston from the caliper **(see illustration)**. Use only enough air pressure to ease the piston out of the

3.7 Remove the dust boot from the caliper bore groove

3.8 The piston seal should be removed with a plastic or wooden tool to avoid damage to the bore and seal groove (a pencil will do the job)

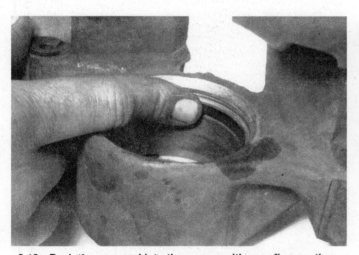

3.13 Push the new seal into the groove with your fingers, then check to see that it isn't twisted or kinked

3.14 Install the dust boot in the upper groove in the caliper bore, making sure it's completely seated

bore. If the piston is blown out, even with the cushion in place, it may be damaged. **Warning:** *Never place your fingers in front of the piston in an attempt to catch or protect it when applying compressed air, as serious injury could occur.*

7   Pull the dust boot out of the caliper bore **(see illustration)**.

8   Using a wood or plastic tool, remove the piston seal from the groove in the caliper bore **(see illustration)**. Metal tools may cause bore damage.

9   Remove the caliper bleeder screw and discard all rubber parts.

10   Clean the remaining parts with brake system cleaner or denatured alcohol, then blow them dry with compressed air.

11   Carefully examine the piston for nicks and burrs and loss of plating. If surface defects are present, the parts must be replaced. Check the caliper bore in a similar way.

12   Discard the caliper pins if they're corroded or damaged.

13   When assembling, lubricate the piston bore and seal with clean brake fluid. Install the seal in the caliper bore groove **(see illustration)**. Make sure the seal does not become twisted and that it is firmly seated in the groove.

14   Install a new boot in the piston groove **(see illustration)**.

15   Lubricate the piston with clean brake fluid, insert the piston squarely into the caliper bore **(see illustration)**, then use a C-clamp and wood

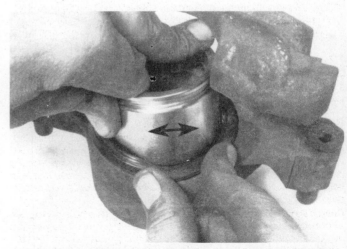

3.15a Insert the piston into the dust boot (NOT the bore) at an angle, then work the piston completely into the dust boot using a rotating motion

3.15b   Use a C-clamp and a block of wood to bottom the piston in the caliper bore – make sure it goes in perfectly straight, or the sides of the piston may be damaged

3.16   Install the lip of the dust boot in the groove in the caliper piston

block to press the piston in until it bottoms out (see illustration).
16   Seat the lip of the dust boot in the groove on the piston (see illustration).
17   Install the bleeder screw.

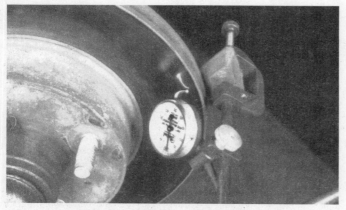

4.4a   Use a dial indicator to check disc runout – if the reading exceeds the maximum allowable runout limit, the disc will have to be machined or replaced

4.4b   Using a swirling motion, remove the glaze from the disc surface with emery cloth or sandpaper

Installation

18   Refer to Section 2 for the caliper installation procedure, as it is part of the brake pad replacement procedure.
19   If the brake hose is the thread-in type, thread it into the caliper. The hose is not designed to thread all the way in, so don't overtighten it. One or two threads should still be exposed when the brake hose is tightened securely.
20   If the brake hose is secured to the caliper by a union bolt, install a new sealing washer on each side of the brake hose fitting, then install the union bolt and tighten it securely.
21   Bleed the brakes as outlined in Section 11. This is not necessary if the inlet hose fitting was not loosened or removed from the caliper.
22   Install the wheels and lower the vehicle. Tighten the lug nuts to the torque listed in Chapter 1.
23   Test the brake operation before placing the vehicle in normal service.

---

4   Brake disc – inspection, removal and installation

Refer to illustrations 4.4a, 4.4b, 4.5a and 4.5b

Inspection

1   Loosen the wheel lug nuts, raise the vehicle and support it securely on jackstands. Remove the wheel(s).
2   Remove the brake caliper (see Section 3). It's not necessary to disconnect the brake hose. After removing the caliper pins, suspend the caliper out of the way with a piece of wire (see illustration 2.7g). Don't let the caliper hang by the hose and don't stretch or twist the hose.
3   Visually check the disc surface for score marks and other damage. Light scratches and shallow grooves are normal after use and may not always be detrimental to brake operation, but deep score marks – over 0.015-inch – require disc removal and refinishing by an automotive machine shop. Be sure to check both sides of the disc. If pulsating has been noticed during application of the brakes, suspect disc runout. Be sure to check the wheel bearings to make sure they're properly adjusted.
4   To check disc runout, place a dial indicator at a point about 1/2-inch from the outer edge of the disc (see illustration). Set the indicator to zero and turn the disc. The indicator reading should not exceed the runout limit listed in this Chapter's Specifications. If it does, the disc should be refinished by an automotive machine shop. **Note:** *Professionals recommend resurfacing of brake discs regardless of the dial indicator reading (to produce a smooth, flat surface that will eliminate brake pedal pulsations and other undesirable symptoms related to questionable discs). At the very least, if you elect not to have the discs resurfaced, deglaze them with sandpaper or emery cloth (use a swirling motion to ensure a nondirectional finish)* (see illustration).
5   The disc must not be machined to a thickness less than the minimum refinish thickness. The minimum wear (or discard) thickness is cast

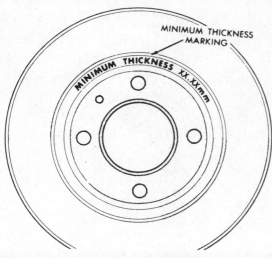

4.5a The minimum thickness limit is cast into the disc

4.5b Use a micrometer to measure the disc thickness at several points near the edge

into the inner surface of the disc (see illustration). The disc thickness can be checked with a micrometer (see illustration).

Removal

6 Refer to Chapter 1, Front wheel bearing check, repack and adjustment for the hub/disc removal procedure.

Installation

7 Install the disc and hub assembly and adjust the wheel bearings (see Chapter 1).
8 Install the caliper and brake pad assembly over the disc and position it on the steering knuckle (see Section 2 for the caliper installation procedure).
9 Install the wheel(s), then lower the vehicle to the ground. Tighten the lug nuts to the torque listed in the Chapter 1 Specifications. Depress the brake pedal a few times to bring the brake pads into contact with the disc. Bleeding of the system isn't necessary unless the brake hose was disconnected from the caliper. Check the operation of the brakes carefully before placing the vehicle into normal service.

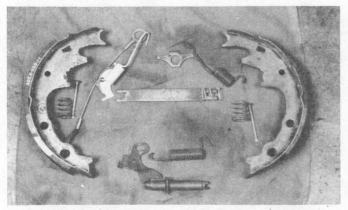

5.1 During removal lay the parts out in their order of removal to keep from getting confused

---

5 Rear brake shoes – replacement and adjustment

Refer to illustrations 5.1 and 5.5a through 5.5y

Warning: Drum brake shoes must be replaced on both wheels at the same time – never replace the shoes on only one wheel. Also, the dust created by the brake system may contain asbestos, which is harmful to your health. Never blow it out with compressed air and don't inhale any of it. An approved filtering mask should be worn when working on the brakes. Do not, under any circumstances, use petroleum-based solvents to clean brake parts. Use brake cleaner or denatured alcohol only!

Caution: Whenever the brake shoes are replaced, the retractor and hold-down springs should also be replaced. Due to the continuous heating/cooling cycle that the springs are subjected to, they lose their tension over a period of time and may allow the shoes to drag on the drum and wear at a much faster rate than normal. When replacing the rear brake shoes, use only high quality nationally recognized brand-name parts.

1 To ease installation of the brake assembly, during the removal procedures lay out all parts in an assembled order on a rag near the work area (see illustration).
2 Loosen the wheel lug nuts, raise the rear of the vehicle and support it securely on jackstands. Block the front wheels to keep the vehicle from rolling.
3 Release the parking brake.
4 Remove the wheels. **Note:** All four rear brake shoes must be replaced at the same time, but to avoid mixing up parts, work on only one brake assembly at a time.
5 Follow the accompanying photos (see illustrations 5.5a through 5.5y) for the inspection and replacement of the brake shoes. Be sure to

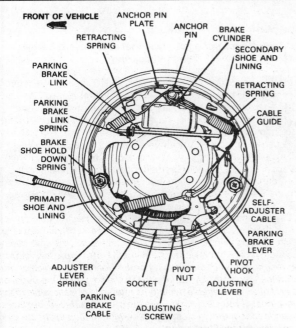

5.5a Components of a typical rear brake assembly (left side shown)

(continued on page 9–14)

9

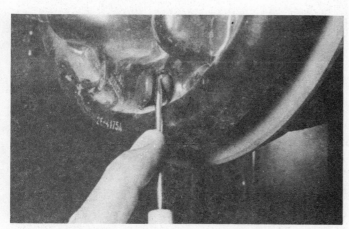

5.5b If, after releasing the parking brake, the drum will not slide off the shoes, remove the rubber plug from the backing plate

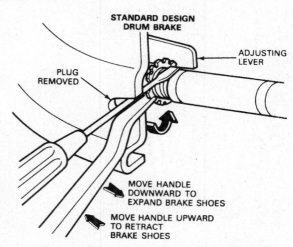

5.5c Use a narrow-bladed screwdriver to push the adjusting lever away from the adjusting screw star wheel so you can turn the star wheel with a brake tool to retract the shoes

5.5d Slide the drum off the shoes

5.5e Use a spring removal tool to remove the shoe retracting springs

5.5f Pull up on the adjusting cable and disconnect the cable eye from the anchor pin

5.5g Remove the anchor pin plate

5.5h   Remove the shoe retaining springs and pins (one on each shoe)

5.5i   Pull the shoes apart and remove the adjusting screw

5.5j   Remove the primary shoe, then slide out the parking brake strut and spring

5.5k   Remove the adjuster pawl

5.5l   Pull the secondary shoe away from the backing plate

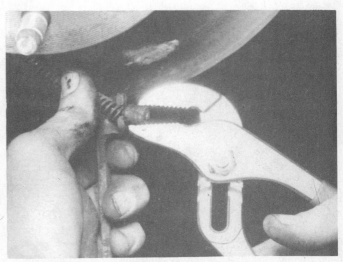

5.5m   Separate the parking brake cable and spring from the actuating lever

9

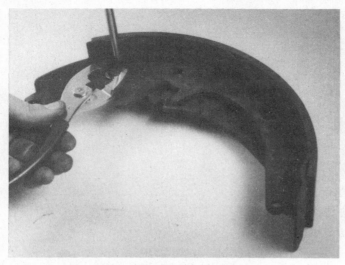

5.5n   Remove the retaining clip which holds the parking brake actuating lever to the brake shoes

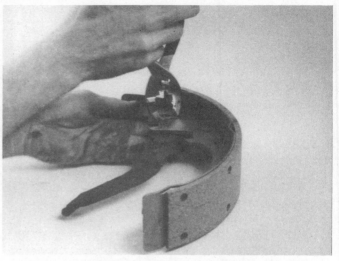

5.5o   Install the parking brake actuator lever on the new brake shoe and install the retaining clip

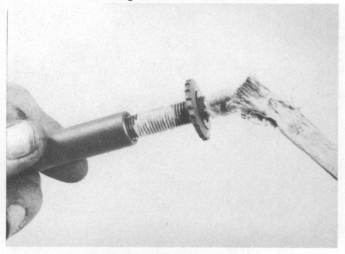

5.5p   Lubricate the adjusting screw assembly with high-temperature brake grease

5.5q   Lightly coat the shoe guide pads on the backing plate with high-temperature brake grease

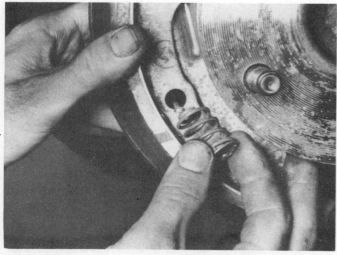

5.5r   Position the shoes on the backing plate, insert the retaining pins through the backing plate and shoes and put the springs over them

5.5s   Install the retaining spring caps

5.5t Make sure the slots in the wheel cylinder plungers and the parking brake strut properly engage the brake shoes

5.5u Install the adjusting screw with the long end pointing towards the front of the vehicle

5.5v Install the adjusting pawl

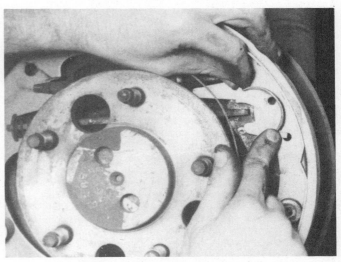

5.5w Install the cable guide and cable

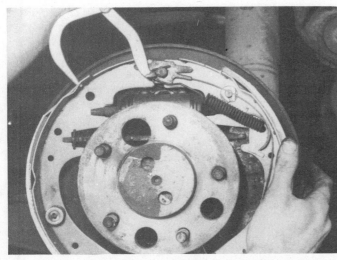

5.5x Install the shoe guide and adjusting cable eye to the anchor pin, then install the shoe retracting springs

5.5y Connect the cable and spring to the lever, then install the drum and adjust the brake shoe-to-drum clearance

9

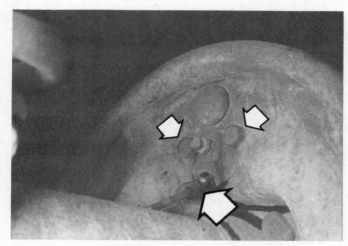

6.4   Disconnect the brake line fitting, then remove the mounting bolts (arrows)

stay in order and read the caption under each illustration. **Note:** *If the brake drum cannot be easily pulled off the axle and shoe assembly, make sure that the parking brake is completely released, then apply some penetrating oil at the hub-to-drum joint. Allow the oil to soak in and try to pull the drum off. If the drum still can't be pulled off, the brake shoes will have to be retracted. This is accomplished by first removing the plug from the backing plate. With the plug removed, pull the lever off the adjusting star wheel with one small screwdriver while turning the adjusting wheel with another small screwdriver, moving the shoes away from the drum. The drum should now come off.*

6   Before reinstalling the drum it should be checked for cracks, score marks, deep scratches and hard spots, which will appear as small discolored areas. If the hard spots cannot be removed with fine emery cloth or if any of the other conditions listed above exist, the drum must be taken to an automotive machine shop to have it turned. **Note:** *Professionals recommend resurfacing the drums whenever a brake job is done. Resurfacing will eliminate the possibility of out-of-round drums. If the drums are worn so much that they can't be resurfaced without exceeding the maximum allowable diameter (cast into the drum), then new ones will be required. At the very least, if you elect not to have the drums resurfaced, remove the glazing from the surface with sandpaper or emery cloth using a swirling motion.*

7   Install the brake drum on the axle flange.
8   Install the wheels and lower the vehicle to the ground. Tighten the lug nuts to the torque listed in Chapter 1.
9   Make a number of forward and reverse stops to adjust the brakes until satisfactory pedal action is obtained.
10   Check brake operation before driving the vehicle in traffic.

6   Wheel cylinder – removal, overhaul and installation

Note: *If an overhaul is indicated (usually because of fluid leakage or sticky operation) explore all options before beginning the job. New wheel cylinders are available, which makes this job quite easy. If it's decided to rebuild the wheel cylinder, make sure that a rebuild kit is available before proceeding. Never overhaul only one wheel cylinder – always rebuild both of them at the same time.*

Removal

Refer to illustration 6.4

1   Loosen the wheel lug nuts, raise the rear of the vehicle and support it securely on jackstands. Block the front wheels to keep the vehicle from rolling.
2   Remove the brake shoe assembly (see Section 5).
3   Remove all dirt and foreign material from around the wheel cylinder.
4   Unscrew the brake line fitting **(see illustration)**. Don't pull the brake line away from the wheel cylinder.
5   Remove the wheel cylinder mounting bolts.
6   Detach the wheel cylinder from the brake backing plate and place it on a clean workbench. Immediately plug the brake line to prevent fluid loss and contamination. **Note:** *If the brake shoe linings are contaminated with brake fluid, install new brake shoes.*

Overhaul

Refer to illustration 6.7

7   Remove the bleeder screw, cups, pistons, boots and spring assembly from the wheel cylinder body **(see illustration)**.
8   Clean the wheel cylinder with brake fluid, denatured alcohol or brake system cleaner. **Warning:** *Do not, under any circumstances, use petroleum-based solvents to clean brake parts!*
9   Use compressed air to remove excess fluid from the wheel cylinder and to blow out the passages.
10   Check the cylinder bore for corrosion and score marks. Crocus cloth can be used to remove light corrosion and stains, but the cylinder must be replaced with a new one if the defects cannot be removed easily, or if the bore is scored.
11   Lubricate the new cups with brake fluid.
12   Assemble the wheel cylinder components. Make sure the cup lips face in.

Installation

13   Place the wheel cylinder in position and install the bolts, but don't tighten the bolts yet.
14   Connect the brake line by hand, being careful not to cross-thread the fitting. Tighten the wheel cylinder mounting bolts to the torque listed in this Chapter's Specifications, then tighten the brake line fitting. Install the brake shoe assembly (see Section 5).
15   Bleed the brakes (see Section 11).
16   Check brake operation before driving the vehicle in traffic.

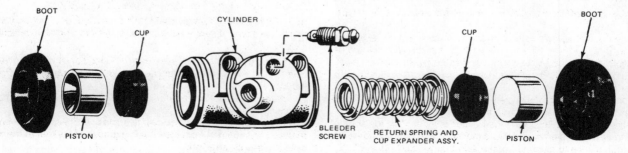

BOOT   CUP   CYLINDER   BLEEDER SCREW   RETURN SPRING AND CUP EXPANDER ASSY.   PISTON   CUP   BOOT

PISTON

6.7   An exploded view of the rear wheel cylinder

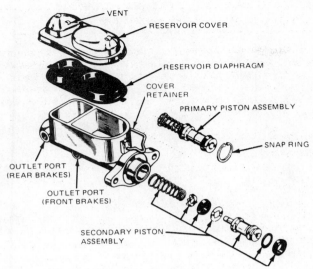

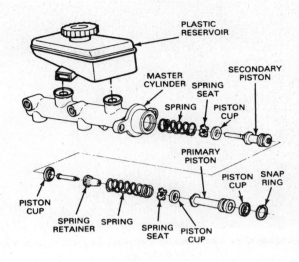

7.7a Exploded view of the master cylinder – 1983 through 1985 models

7.7b Exploded view of the master cylinder – 1986 and later models

7.9 Use a Phillips screwdriver to push the primary piston into the cylinder, then remove the snap-ring

7.10 Remove the primary piston assembly from the cylinder

7 Master cylinder – removal, overhaul and installation

Removal

1 Siphon as much brake fluid as possible from the master cylinder reservoir.

2 On non-power assisted brake systems, disconnect the electrical connector from the brake light switch, under the dash. Remove the retaining clip shoulder bolt and spacers securing the master cylinder pushrod to the brake pedal assembly. Remove the brake light switch from the brake pedal.

3 On power-assisted brake systems, push the brake pedal down several times to expel the vacuum from the brake booster.

4 Unscrew the brake lines from the master cylinder. Plug the ends of the lines to prevent the entry of dirt and moisture. Place newspapers under the connections to catch the brake fluid that will spill out.

5 Unscrew and remove the nuts which secure the master cylinder to the brake booster or to the firewall.

6 Remove the master cylinder from the vehicle. Brake fluid will damage painted surfaces, so don't spill any on the vehicle.

Overhaul

Refer to illustrations 7.7a, 7.7b, 7.9, 7.10, 7.11 and 7.13

Note: *Before deciding to overhaul the master cylinder, check on the availability and cost of a new or factory-rebuilt unit and also the availability of a rebuild kit.*

7 Clean the exterior of the master cylinder and dry it with a lint free rag. Remove the reservoir cover and diaphragm (**see illustrations**). Pour out the hydraulic fluid.

8 Place the master cylinder in a vise with vise jaws clamping on the mounting flange.

9 Use a large Phillips screwdriver to depress the piston assembly, then remove the snap-ring from the retaining groove at the rear of the master cylinder (**see illustration**).

10 Remove the primary piston assembly (**see illustration**). Inspect the seal for damage.

9

7.11 Tap the master cylinder against a block of wood to eject the secondary piston assembly

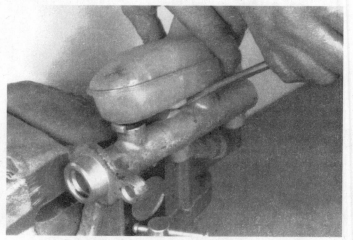

7.13 If you must remove the fluid reservoir (to replace leaking seals or a broken reservoir), gently pry it off with a screwdriver or prybar (1986 and later models only)

11   Remove the secondary piston assembly from the cylinder bore. It may be necessary to remove the master cylinder from the vise and invert it, carefully tapping it against a block of soft wood to expel the piston **(see illustration)**. Inspect the seal for damage.

12   Do not remove the outlet line seats, outlet check valves and outlet check valve springs from the master cylinder body.

13   If fluid has been leaking past the reservoir grommets on 1986 and later models, carefully pry the reservoir from the body with a screwdriver **(see illustration)**. Remove the grommets and discard them.

14   Inspect the cylinder bore and pistons for corrosion, wear and damage. If these are evident, replace the complete master cylinder assembly. Do not hone the master cylinder bore.

15   If these main components are in good condition, then the original assembly is worth overhauling. If the rubber seals are swollen or very loose on the pistons, suspect oil contamination in the system. Oil will swell these rubber seals and if one is found to be swollen it is reasonable to assume that all seals in the brake system need attention.

16   Wash all the internal components in clean brake fluid, brake system cleaner or denatured alcohol. Do not use any other type of fluid. Mineral spirits or solvent must never be allowed to come in contact with hydraulic cylinder components.

17   Purchase a repair kit which contains all the necessary seals and other replaceable parts. Some repair kits will contain a complete primary piston assembly.

18   On 1986 and later models, lubricate the new reservoir grommets with silicone lubricant and press them into the master cylinder body. Make sure they are properly seated.

19   On 1986 and later models, inspect the reservoir cap and reservoir for cracks or damage and replace if necessary.

20   On 1986 and later models, lay the reservoir on a hard surface and press the master cylinder body into the reservoir, using a rocking motion.

21   Lubricate the cylinder bore with clean brake fluid.

22   Dip the secondary piston assembly into clean brake fluid and push the piston into the cylinder, so the spring will seat against the closed end of the cylinder. Ease the seals into the bore taking care that they do not roll over.

23   Grip the master cylinder in a vise so that the open end of the cylinder is facing up. Dip the primary piston assembly into clean brake fluid and then push the piston, spring end first, into the master cylinder.

24   Depress the piston and install the retaining snap-ring. Make sure it is fully seated in its groove.

25   Install the diaphragm and cap.

Installation

26   Installation is the reverse of the removal Steps with the following additions:

a) **Note:** *Whenever the master cylinder is removed, the entire hydraulic system must be bled. The time required to bleed the system can be reduced if the master cylinder is filled with fluid and bench bled (see below) before the master cylinder is installed on the vehicle.*

b) Insert threaded plugs of the correct size into the cylinder outlet holes and fill the reservoirs with fresh brake fluid. The master cylinder should be supported in such a manner that the brake fluid will not spill during the bench bleeding procedure.

c) Loosen one plug at a time, starting with the rear outlet port first, and use a large Phillips screwdriver and push the piston assembly into the bore to force air from the master cylinder. To prevent air from being drawn back into the cylinder, the appropriate plug must be tightened before allowing the piston to return to its original position.

d) Stroke the piston three or four times for each outlet to ensure that all air has been expelled.

e) Since high pressure is not involved in the bench bleeding procedure, an alternative to the removal and installation of the plug with each stroke of the piston is available. Before pushing in on the piston assembly, remove one of the plugs completely. Before releasing the piston, however, instead of installing the plug, simply place your finger tightly over the hole to keep air from being drawn into the master cylinder. Wait several seconds for the brake fluid to be drawn from the reservoir to the piston bore, then repeat the procedure. When you push down on the piston it will force your finger off the hole, allowing air inside to be expelled. When only brake fluid is being ejected from the hole, install the plug and go to the other port.

f) Refill the master cylinder reservoir and install the diaphragm and cap.

g) Bleed the brake system as outlined in Section 11 and test the brakes carefully before driving the vehicle in traffic.

h) On power assisted brake systems, check the distance from the outer end of the booster assembly pushrod to the front face of the brake booster assembly **(see illustration)**. Turn the pushrod adjusting screw in or out as required to obtain the correct length.

8   Power brake booster – removal, installation and adjustment

Refer to illustrations 8.11 and 8.13

1   The power brake booster unit requires no special maintenance apart from periodic inspection of the vacuum hose and the case.

2   Dismantling of the power unit requires special tools and is not ordinarily done by the home mechanic. If a problem develops, install a new or factory rebuilt unit.

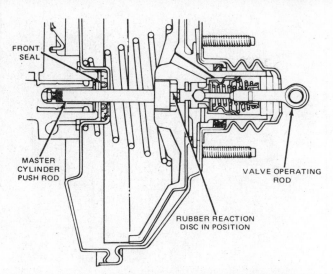

8.11   The reaction disc may become dislodged when the master cylinder pushrod is removed or accidentally pulled out

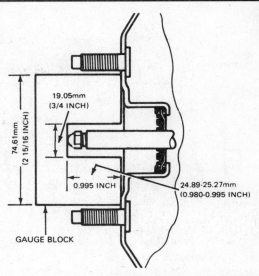

8.13   Place a gauge block against the master cylinder mounting surface of the booster and adjust the end of the pushrod so it jus touches the gauge block

Removal

3   Remove the nuts attaching the master cylinder to the booster and carefully pull the master cylinder forward until it clears the mounting studs. Don't bend or kink the brake lines.

4   Loosen the clamp and disconnect the vacuum hose where it attaches to the check valve on the power brake booster. Remove the check valve from the booster.

5   From inside the passenger compartment, disconnect the electrical connector from the brake light switch.

6   Also from the passenger compartment, disconnect the retaining pin, then slide the brake light switch, booster pushrod, spacers and bushings off the brake pedal arm.

7   Also from this location, remove the bolts securing the booster to the firewall.

8   Carefully lift the booster unit away from the firewall and out of the engine compartment.

Installation

9   Installation is the reverse of the removal Steps with the following additions.

10   Check the pushrod length as described at the end of this section.

11   On 1983 through 1987 models, make sure the booster rubber reaction disc is properly installed if the master cylinder pushrod is removed or accidentally pulled out (**see illustration**). A dislodged disc may cause excessive pedal travel and extreme operation sensitivity. The disc is black, compared to the silver colored valve plunger that will be exposed after the pushrod and front seal is removed. The booster is serviced as a unit and the entire unit must be replaced if the disc cannot be properly installed and aligned, or the disc cannot be located within the booster unit itself.

12   Carefully test the operation of the brakes before placing the vehicle in normal service.

Adjustment (1983 through 1987 models)

13   Some boosters feature an adjustable pushrod. They are matched to the booster at the factory and most likely will not require adjustment, but if a misadjusted pushrod is suspected, a gauge can be fabricated out of a piece of heavy gauge sheet metal (**see illustration**).

14   Some common symptoms caused by a misadjusted pushrod include dragging brakes (if the pushrod is too long) or excessive brake

pedal travel accompanied by a groaning sound from the brake booster (if the pushrod is too short).

15   To check the pushrod length, unbolt the master cylinder from the booster and position it to one side. It isn't necessary to disconnect the hydraulic lines, but be careful not to bend them.

16   Block the front wheels, apply the parking brake and place the transmission in Park or Neutral.

17   Start the engine and place the pushrod gauge against the end of the pushrod (**see illustration 8.13**). The rod should touch the end of the notch in the gauge. If not, adjust the rod by turning the adjusting screws in or out to obtain the correct length.

18   When adjustment is complete, reinstall the master cylinder and check for proper operation before driving the vehicle in traffic.

9   Pressure differential valve assembly (1983 through 1985 models) – removal and installation

Refer to illustration 9.1

On models so equipped, the pressure differential valve senses an unbalanced hydraulic pressure condition existing between the front and rear brake systems. When there is a pressure loss in either system during brake application, the piston will move off center, causing the brake warning lamp to light. The warning lamp will shut off when the brake system is serviced, properly bled and the brakes are applied to center the piston. The brake warning lamp switch is mounted on top of the pressure differential control valve body.

1   Disconnect the brake warning light connector from the warning light switch (**see illustration**).

2   Disconnect the brake line unions from the control valve assembly. Plug the ends of the lines to prevent the loss of brake fluid and the entry of foreign matter and moisture.

3   Remove the two nuts and bolts securing the control valve bracket to the underside of the fender apron. Remove the control valve assembly from the vehicle.

4   To install the assembly, position the control valve assembly on the fender apron holes and install the two mounting bolts and nuts. Tighten the bolts and nuts securely.

5   Reconnect the brake lines and unions to the control valve assembly. Tighten the unions securely.

9

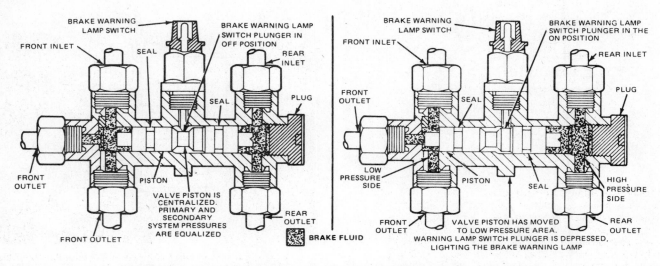

9.1   Operating details of the pressure differential valve (1983 through 1985 models)

6   Connect the brake warning light electrical connector to the switch. Verify this connection by turning the ignition switch to the Start position. The lamp should come on.

7   Bleed the system (see Section 11) and center the piston within the differential valve by applying the brakes.

10   Brake hoses and lines – inspection and replacement

Inspection

1   Brake hoses and lines should be inspected when recommended in the maintenance schedule. See Chapter 1 for inspection intervals and procedures.

Replacement

Front brake hose

2   Using a back-up wrench, disconnect the brake line from the hose fitting, being careful not to bend the frame bracket or brake line.

3   Use a pair of pliers to remove the U-clip from the female fitting at the bracket, then detach the hose from the bracket.

4   Unscrew the brake hose from the caliper.

5   To install the hose, first thread it into the caliper, tightening it securely.

6   Without twisting the hose, install the female fitting in the hose bracket. It will fit the bracket in only one position.

7   Install the U-clip retaining the female fitting to the frame bracket.

8   Using a back-up wrench, attach the brake line to the hose fitting.

9   When the brake hose installation is complete, there should be no kinks in the hose. Make sure the hose doesn't contact any part of the suspension. Check this by turning the wheels to the extreme left and right positions. If the hose makes contact, remove it and correct the installation as necessary. Bleed the system (see Section 11).

Rear brake hose

10   Using a back-up wrench, disconnect the hose at the frame bracket, being careful not to bend the bracket or steel lines.

11   Remove the U-clip with a pair of pliers and separate the female fitting from the bracket.

12   Disconnect the two hydraulic lines at the junction block, then unbolt and remove the hose.

13   Bolt the junction block to the axle housing and connect the lines, tightening them securely. Without twisting the hose, install the female end of the hose in the frame bracket.

14   Install the U-clips retaining the female end to the bracket.

15   Using a back-up wrench, attach the steel line fittings to the female fittings. Again, be careful not to bend the bracket or steel line.

16   Make sure the hose installation did not loosen the frame bracket. Tighten the bracket if necessary.

17   Fill the master cylinder reservoir and bleed the system (see Section 11).

Metal brake lines

18   When replacing brake lines be sure to use the correct parts. Don't use copper tubing for any brake system components. Purchase steel brake lines from a dealer or auto parts store.

19   Prefabricated brake line, with the tube ends already flared and fittings installed, is available at auto parts stores and dealers. These lines are also bent to the proper shapes.

20   When installing the new line make sure it's securely supported in the brackets and has plenty of clearance from moving or hot components.

21   After installation, check the master cylinder fluid level and add fluid as necessary. Bleed the brake system (see Section 11) and test the brakes carefully before driving the vehicle in traffic.

11   Brake hydraulic system – bleeding

Refer to illustration 11.8

Warning: *Wear eye protection when bleeding the brake system. If the fluid comes in contact with your eyes, immediately rinse them with water and seek medical attention.*

Note: *Bleeding the hydraulic system is necessary to remove any air that manages to find its way into the system when it's been opened during removal and installation of a hose, line, caliper or master cylinder.*

1   It will be necessary to bleed the system at all four brakes if air has entered the system due to low fluid level, or if the brake lines have been disconnected at the master cylinder.

2   If a brake line was disconnected only at a wheel, then only that caliper or wheel cylinder must be bled.

3   If a brake line is disconnected at a fitting located between the master cylinder and any of the brakes, that part of the system served by the disconnected line must be bled.

4   On models so equipped, remove any residual vacuum from the brake power booster by applying the brake several times with the engine off.

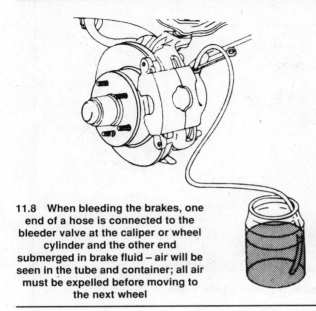

11.8   When bleeding the brakes, one end of a hose is connected to the bleeder valve at the caliper or wheel cylinder and the other end submerged in brake fluid – air will be seen in the tube and container; all air must be expelled before moving to the next wheel

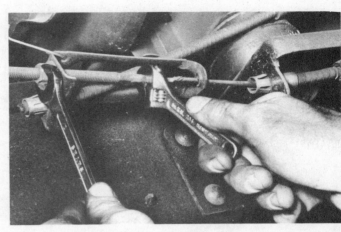

12.2   Hold the tension limiter and tighten the equalizer nut up the rod to adjust the parking brake

5   Remove the master cylinder reservoir cover and fill the reservoir with brake fluid. Reinstall the cover. **Note:** *Check the fluid level often during the bleeding operation and add fluid as necessary to prevent the fluid level from falling low enough to allow air bubbles into the master cylinder.*

6   Have an assistant on hand, as well as a supply of new brake fluid, a clear container partially filled with clean brake fluid, a length of 3/16-inch plastic, rubber or vinyl tubing to fit over the bleeder valve and a wrench to open and close the bleeder valve.

7   Beginning at the right rear wheel, loosen the bleeder valve slightly, then tighten it to a point where it is snug but can still be loosened quickly and easily.

8   Place one end of the tubing over the bleeder valve and submerge the other end in brake fluid in the container **(see illustration)**.

9   Have the assistant pump the brakes slowly a few times to get pressure in the system, then hold the pedal firmly depressed.

10   While the pedal is held depressed, open the bleeder valve just enough to allow a flow of fluid to leave the valve. Watch for air bubbles to exit the submerged end of the tube. When the fluid flow slows after a couple of seconds, close the valve and have your assistant release the pedal.

11   Repeat Steps 9 and 10 until no more air is seen leaving the tube, then tighten the bleeder valve and proceed to the left rear wheel, the right front wheel and the left front wheel, in that order, and perform the same procedure. Be sure to check the fluid in the master cylinder reservoir frequently.

12   Never use old brake fluid. It contains moisture which will deteriorate the brake system components.

13   Refill the master cylinder with fluid at the end of the operation.

14   Tighten the bleeder valves on the calipers and wheel cylinders securely.

15   Check the operation of the brakes. The pedal should feel solid when depressed, with no sponginess. If necessary, repeat the entire process. **Warning:** *Do not operate the vehicle if you are in doubt about the effectiveness of the brake system.*

Centering the pressure differential valve (1983 through 1985 models)

16   After bleeding the system the brake warning light will likely stay lit. Center the pressure differential control valve as follows.

17   Turn the ignition switch to ACC or ON position.

18   Make sure the master cylinder reservoir is filled to 1/4-inch from top.

19   Push the brake pedal down firmly, and the piston will center itself, causing the brake warning light to go off.

12   Parking brake – adjustment

Refer to illustration 12.2

Note: *Adjust the rear brakes prior to adjusting the parking brake cable.*

The parking brake layout is a cable system that incorporates a tension limiter. If the parking brake system is in normal operating condition, depressing the parking brake pedal to the floor will automatically set the proper tension.

Note: *The brake drums must be cold for this adjustment to be correct.*

1   Apply the parking brake.

2   Grip the tension limiter bracket to prevent it from turning and tighten the equalizer nut 2-1/2 inches up the rod **(see illustration)**.

3   Check to make sure the cinch strap has slipped (less than 1-3/8 inch remaining).

4   Position the parking brake pedal to the fully depressed position.

5   Scribe a mark on the threaded rod at the equalizer nut to note the original position.

6   Grip the threaded rod to prevent it from turning and tighten the equalizer nut six full turns past its original position.

7   Release the parking brake and check for rear wheel drag. The cables should be tight enough to provide full application of the rear brake shoes with the pedal fully applied. The cable should be loose enough to ensure complete release of the brake shoes when the lever is in the released position.

13   Brake pedal – removal and installation

Refer to illustrations 13.4, 13.8 and 13.13

1   Disconnect the cable from the negative battery terminal.

2   Disconnect the electrical connector from the brake light switch.

3   Disconnect the cotter pin and spacer connecting the brake pedal assembly, brake light switch assembly and master cylinder pushrod together. Remove the brake light switch and master cylinder pushrod from the pin on the brake pedal.

Manual transmission models

1983 through 1985 models

4   Remove the lockpin from the clutch master cylinder pushrod. Sepa-

9

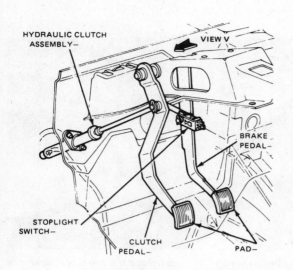

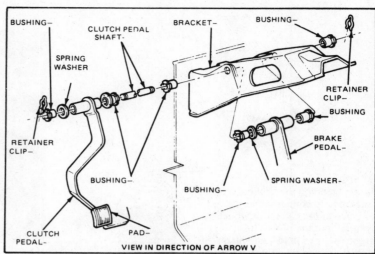

13.4 Brake pedal installation details – 1983 through 1985 models with manual transmission

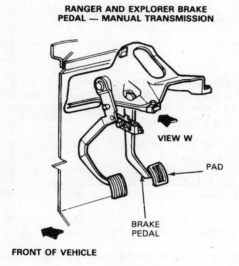

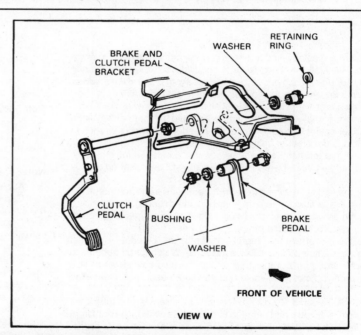

13.8 Brake pedal installation details – 1986 and later models with manual transmission

rate the pushrod from the clutch pedal and remove the bushing **(see illustration)**.

5 Remove the clip retainer from the end of the clutch shaft. Move the clutch pedal assembly to the side allowing space to remove the brake pedal assembly from the shaft.

6 Remove the brake pedal assembly.

7 Installation is the reverse of the removal Steps. Clean, inspect and lubricate the brake shaft bushings with engine oil prior to installation.

1986 and later models

8 Remove the clip securing the clutch/starter switch pushrod to the clutch pedal. Using a screwdriver, pry the pushrod and bushing from the clutch pedal pivot pin **(see illustration)**.

9 Remove the circlip from the end of the clutch shaft. Remove the clutch pedal assembly from the pedal support bracket.

10 Move the clutch pedal assembly to the side allowing space to re-

move the brake pedal assembly from the shaft.

11 Remove the brake pedal assembly.

12 Installation is the reverse of the removal Steps. Clean, inspect and lubricate the brake pedal shaft bushings with engine oil prior to installation.

Automatic transmission models

13 Remove the spring retainer and bushing from the brake pedal shaft **(see illustration)**.

14 From the other end, pull out the shaft and remove the brake pedal assembly including the bushings and spring washer.

15 Installation is the reverse of the removal Steps with the following additions.

16 Clean, inspect and lubricate the brake pedal shaft bushings with engine oil prior to installation.

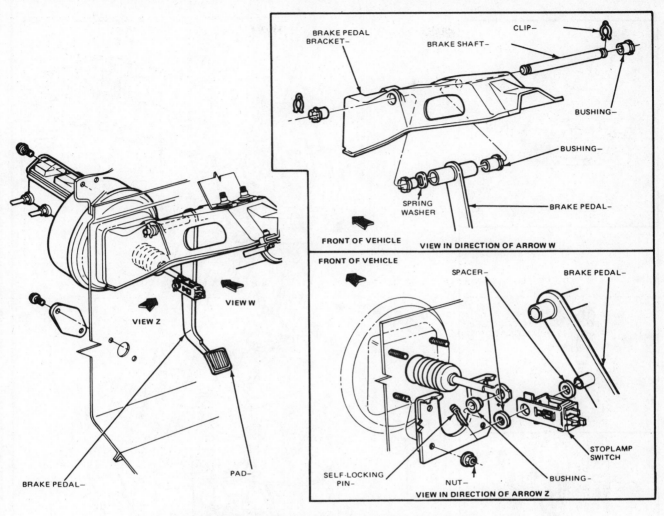

13.13   Brake pedal installation details – automatic transmission models

14   Rear Anti-lock Brakes System (RABS) (1987 and later models) – description, component removal and installation

Description

Refer to illustration 14.1

1   A Rear Anti-lock Brake System (RABS) is optional on 1987 and later models. The system consists of a computer module, anti-lock brake valve and an exciter ring and speed sensor **(see illustration)**.

2   Disconnect the cable from the negative battery terminal.

RAGS module (1987 and 1988 models)

3   Remove the access panel cover over the module on the pillar behind the driver's seat.

4   Disconnect the electrical connector from the RABS module **(see illustration 14.1)**.

5   Remove the two bolts securing the RABS module and remove it from the pillar.

6   Installation is the reverse of the removal Steps.

RABS module (1989 and later models)

7   Working under the instrument panel, depress the plastic tab on the electrical connector and disconnect it from the RABS module **(see illustration)**.

8   Remove the two bolts or nuts securing the RABS module to the instrument panel brace and remove it.

9   Installation is the reverse of the removal Steps.

RABS valve

10   Disconnect the two brake lines from the RABS valve **(see illustrations)**. Plug the ends of the lines to prevent the loss of hydraulic fluid and the entry of foreign matter and moisture.

11   Disconnect the electrical connector from the RABS valve.

12   Remove the nuts or screw securing the RABS valve to the frame rail and remove it.

13   To install, position the RABS valve on the frame rail and install the nuts or screw and tighten to the torque listed in this Chapter's Specifications.

14   Connect the electrical connector to the valve.

15   Install the brake lines and tighten to the torque listed in this Chapter's Specifications. **Caution:** *Do not overtighten the fittings.*

16   Bleed the hydraulic system (see Section 11).

Speed sensor

17   Disconnect the electrical connector from the sensor located on the rear axle housing.

9

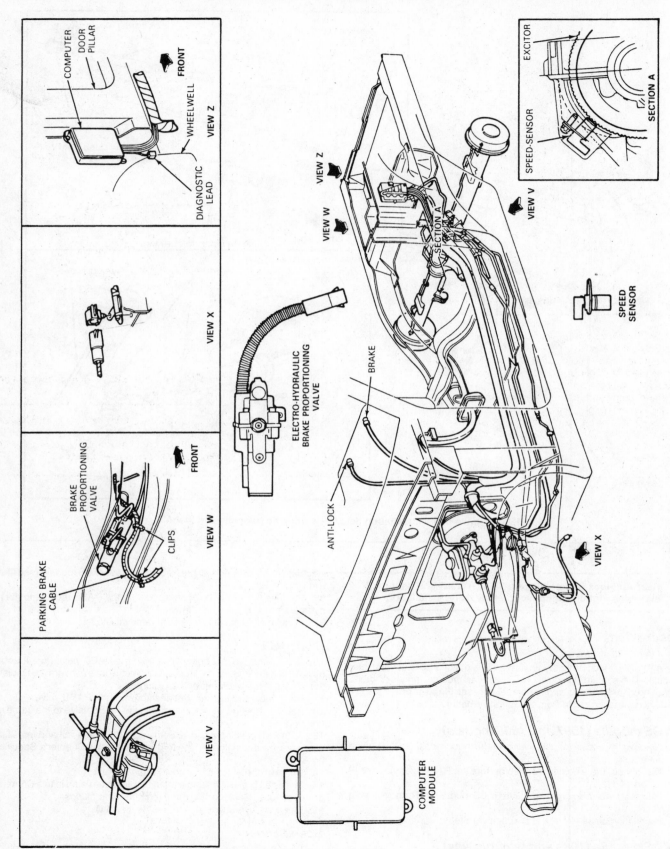

14.1   Rear Anti-lock Brake System (RABS) component layout (1987 and 1988 models shown, later models similar)

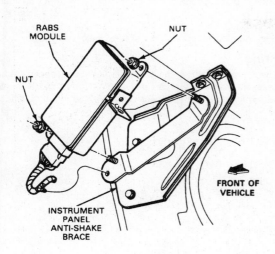

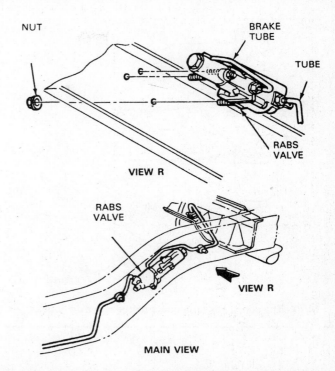

14.7   On 1989 and later models, the RABS module is located under the instrument panel, fastened to a brace

18   Prior to removing the sensor, thoroughly clean the rear axle housing surrounding the sensor.

19   Remove the bolt securing the sensor and remove it from the rear axle housing **(see illustration)**. Do not allow any dirt to fall into the rear axle housing.

20   Thoroughly clean the sensor mounting surface on the rear axle housing.

21   Inspect and clean the magnetized sensor pole piece. Remove any small metal particles that could cause erratic system operation.

22   If installing a new sensor, lightly lubricate the O-ring seal with clean engine oil.

14.10a   On 1987 and 1988 models, the RABS valve is mounted on the rear frame rail

23   If installing an old sensor, remove the old O-ring seal, install a new one and lubricate it with clean engine oil.

24   Firmly grasp the sides of the sensor (do not apply pressure to the electrical connector) and push it into the mounting hole.

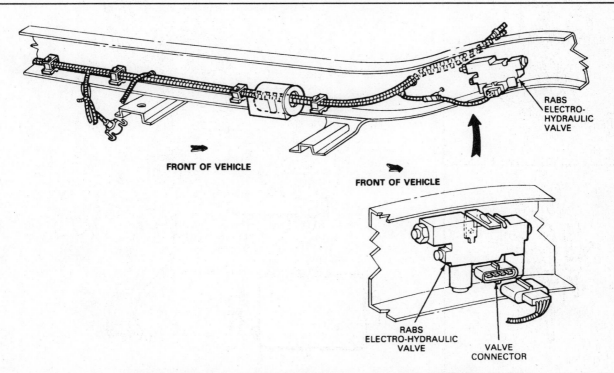

14.10b   On 1989 and later models, the RABS valve is mounted on the rear frame rail

9

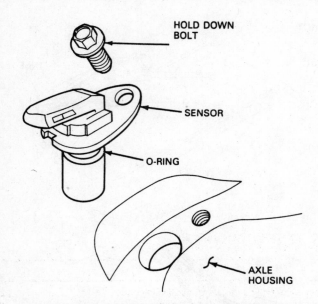

HOLD DOWN
BOLT

SENSOR

O-RING

AXLE
HOUSING

14.19   The speed sensor mounts on the rear axle housing

25   Align the mounting flange bolt hole with that on the rear axle housing and install the hold down bolt. Tighten the bolt to the torque listed in this Chapter's Specifications.
26   Connect the electrical connector to the sensor.

Excitor ring

27   To service the excitor ring the rear axle must be disassembled and the ring gear removed with a press. It is recommended that this procedure be performed by a dealer service department or other qualified repair shop.

Chapter 10
Suspension and steering systems

Contents

Specifications

General

Manual steering gear lubricant type	See Chapter 1
Power steering gear fluid type	See Chapter 1

Torque specifications

Ft-lbs (unless otherwise indicated)

Front suspension

Axle arm-to-pivot bracket nut	120 to 150
Axle arm pivot bracket-to-frame nut	70 to 92
Axle pivot bolt	120 to 150
Axle-to-radius arm bolt and nut	191 to 231
Bumper-to-spring seat bolt	156 to 216 in-lbs
Front shock absorber-to-radius arm bolt and nut	42 to 75
Front shock absorber-to-spring nut	25 to 35
Jounce bumper bolt	132 to 228 in-lbs
Radius arm-to-frame nut	81 to 120
Radius arm bracket-to-frame bolt	77 to 110
Radius arm bracket connecting bolt	35 to 50
Radius arm to rear bracket nut	80 to 120
Radius arm front bracket and axle stud	160 to 220
Radius arm front bracket front bolt	27 to 37
Radius arm front bracket lower bolt	160 to 220
Spring retaining nut	70 to 100
Stabilizer bar-to-radius arm U-bolt nut	48 to 68
Stabilizer bar bushing bracket bolt	35 to 50
Stabilizer bar link bushing bolt and nut	
2WD models	55 to 81
4WD models	30 to 44

Torque specifications (continued)

Ft-lbs (unless otherwise specified)

Front suspension

Tie-rod adjusting sleeve bolt	30 to 42
Tie-rod to spindle nut	51 to 75
Lower balljoint stud nut	
2WD drive models	
Ranger	95 to 110
Bronco II	104 to 146
4WD models (all)	95 to 110
Upper balljoint stud nut	85 to 110
Spindle-to-steering knuckle nuts (4WD only)	35 to 45

Rear suspension

Rear leaf spring U-bolt nut	65 to 75
Drag link-to-connecting rod ball stud nut	50 to 75
Shock-to-lower bracket nut	40 to 60
Shock-to-upper bracket nut	41 to 63
Shackle-to-spring nut	74 to 115
Spring-to-frame nut	74 to 115
Spring shackle-to-rear bracket bolt	74 to 115
Stabilizer-to-mounting bracket bolt	30 to 42
Stabilizer-to-bar and frame bolt	40 to 60

Steering system

Flex coupling-to-steering gear input shaft bolt	25 to 35
Drag link-to-Pitman arm nut	50 to 75
Drag link-to-steering connecting rod nut	50 to 75
Pitman arm-to-steering gear box nut	170 to 230
Tie-rod-to-spindle ball stud nut	50 to 75
Manual steering coupling-to-input shaft bolt	25 to 35
Manual steering gear-to-frame bolt	54 to 66
Power steering gear-to-flex coupling bolt	26 to 34
Power steering gear-to-frame bolt	50 to 62
Power steering pump (four-cylinder engine)	
Pump-to-bracket bolt	30 to 45
Bracket-to-engine block bolt	30 to 45
Bracket bolts	27 to 37
Power steering pump (V6 engine)	
Slider bolt	35 to 47
Front and rear support bracket bolts	35 to 47
Pump-to-bracket bolts	35 to 47
Steering wheel nut	
1983 through 1986 models	30 to 42
1987 and later models	22 to 33

1   General information

The front suspension on vehicles covered in this manual is a twin I-beam type, which is composed of coil springs, I-beam axle arms, radius arms, upper and lower balljoints and spindles, tie-rods, shock absorbers and an optional stabilizer bar. The 4WD model is basically the same except for the addition of two piece driveaxle assembly.

The front suspension consists of two independent axle arm assemblies. One end of the assembly is anchored to the frame and the other is supported by the coil spring and radius arm. The spindle is connected to the axle by upper and lower balljoints. The balljoints are constructed of a special lubricated-for-life bearing material. Lubrication points are found on the tie-rods, steering linkage and U-joints on earlier 4WD models. Movement of the spindles is controlled by the tie-rods and the steering linkage.

Two adjustments can be performed on the axle assembly. Camber is adjusted by removing and replacing an adapter between the upper balljoint stud and the spindle. Adapters are available in 0-degree, 1/2-degree, 1-degree and 1-1/2-degree increments. Toe-in adjustment is accomplished on both models by turning the tie-rod adjusting sleeve.

The hydraulic shock absorbers are of the direct, double acting type, with later models having low pressure gas shocks. Both shock absorbers are of the telescoping design and come equipped with rubber grommets at the mounting points for quiet operation. The low pressure gas shock absorbers are sealed and charged with nitrogen gas to reduce shock absorber fade and improve ride. The shock absorbers are non-adjustable. The shock absorbers are not rebuildable and must be replaced as complete assemblies.

The rear suspension uses shock absorbers and semi-elliptical leaf springs. The forward end of each spring is attached to the bracket on the frame side rail. The rear of each spring is shackled to a bracket on the frame rail. The rear shock absorbers are direct, double acting units with staggered mounting positions. The right shock is mounted forward of the axle and the left mounted behind it.

Since most procedures that are dealt with in this chapter involve jacking up the vehicle and working underneath it, a good pair of jackstands will be needed. A hydraulic floor jack is the preferred type of jack to lift the vehicle, and it can also be used to support certain components during various operations. **Warning:** *Never, under any circumstances, rely on a jack to support the vehicle while working under it.*

Warning: *Whenever any of the suspension or steering fasteners are loosened or removed they must be inspected and, if necessary, replaced with new ones. New fasteners must be of the same part number or of original equipment quality and design. Torque specifications must be followed for proper reassembly and component retention.*

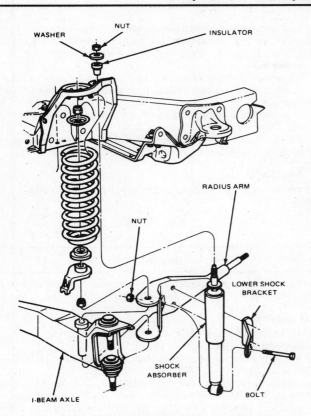

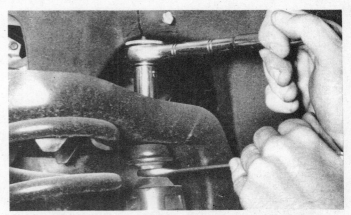

2.3   Hold the shock absorber shaft while turning the top retainer nut

2.2   Mounting details of the front shock absorber and related components (1983 through 1992 models shown, later models similar)

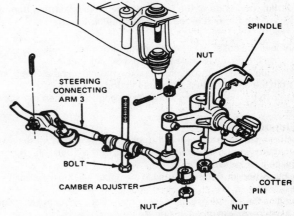

3.4   Exploded view of the front spindle (2WD model)

2.4   The shock absorber lower mounting bracket is attached to the radius arm by a bolt and nut (arrow) (1992 and earlier models only – later models are fastened with a nut)

4   Remove the bolt and nut securing the shock absorber to the radius arm **(see illustration)**.
5   To remove the shock absorber, slightly compress the shock and remove it from its brackets.
6   Installation is the reverse of the removal steps with the following additions.
   a)   Install and tighten the new nuts and bolts to the torque listed in this Chapter's Specifications.
   b)   Install the wheel and lug nuts, lower the vehicle and tighten the lug nuts to the torque listed in the Chapter 1 Specifications.

3   Front wheel spindle (steering knuckle) – removal and installation

Refer to illustrations 3.4 and 3.7

2WD models

Removal

1   Loosen the front wheel lug nuts, raise the front of the vehicle and support it securely on jackstands. Remove the wheel.
2   Remove the brake disc (see Chapter 1, *Front wheel bearing check, repack and adjustment*) and the dust shield.
3   Remove the cotter pin and nut and disconnect the tie-rod end from the spindle (see Section 10).
4   Remove the cotter pin and nut from the upper balljoint stud **(see illustration)**.

2   Front shock absorber – removal and installation

Refer to illustrations 2.2, 2.3 and 2.4
Caution: *The low pressure gas shock absorbers are pressurized to 135 psi with nitrogen gas. Do not attempt to open, puncture or apply heat to the shock absorbers.*

1   Loosen the front wheel lug nuts on the side to be dismantled. Raise the front of the vehicle, support it securely on jackstands, block the rear wheels and set the parking brake. Remove the front wheel.
2   The shock absorbers are mounted next to the coil springs **(see illustration)**. Support the I-beam with a floor jack.
3   Remove the top nut with a deep socket while holding the shaft with an open end wrench **(see illustration)**. Lift off the washer.

3.7   Strike the inside of the front spindle (arrows) with a hammer to break it loose from the balljoint studs

5   Remove the cotter pin from the lower balljoint stud nut.
6   Loosen but do not remove the lower balljoint stud nut.
7   Strike the inside of the spindle near the balljoint to break the spindle loose from the balljoint studs **(see illustration)**.
8   Remove the nut securing the lower balljoint stud, then remove the spindle.

Installation

9   Before installation, check that the upper and lower balljoint seals were not damaged during spindle removal and that they are positioned correctly. Replace if necessary.
10   Apply thread locking compound to the upper and lower balljoint stud threads.
11   Position the spindle over both balljoints. If the camber adjuster came loose, align the marks made in step 4.
12   Install and partially tighten the nut on the lower balljoint stud.

13   Install and tighten the nut on the upper balljoint stud. Tighten the nut to the torque listed in this Chapter's Specifications. Advance the nut to the next castellation, if necessary, to align it with the hole in the stud. Install a new cotter pin.
14   Tighten the lower balljoint stud nut to the torque listed in this Chapter's Specifications and advance the nut to the next castellation, then install a new cotter pin.
15   Install the dust shield and the brake disc and adjust the wheel bearings (see Chapter 1).
16   Install the front wheel and tighten the lug nuts to the torque listed in this Chapter's Specifications.

4WD models

17   Refer to Section 21 of Chapter 8 for spindle and axleshaft removal procedures.

---

4   Balljoints – removal and installation

Caution: *Do not heat the axle or balljoint to aid removal since the temper may be removed from the component(s), leading to premature failure.*

2WD models

Refer to illustrations 4.3, 4.4, 4.5 and 4.8

1   Remove the spindle (see Section 3).
2   Remove the snap-ring from each balljoint. **Note:** *Remove the upper balljoint first.*
3   Install the C-frame assembly tool (Ford part No. T74P-4635-C and receiving cup D81T-3010-A) on the upper balljoint or make a suitable tool out of a C-clamp and piece of thick-walled pipe of the appropriate size **(see illustration)**. Tighten the special tool or C-clamp and press the balljoint out of the I-beam. **Note:** *If the special tools are not available or will not remove the balljoint, remove the I-beam and take it to a dealer service department or other repair shop and have the balljoints pressed out.*
4   Use the same tool setup used in Step 3 on the lower balljoint and press the balljoint out **(see illustration)**.

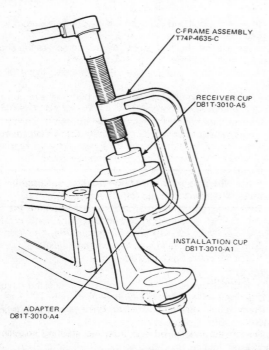

4.3   Use Ford special tools or a C-clamp and a piece of tubing to remove the balljoints (2WD models)

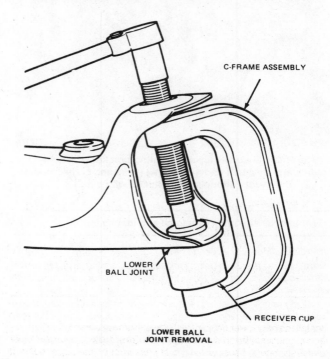

4.4   Removing the lower balljoint (2WD models)

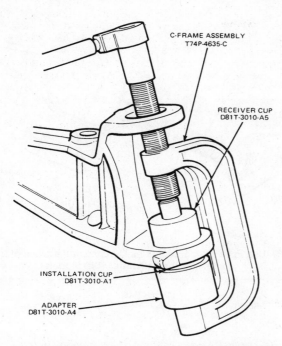

4.5   Note the additional receiver cup required to install the lower balljoint – install the lower balljoint first (2WD models)

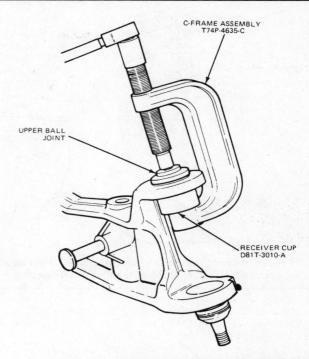

4.8   Installing the upper balljoint (2WD models)

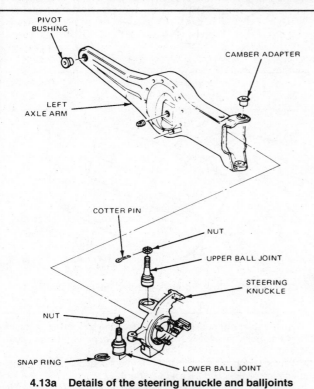

4.13a   Details of the steering knuckle and balljoints (4WD models)

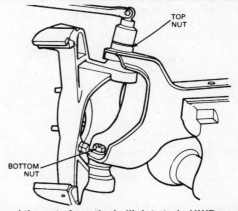

4.13b   Removal the nuts from the balljoint studs (4WD models)

the I-beam until it is completely seated. **Caution:** *Don't heat the axle or balljoint to aid in installation since the temper may be removed from the component(s), which could lead to premature failure.*

7   Install the lower balljoint snap-ring.

8   Install the new upper balljoint with the C-frame assembly, balljoint receiver cup and installation cup **(see illustration).**

9   Turn the screw in the C-frame clockwise and press the balljoint into the I-beam until it is completely seated. **Caution:** *Don't heat the beam or balljoint to aid in installation since the temper may be removed from the component(s), which could lead to premature failure.*

10   Install the upper balljoint snap-ring.

4WD models

Refer to illustrations 4.13a, 4.13b, 4.16, 4.18, 4.19 and 4.21

11   Remove the spindle and shaft and joint assembly (see Section 22 of Chapter 8).

12   Disconnect the tie-rod end from the steering knuckle (see Section 10).

13   Remove the cotter pin from the upper balljoint, then remove the nut **(see illustrations)**.

5   Install the new lower balljoint with the C-frame assembly, balljoint receiver cup and installation cup **(see illustration)**. **Note:** *Install the lower balljoint first since the special tool must pass through the upper balljoint receptacle.*

6   Turn the screw in the C-frame clockwise and press the balljoint into

10

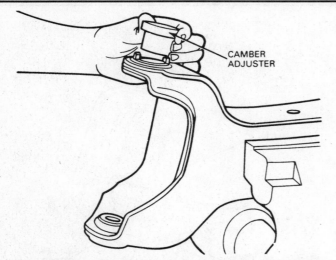

4.16   When removing the camber adjuster, note its orientation so it can be installed in the same position (4WD models)

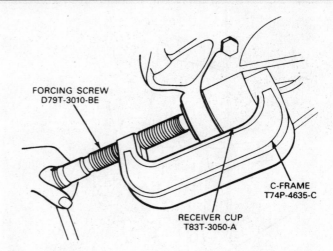

4.18   Use Ford special tools or a C-clamp and a piece of tubing to remove the balljoints (4WD models)

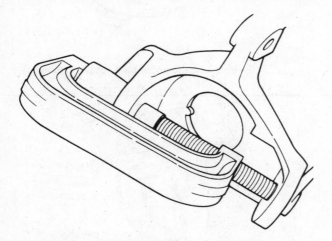

4.19   Using the special tool to remove the upper balljoint (4WD models)

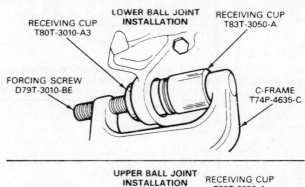

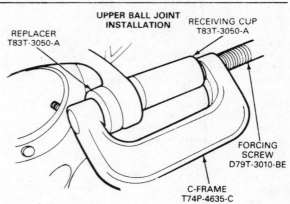

4.21   Balljoint installation details – install the lower balljoint first (4WD models)

14   Loosen the nut on the lower balljoint, but don't remove it at this time.

15   Strike the inside of the steering knuckle near the upper and lower balljoints. This will break the balljoint studs loose from the axle arm. Remove the nut from the lower balljoint and remove the steering knuckle from the axle arm.

16   Remove the camber adjuster sleeve (see illustration). **Note:** *Check the orientation of the sleeve. The slot should be installed in the same manner during installation to maintain the correct alignment.*

17   If so equipped, place the steering knuckle in a vise and remove the snap-ring from the lower balljoint socket. **Note:** *Always remove the lower balljoint first.*

18   Install the C-frame assembly tool (Ford part No. T74P-4635-C), forcing screw (Ford part No. D79T-3010-BE) and balljoint remover (Ford part No. D79T-3010-BE) on the lower balljoint or make a suitable tool out of a C-clamp and piece of thick-walled pipe of the appropriate size (see illustration). Tighten the special tool, or C-clamp, and press the lower balljoint out of the steering knuckle. **Note:** *If the C-frame assembly tool and receiver tool are not available or will not remove the balljoint, then take the steering knuckle assembly to a dealer service department and have the balljoints pressed out.*

19   Use the same tool setup used in Step 18 on the upper balljoint and press the balljoint out (see illustration).

20   Clean the steering knuckle bore and insert the balljoint in the knuckle as straight as possible. **Note:** *The lower balljoint doesn't have a hole in the stud for the cotter pin.*

21   Install the lower balljoint with the C-frame assembly, balljoint receiver cup and installation cup (see illustration).

22   Turn the screw in the C-frame clockwise and press the balljoint into the steering knuckle until it is completely seated. **Caution:** *Do not heat the knuckle or balljoint to aid in installation since some to the temper may be removed from the component(s) leading to premature failure.*

23   If so equipped, install the lower balljoint snap-ring.

24   Install the upper balljoint with the C-frame assembly, balljoint receiver cup and replacer (see illustration 4.21).

25   Turn the screw in the C-frame clockwise and press the balljoint into the knuckle until it is completely seated. **Caution:** *Do not heat the*

5.2   With the vehicle supported on jackstands, use a floor jack to support the front axle

5.5a   Remove the spring retainer nut

knuckle or balljoint to aid in installation since some to the temper may be removed from the component(s) leading to premature failure.

26   Install the camber adjuster into the axle arm. Place the slot in the original position noted during removal. **Note:** *Install the camber adjuster with the arrow pointing toward the outside for positive camber or with the arrow pointing toward the inside of the vehicle for negative camber. Zero camber bushings do not have an arrow and may be rotated in either direction as long as the lugs on the yoke engage the slots in the bushing.* **Caution:** *The following tightening sequence must be followed exactly when securing the spindle. Excessive spindle turning effort may result in reduced steering returnability if this procedure is not followed.*

27   Install the steering knuckle in the axle arm. Do not disrupt the camber adjuster during installation.

28   Install the nut on the bottom balljoint stud and tighten it to the preliminary torque of 40 ft-lbs.

29   Install a new nut on the upper balljoint stud and tighten it to the torque listed in this Chapter's Specifications, then advance the nut until the castellations align with the cotter pin hole in the balljoint. Install a new cotter pin and bend the ends over completely.

30   Finish tightening the lower nut to the torque listed in this Chapter's Specifications. **Note:** *The camber adjuster will seat itself into the steering knuckle at a predetermined position during the tightening sequence. Do not attempt to adjust this position.*

31   For proper front end alignment, take the vehicle to a dealer or alignment shop.

---

5   Coil spring – removal and installation

Removal

Refer to illustrations 5.2, 5.5a and 5.5b

1   Loosen the front wheel lug nuts on the side to be disassembled. Raise the front of the vehicle, support it securely on jackstands, block the rear wheels and set the parking brake. Remove the front wheel.

2   Place a floor jack under the axle **(see illustration)**.

3   Remove the bolt and nut securing the shock absorber to the radius arm **(see illustration 2.4)**.

4   Remove the brake caliper assembly and suspend it with a length of wire to relieve any strain on the brake hose (see Chapter 9).

5   At the lower end of the spring, remove the retaining nut and the retainer securing the spring to the front axle **(see illustration)**. **Note:** *The*

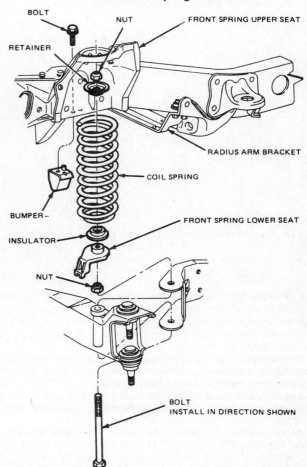

5.5b   An exploded view of the front spring (2WD models)

nut is attached to a stud on 4WD models and on 2WD models it is attached to a bolt that runs through the axle **(see illustration)**.

6   On models so equipped, remove the through bolt securing the stabilizer bar to the front axle.

5.10 Before assembly make sure the lower spring seat and insulator are in place

5.11 Push down on the axle beam to make room to install the spring

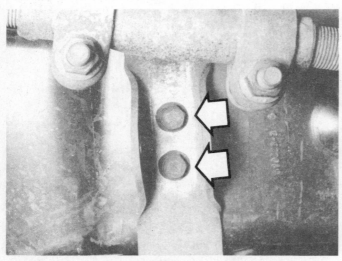

6.3a Remove the two bolts (arrows) securing the radius arm to the front bracket

6.3b On 4WD models, remove the stud and bolt (arrows) securing the radius arm to the axle arm – on 2WD models, a through bolt is used instead of the stud and bolt

7   The front axle should now be free to allow spring removal. Slowly lower the floor jack until the spring is fully extended. **Note:** *If the axle doesn't drop down far enough to allow spring removal, remove the pivot bolt securing the left axle to the frame.*

8   If necessary, use a prybar and lift the spring up and over the bolt or stud that passes through the lower spring seat. Rotate the spring so the upper built-in spring seat retainer is cleared, then remove the spring.

Installation

Refer to illustrations 5.10 and 5.11

9   If removed in Step 7, install the left front axle pivot bolt and tighten the nut to the torque listed in this Chapter's Specifications.

10 Install the spring lower seat and insulator onto the front axle **(see illustration)**.

11 If necessary, push the front axle down to allow installation of the spring. Install the upper end of the spring into the upper seat and rotate

the spring into place **(see illustration)**.

12 If necessary, use a prybar and lift the lower end of the spring up and over the bolt or stud on the axle and into place on the lower spring seat and insulator.

13 Apply pressure on the floor jack and lift the front axle until the spring is correctly seated.

14 Install the lower spring retainer and new nut. Tighten the nut to the torque listed in this Chapter's Specifications.

15 On models so equipped, install the through bolt securing the stabilizer bar to the front axle. Install a new nut and tighten to the torque listed in this Chapter's Specifications.

16 Install the brake caliper assembly (see Chapter 9).

17 Install the bolt and new nut (or nut and washer) securing the shock absorber to the radius arm. Tighten the nut to the torque listed in this Chapter's Specifications.

18 Install the wheel and lug nuts, lower the vehicle and tighten the lug nuts to the torque listed in Chapter 1.

6.4   Remove the nut, washer and insulator and remove the rear radius arm support

6   Radius arm – removal and installation

Removal

Refer to illustrations 6.3a, 6.3b, 6.4, 6.5a and 6.5b

1   Remove the coil spring (see Section 5).
2   Remove the spring lower seat from the radius arm.
3   Remove the fasteners securing the radius arm to the front axle and front bracket **(see illustrations)**.
4   From the rear side of the radius arm bracket, remove the nut, rear washer and insulator **(see illustration)**.
5   Remove the radius arm and remove the inner insulator and retainer from the radius arm threaded end **(see illustrations)**.

Installation

6   Install the front end of the radius arm onto the front axle.
7   On 2WD models, from underneath the axle, install the attaching bolt and a new nut. Tighten the nut only finger tight at this time.
8   On 4WD models, position the front end of the radius arm onto the bracket and axle. Install the bolts and stud (and washer on the left axle only) in the bracket. Tighten the bolts and stud only finger tight at this time.
9   Install the rear retainer and insulator onto the threaded end of the radius arm.

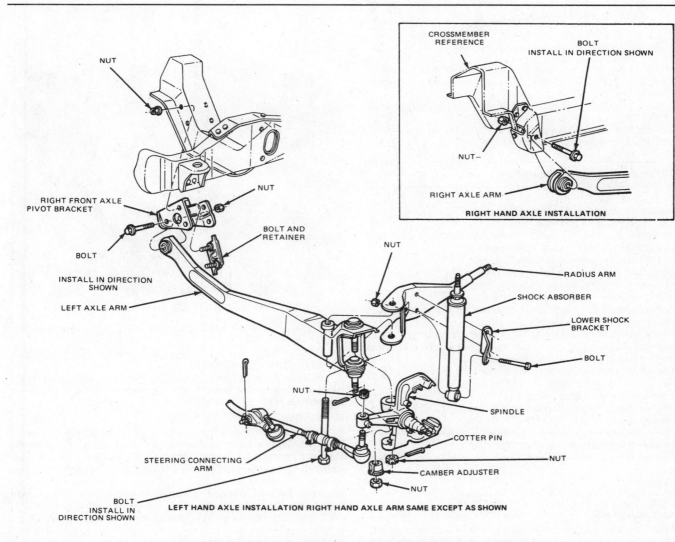

6.5a   An exploded view of the radius arm and related parts (2WD models)

10

6.5b   An exploded view of the radius arm and related parts (4WD models)

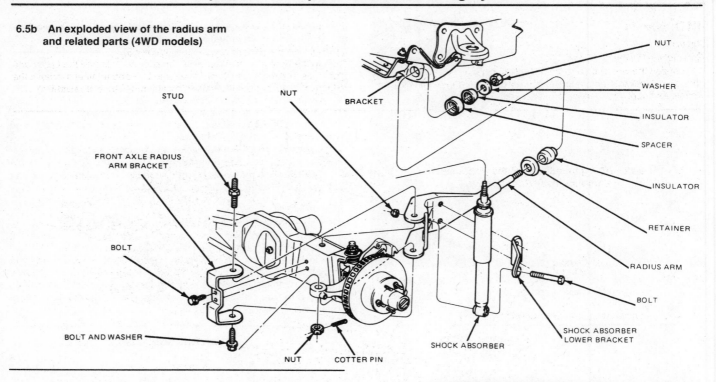

10   Install the radius arm into the rear bracket and install the rear insulator, washer and new nut. Tighten the nut to the torque listed in this Chapter's Specifications.
11   Tighten the bolts and nuts installed in Step 7 and Step 8 to the torque listed in this Chapter's Specifications.
12   Install the spring lower seat and insulator onto the left radius arm.
13   Install the spring assembly (see Section 5).

7   Radius arm insulators – replacement

1   Remove the spring assembly (see Section 5).
2   Loosen the front axle pivot bolt.
3   From the rear side of the radius arm bracket, remove the nut, rear washer, insulator and spacer **(see illustration 6.4)**.
4   On 4WD models, perform the following:
  a) Disconnect the front driveshaft (see Chapter 8).
  b) Loosen the front radius arm retaining bolts.
5   On 2WD models, remove the through bolt.
6   Apply pressure on the floor jack and raise the front axle until the radius arm is level.
7   Pull the radius arm forward until it is free of the radius arm bracket.
8   Remove the front insulator from the radius arm threaded end. Some models also have a shield over the insulator.
9   Installation is the reverse of the removal steps with the following additions:
  a) Install new insulators and nut.
  b) Tighten the bolts and nut to the torque listed in this Chapter's Specifications.

8   Axle pivot bracket – removal and installation

2WD models

Removal

Refer to illustration 8.3

1   Loosen the front wheel lug nuts on the side to be disassembled. Raise the front of the vehicle, support it securely on jackstands, block the rear wheels and set the parking brake. Remove the front wheel.

8.3   Remove the bolt and remove the axle beam

2   Remove the coil spring (see Section 5) and the radius arm (see Section 6).
3   Remove the front axle retaining bolt **(see illustration)** and remove the front axle from the frame.
4   Remove the bolts and nuts securing the axle pivot bracket to the frame and remove the bracket from the frame crossmember **(see illustration 6.5a)**.

Installation

5   Position the front axle bracket onto the frame crossmember. Install the new bolts from within the frame crossmember and out through the bracket, then install the new nuts. After all of the bolts and nuts have been installed, tighten them to the torque listed in this Chapter's Specifications.
6   Install the front axle and new retaining bolt. Tighten to the torque listed in this Chapter's Specifications.
7   Install the radius arm (see Section 6) and the front spring (see Section 5).
8   Install the wheel and lug nuts, lower the vehicle and tighten the lug nuts to the torque listed in Chapter 1.

4WD models

Removal

Refer to illustrations 8.12 and 8.13

9   Loosen the wheel lug nuts on the side to be disassembled, raise the front of the vehicle and support it securely on jackstands. Block the rear wheels and apply the parking brake. Remove the wheel.

10   Remove the coil spring (see Section 5) and the radius arm (see Section 6).

11   Remove the front driveaxle (see Chapter 8).

12   On the right axle pivot bracket, remove the nuts and the upper and side bolts and retainers. Discard the side bolt and retainer. Remove the axle pivot bracket from the frame crossmember **(see illustration)**.

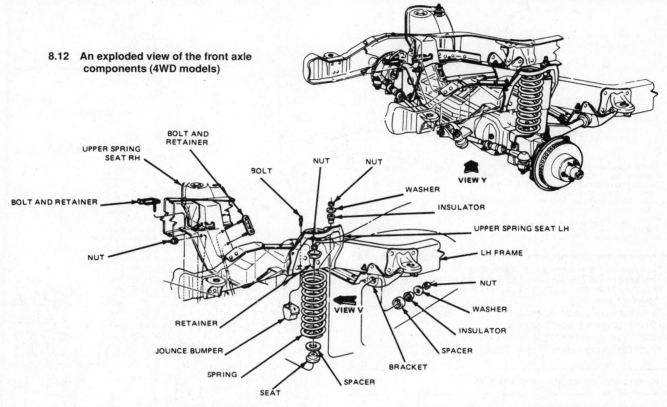

8.12   An exploded view of the front axle components (4WD models)

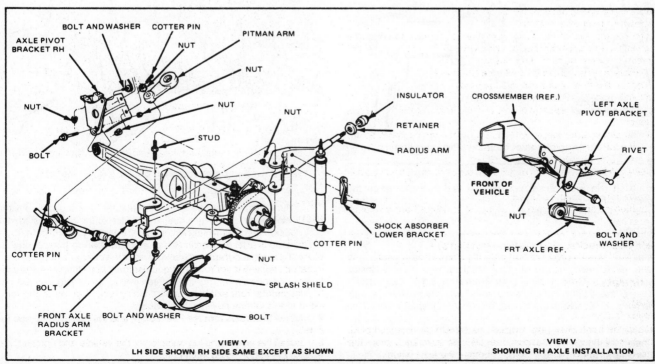

VIEW Y
LH SIDE SHOWN RH SIDE SAME EXCEPT AS SHOWN

VIEW V
SHOWING RH AXLE INSTALLATION

10

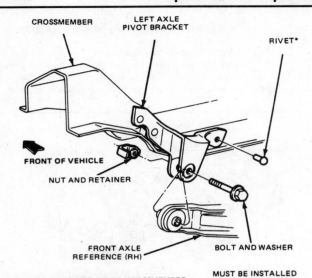

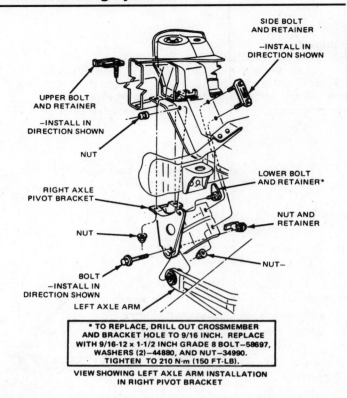

* TO REPLACE RIVET, DRILL CROSSMEMBER AND BRACKET HOLES TO 9/16 INCH. REPLACE RIVET WITH GRADE 8 FASTENERS: BOLT–58697 (9/16-12 x 1-1/2), WASHERS–44880 (2), AND NUT–34990, TIGHTEN TO 210 N·m (150 FT-LB)

VIEW SHOWING RIGHT AXLE ARM INSTALLATION IN LEFT PIVOT BRACKET

8.13   On the left axle pivot bracket, use a 9/16-inch drill bit and drill out the rivets securing the bracket to the frame, then install the bracket with Grade 8 9/16-12 x 1-1/2 inch long bolts with nuts and washers

* TO REPLACE, DRILL OUT CROSSMEMBER AND BRACKET HOLE TO 9/16 INCH. REPLACE WITH 9/16-12 x 1-1/2 INCH GRADE 8 BOLT–58697, WASHERS (2)–44880, AND NUT–34990. TIGHTEN TO 210 N·m (150 FT-LB).

VIEW SHOWING LEFT AXLE ARM INSTALLATION IN RIGHT PIVOT BRACKET

8.15   An exploded view of the right axle pivot bracket

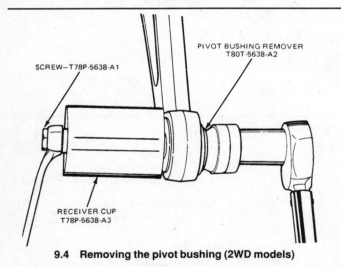

9.4   Removing the pivot bushing (2WD models)

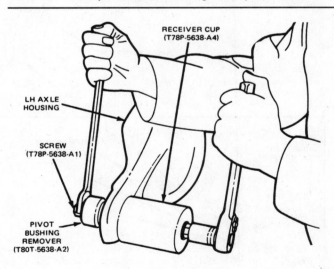

9.6   Removing the pivot bushing (4WD models)

13   On the left axle pivot bracket, use a 9/16-inch drill bit and drill out the rivets securing the bracket to the frame. Remove the axle bracket from the frame crossmember **(see illustration)**.

Installation

Refer to illustration 8.15

14   Install the left axle pivot bracket onto the frame crossmember and align the 9/16 inch holes of the bracket and frame. Install 9/16-12x1-1/2-inch Grade 8 bolts **(see illustration 8.13)**. **Caution:** *Be sure to use Grade 8 bolts, not a lesser grade. Install the washer and nuts onto the bolts and tighten to the torque listed in this Chapter's Specifications.*

15   To install the right axle pivot bracket, perform the following:
   a)   Install the right axle pivot bracket onto the frame crossmember **(see illustration)**. Install the bolts in the direction shown in the il-

lustration so the heads face the engine oil pan giving maximum clearance. Install new nuts and tighten to the torque listed in this Chapter's Specifications.
   b)   Use a 9/16-inch drill bit and drill out the lower mounting hole bracket and frame crossmember.
   c)   Install a 9/16-inch Grade 8 replacement bolt with two flat washers and a new retaining nut. Tighten the nut to the torque listed in this Chapter's Specifications.

16   Install the front driveaxle (see Chapter 8).

17   Install the radius arm (see Section 6) and the front spring (see Section 5 of this chapter).

18   Install the wheel and lug nuts, lower the vehicle and tighten the lug nuts to the torque listed in Chapter 1.

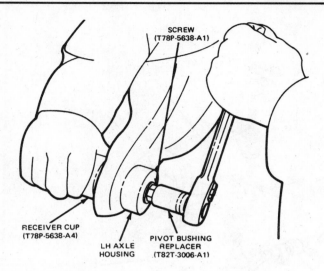

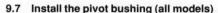

9.7 Install the pivot bushing (all models)

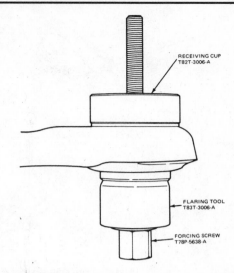

9.8 Flaring the bushing to prevent it from moving within the axle

9   Axle pivot bushing – replacement

Removal
2WD models
Refer to illustration 9.4

1   Loosen the front wheel lug nuts on the side to be dismantled. Raise the front of the vehicle, support it securely on jackstands, block the rear wheels and set the parking brake. Remove the front wheel.

2   To remove the left axle pivot bushing, remove the retaining bolt and nut, then pull the pivot end of the axle down until the bushing is exposed. Proceed to Step 4.

3   To remove the right axle pivot bushing, perform the following:
   a) Remove the coil spring (see Section 5) and the radius arm (see Section 6).
   b) Remove the front axle retaining bolt **(see illustration 8.3)** and remove the front axle from the frame.

4   Install the forcing tool (Ford part No. T78P-5638-A1), bushing remover (Ford part No. T80T-5638-A2) and receiver cup (Ford part No. T78P-5638-A3) or equivalent bushing removal tools onto the bushing. Position the spacer between the walls of the axle, then turn the forcing screw and press the bushing out of the axle **(see illustration)**.

4WD models
Refer to illustration 9.6

5   Remove the front axle (see Chapter 8).

6   Install the forcing tool (Ford part No. T78P-5638-A1), bushing remover (Ford part No. T80T-5638-A2) and receiver cup (Ford part No. T78P-5638-A4) or equivalent bushing removal tools onto the bushing. Turn the forcing screw and press the bushing out of the axle **(see illustration)**.

Installation
Refer to illustrations 9.7 and 9.8

7   Insert the bushing in the axle receptacle. Install the receiver cup, forcing tool and bushing replacer (Ford No. T82T-3006-A1) onto the axle. Turn the forcing screw and press the bushing into the axle **(see illustration)**.

8   The new bushing must be flared to prevent movement within the axle. Install the forcing screw (Ford No. T78P-5638-A1), receiving cup (Ford No. T82T-3006-A1 and flaring tool (Ford No. T82T-3006-A1), or equivalent. Turn the forcing screw and flare the lip of the bushing **(see illustration)**.

9   On 2WD models, move the pivot end of the axle back into position and install the retaining bolt and nut.

10   On 4WD models, install the front axle (see Chapter 8).

11   Tighten all bolts and nuts to the torques listed in this Chapter's Specifications.

12   Remove the jackstands and lower the vehicle.

10   Tie-rod ends – removal and installation

Refer to illustrations 10.5a and 10.5b

Removal

1   Loosen the front wheel lug nuts on the side to be disassembled. Raise the front of the vehicle, support it securely on jackstands, block the rear wheels and set the parking brake. Remove the front wheel.

2   Remove the cotter pin and loosen the nut on the tie-rod end stud. Discard the cotter pin.

3   Loosen the clamp bolts on the tie-rod adjusting sleeve.

4   Unscrew the adjusting sleeve. Count and record the number of turns it takes to back the sleeve off the tie-rod end.

5   Disconnect the tie-rod from the spindle arm with a tie-rod remover (Ford part No. 3290-C), a two-jaw puller or a pickle fork removal tool. **Note:** *On 4WD models the tie-rod end is inserted in from the top of the spindle. On 2WD models the tie-rod is inserted from the bottom of the spindle* **(see illustrations)**. Remove the nut and detach the tie-rod end from the spindle arm.

Installation

6   Install the tie-rod onto the spindle arm. Make sure the front wheels and steering wheel are in the straight ahead position. Make sure the tie-rod stud is seated in the taper to prevent it from rotating while tightening the nut.

7   Install a new nut on the stud and tighten it to the torque listed in this Chapter's Specifications. Install a new cotter pin and bend the ends over completely.

8   Install the adjusting sleeve onto the tie-rod end the same number of turns noted during removal in Step 4.

9   Tighten the clamp bolts on the tie-rod adjusting sleeve to the torque listed in this Chapter's Specifications. Make sure the tie-rod is positioned correctly in the same position as when it was removed.

10   Install the wheel and lug nuts. Lower the vehicle and tighten the lug nuts to the torque listed in the Chapter 1 Specifications.

11   Have the front end alignment checked by a dealer service department or an alignment shop.

10

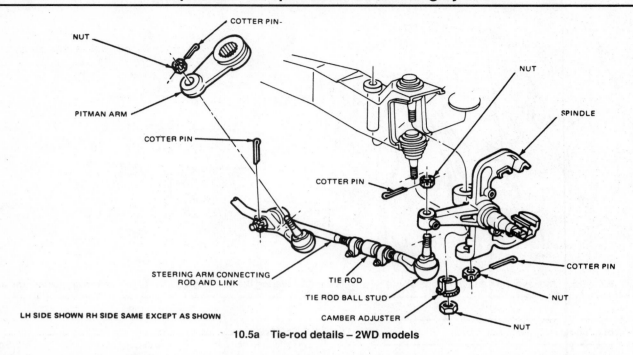

10.5a   Tie-rod details – 2WD models

LH SIDE SHOWN RH SIDE SAME EXCEPT AS SHOWN

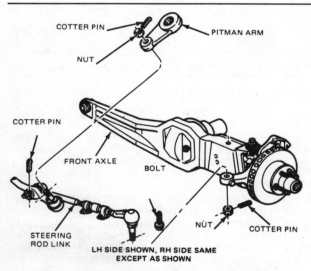

10.5b   Tie-rod details – 4WD models

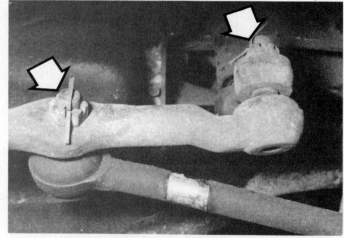

11.2a   Remove the cotter pins, unscrew the nuts and disconnect the ballstuds from the Pitman arm and the drag link (arrows)

11   Drag link – removal and installation

Refer to illustration 11.2

1   Raise the front of the vehicle, support it securely on jackstands, block the rear wheels and set the parking brake. Position the front wheels in the straight ahead position.

2   Remove the cotter pins and nuts securing the drag link to the steering connecting arm and to the Pitman arm **(see illustrations)**. If necessary, separate the components with a two-jaw puller or a pickle fork-type balljoint separator.

3   Loosen the clamp bolts on the tie-rod adjusting sleeve.

Removal

4   Unscrew the adjusting sleeve. Count and record the number of turns it takes to back the sleeve off the drag link.

5   Remove the drag link.

Installation

6   Loosely install the drag link ball stud into the Pitman arm. Position the steering connecting arm ball end into the drag link. Make sure the front wheels and steering wheel are in the straight ahead position. Make sure the ball ends are seated in the taper to prevent them from rotating while tightening the nuts.

7   Install the drag link onto the tie-rod adjusting sleeve and turn it the same number of turns noted during removal in Step 4. Tighten the clamp bolts on the tie-rod adjusting sleeve to the torque listed in this Chapter's Specifications.

8   Install new nuts on the studs of the Pitman arm and steering connecting arm and tighten to the torque listed in this Chapter's Specifications. Install new cotter pins and bend the ends over completely.

9   Install the wheel and lug nuts. Lower the vehicle and tighten the lug nuts to torque listed in the Chapter 1 Specifications.

10   Have the front end alignment checked by a dealer service department or an alignment shop.

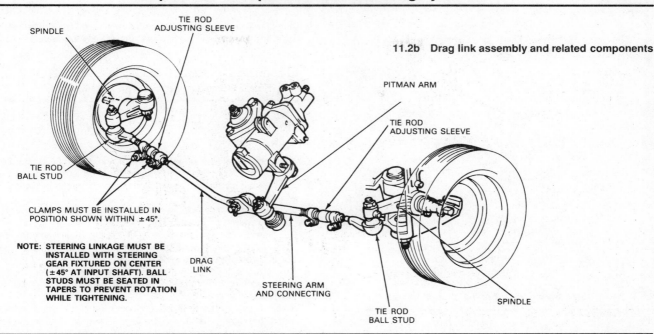

SPINDLE

TIE ROD ADJUSTING SLEEVE

11.2b   Drag link assembly and related components

PITMAN ARM

TIE ROD ADJUSTING SLEEVE

TIE ROD BALL STUD

CLAMPS MUST BE INSTALLED IN POSITION SHOWN WITHIN ±45°.

NOTE: STEERING LINKAGE MUST BE INSTALLED WITH STEERING GEAR FIXTURED ON CENTER (±45° AT INPUT SHAFT). BALL STUDS MUST BE SEATED IN TAPERS TO PREVENT ROTATION WHILE TIGHTENING.

DRAG LINK

STEERING ARM AND CONNECTING

TIE ROD BALL STUD

SPINDLE

12   Steering connecting rod – removal and installation

Removal

1   Raise the front of the vehicle, support it securely on jackstands, block the rear wheels and set the parking brake. Position the front wheels in the straight ahead position.
2   Remove the cotter pin and nut from the ball end of the steering connecting rod **(see illustration 11.2a)**.
3   Use tie-rod remover (Ford part No.3290-D), a two-jaw puller or a pickle fork removal tool and detach the ball end from the drag link.
4   Loosen the clamp bolts on the tie-rod adjusting sleeve.
5   Unscrew the connecting rod from the tie-rod adjusting sleeve. Count and record the number of turns it takes to remove the connecting rod from the tie-rod adjusting sleeve.
6   Remove the steering connecting rod.

Installation

7   Install the steering connecting rod onto the tie-rod and turn it the same number of turns noted during removal in Step 5. Tighten the clamp bolts on the tie-rod adjusting sleeve to the torque listed in this Chapter's Specifications.
8   Install the steering connecting rod end into the drag link. Make sure the front wheels and steering wheel are in the straight ahead position. Make sure the ball end is seated in the taper to prevent them from rotating while tightening the nut.
9   Install a new nut on the stud and tighten to the torque listed in this Chapter's Specifications. Install a new cotter pin and bend the ends over completely.
10   Install the wheel and lug nuts. Lower the vehicle and tighten the lug nuts to torque listed in Chapter 1.
11   Have the alignment checked by a dealer service department or an alignment shop.

13   Front I-beam axle – removal and installation

Note: *Front axle removal and installation for 4WD models is covered in Chapter 8.*

Removal

1   Raise the front of the vehicle, support it securely on jackstands, block the rear wheels and set the parking brake. Position the front wheels in the straight ahead position.
2   Remove the coil spring (see Section 5) and front spindle (see Section 3).
3   Remove the radius arm from the front axle (see Section 6).
4   On models so equipped, remove the front stabilizer bar (see Section 14).
5   Remove the bolt and nut securing the axle to the frame pivot bracket. Remove the front axle.

Installation

6   Install the front axle and new retaining bolt and nut. Tighten the nut only finger tight at this time.
7   On models so equipped, install the front stabilizer bar (see Section 14).
8   Install the front axle onto the radius arm (see Section 6).
9   Install the front spindle (see Section 3) and the coil spring (see Section 5).
10   Tighten the front axle retaining bolt and nut to the torque listed in this Chapter's Specifications.
11   Install the wheel and lug nuts. Lower the vehicle and tighten the lug nuts to torque listed in Chapter 1.
12   Have the front end alignment checked by a dealer service department or an alignment shop.

14   Front stabilizer bar – removal and installation

1   Raise the front of the vehicle, support it securely on jackstands, block the rear wheels and set the parking brake. Position the front wheels in the straight ahead position.

1983 through 1985 Bronco II, 1983 through 1989 Ranger 2WD models and all 1983 through 1988 4WD models

2   Remove the nuts securing both the U-bolts in the lower shock bracket and the stabilizer bar bushing to the radius arm on each side.
3   Remove the bolts securing the stabilizer bar bushing brackets to the frame on each side.
4   Remove the stabilizer bar assembly.
5   Installation is the reverse of the removal steps. Tighten the bolts and nuts to the torque listed in this Chapter's Specifications.

10

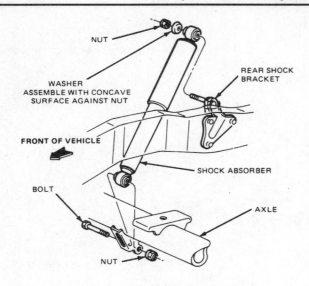

15.2   Shock absorber installation details

1986 and later Bronco II, 1990 and later Ranger 2WD models and all 1989 and later 4WD models

6   Remove the nut and washer securing the stabilizer bar to the stabilizer bar link assembly on each axle arm.
7   Remove the bolts securing the stabilizer bar bushing and retainer to the frame on each side.
8   Remove the mounting bolts from the stabilizer bar link assembly on each axle arm.
9   Remove the stabilizer bar assembly.
10   Installation is the reverse of the removal steps. Tighten the bolts and nuts to the torque listed in this Chapter's Specifications.

15   Rear shock absorber – removal and installation

Refer to illustration 15.2

1   Place a floor jack under the axle adjacent to shock absorber being removed. Apply just enough jack pressure to take the load off the shock absorber.
2   Remove the nuts and bolts securing the lower end of the shock absorber to the spring plate (**see illustration**).
3   Remove the nut securing the top of the shock absorber to the upper mounting bracket on the frame.

4   Installation is the reverse of the removal steps. Tighten the nuts and bolts to the torque listed in this Chapter's Specifications.

16   Rear leaf spring – removal and installation

Refer to illustration 16.4

Removal

1   Loosen the rear wheel lug nuts on the side to be dismantled. Raise the rear of the vehicle, support it securely on jackstands and block the front wheels so the vehicle will not roll in either direction. Remove the rear wheel(s).
2   Place a floor jack under the axle. Apply just enough jack pressure to take the weight off the rear springs.
3   Remove the nuts and bolts securing the lower end of the shock absorber to the spring plate (**see illustration 15.2**). Compress the shock upward and out of the way.
4   Remove the nuts from the U-bolts and remove the U-bolts and the spring plate on top of the spring (**see illustration**). On 4WD models, remove the spacer.
5   Remove the bolts and nuts securing the shackle assembly at the rear of the spring. Let the spring pivot down and rest on the floor.
6   Remove the spring hanger bolt and nut at the front of the spring. Remove the spring.
7   Inspect the spring eye bushings for wear or distortion. If worn or damaged have them replaced by a dealer service department or properly equipped shop.

Installation

8   Place the spring assembly into position and install the shackle bolts and nuts. Tighten the nuts finger tight at this time.
9   Move the front of the spring into position and install the bolt and nut. Tighten the nut finger tight at this time.
10   Slowly lower the floor jack and rest the rear axle on the spring.
11   On 4WD models, install the spacer.
12   Install the U-bolt plate with the flanges facing upward on top of the spring. Install the U-bolts and nuts and tighten the nuts to the torque listed in this Chapter's Specifications.
13   Move the shock absorber down into position and install the nuts and bolts securing the lower end of the shock absorber to the spring plate. Tighten the nuts to the torque listed in this Chapter's Specifications.
14   Lower the floor jack and rear axle until the axle is at its approximate ride height. Tighten the front and rear spring attachment bolts and nuts to the torque listed in this Chapter's Specifications.
15   Install the rear wheel(s) and lug nuts.
16   Lower the vehicle and remove the floor jack. Tighten the lug nuts to the torque listed in Chapter 1.

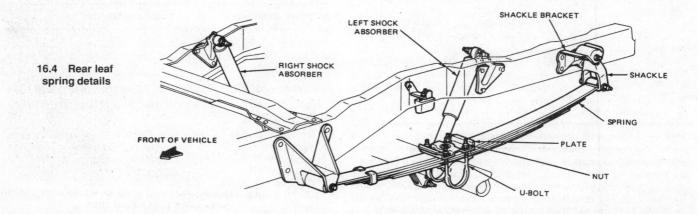

16.4   Rear leaf spring details

19.2 Remove the cover over the steering wheel mounting nut (Bronco II shown)

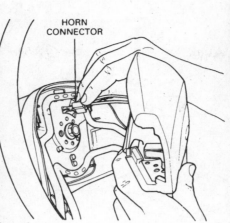

HORN CONNECTOR

19.4 Unplug the wire harness connector(s) then remove the horn pad.

19.5 Mark the relationship of the steering wheel hub to the shaft

17 Rear stabilizer bar – removal and installation

Removal

1 Remove the bolt, nut and washer securing the rear stabilizer bar ends to the link at each end.
2 Remove the nuts from the U-bolts and remove the U-bolts from the mounting brackets on the rear axle housing.
3 Remove the mounting brackets, retainer and the stabilizer bar from the frame.
4 Inspect the rubber isolators on the stabilizer bar and replace if necessary.

Installation

5 Position the stabilizer bar onto the rear axle assembly. Position the retainer with the UP mark facing up.
6 Install the stabilizer bar and retainer onto the mounting brackets. Make sure the UP mark on the retainer is facing up toward the floor pan or bed.
7 Install the U-bolts and nuts. Tighten the nuts finger tight at this time.
8 Move the stabilizer bar ends up into position and connect them to the links. Install the bolt, washer and nut on each end. Tighten the bolts and nuts to the torque listed in this Chapter's Specifications.
9 Tighten the U-bolt and nuts to the torque listed in this Chapter's Specifications.

18 Steering system – general information

The steering system consists of a Pitman arm, drag link, steering connecting rod and tie-rods. The Pitman arm transfers the steering gear movements through the drag link and steering connecting rod to the tie-rods at each end. The tie-rods move the spindles (or knuckle) and front wheels to the desired steering movement. The tie-rods are equipped with an adjusting sleeve for setting the toe-in.

Vehicles with power steering are equipped with the Ford Integral Power Steering gear that consists of a belt-driven Ford C-II pump and associated lines and hoses. The power steering pump reservoir fluid level should be checked periodically (see Chapter 1).

Vehicles with manual steering use a recirculating ball manual steering unit. There are two types of manual ball nut gears with a constant ratio of 24:1 or a variable ratio of 20-24:1. Except for the sector shaft, housing and sector cover all other components are identical to both models. Refer to Ford gear model number to distinguish one model from the other.

The steering wheel operates the steering shaft, which actuates the steering gear through universal joints and the intermediate shaft. Looseness in the steering can be caused by wear in the steering shaft universal joints, the steering gear, the tie-rod ends and loose retaining bolts.

19 Steering wheel – removal and installation

Removal

Refer to illustrations 19.2, 19.4, 19.5 and 19.7

1 Disconnect the negative cable from the battery.
2 On 1983 through 1985 models, perform the following:
   a) On Standard and Sport models, pry off the cover with a small screwdriver **(see illustration)** or remove the two screws securing the horn pad to the steering wheel.
   b) On the optional wheel, lift the top outside edges of the cover and pull it straight back off the steering wheel.
3 On 1986 and later models, perform the following:
   a) On models so equipped, remove the four screws securing the horn pad to the steering wheel.
   b) Partially pull the horn pad away from the steering wheel and remove the foam pad (if so equipped).
4 Unplug the horn and any other related electrical connector(s) **(see illustration)** then remove the horn pad.
5 Make alignment marks on both the steering wheel hub and the steering shaft **(see illustration)**. These marks will be used during installation.
6 Remove the steering wheel mounting nut.
7 Use a puller to remove the steering wheel **(see illustration)**. **Caution:** *Don't hammer on the shaft to remove the steering wheel.*

Installation

8 Align the paint alignment mark on the steering wheel hub with the mark on the steering shaft and slip the wheel onto the shaft. Install the nut

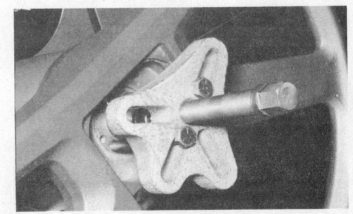

19.7 Use a puller to remove the steering wheel from the steering shaft – don't beat on the shaft

10

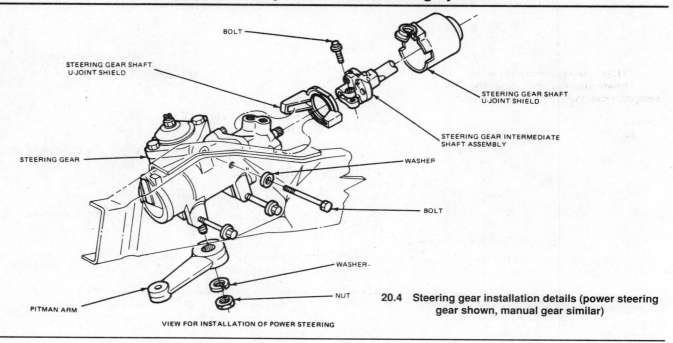

BOLT

STEERING GEAR SHAFT
U-JOINT SHIELD

STEERING GEAR SHAFT
U-JOINT SHIELD

STEERING GEAR INTERMEDIATE
SHAFT ASSEMBLY

STEERING GEAR

WASHER

BOLT

WASHER

NUT

PITMAN ARM

VIEW FOR INSTALLATION OF POWER STEERING

20.4   Steering gear installation details (power steering gear shown, manual gear similar)

and tighten it to the torque listed in this Chapter's Specifications.
9   Reconnect the electrical connector(s) and install the horn pad.
10   Reconnect the negative battery cable.

20   Steering gear – removal and installation

Removal

Refer to illustration 20.4
1   Set the front wheels to the straight-ahead position.
2   Disconnect the negative cable from the battery terminal.
3   Turn the ignition key to the Run position to unlock the steering wheel.
4   Disengage the plastic flex coupling shield from the steering gear input shaft. Carefully pry it rearward and slide it up the intermediate shaft **(see illustration)**.
5   Remove the bolt securing the flex coupling to the steering gear.
6   Loosen the lug nuts from the left front wheel. Raise the front of the vehicle, support it securely on jackstands, block the rear wheels and set the parking brake. Remove the wheel.
7   Remove the large nut and washer securing the Pitman arm to the sector shaft. Use puller (Ford part No. T64P-3590-F) or an equivalent puller and remove the Pitman arm from the sector shaft. **Caution:** *Do not hammer on the end of the puller, as the steering gear will be damaged.*
8   On models equipped with power steering, place a drain pan under the steering gear. Detach the power steering pressure and return lines from the steering gear. Plug the lines and the openings in the steering gear to prevent excessive fluid loss and contamination.
9   Loosen all three bolts securing the steering gear box to the frame. Hold onto the steering gear and remove the bolts and remove the steering gear box.
10   Remove the steering gear input shaft shield.

Installation

11   Make sure the steering gear is centered. Turn the input gear shaft (wormshaft) to full lock in one direction, then count and record the number of turns required to rotate it to the opposite full lock position. Turn the pinion shaft back through one-half of the number of turns just counted to center the assembly.
12   Check that the front wheels are in the straight ahead position.
13   Install the input shaft shield onto the steering gear box. Install the upper shield onto the intermediate shaft.

14   On models with manual steering gear, position the flat on the gear input shaft so it is facing straight up. On models with power steering gear, position the flat on the input shaft facing down. Position the flex coupling on the steering gear input shaft, aligning the flat with the flat on the input shaft.
15   Install all three bolts securing the steering gear box to the frame. Tighten the bolts to the torque listed in this Chapter's Specifications.
16   On models equipped with power steering, connect the pressure and return lines to the steering gear and tighten them securely.
17   Align the two blocked teeth on the Pitman arm with the four missing teeth on the steering gear sector shaft and install the Pitman arm. Install the washer and nut and tighten the nut to the torque listed in this Chapter's Specifications.
18   Install the bolt securing the flex coupling to the steering gear input shaft. Tighten the bolt to the torque listed in this Chapter's Specifications.
19   Move the flex coupling shield into place on the steering gear input shield.
20   Check that there are an equal number of turns from dead center to full lock on each side.
21   Install the front wheel(s) and lug nuts.
22   Lower the vehicle and tighten the lug nuts to the torque listed in the Chapter 1 Specifications.
23   Turn the ignition key Off and connect the negative battery cable.
24   On models equipped with power steering, fill the fluid reservoir with the specified fluid (see Chapter 1) and refer to Section 23 for the power steering bleeding procedure.

21   Power steering pump – removal and installation

Refer to illustrations 21.5a, 21.5b, 21.6 and 21.10
Note: *Refer to Section 22 for information on quick-disconnect fittings used on the power steering system.*

Removal

1   Disconnect the cable from the negative battery terminal.
2   Disconnect the return hose at the reservoir and drain the fluid into a container.
3   Raise the front of the vehicle, support it securely on jackstands, block the rear wheels and set the parking brake.

21.5a   An exploded view of the power steering pump mounting components – four-cylinder models (typical)

ALTERNATOR ADJUSTING BRACKET

POWER STEERING PUMP BRACKET

ALTERNATOR

POWER STEERING PUMP

CLAMP

PRESSURE HOSE

RETURN HOSE

STEERING GEAR

4   Disconnect the pressure hose from the pump.
5   On 4-cylinder engines, loosen the alternator pivot bolt and the adjusting bolt to slacken drive belt tension **(see illustration)**. On V6 engines, loosen the adjustment nut and slider bolts on the pump support and push in on the pump to slacken drive belt tension **(see illustration)**.
6   Remove the pulley from the pump as follows:
   a) Install the pump pulley removal and installation tool (Ford tool no. T69L-10300-B) or equivalent onto the pulley **(see illustration)**.

   b) Hold onto the pump and rotate the tool nut counterclockwise and remove the pulley from the pump. **Caution:** *Do not apply excessive force on the pulley shaft as it may damage the internal parts of the pump.*
7   Remove the bolts securing the pump to the mounting bracket.
8   Remove the pump from the mounting bracket.

Installation

9   Place the pump in the bracket and install the mounting bolts. Tighten the bolts to the torque listed in this Chapter's Specifications.

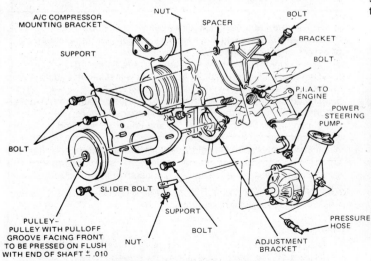

A/C COMPRESSOR MOUNTING BRACKET

NUT

SPACER

BOLT

SUPPORT

BRACKET

BOLT

P.I.A. TO ENGINE

POWER STEERING PUMP

BOLT

SLIDER BOLT

SUPPORT

NUT

BOLT

PRESSURE HOSE

ADJUSTMENT BRACKET

PULLEY–
PULLEY WITH PULLOFF GROOVE FACING FRONT TO BE PRESSED ON FLUSH WITH END OF SHAFT ± .010

21.5b   An exploded view of the power steering pump mounting components – V6 models (typical)

21.6   This special tool designed for removing the power steering pump pulley is available at tool stores and some auto parts stores

10

21.10   This special tool designed for installing the power steering pump pulley is available at tool stores and some auto parts stores

10   Install the pulley onto the pump using Ford tool no. T65P-3A733-C or equivalent (see illustration).
11   Install the pump drive belt and adjust the tension (see Chapter 1).
12   Install the pressure and return hoses to the proper fittings on the pump.
13   Connect the return hose to the reservoir.
14   Fill the pump reservoir with the specified fluid (see Chapter 1) and bleed the system (see Section 23).

22   Power steering line quick-disconnect fittings

Refer to illustration 22.1

The power steering pump return line connection, pressure line connection and both steering gear connections are equipped with fittings that can result in line separation when the line is under pressure. If the line separates from the fitting, or if a leak occurs between the line and the fitting, a new O-ring may be installed to fix the leak (see illustration). If this doesn't solve the problem, a new line or hose assembly must be installed. Service kits are available for the steering gear connections.

If a leak occurs between the threaded part of the fitting (tube end) and the component it threads into, the plastic seal on the tube nut can be replaced with a new one. Use a tapered tool, such as a large centerpunch, to stretch the seal until it fits over the tube nut threads. It will slowly return to its original size.

23   Power steering system bleeding

1   The power steering system must be bled whenever a line is disconnected. Bubbles can be seen in power steering fluid which has air in it and the fluid will often have a tan or milky appearance. On later models, low fluid level can cause air to mix with the fluid, resulting in a noisy pump as well as foaming of the fluid.
2   Open the hood and check the fluid level in the reservoir, adding the specified fluid necessary to bring it up to the proper level (see Chapter 1).
3   Start the engine and slowly turn the steering wheel several times from left-to-right and back again. Do not turn the wheel completely from lock-to-lock. Check the fluid level, topping it up as necessary until it remains steady and no more bubbles are visible.

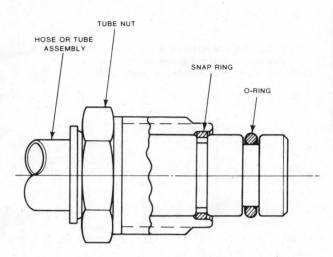

22.1   Quick-disconnect fitting components

24   Steering angles and wheel alignment – general information

Proper wheel alignment is essential for safe steering and even tire wear. Symptoms of alignment problems are pulling of the steering to one side or the other and uneven tire wear.

If these symptoms are present, check for the following before having the alignment adjusted:

Loose steering gear mounting bolts
Damaged or worn steering gear mounts
Worn or damaged wheel bearings
Bent tie-rods
Worn balljoints
Improper tire pressures
Mixing tires of different construction
Front wheel alignment should be left to a dealer service department or an alignment shop.

25   Wheels and tires – general information

1   Check the tire pressures (cold) weekly (see Chapter 1).
2   Inspect the sidewalls and treads periodically for damage and signs of abnormal or uneven wear.
3   Make sure the wheel lug nuts are properly tightened.
4   Don't mix radial and bias ply tires or tires with different tread patterns on the same axle.
5   Periodically inspect the wheels for elongated or damaged lug holes, distortion and nicks in the rim. Replace damaged wheels.
6   Clean the wheels inside and out and check for rust and corrosion, which could lead to wheel failure.
7   If the wheel and tire are balanced on the vehicle, one wheel stud and lug hole should be marked whenever the wheel is removed so it can be reinstalled in the original position. If balanced on the vehicle, the wheel should not be moved to a different axle position.

Chapter 11 Body

Contents

Specifications

Torque specifications

Ft-lbs (unless otherwise indicated)

Door latch-to-door bolt	36 to 72 in-lbs
Door latch attaching bolt	62 to 97 in-lbs
Hood hinge bolt	60 to 96 in-lbs
Hood latch bolt	84 to 120 in-lbs
Folding rear seat-to-floorpan bolt (Ranger Supercab)	156 to 240 in-lbs
Front bumper bolt	17 to 23
Front bumper air deflector bolt	60 to 96 in-lbs
Front bumper guard attaching bolt	17 to 23
Liftgate hinge-to-body nut (Bronco II)	144 to 128 in-lbs
Liftgate hinge-to-liftgate bolt (Bronco II)	60 to 96 in-lbs
Rear bumper inner arm bracket-to-frame bolt (Ranger)	92 to 136
Rear bumper inner arm bracket-to-bumper bolt (Ranger)	92 to 136
Rear bumper outer arm-to-bumper bolt (Bronco II)	17 to 22
Rear bumper outer arm-to-frame nut (Bronco II)	74 to 100
Rear bumper outer arm-to-inner arm bolt	92 to 136
Rear bumper extension assembly bolt (XLS)	72 to 96 in-lbs
Rear bumper extension bolt (Bronco II)	60 to 96 in-lbs
Rear seat cushion-to-floorpan bolt	156 to 228 in-lbs
Rear seat back-to-floorpan and seat bolt	22 to 32
Rear stone deflector bolt (Bronco II)	96 to 168 in-lbs
Seat track-to-floorpan bolts	108 to 216 in-lbs
Tailgate anchor post-to-bed (Ranger)	33 to 51
Tailgate latch release-to-tailgate bolt	84 to 120 in-lbs
Tailgate latch assembly-to-tailgate bolt	16 to 25
Tailgate latch-to-bed bolt	84 to 120
Window glass guide assembly nut	62 to 97 in-lbs

11

1   General information

These models feature a welded body that is attached to a separate frame. Certain components are particularly vulnerable to accident damage and can be unbolted and repaired or replaced. Among these parts are the body moldings, bumpers, hood, doors, tailgate, liftgate and all glass.

Only general body maintenance procedures and body panel repair procedures within the scope of the do-it-yourselfer are included in this Chapter.

2   Body – maintenance

1   The condition of your vehicle's body is very important, because the resale value depends a great deal on it. It's much more difficult to repair a damaged body than it is to repair mechanical components. The hidden areas of the body, such as the wheel wells, the frame and the engine compartment, are equally important, although they don't require as frequent attention as the rest of the body.

2   Once a year, or every 12,000 miles, it's a good idea to have the underside of the body steam cleaned. All traces of dirt and oil will be removed and the area can then be inspected carefully for rust, damaged brake lines, frayed electrical wires, damaged cables and other problems. The front suspension components should be greased after completion of this job.

3   At the same time, clean the engine and the engine compartment with a steam cleaner or water soluble degreaser.

4   The wheel wells should be given close attention, since undercoating can peel away and stones and dirt thrown up by the tires can cause the paint to chip and flake, allowing rust to set in. If rust is found, clean down to the bare metal and apply an anti-rust paint.

5   The body should be washed about once a week (or when dirty). Wet the vehicle thoroughly to soften the dirt, then wash it down with a soft sponge and plenty of clean soapy water. If the surplus dirt is not washed off very carefully, it can wear down the paint.

6   Spots of tar or asphalt thrown up from the road should be removed with a cloth soaked in solvent.

7   Once every six months, wax the body and chrome trim. If a chrome cleaner is used to remove rust from any of the vehicle's plated parts, remember that the cleaner also removes part of the chrome, so use it sparingly.

3   Vinyl trim – maintenance

Don't clean vinyl trim with detergents, caustic soap or petroleum-based cleaners. Plain soap and water works just fine, with a soft brush to clean dirt that may be ingrained. Wash the vinyl as frequently as the rest of the vehicle.

After cleaning, application of a high-quality rubber and vinyl protectant will help prevent oxidation and cracks. The protectant can also be applied to weatherstripping, vacuum lines and rubber hoses, which often fail as a result of chemical degradation, and to the tires.

4   Upholstery and carpets – maintenance

1   Every three months remove the carpets or mats and clean the interior of the vehicle (more frequently if necessary). Vacuum the upholstery and carpets to remove loose dirt and dust.

2   Leather upholstery requires special care. Stains should be removed with warm water and a very mild soap solution. Use a clean, damp cloth to remove the soap, then wipe again with a dry cloth. Never use alcohol, gasoline, nail polish remover or thinner to clean leather upholstery.

3   After cleaning, regularly treat leather upholstery with a leather wax. Never use car wax on leather upholstery.

4   In areas where the interior of the vehicle is subject to bright sunlight, cover leather seats with a sheet if the vehicle is to be left out for any length of time.

5   Body repair – minor damage

See photo sequence

Repair of minor scratches

1   If the scratch is superficial and does not penetrate to the metal of the body, repair is very simple. Lightly rub the scratched area with a fine rubbing compound to remove loose paint and built-up wax. Rinse the area with clean water.

2   Apply touch-up paint to the scratch, using a small brush. Continue to apply thin layers of paint until the surface of the paint in the scratch is level with the surrounding paint. Allow the new paint at least two weeks to harden, then blend it into the surrounding paint by rubbing with a very fine rubbing compound. Finally, apply a coat of wax to the scratch area.

3   If the scratch has penetrated the paint and exposed the metal of the body, causing the metal to rust, a different repair technique is required. Remove all loose rust from the bottom of the scratch with a pocket knife, then apply rust inhibiting paint to prevent the formation of rust in the future. Using a rubber or nylon applicator, coat the scratched area with glaze-type filler. If required, the filler can be mixed with thinner to provide a very thin paste, which is ideal for filling narrow scratches. Before the glaze filler in the scratch hardens, wrap a piece of smooth cotton cloth around the tip of a finger. Dip the cloth in thinner and then quickly wipe it along the surface of the scratch. This will ensure that the surface of the filler is slightly hollow. The scratch can now be painted over as described earlier in this Section.

Repair of dents

4   When repairing dents, the first job is to pull the dent out until the affected area is as close as possible to its original shape. There is no point in trying to restore the original shape completely as the metal in the damaged area will have stretched on impact and cannot be restored to its original contours. It is better to bring the level of the dent up to a point about 1/8-inch below the level of the surrounding metal. In cases where the dent is very shallow, it is not worth trying to pull it back out at all.

5   If the back side of the dent is accessible, it can be hammered out gently from behind using a soft-face hammer. While doing this, hold a block of wood firmly against the opposite side of the metal to absorb the hammer blows and prevent the metal from being stretched.

6   If the dent is in a section of the body which has double layers, or some other factor makes it inaccessible from behind, a different technique is required. Drill several small holes through the metal inside the damaged area, particularly in the deeper sections. Screw long, self tapping screws into the holes just enough for them to get a good grip in the metal. Now the dent can be pulled out by pulling on the protruding heads of the screws with locking pliers.

7   The next stage of repair is the removal of the paint from the damaged area and from an inch or so of the surrounding metal. This is easily done with a wire brush or sanding disk in a drill motor, although it can be done just as effectively by hand with sandpaper. To complete the preparation for filling, score the surface of the bare metal with a screwdriver or the tang of a file or drill small holes in the affected area. This will provide a good grip for the filler material. To complete the repair, see the Section on filling and painting.

Repair of rust holes or gashes

8   Remove all paint from the affected area and from an inch or so of the surrounding metal using a sanding disk or wire brush mounted in a drill motor. If these are not available, a few sheets of sandpaper will do the job just as effectively.

9   With the paint removed, you will be able to determine the severity of the corrosion and decide whether to replace the whole panel, if possible, or repair the affected area. New body panels are not as expensive

as most people think and it is often quicker to install a new panel than to repair large areas of rust.

10   Remove all trim pieces from the affected area except those which will act as a guide to the original shape of the damaged body, such as headlight shells, etc. Using metal snips or a hacksaw blade, remove all loose metal and any other metal that is badly affected by rust. Hammer the edges of the hole inward to create a slight depression for the filler material.

11   Wire brush the affected area to remove the powdery rust from the surface of the metal. If the back of the rusted area is accessible, treat it with rust inhibiting paint.

12   Before filling is done, block the hole in some way. This can be done with sheet metal riveted or screwed into place, or by stuffing the hole with wire mesh.

13   Once the hole is blocked off, the affected area can be filled and painted. See the following subsection on filling and painting.

Filling and painting

14   Many types of body fillers are available, but generally speaking, body repair kits which contain filler paste and a tube of resin hardener are best for this type of repair work. A wide, flexible plastic or nylon applicator will be necessary for imparting a smooth and contoured finish to the surface of the filler material. Mix up a small amount of filler on a clean piece of wood or cardboard (use the hardener sparingly). Follow the manufacturer's instructions on the package, otherwise the filler will set incorrectly.

15   Using the applicator, apply the filler paste to the prepared area. Draw the applicator across the surface of the filler to achieve the desired contour and to level the filler surface. As soon as a contour that approximates the original one is achieved, stop working the paste. If you continue, the paste will begin to stick to the applicator. Continue to add thin layers of paste at 20-minute intervals until the level of the filler is just above the surrounding metal.

16   Once the filler has hardened, the excess can be removed with a body file. From then on, progressively finer grades of sandpaper should be used, starting with a 180-grit paper and finishing with 600-grit wet-or-dry paper. Always wrap the sandpaper around a flat rubber or wooden block, otherwise the surface of the filler will not be completely flat. During the sanding of the filler surface, the wet-or-dry paper should be periodically rinsed in water. This will ensure that a very smooth finish is produced in the final stage.

17   At this point, the repair area should be surrounded by a ring of bare metal, which in turn should be encircled by the finely feathered edge of good paint. Rinse the repair area with clean water until all of the dust produced by the sanding operation is gone.

18   Spray the entire area with a light coat of primer. This will reveal any imperfections in the surface of the filler. Repair the imperfections with fresh filler paste or glaze filler and once more smooth the surface with sandpaper. Repeat this spray-and-repair procedure until you are satisfied that the surface of the filler and the feathered edge of the paint are perfect. Rinse the area with clean water and allow it to dry completely.

19   The repair area is now ready for painting. Spray painting must be carried out in a warm, dry, windless and dust free atmosphere. These conditions can be created if you have access to a large indoor work area, but if you are forced to work in the open, you will have to pick the day very carefully. If you are working indoors, dousing the floor in the work area with water will help settle the dust which would otherwise be in the air. If the repair area is confined to one body panel, mask off the surrounding panels. This will help minimize the effects of a slight mismatch in paint color. Trim pieces such as chrome strips, door handles, etc. will also need to be masked off or removed. Use masking tape and several thicknesses of newspaper for the masking operations.

20   Before spraying, shake the paint can thoroughly, then spray a test area until the spray painting technique is mastered. Cover the repair area with a thick coat of primer. The thickness should be built up using several thin layers of primer rather than one thick one. Using 600-grit wet-or-dry sandpaper, rub down the surface of the primer until it is very smooth. While doing this, the work area should be thoroughly rinsed with water

and the wet-or-dry sandpaper periodically rinsed as well. Allow the primer to dry before spraying additional coats.

21   Spray on the top coat, again building up the thickness by using several layers of paint. Begin spraying in the center of the repair area and then, using a circular motion, work outward until the whole repair area and about two inches of the surrounding original paint is covered. Remove all masking material 10 to 15 minutes after spraying on the final coat of paint. Allow the new paint at least two weeks to harden, then use a very fine rubbing compound to blend the edges of the new paint into the existing paint. Finally, apply a coat of wax.

6   Body repair – major damage

1   Major damage must be repaired by an auto body shop. These shops have the specialized equipment required to do the job properly.

2   If the damage is extensive, the frame must be checked for proper alignment or the vehicle's handling characteristics may be adversely affected and other components may wear at an accelerated rate.

3   Due to the fact that all of the major body components (hood, fenders, etc.) are separate and replaceable units, any seriously damaged components should be replaced rather than repaired. Sometimes the components can be found in a wrecking yard that specializes in used vehicle components, often at a considerable savings over the cost of new parts.

7   Hinges and locks – maintenance

Once every 3,000 miles, or every three months, the hinges and latch assemblies on the doors, hood and the tailgate or the liftgate should be given a few drops of light oil or lock lubricant. The door latch strikers should also be lubricated with a thin coat of grease to reduce wear and ensure free movement. Lubricate the door and the liftgate locks with spray-on graphite lubricant.

8   Hood – removal, installation and adjustment

Note : The hood is heavy and somewhat awkward to remove and install – at least two people should perform this procedure.

Removal and installation

1   Open the hood.

2   Cover the fenders and cowl with blankets or heavy cloths to protect the paint.

3   Use a permanent marker or scribe to make alignment marks around the bolt heads to ensure proper alignment on reinstallation.

4   Have an assistant hold onto the hood and remove the hood-to-hinge assembly bolts.

5   Remove the hood.

6   Installation is the reverse of the removal steps with the following additions:
   a) Align the hood and hinges using the alignment marks made in Step 3.
   b) Tighten the bolts to the torque listed in this Chapter's Specifications.

Adjustment

7   The hood can be adjusted to obtain a flush fit between the hood and fenders.

8   Loosen the hood retaining bolts.

9   Move the hood from side-to-side until the hood is properly aligned with the fenders at the front. Tighten the bolts securely.

10   Loosen the bolts securing the hood latch assembly.

11   Move the latch until alignment is correct with the hood latch striker. Tighten the latch bolts securely.

11

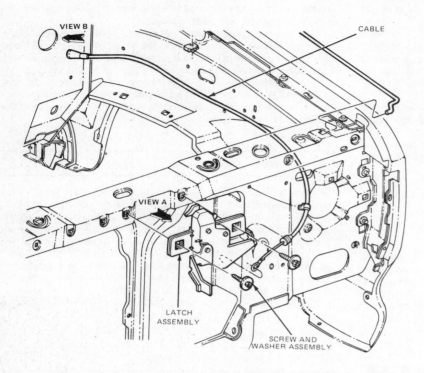

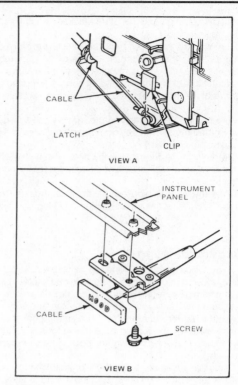

9.10   Hood release cable routing and details

9   Hood latch cable – removal and installation

Refer to illustrations 9.10

1   Open the hood and support it in the open position with a long piece of wood.

2   Use a permanent marker or scribe to make alignment marks around the hood latch to ensure proper alignment on reinstallation.

3   Remove the bolts securing the hood latch and remove it.

4   Turn the latch over and use a small screwdriver to pry the plastic cable retainer off the anchor post).

5   Use a pair of pliers to lift the cable out of the retaining slot in the hood latch.

6   Lift the cable eye off the anchor post).

7   Remove the cover from the fuse panel.

8   Remove the two screws securing the hood release handle bracket to the instrument panel.

9   Remove all cable retaining clips.

10   Carefully withdraw the cable through the rubber grommet in the firewall opening and remove the cable assembly **(see illustration)**.

11   Installation is the reverse of the removal steps with the following additions:
   a) Insert the cable through the grommet in the firewall and make sure the grommet is properly seated within the firewall hole.
   b) Prior to closing the hood, operate the control cable and make sure the latch control operates correctly.

10   Door – removal, installation and alignment

Removal and installation

1   With the door in the open position, place a jack or jackstand under the door or have an assistant hold the door while the hinge bolts are removed. **Note**: *If a jack or jackstand is used, place thick padding on top of the jack to protect the door's painted finish.*

2   On models so equipped, remove the upper and lower hinge access cover plates.

3   Scribe or paint lines around the door hinges to ensure proper alignment on reinstallation.

4   Remove the hinge-to-door bolts and carefully lift off the door.

5   Installation is the reverse of the removal steps. Align the door as described below.

Alignment

Refer to illustration 10.6

6   Check the alignment and adjust if necessary as follows:
   a) Up-and-down and forward-and-backwards adjustments are made by loosening the hinge-to-body bolts and moving the door as necessary **(see illustration)**.
   b) The door lock striker can also be adjusted both up-and-down and sideways to provide positive engagement with the lock mechanism. This is done by loosening the striker and moving the striker as necessary.

7   Tighten the hinge-to-body bolts to the torque listed in this Chapter's Specifications.

11   Door hinge – removal and installation

Note: *If both hinges are to be replaced, it is easier to leave the door in place and replace one hinge at a time.*

1   With the door in the open position, place a jack or jackstand under the door or have an assistant hold the door while the door hinge bolts are removed. **Note:** *If a jack or jackstand is used, place thick padding on top of the jack to protect the door's painted finish.*

2   On models so equipped, remove the upper and lower hinge access cover plates.

3   Scribe or paint lines around the door hinges to ensure proper alignment on reinstallation.

4   Remove the hinge-to-door bolts, then the hinge-to-body bolts. Carefully remove the hinge(s) or lift off the door.

5   Installation is the reverse of the removal steps with the following additions:

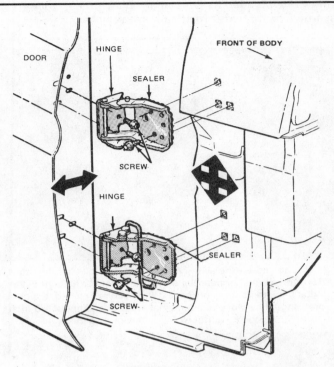

10.6   Door hinge adjustment points

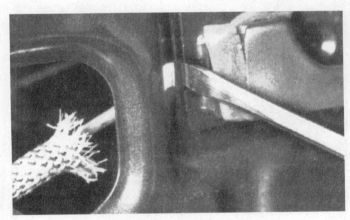

13.3   Pry the latch forward

a)   Apply a sealant (Ford specification ESB-M2G150-A or equivalent) to the hinge before installing it onto the body panel.
b)   Adjust the door if necessary (see Section 10).

12   Door latch striker – removal, installation and adjustment

Removal and installation

1   Use Vise Grip pliers to unscrew the door latch striker stud from the door jamb.
2   Installation is the reverse of removal. Adjust if necessary.

Adjustment

3   The door latch striker can be adjusted vertically and laterally as well as fore-and-aft.
4   Don't use the door latch striker to compensate for door misalignment.
5   The door latch striker can be shimmed to obtain the correct clearance between the latch and the striker.

13.2   Remove the screws securing the inner door handle assembly to the door

13.4   Rotate the inner door handle to release and remove the actuator rod

6   To check the clearance between the latch jamb and the striker area, spread a layer of dark grease on to the striker.
7   Open and close the door several times and note the pattern in the grease.
8   Move the door striker assembly laterally to provide a flush fit at the door and pillar or at the quarter panel.
9   Securely tighten the door latch striker after adjustment is complete.

13   Inner door handle and latch assembly – removal and installation

Inner door handle

Refer to illustrations 13.2, 13.3 and 13.4
1   Remove the door trim panel and watershield (see Section 16).
2   Remove the screws securing the inner door handle assembly to the door (**see illustration**).
3   Insert a screwdriver in the notch on the aft end of the latch and pry the assembly out of the door (**see illustration**).
4   Rotate the inner door handle up 90-degrees and release it from the door latch remote control link assembly (**see illustration**).
5   Installation is the reverse of the removal steps.

11

These photos illustrate a method of repairing simple dents. They are intended to supplement *Body repair - minor damage* in this Chapter and should not be used as the sole instructions for body repair on these vehicles.

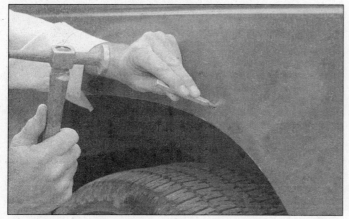

1   If you can't access the backside of the body panel to hammer out the dent, pull it out with a slide-hammer-type dent puller. In the deepest portion of the dent or along the crease line, drill or punch hole(s) at least one inch apart . . .

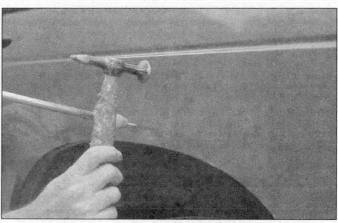

2   . . . then screw the slide-hammer into the hole and operate it. Tap with a hammer near the edge of the dent to help 'pop' the metal back to its original shape. When you're finished, the dent area should be close to its original contour and about 1/8-inch below the surface of the surrounding metal

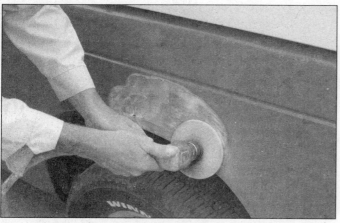

3   Using coarse-grit sandpaper, remove the paint down to the bare metal. Hand sanding works fine, but the disc sander shown here makes the job faster. Use finer (about 320-grit) sandpaper to feather-edge the paint at least one inch around the dent area

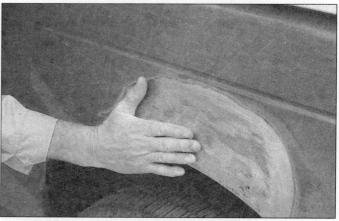

4   When the paint is removed, touch will probably be more helpful than sight for telling if the metal is straight. Hammer down the high spots or raise the low spots as necessary. Clean the repair area with wax/silicone remover

5   Following label instructions, mix up a batch of plastic filler and hardener. The ratio of filler to hardener is critical, and, if you mix it incorrectly, it will either not cure properly or cure too quickly (you won't have time to file and sand it into shape)

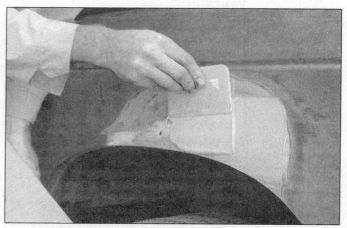

6   Working quickly so the filler doesn't harden, use a plastic applicator to press the body filler firmly into the metal, assuring it bonds completely. Work the filler until it matches the original contour and is slightly above the surrounding metal

7   Let the filler harden until you can just dent it with your fingernail. Use a body file or Surform tool (shown here) to rough-shape the filler

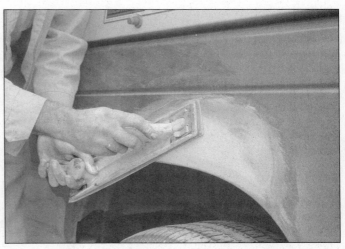

8   Use coarse-grit sandpaper and a sanding board or block to work the filler down until it's smooth and even. Work down to finer grits of sandpaper - always using a board or block - ending up with 360 or 400 grit

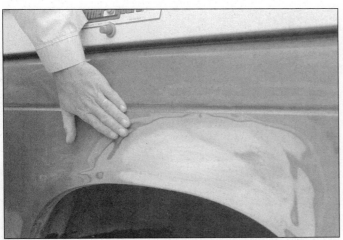

9   You shouldn't be able to feel any ridge at the transition from the filler to the bare metal or from the bare metal to the old paint. As soon as the repair is flat and uniform, remove the dust and mask off the adjacent panels or trim pieces

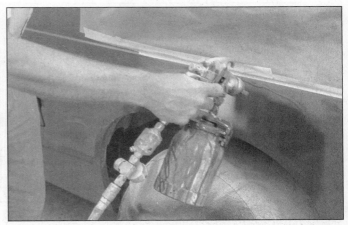

10   Apply several layers of primer to the area. Don't spray the primer on too heavy, so it sags or runs, and make sure each coat is dry before you spray on the next one. A professional-type spray gun is being used here, but aerosol spray primer is available inexpensively from auto parts stores

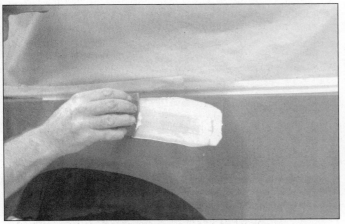

11   The primer will help reveal imperfections or scratches. Fill these with glazing compound. Follow the label instructions and sand it with 360 or 400-grit sandpaper until it's smooth. Repeat the glazing, sanding and respraying until the primer reveals a perfectly smooth surface

12   Finish sand the primer with very fine sandpaper (400 or 600-grit) to remove the primer overspray. Clean the area with water and allow it to dry. Use a tack rag to remove any dust, then apply the finish coat. Don't attempt to rub out or wax the repair area until the paint has dried completely (at least two weeks)

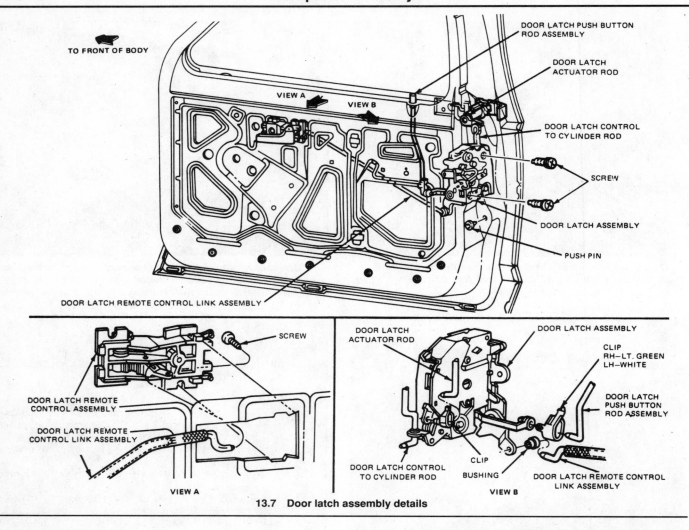

13.7   Door latch assembly details

Door latch assembly

Removal
Refer to illustration 13.7

6   Remove the door trim panel and watershield (see Section 16).
7   Disconnect the rod ends from the latch and disconnect the remote control link assembly **(see illustration)**.
8   Disconnect the handle rod and push button rod from the latch.
9   Remove the screws securing the latch assembly to the door and remove the latch).

Installation
10   Install the rod retaining clips in the new latch assembly.
11   Attach the control rod and lock cylinder rod to the latch before installing the latch assembly.
12   Install the latch assembly in the door and secure with the screws. Tighten the screws securely.
13   Reinstall the rods to the handle, lock cylinder and remote control.
14   Install the handle rod and push button rod to the latch and check for proper latch operation.
15   Install the watershield and door trim panel.

---

14   Outside door handle – removal and installation

Refer to illustration 14.2

1   Remove the access hole cover and/or trim panel and pull away the watershield.

2   Disconnect the door latch actuator rod from the latch **(see illustration)**.
3   Drive out the center of the pop-rivet with a suitable size drift.
4   Use a suitable size drill and drill out the remainder of the rivet. Repeat for the other rivet.
5   Remove the door handle.
6   Installation is the reverse of the removal steps with the following additions:
   a)   Position the handle in the door and install the two pop-rivets.
   b)   Connect the actuator rod to the handle.
   c)   Install the watershield and install the access hole cover and/or trim panel.

---

15   Door lock cylinder – removal and installation

1   Roll the window up all the way.
2   Remove the door trim panel and watershield (see Section 16).
3   Disconnect the door latch control-to-cylinder rod from the retainer clip.
4   Use a pair of pliers to slide the cylinder retainer away from the lock cylinder and door **(see illustration 14.2).**
5   Remove the lock cylinder from the door.
6   Install the lock cylinder into the door opening from the outside and push the retaining clip into place. Make sure it's seated correctly.
7   Reconnect the lock cylinder rod-to-door latch control.
8   Check for proper lock operation, then install the watershield and the door trim panel.

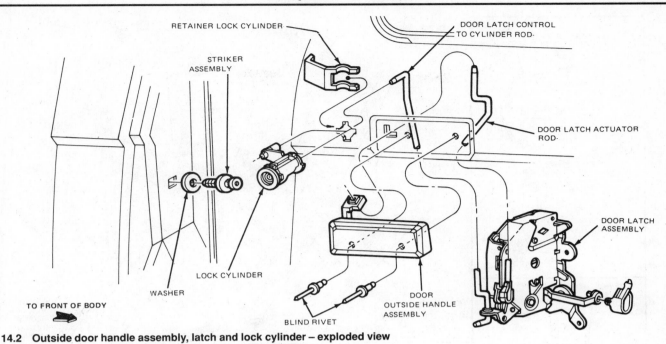

14.2 Outside door handle assembly, latch and lock cylinder – exploded view

16.5 Wedge a flat screwdriver between the door trim panel and the door and disengage the plastic retaining clips to remove the panel – do not pull on the panel or the plastic retainers could pull out of the panel

16 Door trim panel – removal and installation

Door trim panel

Refer to illustration 16.5

1   Remove the three screws securing the arm rest and remove the arm rest.
2   Remove the screw securing the inner door handle trim cup and remove the cup.
3   Remove the screw securing the window crank and remove the crank and washer.
4   On models so equipped, remove the door lock control.
5   Insert a putty knife or flat screwdriver between the door trim panel and the door and disengage the plastic retaining clips **(see illustration)**. Pry around both sides and bottom perimeter of the door trim panel until

the panel is free from the door.
6   Once all of the plastic clips are disengaged, detach the door trim panel and remove the trim panel from the vehicle. **Caution**: *Never pull on the panel to release the plastic clips.*
7   For access to the inner door, carefully peel back the plastic watershield.
8   Installation is the reverse of the removal steps with the following additions:
    a) Be sure to install any clips in the door trim panel which may have come out during the removal procedure.
    b) Position the watershield against the inner door panel, aligning the watershield adhesive with the door panel adhesive, and press it into place.
    c) Make sure all plastic clips are pressed into place correctly.

17 Front door window glass – replacement and adjustment

Refer to illustration 17.2

Replacement

1   Remove the door trim panel and watershield (see Section 16).
2   Reinstall the window regulator crank and lower the glass sufficiently to gain access to the window glass bracket rivets **(see illustration)**.
3   Remove the rivets securing the glass to the regulator as follows:
    a) Place a suitable size block of wood behind the glass at the regulator.
    b) Drive out the center of the pop-rivet with a suitable size drift.
    c) Use a suitable size drill and drill out the remainder of the rivet. Repeat for the other rivet.
4   Remove the window glass from the door. Clean any drilling or rivet remnants or any broken glass from the bottom of the door.
5   Install the plastic retainer and spacer into the holes in the glass. Install the metal retainer on the outside surface of the window glass.
6   Carefully insert the window glass into the door, place the window glass bracket on the regulator and install two 1-inch X 1/4-inch bolts, washers and nuts to secure the glass to the regulator. Tighten the nuts finger-tight at this time.

11

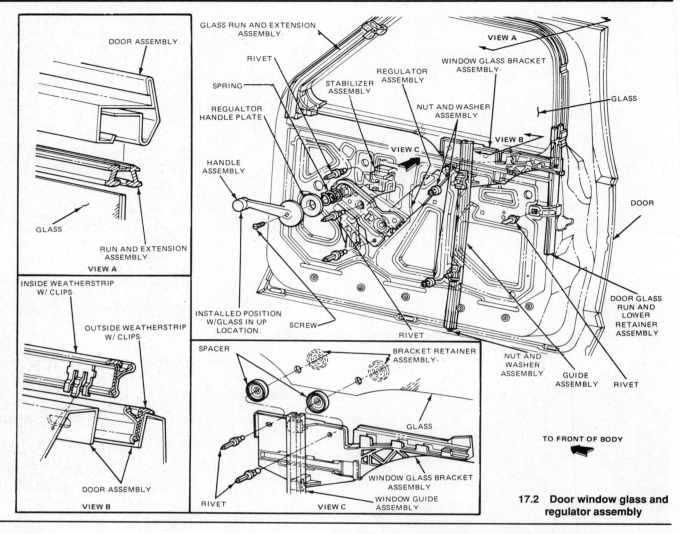

17.2   Door window glass and regulator assembly

Adjustment

7   Lower the glass 2-inches from the full-up position.

8   Loosen the three guide assembly nut and washer assemblies (see illustration 17.2).

9   Push the glass toward the rear, within the glass run assembly until it bottoms out within the door frame.

10   Move the window guide post toward the rear within the retention slot in the door inner panel. Tighten the three guide assembly nuts to the torque listed in this Chapter's Specifications.

11   Cycle the window glass up and down several times and check for proper operation.

12   Install the watershield and door trim panel.

18   Front door window regulator – replacement

1   Remove the door trim panel and watershield (see Section 16).

2   Remove the window glass (see Section 17).

3   Remove the three guide assembly nut and washer assemblies (see illustration 17.2). Remove the window guide from the door belt opening.

4   Remove the glass bracket assembly from the door, sliding the bracket "C" channel off of the regulator arm slider/roller.

5   Drive out the center of the pop-rivet with a suitable size drift.

6   Use a suitable size drill to drill out the remainder of the rivet. Repeat for the other rivet.

7   Remove the regulator assembly through the door access hole.

Clean any drilling or rivet remnants or any broken glass from the bottom of the door.

8   Installation is the reverse of the removal steps with the following additions:

a)   Insert the regulator assembly into the door panel and install new pop-rivets.

b)   Check for proper window glass operation, then install the watershield and door trim panel.

19   Liftgate (Bronco II) – removal and installation

Liftgate gas cylinder assist rod

Refer to illustration 19.2

1   Open the liftgate and secure it in the open position.

2   Use a screwdriver and pry out the spring clip from the ball socket at both ends of the assist rod (see illustration).

3   Remove the liftgate assist rod.

4   Installation is the reverse of the removal steps.

Liftgate

Refer to illustration 19.7

5   Remove the liftgate gas cylinder assist rod as previously described in this Section. Prop the liftgate in the up position.

6   Scribe or paint lines around the liftgate hinges and bolts to ensure proper alignment on reinstallation.

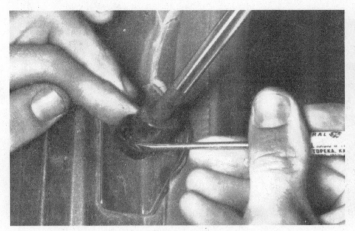

19.2   Pry out the spring clip from the ball socket and lift the rod from the tailgate

19.7   Index the hinge for proper installation before removing the two bolts securing each liftgate hinge (arrows)

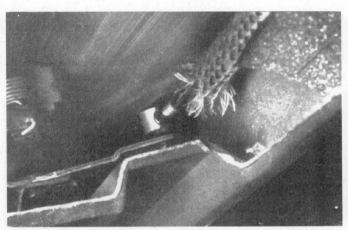

20.7   Pry the retainer from the actuator rod, then slide the rod off the latch assembly

20.13   Disconnect the actuator rods and remove the two bolts securing the latch control assembly

7   Remove the liftgate-to-hinge bolts and carefully remove the liftgate (see illustration).
8   Installation is the reverse of the removal steps. Tighten the hinge bolts to the torque listed in this Chapter's Specifications.

Liftgate hinge

9   Remove the liftgate as previously described in this Section.
10   Remove the interior upper rear garnish molding to gain access to the hinge nuts.
11   If necessary, move the headliner away from the liftgate hinges.
12   Scribe or paint lines around the liftgate hinges and nuts to ensure proper alignment on reinstallation.
13   Remove the nut securing the hinge to the body and remove the hinge.
14   Installation is the reverse of the removal steps. Tighten the hinge nuts to the torque listed in this Chapter's Specifications.

---

20   Liftgate panel, lock cylinder and latches (Bronco II) – removal and installation

---

Liftgate panel removal and installation

1   Remove the six screws securing the panel to the liftgate assembly.
2   Use a putty knife or screwdriver and pry out the plastic retainer clips securing the panel to the liftgate. Caution: Do not pull on the panel as this will rip the plastic retainer clips out of the panel.
3   Installation is the reverse of the removal steps.

Outside lock cylinder latch

4   Use a pair of pliers and slide the cylinder retainer clip away from the lock cylinder and liftgate.
5   Remove the lock cylinder from the liftgate.
6   Install the lock cylinder into the liftgate opening from the outside and push the retaining clip into place. Make sure it's seated correctly.

Liftgate latches

Refer to illustration 20.7

7   Use a screwdriver and pry up on the actuator rod retainers, then slide the rod off the latch assembly (see illustration).
8   Remove the bolts securing the latch to the liftgate and pull the rod and latch out as an assembly,
9   Installation is the reverse of the removal steps.

Liftgate latch control assembly

Refer to illustration 20.13

10   Remove the liftgate panel as previously described in this Section.
11   Remove the outside lock cylinder as previously described in this Section.
12   Remove the latch actuator arms.
13   Remove the two bolts securing the control assembly to the liftgate (see illustration).
14   Remove the latch control assembly.
15   Installation is the reverse of the removal steps.

11

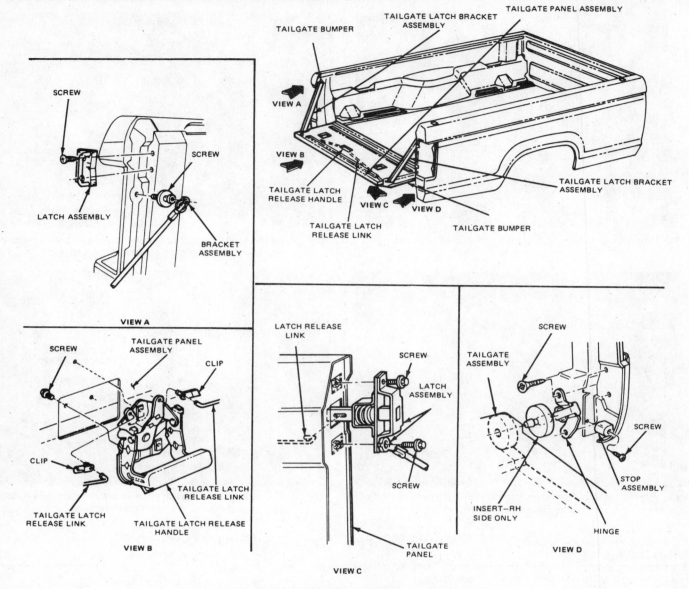

22.7   Tailgate latch and hinge assemblies for Ranger models

---

21   Liftgate flipper glass and hinge (Bronco II) – removal and installation

1   Open the flipper glass and secure it in the open position.
2   Carefully pry both gas cylinder assist rods from the flipper glass.
3   Remove the nut and washer securing the hinge to the flipper glass.
4   Remove the flipper glass assembly.
5   If necessary, remove the screws securing the flipper glass hinge to the liftgate and remove the hinge.
6   Installation is the reverse of the removal steps.

22   Tailgate (Ranger) – removal and installation

Tailgate

1   Open the tailgate.

2   Lift up on the spring retainer securing the cable support onto the support pin. Lift the cables off each support pin.
3   Raise the tailgate off the right side hinge and then off the left side hinge. Remove the tailgate.
4   Installation is the reverse of the removal steps.

Tailgate body latch

Refer to illustration 22.7

5   Open the tailgate.
6   Scribe or paint lines around the tailgate hinge to ensure proper alignment on reinstallation.
7   Remove the two bolts securing the latch to the body **(see illustration)**.
8   Remove the hinge.
9   Installation is the reverse of the removal steps. Tighten the bolts to the torque listed in this Chapter's Specifications.

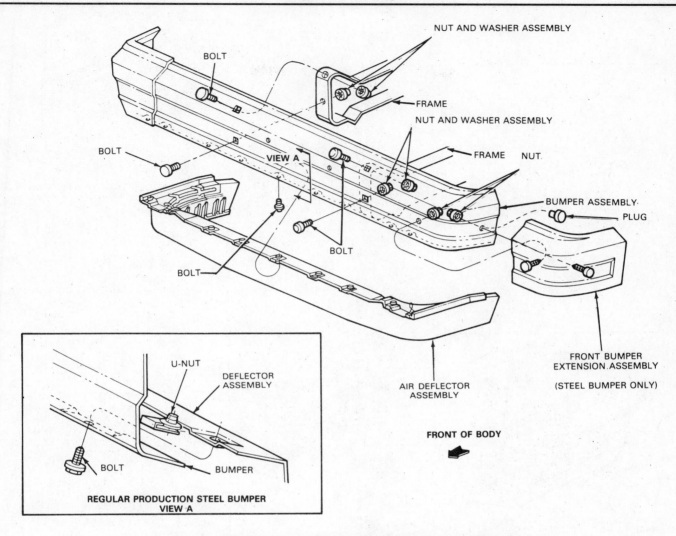

23.1   The front bumper attaches directly to the frame – if equipped with bumper guards, the bolts are located under the guard

Tailgate support, handle and latch support bracket

10   Open the tailgate.

11   Pry out on the spring retainer and lift the support off the pin at the top.

12   If removal is necessary, unscrew the pin with a Torx driver or socket and remove it from the body.

13   To remove the handle assembly, remove the three screws securing the tailgate handle. Disconnect the handle release links from the handle assembly. Remove the handle assembly.

14   Remove the bolts securing the latch support bracket to the tailgate and remove the latch support bracket.

15   Installation is the reverse of the removal steps. Tighten the bolts to the torque listed in this Chapter's Specifications.

23   Front bumper and air deflector – removal and installation

Refer to illustrations 23.1

Air deflector

1   Remove the bolts securing the air deflector to the bumper **(see illustrations)**.

2   Push the air deflector toward the rear of the vehicle and remove it.

3   Installation is the reverse of the removal steps.

Front bumper

Note: *The bumper is heavy and somewhat awkward to remove and install – at least two people should perform this procedure.*

4   Raise the front of the vehicle, support it securely on jackstands, block the rear wheels and set the parking brake.

5   Have an assistant hold onto the bumper assembly and remove the two bolts and nuts on each side securing the bumper to the frame.

6   If equipped with bumper guards, first remove the bumper guards from the bumper, then remove the bumper from the frame.

7   Don't lose the plastic insulators between the bumper and the frame. They must be reinstalled when the bumper is installed.

8   Installation is the reverse of the removal steps with the following additions:

   a)   If installing a new bumper, transfer the bumper guards, license plate holder and any additional items to the new bumper.

   b)   Tighten the bolts to the torque listed in this Chapter's Specifications.

11

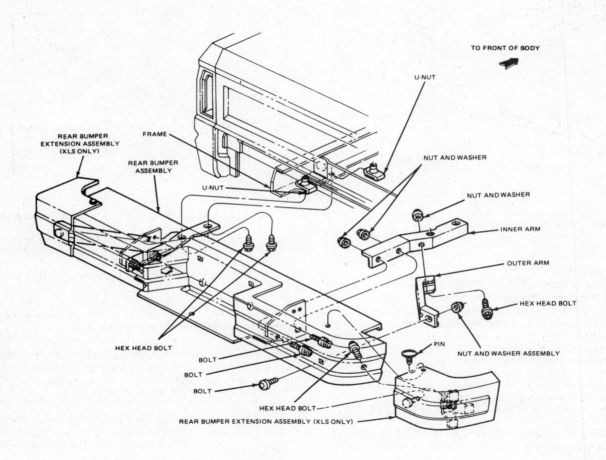

24.2   **An exploded view of a typical bumper (Ranger models)**

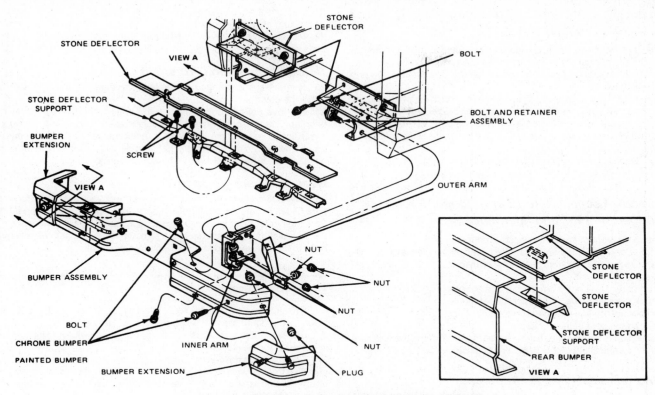

24.7   An exploded view of the rear bumper (Bronco II models)

24   Rear bumper – removal and installation

Ranger

Refer to illustration 24.2

Note: *The bumper is heavy and somewhat awkward to remove and install – at least two people should perform this procedure.*

1   Raise the rear of the vehicle, support it securely on jackstands and block the front wheels so the vehicle will not roll in either direction.
2   Remove the two bolts and nuts on each side securing the bumper to the inner arm **(see illustration)**.
3   Disconnect the license plate light electrical connectors from the main wiring harness.
4   Have an assistant hold onto the bumper assembly and remove the bolt and nut on each side securing the bumper to the outer arm.
5   Installation is the reverse of the removal steps with the following additions:
  a) If installing a new bumper, transfer the brackets and extensions (if equipped), license plate lights and any additional items to the new bumper.
  b) Tighten the bolts to the torque listed in this Chapter's Specifications.

Bronco II

Refer to illustration 24.7

Note: *The bumper is heavy and somewhat awkward to remove and install – at least two people should perform this procedure.*

6   Raise the rear of the vehicle, support it securely on jackstands, block the front wheels so the vehicle will not roll in either direction.
7   Remove the two bolts and nuts on each side securing the bumper to the bracket **(see illustration)**. Use a socket U-joint to gain access to the top nut.
8   Disconnect the license plate light electrical connectors from the main wiring harness.
9   Have an assistant hold onto the bumper assembly and remove the bolt and nut on each side securing the bumper to the outer arm.

10   Installation is the reverse of the removal steps with the following additions:
  a) If installing a new bumper, transfer the brackets and extensions (if equipped), license plate lights and any additional items to the new bumper.
  b) Tighten the bolts to the torque listed in this Chapter's Specifications.

25   Windshield and fixed glass – replacement

Replacement of the windshield and fixed glass requires the use of special fast-setting adhesive/caulk materials and some specialized tools and techniques. These operations should be left to a dealer service department or a shop specializing in automotive glass work.

26   Seats – removal and installation

Front bench seat (Ranger models)

1   On the right side only, remove the pin securing the insulator at the front of the seat track, then remove the seat track insulator.
2   Remove the four bolts securing the seat track to the floorpan and lift the seat track assembly from the vehicle.
3   Installation is the reverse of the removal steps. Tighten the retaining bolts to the torque listed in this Chapter's Specifications.

Front bucket seat (Ranger: driver's and passenger's, Bronco II: driver's only)

4   Remove the pin securing the insulators at the front of the seat track, then remove both seat track insulators.
5   Remove the four bolts securing the seat track to the floorpan and lift the seat track assembly from the vehicle.
6   Installation is the reverse of the removal steps. Tighten the retaining bolts to the torque listed in this Chapter's Specifications.

11

Front bucket seat (Bronco II passenger's only – 1983 through 1986 models)

7   With the seat down in the latched position, remove the two bolts securing the front portion of the seat track to the floorpan.

8   Lift up on the seat support latch release handle. The seat will now pop up and fold forward.

9   Remove the two bolts securing the rear portion of the seat track to the floorpan and lift the seat track assembly from the vehicle. **Warning:** *To ensure your safety, whenever the seat and support assembly is removed from or installed into the vehicle, the support assembly must be in the unlatched position.*

10   Installation is the reverse of the removal steps. Tighten the retaining bolts to the torque listed in this Chapter's Specifications.

Front bucket seat (Bronco II and Ranger Supercab passenger's – 1987 and later models)

11   Unbolt the front of the seat support from the floor.

12   Lift the recliner handle and push the seat back all the way forward.

13   Remove the push pins that secure the rear shields to the seat support and take the shields off.

14   Unbolt the slide bar fromm the support assembly.

15   Unbolt the rear of the seat support from the floor.

16   Disconnect the seat electrical connector (if equipped).

17   Lift the seat oout of the vehicle.

18   Installation is the reverse of the removal steps. Tighten the retaining bolts to the torque listed in this Chapter's Specifications.

Folding rear seat (Ranger Supercab)

19   Remove the three screws securing the cover assembly and remove the cover.

20   Remove the bolt securing the seat belt assembly to the floor.

21   Remove the five bolts securing the seat assembly to the floorpan and lift the seat assembly from the vehicle.

22   Installation is the reverse of the removal steps. Tighten the retaining bolts securely.

Rear seat cushion (Bronco II)

23   Remove the screw securing the outer cover next to the door, then remove the cover.

24   Remove the two bolts securing the seat cushion assembly to the floorpan. Slide the outer edge of the cushion assembly out and disengage it from the center pivot pin. Lift the seat cushion assembly from the vehicle.

25   Installation is the reverse of the removal steps. Tighten the retaining bolts to the torque listed in this Chapter's Specifications.

Rear seat back (Bronco II)

26   Remove the two bolts securing the seat back and seat belt to the floorpan. Slide the outer edge of the seat back assembly out and disengage it from the center pivot pin. Lift the seat back assembly from the vehicle.

27   Installation is the reverse of the removal steps. Tighten the retaining bolts to the torque listed in this Chapter's Specifications.

---

27   Seat belt check

1   Check the seat belts, buckles, latch plates and guide loops for obvious damage and signs of wear.

2   Check that the seat belt reminder light comes on when the ignition key is turned to the Run or Start position.

3   The seat belts are designed to lock up during a sudden stop or impact, yet allow free movement during normal driving. Check that the retractors return the belt against your chest while driving and rewind the belt fully when the buckle is unlatched.

4   If any of the above checks reveal problems with the seat belt system, replace parts as necessary.

Chapter 12   Chassis electrical system

Contents

1   General information

Warning: *To prevent electrical shorts, fires and injury, always disconnect the cable from the negative terminal of the battery before checking, repairing or replacing electrical components.*

The chassis electrical system of this vehicle is a 12-volt, negative ground type. Power for the lights and all electrical accessories is supplied by a lead/acid-type battery which is charged by the alternator.

This chapter covers repair and service procedures for various chassis (non-engine related) electrical components. For information regarding the engine electrical system components (battery, alternator, distributor and starter motor), see Chapter 5.

2   Electrical troubleshooting – general information

A typical electrical circuit consists of an electrical component, any switches, relays, motors, fuses, fusible links or circuit breakers, etc. related to that component and the wiring and connectors that link the components to both the battery and the chassis. To help you pinpoint an electrical circuit problem, wiring diagrams are included at the end of this book.

Before tackling any troublesome electrical circuit, first study the appropriate wiring diagrams to get a complete understanding of what makes up that individual circuit. Trouble spots, for instance, can often be isolated by noting if other components related to that circuit are often routed through the same fuse and ground connections.

Electrical problems usually stem from simple causes such as loose or corroded connectors, a blown fuse, a melted fusible link or a bad relay. Visually inspect the condition of all fuses, wires and connectors in a problem circuit before troubleshooting it.

The basic tools needed for electrical troubleshooting include a circuit tester, a high impedance (10 K-ohm) digital voltmeter, a continuity tester and a jumper wire with an inline circuit breaker for bypassing electrical components. Before attempting to locate or define a problem with electrical test instruments, use the wiring diagrams to decide where to make the necessary connections.

Voltage checks

Perform a voltage check first when a circuit is not functioning properly. Connect one lead of a circuit tester to either the negative battery terminal or a known good ground.

Connect the other lead to a connector in the circuit being tested, preferably nearest to the battery or fuse. If the bulb of the tester lights up, voltage is present, which means that the part of the circuit between the connector and the battery is problem free. Continue checking the rest of the circuit in the same fashion.

When you reach a point at which no voltage is present, the problem lies between that point and the last test point with voltage. Most of the time the problem can be traced to a loose connection. **Note:** *Keep in mind that some circuits receive voltage only when the ignition key is in the Accessory or Run position.*

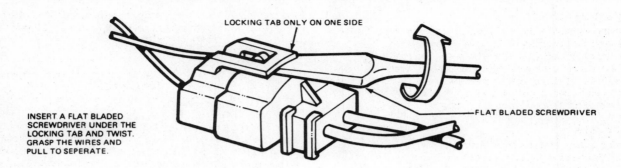

LOCKING TAB ONLY ON ONE SIDE

FLAT BLADED SCREWDRIVER

INSERT A FLAT BLADED
SCREWDRIVER UNDER THE
LOCKING TAB AND TWIST.
GRASP THE WIRES AND
PULL TO SEPERATE.

PLACE A THUMB UNDER THE LOCKING TAB AND PUSH UP. GRASP THE WIRES AND PULL TO SEPARATE.

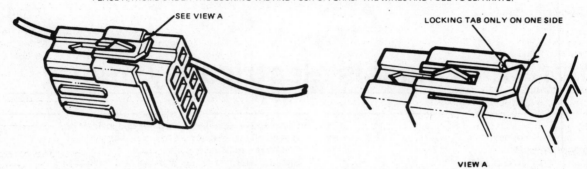

SEE VIEW A

LOCKING TAB ONLY ON ONE SIDE

VIEW A

INSERT A FLAT BLADED SCREWDRIVER UNDER THE LOCKING TAB AND TWIST. GRASP
THE WIRES AND PULL UNTIL THE LOCKING TAB IS ON THE RAMP. TURN THE
CONNECTOR OVER AND REPEAT THE PROCEDURE ON THE OPPOSITE SIDE OF THE
CONNECTOR. THEN GRASP THE WIRES AND PULL APART.

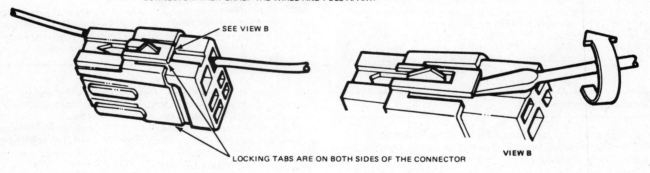

SEE VIEW B

LOCKING TABS ARE ON BOTH SIDES OF THE CONNECTOR

VIEW B

GRASP THE WIRES WITH BOTH HANDS AND PULL THE CONNECTOR APART

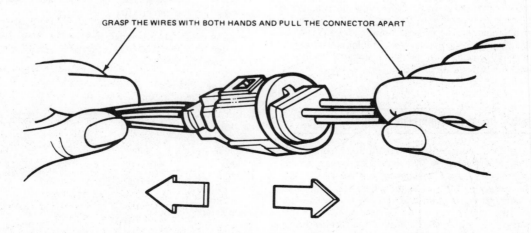

3.1   **Some of the various types of inline connectors used on these models**

Finding a short circuit

One method of finding shorts in a circuit is to remove the fuse and connect a test light or voltmeter in its place. There should be no voltage present in the circuit. Move the wiring harness from side-to-side while watching the test light. If the bulb goes on, there is a short to ground somewhere in that area, probably where the insulation has been rubbed through. The same test can be performed on each component in a circuit, even a switch.

Ground check

Perform a ground test to check whether a component is properly grounded. Disconnect the battery and connect one lead of a self-powered test light, known as a continuity tester, to a known good ground. Connect the other lead to the wire or ground connection being tested. If the bulb goes on, the ground is good.

If the bulb does not go on, the ground is not good.

Continuity check

A continuity check determines if there are any breaks in a circuit – if it is conducting electricity properly. With the circuit off (no power in the circuit), a self-powered continuity tester can be used to check the circuit. Connect the test leads to both ends of the circuit, and if the test light comes on the circuit is passing current properly. If the light doesn't come on, there is a break somewhere in the circuit. The same procedure can be used to test a switch, by connecting the continuity tester to the power in and power out sides of the switch. With the switch turned on, the test light should come on.

Finding an open circuit

When diagnosing for possible open circuits it is often difficult to locate them by sight because oxidation or terminal misalignment are hidden by the connectors. Merely wiggling a connector on a sensor or in the wiring harness may correct the open circuit condition. Remember this if an open circuit is indicated when troubleshooting a circuit. Intermittent problems may also be caused by oxidized or loose connections.

Electrical troubleshooting is simple if you keep in mind that all electrical circuits are basically electricity running from the battery, through the wires, switches, relays, fuses and fusible links to each electrical compo-nent (light bulb, motor, etc.) and then to ground, from which it is passed back to the battery. Any electrical problem is an interruption in the flow of electricity to and from the battery.

---

3   Connectors – general information

Refer to illustration 3.1

Always release the locking tab(s) before attempting to unplug inline type connectors. There are a variety of locking tab configurations (**see illustration**). Although nothing more than a finger is usually necessary to pry locking tabs open, a small pocket screwdriver is effective for hard-to-release tabs. Once the tabs are released, try to pull on the connectors themselves, not the wires, when unplugging two connector halves (there are times, however, when this is not possible – use good judgment).

It is usually necessary to know which side, male or female, of the connector you're checking. Male connectors are easily distinguished from females by the shape of their internal pins.

When checking continuity or voltage with a circuit tester, insertion of the test probe into the receptacle may open the fitting to the connector and result in poor contact. Instead, insert the test probe from the wire harness side of the connector (known as "backprobing").

---

4   Fuses – general information

Refer to illustrations 4.3a, 4.3b, 4.4 and 4.6

The electrical circuits are protected by a combination of fuses, fusible links and circuit breakers. The fuse panel is located in the left end of the instrument panel.

The fuse block is equipped with miniaturized fuses because their compact dimensions and convenient blade-type terminal design allow fingertip removal and installation.

Each fuse protects one or more circuits. The protected circuit is identified on the face of the fuse panel cover above each fuse. Fuse guides are included here (**see illustrations**), but consult your owner's manual – it will have the most accurate guide for your vehicle.

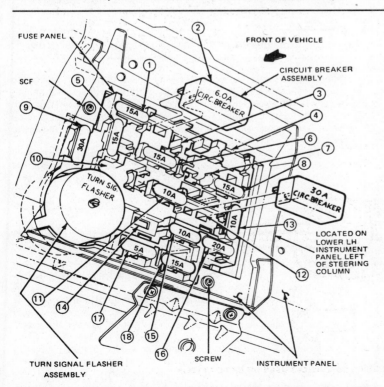

4.3a   Fuse and circuit breaker panel (1983 through 1988 models)

1   Stop lights, hazard warning light fan – 15-amp fuse
2   Windshield wiper, washer pump - 6-amp circuit breaker
3   Not used
4   Tail, parking, side marker lights, instru-ment cluster illumination light, license plate light, trailer lights relay – 15-amp fuse
5   Turn signal, back-up lights – 15-amp fuse
6   4WD indicator, clock display, speed control, rear window washer/wiper/de-froster, light out warning – 15-amp fuse
7   Not used
8   Courtesy lights, dome light, clock, glove compartment light, "Head lights On" indicator – 15-amp fuse
9   Heater and A/C motor blower motor, A/C clutch – 30-amp fuse
10   Rear anti-lock brakes module - 20-amp fuse
11   Radio/tape player – 15-amp fuse
12   Power lumbar seat – 30-amp circuit breaker
13   Not used
14   Power windows – 20-amp circuit breaker
15   Fuel tank selector – 10-amp fuse
16   Horn, cigar lighter – 20-amp fuse
17   Instrument panel illumination lights, automatic transmission floor shift illumination – 5-amps
18   Carburetor circuits, low fuel warning, shift indicator, seat belt buzzer - 15-amp fuse

12

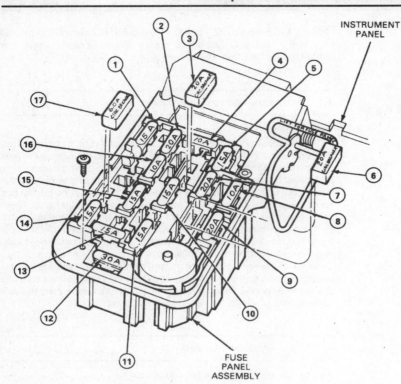

INSTRUMENT
PANEL

FUSE
PANEL
ASSEMBLY

4.3b   Fuse and circuit breaker panel (1989 and later models)

1   *Stop lights, hazard warning lights, speed control inhibit – 15-amp fuse*
2   *Horns – 20-amp fuse*
3   *Cigar lighter, flash to pass – 20-amp circuit breaker*
4   *Instrument panel illumination lights, park/H light hot – 10-amp fuse*
5   *Premium radio amplifier – 20-amp fuse*
6   *Rear window heater relay, power lumbar seat – 30-amp circuit breaker*
7   *Rear anti-lock brakes module - 20-amp fuse*
8   *Heater – 10-amp fuse*
9   *Instrument panel warning lights, electronic all wheel drive - 20-amp fuse*
1 0   *Speed control amplifier, radio - 15-amp fuse*
11   *Park/license lights – 15-amp fuse*
12   *Heater and A/C blower motor – 30-amp fuse*
13   *Turn signal lights, backup la,ps, turn indicator, rear window defroster control - 15-amp fuse*
14   *Dome/courtesy light – 15-amp fuse*
15   *Rear window/washer/wiper – 15-amp fuse*
16   *Air conditioner switches and clutch - 15-amp fuse*
17   *Windshield wiper/washer – 6-amp circuit breaker*

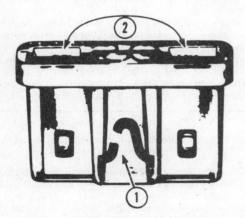

4.4   To test for a blown fuse, pull it out and inspect it for a broken element (1), then, with the circuit activated, use a test light between ground and each of the terminals (2)

Fuse Value Amps	Color Code
4	Pink
5	Tan
10	Red
15	Light Blue
20	Yellow
25	Natural
30	Light Green

4.6   Each fuse amp value has a corresponding color code

If an electrical component fails, always check the fuse first. A blown fuse, which is nothing more than a broken element, is easily identified through the clear plastic body **(see illustration)**. Visually inspect the element for evidence of damage. If you aren't sure about a fuse's condition, you can easily check the fuse with it in place in the fuse block: Connect a test light between ground and each of the exposed fuse terminals **(see illustration 4.4)**. If the fuse is good, the light will light when connected to each terminal. If the fuse is no good, the light will light on only one terminal.

Remove and insert fuses straight in and out without twisting. Twisting could force the terminal open too far, resulting in a bad connection.

Be sure to replace blown fuses with the correct type and amp rating. Fuses of different ratings are physically interchangeable, but replacing a fuse with one of a higher or lower value than specified is not recommended. Each electrical circuit needs a specific amount of protection. The amperage value of each fuse is usually molded into the fuse body.

Different colors are also used to denote fuses of different amperage types. The accompanying color code **(see illustration)** shows common amperage values and their corresponding colors. **Caution:** *Always turn off all electrical components and the ignition switch before replacing a fuse. Never bypass a fuse with pieces of metal or foil. Serious damage to the electrical system could result.*

If the replacement fuse immediately fails, do not replace it again until the cause of the problem is isolated and corrected. In most cases, this will be a short circuit in the wiring caused by a broken or deteriorated wire.

5   Fusible links – general information

Refer to illustrations 5.1

Some circuits are protected by fusible links. These links are used in circuits which are not ordinarily fused, such as the ignition circuit **(see illustration)**.

Although fusible links appear to be of heavier gauge that the wire they are protecting, their appearance is due to thicker insulation. All fusible links are four wire gauges smaller than the wire they are designed to protect.

Fusible links cannot be repaired, but a new link of the same size wire can be put in its place. The procedure is as follows:

a)   Disconnect the negative cable at the battery.

WIRING ASSEMBLY — FUSE LINK
(WITH INSULATION STRIPPED BOTH ENDS)

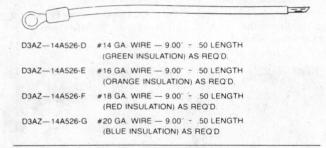

D3AZ—14A526-H #14 GA. WIRE — 9.00" ± .50 LENGTH
(GREEN INSULATION)

D3AZ—14A526-J #16 GA. WIRE — 9.00" ± .50 LENGTH
(ORANGE INSULATION) AS REQ'D.

D3AZ—14A526-K #17 GA. WIRE — 9.00" ± .50 LENGTH
(YELLOW INSULATION) AS REQ'D.
(SPECIAL USED WITH AIR CONDITIONING SYSTEM)

D3AZ—14A526-L #18 GA. WIRE — 9.00" ± .50 LENGTH
(RED INSULATION) AS REQ'D.

D3AZ—14A526-M #20 GA. WIRE — 9.00" ± .50 LENGTH
(BLUE INSULATION) AS REQ'D.

WIRING ASSEMBLY — FUSE LINK
(WITH EYELET TERMINAL AND ONE END STRIPPED)

D3AZ—14A526-D #14 GA. WIRE — 9.00" ± .50 LENGTH
(GREEN INSULATION) AS REQ'D.

D3AZ—14A526-E #16 GA. WIRE — 9.00" ± .50 LENGTH
(ORANGE INSULATION) AS REQ'D.

D3AZ—14A526-F #18 GA. WIRE — 9.00" ± .50 LENGTH
(RED INSULATION) AS REQ'D.

D3AZ—14A526-G #20 GA. WIRE — 9.00" ± .50 LENGTH
(BLUE INSULATION) AS REQ'D

BUTT CONNECTOR — WIRING SPLICE

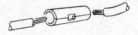

D3AZ—14488-Y FOR #10 AND 12 GA. WIRE (LOAD CIRCUIT) AS REQ'D.
D3AZ—14488-Z FOR #14 AND 16 GA. WIRE (LOAD CIRCUIT) AS REQ'D.

5.1a Fusible link and connector types

b) Disconnect the fusible link from the wiring harness.
c) Cut the damaged fusible link out of the wiring just behind the connector.
d) Strip the insulation back approximately 1/2-inch.
e) Position the connector on the new fusible link and crimp it into place.
f) Splice and solder the new fusible link to the wires from which the

old link was cut. Use rosin-core solder at each end of the new link to obtain a good solder joint.
g) Wrap the splices completely with vinyl electrical tape around the soldered joint. No wires should be exposed.
h) Install the repaired wiring as before, using existing clips, if provided.
i) Connect the battery ground cable.
j) Test the circuit for proper operation.

6 Circuit breakers – general information

Circuit breakers protect accessories such as the windshield wipers, windshield washer pump, interval wiper, low washer fluid indicator, etc. Circuit breakers are located in the fuse box. Refer to the fuse panel guide in Section 4 or the fuse panel guide in your owner's manual for the locations of the circuit breakers used in your vehicle.

Because a circuit breaker resets itself automatically, an electrical overload in a circuit breaker-protected system will cause the circuit to fail momentarily, then come back on. If the circuit does not come back on, check it immediately.

a) Remove the circuit breaker from the fuse panel **(see illustrations 4.3a and 4.3b).**
b) Using an ohmmeter, verify that there is continuity between both terminals of the circuit breaker. If there is no continuity, replace the circuit breaker.
c) Install the old or new circuit breaker. If it continues to cut out, a short circuit is indicated. Troubleshoot the appropriate circuit (see the wiring diagrams at the back of this book) or have the system checked by a professional mechanic.

7 Steering column switches – replacement

Refer to illustration 7.3, 7.5a, 7.5b and 7.6
1 Disconnect the negative cable from the battery.
2 On models equipped with a tilt steering wheel, squeeze the upper extension shroud at the six and twelve o'clock positions and pop it free of the retaining plate.
3 On non-tilt steering wheel models, remove the two screws securing the steering column upper and lower shrouds and remove both shrouds **(see illustration)**.
4 Carefully peel the foam covering from the steering column switch assemblies.
5 To remove the turn signal/high beam/horn switch assembly, perform the following:
a) Remove the two screws securing the switch assembly to the steering column **(see illustration)**.

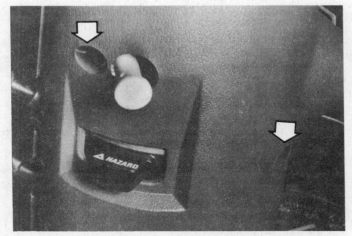

7.3 On models without a tilt steering wheel, the steering column upper and lower shrouds are attached with screws (arrows)

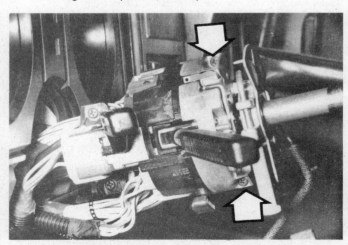

7.5a Two screws (arrows) secure the combination turn signal/high beam/horn switch assembly to the steering column

12

7.5b   Use a screwdriver to pry up on the locking tabs, then remove the electrical connector from the turn signal/high beam/horn switch

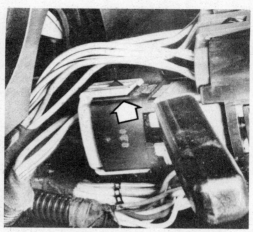

7.6   Pry up on the tab (arrow), then remove the electrical connector from the windshield wiper/washer switch assembly

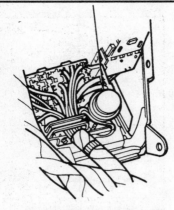

REAR VIEW OF FUSE PANEL

8.3   The hazard flasher relay is located on the rear of the fuse panel

b) Use a small screwdriver to release the tangs, then pull the electrical connector from the turn signal/high beam/horn switch assembly **(see illustration)**.
c) Remove the switch assembly.
6   To remove the windshield wiper/washer switch assembly, perform the following:
a) Remove the two screws securing the switch assembly to the steering column.
b) Use a small screwdriver to pry up on the electrical connector tang, then pull the electrical connector from the windshield wiper/washer switch assembly **(see illustration)**.
c) Remove the switch assembly.
7   Installation is the reverse of the removal steps. Check the steering column and switch for proper operation.

8   Turn signal/hazard flasher relays – replacement

Refer to illustration 8.3
Note: *No functional or operation check of the hazard/turn signal flashers is necessary. If they stop working, replace them.*
1   Disconnect the negative cable from the battery.
2   The turn signal flasher relay is located on the front of the fuse panel **(see illustrations 4.3a and 4.3b)**. Remove the flasher by turning it 90-degrees counterclockwise, then pulling straight out.
3   The hazard flasher is located on the back of the fuse panel **(see illustration)**. Remove the flasher by turning it 90-degrees counterclockwise, then pulling straight out.
4   Install the new flasher unit. Be sure to line up the metal contacts with the slots in the fuse panel. Press the flasher firmly into place and turn it 90-degrees clockwise to lock it.

9   Ignition key lock cylinder – replacement

Refer to illustration 9.6
1   Disconnect the negative cable from the battery.
2   Turn the ignition key lock cylinder to the Run position.
3   On models equipped with a tilt steering wheel, squeeze the upper extension shroud at the six and twelve o'clock positions and pop it free from the retaining plate.
4   On non-tilt steering wheel models, remove the two screws securing the steering column upper and lower shroud and remove both shrouds **(see illustration 7.3)**.
5   Pry up on the tab on the electrical connector and disconnect.

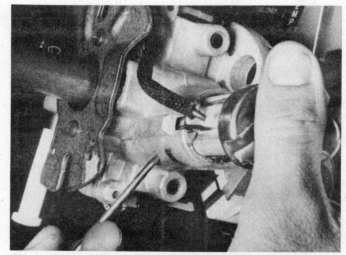

9.6   Release the actuator pin while pulling out on the cylinder

6   Insert a small screwdriver into the lock cylinder housing and release the actuator pin while pulling out on the switch **(see illustration)**.
7   Installation is the reverse of the removal steps. Install the lock cylinder onto the actuator pin. It may be necessary to slightly move the cylinder back and forth to align the mounting holes.

10   Windshield wiper motor – removal and installation

Refer to illustration 10.10
1   Turn the windshield wiper switch On.
2   Turn the ignition switch on and keep your hand on the key. When the wiper arms move to the straight-up position, turn the ignition switch Off.
3   Disconnect the negative cable from the battery.
4   Remove the right side wiper arm and blade assembly (see Section 11).
5   Remove the pivot nut from the right side linkage post. Allow the linkage to drop down into the cowl.
6   Remove the wiper linkage access cover. Reach through the access opening and unsnap the wiper motor clip.
7   Push the clip away from the linkage until it clears the crank pin nib, then push the clip off the linkage.
8   Remove the wiper linkage from the motor crankpin.
9   Disconnect the electrical connector from the motor.

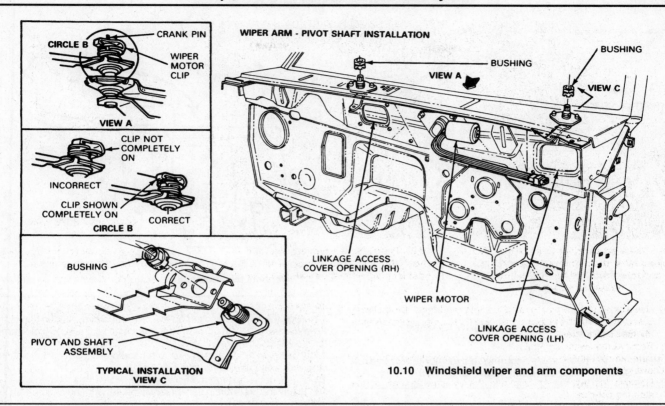

10.10   Windshield wiper and arm components

10   Remove the screws securing the motor and remove the motor **(see illustration)**.

11   Installation is the reverse of the removal steps. Make sure the wiper blades are in the parked position before attaching the linkage to the motor.

11   Windshield wiper arm – removal and installation

Refer to illustration 11.2

1   **Note:** *To prevent damage to the windshield and also to make sure the wipers are operating under normal conditions, keep the windshield wet during this step. Prior to removing the wiper arm, turn the windshield wiper switch On, allow the wipers to travel through several cycles, then turn it Off. This will ensure that the wiper arm is in the parked position parallel to the base of the windshield.*

2   Swing the wiper arm and blade away from the windshield. Slide the latch away from the wiper spindle **(see illustration)**, then pull the wiper arm assembly off the spindle.

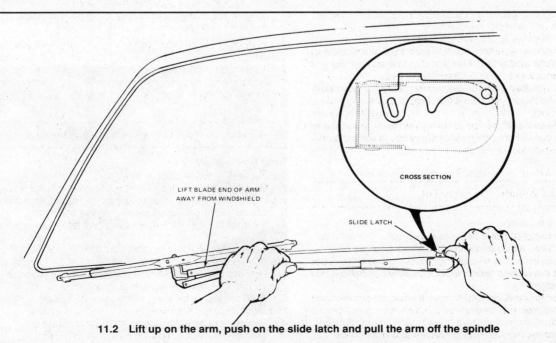

11.2   Lift up on the arm, push on the slide latch and pull the arm off the spindle

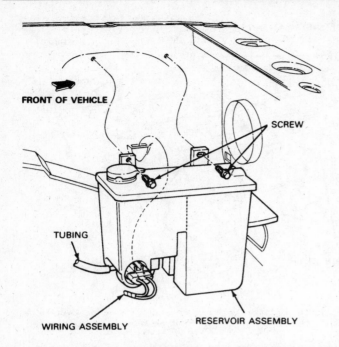

FRONT OF VEHICLE

SCREW

TUBING

WIRING ASSEMBLY

RESERVOIR ASSEMBLY

12.2   Remove the two screws securing the washer reservoir and pump motor assembly to the fenderwell

3   Installation is the reverse of the removal steps with the following additions.
   a) Position the arm back onto the post in the parked position. Do not position the arm too low as it will hit the base of the windshield during normal wiper operation.
   b) Make sure the latch is correctly seated in the groove in the wiper spindle.

12   Windshield washer reservoir and pump assembly – removal and installation

Refer to illustration 12.2

1   Disconnect the negative battery cable. Use a small screwdriver to unlock the electrical connector tabs, then unplug the washer pump's electrical connector.
2   Remove the two screws securing the washer reservoir and pump motor assembly to the fenderwell **(see illustration)**.
3   Remove the coolant hose from the reservoir, lift the washer reservoir up and disconnect the small hose from the base of the reservoir. Place your finger over the end of the small hose fitting on the reservoir to prevent spilling the washer fluid in the engine compartment. Remove the reservoir.
4   Drain the washer fluid and coolant from the reservoir into separate clean containers. If the fluid is kept clean it can be reused.
5   Use a small screwdriver to carefully pry out the retaining ring securing the pump motor in the reservoir receptacle.
6   Grasp one wall surrounding the electrical terminal with a pair of pliers, then pull the motor, seal and impeller assembly out of the reservoir.
Note: *If the impeller and seal separate from the motor they can be reassembled after removal.*
7   Flush out the reservoir with clean water to remove any residue. Inspect it for any foreign matter.
8   Inspect the reservoir pump chamber prior to installing an old motor into a new reservoir. Clean if necessary.
9   Lubricate the outer surface of the seal with powdered graphite to make installation easier.

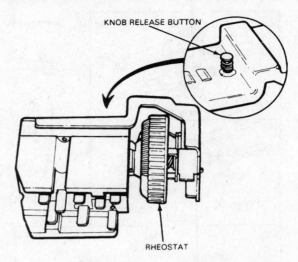

KNOB RELEASE BUTTON

RHEOSTAT

13.4   Depress the knob release button on the switch assembly

10   Align the small projection on the motor end cap with the slot in the reservoir and push it in until the seal seats against the bottom of the motor receptacle in the reservoir.
11   Use a 1-inch 12-point socket and hand press the retaining ring securely against the motor and plate.
12   Connect the hose to the fitting on the base of the reservoir.
13   Install the reservoir in the engine compartment and secure with the two screws.
14   Connect the electrical connector and the negative battery cable..
15   **Caution:** *Do not operate the pump without fluid in the reservoir as it would be damaged. Fill the reservoir with fluid, operate the pump and check for leaks.*

13   Headlight switch – replacement

1983 through 1988
Refer to illustrations 13.4, 13.6 and 13.7
1   Disconnect the negative battery cable from the battery.
2   Pull the headlight switch out as far as it will go.
3   Use needle-nose pliers to unscrew the retaining nut securing the light switch shaft to the instrument panel.

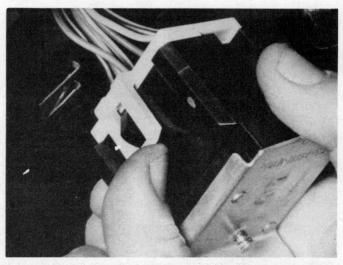

13.6   Lift the tangs and disconnect the connector from the switch

13.7 Align the switch tab (arrow) with the notch in the instrument panel

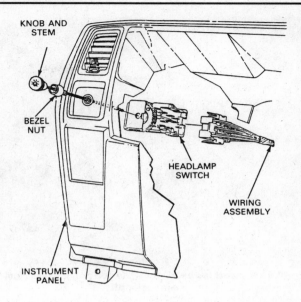

13.14 Unscrew the bezel nut securing the light switch shaft to the instrument panel

4   Depress the knob release button on the switch assembly (**see illustration**) and remove the shaft.

5   Push the switch assembly back into the instrument panel, then bring it out through the instrument cluster opening.

6   Lift the tangs on the electrical connector, disconnect the connector from the switch and remove the switch (**see illustration**).

7   Installation is the reverse of the removal steps. Insert the switch assembly shaft through the hole in the instrument panel and align the switch tab with the notch in the instrument panel (**see illustration**).

1989 on

Refer to illustration 13.14

8   Disconnect the negative battery cable from the battery.

9   Remove the ashtray assembly.

10   Remove the screws securing the finish trim panel, then remove the trim panel (it snaps off).

11   On Bronco II models, carefully snap out and remove the rear window washer/wiper and heated rear window switch assembly. On Ranger models, carefully snap out and remove the storage bin.

12   Pull the headlight switch out as far as it will go.

13   Depress the shaft release button on the switch assembly (**see illustration 13.4**).

14   Unscrew the bezel nut securing the light switch shaft to the instrument panel (**see illustration**).

15   Push the switch assembly back into the instrument panel, then bring it out through the instrument cluster opening.

16   Lift the tangs on the electrical connector and disconnect the connector from the switch and remove the switch.

17   Installation is the reverse of the removal steps.

---

14   Headlights – removal and installation

Sealed beam headlights (1983 through 1988)

Refer to illustrations 14.3, 14.4 and 14.5

Note: *Due to the stiffness of the rubber around the headlight rim, we found it necessary to first remove the grille to replace the headlight.*

1   Disconnect the negative battery cable from the battery.

2   Remove the screws securing the grille.

3   Tilt the top of the grille forward to reveal two additional screws located under the headlight (**see illustration**). Remove these two screws and remove the grille.

4   Remove the four screws securing the headlight retaining ring and remove the ring. Do not remove the headlight adjusting screws (**see illustration**).

14.3   These grille screws are hidden under the headlight

14.4   Don't confuse the headlight retaining ring screws with the two adjusting screws (arrows)

12

14.5 Support the headlight while you pull the electrical connector off

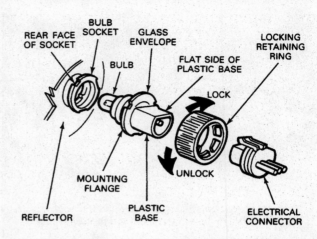

14.13   Rotate the retaining ring about 1/8-turn counterclockwise (viewed from the rear) and slide it off the base

5   Pull the headlight out enough to reach the electrical connector and disconnect it from the backside of the headlight **(see illustration)**.
6   Remove the headlight.
7   To install the headlight, plug in the electrical connector, place the headlight in position and install the retaining ring and screws.
8   Install the grille and reconnect the battery negative cable.
9   Have the headlights adjusted by a dealer service department or service station at the earliest opportunity.

Halogen bulb-type (1989 and later models)

Refer to illustration 14.13
Warning: *Halogen gas filled bulbs are under pressure and may shatter if the surface is scratched or the bulb is dropped. Wear eye protection and handle the bulbs carefully, grasping only the base whenever possible. Do not touch the surface of the bulb with your fingers because the oil from your skin could cause the bulb to overheat and fail prematurely. If you do touch the bulb surface, clean it with rubbing alcohol.*

10   Open the hood.
11   Disconnect the negative battery cable from the battery.
12   Disconnect the electrical connector from the back of the headlight reflector.
13   Rotate the retaining ring about 1/8-turn counterclockwise (viewed from the rear) and slide it off the base **(see illustration)**.
14   Carefully pull the bulb straight out of the socket. Do not rotate the bulb during removal.
15   Insert the bulb into the socket. Position the flat on the plastic base up.
16   Align the socket locating tabs with the grooves in the forward part of the plastic base, then push the socket firmly into the base. Make sure the base mounting flange contacts the socket.
17   Slide the retaining ring on. Turn it clockwise until it hits the stop.
18   Connect the electrical connector. Test headlight operation, then close the hood.
19   Have the headlights adjusted by a dealer service department or service station at the earliest opportunity.

---

15   Headlights – adjusting

Refer to illustration 15.6
Note: *The headlights must be aimed correctly. If adjusted incorrectly, they could blind the driver of an oncoming vehicle and cause a serious accident or seriously reduce your ability to see the road. The headlights should be checked for proper aim every 12 months and any time a new headlight is installed or front end body work is performed. It should be emphasized*

that the following procedure is only an interim step which will provide temporary adjustment until the headlights can be adjusted by a properly equipped shop.

1   Headlights have two spring-loaded adjusting screws, one on the top controlling up-and-down movement and one on the side controlling left-and-right movement **(see illustration 14.4)**. Late-model "aerodynamic" style headlights have metal rods that are accessible above the headlight, near the radiator support.
2   There are several methods of adjusting the headlights. The simplest method requires a blank wall 25 feet in front of the vehicle and a level floor.
3   Position masking tape vertically on the wall in reference to the vehicle centerline and the centerline of both headlights.
4   Position a horizontal line in reference to the centerline of all headlights. **Note:** *It may be easier to position the tape on the wall with the vehicle parked only a few inches away.*
5   Adjustment should be made with the vehicle sitting level, the gas tank half-full and no unusually heavy load in the vehicle.
6   Starting with the low beam adjustment, position the high intensity zone so it is two inches below the horizontal line and two inches to the right of the headlight vertical line. Adjustment is made by turning the top adjusting screw clockwise to raise the beam and counterclockwise to lower the beam **(see illustration)**. The adjusting screw on the side should be used in the same manner to move the beam left or right.
7   With the high beams on, the high intensity zone should be vertically centered with the exact center just below the horizontal line. **Note:** *It may*

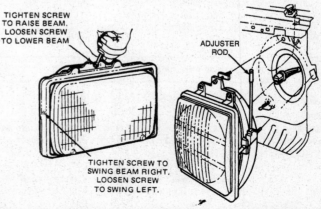

15.6   The top screw adjusts the headlight up and down while the screw on the side adjusts the headlight left or right

16.1   Remove these two screws securing the parking/turn signal light assembly to the body (1983 through 1988 models)

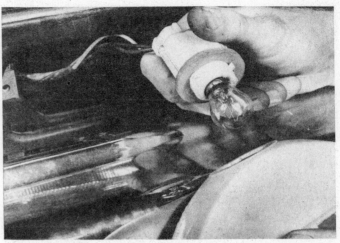

16.3   Rotate the socket while holding onto the lens and remove the socket

not be possible to position the headlight aim exactly for both high and low beams. If a compromise must be made, keep in mind that the low beams are the most used and have the greatest effect on driver safety.

8   Have the headlights adjusted by a dealer service department or service station at the earliest opportunity.

16   Bulb replacement

Parking/turn signal light (1983 through 1988)
Refer to illustrations 16.1 and 16.3

1   Remove the screws securing the parking/turn signal light assembly **(see illustration)**.

2   Pull the parking/turn signal light assembly partially out.

3   Rotate the socket assembly while holding onto the lens assembly and remove the socket assembly **(see illustration)**.

4   Push the bulb in, turn it counterclockwise and remove it.

5   Installation is the reverse of the removal steps.

Parking/turn signal/front side marker light (1989 on)

6   Open the hood.

7   On the backside of the headlight assembly rotate the bulb socket in either direction until the lugs are aligned with the notches in the housing.

8   Pull the socket and bulb assembly out of the headlight assembly housing.

9   Pull or turn the parking light bulb socket and remove it from the socket assembly.

10   Installation is the reverse of the removal steps.

Front side marker light (1983 through 1988 models)

11   Remove the screw at the top of the lens.

12   Pull the light assembly out at the top and lift it up to disengage the tab at the bottom. Pull the assembly out of the fender.

13   Pull the bulb from the socket and remove it.

14   Installation is the reverse of the removal steps.

Rear combination lights (stop, tail, turn and back-up)
Refer to illustrations 16.15 and 16.17

15   Remove the four screws securing the rear combination light lens **(see illustration)**.

16   Rotate the bulb socket and remove it from the combination light assembly.

17   Push in on the bulb and turn it counterclockwise, then pull the bulb out of the socket, then reverse the procedure to install a new bulb **(see illustration)**.

18   Installation is the reverse of the removal steps.

License plate bulb
Refer to illustration 16.20

19   Rotate the socket 1/4-turn in either direction and remove the bulb socket assembly away from the bumper.

20   Twist the socket assembly and remove it from the housing **(see illustration)**.

16.15   Remove the four screws and remove the taillight assembly

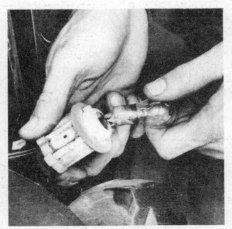

16.17   Hold the socket, insert the new bulb and turn it clockwise

16.20   Twist the socket and remove it from the housing

12

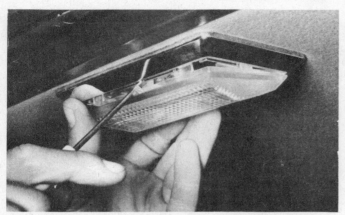

16.23   Carefully pry the plastic lens away from the chrome base to gain access to the bulb

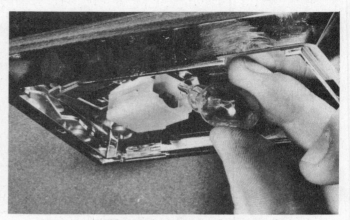

16.24   Pull the bulb straight out of the socket

21   Pull the bulb out of the socket.
22   Installation is the reverse of the removal steps.

Dome light

Refer to illustrations 16.23 and 16.24

23   Use a small screwdriver and carefully pry the dome light lens away from the chrome base **(see illustration)**. Remove the lens.
24   Pull the bulb straight out of the socket **(see illustration)**.

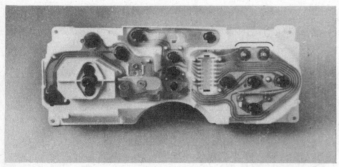

16.27   The instrument cluster bulbs (black connectors) have no wires connected to them – to replace a bulb, simply turn it 1/4-turn counterclockwise and remove it from the instrument cluster printed circuit board

25   Install a new bulb and press it in all the way, then install the dome light lens assembly.

Instrument cluster bulbs

Refer to illustration 16.27

26   **Note:** *The instrument cluster printed circuit board is fragile. Be careful when removing the bulb assemblies. Reach up under the instrument panel and turn the bulb/socket assembly 1/4-turn counterclockwise.*
27   Remove the bulb from the socket and install a new bulb **(see illustration)**. **Note:** *If you cannot reach some of the bulb/sockets, remove the instrument cluster to gain access to the bulbs (see Section 20).*

---

17   Radio and/or tape deck – removal and installation

1983 through 1988

Refer to illustration 17.4

1   Disconnect the negative battery cable from the battery.
2   Remove the control knobs and discs by pulling them straight off.
3   Remove the instrument panel trim panels (see Section 20 of this Chapter).
4   Remove the four screws securing the radio mounting bracket to the instrument panel **(see illustration)**.

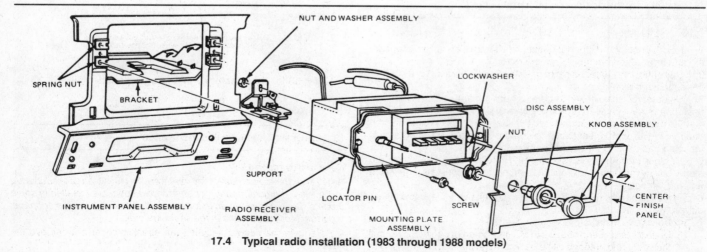

SPRING NUT
BRACKET
INSTRUMENT PANEL ASSEMBLY
SUPPORT
RADIO RECEIVER ASSEMBLY
NUT AND WASHER ASSEMBLY
LOCATOR PIN
MOUNTING PLATE ASSEMBLY
SCREW
NUT
LOCKWASHER
DISC ASSEMBLY
KNOB ASSEMBLY
CENTER FINISH PANEL

17.4   Typical radio installation (1983 through 1988 models)

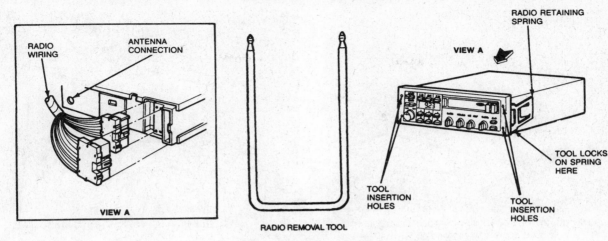

17.10   Special tool used for radio removal (1989 and later models)

5   Pull the radio and mounting bracket partially out of the instrument panel, then disconnect the power, speaker and antenna wires from the radio.
6   Pull the radio assembly out of the instrument panel.
7   If necessary, remove the nut on each control knob shaft and remove the mounting bracket from the radio.
8   Installation is the reverse of the removal steps.

1989 on

Refer to illustration 17.10

9   Remove the instrument panel trim panels (see Section 20 of this Chapter).
10   Insert radio removal tool (Ford part No. T87P-19061-A) or equivalent into the radio face plate **(see illustration)**. Push the tool in about 1-inch to release the retaining clips on each side.
11   Using the special tool, pull the radio partially out of the instrument panel, then disconnect the power, speaker and antenna wires from the radio.
12   Pull the radio assembly out of the instrument panel.
13   Installation is the reverse of the removal steps.

---

18   Radio antenna – removal and installation

Refer to illustration 18.3

1   Reach under the instrument panel, pull straight out and disconnect the antenna cable from the rear of the radio.
2   Disconnect the antenna cable from the plastic clips along the top of the defroster nozzle.
3   Use a small screwdriver to carefully pry the antenna cap from the base and remove the cap **(see illustration)**.
4   Tie a piece of string onto the radio end of the antenna cable and the other end to the instrument panel. This will be used to pull the new antenna cable back through the same path as the old one.
5   Remove the four screws securing the antenna base to the body and slowly pull the antenna cable out through the body opening. Remove the antenna and gasket.
6   Installation is the reverse of the removal steps with the following additions.
   a)   Be sure to install a new gasket.
   b)   Untie the string and attach it to the new antenna cable. Slowly pull the string and antenna cable back through the body opening. Discard the string.

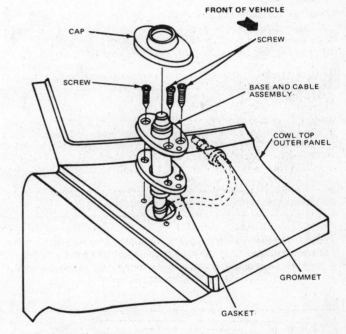

18.3   Radio antenna mounting – exploded view

---

19   Speakers – removal and installation

Refer to illustration 19.2

Note: *Your particular model may vary from the following procedure due to the size and configuration of aftermarket speakers installed in some models. Speakers mounted in locations other than the instrument panel are removed and installed in the same manner.*

1   Remove the screws securing the speaker cover and remove the cover.
2   Remove the three screws securing the speaker to the instrument

12

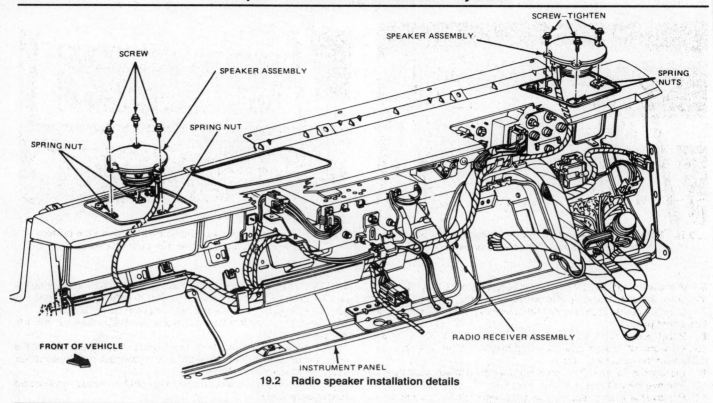

19.2   Radio speaker installation details

panel **(see illustration)**.

3   Lift out the speaker and disconnect the wiring connector at the speaker. **Note:** *Do not operate the radio with the speakers disconnected.*

4   Installation is the reverse of the removal steps.

---

20   Instrument cluster – removal and installation

1983 through 1988

Refer to illustrations 20.3, 20.4, 20.5, 20.6a and 20.6b

1   Disconnect the negative battery cable from the battery.

2   On models equipped with a tilt steering wheel, squeeze the upper extension shroud at the six and twelve o'clock positions and pop it free from the retaining plate.

3   On non-tilt steering wheel models, remove the two screws securing the steering column upper and lower shroud and remove both shrouds **(see illustration)**.

4   Insert a small screwdriver behind the trim panel and carefully pry off all three face panels **(see illustration)**.

5   To remove the trim panel where the headlight switch is mounted, perform the following:

     a)   Insert a small screwdriver into the slot in the light switch knob and push in on the retaining clip **(see illustration)**.

     b)   Pull the knob off the shaft, then remove the trim panel.

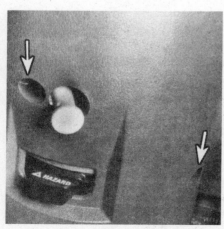

20.3   Remove these two steering column cover screws

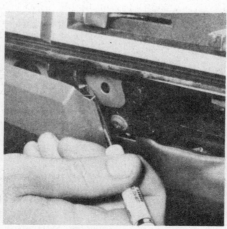

20.4   The instrument panel lower trim panels are secured with spring clips

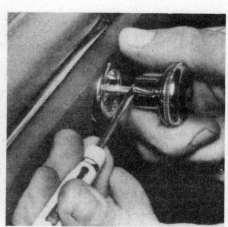

20.5   Remove the headlight switch knob by inserting a small screwdriver into the slot and pushing in on the retaining clip while pulling on the knob

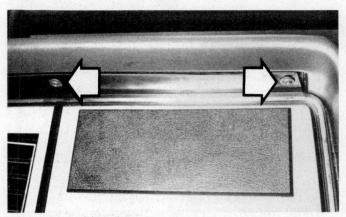

20.6a   Note the locations of the screws securing the top of the instrument cluster trim cover (arrows)

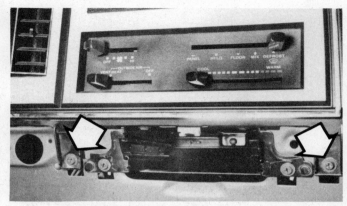

20.6b   Note the locations of the screws securing the bottom of the instrument cluster trim cover (arrows)

6   Remove the top and bottom screws securing the instrument cluster trim cover to the instrument panel (**see illustrations**).
7   Carefully pull the instrument cluster assembly partially out from the instrument panel.
8   Reach under the instrument panel, press on the flat portion of the quick-disconnect plastic connector and disconnect the speedometer cable from the instrument cluster.
9   Disconnect the electrical connector from the printed circuit board.
10   Remove the instrument cluster assembly.
11   Remove the screws securing the instrument cluster to the trim cover and remove the cluster.
12   Installation is the reverse of the removal Steps. Apply a 3/16-inch diameter ball of silicone dielectric compound to the drive hole of the speedometer head prior to installing the cable.

1989 on
Refer to illustration 20.16 and 20.20

13   Disconnect the negative battery cable from the battery.
14   Remove the ashtray.
15   Carefully pull rearward around the edge and unsnap the trim panel surrounding the instrument cluster. Depress the hazard warning switch on the steering column and remove the trim panel.
16   Remove the four screws securing the instrument cluster (**see illustration**).

17   On automatic transmission models, remove the screws securing the gear indicator to the instrument cluster and slide the indicator down and out of the cluster. It is not necessary to disconnect the indicator.
18   Carefully pull the instrument cluster assembly partially out from the instrument panel.
19   Reach under the instrument panel, press on the flat portion of the quick-disconnect plastic connector and disconnect the speedometer cable from the instrument cluster.
20   Disconnect the electrical connectors from the printed circuit board (**see illustration**).
21   Remove the instrument cluster assembly.
22   Installation is the reverse of the removal steps. Apply a 3/16-inch diameter ball of silicone dielectric compound to the drive hole of the speedometer head prior to installing the cable.

---

21   Speedometer and cable – removal and installation

Cable and casing

1   On 1983 through 1988 models, perform Steps 1 through 7 of Section 20. On 1989 and later models perform Steps 13 through 18 of Section 20.
2   Reach under the instrument panel, press on the flat portion of the quick-disconnect plastic connector and disconnect the speedometer cable from the speedometer head.

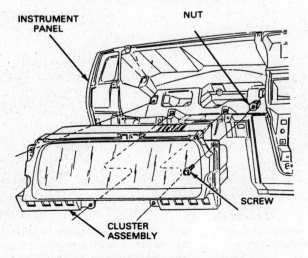

20.16   Instrument cluster mounting screws

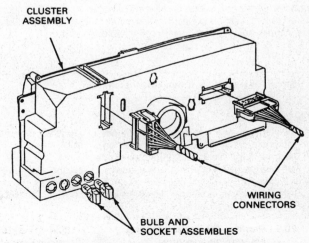

20.20   Electrical connector locations on the printed circuit board

12

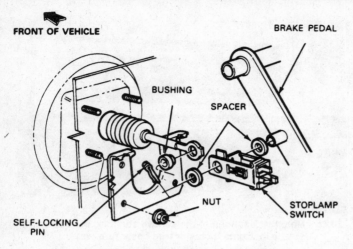

FRONT OF VEHICLE

BRAKE PEDAL

BUSHING

SPACER

NUT

STOPLAMP SWITCH

SELF-LOCKING PIN

22.1   A typical stoplight switch – exploded view

3   To remove the inner cable only, pull it out of the casing and install a new one by reversing the removal steps. Twist the inner cable back and forth while pushing down until the cable is completely seated (it will resist twisting when it's seated).

4   To remove the casing, perform the following:
  a) Remove the screw and clamp securing the speedometer cable to the firewall.
  b) Working under the vehicle, remove the clamp screw and remove the cable and casing from the transmission case. Pull the cable down, out of the passenger compartment.

5   Connect the speedometer casing to the head, applying a 3/16-inch ball of silicone dielectric compound to the speedometer drive hole. If removed, install the casing to the transmission, using a new O-ring (see Chapter 7A) and re-secure the cable to the firewall.

6   Install the instrument cluster (see Section 20).

Speedometer head

Note: *US Federal law requires that the odometer in any replacement speedometer must register the same mileage as that on the removed speedometer.*

7   Perform Steps 1 and 2.

8   Remove the lens and mask from the instrument cluster.

9   Remove the two screws securing the speedometer to the instrument cluster and remove it.

10   Installation is the reverse of the removal steps. Apply a 3/16-inch diameter ball of silicone dielectric compound to the drive hole of the speedometer head prior to installing the cable.

---

22   Stoplight switch – removal and installation

Refer to illustrations 22.1

1   The stoplight switch is located on a flange or a bracket protruding from the brake pedal support **(see illustration)**.

2   Disconnect the electrical connector from the switch.

3   Remove the hairpin retainer and spacer securing the switch to the brake pedal arm.

4   Slide the switch, pushrod, nylon washers and bushing away from the pedal, then remove the switch.

5   To install, place the switch with the U-shaped side nearest the pedal and directly over or under the pin. The bushing must be in the pushrod eyelet with the washer face on the side closest to the retaining pin.

6   Slide the switch up or down so that the master cylinder pushrod and bushing are trapped, then push the switch firmly downward.

7   Install the plastic washer and hairpin retainer.

8   Connect the electrical wire connector to the switch. Make sure the wiring harness is routed correctly and will travel the full swing of the pedal without binding.

---

23   Power window system – description and check

The power window system operates the electric motors mounted in the doors which lower and raise the windows. The system consists of the control switches, the motors, glass mechanisms (regulators) and associated wiring.

Diagnosis can usually be limited to simple checks of the wiring connections and motors for minor faults which can be easily repaired. These are:
  a) Inspect the power window actuating switches for broken wires and loose connections.
  b) Check the power window fuse/and or circuit breaker.
  c) Remove the door panel(s) and check the power window motor wires to see if they're loose or damaged. Inspect the glass mechanisms for damage which could cause binding.

---

24   Wiring diagrams – general information

Since it isn't possible to include all wiring diagrams for every year covered by this manual, the following diagrams are those that are typical and most commonly needed.

Prior to troubleshooting any circuits, check the fuse and circuit breakers (if equipped) to make sure they're in good condition. Make sure the battery is properly charged and check the cable connections (see Chapter 1).

When checking a circuit, make sure that all connectors are clean, with no broken or loose terminals. When unplugging a connector, do not pull on the wires. Pull only on the connector housings themselves.

Refer to the accompanying table for the wire color codes applicable to your vehicle.

Wiring diagram color codes

BK	=	Black	P	= Purple
BR	=	Brown	PK	= Pink
DB	=	Dark blue	R	= Red
DG	=	Dark green	T	= Tan
GY	=	Gray	W	= White
LB	=	Light blue	Y	= Yellow
LG	=	Light green		
N	=	Natural	(H)	= Hash
O	=	Orange	(D)	= Dot

Note: *The presence of a tracer on the wire is indicated by a secondary color followed by an "H" for hash or "D" for dot. A stripe is understood if no letter follows.*

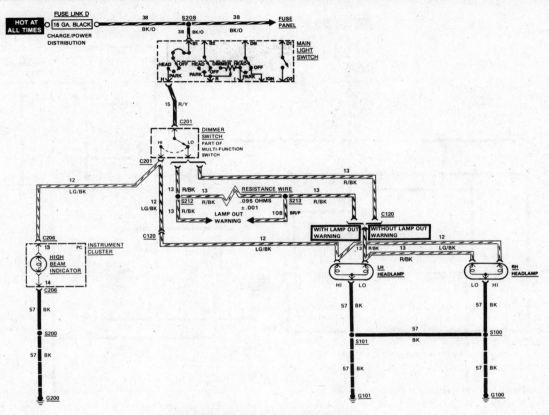

Headlights – 1983 through 1989 models

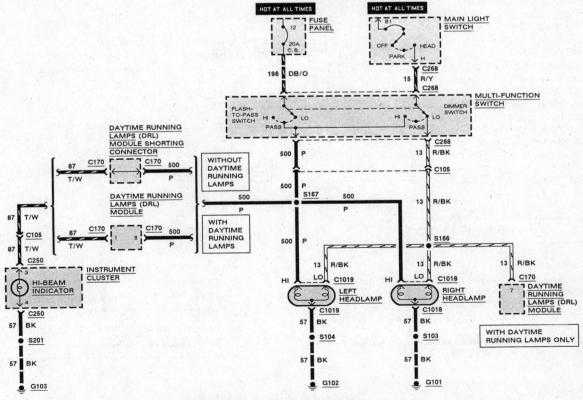

Headlights – 1990 and later models

12

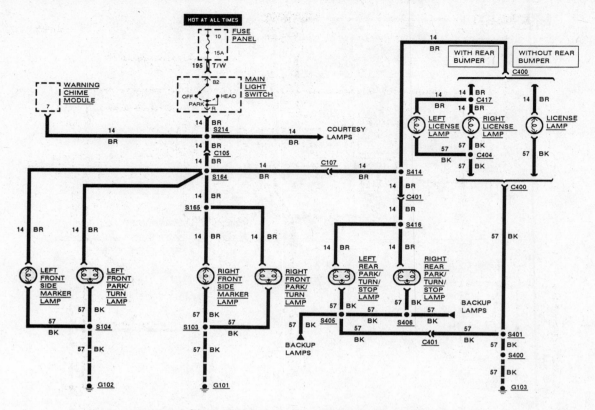

Exterior lights – 1983 through 1989 models, typical (Ranger shown Bronco II similar)

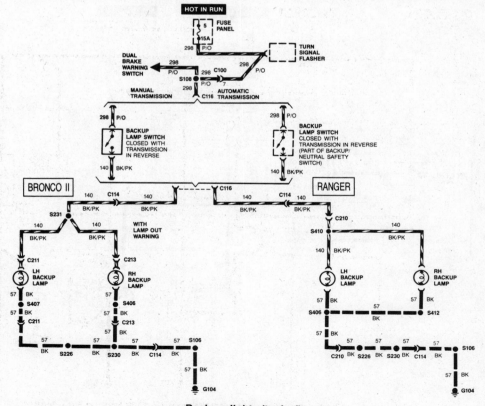

Back-up lights (typical)

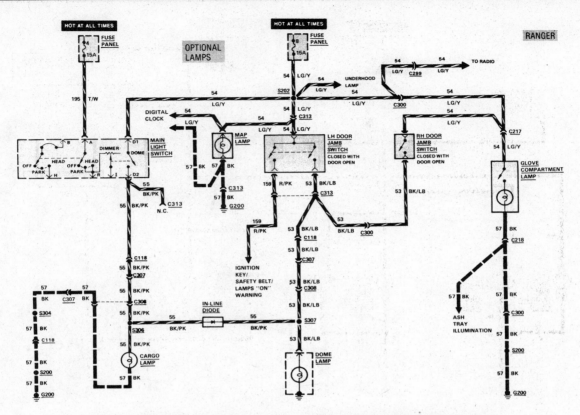

Dome/cargo lights with "lights on" warning – 1983 through 1988 Ranger (typical)

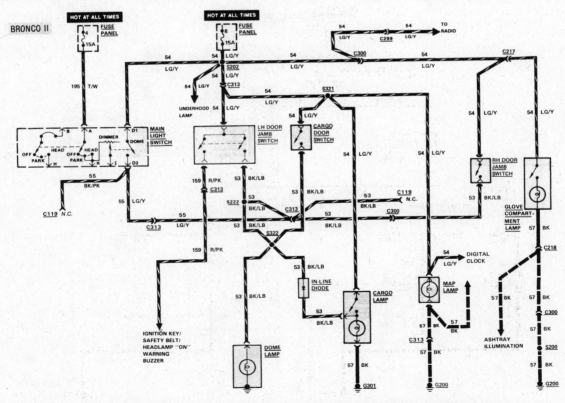

Dome/cargo lights with "lights on" warning – 1984 through 1988 Bronco II (typical)

12

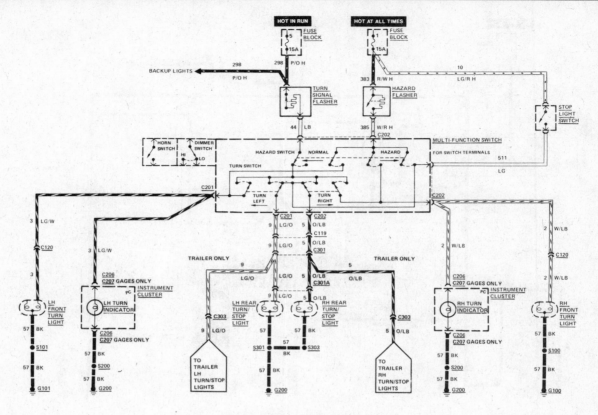

Turn/stop/hazard lights (typical)

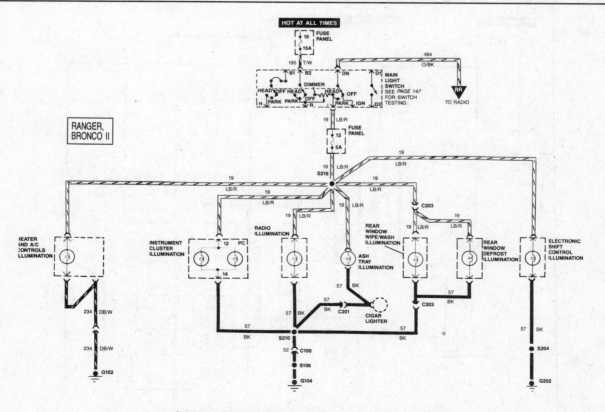

Instrument panel lights – 1983 through 1989 (typical)

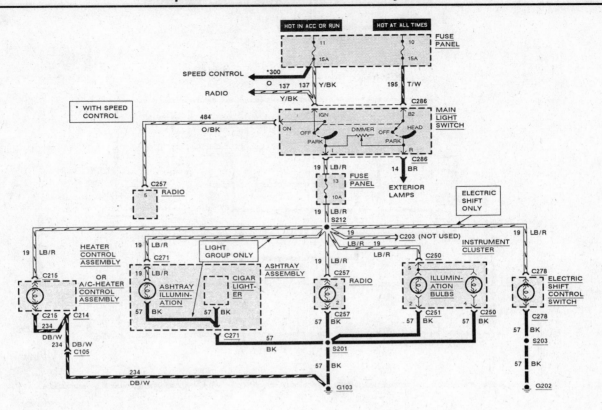

Instrument panel lights – 1990 on (typical)

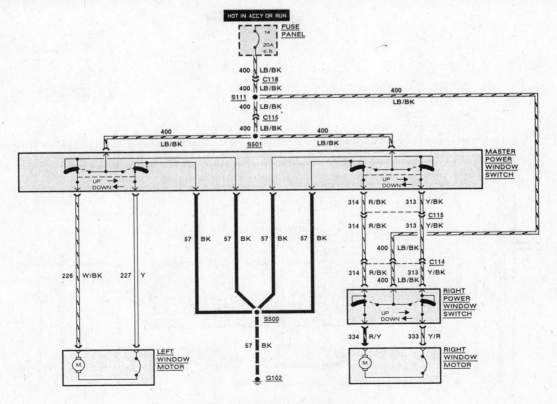

Power windows (typical)

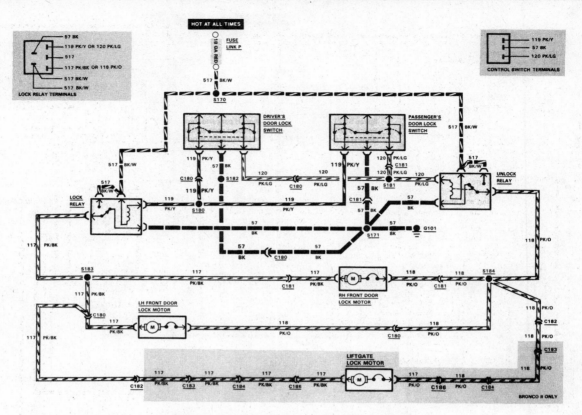

Power door locks – 1985 through 1988 (typical)

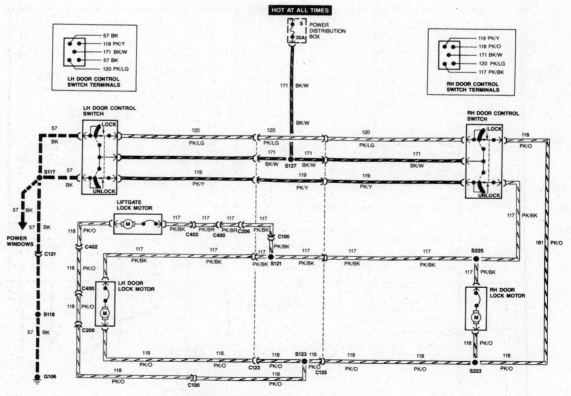

Power door locks – 1989 on (typical)

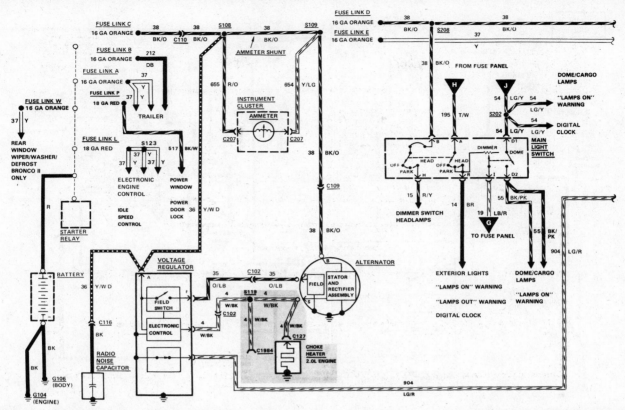

Charging system/power distribution – 1983 through 1985 (part 1 of 2) (ammeter type shown – warning indicator light type similar)

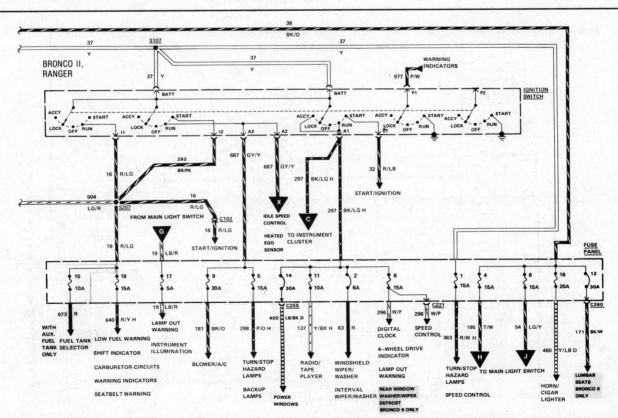

Charging system/power distribution – 1983 through 1985 (part 2 of 2) (ammeter type shown – warning indicator light type similar)

12

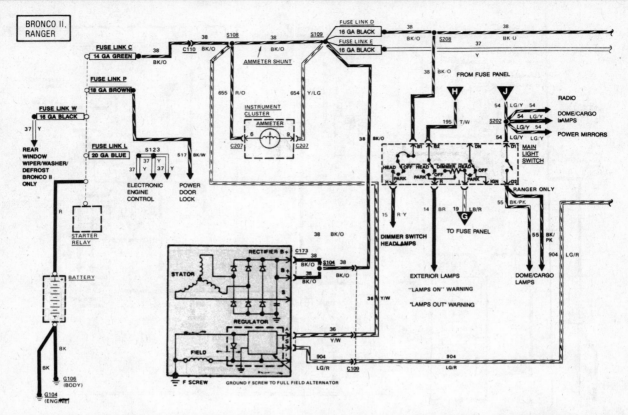

Charging system/power distribution – 1986 through 1988 (part 1 of 2) (ammeter type shown – warning indicator light type similar)

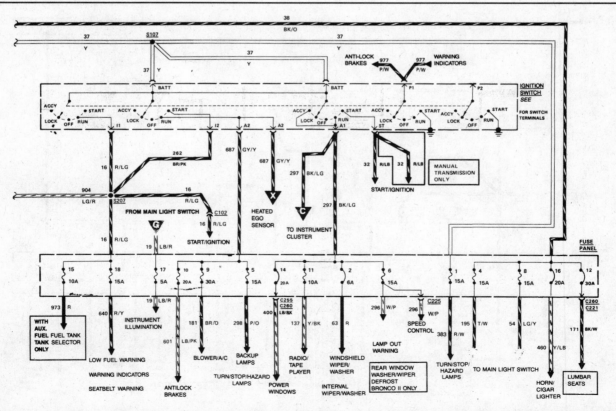

Charging system/power distribution – 1986 through 1988 (part 2 of 2) (ammeter type shown – warning indicator light type similar)

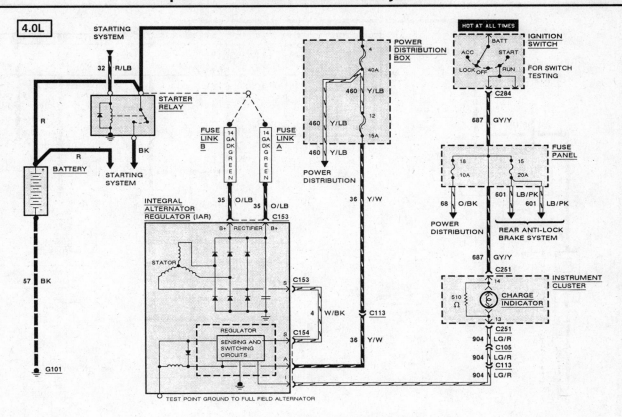

Charging system – late models (typical – 1991 shown) (part 1 of 2)

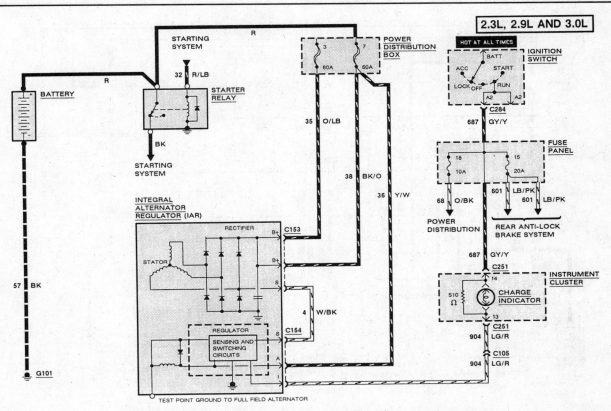

Charging system – late models (typical – 1991 shown) (part 2 of 2)

12

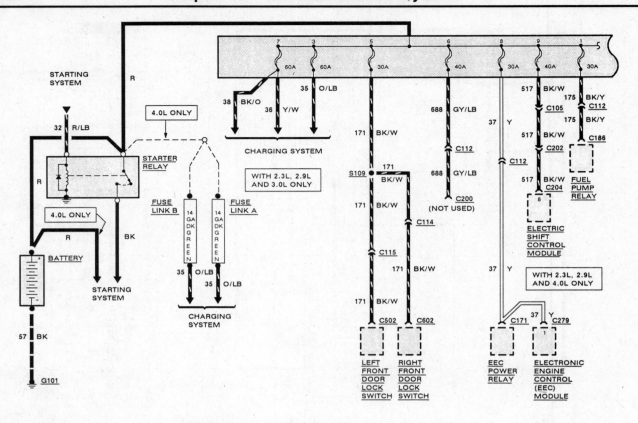

Power distribution – (typical – 1991 shown) (part 1 of 7)

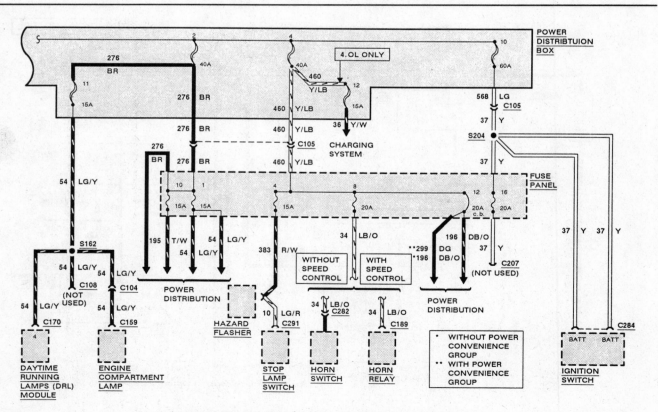

Power distribution – (typical – 1991 shown) (part 2 of 7)

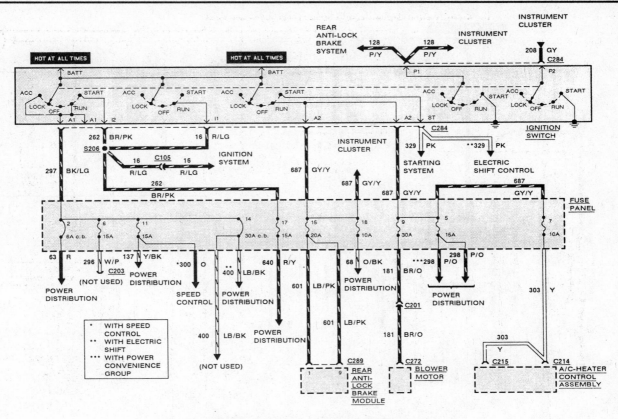

Power distribution – (typical – 1991 shown) (part 3 of 7)

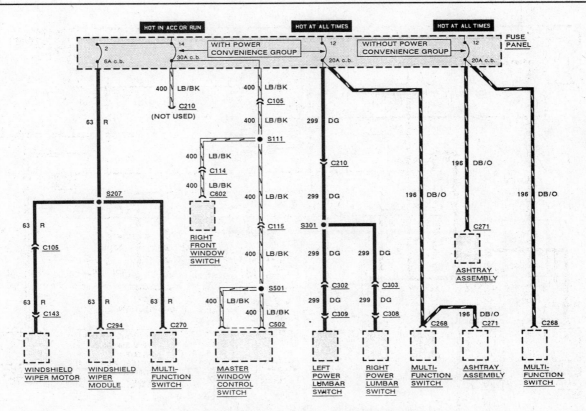

Power distribution – (typical – 1991 shown) (part 4 of 7)

12

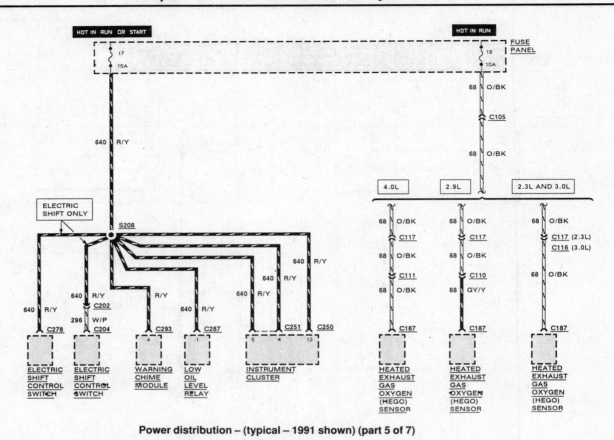

Power distribution – (typical – 1991 shown) (part 5 of 7)

Power distribution – (typical – 1991 shown) (part 6 of 7)

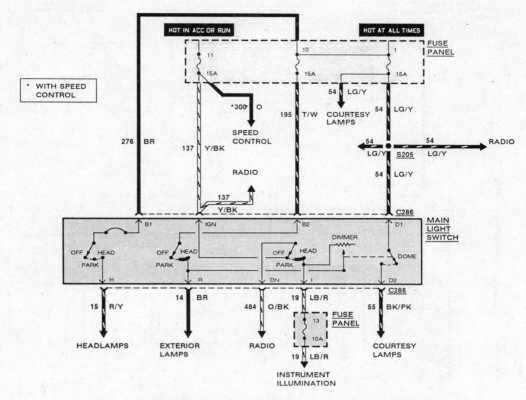

Power distribution – (typical – 1991 shown)(part 7 of 7)

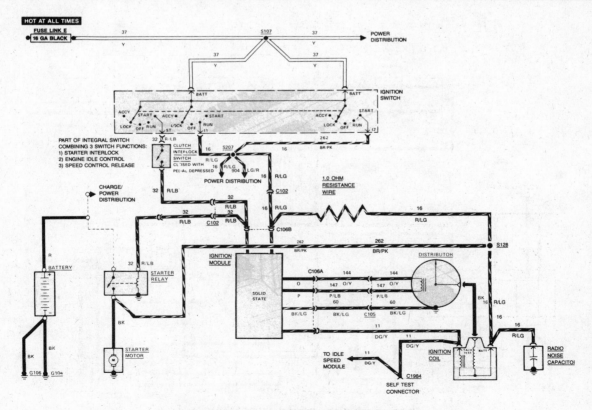

Start/ignition – 2.0L engine (typical)

12

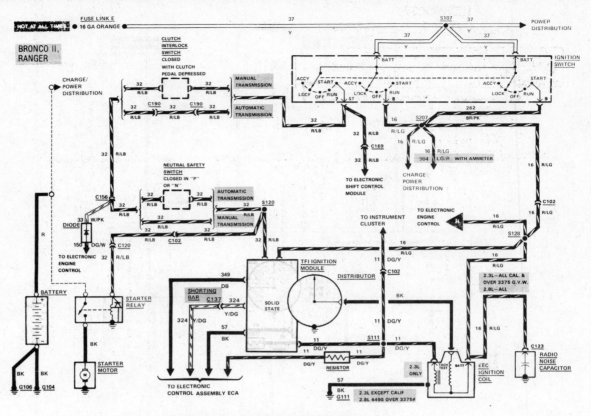

Start/ignition – 1983 through 1988 2.3L engine

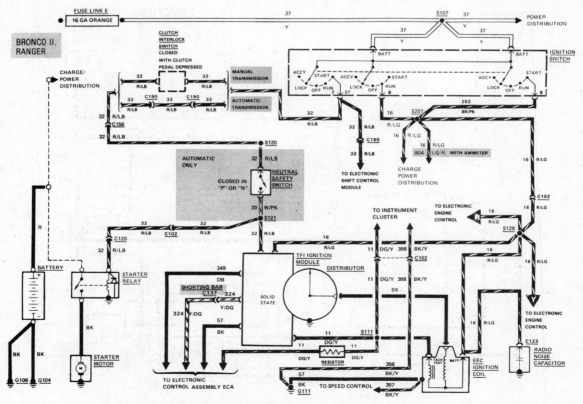

Start/ignition – 1983 through 1988 2.8L and 2.9L engines

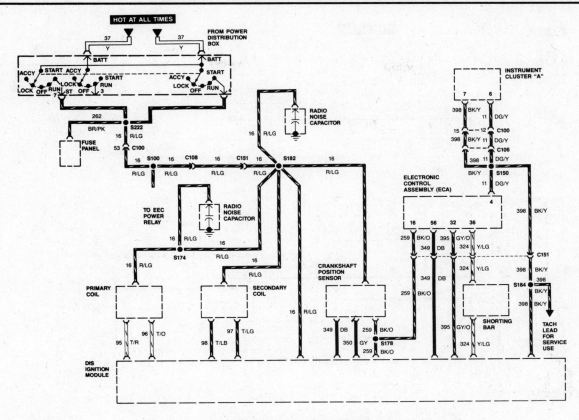

Ignition system – 1989 2.3L engine

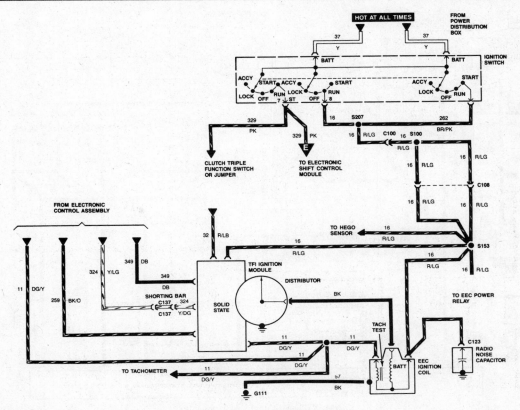

Ignition system – 1989 2.9L engine

12

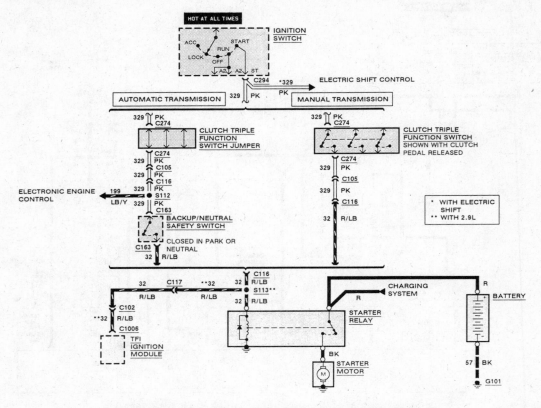

Starting system – 1990 on (2.3L engine shown, others similar)

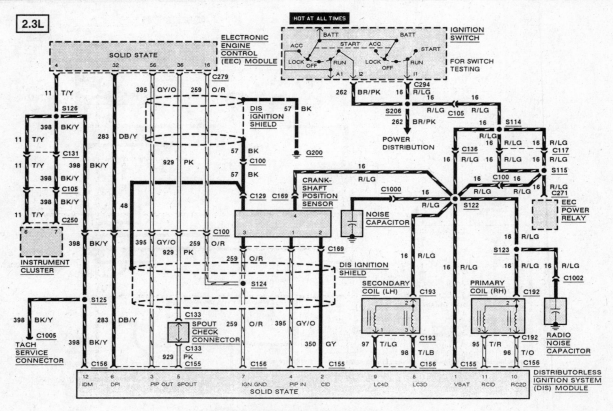

Ignition system – 1990 on 2.3L engine

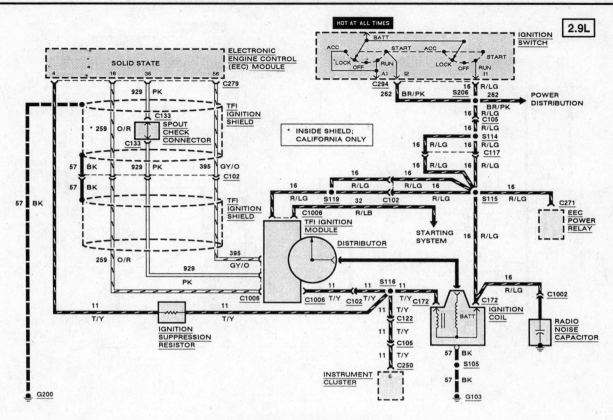

Ignition system – 1990 on 2.9L engine

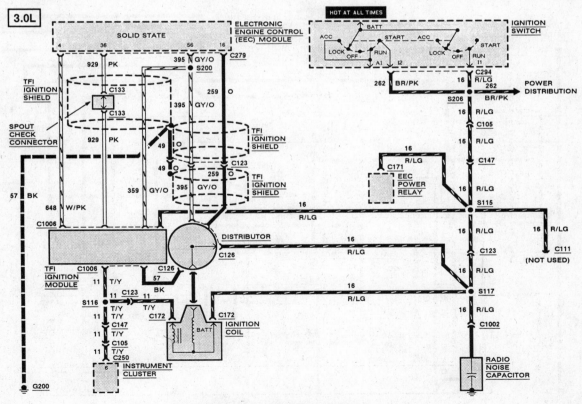

Ignition system – 1990 on 3.0L engine

12

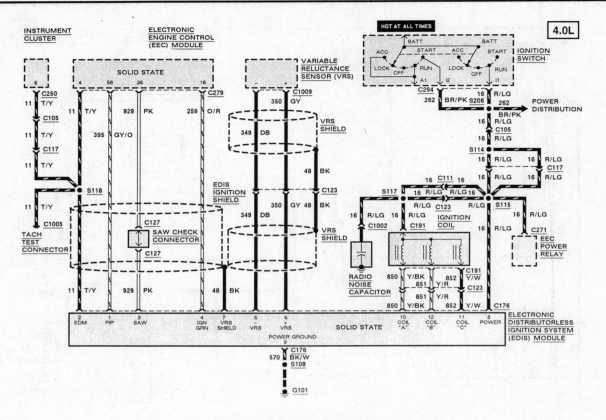

Ignition system – 1990 on 4.0L engine

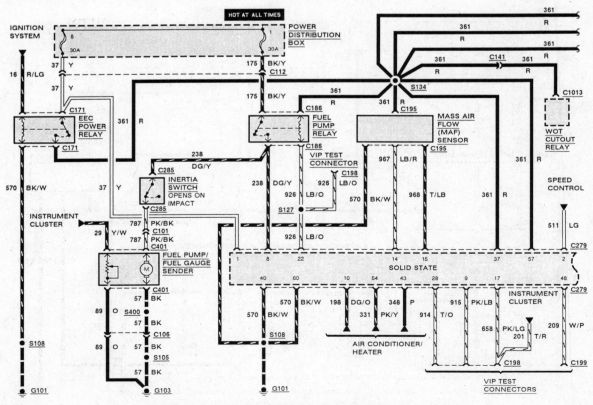

Electronic engine controls, 2.3L engine (typical – part 1 of 3)

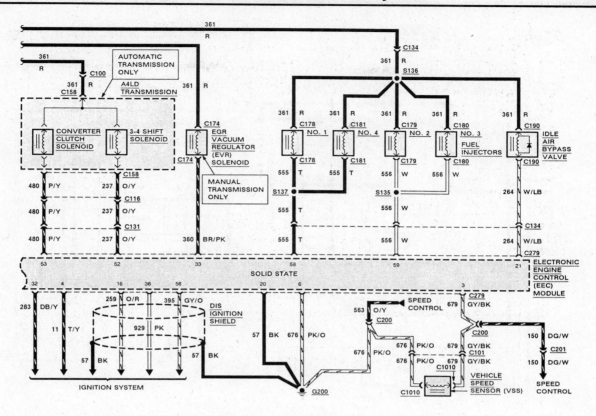

Electronic engine controls, 2.3L engine (typical – part 2 of 3)

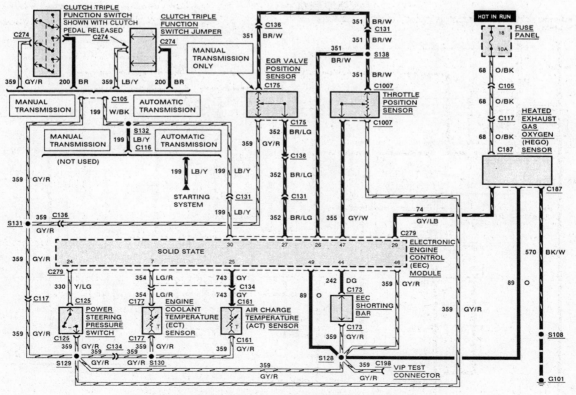

Electronic engine controls, 2.3L engine (typical – part 3 of 3)

12

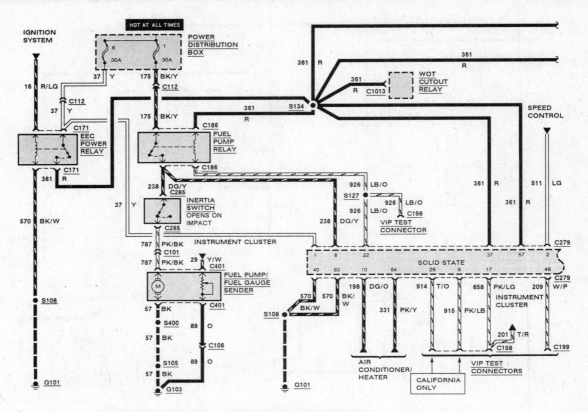

Electronic engine controls, 2.9L engine (typical – part 1 of 3)

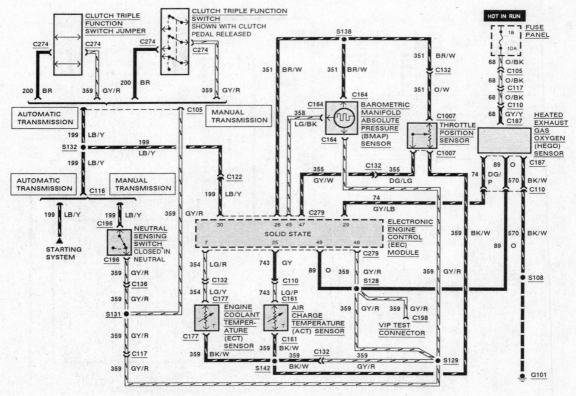

Electronic engine controls, 2.9L engine (typical – part 2 of 3)

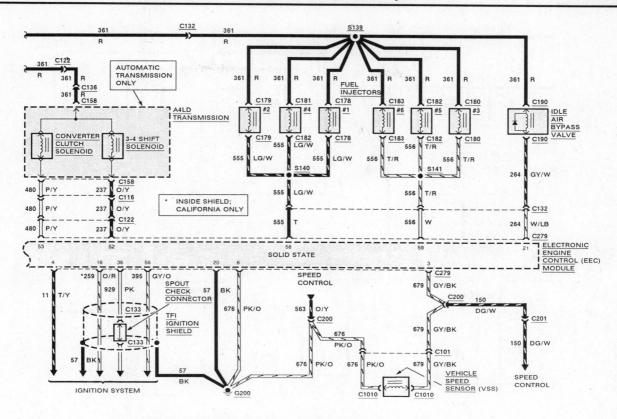

Electronic engine controls, 2.9L engine (typical – part 3 of 3)

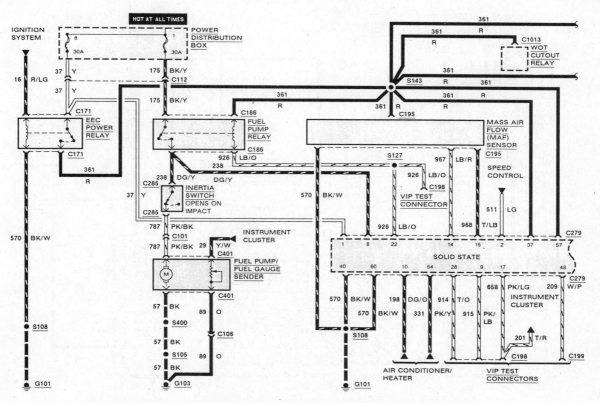

Electronic engine controls, 4.0L engine; 3.0L similar (typical – part 1 of 3)

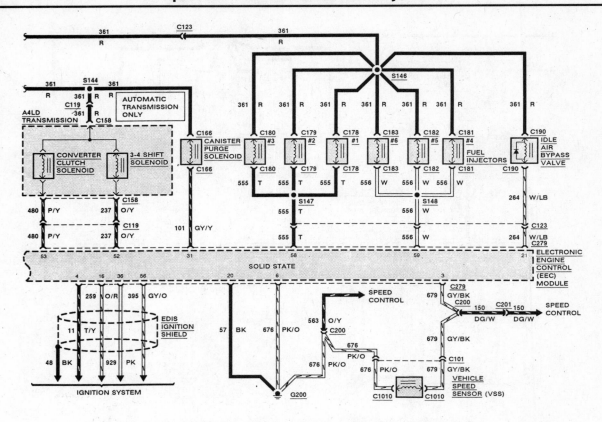

Electronic engine controls, 4.0L engine; 3.0L similar (typical – part 2 of 3)

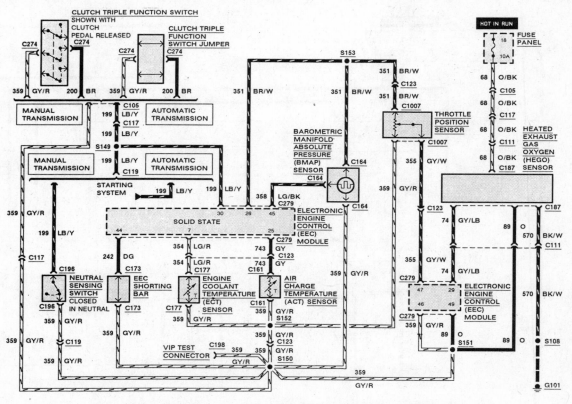

Electronic engine controls, 4.0L engine; 3.0L similar (typical – part 3 of 3)

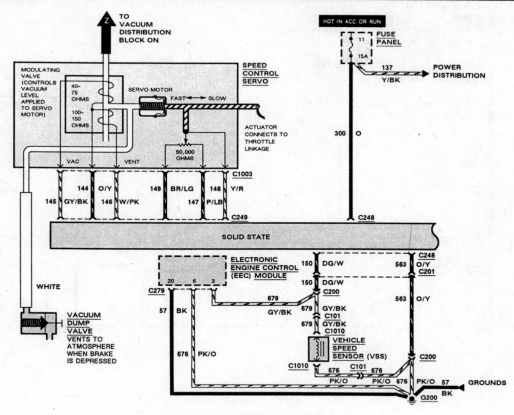

Cruise control (typical) – part 1 of 2

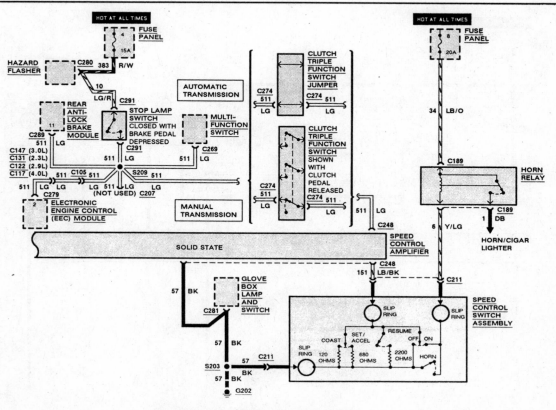

Cruise control (typical) – part 2 of 2

12

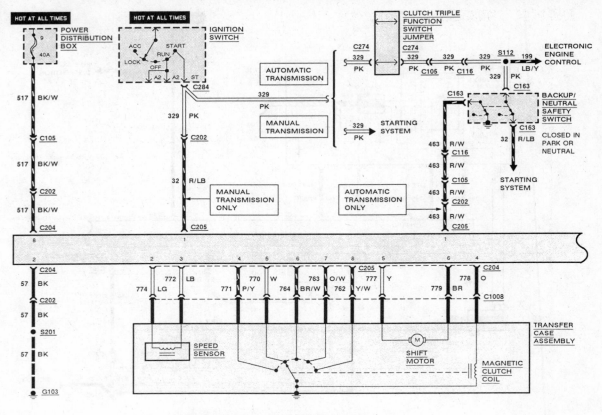

Electric shift control (typical) – part 1 of 2

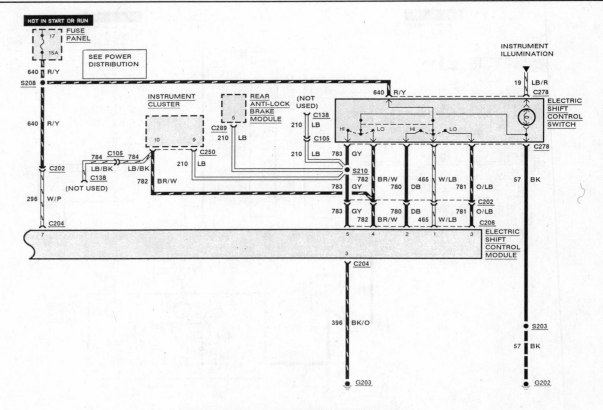

Electric shift control (typical) – part 2 of 2

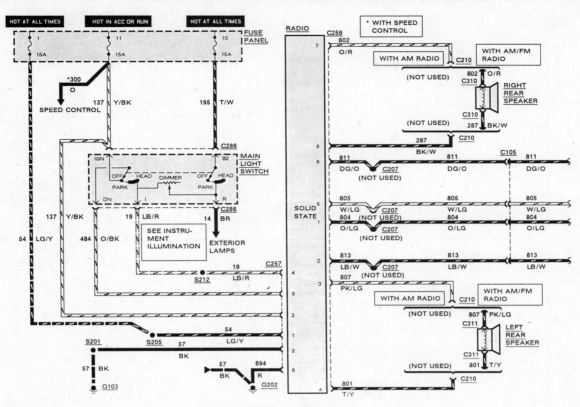

Radio (typical) (part 1 of 2)

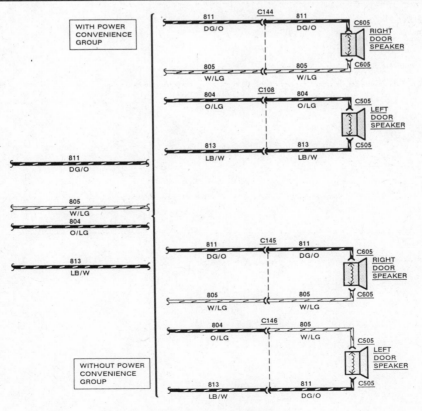

Radio (typical) (part 2 of 2)

12

Index

Haynes Automotive Manuals

ACURA
*1776   **Integra** '86 thru '89 & **Legend** '86 thru '90

AMC
  Jeep CJ - see JEEP (412)
694   **Mid-size models,** Concord, Hornet, Gremlin & Spirit '70 thru '83
934   **(Renault) Alliance & Encore** '83 thru '87

AUDI
615   **4000** all models '80 thru '87
428   **5000** all models '77 thru '83
1117   **5000** all models '84 thru '88

AUSTIN-HEALEY
  Sprite - see MG Midget (265)

BMW
*2020   **3/5 Series** not including diesel or all-wheel drive models '82 thru '92
276   **320i** all 4 cyl models '75 thru '83
632   **528i & 530i** all models '75 thru '80
240   **1500 thru 2002** except Turbo '59 thru '77

BUICK
  Century (front wheel drive) - see GM (829)
*1627   **Buick, Oldsmobile & Pontiac Full-size (Front wheel drive)** all models '85 thru '95 **Buick** Electra, LeSabre and Park Avenue; **Oldsmobile** Delta 88 Royale, Ninety Eight and Regency; **Pontiac** Bonneville
1551   **Buick Oldsmobile & Pontiac Full-size (Rear wheel drive)** **Buick** Estate '70 thru '90, Electra'70 thru '84, LeSabre '70 thru '85, Limited '74 thru '79 **Oldsmobile** Custom Cruiser '70 thru '90, Delta 88 '70 thru '85,Ninety-eight '70 thru '84 **Pontiac** Bonneville '70 thru '81, Catalina '70 thru '81, Grandville '70 thru '75, Parisienne '83 thru '86
627   **Mid-size Regal & Century** all rear-drive models with V6, V8 and Turbo '74 thru '87 **Regal** - see GENERAL MOTORS (1671) **Riviera** - see GENERAL MOTORS (38030) **Skyhawk** - see GENERAL MOTORS (766) **Skylark** '80 thru '85 - see GM (38020) **Skylark** '86 on - see GM (1420) **Somerset** - see GENERAL MOTORS (1420)

CADILLAC
*751   **Cadillac Rear Wheel Drive** all gasoline models '70 thru '93 **Cimarron** - see GENERAL MOTORS (766) **Eldorado** - see GENERAL MOTORS (38030) **Seville** '80 thru '85 - see GM (38030)

CHEVROLET
*1477   **Astro & GMC Safari Mini-vans** '85 thru '93
554   **Camaro V8** all models '70 thru '81
866   **Camaro** all models '82 thru '92 **Cavalier** - see GENERAL MOTORS (766) **Celebrity** - see GENERAL MOTORS (829)
24017   **Camaro & Firebird** '93 thru '96
625   **Chevelle, Malibu & El Camino** all V6 & V8 models '69 thru '87
449   **Chevette & Pontiac T1000** '76 thru '87
550   **Citation** all models '80 thru '85
*1628   **Corsica/Beretta** all models '87 thru '96
274   **Corvette** all V8 models '68 thru '82
*1336   **Corvette** all models '84 thru '91
1762   **Chevrolet Engine Overhaul Manual**
704   **Full-size Sedans** Caprice, Impala, Biscayne, Bel Air & Wagons '69 thru '90 **Lumina** - see GENERAL MOTORS (1671) **Lumina APV** - see GENERAL MOTORS (2035)
319   **Luv Pick-up** all 2WD & 4WD '72 thru '82
626   **Monte Carlo** all models '70 thru '88

241   **Nova** all V8 models '69 thru '79
*1642   **Nova and Geo Prizm** all front wheel drive models, '85 thru '92
420   **Pick-ups '67 thru '87** - Chevrolet & GMC, all V8 & in-line 6 cyl, 2WD & 4WD '67 thru '87; Suburbans, Blazers & Jimmys '67 thru '91
*1664   **Pick-ups '88 thru '95** - Chevrolet & GMC, all full-size pick-ups, '88 thru '95; Blazer & Jimmy '92 thru '94; Suburban '92 thru '95; Tahoe & Yukon '95
831   **S-10 & GMC S-15 Pick-ups** '82 thru '93
*24071   **S-10 & GMC S-15 Pick-ups** '94 thru '96
*1727   **Sprint & Geo Metro** '85 thru '94
*345   **Vans - Chevrolet & GMC,** V8 & in-line 6 cylinder models '68 thru '96

CHRYSLER
25025   **Chrysler Concorde, New Yorker & LHS, Dodge** Intrepid, **Eagle** Vision, '93 thru '96
2114   **Chrysler Engine Overhaul Manual**
*2058   **Full-size Front-Wheel Drive** '88 thru '93 **K-Cars** - see DODGE Aries (723) **Laser** - see DODGE Daytona (1140)
*1337   **Chrysler & Plymouth Mid-size** front wheel drive '82 thru '95 **Rear-wheel Drive** - see Dodge (2098)

DATSUN
647   **200SX** all models '80 thru '83
228   **B - 210** all models '73 thru '78
525   **210** all models '79 thru '82
206   **240Z, 260Z & 280Z** Coupe '70 thru '78
563   **280ZX** Coupe & 2+2 '79 thru '83 **300ZX** - see NISSAN (1137)
679   **310** all models '78 thru '82
123   **510 & PL521 Pick-up** '68 thru '73
430   **510** all models '78 thru '81
372   **610** all models '72 thru '76
277   **620 Series Pick-up** all models '73 thru '79 **720 Series Pick-up** - see NISSAN (771)
376   **810/Maxima** all gasoline models, '77 thru '84 **Pulsar** - see NISSAN (876) **Sentra** - see NISSAN (982) **Stanza** - see NISSAN (981)

DODGE
  400 & 600 - see CHRYSLER Mid-size (1337)
*723   **Aries & Plymouth Reliant** '81 thru '89
1231   **Caravan & Plymouth Voyager Mini-Vans** all models '84 thru '95
699   **Challenger/Plymouth Saporro** '78 thru '83 **Challenger** '67-'76 - see DODGE Dart (234)
610   **Colt & Plymouth Champ (front wheel drive)** all models '78 thru '87
*1668   **Dakota Pick-ups** all models '87 thru '96
234   **Dart, Challenger/Plymouth Barracuda & Valiant** 6 cyl models '67 thru '76
*1140   **Daytona & Chrysler Laser** '84 thru '89 **Intrepid** - see CHRYSLER (25025)
*30034   **Neon** all models '94 thru '97
*545   **Omni & Plymouth Horizon** '78 thru '90
*912   **Pick-ups** all full-size models '74 thru '93
*30041   **Pick-ups** all full-size models '94 thru '96
*556   **Ram 50/D50 Pick-ups & Raider and Plymouth Arrow Pick-ups** '79 thru '93
2098   **Dodge/Plymouth/Chrysler** rear wheel drive '71 thru '89
*1726   **Shadow & Plymouth Sundance** '87 thru '94
*1779   **Spirit & Plymouth Acclaim** '89 thru '95
*349   **Vans - Dodge & Plymouth** V8 & 6 cyl models '71 thru '96

EAGLE
  Talon - see Mitsubishi Eclipse (2097)
  Vision - see CHRYSLER (25025)

FIAT
094   **124 Sport Coupe & Spider** '68 thru '78
273   **X1/9** all models '74 thru '80

FORD
10355   **Ford Automatic Trans. Overhaul**
*1476   **Aerostar Mini-vans** all models '86 thru '96

268   **Courier Pick-up** all models '72 thru '82
2105   **Crown Victoria & Mercury Grand Marquis** '88 thru '96
1763   **Ford Engine Overhaul Manual**
789   **Escort/Mercury Lynx** all models '81 thru '90
*2046   **Escort/Mercury Tracer** '91 thru '96
*2021   **Explorer & Mazda Navajo** '91 thru '95
560   **Fairmont & Mercury Zephyr** '78 thru '83
334   **Fiesta** all models '77 thru '80
754   **Ford & Mercury Full-size,** Ford LTD & Mercury Marquis ('75 thru '82); Ford Custom 500,Country Squire, Crown Victoria & Mercury Colony Park ('75 thru '87); Ford LTD Crown Victoria & Mercury Gran Marquis ('83 thru '87)
359   **Granada & Mercury Monarch** all in-line, 6 cyl & V8 models '75 thru '80
773   **Ford & Mercury Mid-size,** Ford Thunderbird & Mercury Cougar ('75 thru '82); Ford LTD & Mercury Marquis ('83 thru '86); Ford Torino,Gran Torino, Elite, Ranchero pick-up, LTD II, Mercury Montego, Comet, XR-7 & Lincoln Versailles ('75 thru '86)
231   **Mustang II** 4 cyl, V6 & V8 models '74 thru '78
357   **Mustang V8** all models '64-1/2 thru '73
*654   **Mustang & Mercury Capri** all models Mustang, '79 thru '93; Capri, '79 thru '86
*36051   **Mustang** all models '94 thru '97
788   **Pick-ups & Bronco** '73 thru '79
*880   **Pick-ups & Bronco** '80 thru '96
649   **Pinto & Mercury Bobcat** '75 thru '80
1670   **Probe** all models '89 thru '92
*1026   **Ranger/Bronco II** gasoline models '83 thru '92
*36071   **Ranger** '93 thru '96 & **Mazda Pick-ups** '94 thru '96
*1421   **Taurus & Mercury Sable** '86 thru '95
*1418   **Tempo & Mercury Topaz** all gasoline models '84 thru '94
1338   **Thunderbird/Mercury Cougar** '83 thru '88
*1725   **Thunderbird/Mercury Cougar** '89 and '96
344   **Vans** all V8 Econoline models '69 thru '91
*2119   **Vans** full size '92-'95

GENERAL MOTORS
*10360   **GM Automatic Transmission Overhaul**
*829   **Buick Century, Chevrolet Celebrity, Oldsmobile Cutlass Ciera & Pontiac 6000** all models '82 thru '96
*1671   **Buick Regal, Chevrolet Lumina, Oldsmobile Cutlass Supreme & Pontiac Grand Prix** front wheel drive models '88 thru '95
*766   **Buick Skyhawk, Cadillac Cimarron, Chevrolet Cavalier, Oldsmobile Firenza & Pontiac J-2000 & Sunbird** '82 thru '94
38020   **Buick Skylark, Chevrolet Citation, Olds Omega, Pontiac Phoenix** '80 thru '85
1420   **Buick Skylark & Somerset, Oldsmobile Achieva & Calais and Pontiac Grand Am** all models '85 thru '95
38030   **Cadillac Eldorado** '71 thru '85, **Seville** '80 thru '85, **Oldsmobile Toronado** '71 thru '85 & **Buick Riviera** '79 thru '85
*2035   **Chevrolet Lumina APV, Olds Silhouette & Pontiac Trans Sport** all models '90 thru '95 **General Motors Full-size Rear-wheel Drive** - see BUICK (1551)

GEO
  Metro - see CHEVROLET Sprint (1727)
  Prizm - '85 thru '92 see CHEVY Nova (1642), '93 thru '96 see TOYOTA Corolla (1642)
*2039   **Storm** all models '90 thru '93 **Tracker** - see SUZUKI Samurai (1626)

GMC
  Safari - see CHEVROLET ASTRO (1477) **Vans & Pick-ups** - see CHEVROLET (420, 831, 345, 1664 & 24071)

(Continued on other side)

Haynes North America, Inc., 861 Lawrence Drive, Newbury Park, CA 91320 • (805) 498-6703

Haynes Automotive Manuals (continued)

NOTE: New manuals are added to this list on a periodic basis. If you do not see a listing for your vehicle, consult your local Haynes dealer for the latest product information.

HONDA
351	**Accord CVCC** all models '76 thru '83
1221	**Accord** all models '84 thru '89
2067	**Accord** all models '90 thru '93
42013	**Accord** all models '94 thru '95
160	**Civic 1200** all models '73 thru '79
633	**Civic 1300 & 1500 CVCC** '80 thru '83
297	**Civic 1500 CVCC** all models '75 thru '79
1227	**Civic** all models '84 thru '91
*2118	**Civic & del Sol** '92 thru '95
*601	**Prelude CVCC** all models '79 thru '89

HYUNDAI
*1552	**Excel** all models '86 thru '94

ISUZU
*1641	**Trooper & Pick-up,** all gasoline models Pick-up, '81 thru '93; Trooper, '84 thru '91
	Hombre - see *CHEVROLET S-10 (24071)*

JAGUAR
*242	**XJ6** all 6 cyl models '68 thru '86
*49011	**XJ6** all models '88 thru '94
*478	**XJ12 & XJS** all 12 cyl models '72 thru '85

JEEP
*1553	**Cherokee, Comanche & Wagoneer Limited** all models '84 thru '96
412	**CJ** all models '49 thru '86
50025	**Grand Cherokee** all models '93 thru '95
50029	**Grand Wagoneer & Pick-up** '72 thru '91 Grand Wagoneer '84 thru '91, Cherokee & Wagoneer '72 thru '83, Pick-up '72 thru '88
*1777	**Wrangler** all models '87 thru '95

LINCOLN
2117	**Rear Wheel Drive** all models '70 thru '96

MAZDA
648	**626** (rear wheel drive) all models '79 thru '82
*1082	**626/MX-6 (front wheel drive)** '83 thru '91
370	**GLC Hatchback (rear wheel drive)** '77 thru '83
757	**GLC (front wheel drive)** '81 thru '85
*2047	**MPV** all models '89 thru '94
	Navajo - see *Ford Explorer (2021)*
267	**Pick-ups** '72 thru '93
	Pick-ups '94 thru '96 - see *Ford Ranger (36071)*
460	**RX-7** all models '79 thru '85
*1419	**RX-7** all models '86 thru '91

MERCEDES-BENZ
*1643	**190 Series** four-cyl gas models, '84 thru '88
346	**230/250/280** 6 cyl sohc models '68 thru '72
983	**280 123 Series** gasoline models '77 thru '81
698	**350 & 450** all models '71 thru '80
697	**Diesel 123 Series** '76 thru '85

MERCURY
See FORD Listing

MG
111	**MGB** Roadster & GT Coupe '62 thru '80
265	**MG Midget, Austin Healey Sprite** '58 thru '80

MITSUBISHI
*1669	**Cordia, Tredia, Galant, Precis & Mirage** '83 thru '93
*2097	**Eclipse, Eagle Talon & Plymouth Laser** '90 thru '94
*2022	**Pick-up** '83 thru '96 & **Montero** '83 thru '93

NISSAN
1137	**300ZX** all models including Turbo '84 thru '89
*72015	**Altima** all models '93 thru '97
*1341	**Maxima** all models '85 thru '91
*771	**Pick-ups** '80 thru '96 **Pathfinder** '87 thru '95
876	**Pulsar** all models '83 thru '86
*982	**Sentra** all models '82 thru '94
*981	**Stanza** all models '82 thru '90

OLDSMOBILE
	Achieva - see *GENERAL MOTORS (1420)*
	Bravada - see *CHEVROLET S-10 (831)*
	Calais - see *GENERAL MOTORS (1420)*
	Custom Cruiser - see *BUICK RWD (1551)*
*658	**Cutlass V6 & V8 gas models** '74 thru '88
	Cutlass Ciera - see *GENERAL MOTORS (829)*
	Cutlass Supreme - see *GM (1671)*
	Delta 88 - see *BUICK Full-size RWD (1551)*
	Delta 88 Brougham - see *BUICK Full-size FWD (1551), RWD (1627)*
	Delta 88 Royale - see *BUICK RWD (1551)*
	Firenza - see *GENERAL MOTORS (766)*
	Ninety-eight Regency - see *BUICK Full-size RWD (1551), FWD (1627)*
	Ninety-eight Regency Brougham - see *BUICK Full-size RWD (1551)*
	Omega - see *GENERAL MOTORS (38020)*
	Silhouette - see *GENERAL MOTORS (2035)*
	Toronado - see *GENERAL MOTORS (38030)*

PEUGEOT
663	**504** all diesel models '74 thru '83

PLYMOUTH
	Laser - see *MITSUBISHI Eclipse (2097)*
	For other PLYMOUTH titles, see DODGE.

PONTIAC
	T1000 - see *CHEVROLET Chevette (449)*
	J-2000 - see *GENERAL MOTORS (766)*
	6000 - see *GENERAL MOTORS (829)*
	Bonneville - see *Buick FWD (1627), RWD (1551)*
	Bonneville Brougham - see *Buick (1551)*
	Catalina - see *Buick Full-size (1551)*
1232	**Fiero** all models '84 thru '88
555	**Firebird V8** models except Turbo '70 thru '81
867	**Firebird** all models '82 thru '92
	Firebird '93 thru '96 - see *CHEVY Camaro (24017)*
	Full-size Front Wheel Drive - see *BUICK, Oldsmobile, Pontiac Full-size FWD (1627)*
	Full-size Rear Wheel Drive - see *BUICK Oldsmobile, Pontiac Full-size RWD (1551)*
	Grand Am - see *GENERAL MOTORS (1420)*
	Grand Prix - see *GENERAL MOTORS (1671)*
	Grandville - see *BUICK Full-size (1551)*
	Parisienne - see *BUICK Full-size (1551)*
	Phoenix - see *GENERAL MOTORS (38020)*
	Sunbird - see *GENERAL MOTORS (766)*
	Trans Sport - see *GENERAL MOTORS (2035)*

PORSCHE
*264	**911** except Turbo & Carrera 4 '65 thru '89
239	**914** all 4 cyl models '69 thru '76
397	**924** all models including Turbo '76 thru '82
*1027	**944** all models including Turbo '83 thru '89

RENAULT
141	**5 Le Car** all models '76 thru '83
	Alliance & Encore - see *AMC (934)*

SAAB
247	**99** all models including Turbo '69 thru '80
*980	**900** all models including Turbo '79 thru '88

SATURN
2083	**Saturn** all models '91 thru '96

SUBARU
237	**1100, 1300, 1400 & 1600** '71 thru '79
*681	**1600 & 1800** 2WD & 4WD '80 thru '89

SUZUKI
*1626	**Samurai/Sidekick & Geo Tracker** '86 thru '96

TOYOTA
1023	**Camry** all models '83 thru '91
92006	**Camry** all models '92 thru '95
935	**Celica Rear Wheel Drive** '71 thru '85
*2038	**Celica Front Wheel Drive** '86 thru '93
1139	**Celica Supra** all models '79 thru '92
361	**Corolla** all models '75 thru '79
961	**Corolla** all rear wheel drive models '80 thru '87
1025	**Corolla** all front wheel drive models '84 thru '92
*92036	**Corolla & Geo Prizm** '93 thru '96
636	**Corolla Tercel** all models '80 thru '82
360	**Corona** all models '74 thru '82
532	**Cressida** all models '78 thru '82
313	**Land Cruiser** all models '68 thru '82
*1339	**MR2** all models '85 thru '87
304	**Pick-up** all models '69 thru '78
*656	**Pick-up** all models '79 thru '95
*2048	**Previa** all models '91 thru '95
2106	**Tercel** all models '87 thru '94

TRIUMPH
113	**Spitfire** all models '62 thru '81
322	**TR7** all models '75 thru '81

VW
159	**Beetle & Karmann Ghia** '54 thru '79
238	**Dasher** all gasoline models '74 thru '81
96017	**Golf & Jetta** all models '93 thru '97
*884	**Rabbit, Jetta, Scirocco, & Pick-up** gas models '74 thru '91 & Convertible '80 thru '92
451	**Rabbit, Jetta & Pick-up** diesel '77 thru '84
082	**Transporter 1600** all models '68 thru '79
226	**Transporter 1700, 1800 & 2000** '72 thru '79
084	**Type 3 1500 & 1600** all models '63 thru '73
1029	**Vanagon** all air-cooled models '80 thru '83

VOLVO
203	**120, 130 Series & 1800 Sports** '61 thru '73
129	**140 Series** all models '66 thru '74
*270	**240 Series** all models '76 thru '93
400	**260 Series** all models '75 thru '82
*1550	**740 & 760 Series** all models '82 thru '88

TECHBOOK MANUALS
2108	**Automotive Computer Codes**
1667	**Automotive Emissions Control Manual**
482	**Fuel Injection Manual, 1978 thru 1985**
2111	**Fuel Injection Manual, 1986 thru 1996**
2069	**Holley Carburetor Manual**
2068	**Rochester Carburetor Manual**
10240	**Weber/Zenith/Stromberg/SU Carburetors**
1762	**Chevrolet Engine Overhaul Manual**
2114	**Chrysler Engine Overhaul Manual**
1763	**Ford Engine Overhaul Manual**
1736	**GM and Ford Diesel Engine Repair Manual**
1666	**Small Engine Repair Manual**
10355	**Ford Automatic Transmission Overhaul**
10360	**GM Automatic Transmission Overhaul**
1479	**Automotive Body Repair & Painting**
2112	**Automotive Brake Manual**
2113	**Automotive Detailing Manual**
1654	**Automotive Eelectrical Manual**
1480	**Automotive Heating & Air Conditioning**
2109	**Automotive Reference Manual & Dictionary**
2107	**Automotive Tools Manual**
10440	**Used Car Buying Guide**
2110	**Welding Manual**
10450	**ATV Basics**

SPANISH MANUALS
98903	**Reparación de Carrocería & Pintura**
98905	**Códigos Automotrices de la Computadora**
98910	**Frenos Automotriz**
98915	**Inyección de Combustible 1986 al 1994**
99040	**Chevrolet & GMC Camionetas** '67 al '87 Incluye Suburban, Blazer & Jimmy '67 al '91
99041	**Chevrolet & GMC Camionetas** '88 al '95 Incluye Suburban '92 al '95, Blazer & Jimmy '92 al '94, Tahoe & Yukon '95
99042	**Chevrolet & GMC Camionetas Cerradas** '68 al '95
99055	**Dodge Caravan & Plymouth Voyager** '84 al '95
99075	**Ford Camionetas y Bronco** '80 al '94
99077	**Ford Camionetas Cerradas** '69 al '91
99083	**Ford Modelos de Tamaño Grande** '75 al '87
99088	**Ford Modelos de Tamaño Mediano** '75 al '86
99095	**GM Modelos de Tamaño Grande** '70 al '90
99118	**Nissan Sentra** '82 al '94
99125	**Toyota Camionetas y 4-Runner** '79 al '95

---

* Listings shown with an asterisk (*) indicate model coverage as of this printing. These titles will be periodically updated to include later model years - consult your Haynes dealer for more information.

Over 100 Haynes
motorcycle manuals
also available

5-97

Haynes North America, Inc., 861 Lawrence Drive, Newbury Park, CA 91320 • (805) 498-6703

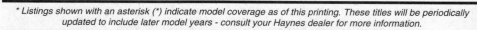